Oxford Studies in Philosophy of Mind

Oxford Studies in Philosophy of Mind

Volume 3

Edited By
URIAH KRIEGEL

Great Clarendon Street, Oxford, OX2 6DP,
United Kingdom

Oxford University Press is a department of the University of Oxford.
It furthers the University's objective of excellence in research, scholarship,
and education by publishing worldwide. Oxford is a registered trade mark of
Oxford University Press in the UK and in certain other countries

© the several contributors 2023

The moral rights of the authors have been asserted

All rights reserved. No part of this publication may be reproduced, stored in
a retrieval system, or transmitted, in any form or by any means, without the
prior permission in writing of Oxford University Press, or as expressly permitted
by law, by licence or under terms agreed with the appropriate reprographics
rights organization. Enquiries concerning reproduction outside the scope of the
above should be sent to the Rights Department, Oxford University Press, at the
address above

You must not circulate this work in any other form
and you must impose this same condition on any acquirer

Published in the United States of America by Oxford University Press
198 Madison Avenue, New York, NY 10016, United States of America

British Library Cataloguing in Publication Data
Data available

Library of Congress Control Number: 2022952227

ISBN 978-0-19-887946-6

DOI: 10.1093/oso/9780198879466.001.0001

Printed and bound in the UK by
TJ Books Limited

Links to third party websites are provided by Oxford in good faith and
for information only. Oxford disclaims any responsibility for the materials
contained in any third party website referenced in this work.

Contents

Preface   vii
List of Contributors   xi

PART I. MIND AND SCIENCE

1. The Parts of an Imperfect Agent   3
   Sara Aronowitz

2. The Average Isn't Normal: The History and Cognitive Science of an Everyday Scientific Practice   29
   Henry M. Cowles and Joshua Knobe

3. Correspondence and Construction: The Representational Theory of Mind and Internally Driven Classificatory Schemes   57
   Gabe Dupre

4. Unconscious Perception and Unconscious Bias: Parallel Debates about Unconscious Content   87
   Gabbrielle M. Johnson

5. Aphantasia and Conscious Thought   131
   Preston Lennon

6. The Introspective Method   156
   Maja Spener

PART II. SENSORY EXPERIENCE: PERCEPTION, IMAGINATION, PLEASURE

7. Right Here, Right Now: On the Eudaimonic Value of Perceptual Awareness   191
   Dorothea Debus

8. Imagination, Fiction, and Perspectival Displacement   219
   Justin D'Ambrosio and Daniel Stoljar

9. The Dilemma for Attitude Theories of Pleasure 241
   Daniel Pallies and Alexander Dietz

10. Seeing through Transparency 263
    Davide Bordini

PART III. BOOK SYMPOSIUM ON DAVID PAPINEAU'S *THE METAPHYSICS OF SENSORY EXPERIENCE*

11. Précis of *The Metaphysics of Sensory Experience* 299
    David Papineau

12. Papineau on Sensory Experience 308
    Alex Byrne

13. Truth and Content in Sensory Experience 318
    Angela Mendelovici

14. An Argument against Papineau's Qualitative View of Sensory Experience 339
    Adam Pautz

15. Responses to Mendelovici, Pautz, and Byrne 352
    David Papineau

PART IV. HISTORY OF PHILOSOPHY OF MIND: CAVENDISH AND STRONG

16. Cavendish and Strawson on Emergence, Mind, and Self 369
    David Cunning

17. 'Actions of a Body Sentient': Cavendish on the Mind (and against Panpsychism) 399
    Alison Peterman

18. C. A. Strong—Real Materialism, Evolutionary Naturalism, Panpsychism 432
    Galen Strawson

Index 463

Preface

This third volume of *Oxford Studies in Philosophy of Mind* features a cluster of chapters on the theme "mind and science," a second cluster on the theme "sensory experience," and a third on the philosophy of mind of Margaret Cavendish and C.A. Strong. It also features a book symposium on David Papineau's important *The Metaphysics of Sensory Experience*.

In the first cluster are six chapters that address the relationship between mind and science from a variety of angles. In "The Parts of an Imperfect Agent," Sara Aronowitz discusses the need for, and challenges facing, a theory of human rationality that is sensitive both to (a) the ideal/normative truths about reasoning and decision-making that we get from such formal disciplines as confirmation and decision theory and (b) the empirical/descriptive reality of human agents as we understand it from cognitive science. In "The Average Isn't Normal," Henry Cowles and Joshua Knobe reconstruct the development of comparison to an average as a central scientific tool for understanding certain phenomena and point out the risk this poses in the folk reception of scientific results, given that the folk tend to spontaneously interpret the notion of average in teleological terms, as amounting to what is *normal*. In "Correspondence and Construction: The Representational Theory of Mind and Internally Driven Classificatory Schemes," Gabe Dupre argues that a central motivation for the widespread notion that mental states function as internal proxies for external items is undermined by the repeated discoveries of ways in which objective divisions in nature are distorted in mental classificatory schemes in various perceptual and cognitive domains. In "Unconscious Perception and Unconscious Bias: Parallel Debates about Unconscious Content," Gabbrielle Johnson brings out certain dialectical patterns in debates about empirical inquiry into the unconscious mind: in particular, the way it is unclear in research about both unconscious perception and unconscious bias whether the phenomena at play really qualify as unconscious or really qualify as perception/bias. In "Aphantasia and Conscious Thought," Preston Lennon develops a sustained empirical argument for a "cognitive phenomenology" irreducible to the sensory phenomenology associated with imagery and silent speech: subjects suffering from aphantasia—an incapacity to form mental imagery—are nonetheless capable, he argues, of having phenomenally conscious thoughts. In "The Introspective Method," Maja Spener discusses the highly sophisticated methodological awareness about the methodical use of introspection in early consciousness science.

The second cluster features chapters on three varieties of sensory experience—perception, imagination, and pleasure—as well as a review articleon the so-called transparency of experience, an idea that has structured much of the debate on the nature of sensory experience over the past three decades. In "Right Here, Right Now: On the Eudaimonic Value of Perceptual Awareness," Dorothea Debus argues that perceptual experience enhances our wellbeing by offering direct contact with external reality, and that naïve realism is the only account of perception that can do justice to this. In "Imagination, Fiction, and Perspectival Displacement," Justin D'Ambrosio and Daniel Stoljar draw lessons about the nature of imagining, and imagination reports, from the fact that "imagines" admits of perspectival modifications (as in "she imagines how the airport looks *from above*," where "from above" is the perspectival modifier) even though no real or imagined perspective needs to be implicated. In "The Dilemma for Attitude Theories of Pleasure," Daniel Pallies and Alexander Dietz present a destructive-dilemma argument against the view that taking pleasure in X is not a matter of experiencing a distinctive pleasurish phenomenology, but a matter of bearing a pro attitude toward X. The argument is, very roughly, that if the relevant pro attitude is construed as phenomenally conscious, then the alleged advantages of the attitudinal theory over the phenomenological theory disappear; but if the pro attitude is *not* phenomenally conscious, certain absurd scenarios would become possible in which a subject would qualify as taking pleasure in something who doesn't experience any remotely relevant phenomenology. In the final contribution to this part of the volume, "Seeing through Transparency," Davide Bordini reviews the many distinctions between types of transparency that might allegedly characterize sensory experience (and perhaps all experience) and attempts to construct a unified multidimensional logical space in which highly specific transparency theses might be placed.

Every volume of *Oxford Studies in Philosophy of Mind* has a "history corner" featuring studies in the history of the philosophy of mind. The first volume focused on Islamic philosophy of mind, the second on Spinoza's philosophy of mind; this third volume focuses on two lesser-known alleged proponents of panprotopsychist approaches to the mind-body problem: Margaret Cavendish in the mid-17th century and C.A. Strong in the first half of the 20th century. Because of her repeated and central claim, against Descartes, that matter is intelligent, Cavendish is standardly interpreted to have defended a panpsychist philosophy of mind. In his contribution, David Cunning develops the case for this via comparison with Galen Strawson's "real materialism" view ("Cavendish and Strawson on Emergence, Mind, and Self"). However, in her "'Actions of a Body Sentient': Cavendish on the Mind (and against Panpsychism)," Alison Peterman argues that current-day philosophers have (mis)read panpsychism into Cavendish: although Cavendish says that inanimate beings engage in perception and cognition, her use of these terms is different from ours and ultimately only means that these beings have certain characteristic ways of interacting with their environments. The volume closes with a contribution by Galen Strawson himself—a study of C.A. Strong's philosophy of mind, highlighting Strong's case for panpsychism and "real materialism."

In addition to these three clusters of research articles, the volume features a book symposium on David Papineau's *The Metaphysics of Sensory Experience*, which goes against the representationalist and direct-realist grain in current philosophy of perception and argues for a "qualitative view" of sensory experience according to which experience's relation to the ambient environment is entirely contingent and its only *essential* properties are intrinsic, qualitative, and ultimately (given Papineau's physicalism) neural. Various aspects of this picture are challenged by Alex Byrne (as an externalist representationalist), Angela Mendelovici (as a phenomenal intentionalist), and Adam Pautz, who develops a sustained argument that Papineau's qualitative view cannot account for central aspects of *spatial* experience. Papineau's responses conclude the symposium.

List of Contributors

Sara Aronowitz University of Toronto

Davide Bordini University of Fribourg

Alex Byrne MIT

Henry M. Cowles University of Michigan

David Cunning University of Iowa

Justin D'Ambrosio University of St. Andrews

Dorothea Debus University of Konstanz

Alexander Dietz Cardiff University

Gabe Dupre Keele University

Gabbrielle Johnson Claremont McKenna College

Joshua Knobe Yale University

Preston Lennon Rutgers University

Angela Mendelovici Western University

Daniel Pallies Lingnan University

David Papineau Kings' College London

Adam Pautz Brown University

Alison Peterman University of Rochester

Maja Spener University of Birmingham

Daniel Stoljar The Australian National University

Galen Strawson University of Texas—Austin

PART I
MIND AND SCIENCE

1
The Parts of an Imperfect Agent

Sara Aronowitz

Introduction

Understanding when we meet and fail to meet the standards of rationality is an important part of understanding human cognition. To this end, formal theories of ideal rationality—such as decision theory—hold promise as ways of making precise what these standards might be. These models have, of course, a wide domain of application in laying a standard of rationality for communities, artificial agents, and the process of science. But our use of such idealized accounts often goes beyond creating a measuring-stick for human progress. We sometimes take these models to provide insight into the representations and computations with which we produce beliefs and behaviors. In doing so, I'll argue, we sometimes misstep in an interesting way: taking the ideal model too literally, we rely on it to adjudicate fine-grained debates about inner workings. Revealing these kinds of mistakes opens up a gap. As we move away from perfectly rational agents, questions emerge that, on the one hand, cannot be settled by the ideal model, and on the other hand, have deep implications for whether and how imperfect agents might be rational.

A wide variety of recent work, such as books by Julia Staffel (2020) and Richard Bradley (2017), has focused on how to relax the standards of ideal rationality to *evaluate* less perfect agents. In this chapter, I'll instead take a step back. Before we can face these problems of evaluation, we need to first apply concepts such as credences, preferences, and inferences. Already, as I'll argue, difficulties arise in assessing which part, if any, of an imperfect agent should be brought under these labels. This question starts with one way in which philosophy of mind has relied on philosophy of science: to lend idealized formal models. We end up with a lesson that philosophy of mind might in turn share: to attend closely to the connection between standards of evaluation and the nature of the states which are being evaluated.

Sara Aronowitz, *The Parts of an Imperfect Agent* In: *Oxford Studies in Philosophy of Mind Volume 3*. Edited by: Uriah Kriegel, Oxford University Press. © Sara Aronowitz 2023. DOI: 10.1093/oso/9780198879466.003.0001

In Section 1, I introduce and motivate the project of 'approximate rationality', a mix of normative and descriptive inquiry which will be the target of this chapter. Section 2 presents two approximate rationality models of decision-making that use the same formal machinery and yet make substantially different commitments about inner workings, and consequently rationality. Could this problem be solved by picking the model closest to the ideal? I argue that this impasse is genuinely hard to solve, even in principle, in Section 3. Section 4 aims to extend this impasse to related debates.

1. Approximate Rationality: What and Why

The project I'll call 'approximate rationality'[1] is an attempt to combine two forms of theorizing: descriptive psychological work on how we function, and normative work on what rational functioning amounts to. In combining these two, the approximate rationality project does not merely aim to conduct two lines of inquiry simultaneously, but to allow each to inform the other in creating a theory that is in some sense a united whole. Within this umbrella, we find several significantly different forms of combination.

One version (arguably what was suggested by John Anderson (1990) under the heading of 'rational analysis') might start from the empirical observation that humans are surprisingly successful in various domains, and then ask how this might be possible given psychological constraints and principles of rationality. This project may ask about success across any environment consistent with our evidence, or instead understand our success as built upon the particular environments we tend to encounter (the latter being a version of Herbert Simon's ecological rationality (1955)). We might instead accept that humans are not on the whole rational or irrational, but place greater scientific value on explanations of how we are rational, when we are, than explanations of irrationality or a-rationality.

Alternately, we might use descriptive psychological findings to provide insight into a question about rationality, such as: how is it possible to learn new theories selectively, that is without brute-force enumerative search? Along these lines, Dedre Gentner has built a theory of the rationality of

---

[1] I use this term instead of ones like 'bounded rationality' (Simon, 1990; Gigerenzer & Selton, 2002) or 'rational analysis' (Anderson, 1990; Lewis, Howes &, and Singh, 2013) in order to signal that I mean a very broad set of approaches, including those that focus on explaining how we fail to be fully rational.

analogical reasoning based on historical (Gentner et al. 1997) and lab-based (e.g. Markman and Gentner 1993; Gentner 2010) observations about how humans come up with new ideas. For instance, she uses the example of Kepler's development of an analogy between light and 'the motive power' to refine and illustrate a theory of conceptual change where we map structures from one domain onto a novel hypothesis in a target domain, and then adjust the comparison along with our understanding of both domains. Here, findings about how we think emerge alongside analysis of the rationality of discovery of new concepts, both supporting one another: the more it appears a way of thinking is characteristic of actual human discoveries, the more it would seem to be a candidate for a rational mode of discovery, and vice versa. Her resulting theory, the structure-mapping theory, is a theory of how we solve a problem (inventing a new theory) that the most ideal of agents never need to solve; with an unlimited ability to construct possible hypotheses, it is no longer necessary to be economical in adding just the new theories that can be constructed most handily out of current ones through analogy and other forms of bootstrapping.

Gentner's work tells us a lot about human reasoning, of course, but it also illuminates something about the problem of new hypotheses itself, and consequently has been extended to artificial contexts where conformity to actual human reasoning is not a major aim (Falkenhainer et al. 1989). That is, both Anderson's approach and Gentner's aim to understand approximate rationality through psychology as well as psychology through approximate rationality, though I separate out these two directions to make the conceptual point that each direction is a distinguishable form of inquiry.

There are many approximate rationality projects beyond the ones I've sketched here. But for the purposes of this chapter, these differences are for the most part irrelevant. All of these projects aim to carry out a kind of combination and integration of two very different forms of theorizing, and the challenge I'll raise picks up on that feature. Before presenting the challenge, however, it's worth saying something about why this form of theorizing is attractive and important.

First, imagine that we can derive a theory of ideal rationality on purely *a priori* grounds. Even so, this may not be enough to determine a hierarchy of approximations without descriptive input. This could simply be because of our limited scientific imagination. But in some cases, determining closeness to the ideal is underdetermined without first specifying at least some features of the environment, such as an ecological hierarchy that evaluates success in the actual world and its near modal neighbors as closer to rationality than success in an equally sized range of distantly possible environments. In either case, without such a hierarchy, and provided that humans are never fully ideally rational, we would be unable to ever classify our behavior as more or less rational. Presumably this would fall far short of a central explanatory aim of both philosophy and psychology.

Second, we may not even be able to understand ideal rationality without leaning on descriptive findings. This might be a contingent fact about human inquiry, or a deeper fact about conceptual priority. In the first case, looking at descriptive data on human successes might be important in getting inspiration for even purely normative inquiry—after all, we might have left out key possibilities for rational optimization that might only emerge when presented through actual behavior. In the second case, some meta-epistemological views support the dependence of the ideal on the non-ideal, such that what defines the ideal thinker is dependent on empirical facts (Kornblith 2002). On this view, the normative theory is an idealization that might differ depending on the empirical starting point and be underdetermined in lieu of a connection to empirical inquiry.

Finally, purely descriptive psychology may likewise be hard to understand on its own, without drawing to some degree on theories of rationality. Following Gibbard (2012), we might take the idea of meaning, including the cognitive significance we appeal to in psychology, as essentially normative. Or drawing from Dennett (1988) or Davidson (1980), it may be that minds, intentions, beliefs, and so on only emerge once we're in the business of interpreting behavior as oriented toward goals. On these projects, we don't just fit any model of beliefs and desires to an agent's actions, but our understanding is constrained by a (defeasible) preference for models that make *sense* of the agent's behavior by aligning actions with mental states in a normative way. That is, we might be able to imagine a world where the only way we study humans is using the same descriptive orientation we currently take toward studying volcanoes—but in that world, there might be no psychology nor any science of the mind. At a minimum, it would be a very different kind of science.

Approximate rationality comes in a variety of different forms. In all cases, it is committed to a genuine synthesis of normative and descriptive inputs to produce a theory that explores rationality in realistic agents. While I will now raise a challenge for this synthesis, it's important to note that approximate rationality is well-motivated on both psychological and philosophical grounds and, far from being an optional add-on, may even be essential for 'pure' normative and descriptive projects.

2. Two Competing Approximate Rationality Models

2.1 The Structural Model

We'll start with an example. I've modified two approximate rationality models in the literature to be mathematically identical. However, they disagree about how parts of their approximate agent map onto the ideal decision-theoretic agent, and thereby have a substantial disagreement about in what sense the approximate agent is rational. The first of these, which I'll call the structural model, turns up in many recent projects in various forms, but I'll present it through the account given by Howes et al. (2016). Like many approximate rationality proponents in the rational analysis tradition, the authors present their framework as making rational sense of a common behavior previously understood as irrational—in this case, preference reversals. To illustrate this phenomenon, let's take an example. Suppose you are going to a restaurant which has a menu of two items, Xi'an noodles and eggplant. You find yourself more or less indifferent between these options, but on reflection, the eggplant sounds a little more tasty. Before you go to order, however, you realize you were mistaken. The menu actually contains three options, Xi'an noodles, Lanzhou noodles, and eggplant. You've always thought Xi'an noodles were tastier than Lanzhou—they have more interesting spices. Considering these three options, you find yourself drifting toward the Xi'an noodles.

This shift in choices should not seem outlandish: it's been well documented in various forms of behavioral experiments. In particular, it's not just that people sometimes change their minds when presented with a third (inferior) option. The key feature of this phenomenon is that the third, unchosen, option is a 'decoy' (also called phantom or phantom decoy)—it's somehow similar to but worse than one of the original options, and the presentation of the decoy tends to shift preference toward that similar, but better, option.

This form of contextual preference reversal is on its face irrational. The option of Lanzhou noodles, given that you're not going to choose them, should not change your preference among the other two options. Unless we get very creative with the way to understand the choice problem, an agent who exhibits preference reversals will violate the Independence of Irrelevant Alternatives (IIA). I'll define IIA as follows, where '$x > y$' stands for a strict preference for x over y:

IIA If A and B are two options such that A > B in choice set {A, B}, then it cannot be the case that B > A in any larger set that contains A and B.[2]

IIA can be thought of intuitively as guaranteeing that no independent third option can reverse the relationship between A and B. It's also worth noting that if we treat the value of every option as fixed and absolute (and apply a suitably straightforward decision-making rule), IIA follows automatically. Conversely, violations of IIA force us away from frameworks where we represent your desire for each option as a fixed value, and your behavior as flowing consistently from those values. Note that IIA itself, as I've defined it, is a constraint on preferences. If we allow our agent to act in a way that doesn't reflect her preferences, then a preference reversal does not necessarily imply a violation of IIA. So while preference reversals are *prima facie* evidence of IIA violations, they do not necessarily imply such a violation.

Howes et al. develop a psychological theory that rationalizes preference reversals, showing how they are consistent with IIA. Their model takes a standard decision-theoretic idealized agent and breaks the informational connection between her decision algorithm and her underlying preferences and utilities. This approximately rational agent possesses a classical, well-behaved utility distribution that respects IIA, but she only has partial access to this distribution through a noisy sampling process. The key here is that since she's uncertain about her own preferences, features of the decision problem itself can give her information pertinent to estimating those preferences. This generates a sensitivity to context in decision behavior without sensitivity to context in the preferences or credences themselves. And so, in the case of preference reversals, the rough idea is that the presentation of the Lanzhou noodles, and your subsequent feeling that the Xi'an noodles were similar but much better, gives you a bit of information about the absolute value of the Xi'an noodles. It suggests they must be pretty good, if a (randomly generated) alternative is definitely worse. And thus the presentation of the decoy shifts your choice behavior, not because you've changed what you value, but because you've gotten a hint about what you value.

---

[2] As has become standard outside of voting theory, this property is not actually Arrow's (1951) original IIA, but Sen's (2017) principles α and β (see Eells and Harper 1991). For present purposes, the difference between these principles is not important, since in any case, the principle is incompatible with a standard reading of preference reversals where the addition of the decoy causes the person to prefer the initially dispreferred option. For that reason, I have formulated a weak version of IIA such that violations of this principle will necessarily be violations of the stronger versions.

THE PARTS OF AN IMPERFECT AGENT   9

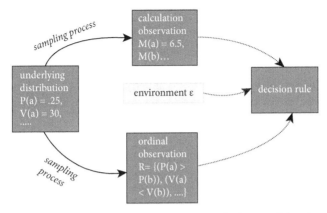

Figure 1.1 The model agent developed by Howes et al. Their model makes two kinds of observations of its own underlying state (left). The calculation observation is a noisy sample of the expected utility of an act, and the ordinal observation is a noisy sample of the value ordering over outcomes in the decision set, along with a second ordering representing the relative probability of these outcomes. The agent uses these two observations as inputs to a decision rule along with an expectation of the environment E. (Figure based on the original paper.)

Howes et al. provide a model that is intended to capture human behavior as well as to show that the occurrence of preference reversals in certain contexts is rational (Figure 1.1). The details of their model are mostly not pertinent to the aim of this chapter. However, several features will be relevant: first, their model uses a sampling process to determine its own utilities and probabilities. Second, the underlying distributions from which the samples are taken are identified with the agent's actual utilities, probabilities, and preferences. Finally, their model actually samples both an expected utility value, and ordinal rankings over both utilities and probabilities.

The ordinal observation is crucial for generating preference reversals, as can be seen in the informal gloss given in the preceding paragraph.

Howes et al. take their model, if accurate, to vindicate human rationality:

In summary, our analysis of the effect of the phantom decoy suggests that the average behavior of the participants studied by Soltani et al. (2012) was rational; by making ordinal observations relative to an unavailable option suppresses the selection of options dominated by a phantom, these participants were behaving in a way that is consistent with an observer that seeks to maximize the expected value of selected gambles given noise.

Here, they take the way in which their agent is rational to be that she is doing what even the best possible observer would suggest given her *evidential limitations*. But these are not standard evidential limitations. They are limits in knowing one's own values and beliefs—internal informational barriers, rather than limited access to underlying facts in the environment. In fact, this is one of two ways their agent might be deemed rational. She's also rational insofar as her preferences satisfy IIA.[3]

To generalize, structural models preserve rationality in the face of limitations by inserting informational barriers inside the agent. These barriers allow the structural agent to preserve two forms of rationality: first, she is what I'll call intra-internally rational. There's a sort of built-in mini agent, in our case the decision-maker, who is classically rational in the internalist sense, but merely lacks access to pertinent information on the other side of the barrier. Second, the structural agent is rational in the sense that her buried representations, on the far side of the barrier, may themselves be well-behaved, coherent, or otherwise classical. In this case, the underlying preferences satisfy IIA, and in fact presumably satisfy other constraints. On the other hand, there are ways in which the structural agent fails to be rational, which will be brought out via a contrast with our second model.

2.2 The Dispositional Model

I'll now discuss an account which is in some sense a rival to the structural model. This account is essentially the one presented by Icard (2016)—however, for dialectical purposes, I'll present a version of Icard's picture that adheres as closely as possible to the details of the Howes et al. model. In fact, this involves making just one simple change. Instead of thinking of the utilities and probabilities of the agent as the underlying distribution from which samples are drawn, as Howes et al. do, this dispositional model takes the probabilities and utilities of the agent to be her dispositions to sample from those distributions. In the previous section, our agent really took the value of choosing the Xi'an noodle to be always greater than choosing the eggplant, but her behavior varied due to her lack of consistent access to those preferences. On the dispositional model, we would treat an agent expressing these preferences as having a more complex preference ranking.

---

[3] See Rulli and Worsnip (2016) for a discussion of the place of IIA in rationality.

Icard argues for an understanding of credences as dispositions to sample, and so our modified understanding will be as of preferences as dispositions to sample.

First, a technical qualification. Because the Howes et al. model involved a few different noisy observations, we could in principle discuss a few different forms of the dispositional model. That is, using exactly the same model, we have three sampling processes, and so we can talk about a disposition to sample from the expected utility calculation, the probability ranking, and the value ranking. However, since the vindication relies on the ordinal rankings, and in fact Howes et al. demonstrate that many other agents who use noisy ordinal sampling will exhibit the same behavior, it seems most pertinent to focus on the ordinal observations. And since the preference reversal decision problems do not involve much or any uncertainty about which outcome will occur given which act is chosen, it's simpler to just focus on the ordinal observation of utilities as an expression of preference.

Icard's idea, in brief, is that treating credences as these dispositions sidesteps a lot of difficult issues about how credence distributions, which are massively complex, could be represented in the brain as well as reflected in our sometimes quite inconsistent behaviors. It might initially appear odd to talk about a disposition to sample without a representation of the underlying distribution from which samples are taken. But Icard brings out that this oddness relies on an incorrect understanding of how sampling works. Not only do many sampling algorithms operate without such an explicit representation, but this even applies to simple sampling machines. In his example, the Galton box (Figure 1.2) is a device where balls are dropped over a set of evenly distributed pegs through an opening which tapers outwards. Balls dropped through the Galton box land in the bottom in a pattern which approximates a Gaussian curve. Since this is a random process (more or less), each dropped ball is a sample from the Gaussian distribution. But of course nowhere is there a representation or explicit encoding of that distribution, there is just a bunch of pegs spaced evenly on a board. The lesson of this example is that there are cases where the sample is the 'real' thing, and the underlying distribution is the abstraction.

Our version of Icard's picture, then, takes exactly the same formal machinery as the structural model of Howes et al. But instead of identifying preference with the underlying, noisily observed, ordering, we identify the preference with the disposition or propensity to sample from that ordering (see Figure 1.3). This change has a few significant ramifications.

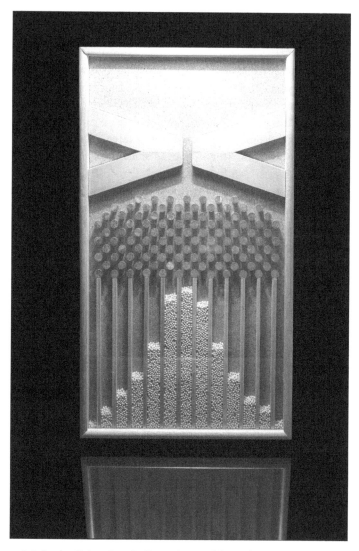

Figure 1.2 In the Galton box, balls are dropped from the top, and each ball, once it comes to rest in the slots at the bottom, acts as a sample from an approximately Gaussian distribution.
Source: Wikimedia/Matemateca (IME/USP). CC BY-SA 4.0.

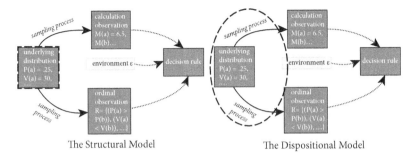

Figure 1.3 The structural and dispositional models. Heavy dashed lines locate the representation of credences and utilities. On the structural model, these are identical to the underlying distribution. In the dispositional model, utilities and credences are instead represented by a disposition to sample.

The structural model satisfied IIA, and the dispositional model does not. It might be more accurate to say that the dispositional model is not evaluable with respect to IIA, because treating the preferences as a disposition rather than an ordering means it is something of a category mistake to apply the criterion. But this is not merely a syntactic problem. Consider the fact that many sampling methods are predictably biased. An agent's disposition, and hence her actual preferences, will take into account her method of sampling. So assuming a relatively small number of samples, an agent with a propensity to use biased sampling methods will have preferences that are not particularly well described by the underlying distribution. In fact, this is the move Icard relies on to accommodate inconsistent behaviors. So even if we are allowed to find a unique ordering that reflects the disposition, that ordering would not be identical with the ordering given by the underlying distribution. Therefore, the dispositional agent does not typically meet IIA, even on a very liberal interpretation.

The structural model was intra-internally rational, in that the agent was doing its best given informational limitations. The dispositional model doesn't make use of a barrier beyond which the agent cannot 'see'. Instead, the underlying distribution is conceived of as implicit. So while it was true for the structural agent that some observer could do no better than the agent herself when it came to making decisions based on available information, this will not be true of the dispositional agent. Presumably, some ideal observer could extract the underlying distribution, given that it is implicit. Then, this observer could in some sense do better than the dispositional agent herself. In what sense could the observer do better? She could produce a consistent set of responses that reflect the performance of the dispositional agent if she was able to take *infinitely many samples*. There are some thorny issues about whether this counts as doing better by the agent's own lights, but I will tentatively suggest that it does—at least internal to the notion of sampling, if more samples in the limit does not result in 'better' behavior, something seems to have gone very wrong.

So the dispositional agent seems less rational than the structural agent in terms of consistency constraints like IIA and intra-internal rationality. But the dispositional agent has a form of rationality that the structural agent lacks. The dispositional agent always acts (or at least chooses) in a way that reflects her preferences. This is clearly false of the structural agent: the barrier trick which allowed her to preserve rationality of the other sort is her undoing here.

3. The Individuation Problem

This brings us to the problem. We have two agents, who have all of the same formal machinery. They input the same information and output the same choices according to the same mathematical operations. But we have moved the labels of 'utilities', 'credences', and 'preferences', and each agent comes along with an interpretation of what is accessible and inaccessible (this is in effect just another label, the 'barrier' that distinguishes the inner agent from the outer agent). This seemingly trivial adjustment had significant consequences for how we understand the rationality of the two agents. The classical ideal agent satisfies IIA, she is intra-internally rational, and her choices always directly reflect her preferences. The structural agent is only rational in the first two ways, and the dispositional agent only in the last way.

The problem is this. Approximate rationality accounts must answer questions like: in what way are people rational? Otherwise, they do not make good on their promises to bridge between ideal and descriptive. But in this example, we've seen how a pair of such accounts differ dramatically in how they would answer this question. So there must be a way to determine which account is correct, at least in principle. Otherwise, the question cannot be answered.

However, I'll now argue that there are serious difficulties in even imagining how we could decide between the structural and dispositional accounts in this case. In the next section, I show that this problem is not unique to this context, but generalizes within approximate rationality projects and perhaps to other domains which aim to bridge the ideal and descriptive.

I will not offer an exhaustive and conclusive argument to the effect that adjudicating between the structural and dispositional accounts is impossible: indeed, I hope that it is possible. But I will consider three avenues of evidence, and suggest some difficulties with each: normative theorizing, descriptive evidence, and theoretical virtues.

3.1 Drawing on the Purely Normative

Can we appeal to considerations in the ideal version of decision theory to decide between the two? One obvious way to do so would be if decision theory itself had an opinion about what kind of object preferences (or credences) are, such that we could compare the ideal mental objects to the non-ideal, even absent differences in behavior.

I'll now argue that ideal agents, as understood in decision theory, do not have inner workings. My argument will have two parts. First, the considerations that determine the features of an ideal agent are not such that, even in principle, they could have anything substantial to say about one set of inner workings over another. Second, since an ideal agent is merely an idealization and not an actual creature, the agent doesn't strictly speaking possess any more precise characteristics than can be specified by their theoretical role.

What do I mean by 'inner workings'? The difference in the two models in Section 2 highlights a disagreement between understanding the sampling process as part of the agent's preferences or merely a reflection of deeper preferences—a disagreement about where the preferences are in the model, rather than anything about the inputs or outputs of the agent (since these, in our example, are completely identical). More generally, descriptions of inner workings answer questions such as: how many parts does the agent have? Does she represent possibilities by numbers, symbols, or something else? Does she have a single representation of utilities, or more than one? By saying that ideal decision-theoretic agents have no inner workings, I mean that such questions have no answers or are poorly posed with respect to these agents.

To start, it's worth noting that this lack of inner workings is implied by the way ideal agents are discussed generally, and particularly in early writing on decision theory. For example, Savage (1972) introduces the decision-theoretic agent as a means to determine 'criteria for deciding among possible courses of action'. That is, the discussion of the agent is merely in service of determining standards for rational action. Ramsey (1931) likewise contrasts a notion of beliefs as real mental states knowable through introspection with one on which beliefs are merely the causes of action, concluding 'the kind of measurement of belief with which probability is concerned is not this kind [i.e. the introspectable kind] but is a measurement of belief qua basis of action' (171). Humans, then, presumably have some actual internal workings that correspond to causes of action.

But how to go from causes to reasons? In humans, these things can be far apart. For instance, Railton (2017) provides a complex set of criteria to separate 'causal-explanatory reasons' (a subset of causes) from 'putative-rationale reasons'. Railton explains how these come apart when we act without engaging our capacity to act *for* a reason and are thereby merely caused to act, which sets up a puzzle about a naturalistic account of what that capacity might be. Railton's discussion is in contrast to our ideal agent. For instance, the ideal agent never chooses to gamble just because they are feeling stressed; or opens the fridge out of habit. This creature whose actions are always determined rationally has no further sense of internal workings as causal-explanatory reasons beyond whatever provides reasons to act, since there are no merely caused actions for such an agent. The ideal decision-theoretic agent, thus, only acts when they have reason to, and only from that reason (as opposed to by accident, from pure habit, and so on) and thereby can't be said to have causal-explanatory reasons as distinct from putative-rationale reasons.[4]

Of course, in the variety of literature on decision theory, constructs such as preferences and credences are taken literally (that is, taken to designate inner workings) to various degrees. I am not aiming to argue that theorists never take the more literal stance. Instead, we should ask: do the reasons why we take decision-theoretic agents to be ideal have anything to do with inner workings? If the arguments for these agents as models of the ideal, or for certain properties being ascribed to the agents on ideal grounds, do not depend on inner workings at all, we can then conclude that these agents *as ideals* do not have inner workings. That is, if they would do their job in the ideal theory just as well without any particular inner workings, we can consider the inner workings dispensable. Let's turn to some of these arguments.

---

[4] Of course, an ideal agent can be caused to behave, where behaving designates non-intentional activity, but when they act (where action is understood to require intention), their causal-explanatory reasons are inseparable from putative-rationale reasons.

First, Dutch book arguments are a family of arguments that aim to discredit a particular version of ideal agency. The targeted agents are shown to be potential victims of a series of bad bets, such that the agent herself will agree to the bets, and that once she takes these bets, she's guaranteed to lose money. While interesting differences exist between arguments in this family, they all implicitly target any internal operations that would lead to the bad bets.

But these arguments target the downstream (hypothetical) consequences of a decision-making algorithm: what about arguments that point to an intrinsic problem? One example of such an argument comes from Joyce (2005) who sets up an example of an urn which could spit out coins that have any possible bias, and you have no information about the distribution of such biases among the coins. Joyce suggests that there is something different about your evidential situation with respect to a coin from that mysterious urn as compared to an ordinary coin, and uses this intuition to support the claim that a good theory of credal states ought to treat the two situations as requiring different epistemic responses. Unlike the Dutch book argument, this argument does not target the distal consequences of internal states but instead places a constraint on credal representations. So it should be a favorable case for someone who disagrees with my claim and holds that decision theory does actually concern itself with inner workings.

However, looking more closely, we see that what Joyce is targeting is the degree of information contained in precise credences. The problem with various precise ways of accommodating the urn example is that they represent the situation as if the agent had far more evidence than she actually had: even if the principle of indifference could give us the least informative precise credences to adopt, Joyce argues, such credences would still be far too informative. This critique, then, does not reach as far into the inner workings of the agent as it might have appeared. Informativeness of a mental representation, for an ideal agent, is *transparent*—her credences are informative with respect to distinguishing situation x from y if and only if they allow her (or someone with those credences) to in principle act differently in x than in y.

Of course, we often talk as if the inner workings of these agents are real. We say, for instance, decision-theoretic agents have two distributions, one of utilities and the other of probabilities. And especially when discussing rational credences, we abstract away from Ramsey's idea that beliefs (and degrees thereof) are just the things that make the right kind of causal contribution to action. But given that the kind of arguments we rely on for such theories are almost always indifferent to inner workings, it would be uncharitable to take this talk too literally. Instead, we should accept that the notions of utilities, probabilities, decision algorithms, and so on are in the ideal case merely *functional* at the agent level: they individuate only as finely as a function from possible environmental inputs to possible behavioral outputs. This means that any finer-grained question about two kinds of inner working that in the ideal case would amount to the same function are not answerable.

None of this should be particularly surprising, given that, for instance, we also don't think there are real differences between Turing machines and Abacus machines—two idealizations that are capable of computing exactly the same set of functions. This analogy, however, also suggests a warning with respect to the point I've made in this section. Consider the comparison between standard, deterministic Turing machines and non-deterministic Turing machines. The latter can be simulated on the former, such that the set of computable functions will be the same for both. However, this deterministic simulation massively increases the number of steps that the machine would take to compute some functions relative to the non-deterministic machine. Since these steps are really just the same steps, it seems reasonable to talk about this difference in terms of time, since any assignment of time to steps would result in the non-deterministic machine being faster. The moral of this comparison, I take it, is that even the slightest de-idealization (in this case, allowing in a very generic notion of time costs such that the same steps take the same amount of time) starts to make differences in inner workings consequential, and hence real.

Even if I've shown that ideal decision theory does not directly mandate inner workings, it might seem as though we could, for instance, measure the 'distance' between each of the two and the ideal version, and take a shorter distance to be a mark in favor. The issue with this idea is that the three elements of rationality are not obviously comparable. Is it more rational to have preferences that are consistent with each other, or to have choices that are consistent with one's preferences? These are both consistency requirements, of a sort, and it seems quite arbitrary to establish precise weights to accord them.

Further, even if such a comparison were possible, a second problem would follow: if there were pairs of rational approximation accounts, such that they differed significantly in their degree of rationality, would it really be acceptable to use this as a deciding factor or even a tiebreaker? This would entail a form of bias toward rationality that, depending on the degree of difference, could be quite substantial. There's a difficult line to walk here: the smaller the degree of difference, the less such a difference should be used to decide between theories, but the larger the degree of difference, the more problematic a rationality bias would be.

One might make the case that a rationality bias is relatively innocent. Along these lines, I once heard a proponent of this approach justify it by saying: 'is a psychological theory even an explanation if it doesn't explain why a behavior is rational?'. That is, in this domain, we might think a good explanation (often) just must be a rational explanation. In other domains, we find a preference for explanatory over non-explanatory accounts to be benign, and even optimal. So we might seek to assimilate a preference for theories on which subjects are more rational to this more general category of preference for explanatory theories. But scientific theories do not in general seek to determine *whether* things in nature should have an explanation, but *how* they can be explained. Were these theories to attempt to discover the boundaries of what should be explained, it would indeed be illegitimate to prefer explanatory theories. On the other hand, a common debate among approximate rationality accounts is which behaviors of ours are rational and which are irrational. In the background lurks a more general disagreement about whether on the whole we usually meet the standards of rationality. So it seems like positioning rational explanations as especially explanatory does not justify a preference for rationality when engaged in at least one substantial debate within approximate rationality. Thus even if we could assess whether the structural or dispositional model is more rational, we would still face obstacles in using that difference in favor of one or the other theory.

3.2 Drawing on Descriptive Data

The use of descriptive data to adjudicate between models seems more promising. Could we not, for example, identify a neural system that resembles an underlying distribution, or one that is closer to a Galton box? After all, the two accounts differ in what they claim is explicitly represented, even though they use all the same numerical machinery.

I think there is something both right and wrong with this line of thought. The correct part is that the plausibility of the dispositional model rests on empirical findings: it cannot be that the underlying distribution, a set of well-behaved relations among outcomes individuated in some suitable way, is genuinely explicitly neurally represented, since if that were the case, there would be something overly complex about relying on the disposition to explain behavior over time when we could instead talk about this tidy neural representation.

However, the structural account need not be committed to any particular explicit representation. Why not? The idea that we would find a list of outcomes with an ordering relation somehow written in the brain takes decision theory far too literally. That is, we've already seen that ideal theory is not concerned with inner workings. This means that the particular way we describe utility distributions is one out of a vast set of internal workings that function the same. There is nothing special about the one we have chosen. From this we can conclude two things: first, it would be quite surprising if we found anything like the particular conventional representation in the brain; and, second, since the criteria for identifying an 'explicit' representation of preference in the brain cannot be any finer in grain than the notion of what a preference is, there is really no support from ideal theory for thinking a so-called explicit representation is more psychologically real or even more explicit than a so-called 'implicit' one.

Thus, there is no ready account of what kind of neural finding could favor one of these accounts over the other. The fundamental problem is that these accounts deal in concepts taken from the ideal theory, and yet accord them a kind of representational commitment that cannot come along with the concept. This is not to say that these representational questions are vacuous. It's just that however much we learn about rational choice, and however much we learn about brains, we will not amass a theory of whether preferences, utilities, or credences are represented in the brain, *ceteris paribus*. What we need is a theory of preference representations, utility representations, and so on that *add* to the ideal concepts further constraints on inner workings. Empirical evidence alone cannot do this.

3.3 Drawing on Theoretical Virtues

Finally, could theoretical virtues such as simplicity, depth, and so on close this gap? Let's consider an extreme form of the structural account. We'll assume there is so much variability in human behavior that the best structural explanation is that the barrier is very opaque, and the ability to sample both limited and inconsistent. On this model, we've put so much information beyond the barrier, and allowed so little of it to be accessed that our inner agent has become quite 'small': she has little information, and her influence on decision-making is dwarfed by that of the variability in the input she receives from across the barrier. Call this the tiny agent model. It strikes me that some of the theoretical virtues count against the tiny agent model. It seems less explanatory than the original structural model, less deep, and perhaps even less parsimonious.

Conversely, imagine a version of the dispositional model that is fit to human behavior, that is very consistent and representable with a neat and unique preference ordering. This dispositional model still identifies preferences with a propensity to sample as opposed to an explicitly represented distribution, but of course the disposition now explains very little beyond what can be explained by saying that the preference ordering is represented implicitly. Presumably the best fitting dispositional model would take this agent to be using massive numbers of samples, so I'll call this the massive sampling model. Just like the tiny agent model, the massive sampling model seems unexplanatory: the variance in context that dispositions were meant to explain has been nearly eliminated. This makes the sampling algorithm itself look overly complex and unparsimonious.

The point of these two examples is this: as we move from more consistent, classical behaviors to more sporadic, variable behaviors, we see that at the extremes, theoretical virtues do make a difference. These considerations seem to favor the structural model over the dispositional at the classical and consistent end, and the dispositional over the structural at the sporadic and variable end (*ceteris paribus*). But the difference between the extremes mentioned above and the case of preference reversal shows that in this case we're somewhere in the middle of the spectrum: the documentation of preference reversals in many domains of decision-making is evidence enough that our behavior is not deeply classical, but the optimality of human choice in general would suggest we are not fully sporadic either. We can also raise an epistemic obstacle to the application of theoretical virtues. Given persistent disagreement between psychologists who think of humans as highly sporadic and those who model us as nearly perfectly rational (and everything in between), we may even be unable to locate where humans are on the spectrum of consistency, whether in the case of preference reversals or more generally. This would suggest that theoretical virtues are unlikely to provide a neat fix for our problem.

In summary, in the case of fitting ideal rational choice models to understand actual human behavior, we find that the structural model and the dispositional model are not just two theories waiting on a decisive piece of neural or psychological evidence. Because this debate rests on the representational encoding of concepts that are merely functional in their original ideal formulations, more ideal decision theory cannot help determine these representational nuances. And while some empirical evidence might help make one or both of these theories look overly complex or otherwise off, there's a wide swath of empirical possibilities that seem consistent with both. In fact, this difficulty seems to also originate in underspecification from the ideal level: the concepts we're trying to apply are just not fine-grained enough to make decisive predictions.

4. Generalizing the Problem

Is this problem unique to the current debate about preferences, or to the slightly broader one about applying ideal decision theory to psychology? I'll now suggest that the structural/dispositional divide occurs all over in different sorts of approximate rationality debates, and that at a more general level, the problem of stretching ideal concepts beyond their intended commitments also recurs in other ideal/descriptive interfaces beyond rationality.

In the context of approximate rationality, the structural and dispositional theories can be juxtaposed in a few different versions: centering on preferences, as I've developed them here, or credences, as in Icard's actual account, as well as various related permutations. In each of these cases, sampling models will have a structural and a dispositional interpretation. Further, these elements of a decision-theoretic agent are closely connected, and so it might be somewhat unnatural to adopt a structural interpretation for credences and a dispositional interpretation for utilities, for instance. Credences are also typically evaluated according to synchronic and diachronic coherence, and these properties are rationally significant. We can replace IIA, then, with a corresponding credal coherence principle: the structural model in this case explains the appearance of contextual credal change (or 'reversal') by the inaccessibility of the underlying, coherent credence function, whereas a dispositional account explains the contextual shift by appeal to features of the disposition to sample. As before, these differences would lead to evaluatively significant consequences. To simplify a bit, the issue becomes: are we sadly unable to access our true, hidden, credence function or do we have somewhat complex credences that depend on context? And we might find similar reasons on either side as well: perhaps the structural account is too humuncular, or the dispositional account insufficiently representational.

Further, cases where theorists employ sampling models could in principle always be interpreted according to the dispositional or structural model. This is because there is nothing special about the application of the model in the context we started with: sampling can always be thought of as uncovering a 'real' underlying distribution or a convenient expression of a disposition. However, the two interpretations will not always be similarly plausible: the balance can shift based on context, or on the mathematical implementation.

First, the context of application can shift the balance of plausibility away from a true impasse. For example, sampling models of various kinds have been applied to the problem of learning new theories, such that an agent is modeled as sampling from the space of possible theories during learning. In this application, the dispositional interpretation seems clearly better than the structural interpretation: it's more natural to think of the space of all possible states as implicit and merely instantiated in a disposition than to think of it as really encoded or otherwise there in the agent. This is in part because the space of possibilities is usually massively complex, but also because if it's not 'in' the agent, this space still has an independent reality. The pressure to adopt the structural model is thus reduced. Subjective preferences, on the other hand, in a sense should be in the agent if they are to be anywhere.

Second, sampling processes can have different mathematical forms, and different degrees of noise and bias. For example, comparing Slice sampling and Metropolis-Hastings sampling (two forms of Markov Chain Monte Carlo (MCMC) sampling[5]), we find that Metropolis, unlike Slice, produces results sensitive to an initial choice of step size (i.e. how far apart steps are in the random walk process, a quantity that is fixed in Metropolis but dynamic in Slice). In Metropolis, a greater share of the output will be explained by features of the algorithm rather than features of the underlying distribution. This difference makes the dispositional interpretation for Metropolis comparatively more attractive than for Slice, *ceteris paribus*.[6] Likewise, the more

---

[5] MCMC sampling is a way of taking a random walk through a potential situation and drawing an inference about the underlying features as you go. It uses linked samples that have the Markov property, that is it treats the likelihood of each next point in the walk as independent of the past conditional on the present. In these algorithms, we try to estimate the properties of an underlying distribution through many iterations of these walks. Each walk is divided into steps that go from the current location of sampling to a new one, and these two versions of MCMC differ on how these step sizes are determined.

[6] There are ways in which Metropolis differs from slice that might cut in the other direction, which I ignore here.

biased an algorithm, the greater the distance between an explanation based solely on the underlying distribution and the best explanation. Noise is a bit different than bias, however, since noise will always reduce on repeated sampling whereas some biases may remain—the structural model is at home in cases where repeated sampling gets closer and closer to the underlying disposition, since the epistemic barrier between the agent and her underlying distribution is in the simplest case increasingly eroded by the acquisition of more information. Of course, many epistemic barriers induce bias in addition to noise, but when we have either an immense amount of bias or a bias that is complex, more bells and whistles will need to be added to the structural account. So not all uses of sampling processes in approximate rationality will give rise to a troubling impasse, though in principle the pair of interpretations will be available.

Another area where ideal frameworks stop short is in modeling agents over time. Here we see a re-capitulation of the individuation problem. Most people come to want different things over time. One way to describe this is epistemic: people come to learn what they really want over time. As in the structural model, this approach takes the underlying values to be constant, but separated from the decision-maker by some sort of barrier. This is the view Richard Pettigrew (2020) calls the One True Utility Solution to the problem of choice over time. In this debate, the dispositional model could take a few different forms: we might take the relevant disposition to be so contextual so as to support talking about agents in vastly different contexts as having different values. Or we might adopt a view on which preferences are not uncovered over time, but are instead the same dispositions they always were, just leading to different behaviors in different contexts: what Pettigrew calls the Unchanging Utility Solution. Emphasizing the rational significance of this debate, the choice of what to identify as the utilities drives a choice in how to understand norms for choice in these temporal problems, the project of Pettigrew's book.

A second context where the structural/dispositional dichotomy appears is in the rational analysis of memory. Gershman (2021) lays out the memory problem as one of encoding traces that must subsequently be decoded. This is clearly a structural interpretation. The trace to be decoded is really there, it's not that we're merely disposed to come up with it in the right context. A dispositional interpretation here might be built around the constructive episodic simulation theory of memory (Addis and Schacter 2008). This account holds that rather than being encoding, episodic memories are constructions that are generated at recall. And yet, we presumably have some standing disposition to construct this or that simulation that exists over time, explaining individual constructive episodes. In this case, the two competing models can be thought of as structural and dispositional, but it would take some work to bring them under the same formalism as I have with the two models in the present chapter.

Outside of individual rationality, other contexts in which the ideal meets the descriptive include political philosophy and evolutionary science. In the former, notions such as 'justice' are sometimes formulated in a purely normative context, and then applied to actual circumstances. In the latter, an idealized model of how traits are selected for is sometimes stretched downwards to fit real natural history. It is unfortunately beyond the scope of this chapter to tackle these contexts. However, I note the abstract similarity in structure as an invitation to the reader to consider whether similar impasses may arise in these disparate domains.

The individuation problem I initially described can be formulated whenever we move from a classical representation of a distribution smoothly connected to decision-making and action, to a setting where a sampling process intercedes between the underlying distribution and the decision rule. Except at the extremes of minimal or maximal contextual variation in decision-making, both the structural and the dispositional model have claims to correctly describe the representational structure, and both will have distinct rational implications. A more general version of the problem occurs where noise is inserted between the joints of canonical representations—in these cases, including representational debates in memory and preference change, we can recognize a related structural/dispositional standoff even without the device of the sampling process.

5. Conclusion

I've presented an impasse between two ways of interpreting exactly the same formalism. These two ways are not trivially different: they entail significant differences in understanding the rationality of the agent being modeled. I've argued that purely ideal considerations are too coarse-grained to adjudicate between these competing theories, and that without a suitable criterion for applying concepts like 'preferences', empirical data will not be of any help either.

This problem illustrates the double-edged sword of the breadth of ideal, formal methods. On the one hand, the lack of constraint on internal workings is what enables decision theory to be employed as a model of agents who are composed in varied ways, giving us a way to evaluate a biology lab determining which experiments to pursue and a traffic control system under the same umbrella. On the other hand, precisely this lack of specificity opens up a gap between the sparse nature of the categories and the work we want to put them to in determining which part, if any, of an imperfect agent is the best fit. An imperfect agent is one whose operations fall short of a rational standard. But along with this, an imperfect agent almost always differs from a perfect agent in terms of internal composition: the imperfect agent's inner workings are divided into pieces that are separated by noise, and biased approximations such as sampling methods create newly distinct categories, such as the disposition to sample. To understand these imperfect agents and even to hold them up to a rational standard requires determining how their parts correspond to the parts of an ideal agent, what counts as the utilities, preferences, and credences. The dispositional and structural models are two families of such an assignment that show up all over as rival descriptions of an imperfect agent beyond the case of sampling models.

Approximate rationality is an important and perhaps even essential project. But we need a further source of constraint in order to move forward without making the mistake of fetishizing the merely notational features of our mathematical models or being lost in a sea of incomparable but distinct theories. Where could further constraints come from? Not from purely ideal analysis, nor from descriptive science alone. Instead, I want to suggest that this problem can only be solved by bringing in new considerations that are in part normative—but not fully ideally so. These normative constraints would in that sense be *sui generis* to approximate rationality. They would tell us something about efficiency, partial coherence, learning trajectories, and so on. Perhaps these constraints are even already part of our philosophical arsenal, but we have yet to recognize their character.[7]

References

Addis, Donna Rose and Daniel L. Schacter. 2008. Constructive episodic simulation: Temporal distance and detail of past and future events modulate hippocampal engagement. *Hippocampus*, 18(2):227–237.

Anderson, John R. 1990. *The adaptive character of thought*. Erlbaum.

---

[7] Thanks to audiences at York University and UT Austin, as well as Daniel Drucker, Mark Ho, Uriah Kriegel, Emily Liquin, and Tania Lombrozo.

Arrow, Kenneth J. 1951/2012. *Social choice and individual values*. Yale University Press.

Bradley, Richard. 2017. *Decision theory with a human face*. Cambridge University Press.

Davidson, David. 1980/2001. *Essays on actions and events: Philosophical essays*, Volume 1. Clarendon Press.

Dennett, Daniel C. 1988. Précis of the intentional stance. *Behavioral and Brain Sciences*, 11(3):495–505.

Eells, Ellory and William L. Harper. 1991. Ratifiability, game theory, and the principle of independence of irrelevant alternatives. *Australasian Journal of Philosophy*, 69(1):1–19.

Falkenhainer, Brian, Kenneth D. Forbus, and Dedre Gentner. 1989. The structure-mapping engine: Algorithm and examples. *Artificial Intelligence*, 41(1):1–63.

Gentner, Dedre, Sarah Brem, Ronald W. Ferguson, Arthur B. Markman, Bjorn B. Levidow, Phillip Wolff, and Kenneth D. Forbus. 1997. Analogical reasoning and conceptual change: A case study of Johannes Kepler. *The Journal of the Learning Sciences*, 6(1):3–40.

Gentner, Dedre. 2010. Bootstrapping the mind: Analogical processes and symbol systems. *Cognitive Science*, 34(5):752–775.

Gershman, Samuel J. 2021. The rational analysis of memory. *Oxford handbook of human memory*. Oxford University Press.

Gibbard, Allan. 2012. *Meaning and normativity*. Oxford University Press.

Gigerenzer, G., and R. Selten (Eds.). 2002. *Bounded rationality: The adaptive toolbox*. MIT Press.

Howes, Andrew, Paul A. Warren, George Farmer, Wael El-Deredy, and Richard L. Lewis. 2016. Why contextual preference reversals maximize expected value. *Psychological Review*, 123(4):368.

Icard, Thomas. 2016. Subjective probability as sampling propensity. *Review of Philosophy and Psychology*, 7(4):863–903.

Joyce, James M. 2005. How probabilities reflect evidence. *Philosophical Perspectives*, 19:153–178.

Kornblith, Hilary. 2002. *Knowledge and its place in nature*. Oxford University Press.

Lewis, R. L., A. Howes, and S. Singh. 2014. Computational rationality: Linking mechanism and behavior through bounded utility maximization. *Topics in Cognitive Science*, 6(2):279–311.

Markman, Andrew B. and Dedre Gentner. 1993. Structural alignment during similarity comparisons. *Cognitive Psychology*, 25(4):431–467.

Pettigrew, Richard. 2020. *Choosing for changing selves*. Oxford University Press.

Railton, Peter. 2017. At the core of our capacity to act for a reason: The affective system and evaluative model-based learning and control. *Emotion Review*, 9(4):335–342.

Ramsey, Frank P. 1931. *The foundations of mathematics and other logical essays: Number 214*. K. Paul, Trench, Trubner & Company, Limited.

Rulli, Tina and Alex Worsnip. 2016. IIA, rationality, and the individuation of options. *Philosophical Studies*, 173(1):205–221.

Savage, Leonard J. 1972. *The foundations of statistics*. Courier Corporation.

Sen, Amartya. 2017. *Collective choice and social welfare*. Harvard University Press.

Simon, Herbert A. 1955. A behavioral model of rational choice. *The Quarterly Journal of Economics*, 69(1):99–118.

Simon, Herbert A. 1990. Invariants of human behavior. *Annual Review of Psychology*, 41:1–19.

Soltani, Alireza, Benedetto De Martino, and Colin Camerer. 2012. A range-normalization model of context-dependent choice: a new model and evidence. *PLoS Computational Biology*, 8(7):e1002607.

Staffel, Julia. 2020. *Unsettled thoughts: A theory of degrees of rationality*. Oxford University Press.

2
The Average Isn't Normal
The History and Cognitive Science of an Everyday Scientific Practice

Henry M. Cowles and Joshua Knobe

Looking at the practices at work in contemporary science, one obvious and seemingly unremarkable fact is that scientists often compare data points to the *average*, i.e., to the statistical mean. This practice plays an absolutely central role in everyday statistical analysis. Indeed, it is such a commonplace part of scientific practice that it is easy to find oneself taking it for granted and not regarding it as worthy of explanation or exploration.

But now suppose we look instead at cognitive science research on the processes that take place within people's minds ordinarily as they are trying to make sense of the world. Strikingly, this research indicates that people do not ordinarily understand data points by comparing them to the statistical average. Instead, people seem to employ an importantly different notion: namely, the notion of the *normal*. As we will see, existing research suggests that this notion differs in important respects from the notion of the statistical average. That is, people's notion of the average is not a purely statistical one but also involves a key role for value judgments—judgments about whether certain things are good or bad, right or wrong.

Looking to work in the history of science, one finds a striking convergence with this research on ordinary cognition. Research in the history of science points to profound changes in scientific practices over the course of the nineteenth century. We will argue that the practice of comparing data points to the average arose as part of that much larger change. At the beginning of the nineteenth century, scientific reasoning across a range of fields often relied on notions that were *overtly* value-laden, but by the end, things had changed considerably. Innovations both statistical and social across that time period made possible an importantly different set of practices, paving the way for the self-evidence of comparing data points to the statistical mean that is now so central to scientific research.

Bringing together research in cognitive science and the history of science, this chapter argues that we should see the scientific notion of average as surprising, if not strange. Given what we know about how most people think in their everyday lives *and* how scientific researchers worked not all that long ago, the relative value-neutrality of contemporary comparison to the average is anything but normal. While it has become so common as to be almost invisible, we hope to restore this practice to visibility in order to raise new questions for history, philosophy, and cognitive science.

In what follows, we will explore some possible ways of explaining how scientists' current use of the statistical average arose when it did (a historical question) and how it is sustained in ongoing practice (a question for cognitive science). The goal is not so much to defend a specific account of the origins or sustaining conditions of this practice but just to argue that its existence should be regarded as a surprising fact, the sort of thing that calls for explanation.

Although we will be focusing specifically on questions about the average and the normal, our inquiry is clearly related to broader issues. Chief among these is the role of values in contemporary science. Decades of important work in the philosophy of science has made clear that science today is laden with values in ways that often go unacknowledged. But this stream of research may have inadvertently produced the assumption we interrogate in this chapter. By suggesting that we should find contemporary invocations of the average surprising in their relative value-neutrality, we are not arguing that science is value-free. Rather, we are opening up new space for understanding how its *relative* value-neutrality arose and is sustained in quotidian practices.

1. Two Approaches to the Study of Values in Science

Let's begin, then, by situating our exploration within a broader context in the history and philosophy of science. We will be concerned here with questions about the role of value judgments in the practice of science, but will be pursuing this question in a slightly different way from the one that has become most common within existing research. We therefore begin by drawing a distinction between the traditional approach to research on this topic (what we call the "direct approach") and the approach we will be pursuing here (which we will call the "indirect approach").

1.1 The Direct Approach

The direct approach aims to characterize the way that contemporary science actually works. Research conducted via this approach has uncovered numerous important features of contemporary science. These features have often come as a surprise to people who are not already intimately familiar with the workings of contemporary science, and in many cases, they would be extremely difficult to discern even for people who are engaged in the practice of science every day.

Work within this first approach has provided a series of powerful arguments for the claim that value judgments play an important role in contemporary science. Researchers have argued that value judgments play a role in deciding how much evidence one needs before arriving at a conclusion in a given domain (Hempel, 1965; Rudner, 1953); that some of the concepts used in social science are irreducibly value-related (e.g., Dupré, 2012); that values (help) determine how one makes sense of scientific results (Barnes, 1977); that value judgments play a role in how scientists choose between different modes of explanation (Longino, 1990); and that epistemic and non-epistemic values cannot be cleanly separated, and inevitably end up influencing each other (Kitcher, 2003). Work in this vein continues up until the present day. For a sophisticated recent discussion, see Douglas (2009).

Abstracting away from the details of the individual arguments, let's offer a brief characterization of the importance of the direct approach to values in contemporary science as a whole. Much of the work in this area provides arguments for the thesis:

(Value-Ladenness) Value judgments play an important role in contemporary science.

This thesis can be contrasted with an opposing opinion about the lack of a role for value judgments in science:

(Value-Freedom) Value judgments do not play an important role in contemporary science.

To the extent that one started out with the assumption of Value-Freedom, it would be quite surprising to read work motivating Value-Ladenness. The history of the philosophy of science suggests that this assumption was prevalent among practitioners as recently as the mid-twentieth century, and that the arguments for Value-Ladenness cited above were surprising and controversial when published (Zammito 2004). Indeed, insofar as many people presume or expect Value-Freedom, arguments for Value-Ladenness remain both surprising and important (Oreskes & Conway 2010).

We mention this direct approach to values in contemporary science only to distinguish it from the project we will be pursuing here. Our project will not contribute anything new to this first stream of research. We will not be arguing either that the contemporary scientific notion of the average is value-free or that it is value-laden. Instead, we pursue an indirect approach.

1.2 The Indirect Approach

The indirect approach aims to shed light on the workings of contemporary science by exploring *other* ways of making sense of the world, in particular by contrasting scientific cognition with ordinary, pre-scientific (or non-scientific) cognition. While such work could take a number of forms, we will be focusing especially on cognitive science and history of science.

In a certain sense, the indirect approach also reveals surprising facts about contemporary science, but it does so in a very different way. It is not that the indirect approach teaches us new facts about how contemporary science works. Rather, the indirect approach addresses the modes of thought against which contemporary science is most often compared: contemporary non-scientific thought, on the one hand, and past scientific thought on the other. By synthesizing work on adjacent modes of thinking to which contemporary science is frequently compared, we get a sense of which aspects of contemporary science call out for explanation or should even surprise us.

The best way to get a sense for this kind of research is not to describe it in general but rather to consider a prominent example. Consider work on *teleological explanation*. People tend to explain some things in terms of purposes while explaining other things in ways that do not involve purposes. In contemporary science, it is considered appropriate to explain certain objects—such as chairs or buildings—in terms of their purpose, or *telos*, while others—such as mountains or oceans—are not generally considered teleologically in this way. While philosophers of science have done good work revealing the persistence of teleological thinking in some aspects of contemporary science, it is still the case that this is one area in which scientists seem to diverge from other thinkers.

Research within cognitive science and history of science helps highlight this gap. Cognitive scientists find that non-scientists seem drawn to give teleological explanations for phenomena that scientists explain non-teleologically. For example, one finds such explanations in children, in people with Alzheimer's, and even in trained scientists when they are forced to respond under extreme time pressure (Kelemen, Rottman, & Seston, 2013; Lombrozo, Kelemen, & Zaitchik, 2007). Similarly, historians of science have shown that teleology gave way to alternatives only recently, in the life sciences and elsewhere (Lenoir, 1982; Riskin, 2016).

Taken together, this information leaves us with a very different understanding of the non-teleological explanations that are so often found in contemporary science. In other words, we might already have known that contemporary science attempts to explain the existence of mountains in ways that do not involve purposes (even if it sometimes fails). But after learning more about cognitive science and the history of science, we come to see that it is actually surprising that scientists use non-teleological explanations—and that we might want to figure out how, and why, they do so. (It is "surprising" not in the sense that it calls for vindication, but in the sense that it does not characterize pre-scientific or non-scientific modes of knowledge-acquisition.)

Our project adopts a similar approach to the use of the statistical average in contemporary science. We argue that, while values do persist in contemporary science, the widespread use of the average *as opposed to the normal* by scientists today should be regarded with more surprise than it has tended to be. Given how prominent the value-laden notion of the normal is in ordinary cognition today and in past scientific work, the relative importance of the more value-neutral statistical average calls out for more attention than it has tended to receive in recent decades.

Although our focus will be specifically on questions about the average and the normal, we will be drawing heavily on ideas from broader literatures on how contemporary science differs from other modes of thought. On one hand, we draw from the literature in cognitive science on the ways in which value judgments can impact a wide variety of different ordinary judgments. On the other, we draw from a broader literature in the history of science on the ways in which the role of value judgment in the practice of science changed over the course of the nineteenth century.

Recent work in cognitive science on the role of value judgments has shown that they have a far greater and more pervasive impact on cognition than one might initially suppose. For example, one might initially think that people's moral values would impact their judgments about a certain range of questions (questions about how to live, questions about whether agents deserve praise or blame) but that there would be plenty of questions that people answer using cognitive processes that are unaffected by moral values (e.g., straightforwardly factual questions about whether one event caused another). Of course, one would not be surprised to find occasional exceptions to this generalization. There might be various unusual circumstances in which people's value judgments do end up impacting their intuitions about what seem like purely factual questions. Still, one might expect that, for the most part, the role of value judgment would be relatively circumscribed, with value judgments having an impact on the way people think about some questions but not others.

A large body of research over the past decade or so has challenged this assumption. This research suggests that people's moral judgments can actually impact their way of thinking about a wide variety of questions that might initially appear to be purely factual or value-neutral. Such questions include: whether one event caused another (Halpern & Hitchcock, 2014; Hitchcock & Knobe, 2009; Kominsky, Phillips, Gerstenberg, Lagnado, & Knobe, 2015), whether an agent acted intentionally (Knobe, 2010), whether an agent has knowledge of a proposition (Beebe & Buckwalter, 2010), whether an agent is happy (Phillips, De Freitas, Mott, Gruber, & Knobe, 2017), whether an event is possible (Phillips & Cushman, 2017) or probable (Dalbauer & Hergovich, 2013).

Considerable controversy remains about how to explain these effects (e.g., Alicke, Rose, & Bloom, 2011; Samland & Waldmann, 2016; Uttich & Lombrozo, 2010), but we will not be weighing in on that controversy here. For our purposes, the key point is not that these effects are best explained by one or another specific cognitive process, but rather just that the effects themselves truly do exist. This point has by now been amply confirmed by a wide-ranging research program in psychology and experimental philosophy.

Historians of science have tended to highlight a similar ubiquity of value-laden notions in the scientific practices of past eras. From debates about experimentalists during the Scientific Revolution (Shapin & Schaffer, 2011 [1985]) and public enthusiasm around Enlightenment chemistry (Golinski, 1992) to the practices of Victorian physics (Smith, 1999) and even the priorities of early cognitive scientists (Cohen-Cole, 2014), historians have done a remarkable job of showing just how important value-laden concepts and indeed social values have been not just to the public position of science at different moments, but to its practices and theories as well.

Of course, these same historians have also done a good job of documenting how the role of values has *changed* over the last few centuries. While scholars hold different views on the subject, most seem to agree that a major shift toward explicit attempts to address the role of values *qua* values had increased markedly by the end of the nineteenth century (Proctor, 1991). Part of this shift in the role of values was the rise of widespread "trust in numbers" (Porter, 1995b) as well as a form of self-abnegation among scientists that has been called "mechanical objectivity" (Daston & Galison, 2007). While these and other authors are not arguing that values have completely disappeared from science today—indeed, far from it—they have laid the groundwork for an indirect approach to the relative decline of explicit appeals to value-laden notions starting in the nineteenth century.

In terms of the indirect approach, we can see in this large body of work a fundamental shift that can help explain what we see today. At the beginning of the nineteenth century, it was still common for scientific thinkers to invoke value-laden notions of divine power; by the end of the century, this was much less common in scientific circles and at the research universities that emerged over this same period (Gregory, 1992; Lenoir, 1997). This shift is perhaps clearest in Max Weber's famous essay on "Science as a Vocation," in which he argued for the separation of science and religion and insisted that "whenever the man of science introduces his personal value judgment, a full understanding of the facts ceases" (Weber 1946 [1917]). Whatever one thinks of Weber's claim, it encapsulated a view that dominated scientific thinking by the early twentieth century and that, we argue, can help us work toward an explanation of science's relative value-neutrality today.

In short, existing research provides powerful evidence for the claim that there is some important difference between the role that value judgments play in contemporary science and the role they play in ordinary cognition and in the science of earlier periods. Our aim now is to apply this more general idea to the specific case of the average and the normal.

2. The Average and Normal

It is common practice within contemporary science to compare quantities to some measure of central tendency. One can compare quantities to the median or to the mode, but the most common approach is to compare quantities to the average (the mean). Thus, when one wants to make sense of the values of a given variable, one often proceeds by representing them in terms of the degree to which they are higher or lower than the average.

To illustrate, suppose that you have collected information about how much TV certain people watched yesterday. One way to represent this information would be just to list out the raw amounts:

4 hours
0.5 hours
2.5 hours
7 hours

Another approach, however, would be to represent each amount in comparison to the average. To do this, one computes the average and then subtracts that amount from each data point. In the present example, that approach would involve transforming our four numbers as follows:

0.5 hours
−3 hours
−1 hours
3.5 hours

This transformation is referred to as "centering," and scientists use it all the time when trying to understand patterns of data.

Taking things just a little bit farther, we might then divide each number by the standard deviation. This involves transforming each number into a *z-score*:

0.2
−1.1
−0.4
1.3

This transformation is known as "standardizing" or, in a telling phrase, "normalizing." It plays an absolutely foundational role in the field of statistics as currently practiced.

Before proceeding any further, it might be helpful to emphasize that the point we are making here is very different from the kinds of points one usually finds in philosophical work on values in science. Within the existing literature, there is a tendency to focus on aspects of scientific practice that are not at all obvious and can only be revealed through serious empirical and conceptual research (e.g., Douglas, 2009). By contrast, the point we are making is one that would usually be regarded as entirely uninteresting. All we are saying is that scientists often make use of a particular statistical procedure. This procedure is widely taught in introductory statistics courses, and scientists invoke it quite explicitly all the time. No real insight or sophistication is required to see it at work.

Our aim is to show that this seemingly uninteresting aspect of contemporary science should be regarded as highly surprising and worthy of further exploration. The argument relies on a comparison between contemporary science and two other modes of thought.

2.1 Normality in Cognitive Science

To begin with, we can ask about the relationship between the precise statistical concept of the average and people's ordinary ways of making sense of the world. One possible hypothesis would be that the precise statistical concept is best understood as providing a more formal version of the sorts of notions people use in ordinary cognition. People might not ordinarily go through the steps necessary to precisely calculate the average, but they do have an intuitive sense that certain quantities are *normal*. For example, we might have an intuitive sense for the "normal amount of TV." Then we might classify other amounts in terms of their relationship to the normal ("a little bit less than normal," "far greater than normal"). So this hypothesis would be that statistical concepts just give us a more precise, formal way of spelling out these ordinary notions. Thus, one might think that a statistical concept like a z-score of 2 (i.e., two standard deviations above the mean) is best understood as simply spelling out more precisely the very same thing we might express in a vague, intuitive manner by using an expression like "much more than normal."

Recent work in cognitive science shows that this hypothesis is mistaken. People's ordinary thought does seem to include a notion of the normal that in some ways resembles a statistical measure of central tendency, but this ordinary notion appears to differ from the average in one very important respect. Specifically, recent empirical studies suggest that the ordinary (as opposed to the scientific) understanding of normality is *value-laden* (Bear & Knobe, 2017; Egré & Cova, 2015; Halpern & Hitchcock, 2014; Hitchcock & Knobe, 2009; Icard, Kominsky, & Knobe, 2017; Kominsky, Phillips, Gerstenberg, Lagnado, & Knobe, 2015; Wysocki, 2020). People's intuitions about which quantity counts as normal are not simply sensitive to their statistical beliefs—"normal" is not simply a synonym for "average"—but are also sensitive to people's beliefs about the degree to which quantities would be good or bad from a more evaluative standpoint.

To get a sense for this phenomenon, consider again the case of amounts of TV. In a recent study, one group of participants were asked to guess the average amount of TV people watch per day (a statistical judgment), while another was asked about the ideal amount of TV to watch per day (a value judgment). Unsurprisingly, participants gave a quite high amount for the average and a much lower amount for the ideal. A third group of participants was then asked about the *normal* amount of TV to watch in a day. The results show that people's judgments about the normal were not simply identical to their judgments about the average. Rather, the perceived normal amount was intermediate between the average and the ideal. This pattern of judgments did not arise only for the case of TV; it arose systematically across a wide variety of quantities, including everything from amounts of exercise for a person to do in a week to percentages of students to be bullied in a middle school (Bear & Knobe, 2017). The pattern as a whole suggests that people's notion of the normal is shaped by a mixture of statistical and evaluative considerations.

This same basic effect has emerged in studies using many other methodologies. For example, another study showed that participants' judgments about whether a particular political view was normal do not depend only on the statistical prevalence of that view. Rather, each participant's judgment depends in part on whether that participant regards the view itself as good or bad (Wysocki, 2020).

Difficult questions arise about precisely how people integrate statistical judgments and value judgments into an overall judgment of normality. It is clear that people's ordinary notion of normality somehow brings together judgments about what is statistically average with judgments about what is evaluatively ideal, but it is not yet clear exactly how to understand this more integrated notion. Yet, regardless of how these difficult questions are resolved, it seems that the scientific concept of the average is importantly different from the ordinary notion of normality. Perhaps it can be shown that value judgments play some role in people's way of understanding the average, but they do not seem to play the role that is characteristic of normality judgments. To the extent that a person has the relevant knowledge, she can take a list of numbers and, without making any further value judgment, calculate the average using a straightforward mathematical procedure.

With this framework in place, let's consider again people's ordinary ways of comparing quantities to a standard. To say that a quantity counts as (for example) "large" or "small," we need to compare the quantity in question to some standard (Kennedy, 2013). But what standard do people use? One obvious hypothesis would be that people compare quantities to the average. For example, it might be thought that people would see someone as watching a "large amount of TV" when the amount that person watches is sufficiently above the average (say, anything higher than $z = 1$). However, existing studies suggest that this is not the case. Instead, people seem to regard a quantity as large when it is larger than their undifferentiated representation of the *normal* (Egré & Cova, 2015). Thus, the threshold one needs to surpass to count as watching a "large amount of TV" is not the statistical average but a value-laden notion of the normal (Bear & Knobe, 2017). Similar effects have been observed for numerous other psychological phenomena. The notion of normality has been implicated in people's intuitions about prototypicality, causation, and even the folk-biological concept of innateness (Barsalou, 1985; Bear & Knobe, 2017; Icard et al., 2017; Knobe & Samuels, 2013; Kominsky et al., 2015). In all of these cases, studies show that people's intuitions are not shaped solely by statistical considerations. Rather, people's intuitions appear to be shaped in each case by a mixture of statistical and evaluative considerations. Thus, the available evidence suggests that people's integrated statistical/evaluative notion of normality plays a pervasive role in cognition.

These facts about people's ordinary understanding give us reason to adopt a different view of the scientific practice of comparing data points to the average. This concept plays such an important role in our scientific practices that it is easy to take it for granted, and it might be difficult to see this concept as involving any kind of important innovation. However, existing studies suggest that the concept of an average actually involves a fundamental departure from people's ordinary mode of thought.

2.2 Normality in the History of Science

To understand how the descriptive notion of the average departs from the evaluative notion of the normal, it is instructive to study not only how far apart they are in the present, but also how they came apart in the past. As with the case of cognitive science, history suggests that ideas about normality in contemporary science are *relatively* value-free and should be regarded as surprising, given the value-laden history of their usage and development in the nineteenth century.

Historians of science have highlighted stages in the history of normality, from the early development of "political arithmetic" in the seventeenth century (Deringer, 2018) through the advent of classical probability in the eighteenth century (Daston, 1988) and the rise of statistical thinking in the nineteenth century (Porter, 1986). In 1800, depending on the field you were in and the questions you asked, it might have made sense to invoke value-laden ideas of "normality" when describing the natural world, but by 1900 a more value-neutral statistical notion of "the average" had taken over in most fields. This transformation occurred in different ways in different areas, but the general trend was to invoke a value-neutral meaning of "normal" as part of a more general movement to scrub values from science. Ian Hacking has called this process "the taming of chance": that is, the separation of statistical terms for describing the world from value judgments of (and value-laden terms for) whatever was being described (Hacking, 1990).

It can be instructive to review a specific case. Evaluative and descriptive meanings of "normality" were intertwined in the field of medicine during the nineteenth century. Physicians held "the normal state" to be a healthy one—bodies operating at a temperature and a rhythm conducive to the functions of whatever organ or organism was being observed. The opposite of "the normal," as Georges Canguilhem famously showed, was "the pathological," and in this context it was clear that one was to be preferred and one avoided (1991 [1943]). In medicine, this value-laden meaning has stuck with "normality." This persistence is illustrated by the common question: "Doc, is this normal?" A positive answer is calming, a negative one cause for concern. According to Canguilhem, this value-laden sense of "normality" is inevitable in both medicine and physiology. "It seems to us," he concluded, "that physiology has better to do than to search for an objective definition of the normal, and that is to recognize the original normative character of life" (Canguilhem 1991 [1943]: 177).

Even if the value-laden meaning of "normal" played an important role in medicine through the twentieth century (Wellman, 1958) up to the present (Manrai et al., 2018), its importance and role changed during the nineteenth century. The rise of "scientific medicine" meant, in part, aspirational identification with an approach to the "normal" that was increasingly statistical alone. Whether or not this was achieved (Tiles, 1993), normality's evolving meaning produced tension and debate in the changing medical landscape of the nineteenth century.

One way to trace this is in the development of so-called "normal curves" and their application to human affairs. The use of "normal curves" originated with Pierre-Simon Laplace and Johann Carl Friedrich Gauss, two mathematicians who plotted the distribution of observations of a given data point in order to reduce error and arrive at the true value. The original "normal curve" was thus a plot of human errors, not of natural phenomena. Gradually, however, this pattern was reimagined as a part of nature itself—the distribution of observational errors was transposed onto the things that were being observed, natural and human alike (Hacking, 1990).

It was Francis Galton (1895) who argued that the "normal curve" captured something out there in the real world, and in his hands descriptive statistics was joined to probability theory and the mathematical prediction of complex patterns (Porter, 1986). This marriage of statistics and mathematics, achieved during the nineteenth century, seemed to help scientists separate the descriptive and evaluative senses of "normal." If "the normal heart" still meant the one that pumped blood like it should, it also became possible for it to mean something else: the average heart, which in a given population (under specific stresses) might actually be a poor pump indeed. Galton's status as a leader of the eugenics movement (a term he coined) and a scientific racist make his attention to the role of values in science especially significant. While historians have done well to highlight how thoroughly his scientific program was shot through with often deplorable values (Kevles, 1985), this has in some ways obscured his *simultaneous* role in separating out the average and the normal in the day-to-day statistical practices that were quickly adopted in a range of scientific fields.

Importantly, scientific authors recognized early on that the term "normal" blurred the very boundary they sought to shore up. This applied both to particular data on distribution curves and to those curves themselves. Thus, in 1920 Pearson could invoke "the *normal* curve, which name, while it avoids an international question of priority, has the disadvantage of leading people to believe that all other distributions of frequency are in one sense or another 'abnormal'" (Pearson, 1920: 25). Pearson worried about how descriptive and evaluative notions of "normal" ran together.

Here we see the emergence of statistical "curve fitting" in two competing senses. First, there is the sense pursued by Pearson: the effort to fit statistical curves to the data at hand. Second, however, there is another sense: the effort to fit the data themselves to an idealized "normal" curve. This latter sense is controversial, of course. Its most persistent critic was Michel Foucault, a student of Canguilhem. Foucault argued that the term "normal" carried with it a value-laden weight that had the power to shape the contexts in which it was used, even if those who wielded the term insisted it had only statistical meaning. Over the course of the nineteenth century, this power increased as ideas of "normality" were enforced in places like hospitals, schools, and—most famously—prisons (Foucault, 1977 [1975]). It was to Foucault that scholars like Porter and (more explicitly) Hacking looked as they unearthed the moral history of "normal" in statistics and everyday life.

Subsequent work in this vein has proven Pearson's worries correct. Confusion about what "normal" means continued well into the twentieth century. Public opinion polls, for example, built "the average American" out of values associated with American-ness in the early to mid-twentieth century (Igo, 2007). Other, related developments confirm this continued confusion. The rise of "normal controls" in biomedical research, for example, were *meant* to be "average" but came with their own assumptions about ideal body types and the generalizability of male bodies (Stark, forthcoming). Such studies highlight how difficult it has been to separate the evaluative and descriptive aspects of "normality"—which has led some, echoing Canguilhem, to insist that there is no such distinction in any meaningful sense (Sholl, 2017).

And yet, something *did* change in the nineteenth century. This can be illustrated by the gradual success of applying statistical methods to the interpretation of social issues. At the start of the nineteenth century, the idea that human behaviors—including crime and suicide—were regular or predictable seemed to challenge the idea of free will (Porter, 1986). In part, this was because laws like those governing astronomical phenomena were thought to be divine expressions of an ideal order (hence the very notion of "law"). How could this hold true of suicide? Adolphe Quetelet (1835) broke the taboo idea of laws governing human behavior in the 1830s, but he did so by applying such laws only to "the average man" (*l'homme moyen*), not to individual men. This idea, perhaps ironic, shielded Quetelet and his "social physics" from charges of immorality and blasphemy (Porter, 1985, 1995a). But the door was open for purportedly value-free tools to be used on the ultimate value-laden object: society itself.

By the end of the century, Emile Durkheim could dispense with Quetelet's circumspection. In his canonical study, *Suicide* (2002 [1897]), he attributed regularities in this tragic behavior to the "normal" distribution of happiness and family values, with "normal" encompassing both positive and negative emotions. While this may *seem* value-laden—and in certain ways, it surely was—it is important to note that Durkheim was able to describe a "normal" rate of suicide without running afoul of ideas about divine laws or seeming to imply that suicide was "good." It was a distribution, he could argue, and nothing more. What is surprising is that, eventually, people agreed.

Galton took this one step further. If Quetelet and Durkheim had made it possible to include both good and bad under the "normal" umbrella, Galton claimed to identify "normal" ranges that were *only* bad. As one of the founders of the eugenics movement, Galton saw something like "normal intelligence" as decidedly less than ideal. Being "only average" was something to be improved upon (Hacking, 1990). Thus, by the end of the nineteenth century it was possible not only to imagine "the normal" as a descriptive, rather than evaluative, claim, but even to imagine it as evaluative *in a new sense*—as less than you might hope for, assuming you wanted to fall further down the curve.

The point is that, by 1900, the meaning of "normal" had bifurcated. While "normal" still implied—and indeed, still implies (Metzl & Kirkland, 2010)—a value judgment about bodily health, it could also indicate something like "average." Then, as now, the task was to distinguish between the two in scientific contexts, such that statistical tools could be applied for descriptive purposes without introducing (or seeming to introduce) value judgments that, by then, seemed to have no place in science. While we can identify breaches of these standards today, it is worth noting their emergence as a means of indirectly analyzing the role of values in contemporary science by comparison with their historical role.

2.3 Summary and Interim Conclusion

Within contemporary science, we find a practice of "normalizing" data that involves comparing each data point to the mean. This aspect of contemporary science might at first seem perfectly straightforward, but we have argued that it contrasts sharply with what is found in other modes of thought. Both in people's ordinary intuitions and in earlier periods in the history of science, we find a notion of normality that is determined by a mixture of statistical and evaluative considerations. The idea of comparing each data point to a level determined by purely statistical considerations, we have suggested, is best understood as a striking innovation, first introduced in the nineteenth century.

So then, what implications might this claim have for the study of contemporary science? One possible answer would be that we could use it as an additional piece of evidence within the kind of inquiry that is already quite well-established in the philosophy of science literature. As noted above, research in this area has uncovered numerous subtle ways in which value judgments play a role in scientific practice. In keeping with this tradition, we might now try to uncover a subtle yet important respect in which contemporary science actually *does* use a value-laden notion of normality. For example, existing work in the philosophy of psychiatry has wrestled with how to understand the notion of normality used within psychiatry and whether this notion is best understood as a value-laden one (see, e.g., Washington, 2016). Perhaps a study of value-laden notions of normality within other modes of thought could help to illuminate some of the difficult issues that arise here.

Now, one possible view would be that it is only when we begin investigating these more subtle aspects of scientific practice that our inquiry truly becomes philosophically interesting. After all, it was perfectly obvious all along that scientists often normalize their data by comparing each data point to the mean. The more interesting question, one might think, is whether scientists sometimes depart from this straightforward statistical procedure and begin employing a more value-laden notion.

There is certainly something right in this view, but we have been trying to show that there is also something right in going against it. In a certain sense, it is not surprising at all that scientists sometimes make use of a value-laden notion of normality. If we discover, e.g., that the practice of psychiatry involves comparing each person to a value-laden standard that is intermediate between the statistical average and the prescriptive ideal, we are basically just discovering that psychiatrists do the same thing that people do all the time. They are human, after all.

As such, it is remarkable that scientists even come close to normalizing data using statistics alone. For example, it should be seen as remarkable that scientists are able to consider a person who watches four hours of TV per day and think of the quantity not as "higher than the normal" but rather "about average." In doing this, they are engaged in a practice that involves a very serious departure from ordinary cognition and earlier forms of scientific thought. Somehow scientists are able to use a set of procedures that makes it possible for them to compare each data point to a standard that is derived simply by considering the statistical distribution of the data and does not take into account the degree to which various quantities are good or bad.

3. Explaining Use of the Statistical Average

We have been arguing for a change in perspective about what should be taken for granted and what calls for explanation. An obvious view would be that we can simply take for granted the fact that people sometimes compare data points to the average, and that the only thing that calls for explanation is the fact that people sometimes compare data points to a value-laden notion of the normal. We have argued against that view. In its place, we argued for a view on which the fact that people ever compare data points to the statistical average is what calls for explanation. We now ask what that explanation might be.

The thing that requires explanation here is a certain sort of divergence between the practices found in systematic scientific research today and the processes found in people's more intuitive, ordinary cognition or in past scientific research. We will be taking up the effort to explain that divergence on two different levels. On a *historical* level, we want to understand how scientific practice diverged in this way from people's ordinary understanding. Then, at a more *contemporary* level, we want to understand the processes that sustain that divergence today.

Clearly, the questions we are taking up here touch on some extremely abstract issues about the relationship between complex practices sustained by large-scale institutions and the ordinary intuitions generated by cognitive processes that take place within individual human minds. Our question is about one specific case in which the two appear to diverge, and in what follows, we will be focusing entirely on this one specific case. Still, a close examination of this one case has some potential to shed light on the more general issue.

While there are many strands of existing research—both historical and cognitive—that can help explain the divergence in this specific case, no single explanation dominates. In what follows, we explore a number of different plausible accounts of this divergence that could contribute to the indirect approach to values in contemporary science toward which we are pointing.

3.1 Diachronic: How the Average Took Over

Our first question is historical. As our case study shows, scholars have documented a change over the course of the nineteenth century—a shift in invocations of "the normal," away from a value-laden notion to something more like the statistical average. However, this account was purely descriptive. That is, our claim was simply that, with respect to normality, the role of values that one finds at the beginning of the nineteenth century differs from the one found at century's end. But one might pose a deeper question: *why* did scientific practice change in this way?

We have already seen two approaches to answering such a question. One is political: Porter, for example, argued that the rise of quantification was less about its scientific superiority and more about the *political* power of statistical arguments. Applied to explain the changing meaning of "the normal," this approach would link increasing references to the statistical mean to the rise of a "trust in numbers" within political culture. The other is epistemological: Daston & Galison's "mechanical objectivity" stemmed from the impact of Kant's account of the limits of human knowledge. In order to extend this claim to our specific case, Daston & Galison might link the rise of the statistical mean (and the fall of more value-laden notions of normality) to a broader distrust of the individual as the source of knowledge of ultimate causes. Both approaches would link the shift we have documented to shifts in political or epistemological attitudes in the broader culture.

Of course, one could also look more narrowly at how practices and pedagogy themselves were changing in this period. For example, the relative reduction in value-ladenness could be linked to technological shifts. The development and spread of tabulating machines, mechanical calculators, and other aids to computation during the nineteenth century would have made the statistical mean of large datasets easier to compute and, eventually, practically ready to hand. Indeed, even the *dream* of such machines played a role in how the human mind was understood and the value placed on a range of scientific practices (Jones, 2016). The spread of what Ursula Klein has called "paper tools"—including specific inscription practices and mathematical formulae shared by communities of researchers—no doubt helped make arriving at the statistical mean not only easier but also a matter of course as researchers performed specific computations without thinking twice (Klein, 2001). Such technological shifts explain how value-laden notions of normality could give way to more statistical notions *without* requiring recourse to the kinds of conscious rejection of values implied by the political and epistemological shifts traced above.

Changes in *publishing* would also have contributed to the shift we are exploring. From the rise of the scientific journal as a specific site for publishing (Csiszar, 2018) to the development of peer review and other mechanisms for standardizing practices in the field (Baldwin, 2015), methods such as comparing data points to the mean and—eventually—computing z-scores would have become expected elements of the scientific paper, a genre that was gradually taking more or less its modern form. The same goes for calls for replicability in the sciences. As replication became central to adjudicating matters of trust and truth, notions of "the normal" that depended upon unarticulated values would have been less acceptable than those (supposedly) shorn of those values and limited to comparisons one's colleagues could repeat with their own pen and paper (Cantor & Shuttleworth, 2004; Fyfe, 2012). As science came to be seen as "out there," embodied in journals and groups but not in individuals, it also came to be seen as natural—and, thus, in the minds of many, value-free (Cowles, 2017). It is easy to see how the standardization of publishing forms would have naturalized procedures like comparing data to a statistical mean and denaturalized the reliance on value-laden notions of "the normal."

The same goes, to take one final example, for changes in scientific training in particular and science education in general. Scholars have shown how a new secularism in university education (Reuben, 1996) and debates over the place of science in such a context (Jewett, 2012) paved the way for the decline in value-ladenness we have sketched. From the rise of state-based science curricula in the nineteenth century to the so-called "general science" movement in the early twentieth century, there emerged a felt need for the kind of standardized practices that anyone could replicate on the way to gaining familiarity with scientific fields or specific scientific credentials (Rudolph, 2005a, 2005b; White, 2003). One notion that gained traction during this shift was the idea of a single, shared scientific method based on hypothesis testing (Cowles, 2020), which went on to structure how basic scientific norms have been taught to children ever since (Rudolph, 2019). Something similar may well have occurred with regard to the question of comparing data to the average, such that—by the turn of the twentieth century—the performance of such computations became definitional for rigorous science. Such an explanation could also help explain why this practice became, for practitioners but relatively rare among others: by *identifying* science with such a practice, other ways of imagining "the normal" would be allowed to persist in areas (including everyday life) not held to the same standard.

In presenting these three specific hypotheses from the work of others, we certainly don't mean to suggest that we already have in hand a complete and accurate explanation of the change over time in the role that value judgments play in science in general or the rise of statistical notions of the average in particular. Rather, we present these hypotheses to illustrate the sorts of ideas that might be pursued in further work. Specifically, these explanations would help texture the larger scale accounts of the rise of objectivity (understood as a means of limiting human subjectivity) over the last two centuries (e.g., Daston & Galison, 2007; Porter, 1995b).

3.2 Synchronic: How the Average Is Enforced

Another question arises about how to understand the ways in which this departure from other modes of thought is sustained within the day-to-day practice of science. Given that people's ordinary intuitive mode of thought seems to involve comparing data points to the normal, the use of the statistical average—and other relatively technical mathematical practices—is neither natural nor pre-ordained. Anthropologists have shown how the decision to use such techniques is just that—a *decision*, one that is socially inflected and community based (Carraher et al., 1985; Lave, 1986). How are such decisions made and what are the structures that enable and enforce them?

One possible view would be that this phenomenon is to be explained in large part in terms of cognitive processes taking place *within the minds of individual scientists*. In existing work on other phenomena, it has often been suggested that even trained scientists retain the same intuitions found in non-scientists but that they are able to override these intuitions and rely instead on a process of more controlled conscious reasoning (Kelemen, Rottman, & Seston, 2013; Shtulman & Valcarcel, 2012). A similar process might explain scientists' thinking about the average and the normal. Perhaps scientists have an intuitive tendency to compare data points to the normal, but they are sometimes able to override this tendency and instead compare data points to the statistical average. Of course, this type of overriding can only take us so far. Scientists are human beings, and they will inevitably be guided in many cases by more ordinary modes of thought. Still, even if scientists only occasionally override their ordinary way of applying value judgments, this occasional occurrence should be seen as a remarkable and deeply important aspect of scientific practice.

A second possible factor would be the role of *technology* in sustaining divergences from ordinary thought. Contemporary scientific work involves a complex interplay between individual scientists' minds and external technologies. Indeed, scientific work always has. But the nature of that relationship has shifted over time, and specific practices that were once done by hand have been offloaded to technologies like computers, with major consequences for the nature of scientific thinking. An obvious hypothesis would be that it is in part this interplay that more generally makes possible certain kinds of divergence from more ordinary modes of thought. Perhaps this type of hypothesis can also explain people's use of the statistical average.

At the most basic level, there is the fact that people do not need to calculate the average in their heads; they can do the calculations using a pencil and paper. Thus, a person might determine that a given data point is above the average, but the process used to make that determination does not take place entirely within the person's own head. Rather, the determination is a product of an interplay between processes taking place within the person's head and processes taking place in an external technology (the pencil and paper). In this way, the process of comparing data points to the statistical average is quite different from the process usually used to determine whether something falls above or below the normal.

But of course, in much work within contemporary science, the reliance on external technology is far more extensive. For example, to calculate a correlation coefficient, one needs to compare each data point to the average, but it is not as though scientists typically go through this process using pencil and paper. Almost always, the process is executed by a computer, and on many occasions, the scientists aren't thinking at all about the actual computations the computer is carrying out. The result is a striking divergence between what is happening within science and what is happening within the heads of individual scientists. Science relies on a procedure that involves comparing data points to the average, but this does not mean that there needs to be any process at all in which individual scientists compare data points to the average in their own heads.

Third, and perhaps most importantly, there is the *social* character of science. Scientific progress is not usually the product of an individual scientist working in isolation. Instead, scientists typically work in teams, and there is usually a structure set up such that each team will not be successful unless its work is accepted by other teams. An individual scientist may have her own cherished values, but she will also be embedded in a larger structure that is set up in such a way that her work cannot succeed without the blessing of various other people, many of whom will have quite different values.

Suppose now that each individual scientist has certain values but that different scientists have different values. Each individual scientist might show a tendency to develop an understanding of the normal that is deeply informed by her own values, but as long as other scientists do not share those values, the social character of science may lead to an outcome in which her published work is not simply a reflection of her own tendencies. Thus, even if each individual scientist shows a tendency to use something like the ordinary notion of the normal, science as a whole might be drawn toward practices that more closely approximate a purely statistical notion of the average.

Finally, we might consider hypotheses that combine a number of these factors together. One of the most appealing such hypotheses would be that (a) there is a mechanism within the minds of individual scientists that allows them to use a purely statistical notion of the average; but that (b) this mechanism is created or sustained by a process that requires either external technology or the social character of science.

To give a simple analogy, studies have shown that people who frequently do arithmetic by using an abacus eventually acquire the ability to do arithmetic in their minds using what is called a "mental abacus" (Frank & Barner, 2012). In much the same way, it might be that people first acquire the ability to think in terms of a purely statistical average either by using technology or by relying on the social character of science. However, as people continue using this method, it might be that they eventually come to be able to conceptualize things in a purely statistical way even without relying in the moment on either extra technology or external social connections. The extent to which scientists actually are able to do this is, of course, an open and very interesting empirical question.

4. Conclusion

Our inquiry has been concerned with the practice of comparing data points to the statistical average. We have argued that evidence from cognitive science and from the history of science gives us reason to regard this practice as highly surprising. The fact that this practice exists at all should be seen as something that calls for explanation, and we have sketched a number of possible ways to explain it.

Although we have focused very narrowly just on questions about the use of the statistical average, the approach introduced here could potentially be applied to numerous other problems. To give just one example, consider the notion of *essence*. Work on contemporary science suggests that scientists might make use of a notion of "causal essentialism," in which essences are understood as hidden factors that causally explain observable features (Putnam, 1975). But within work in the cognitive science of ordinary judgments and in the history of science, there is growing evidence of a more value-laden notion of essentialism (for cognitive science evidence, see Bailey, Knobe, & Newman, forthcoming, Gelman & Rhodes, 2012, Newman & Knobe, 2018; for historical evidence, see Daston & Galison, 2007; Dear, 2014; Hacking, 2007; Müller-Wille, 2013). Thus, there is at least some reason to think that we might face a real question as to why the understanding of essence at work in contemporary science departs from people's ordinary understanding of essence.

More generally, there is immense potential for convergence between, on the one hand, work on values in contemporary science and, on the other, work on values in ordinary cognition and on their role in the history of science. A key task now will be to bring those two literatures together. Looking across a whole range of different concepts, we need to explore the ways in which the role of value in contemporary science might depart from the role of value in other modes of thinking. Ultimately, then, our inquiry into the average and the normal is perhaps best understood as a model for the indirect approach to values in contemporary science.[1]

References

Alicke, M. D., Rose, D., & Bloom, D. (2011). Causation, norm violation, and culpable control. *Journal of Philosophy*, 108, 670–696.

Bailey, A. H., Knobe, J., & Newman, G. E. (forthcoming). Value-based essentialism: Essentialist beliefs about social groups with shared values. *Journal of Experimental Psychology: General*.

Baldwin, M. C. (2015). *Making Nature: The History of a Scientific Journal*. University of Chicago Press.

Barnes, B. (1977). *Interests and the Growth of Knowledge*. Routledge.

Barsalou, L. W. (1985). Ideals, central tendency, and frequency of instantiation as determinants of graded structure in categories. *Journal of Experimental Psychology: Learning, Memory, and Cognition*, 11(4), 629.

---

[1] We are very grateful to Kathryn Tabb, Alexander Klein, and Uriah Kriegel for their comments on previous drafts.

Bear, A., & Knobe, J. (2017). Normality: Part descriptive, part prescriptive. *Cognition*, 167, 25–37.

Beebe, J. R., & Buckwalter, W. (2010). The epistemic side-effect effect. *Mind & Language*, 25, 474–498.

Canguilhem, G. (1991 [1943]). *The Normal and the Pathological*. Zone Books.

Cantor, G. N., and Shuttleworth, S. eds. (2004). *Science Serialized: Representations of the Sciences in Nineteenth-Century Periodicals*. MIT Press.

Carraher, T. N., et al. (1985). Mathematics in the streets and in schools. *British Journal of Developmental Psychology*, 3, 21–29.

Cohen-Cole, J. (2014). The open mind. In *The Open Mind*. University of Chicago Press.

Cowles, H. M. (2017). History naturalized. *Historical Studies in the Natural Sciences*, 47(1), 107–16.

Cowles, H. M. (2020). *The Scientific Method: An Evolution of Thinking from Darwin to Dewey*. Harvard University Press.

Csiszar, A. (2018). *The Scientific Journal: Authorship and the Politics of Knowledge in the Nineteenth Century*. University of Chicago Press.

Dalbauer, N., & Hergovich, A. (2013). Is what is worse more likely? The probabilistic explanation of the epistemic side-effect effect. *Review of Philosophy and Psychology*, 4, 639–657.

Daston, L. (1988). *Classical Probability in the Enlightenment*. Princeton University Press.

Daston, L., & Galison, P. (2007). *Objectivity*. Zone Books.

Dear, P. (2014). Darwin's sleepwalkers: Naturalists, nature, and the practices of classification. *Historical Studies in the Natural Sciences*, 44, 297–318.

Deringer, W. P. (2018). *Calculated Values: Finance, Politics, and the Quantitative Age*. Harvard University Press.

Douglas, H. (2009). *Science, Policy, and the Value-Free Ideal*. University of Pittsburgh Press.

Dupré, J. (2012). The inseparability of science and values. *Drunk on Capitalism: An Interdisciplinary Reflection on Market Economy, Art and Science* (pp. 13–24). Springer.

Durkheim, E. (2002 [1897]). *Suicide: A Study in Sociology*. Routledge.

Egré, P., & Cova, F. (2015). Moral asymmetries and the semantics of many. *Semantics and Pragmatics*, 8, 13–1.

Foucault, M. (1977 [1975]). *Discipline and Punish: The Birth of the Prison*. Pantheon Books.

Frank, M. C., & Barner, D. (2012). Representing exact number visually using mental abacus. *Journal of Experimental Psychology: General*, 141, 134.

Fyfe, A. (2012). *Steam-Powered Knowledge: William Chambers and the Business of Publishing, 1820–1860*. University of Chicago Press.

Galton, F. (1895). A new step in statistical science. *Nature*, 51, 319.

Gelman, S. A., & Rhodes, M. (2012). Two-thousand years of stasis: How psychological essentialism impedes evolutionary understanding. *Evolution Challenges: Integrating Research and Practice in Teaching and Learning about Evolution*, 1–26.

Golinski, J. (1992). The chemical revolution and the politics of language. *The Eighteenth Century*, 33(3), 238–251.

Gregory, F. (1992). *Nature lost? Natural science and the German theological traditions of the nineteenth century*. Harvard University Press.

Hacking, I. (1990). *The Taming of Chance*. Cambridge University Press.

Hacking, I. (2007). Natural kinds: Rosy dawn, scholastic twilight. *Royal Institute of Philosophy Supplement*, 61, 203–239.

Halpern, J. Y., & Hitchcock, C. (2014). Graded causation and defaults. *The British Journal for the Philosophy of Science*, 66(2), 413–457.

Hempel, C. (1965). Science and human values. *Aspects of Scientific Explanation and other Essays in the Philosophy of Science* (pp. 81–96). New York: The Free Press.

Hitchcock, C., & Knobe, J. (2009). Cause and norm. *Journal of Philosophy*, 106(11), 587–612.

Icard, T. F., Kominsky, J. F., & Knobe, J. (2017). Normality and actual causal strength. *Cognition*, 161, 80–93.

Igo, S. E. (2007). *The Averaged American: Surveys, Citizens, and the Making of a Mass Public*. Harvard University Press.

Jewett, A. (2012). *Science, Democracy, and the American University: From the Civil War to the Cold War*. Cambridge University Press.

Jones, M. L. (2016). *Reckoning with Matter: Calculating Machines, Innovation, and Thinking about Thinking from Pascal to Babbage*. University of Chicago Press.

Kelemen, D., Rottman, J., & Seston, R. (2013). Professional physical scientists display tenacious teleological tendencies: Purpose-based reasoning as a cognitive default. *Journal of Experimental Psychology: General*, 142(4), 1074.

Kennedy, C. (2013). *Projecting the Adjective: The Syntax and Semantics of Gradability and Comparison*. Routledge.

Kevles, D. (1985). *In the Name of Eugenics: Genetics and the Uses of Human Heredity*. Knopf.

Kitcher, P. (2003). *Science, Truth, and Democracy*. Oxford University Press.

Klein, U. (2001). Paper tools in experimental cultures. *Studies in History and Philosophy of Science Part A*, 32(2), 265–302.

Knobe, J. (2010). Person as scientist, person as moralist. *Behavioral and Brain Sciences*, 33, 315–329.

Knobe, J., & Samuels, R. (2013). Thinking like a scientist: Innateness as a case study. *Cognition*, 126(1), 72–86.

Kominsky, J. F., Phillips, J., Gerstenberg, T., Lagnado, D., & Knobe, J. (2015). Causal superseding. *Cognition*, 137, 196–209.

Lave, J. (1986). The values of quantification. *The Sociological Review Monograph*, 32(2), 88–111.

Lenoir, T. (1982). *The Strategy of Life: Teleology and Mechanics in Nineteenth-Century German Biology*. University of Chicago Press.

Lenoir, T. (1997). *Instituting science: The cultural production of scientific disciplines*. Stanford University Press.

Lombrozo, T., Kelemen, D., & Zaitchik, D. (2007). Inferring design: Evidence of a preference for teleological explanations in patients with Alzheimer's disease. *Psychological Science*, 18, 999–1006.

Longino, H. E. (1990). *Science as Social Knowledge: Values and Objectivity in Scientific Inquiry*. Princeton University Press.

Manrai, A. K., Patel, C. J., & Ioannidis, J. P. A. (2018). In the era of precision medicine and big data, who is normal? *Journal of the American Medical Association*, 319(19), 1981–1982.

Metzl, J., & A. Kirkland. (2010). *Against Health: How Health Became the New Morality*. NYU Press, USA.

Müller-Wille, S. (2013). Systems and how Linnaeus looked at them in retrospect. *Annals of Science*, 70(3), 305–317.

Newman, G. E., & Knobe, J. (2019). The essence of essentialism. *Mind & Language*. 34, 585–605.

Oreskes, N., & Conway, E. M. (2010). *How a Handful of Scientists Obscured the Truth on Issues from Tobacco Smoke to Global Warming*. Bloomsbury Press.

Pearson, K. (1920). Notes on the history of correlation. *Biometrika*, 13(1), 25–45.

Phillips, J., & Cushman, F. (2017). Morality constrains the default representation of what is possible. *Proceedings of the National Academy of Sciences*, 114, 4649–4654.

Phillips, J., De Freitas, J., Mott, C., Gruber, J., & Knobe, J. (2017). True happiness: The role of morality in the folk concept of happiness. *Journal of Experimental Psychology: General*, 146, 165.

Porter, T. M. (1985). The mathematics of society: Variation and error in Quetelet's statistics. *The British Journal for the History of Science*, 18(1), 51–69.

Porter, T. M. (1986). *The Rise of Statistical Thinking, 1820–1900*. Princeton University Press.

Porter, T. M. (1995a). Statistical and social facts from Quetelet to Durkheim. *Sociological Perspectives*, 38(1), 15–26.

Porter, T. M. (1995b). *Trust in Numbers: The Pursuit of Objectivity in Science and Public Life*. Princeton University Press.

Proctor, R. N., & Proctor, R. (1991). *Value-free science? Purity and power in modern knowledge*. Harvard University Press.

Putnam, H. (1975). The meaning of 'meaning'. In *Mind, Language and Reality: Philosophical Papers, Vol. 2, Cambridge University Press, Cambridge*.

Quetelet, A. (1835). *Sur l'homme et le développement de ses facultés*. Bachelier.

Reuben, J. A. (1996). *The Making of the Modern University: Intellectual Transformation and the Marginalization of Morality*. University of Chicago Press.

Riskin, J. (2016). *The Restless Clock: A History of the Centuries-Long Argument over What Makes Living Things Tick*. University of Chicago Press.

Rudner, R. (1953). The scientist qua scientist makes value judgments. *Philosophy of Science*, 20(1), 1–6.

Rudolph, J. L. (2005a). Epistemology for the masses: The origins of 'the scientific method' in American schools. *History of Education Quarterly*, 45(3), 341–376.

Rudolph, J. L. (2005b). Turning science to account: Chicago and the general science movement in secondary education, 1905–1920. *Isis*, 96(3), 353–389.

Rudolph, J. L. (2019). *How We Teach Science: What's Changed, and Why It Matters*. Harvard University Press.

Samland, J., & Waldmann, M. R. (2016). How prescriptive norms influence causal inferences. *Cognition*, 156, 164–176.

Shapin, S., & Schaffer, S. (2011 [1985]). Leviathan and the air-pump. In *Leviathan and the Air-Pump*. Princeton University Press.

Sholl, J. (2017). Nobody is normal. *Aeon*, 31 January.

Shtulman, A., & Valcarcel, J. (2012). Scientific knowledge suppresses but does not supplant earlier intuitions. *Cognition*, 124, 209–215.

Smith, C. (1998). *The Science of Energy: A Cultural History of Energy Physics in Victorian Britain*. University of Chicago Press.

Stark, L. J. (forthcoming). *The Normals: A People's History of Human Experiment*. University of Chicago Press.

Tiles, M. (1993). The normal and the pathological: The concept of a scientific medicine. *British Journal of the Philosophy of Science*, 44(4), 729–742.

Uttich, K., & Lombrozo, T. (2010). Norms inform mental state ascriptions: A rational explanation for the side-effect effect. *Cognition*, 116(1), 87–100.

Washington, N. (2016). Culturally unbound: Cross-cultural cognitive diversity and the science of psychopathology. *Philosophy, Psychiatry, & Psychology*, 23(2), 165–179.

Weber, M. (1946 [1917]). Science as a vocation. *Science as a Vocation*, trans. H. H. Gerth and C. W. Mills. The Free Press.

Wellman, M. (1958). The concept of normal in medicine. *Canadian Medical Association Journal*, 79(1), 43–44.

White, Paul. (2003). *Thomas Huxley: Making the 'Man of Science'*. Cambridge University Press.

Wysocki, T. (2020). Normality: A two-faced concept. *Review of Philosophy and Psychology*, 11, 689–716.

Zammito, J. H. (2004). *A nice derangement of epistemes: Post-positivism in the study of science from Quine to Latour*. University of Chicago Press.

3
Correspondence and Construction
The Representational Theory of Mind and Internally Driven Classificatory Schemes

Gabe Dupre

1. Introduction

There is a tension at the heart of much contemporary work in philosophy of psychology—specifically, within *representational* theories of mind. On the one hand, the central insight of this tradition is that mental and behavioral processes are understood by appeal to mental representations: mental tokens which function as internal proxies for some aspect of the environment, on which behavioral interaction with the environment can depend. On the other, it has long been noted that many purported representations seriously distort, or even simply fabricate, those aspects of the environment they are alleged to represent. I will focus on the examples of color vision and speech perception. At a minimum, this puts pressure on the explanatory goals of representationalism. Many representational theories explain behavior with reference to *accurate* representation, but if we can seemingly function perfectly well with wildly inaccurate representations, the centrality of this strategy is threatened. At worst, this undermines the representationalist project itself, posing insuperable worries for any account that seeks to ground mental content in relations to the environment.

2. Representation as Correspondence

The core idea of the representational theory of mind is that mental states function to correspond to the extra-mental world. Having an internal state which represents the external world allows organisms to better navigate their environments, as they can make their behavior sensitive to the properties of this internal state. Conditioning behavior on such internal representations brings with it many benefits. For one thing, it increases the range of environmental properties behavior can be sensitive to. Organisms' sensory transducers are sensitive only to a small subset of the properties of the environment (wavelength, intensity, and polarization of light, chemical structure of odorants, pressure on the skin, etc.). Interposing a system of representations between these sensory transducers and behavioral responses grants the latter sensitivity to non-transducible properties: I can run from predators, and towards food, rather than simply respond to light and sound. Further, representations provide stability. The ways the environment causally impinges on the body are hyper-sensitive to minor changes in the body, the environment, or their relation. Conditioning behavior directly on such interactions would thus be likely detrimental. While the retinal projection from an object may shift radically as I move my head, my representation of the object can remain the same, allowing me to continue interacting with it. On a longer timescale, forming a representation of the spatial layout of a maze means that the next time it is encountered it can be run efficiently rather than painstakingly explored. And so on.

In these ways, mental representations can be thought of analogously to public representations, like maps. If I want to get from Shepherd's Bush to Elephant & Castle, my best bet is to condition my behavior on the spatial relationships schematically depicted in the Tube map. The map in this case serves as a proxy for the real-world connectivity relationships between the stations. The crucial information contained in the map (e.g. that I need to change at Oxford Circus) is not easily accessible without such an intermediate representation. And to the extent that the map is accurate, my behavior will likely be successful (assuming normal service). The representational theory of mind thus views mental states as functioning similarly to these external representations: serving as stable stand-ins for the environmental properties of interest.[1]

---

[1] The claim is not that *all* representations must function in this way. Clearly, not all do. The hope is that an account of representation can be provided for some basic kinds of perceptual and cognitive processes, which can serve as a sort of "base case" from which other representational capacities and structures can be constructed. One key question here is how we get from the sorts of iconic representational capacities provided as paradigm cases here, for which structural relations in the representation (function to) correspond to structural relations in the represented target, to non-iconic representational systems, such as natural language. I will not take a stand on this issue in this chapter, but will confine my discussion to cases that, at least *prima facie*, constitute this "lower level" of representational complexity.

While details vary, in broad outline this view has [been endorsed by] theorists of quite different orientations:

> The term representation focuses attention on the image of the o... in the symbolic structure which represents it. The analysis...presen... here, focuses on the adequacy of constructing functions from the distal object to the behavior of the system, which works through the representations as an intermediate structure. (Newell, 1980, p. 176)

> A mental representation is a functioning isomorphism between a set of processes in the brain and a behaviorally important aspect of the world.
> (Gallistel, 1998, p. 13)

> To a first approximation, a given kind of animal comes to have an internal model of its world; that is, of its relevant-to-my-life-style world.
> (Churchland et al., 1994, p. 56)

> I have argued here that a particular type of representation, referring to patterns of activity that bear a systematic relationship to the structure of the external world and play a causal role in behavior, is fundamentally necessary for any intelligent organism. (Poldrack, 2020, p. 16)

As these quotes make clear, the representationalist strategy is widespread in philosophy and the cognitive sciences. However, on pain of vacuity, there must be constraints on when representations are profitably posited. I believe the following simplified schema (drawing primarily on aspects of Fodor, 1986; Burge, 2010; and Shea, 2018) identifies the crucial features of inquiry which justify such posits.

1. An organism is observed to display behavioral plasticity.
2. This plasticity cannot be adequately explained merely with reference to differences at the sensory periphery.
3. This plasticity can be adequately explained with reference to differences in distal features of the environment.

When these three conditions are met, we can reasonably conclude that the organism mentally represents the distal features their behavior is sensitive to.

By condition 1, it is meant that an organism shows a range of different behaviors across different environments. Of course, there is vagueness in s statement (how big a range? how different must the environments be? etc.), but not I think in a way that undermines what is intended. This condition is relatively uncontroversial: I think every major account of representation takes the explanation of differential response to a changing environment as central. It is also very weak. Most organisms, including relatively behaviorally restricted ones such as plants and microbes, can be claimed to meet this condition, and even extreme non-representational theories (e.g. behaviorism) view behavioral flexibility as a central explanandum.[2]

Condition 2 is more substantive. It ensures that we do not explain with appeal to representation that which can be explained solely as a matter of causal response to sensory information. Representational theories get their bite by positing an extra, intermediary layer between sensation and behavior. A system which fails to meet condition 2 will thereby not call for such explanation. Phototropism in plants and chemotaxis in some microbes seem like paradigm cases here. An *E. coli* bacterium will display characteristically different movements depending on the chemical gradients of attractants and repellants in its local environment, but this behavior is strictly conditional on the impact of these chemical stimuli on its receptors over short time scales. For this reason, there seems to be little call to view these organisms as representing, rather than merely sensing and responding to, chemical stimuli. One can think of this as an application of Morgan's Canon, which warns against attributing "higher" psychological capacities to organisms when "lower" capacities are sufficient. Early defenders of the representationalist approach such as Chomsky (1959) and Fodor (1968) argued for representations precisely on the grounds that many human behaviors did meet condition 2, and thus were not susceptible to behaviorist-style explanation.

Paradigmatically, organisms will meet condition 2 when there is a "mismatch" between sensory input and behavior. That is, either the same input causes different behaviors or different kinds of input cause the same behaviors.[3] This degree of freedom between sensation and behavior is filled in by intervening representational systems. This is a nomological condition: when there are *laws* mapping sensation onto behavior, there will be no

---

[2] What is controversial, and I deliberately leave open, is the status of this condition. Is it merely evidential, as Fodor (2003) suggests, or is the connection to different behavioral options constitutive of representation, as in Shea, following Millikan (1984) and Sterelny (2003)?

[3] Burge's focus on perceptual constancies stresses this aspect of representational psychology.

benefit to positing representations.[4] Condition 2 is thus necessary for positing representations, but it is not sufficient. There can be gaps between sensation and behavior which are not best accounted for by representational systems. Most obviously, a system which acted randomly would meet conditions 1 and 2, displaying different behavior in different contexts in a way not explicable with reference to sensory input. But the behavior would be no more explicable with reference to representational systems.

For this reason, condition 3 is required as well. The behavior of interest is *appropriate*, in light of the distal environment the organism is in. Objective properties of the environment, which outstrip the information conveyed to the organism in its sensory channels, explain why a certain behavior was successful. We say that the creature represents *depth* because its behavior is appropriately related to the depth of the objects in its environment, even though depth is conflated with, among other things, size in the information made available by its sensory systems.

When these three conditions are met, positing representations is explanatorily powerful. Representations interposed between sensation and behavior allow for the complex causal pathways between the former and the latter. And appeal to distal features of the environment specifies what role this intermediate system plays and why playing this role is useful to the organism: the representations stand in for these distal features, and this is useful because conditioning behavior on these features rationalizes the organism's actions.

This is, of course, an inference to the best explanation, and thus a fallible, ampliative inference.[5] Specifically, positing representations generates predictions for neuro-biological accounts of the mind. Internal representations

---

[4] I do not assume anything too metaphysically robust here. I will count as sufficiently "lawlike" any connections between sensation and behavior which enable scientific theories or models to explain the latter with reference to the former without appealing to distal features of the environment. What I will assume is that such a notion of "law" is intransitive, so that the existence of laws mapping sensation to representation (as posited in psychophysics) and mapping representations to behavior (in line with the standard Fodorian view of psychological explanation) will not entail the existence of laws mapping sensation onto behavior.

[5] I say that positing representations is the *best* explanation of these capacities, not that it is the only possible explanation. Alternative proposals, such as *relationalism* (Campbell, 2002) instead explain such behavioral capacities with reference to the relations between the agent and the perceived distal object. This is not the place to enter into such debates, but I believe that the positing of *inaccurate* and *non-referring* representational states offers representationalism explanatory purchase not available to the relationalist. See Burge (2005) for extended discussion of this point.

of distal states of affairs require physical vehicles capable of acquiring, storing, and making available information concerning whatever aspects of these distal properties downstream behavior is sensitive to. While it is far from straightforward to figure out how such information is stored in the brain, it is clear that it must be, for the representationalist project to succeed, and some physical systems will be more plausibly suited for this than others. As always, our scientific theories must be evaluated for both their successes within their proprietary domains and also their fit with other disciplines.

These are then quite stringent conditions. However, there are ample cases in the literature of psychological systems meeting them. Some of the clearest come from visual perception of "physical" properties (such as distance, size, and motion), and from the navigatory capacities of various creatures.

One of the basic tasks for any visual system is locating local objects in space, relative to the location of the organism. One way to determine the location of an object in three-dimensional space, relative to a perceiver, is by identifying a line between object and perceiver and then determining the distance along this line between the two. The former is relatively straightforward: that light travels in a straight line means that this information is generally extractable from the retinal image. However, the latter is complex. There are no laws that guarantee that a certain retinal image corresponds to an object of a certain distance from the viewer. That this is so is evidenced by the conflation of size and distance in retinal projections: big objects far away can project retinal images of the same size and shape as small objects nearby. For these reasons, visual systems have developed multiple complex and subtle strategies for inferring distance from retinal cues. One such strategy is reliance on *texture gradients*. Many distal scenes contain surfaces featuring repeated patterns. Checkerboard-tiled floors are paradigms here, but similar examples can be found in natural scenes, such as the roughly evenly sized pebbles covering the ground on a beach. When such surfaces extend away from the perceiver, despite their intrinsic regularity, they project non-repeating patterns onto the viewer's retina. "Units" of the pattern (individual tiles, pebbles, blades of grass) near the perceiver project distinct shapes, with clear demarcation between them, whereas those far away blur together; nearby units will project bigger images compared to those far away; and so on. Gradients of size, distinctness, distortion, and other retinal features can thus be reliably correlated with regularly patterned surfaces extending away into the distance. The visual system can thus rely on this correlation, and infer that the distal scene in front of them contains a regular surface with parts at varying distances, rather than other alternatives physically consistent with this retinal image, such as a two-dimensional surface perpendicular to the viewer's line of sight, with large, well-defined units of a pattern at the bottom and smaller, less-defined units at the top. This preference for one distal scene over another, despite their both conforming equally well to the proximal projection, is achieved due to what Tyler Burge calls "formation principles": psychological rules which govern the transition from proximal stimulation to perceptual representation. The rule that generates a representation as of a surface extending away from the viewer on the basis of texture gradients in the retinal image provides a paradigmatic example of a formation principle.[6] Similar stories can be told for other kinds of environmental property, such as size or motion, in terms of reliable (but imperfect) correlations between distal properties and retinal projections, which are reflected in formation principles.

Crucially, while such formation principles allow the possibility of error (as when well-constructed paintings give an "illusion of depth" through just such depth cues as texture gradient), the correlations they depend on are generally environmentally valid, and so in most cases they enable us to accurately perceive our environment. The reliance on such principles thus enables internal states to accurately report properties (e.g. depth) of distal objects. These accurate reports can then guide action, as when we successfully manage to grab a nearby object. Thus, depth perception seems to perfectly fit our schema for representational explanation. Proximal stimuli seem unable to explain why we reached for the object at the depth that we did, given that they are consistent with objects at different depths. But the distal property (i.e. the actual depth of the object) does seem to explain why we reached where we did, as we reached successfully. So, this distal property must be represented by some internal state suitable for guiding behavior.

Another relatively well-understood case comes from accounts of animal navigation. Again in such cases, we see the computation of (generally) accurate information about distal features, partly on the basis of variable proximal stimulation. Gallistel (1998) provides a comprehensive review of the capacities of ants, bees, and wasps to generate internal "maps" of their surroundings, incorporating both egocentric and allocentric information (the latter identified relative to the movements of the Sun) about the relative distances and directions of landmarks and locations of interest such as

---

[6] This is of course massively simplified, both in the description of how texture gradients serve as cues for depth, and in abstracting from the way that texture along with many other cues are integrated. The point is merely to illustrate how paradigmatic representational explanation works.

hives/nests and food sources. The information contained in such a map can then be used to solve novel navigatory tasks, such as returning home from novel locations, and orienting towards landmarks seen from novel directions. These insects rely on processing principles reflecting geometric laws, analogous to those used by human navigators when determining location on a map from the angles generated between their position and three landmarks.

In these and related cases, it is relatively straightforward to identify the environmental property that such systems serve to identify, and on which subsequent processing then comes to rely. These cases thus provide paradigmatic examples of the representationalist schema. The bee identifying its location on a map using a "three-point fix" cannot, of course, apply geometric inference rules to the angles in fact found in the environment, so must generate internal symbols that correspond to them and compute its location on the basis of these symbols. To the extent that such symbols correctly correspond to the angles in the environment they represent, the bee's subsequent navigations will be successful. As these environmental correlates are objective, i.e. identifiable without reference to the bee's internal states, these correlations can be verified. The internal, computational story, appealing to re-usable mental symbols being manipulated in lawlike ways, and the representational story, appealing to the distal properties such symbols represent, thus go hand-in-hand.

These systems, then, will serve for me as paradigmatic examples of the standard story about mental representation as serving to provide an internal proxy for a distal property, object, or state of affairs, on which organismic behavior can be conditioned. If I generate an internal state which accurately corresponds to the distance between my body and my coffee cup, I am able to pick the cup up safely. If I misjudge this, I am liable to knock it over. Likewise, we can explain how the ant makes it home from a novel location by appealing to the accuracy of its internal map and its self-placement on this map. Thus, these cases provide paradigmatic examples of what Shea (2018) calls the "explanatory grammar" of representational explanation, according to which successful behavior is explained with reference to accurate representation, and unsuccessful behavior is explained with reference to inaccurate representation.

3. Representation without Correspondence?

Despite these clear cases, and the fairly widespread view that representations serve as proxies for distal features, and are explanatory precisely in virtue of this, various theorists have pointed to a range of cases which don't seem to fit this mold. In particular, there are cases which are commonly described as representations by both philosophers and psychologists, but which do not seem to correspond to anything in the creature's environment. The point is made forcefully by Akins (1996) who says that "In general, sensory systems both make and ignore distinctions in nature when it suits the organism's motor needs" (p. 369).

To generate a difficulty for representational theories, we need to find cases which seem to be representational, in that behavior seems to be conditioned on an internal symbol which is not explicable solely as a response to proximal stimulation, but for which there are no plausible external states for them to represent. This is made tricky by substantial disagreements about which sensory systems should be viewed as generating representations. For example, Barwich (2019) argues compellingly that olfactory sensation should not be understood as functioning to internally reproduce environmental states. Whether this is a worry for an account of *representation*, however, depends on whether we agree with Lycan (2014) that olfaction is representational, or side with Barwich and Burge (2010) in denying this status to the chemical senses. Similarly, Akins (1996) argued that thermoception radically distorts environmental signals, on the basis of biological relevance to the organism, thus posing problems for an intentional theory of the sort outlined above for our detection of environmental temperature. However, again Burge (2010) has argued that what this shows is not that representation is not a matter of reliably standing in for some distal state, but rather that thermoception is not representational.

At the other end of the scale, "higher" forms of cognition appear to provide novel ways of determining mental content. Our abilities to think, and talk, about fictional entities, and to develop abstract scientific theories, for example, outstrip the explanatory resources of the above account of representation. Following Burge (2010) and Shea (2018), I shall thus restrict my attention to (purportedly) representational systems that do not depend for their functioning on complex propositional or linguistic reasoning.

For these reasons, I will focus my attention on two problem cases that are both (i) widely agreed to be representational and which (ii) display many of the characteristics of the genuinely representational systems discussed in the previous section, which (iii) do not depend on conscious, non-modular, reasoning, but for which (iv) there seem to be no external entities, states, or processes which they function to represent: namely, perception of color and of speech. My discussion will be quite brief and highly simplified, serving mainly to give a flavor of the ways in which the mind creates and imposes structure of its own on stimuli, rather than seeking to reproduce the properties of these stimuli.

While I will get into some detail with these examples, I do not mean to suggest that these are the sole cases which generate the issues discussed in this chapter. I believe similar arguments could be made with appeal to a variety of other psychological capacities. Further, even if all such cases can be resolved in ways amenable to the representationalist style of explanation adumbrated in the previous section, this would be a significant empirical result. As I will discuss them, color and speech perception represent the empirical possibility that psychological systems could function internally *as if* they were tracking environmental properties, without such properties being present.

Both color and speech perception pose various distinct puzzles for representationalist theorizing. The general point is that in perceiving color and speech, the mind creates its own structure. On one standard way of talking, perceptual categories of color and speech are mental *constructs*. Classifying something as red, or as a /b/, is not a matter of determining which category the external stimulus antecedently exemplifies, but rather of imposing an internally driven classificatory scheme onto the stimulus.

The first thing to notice is that both color and speech exemplify *categorical perception*. This is the phenomenon of perception imposing a discrete grouping onto continuously variable stimuli, and treating those members within a given grouping as more closely related to each other than they are to those outside of the grouping, even if the "objective" distance between the in-group and out-group stimuli is equal to or even less than that between in-group stimuli. For example, consider a beam of white light being dispersed by an optical prism. The prism will produce a spectrum of rays of continuously varying wavelength. However, when we look at this spectrum, it will not look continuously varying to us. Rather, it will look to be composed of a relatively small number of bands of color, with blurry edges between them. Perceived similarities between locations along the spectrum will not be determined by "objective" similarities of wavelength, but rather by their place in these color bands. So a blueish green will look more similar to a yellowish green than it will to a greenish blue, due to the former both being classified as *green*, even if the wavelengths of light responsible for these percepts are more similar in the latter case than the former.

The same thing is observed in speech perception. Most famously, plosive, or stop, consonants like /b/ and /p/, generated by the blockage and then release of air in the oral cavity, may differ continuously in their

Voice-Onset-Time (VOT), the time between the start of airflow after the blockage of the airway and the vibration of the vocal cords. However, despite this continuous variation in their articulation, these sounds are not perceived as forming a spectrum, but as discrete categories. For example, bilabial plosives, formed by stopping airflow by closing both lips together, are differentiated according to VOT: those with a VOT of 30 milliseconds (ms) or less tend to be perceived as /b/, while those with VOT of over 30ms are perceived as /p/. A consonant with a VOT of 28ms will typically be perceived as more similar to one with a VOT of 15ms, due to both being /b/s, than to one with a VOT of 32ms, despite the latter being more "objectively" similar. So, we could arrange a series of stimuli ordered by VOT, with arbitrarily small gaps between each instance. From the perspective of articulation, we have a roughly continuous series, with VOT increasing steadily. However, perceptually, what we hear is not a /b/ sound gradually changing into a /p/ sound, with some intermediate cases along the way. Rather, we hear this as a series of definite /b/ sounds, and then suddenly a series of definite /p/ sounds. This sudden transition must thus be imposed on the stimulus by the mind, rather than correspond to some pre-existing environmental change.[7]

Categorical perception provides an initial illustration of the difficulties posed for representationalist accounts. The categories, and thus the perceived "similarity space" imposed by our perceptual systems, do not seem to correspond to any objective feature of the stimulus. Unlike in the case of, say, depth perception, where we could look to the environment to see whether a percept was accurate or not, in cases of categorical perception we cannot do this. The physical facts about the environment, wavelength or VOT, do not determine whether a stimulus will be perceived as green or as a /b/. Information about the internal classificatory system, about where these lines are drawn, is needed in addition.

While illustrative, I don't view categorical perception on its own as damning. While the categories seem to be internally determined, that some stimulus falls into one category or another could still be viewed as an objective fact about the environment, which perceptual systems function to track. *Merely* imposing a classificatory scheme on environmental variation may be compatible with the general representationalist account identified above.

---

[7] That color and speech are perceived categorically is about as close to consensus as one gets in psychology, but even here there are detractors. See e.g. Schouten et al. (2003) and Witzel (2019).

What will pose a problem is if such classification schemes go beyond merely dividing up the objective stimuli and distort the objective relationships, or even invent classifications *de novo* with minimal input from the environment. Discussing examples of just this phenomenon will require presenting a bit more of the details of color and speech perception.

"Color vision" refers to the collection of capacities of organisms to differentially respond to different wavelengths of light. Wavelength provides a valuable source of information concerning the organism's environment. However, making use of this information typically requires significant processing due to the fact that wavelength conflates a variety of different environmental sources. Most significantly, wavelength reflected from a surface is a product of both the surface reflectance properties of the object and the wavelength of the light illuminating it. A white wall in red lighting may thus reflect light with the same wavelength as a red wall in white lighting. It has traditionally been assumed that the purpose of color vision was to extract information about the color (i.e. surface reflectance) of distal objects, and thus the goal is to control for variations in such confounding influences as variation in illumination. Such a picture fits nicely with the view of representation as correspondence detailed above.

However, much work in color science tells against this view. Many features of color vision would be unexpected on the basis solely of examination of the reflectance properties of distal objects. For example, human color vision identifies four colors as "unitary," i.e. as not decomposable into mixtures of other colors. So, while orange and purple *look* to us like mixtures of red and yellow and red and blue, respectively, red, green, yellow, and blue look to be basic.[8] Our judgements of color similarity and difference are strongly influenced by such classifications. While the neurobiology and psychology are complex, it is widely accepted that this classification is explained at least partially with reference to internal features of the trichromat visual system, especially the post-receptoral "opponent coding" system which is traditionally understood to respond on the basis of the ratios of red to green and blue to yellow light. That is to say that the representational system used by the color vision system is not explained with reference to the properties it tracks in the environment, but rather by the physical channels involved in sensation.

---

[8] While the precise location of the unitary hues varies from subject to subject, that each individual takes some instance of red, yellow, green, and blue to be basic is widely accepted in the vision science literature. This observation dates back to Hering (1878/1964). See Hardin (1988, pp. 39–45) for discussion; and Fuld et al. (1981) for experimental results.

Of course, providing a neurobiological explanation of our visual classification schemes doesn't *preclude* a correspondence-based account. Indeed, one might be tempted to think that standard "methodological adaptationist" (Godfrey-Smith, 2001) assumptions about the evolution of mental capacities might tie them together nicely: our visual systems make the distinctions they do because latching onto certain environmental properties was beneficial for our ancestors. However, even if we accept this adaptationist explanatory scheme, we cannot simply infer that the function of such mental capacities is to correspond to environmental distinctions. One can accept that color vision is useful without accepting that it is useful for tracking, as do Akins & Hahn (2014) and Chirimuuta (2015). And given the above arguments that color vision doesn't seem to involve tracking distinctions in our present environment, we seem to have strong reasons to deny that any phylogenetic story will be able to save the correspondence-based approach to color vision.

A related worry for representationalist approaches comes from metamers: surfaces with radically different reflectances which, in a particular context (e.g. under specific illumination, or viewed from a specific angle), appear to be identically colored to an observer. Metamers raise worries for any account which views color vision as functioning to track environmental properties, as it seems these quite distinct environmental properties (surface reflectances) are generating identical representations (as of the same color). Unless the representationalist is willing to say that in each class of metamers, all but one systematically leads to inaccurate perception, this suggests that the represented category is one that does not correspond to any objective, or mind-independent, feature of the environment.

Turning now to speech perception, we see the same sorts of problems arising, wherein the categories utilized by the system seem to be internally driven, rather than reflective of any objective environmental attributes. Speech perception involves categorizing a speech stimulus with respect to a hierarchy of linguistic properties: sounds must be classified phonetically and phonologically; sequences of phonemes must be grouped into syllables, morphemes, and words; words must be grouped syntactically into phrases, and semantic values must be assigned at both the morphemic and syntactic level. At every stage of this process, there are vast gaps between the imposed mental classification and any properties of the stimulus.

Consider first the lowest levels of identifying phonological properties of an uttered string. Each language determines a set of phonemes, usually around a few dozen, out of which the legitimate sounds of the language can be composed. Identifying the words one hears depends on identifying the phonemes composing them (*did she just say 'bin' or 'pin'?*). Further, these phonemic inventories vary from language to language (e.g. dental fricatives, as in English *this* and *brother*, are absent in French), and so must depend on early exposure to native language. So both in use and development, the phonemic inventory for a given language must be, in some sense, identified by the child on the basis of environmental stimuli. This is, however, a notoriously difficult computational problem due to the very messy relationship between phonology and physical stimuli. The phonological perception system must be able to abstract from variation due to factors such as age, sex, (some aspects of) dialect, conversational focus and carefulness, etc., and group together the same phonemes despite significant variation in physical properties of the stimulus.

One well-studied example of this sort of computation stems from the fact that the anatomical features of the vocal apparatus impose constraints on how phonological forms can be efficiently produced. Different phonemes are (generally) individuated by the way they are produced by the tongue, vocal cords, and other parts of the oral cavity. In the rapid process of speech, however, the different features of such productions can be run together, in often predictable ways. For example, in English, when (what would normally be) a dental plosive (/d/) is immediately followed by a bilabial consonant (e.g. /m/, /p/, or /b/), it is typically transformed into a bilabial plosive. In most spoken English (i.e. as long as the speaker isn't taking special care to speak slowly and enunciate), the final consonant of 'could', in 'I could make more', 'He could pass the salt', and 'You could buy some' will be realized not as a /d/ as it is written and would be produced in default contexts, but as a /b/. It is difficult to quickly transition from having one's lips apart as needed for the production of /d/ to pursing them as needed for subsequent bilabial consonants, and so the system uses a "shortcut" and simply turns the /d/ into a /b/ to make production easier. This process is called assimilation.

What matters for our purposes is that assimilation appears (see e.g. Mitterer & Blomert, 2003) to be "corrected for" early in speech perception. That is, despite the different ways that 'could' is pronounced in different contexts (with or without assimilation), it is perceived as the same word, with the same, default, final consonant. Whether the stimulus is /kΩd/ or /kΩb/, it is *heard* as if it is the former. This mental correction of the assimilation imposed by speech mechanics provides a case of an internal classification system being imposed on an external stimulus, rather than the perceptual system functioning to correctly reproduce what is in the environment.

Any perception in a noisy environment is liable to generate cases of misrepresentation. Indeed, that such misrepresentation is possible has long been one of the central desiderata for a philosophical theory of mental content (Fodor, 1990). However, assimilation does not seem to be merely another example of misrepresentation. On standard, hierarchical, models of speech perception, phonological representation of the stimulus feeds into lexical identification (which then feeds into syntactic and semantic parsing). Assimilation generates a tension between these two processing pressures: if we failed to correct for assimilation, and heard the spoken word as /kΩb/, this would impede our ability to identify it as a token of the word 'could'. So, unlike paradigmatic instances of misrepresentation which reflect (perhaps necessary) computational shortcomings in our perceptual systems, in cases like assimilation what we see is a competition between the goal of representational accuracy (which would favour correctly representing the produced /b/ sound) and the internal usefulness of classification (which favours incorrectly representing the stimulus so as to make lexical identification easier), and in which the latter virtue wins out. Thus again we have a case in which the functioning of the system does not seem to be a matter of tracking environmental properties, but instead of classifying according to an internally motivated scheme.

One final example comes from the process of syllabification, which groups phonemes together to form pronounceable sounds. As with phonological inventories, syllabification differs from language to language. A major driver of inter-linguistic variation in syllabification is phonotactics, the rules governing which sequences of phonemes can appear in which contexts. For example, languages typically place more constraints on the presence of consonant clusters at the beginning of a syllable than at the end. In English, many sounds which are fine syllable-finally are prohibited syllable-initially, such as /rt/ and /ts/ ('cart' and 'bats', but not *'rtac' or *'tsab').[9] In perception, the string of phonemes must be divided up to form syllables. Phonotactics plays a central role here: syllables can't be formed which would violate phonotactic rules of this sort. And this leads to inter-linguistic

---

[9] This prohibition can be overridden by adoption of words from other languages, such as 'Tsunami', 'Tsar', or 'Tsetse', but such words are easily recognizable as loan words and further the initial consonant is often dropped either as a matter of policy or in rapid speech.

variation in how the same speech stimulus will be perceived. In Japanese, unlike English, /ts/ is legitimate syllable-initially (in the "onset").[10] Further, consonants are generally (with a few exceptions) precluded from appearing at the end of a syllable (in the "coda"), so that Japanese syllables almost always end with a vowel. Thus, certain words will be syllabified quite differently by native speakers of English and Japanese. The name of the car company, Mitsubishi, for example will be syllabified as Mit-su-bi-shi by English speakers, due to the prohibition of syllable-initial /ts/, whereas Japanese speakers will hear it as Mi-tsu-bi-shi, with the syllable-initial /ts/ allowed, and indeed required to prevent a prohibited syllable-final /t/.

Thus we again have a case wherein how an environmental stimulus is characterized seems to involve imposing an internally driven classificatory scheme onto it, rather than seeking to identify its mind-independent features. That one and the same stimulus (e.g. a spoken token of the word 'Mitsubishi') can be classified quite differently by different speakers, without any pressing reason to determine that one of them is *misrepresenting*, problematizes the idea that mental representation is a matter of reproducing environmental properties.

Note that these cases are arising in the lower levels of speech perception, wherein what is being classified does seem, intuitively at least, relatively close to the physical properties of the stimulus: sounds and sound-groupings. The problem of course gets much worse as we turn to higher levels of perception, such as syntax and semantics. Syntactic theory says that 'the guests are eager to eat' and 'the guests are easy to eat' have radically different grammatical structures, and psycholinguistic theories of human parsing provide theories of how such structures are generated as representations of speech stimuli. But whatever this difference consists in, it doesn't seem to be an independently identifiable (i.e. identifiable without actually using the very perceptual categories under investigation) property of the stimulus in the way that relative spatial locations were in the examples discussed above. It certainly won't be identified through spectrographic analysis. Likewise for the quite different semantic properties of such examples.[11]

---

[10] Strictly, Japanese is typically viewed as based not around syllables, but around *moras*, a slightly different notion incorporating constraints on speech rhythm in addition to phoneme grouping. The difference shouldn't matter for my purposes, and so I will stick to the more familiar notion of the syllable.

[11] For my purposes, I can remain silent on the question of whether there is a more abstract way in which these stimuli can be said to have these properties. Devitt (2006), for example, argues that syntactic and semantic properties are genuinely properties of public linguistic objects, but they are "high level" relational properties held in virtue of a given public symbol's

Despite these stark differences between color and speech perception, on the one hand, and the perception of physical features of the environment and animal navigation, on the other, from a particular perspective we can note significant similarities. These differences consist exclusively in the relationships between these symbols and the outside world. The differences disappear when we view these systems from an "internalist" perspective, focusing only on the ways that internal states are formed, manipulated, stored, and relied on in controlling action. The "symbolic system" approach discussed in the previous section applies equally well to paradigmatic work in color perception and psycholinguistics, involving the lawlike generation of internal tokens on the basis of these tokens' membership in various equivalence classes, and subsequent processing determined by which such class they are in.

Before concluding this section it is worth briefly driving home the point that these systems cannot easily be dismissed as "merely sensory," as opposed to full-blown representational systems. Burge (2010) has argued that perceptual constancy mechanisms should be viewed as the defining feature of representational systems: systems with constancies represent, sensory systems without constancies do not (in Burge's terms, they merely "register information"). Constancy mechanisms, for Burge, are 'capacities to represent environmental attributes, or environmental particulars, as the same, despite radically different proximal stimulations' (2010, p. 114). It is near-uncontroversial that this applies to both speech and color perception (indeed, Burge discusses color constancies alongside other constancy mechanisms). We see objects as having stable colors despite changing illumination or distance from the perceiver. And we hear speech sounds as consisting of the same phonemes despite varying features of the speaker. Relatedly, it is clear that what is involved in speech and color perception goes far beyond mere averaging, aggregation, etc., of properties of the sensory stimulus. What these cases bring out is that the existence of a constancy is neutral on whether the environmental particular in question is being stably represented as having a property that it actually has or not. Size constancies enable us to accurately gauge the size of an object, despite the changing projection it produces on our retina. Color constancy, on the other hand,

---

relationship to the standing linguistic conventions of a linguistic community. Whatever the merits of this proposal, I can grant it here and still make the point that such properties are not plausibly causally responsible for the representational functioning of the speech perception systems, and so such properties seem ill-suited for featuring in the sort of correspondence-based views discussed above.

enables us to stably impose internally driven color categories on distal stimuli, despite the variable ways such stimuli causally interact with our sensory systems. But this does not seem to require that the imposed category functions to track a genuine property of the stimulus. But if even someone as stingy with their attributions of "representational" as Burge seems forced to accept that speech and color perception are representational systems, the fact that these systems *impose* their classificatory scheme on environmental stimuli, rather than functioning to track antecedently existent environmental categories, seems to suggest a deep conflict with the above-described account of when and why representations are to be posited.

Color and speech perception, then, pose a stark worry for representationalist accounts of mind. On the one hand, these accounts are primarily motivated by the thought that internal proxies for inaccessible features of the environment play central roles in explaining organismic behavior within such an environment. Representational contents are posited essentially as part of this explanatory project. But in the cases described here, there seems to be no aspect of the environment that these representations function to reproduce, or correspond to. The properties of color vision, such as color similarity and difference, are not properties of distal objects' surfaces. And properties of heard speech do not, generally, track properties of speech stimuli, but internally driven features of linguistic competence. However, these are often given as paradigms of representationalist psychology. This tension between the explanatory schema invoked in philosophical accounts of scientific methodology and between the empirical facts of the science must be resolved somehow.

4. Possible Responses

While my main goal in this chapter is to identify a foundational worry for standard representational theories of mind, I will close by briefly outlining the various strategies one could take to resolve the problem outlined above. I will discuss them separately, but it is likely that a solution will involve elements of each.

Firstly, there are attempts in the literature to show how both color and linguistic properties are genuinely found in our environments. Perhaps most famously, Byrne & Hilbert (2003) argue that colors are simply surface reflectances, color vision functions to represent surface reflectances, and that the representations formed are often accurate. If this can be made to work, despite the criticism raised in e.g. Hardin (2003), then it would be possible to assimilate color to the physical properties for which representational theories worked so well. A similar account could be offered for language. Pereplyotchik (2017), for example, defends a possible combination of Devitt's (2006) view that public linguistic symbols have the phonological and syntactic properties posited by linguistic theories in virtue of conventions among speakers with a representational theory of speech perception. Here too, these proposals have received strong pushback—see for example Rey (2006) and Collins (2008) for worries about Devitt's claims about the ontology of linguistics. If these respective worries can be overcome, this would provide a first step towards solving the puzzle discussed above, and showing how the standard representation-as-correspondence account could apply to color and language.

While these strategies are available, I wouldn't bet on them. For whatever it's worth, within philosophy, they are not hugely popular, and within vision science and linguistics they seem to be vanishingly rare. Perhaps the central reason is that even if we can make ontological sense of an environment populated with reds and blues and nouns and verbs, it has often seemed that doing so is a sort of metaphysical third wheel. That is, the ontology does not seem to play a central role in the explanatory projects of the sciences. If the proposed identification of colors with reflectances failed, vision science would not, it seems, have to change anything. Likewise, the success of psycholinguistics does not seem to turn on the question of whether there are unarticulated constituents in our environments. As the motivation for positing mental representations, at least in the tradition I have been focusing on, has centrally been an explanatory one, it would be an uneasy marriage between this general approach to mind and these apparently non-explanatory ontological doctrines. Further, as mentioned, speech and color are illustrative examples, but there is no reason to think they are the only problem cases. Any account which aims to solve the problem by populating the environment with suitable targets for representation would thus have to generalize to cover all such cases.

Further, I said that this would be a key *first step* in resolving the problem. But more would be needed. In the terms of Quine (1951), this would account for the *ontology* of our theories of color and speech perception, but not necessarily for their *ideology*. That is, it could ground claims that color and speech perception function to identify examples of color and speech in the environment, but it may leave unchanged the central point of my argument: that the categories involved in classifying such stimuli are internally generated. Take the case of color, and allow with Byrne and Hilbert that surface reflectances are colors.[12] From this fact alone, it doesn't follow that when we classify some environmental color as *red*, we are thereby identifying a property that it has independently of our so classifying it. For that, we would also need to show that there is some mind-independent reality to the property *redness*, instantiated by objects with quite different surface reflectances. But, as Byrne and Hilbert allow, such a property 'will be quite uninteresting from the point of view of physics or any other branch of science unconcerned with the reactions of human perceivers' (2003, p. 11). But this seems to be just another way of saying that such a classificatory scheme is internally determined, not a matter of identifying or tracking a pre-existing environmental distinction. Likewise with linguistic properties: saying that there are linguistic properties in the environment is one thing, and saying that our perceptual classification of them involves placing them into categories they instantiate independently of such a classification is another. For these reasons, I will assume that the problem above is a real one, and will turn to more radical approaches to resolving it.

One approach starts from the observation that misrepresentation is a central feature of any account of representation. From a theoretical perspective, it is often recognized that there can be no representation without the possibility of misrepresentation (Fodor, 1990). And more prosaically, it is a commonplace that many of our representational states are misguided in some way or other, from perceptual illusions to cognitive delusions. One possibility for resolving the above worries then amounts to viewing perception of speech and color as simply misrepresentation on a grand scale. Mendelovici (2013) argues for this with respect to color, and Rey (2008, 2020) applies it to both of the cases I discuss. On this view, mental representations do indeed function to correspond to environmental properties, but that provides no guarantee that they succeed in so corresponding. So just as illusions of depth provide no objection to accounts of depth perception as representational, we should not view the fact that there are no colors or linguistic properties in our environments as reason to doubt that our perceptual systems represent these properties.

---

[12] Byrne and Hilbert go on to precisify their view, and argue that reflectances are one "flavor" (of color), so as to allow for the existence of colored light sources and colored translucent volumes. They dub this larger category 'productances'. This wrinkle will not matter for my purposes.

The main obstacle to a view of this kind is that it is in need of a metasemantic account of what makes these representations the representations they are. The standard representational theory of mind discussed above provides a neat answer here: mental states represent those aspects of the environment which cause them, and to which behavior is sensitive. Depth perception represents depth because different representations are formed in response to interaction with objects at different depths and it enables creatures to interact successfully with objects at different depths. Once it is admitted that there are no colors or linguistic properties in the environment, this opens up the question of why we view these properties as the represented contents, rather than some others. As Stalnaker (1989) argues compellingly, it is often not possible to individuate a mental content other than with respect to its causal antecedents. This may be compatible with occasional misrepresentation: representations of depth typically correspond to environmental depth, which suffices to ground their representational content, even if on certain occasions this correspondence fails. But it is much more difficult to see how it is compatible with *across-the-board* misrepresentation as we see in the cases described above.

A closely related concern is that such accounts seem to undermine core motivations for representational theories. As noted above, Shea (2018) points out that one central role for representational content in cognitive science is in licensing a particular "explanatory grammar": 'Representing correctly explains successful behavior and misrepresentation explains failure' (p. 28). If representations of color and speech are inevitably misrepresentations, then such an explanatory strategy cannot apply. Representational explanations paradigmatically function to show how an organism can engage successfully with its environment, but if my hallucinatory representations of the banana in front of me as blue are no less accurate than would be representations of it as yellow, what explanatory purchase does this content have?[13]

Rey (2020) proposes a dispositionalist account here: representations of color/speech have the content they do because *were* we to interact with genuine colors or Verb Phrases, our perceptual systems would track them, even if we never in fact encounter such things and so all of our representations of them are misrepresentations. I believe such an account similarly

---

[13] See also Johnson (this volume, section 3.1) for a clear discussion of the ways that color vision science centrally involves appeal to perceptual *successes* and *failures*, defined in terms of the system's ability to keep track of distal and objective properties.

suffers from the above-mentioned worry that it is *actual* behavioral success and failure that we want our cognitive theories to explain, and any account on which our representations are uniformly inaccurate will not be equipped to provide this. A further problem is that no particular reason to believe such a counterfactual is given. Our perceptual systems are designed to respond to the physical stimuli they in fact encounter and have encountered over evolutionary time. It is thus not clear that they would recognize a genuine instance of redness or of a controlled unarticulated subject if they were to encounter them (if such objects/properties can even be made sense of). Given that Rey admits that we don't encounter such entities, it is not clear why he is entitled to make claims about what we would perceive if we did.

Other sorts of metasemantic accounts could step in here, providing an alternative solution. While the representation-as-correspondence approach is fairly dominant within the cognitive sciences, within philosophy there is a significant tradition viewing representational content as determined in other ways. One widely discussed alternative is the inferentialist tradition, according to which the meaning of a symbol is determined primarily by its relations to other symbols within a broader representational system. In different ways, this idea has been developed by Loar (1981), Block (1986), Brandom (1994), and Greenberg & Harman (2008) (although see Fodor & Lepore, 2007, 1992, for criticism). Representing a stimulus as *red*, or as a *rounded vowel*, on this view, would be a matter just of applying to it a representational token which plays a specified role within the overall perceptual systems of color or speech. Such an account again faces the problem that it fails to explain why certain actions are successful and others are unsuccessful, as this seems to rely on correspondence, or lack thereof, between environmental and internal states. More generally, one could worry that such approaches are unsuited for behavioral explanation on the grounds that content is simply an abstraction over the causally significant mental symbols and processes. On the standard view, a state's being an edge-representation depends on its corresponding to environmental edges (Burge, 1986), and appealing to this mind-world relationship explains why having such internal states would be useful to an organism. But this style of explanation is unavailable to the inferentialist. If what makes something an edge-representation is simply standing in causal relationships to other sorts of representations, it doesn't seem that classifying something as such a representation adds anything of explanatory value to the pre-existing causal/syntactic story. So one major challenge for the view that mental content can be grounded other than with reference to correspondence is to show how such content is explanatorily pertinent to cognitive and behavioral science.

Of course, there are also other metasemantic options one could take, complicating the relations between content, environment, and computational role.[14] But I hope what I have argued above is enough to show that simply moving away from the content-as-correspondence view is not sufficient to avoid these worries. That there must be at least a plausible story, if not a fleshed-out theory, of what makes representations of color and speech contentful, and that such a story must contribute to the explanatory goals of the cognitive sciences, together provide powerful constraints on a theory of mental content. So powerful that to my knowledge, no proposal in the literature has yet managed to meet them.

Given these worries about a suitably general and explanatory representational theory of mind, one could take these cases as demonstrations that this is simply the wrong way to think about the mind. That is, one could argue that color and speech are just instances of the larger, "internalist," idea that the mind should be studied on its own terms, rather than as relating to or reflecting its environment. This idea has been prominently defended in philosophy by Stich (1983), who argues for a "syntactic theory of mind," according to which mental states are individuated by their computational roles, not by their representational contents. Within the cognitive sciences, Chomsky (2000) has consistently argued, centrally from the linguistic case discussed above, that one's environment can play no role in individuating mental states, and thus that notions of representational content in the robust sense endorsed by the standard account should be rejected. Collins (2014) develops an "algebraic" approach along these lines.

If taken as general accounts of the mind, the standard worry for such approaches is that the assumption that we can provide equally good explanations of behavior without reference to the environment is simply mistaken. As Pylyshyn (1984), Fodor (1987), Burge (2003), and others have argued forcefully, genuine cognitive-scientific explanations take patterns of mind-world interaction as both explanantia and explananda. Further, certain philosophically significant properties of mental life and behavior, such as "objectivity"—drawing a boundary between the world and the way the world appears to us (Burge)—and rationality—explaining how our behavior is

---

[14] One prominent alternative is Mendelovici's (2018) "phenomenal intentionality" approach, which aims to derive representational properties from properties of phenomenal experience. While discussion of this approach would take me too far afield for the purposes of this chapter, it is worth noting that, especially in the case of speech perception, many of the purported representational properties (e.g. representation of a stimulus as an unpronounced subject, such as the subject of 'dance' in 'Asher wants to dance') are not consciously accessible, and so this strategy will not be available here.

appropriately responsive to our environmental conditions (Newell)—seem constituted by relationships between internal states and the surrounding environment. Any account of the mind which abstracts entirely from relations to the environment seems intrinsically unable to shed light on these phenomena.

To address this worry, the internalist position has more recently been developed in a series of papers by Egan (1989, 1995, 2009, 2014, 2018), who follows Stich and Chomsky in viewing mental states as individuated by their internal, computational role, while allowing that relations to the environment may play an explanatory, but non-individuating role. Rescorla (2017), however, argues that, in actual practice, empirical psychology individuates mental states precisely by their representational roles, and not, in general, by any syntactic categories that they may instantiate.

If these worries can be overcome, one nice feature of Egan's proposal is that it allows room for a pluralism about cognitive explanation. If mental states have their representational properties only contingently, if at all, we can allow that these properties play an essential role in explaining cognitive capacities and behavior in the cases in which correspondence does play a role, such as spatial perception. That some such connections to objective aspects of the environment are featured in our descriptions and explanations of the mind and behavior can thus provide the raw materials for accounts of rationality mentioned above. But we may still view such states as members of a broader computational kind which contains also states like color and speech "representations," for which there seems to be no possibility of correspondence.[15]

Such a pluralism would take seriously Marr's (1982) observation that a computational theory of any aspect of mind must tell us both *what* is computed, and also *why* it is this computation rather than some other that is found in a given psychological system (pp. 22–23). What the cases above then point to is the fact that answers to this latter question can take forms other than those Marr described, which involved computations for extracting distal information from an impoverished proximal stimulus. Much work in psychology provides alternative styles of explanation, but within the same information processing framework. For example, Averill (2005) claims that opponent coding models of color vision can explain why we classify colors

---

[15] One could of course endorse a pluralism about mental representation without agreeing with Egan that states in, say, the visual system were generally individuated without reference to the environment. Plausibly, states representing depth or object boundaries might be externalistically individuated, while states representing color and speech were individuated purely with reference to their computational roles.

as we do, despite such classifications not tracking any external properties. Chirimuuta (2015, ch. 3) points out that Averill is here relying on a scientific conjecture, rather than accepted results, but for my purposes the possibility of such a model is sufficient. If the underlying neurobiology can provide an explanation for the ways that information is processed without appeal to estimating distal properties, then the pluralism I am here suggesting could go some way towards resolving the problem raised by representations without correspondence.

Alongside these explanations from neurobiological constraints, functional, but not correspondence-based, accounts of color vision have been provided by Akins & Hahn (2014) and Chirimuuta (2015). On these views, color vision is functional, but its function is not to reproduce external color. Rather, color vision provides us with information about a whole host of other environmentally useful properties, such as object boundaries and distance.

One sees such alternative models of explanations in linguistics as well, such as Chomsky's (2001) explanation for wh-island effects which appeals to computational efficiency.[16] Such an account explains why we perceive certain stimuli as having the linguistic properties they have (e.g. grammaticality, or the availability of a given reading) not with reference to them actually having such properties, but instead by claiming that representational systems which allowed for different grammatical structures (e.g. with long-distance wh-movement) would be too computationally costly.

By carefully distinguishing the computational story concerning what role mental symbols play within a cognitive system from the explanatory story concerning why such symbols are found with the properties they have, we can thus highlight the reasons why we felt compelled to group color and speech with paradigmatic cases of representation as correspondence as well as the key differences between them.

While there is of course much more to say here, my aim has been to reasonably clearly identify the major strategies for resolving the problem raised by representation without correspondence. The hope is that some, likely pluralistic, combination of the following will provide the tools for resolving

---

[16] Wh-islands are sentential contexts which preclude certain sorts of grammatical dependencies. For example, conjunctions generally preclude the extraction of a question-particle from only one of their conjuncts. Witness: *'Who did Matthieu and ___ see at the bar?'. The core idea of Chomsky's proposal is that computational efficiency is increased if our linguistic system identifies certain structures as complete, and thus do not allow any further operations on them. Without this constraint on interpretive dependencies, increases in sentence length will lead to explosions in computational complexity as each structural constituent could potentially depend on arbitrarily many others. Although see Sprouse & Hornstein (2013) and Asoulin (2020) for discussion and alternative accounts.

the problem: (i) identifying suitable targets for apparently constructive representational systems in the environment, (ii) providing a metasemantics for such systems which allows for widespread misrepresentation, (iii) providing non-representational explanations for such capacities, and (iv) providing an account of representational content which does not rely on correspondence. Such a solution would ideally retain the explanatory successes of the standard, correspondence-based approach, while showing how to generalize to cases like color and speech.

5. Conclusion

In this chapter, I have argued that there is a deep tension at the heart of contemporary representational approaches to philosophy of mind and cognitive science. On the one hand, the explanatory apparatus of these disciplines seems to essentially involve appeal to correspondences between mind and environment. On the other, paradigmatic representational systems, such as color vision and speech perception, seem to lack any suitable environmental correlates. In the last section, I briefly canvassed what I take to be the most plausible ways out of this puzzle, but more work must be done to concretize, evaluate, and combine these proposals so as to reinforce the foundations of the representational theory of mind. I hope that setting the puzzle and the possible solutions out as explicitly as possible will spur research by philosophers and cognitive scientists aimed at just this.[17]

References

Akins, Kathleen. (1996). Of sensory systems and the "aboutness" of mental states. *The Journal of Philosophy*, 93(7), 337–372.

Akins, Kathleen A., & Hahn, Martin. (2014). More than mere coloring: The role of spectral information in human vision. *The British Journal for the Philosophy of Science*, 65(1), 125–171.

Asoulin, Eran. (2020). Why should syntactic islands exist? *Mind & Language*, 37(1), 114–131.

Averill, Edward Wilson. (2005). Toward a projectivist account of color. *The Journal of Philosophy*, 102(5), 217–234.

---

[17] This chapter benefited from feedback from Zed Adams, John Dupré, Gabbrielle Johnson, Uriah Kriegel, and Kevin Lande, as well as an audience at the British Society for the Philosophy of Science.

Barwich, Ann-Sophie. (2019). A critique of olfactory objects. *Frontiers in Psychology*, *10*, 1337.

Block, Ned. (1986). Advertisement for a semantics for psychology. *Midwest Studies in Philosophy*, *10*, 615–678.

Brandom, Robert. (1994). *Making It Explicit: Reasoning, Representing, and Discursive Commitment*. Harvard University Press.

Burge, Tyler. (1986). Cartesian error and the objectivity of perception. In P. Pettit & J. McDowell (eds.) *Subject, Thought and Context* (pp. 117–136). Oxford University Press.

Burge, Tyler. (2003). Psychology and the environment: Reply to chomsky. In M. Hahn & B. Ramberg (eds.) *Reflections and Replies: Essays on the Philosophy of Tyler Burge*. MIT Press.

Burge, Tyler. (2005). Disjunctivism and perceptual psychology. *Philosophical Topics*, *33*(1), 1–78.

Burge, Tyler. (2010). *Origins of Objectivity*. Oxford University Press.

Byrne, Alex, & Hilbert, David R. (2003). Color realism and color science. *Behavioral and Brain Sciences*, *26*(1), 3–21.

Campbell, John. (2002). *Reference and Consciousness*. Oxford University Press.

Chirimuuta, Mazviita. (2015). *Outside Color: Perceptual Science and the Puzzle of Color in Philosophy*. MIT Press.

Chomsky, Noam. (1959). A review of BF Skinner's Verbal Behavior. *Language*, *35*(1), 26–58.

Chomsky, Noam. (2000). *New Horizons in the Study of Language and Mind*. Cambridge University Press.

Chomsky, Noam. (2001). Derivation by phase. In M. Kenstowicz (ed.) *Ken Hale: A Life in Language* (pp. 1–52). MIT Press.

Churchland, Patricia S., Ramachandran, V.S., & Sejnowski, Terrence J. (1994). A critique of pure vision. in C. Koch and J.L. Davis (eds.) Large-Scale Neuronal Theories of the Brain. MIT Press.

Collins, John. (2008). A note on conventions and unvoiced syntax. *Croatian Journal of Philosophy*, *8*(23), 241–247.

Collins, John. (2014). Representations without representata: Content and illusion in linguistic theory. In P. Stalmaszczyk (ed.) *Semantics and Beyond: Philosophical and Linguistic Inquiries* (pp. 27–64). Walter de Gruyter.

Devitt, Michael. (2006). *Ignorance of Language*. Oxford University Press.

Egan, Frances. (1995). Computation and content. *The Philosophical Review*, *104*(2), 181–203.

Egan, Frances. (2009). Is there a role for representational content in scientific psychology? *Stich and His Critics*, *14*, 14.

Egan, Frances. (2014). How to think about mental content. *Philosophical Studies*, *170*(1), 115–135.

Egan, Frances. (2018). The nature and function of content in computational models. In *The Routledge Handbook of the Computational Mind* (pp. 247–258). Routledge.

Egan, Frances. (1989). What's wrong with the syntactic theory of mind. *Philosophy of Science*, *56*(4), 664–674.

Fodor, Jerry A. (1968). *Psychological Explanation: An Introduction to the Philosophy of Psychology*. Random House.

Fodor, Jerry A. (1986). Why paramecia don't have mental representations. *Midwest Studies in Philosophy*, *10*(1), 3–23.

Fodor, Jerry A. (1987). The persistence of the attitudes. *Psychosemantics: The Problem of Meaning in the Philosophy of Mind*. MIT Press.

Fodor, Jerry A. (1990). *A Theory of Content and Other Essays*. MIT Press.

Fodor, Jerry A. (2003). *Hume Variations*. Clarendon Press.

Fodor, Jerry A., & Lepore, Ernest. (1992). *Holism: A Shopper's Guide*. Wiley-Blackwell.

Fodor, Jerry, & Lepore, Ernie. (2007). Brandom beleaguered. *Philosophy and Phenomenological Research*, *74*(3), 677–691.

Fuld, Kenneth, Wooten, Billy R., & Whalen, James J. (1981). The elemental hues of short-wave and extraspectral lights. *Perception & Psychophysics*, *29*(4), 317–322.

Gallistel, Charles R. (1998). Symbolic processes in the brain: The case of insect navigation. *An Invitation to Cognitive Science*, *4*, 1–51.

Godfrey-Smith, Peter. (2001). Three kinds of adaptationism. In S. Orzack & E. Sober (eds.) *Adaptationism and Optimality*. Cambridge University Press.

Greenberg, Mark., & Harman, Gilbert. (2008). Conceptual role semantics. In E. Lepore & B. Smith (eds.) *The Oxford Handbook of Philosophy of Language* (pp. 295–322). Oxford University Press.

Hardin, C. L. (2003). A spectral reflectance doth not a color make. *The Journal of Philosophy*, *100*(4), 191–202.

Hardin, C. L. (1988). *Color for Philosophers: Unweaving the Rainbow*. Hackett Publishing.

Hering, Ewald. (1878/1964). *Outlines of a Theory of the Light Sense*, trans. L. M. Hurvich and D. Jameson. Harvard University Press.

Johnson, Gabbrielle (this volume). *Unconscious Perception and Unconscious Bias: Parallel Debates About Unconscious Content*. In Kriegel, U. (ed.) *Oxford Studies in Philosophy of Mind vol. 3*. Oxford University Press.

Loar, Brian. (1981). *Meaning and Mind*. Cambridge University Press.

Lycan, William G. (2014). The intentionality of smell. *Frontiers in Psychology*, 5, 436.

Marr, David. (1982). *Vision: A Computational Investigation into the Human Representation and Processing of Visual Information*. MIT Press.

Mendelovici, Angela. (2013). Reliable misrepresentation and tracking theories of mental representation. *Philosophical Studies*, 165(2), 421–443.

Mendelovici, Angela A. (2018). *The Phenomenal Basis of Intentionality*. Oxford University Press.

Millikan, Ruth Garrett. (1984). *Language, Thought, and Other Biological Categories: New Foundations for Realism*. MIT Press.

Mitterer, Holger, & Blomert, Leo. (2003). Coping with phonological assimilation in speech perception: Evidence for early compensation. *Perception & Psychophysics*, 65(6), 956–969.

Newell, Allen. (1980). Physical symbol systems. *Cognitive Science*, 4(2), 135–183.

Pereplyotchik, David. (2017). *Psychosyntax: The Nature of Grammar and Its Place in the Mind*, vol. 129. Springer.

Poldrack, Russell A. (2020). The physics of representation. *Synthese*, 199 (1–2), 1307–1325.

Pylyshyn, Zenon Walter. (1984). *Computation and Cognition*. MIT Press.

Quine, W. V. O. (1951). Ontology and ideology. *Philosophical Studies*, 2(1), 11–15.

Rescorla, Michael. (2017). Levels of computational explanation. *Philosophy and Computing* (pp. 5–28). Springer.

Rey, Georges. (2006). Conventions, intuitions and linguistic inexistents: A reply to Devitt. *Croatian Journal of Philosophy*, 6(18), 549–569.

Rey, Georges. (2008). In defense of Folieism: Replies to critics. *Croatian Journal of Philosophy*, 8(23), 177–202.

Rey, Georges. (2020). *Representation of Language: Philosophical Issues in a Chomskyan Linguistics*. Oxford University Press.

Schouten, Bert, Gerrits, Ellen, & Van Hessen, Arjan. (2003). The end of categorical perception as we know it. *Speech Communication*, 41(1), 71–80.

Shea, Nicholas. (2018). *Representation in Cognitive Science*. Oxford University Press.

Sprouse, Jon, & Hornstein, Norbert. (2013). *Experimental Syntax and Island Effects*. Cambridge University Press.

Stalnaker, Robert. (1989). On what's in the head. *Philosophical Perspectives*, 3, 287–316.

Sterelny, Kim. (2003). *Thought in a Hostile World: The Evolution of Human Cognition*. Blackwell.

Stich, Stephen P. (1983). *From Folk Psychology to Cognitive Science: The Case against Belief.* MIT Press.

Witzel, Christoph. (2019). Misconceptions about color categories. *Review of Philosophy and Psychology, 10*(3), 499–540.

4
Unconscious Perception and Unconscious Bias
Parallel Debates about Unconscious Content

Gabbrielle M. Johnson

1. Introduction

Two parallel debates about unconscious mental content serve as fruitful domains in which to study the relationship between philosophy and empirical science. The first debate, about unconscious perception, highlights conceptual confusion regarding its two central notions of *consciousness* and *perception*. Progress in understanding the nature of unconscious perception is due to a mutual exchange between philosophers and psychologists working in tandem to clarify concepts, test those concepts using empirical methods, and use the combined conceptual-empirical methods to make progress on a general theory of unconscious content. A second debate, emerging more recently, concerns the existence of unconscious social bias. Though still in early stages, comparatively less attention has been paid to the possible exchange between philosophy and social psychology. But, as I'll argue, here too empirical science and philosophy have much to gain from one another.

In this chapter, I zoom in on these two contemporary debates concerning unconscious content in order to illustrate the benefits of exchange between philosophy and empirical science. I begin, in section 2, with some conceptual groundwork, introducing two philosophical marks of the mental that will be central to each debate to follow—consciousness and representational content—and associated problems that accompany empirical study of both. Then, in section 3, I investigate the debate around unconscious perception, demonstrating how it has clarified the conceptual problems facing any debate about unconscious content and how it has attempted to overcome these problems. In section 4, I investigate the debate of unconscious social bias, demonstrating how it is subject to these same conceptual problems and arguing that progress on them can be made by adopting lessons learned from the debate about unconscious perception.

2. Consciousness and Content

Historically, philosophers have found it helpful to distinguish between two so-called "marks of the mental": *consciousness* and *intentional content*. Consciousness is paradoxically the most familiar and the most mysterious mark of the mental. Most famously, the notion of consciousness is thought to be captured by "the feeling of what it's like." If some creature is conscious, then there is a feeling of what it is like to be that creature. If some state of the creature is conscious, then there is something it is like for the creature to be in that state. That is, when in this state, the creature has some unique, subjective perspective on how the world is presented to them. Consider the feeling of what it's like to stub your toe, to wake up to the rich smell of coffee, to stare intently at a perfectly ripe tomato, to fall in love. Each of these experiences is accompanied by a rich host of phenomenal qualities (or "qualia") that are presented to you and only you through your subjective experience.[1] In a nutshell, consciousness corresponds roughly to the inward-directed, subjective aspects of mental life: how things feel *for you*.[2]

Intentional content, on the other hand, corresponds roughly to the mind's ability to reach out into the world, bringing outward objects into the mind to think about (and, perhaps, present through conscious experience). Historically, philosophers have associated intentional content with *aboutness*. My belief that Barack Obama attended Harvard Law School has this quality: it is about things out there in the world, most centrally a person named

---

[1] More precisely, we might follow Kriegel (2009) in distinguishing between the "subjective character" of there being something it's like to be in the state and the "qualitative character" of what it's like to be in the state.

[2] As much as possible, I avoid making distinctions between different kinds of consciousness (access, phenomenal, introspective, etc.). See Block (1995) and Berger (2022) for further, helpful distinctions. I likewise avoid spelling out theories of what makes something consciously accessible. This unfortunately includes interesting theories specifically with respect to the debates at hand, e.g., HOT theories (Rosenthal 2005; Berger 2020), inferential/interpretive awareness theories (Carruthers 2017), and attention, categorization, and control of action theories (Krickel 2018), all of which are developed in the context of the debate about unconscious social bias. Questions about what makes some state consciously accessible are different from the question of how we might empirically test for consciousness, the latter of which will be a central theme of the chapter.

"Barack Obama," a law school named "Harvard Law School," and the relation of *attending*. We might say that the representational content of my belief is, again roughly, the proposition that "Barack Obama attended Harvard Law School." Crucially, the way the world is represented might not be how the world actually is—perhaps Barack Obama attended Yale. In these cases, the representational content is false or inaccurate.[3]

The view of the mind we're left with is one where the mind is conceptually split into two capacities: consciousness (i.e., subjective experience) and cognition (i.e., mental calculation involving representational contents). Purported cases of unconscious content to be discussed will involve states that allegedly have just one of these marks: content. That is, they lack consciousness but have representational content. This involves two separate arguments: first, that they're unconscious; and, second, that they're representational. Each debate to follow presents challenges to each step.

In what follows, I walk through each of these debates (about consciousness and content) for each case study (about perception and bias) totaling four dialectical touchstones. This will highlight the extensions from one to the other: arguments surrounding consciousness of perception will be similar to, and help to inform, arguments surrounding consciousness for bias, likewise for arguments surrounding content for both.

Regarding consciousness, the debates in both domains will boil down to the difficulty in establishing that some state is truly unconscious. This is partly due to there being no universally agreed-upon empirical methods for studying consciousness.[4] In most cases, empirical methods purporting to study consciousness rely on subjective reports. However, notoriously, subjective reports are prone to response bias. Thus, in any particular case, critics of unconscious content will argue that purported cases are not truly unconscious, but rather cases where subjective report is in some sense obscuring the conscious accessibility of the state. I'll call the broad collection of these sorts of issues "the Conscious Criterion Problem":[5]

---

[3] Here I am presenting a view that roughly accords with a representational theory of mind. Not all philosophers subscribe to such a view of the mind, but the framework is nearly ubiquitous in empirical psychology and cognitive science. So adopting it here has the additional advantage of facilitating communication between the two domains, which is a primary goal of the chapter.

[4] Some question whether there can ever be a satisfying scientific explanation of consciousness. See Irvine (2013) for a comprehensive discussion. I avoid such extreme skepticism here.

[5] My Conscious Criterion Problem and Content Attribution Problem are modeled roughly on Ian Phillips's Criterion and Attribution Problems to be discussed below. Phillips's Attribution problem focuses more on so-called "attributability to the individual" than mine does. My reasons for this departure will become clear as the debates unfold.

The Conscious Criterion Problem: Some purported unconscious representational content might in fact not be unconscious (because it is a conscious state registering below a subjective response criterion).

Likewise, in the absence of consciousness, establishing that a state has representational content is not a straightforward matter. This is because we standardly distinguish between a robust sort of intentionality, exhibited by mental states that are attributable to individuals, and weaker statistical notions, exhibited when parts of the natural world carry information about other parts of the natural world. The natural world finds plenty of ways for some things to carry information about other things. This can be as mundane as the angle of a rock's shadow carrying information about the time of day. If this is all there were to intentional content, then it might seem that the mind's capacity for *aboutness* is not all that unique, i.e., it is no longer a mark of the mental. Thus, in any particular case, critics of unconscious content will argue that purported cases are not truly representational contents attributable as mental states to the individuals that harbor them, but rather cases where there is some low-level, non-representational information processing occurring. In essence, they're arguing that such processes' lacking consciousness is theoretically uninteresting, as it's tantamount to a rock's shadow not being accompanied by subjective experience. I'll call the broad collection of these sorts of issues, "the Content Attribution Problem":

The Content Attribution Problem: Some purported unconscious representational content might in fact not be representational content (because it does not differ significantly from low-level, non-representational information processing).

I now turn to the two parallel debates on unconscious content that center around these two concepts and their associated problems.

3. Is Unconscious Perception Unconscious Content?

The first purported case of an unconscious representational content is unconscious perception. Following tradition in philosophy and psychology, the focus here will be almost exclusively on visual perception. Exploration of this case will serve as an exemplary model of how philosophers and scientists can mutually inform our understanding of unconscious content.

3.1 What Is Perception?

For the question of whether perception can be unconscious to make sense, we need some characterization of perception that does not presuppose conscious accessibility. If we were to define visual perception as conscious visual awareness, then since there can be no unconscious conscious visual awareness, there could be no unconscious perception. Thus, we need some characterization that is independent of consciousness.

One such independent characterization utilized in debates about unconscious perception originates in the work of Tyler Burge. Burge (2010, 2022) characterizes perception as objective sensory representation, paradigmatically by the individual. In what follows, I summarize each element of this characterization using a concrete (though idealized) example.

Suppose I have an accurate visual perception of a white berry under blue light. The basic mechanics of how this visual perception comes to fruition begins with the distal cause of my perception (the white berry) and culminates in the perceptual state itself (with the content "white berry"). In between, there is a complex chain of non-perceptual, causal processes linking the two. The chain begins with blue light streaming down and coming into contact with the surface of the berry (what we'll call *the distal cause*). At that point, a combination of light bounces off the berry. To keep track, we'll call the initial blue light *the illuminance*, the white *the reflectance*, and the combination of blue and white *the luminance*. The luminance is what the eyes register initially, on a two-dimensional array constituting the retina. We regard it as the *proximal stimulus* because it is closer than the *distal cause*. When the luminance makes contact with the array, the sensory registrations responsible for activating when hit with the appropriate kind of stimulus (in this case, the mostly blue light) activate. Thus, the sensory array registers information about the luminance. But notice the puzzle here: what we've registered is the mostly blue light of the proximal stimulus, but what we're really interested in is the color of the distal berry itself, which is white. So, the visual system's primary function is to get us from proximal to distal. It does this by processing the initial sensory information through a series of rule-governed calculations, one of which will subtract surrounding light for the purpose of getting at the true color of the berry. Thus, this calculation takes as an input the luminance (blue + white) and subtracts the illuminance (blue) so as to produce an output of the reflectance (white). The whole process is a paradigm instance of cognition (mental calculation involving representational contents) (see Figure 4.1).

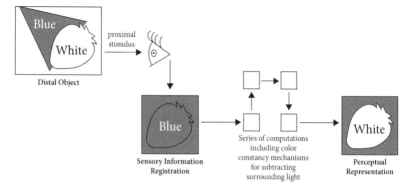

Figure 4.1 An idealized model of seeing a white berry under blue light.

Crucially, the same type of sensory information registration could be the result of many possible distal objects. For example, the same registration of blue could be the result of a blue berry under blue light or a magenta berry under blue light (and there are indefinitely many other combinations as well). So there are many other cues and rule-governed processes that the visual system uses to make a best guess as to how to perform the calculation correctly. Discovering which cues are important and what rules govern the processes is the primary aim of vision science. This is a difficult task and made possible only by exploring a myriad of cases where things go awry. While the visual system is astonishingly good at getting things right, exploring cases where it gets things wrong gives psychologists hints about what sorts of cues and assumptions it relies on.

In the berry example, a non-standard visual scene, such as an image cleverly designed to seem like uniform blue illumination, but that in fact has an illumination gap just where the berry is, will result in a perceptual illusion. In this case, the visual system's assumption that illuminance is uniform will cause it to subtract blue light from the berry. But since there is no illumination on the berry, subtracting blue will lead it astray. Subtracting in this context makes the distal object appear yellower than it actually is, resulting in visual illusions.[6] Working backwards, scientists observe that we're systematically prone to illusions in these sorts of contexts, and so infer to internal workings of the visual system, i.e., the assumption that illumination is uniform and the process that subtracts it. Thus, knowing the cases of

---

[6] You can explore these sorts of illusions for yourself here: https://www.echalk.co.uk/amusements/OpticalIllusions/colourPerception/colourPerception.html

when the visual system gets things right (produces accurate representations) and when it gets things wrong (produces inaccurate representations) is crucial to vision science. In this way, a notion of intentional or representational content is baked into the very heart of contemporary cognitive psychology.

With this example in hand, we can inspect each of the four aspects of Burge's characterization: that perception is objective, sensory, representational, and paradigmatically by the individual. Importantly, this characterization is not meant to give collective necessary or sufficient conditions for some psychological state's being perception.[7] The notions of *objective* and *representational* are most central to Burge's understanding of perception, and are most important for our purposes of extending lessons from the debate about perception to the debate about bias.

Let's start with the claim that perceptual states are sensory. This means that perceptual states, unlike other higher level cognitive states, are constitutively tied to sensory modalities. Visual perception is tied to vision, auditory perception to audition, etc. A state's being tied to sensory modalities in this way can be contrasted with higher level cognitive states that are amodal. Propositional attitudes like belief and desire seem not tied to any specific modality. Some states can be sensory but not be perception. The information registrations at the retina are an example. These states are not perception because they do not rise to the status of objective representation.

Which bring us to the two most central notions of the characterization: objectivity and representation. For a state to be representational is, for Burge, for veridicality conditions (namely, conditions under which we would say the state is true or accurate) to feature as an essential aspect of its nature. In other words, veridicality conditions are essential to that state's being the state that it is. Contrasts are helpful. In the case of the information registration, that state is characterized in straightforward causal terms: the registrations were directly caused by the light hitting the retina. Of course, we can talk about the state *as if* it had veridicality conditions (we could say that the retina "represents" blue light), but we don't have to. In this case, simpler non-representational, mere causal statements can do the trick. Contrast that with the representation of white at the end of the process. Here, a direct causal story won't do. This is partly because the white berry is

---

[7] Burge (2022, 19). There are some psychological states that are objective sensory representations by the individual that are not perception, such as states of perceptual memory and anticipation (these are perceptual, but not perception, according to Burge). However, it will be impossible that some state is not objective or representational, but is still perception.

not a direct cause of the perception; rather, it is mediated by a variety of other causal links (including the sensory registration). Likewise, while it might be true in some cases to say that the representation was distally caused by the white reflectance of the berry, it needn't always be caused in this way. As we saw in the case of optical illusions, the very same type of sensory registration, producing the very same type of representational state, could be formed by very different distal causes. Notice that in these cases, e.g. where the reflectance of the berry is white but we inaccurately form the representation of a yellow reflectance, we cannot point to a yellow reflectance as the cause (not even distally). Thus, to characterize the nature of the representational state, we *must* go beyond reference to direct, proximal causes. We *must* make use of veridicality conditions, saying what the state was aiming to pick out (even in the absence of that thing). This is roughly what it means for the state to have veridicality conditions as an aspect of the state's nature, i.e. for the state to be representational.

This discussion also helpfully elucidates what it means for the state to be objective. In this case, the representational state is objective insofar as it captures features of the distal object that go beyond idiosyncratic features of the subject's registrational capacities. In other words, the representation can continue to represent the distal berry as white, despite the ever-changing idiosyncratic registrations at the retina. Were we to move the white berry out of blue light and into yellow light, the proximal registrations would change dramatically (shifting from blue to yellow). However, we wouldn't thereby see the berry as drastically changing color. Instead, we continue to see the berry as white. Our visual system first subtracts the blue, and then subtracts the yellow, keeping the representation white. This ability to keep distal features constant despite ever-changing proximal stimulations is precisely the function of what are called "perceptual constancy mechanisms." Because of their ability to facilitate the tracking of distal features, resulting in the formation of objective representational states, the constancy mechanisms posited by visual psychology feature centrally in Burge's theory of perception. They take us from sensory informational registrations that are non-representational and merely causal to rich representational states that are of (or *as of*, in the case of misrepresentation) constant, distal features of the environment. They are, according to Burge, the origins of objectivity in the mind. They are what allow representational mind to begin.

What of the last element of the characterization, that perception is paradigmatically by the individual? One might think this is the most central aspect of the characterization given how prominently it figures in the debates to follow. However, I'll argue that this emphasis is misplaced, and that rather we should maintain a focus on the two most central notions of the characterization: objectivity and representation. Still, it will help to give a brief gloss of what is meant by the idea.

Formally, a state's being *by the individual* means that it is "functionally integrated with the exercises of whole individual functions."[8] The basic distinction Burge is interested in is between states and processes that it is natural to attribute to the individual as opposed to those it is natural to attribute merely to an individual's subsystems. Some cases can be illustrated by consideration of simple intuitions. For example, does it make more sense to say that I subtract surrounding light from the information registration or that my visual system does? Does it make more sense to say that I perceive a white berry or that my visual system does? Following these intuitions, perceptual constancies are attributed to the perceptual system whereas the representational states themselves are attributed to the individual.[9] Perception, according to Burge, is sometimes (and paradigmatically) by the individual, but he allows that some perceptual states could occur that are not by the individual, e.g. some lower levels of visual processing might be better attributed only to the visual system. We will return to these issues in the debates to follow.

---

[8] Burge (2020, 69, fn. 45).
[9] Burge never gives clear criteria for attribution to the individual. Other considerations beyond intuition are varied and show up primarily in orthogonal discussions regarding behavior and primitive agency (see Burge 2010, 333–341, 369–376, for full discussion). Some considerations (Burge 2010, 331, 333) rest on a state or process issuing from "central [behavioral/coordinating] capacities," a feature Phillips (Phillips and Block 2017, 169, 174, 181; Phillips 2018, 494, 497–499) places a lot of weight on in the debate to follow, but is ultimately inessential to Burge's notion. Other considerations of Burge's involve whether the state involves the whole body of the individual or, more intuitively, just the head (Burge 2010, 332, fn. 60). Some states and processes can be attributed to the individual without being representational or perceptual. For example, a feeling of pain might be entirely sensory (non-representational), but it is felt by the individual. Crucially, some states and processes can be attributable to the individual without being guided by the individual (i.e., under conscious, deliberative control of the individual). Burge (2010, 332) gives the example of a creature writhing in pain as a pure reflex that is nevertheless attributable to the individual. Burge says explicitly that action guided by perception need not be under the control or guidance of the individual, insofar as "the individual could not monitor or adjust" the action (Burge 2010, 335, fn. 62). In the surrounding context of that footnote, Burge provides an extensive discussion of a grouse's reflexive, instinctual behavior to mate. This behavior is guided purely by visual perception and not the grouse in some voluntary way, but attributable to the grouse nevertheless. Likewise, he gives the example of an individual's ducking reflex being attributable to them, but not under voluntary control (Burge 2010, 335). Burge (2010, 369) is also explicit that not all perception is by the individual. Rather, he says, perception is *fundamentally* by the individual, meaning that all perceptions either are themselves—or contribute to other perceptions that are themselves—attributable to the individual. For more discussion, see Burge (2020, fn. 45).

With this characterization of perception in hand, we can now turn to evidence for the existence of unconscious perception.

3.2 What Is Unconscious Perception?

I begin with two cases frequently offered to support the claim that unconscious visual perception exists—blindsight (or neglect) and continuous flash suppression (involving subliminal priming). I will follow the trajectory of the debate as it has been laid out by Ian Phillips and Ned Block, two empirically oriented philosophers of mind. Block defends the position that unconscious perception exists and is well-established by scientific findings. Phillips denies the existence of unconscious perception, providing both a systematic critique of the purported evidence as well as philosophical grounds on which to doubt convincing evidence could ever be marshaled.[10]

The first purported cases of unconscious perception, blindsight and neglect, involve partial damage to areas of the brain responsible for visual processing. This results in instances where subjects report having no conscious awareness of at least some part of their visual field but are nevertheless able to perform behaviors similar to normally sighted individuals.

Consider a famous case of neglect studied by Marshall and Halligan (1988). The subject P.S. was presented with the following image, aligned in such a way that the left sides of both houses fell into her left visual field (her "blind" side) (see Figure 4.2).

P.S.'s reports suggested that she lacked conscious access to the left side of both houses. When asked whether the houses are the same or different, she responded that they are the same. When asked if there was anything wrong with either of the houses, she responded no. These responses seem to vindicate claims that she lacked conscious awareness on this side. However, when she was asked which house she would prefer to live in, she chose the house without fire well above chance (on nine out of eleven trials).[11] This seems to indicate that she represented features of the left side of the visual scene, despite purportedly lacking conscious awareness of it. Thus it seems a candidate case of perceptual representation without consciousness.

---

[10] The debate ranges over a series of articles including, but not limited to, Block (2015); Phillips (2015, 2018, 2021); and Phillips and Block (2017).

[11] Marshall and Halligan (1988, 766); see also Phillips (2015, 15).

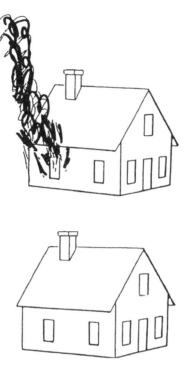

Figure 4.2 Stimulus used by Marshall and Halligan (1988) to demonstrate neglect.

Some, like Block, are suspicious of relying on cases of blindsight and neglect to defend unconscious perception because they involve damage resulting in neuro-atypicality. It's difficult to tell in these cases if the damage has truly resulted in a lack of conscious awareness, as opposed to full-blown conscious awareness coupled with an inability to report.[12] Block prefers to defend cases of unconscious perception from our second category. These involve neurotypical individuals whose perceptual contents are purportedly rendered unconscious due to suppression techniques, including masking, binocular rivalry, and continuous flash suppression (Phillips and Block 2017, 174).

---

[12] One might also find it suspicious if cases of unconscious perception were possible only in patients with brain damage. Here, we are minimally exploring the possibility of unconscious content, not pursuing the stronger claim that it is normal or even frequent. In any case, other instances of purported cases involve neurotypical subjects.

In cases of continuous flash suppression, the two eyes are presented with different stimuli, one of which is a flashing, high-contrast image called a "Mondrian" and the other a normal image of, say, a house or face. The flashing image allegedly suppresses the ordinary image from the subject's conscious awareness, resulting in subjects reporting near total unawareness of it. Nevertheless, evidence suggests some processing of the content of the suppressed image must be taking place. Block cites studies by Jiang et al. (2007) where images of nude bodies presented to subjects appeared to be suppressed from conscious awareness by Mondrians. When subjects were asked questions about the location of the nude body image, they were at chance in responding, suggesting the images were unconscious. Still, after viewing these images, the subjects were faster at identifying properties of the next stimulus provided it appeared on the same side as the nude image and the nude matched the gender that was desirable given the subject's reported sexual orientation (a point that will be important later in the debate).[13] Again, this seems to indicate that the subjects perceptually represented the nude images, despite purportedly lacking conscious awareness of them.

In both of these cases, we have evidence for visual perceptual representation in the absence of consciousness. Critics of these cases, most notably Phillips, object to them on one of two grounds, presenting a dilemma for the proponent of unconscious perception. The first objection is that these findings are arguably not the result of unconscious mental states (as opposed to conscious mental states that the subject fails to report due to personal biases in their responses); while the second objection is that these findings arguably lack genuine perception (as opposed to non-perceptual, mere information processing). The first Phillips labels *the problem of the criterion* and the second, *the problem of attribution*. (It is from these more narrow characterizations that I derived the more general characterizations of the problems defined above.)

3.3 Is Perception Really Unconscious?

The first critique of purported cases of unconscious perception is that they are not clearly cases lacking consciousness. It seems our best evidence as to

---

[13] Phillips and Block (2017, 177–178).

whether some state is conscious or unconscious for some individual is through the individual's own verbal reports. As Block (2007, 535) states, "introspective reports do have a certain priority: we have no choice but to start with reports in investigating consciousness." This makes sense since consciousness is ultimately a matter of subjective experience, and who better to report those experiences than the subject. However, notoriously, such reports are also subject to response bias.

Recall the questions asked in the neglect study:

1) Are the houses the same or different?
2) Is there anything wrong with one of them?
3) Which would you want to live in?

The worry is that some of these questions might prompt conservative responses in light of, say, uncertainty or lack of confidence, which themselves could be the result of degraded or fragmented conscious perception rather than from unconscious perception. In these cases, we might say that the subject is only "dimly conscious" of the relevant stimulus, and that conscious awareness is so dim that they hesitate to rely on it when producing subjective reports.[14]

We can imagine that P.S. does have *some* conscious awareness of what's occurring on the left side of her visual field, it's just that this awareness is weak, perhaps even incomplete—she is merely "dimly conscious" of it.[15] This would give her an inkling that something is different between the two houses, but she might be hesitant to trust that inkling. Thus, in response to questions (1) and (2), she might decide not to trust her inkling, instead preferring to err conservatively on the side of reporting no difference. One can

---

[14] Response bias can be due to many factors outside of mere uncertainty. It might be that subjects are aware of what the experiment is intended to study, and so (wittingly or unwittingly) conform their responses to them; or they might simply have other personal motivations for responding in particular ways, like to preserve certain self-conceptions. These other ways response bias thwarts measures of consciousness will be especially relevant in the discussion of unconscious social bias.

[15] Likewise, blindsight subjects often state that although they cannot precisely identify the stimulus in front of them, they are aware that something is happening. Consider, for example, what's often called *type-2 blindsight*, which differs from *type-1 blindsight* in that patients with the former but not the latter "under some circumstances, report some kind of experiences associated with stimuli presented in their regions of blindness" (Kentridge 2015, 41). These cases are typically instances wherein blindsight patients can detect sharp changes in contrast or motion, but are not able to discriminate what sorts of changes they're detecting. In other words, they have a feeling that something happened, but they can't say what it is.

imagine her reasoning that if, say in response to question (1), she reports the houses are different, then she might then be on the hook for saying in what way they differ—a question she doesn't feel confident she can provide a precise answer to. However, when confronted with question (3), it's not clear which option would be more conservative than the other. No matter what she chooses, she can always fall back on claiming she just picked one at random. Therefore, her responses to this question seem free from response bias and are taken to more accurately reflect her conscious experience. If this story is right, then what appeared evidence for unconscious perception can be explained away by response bias.

Phillips puts these points in terms of Signal Detection Theory (SDT). Here, I summarize the theory in order to highlight two advantages it provides in engaging with the conscious criterion problem. First, SDT has the advantage of distinguishing between measures of tasks that are and are not subject to response bias. Returning again to P.S., her ability to discriminate between the houses revealed by question (3) is taken to be free of response bias. In SDT, this ability is measured by d', where a value of d' greater than zero indicates some ability to discriminate between signal and noise. That said, her willingness to report same/different or yes/no revealed by questions (1) and (2) was taken to be subject to response bias. Thus, it is a product of some combination of d' and her particular subjective response criterion c. Think of c as a threshold set by each subject (not necessarily deliberatively) for responding. If the subject has some discriminative capacity (d' > 0) *and* that capacity has exceeded their personal threshold (c), then their reports are likely to reflect their discriminative capacity. However, it's possible that they have some discriminative capacity (d' > 0) that falls below their personal threshold c, in which case their reports will not reveal the full range of their capacity to detect signal from noise. Looking at extremes, one can imagine a subject that has an extremely conservative response bias (say they, for whatever reason, refuse to ever report seeing a stimulus), which would result in learning almost nothing about their discriminative capacities.

The second advantage of SDT, related to the first, is that it helps keep track of four possibilities that can occur for any discriminative task involving a combination of signal and noise: first, a subject can say there's a signal when there is (a true positive); second, they can say there's no signal when there isn't (a true negative); third, they can say there's a signal when there isn't (a false positive); and finally, they can say there's no signal when there is (a false negative). Notice how these might intersect in interesting ways with c. If there is never a signal present and the subject has an extremely conservative response bias, they might accidentally register a lot of true negatives. Likewise, if there's always a signal present and the subject has an extremely liberal response bias, they might accidentally register a lot of true positives. Both would give the appearance that the subject is quite accurate in their discriminative abilities even if they're not; were the signal to fluctuate, we would see that they have many false positives and false negatives, respectively. Thus, the base-rates of the stimulus are important for measuring overall accuracy.[16] Reading discriminative capacity off of results becomes even more complicated if we allow for the possibility of subjects changing their response criterion c from trial to trial.

In sum, some observed behaviors that seemed evidence of unconscious perception might not in fact be tracking conscious awareness. This is because those measures track behaviors that are a combination of many features, including subjective response criteria. All behavioral responses that are not free of potential response bias—which includes all subjective reports about what a subject sees—will be subject to what we (partly following Phillips) call "the conscious criterion problem." In all cases we can ask: is this person really not conscious of what they see, or are they merely not confident enough to report it to others?

What's important for our purposes is that progress can be made on this issue by relying on sophisticated (psychophysical) metrics that can tease apart objective and subjective criterion influences. According to Phillips, SDT is one metric that shows promise in this domain. In the end, Phillips and Block agree that there are empirical tests where sophisticated metrics have arguably been used to measure objective discrimination capacities that operate below conscious awareness. However, Phillips will respond that in all such cases where we have a good candidate for unconsciousness using such methods, such cases will not involve genuine attributable content. They lack the relevant conditions that would distinguish these cases from mere low-level, non-representational information processing. In other words, they fall victim to the content attribution problem, which I turn to next.

---

[16] This point will be important later when discussing recent evidence for unconscious social bias.

3.4 Is Unconscious Perception Really Attributable Content?

According to Phillips, the attribution problem distills into a problem about individual-level attributability. Attributability to the individual will, for him, require some connection to voluntary control. On this, Phillips at various times contrasts, on the one hand, states and processes that are attributable to the individual by dint of being "available to central agency," being within "voluntary, agentive control," being those that "the subjects can themselves use," being those that can be "exploited by subjects to guide and control their actions," and being those that operate in accordance with "subject's knowledge and intentions"; while on the other hand, states that are not attributable to the individual by dint of being "completely stimulus-driven reflexes," of operating "entirely outside of voluntary control," and outside of "direct control."[17] Crucially, according to Phillips, all of the cases of unconscious perception that do not fall victim to the criterion problem (and some that do), fall victim to this attribution problem, because they fail to meet these standards for attribution to the individual.[18]

Block, like Burge, denies that availability to central agency is a necessary condition for attributability to the individual. Likewise, he argues that his preferred cases of unconscious perception are attributable to the individual, since the representational contents they involve are high-level contents connected to whole-individual aims. Consider again the Jiang et al. (2007) study. Because the nude images only primed identification in cases where they matched the sexual orientation of the subject, the study suggests that the subjects were registering high-level content (the gender of the individual in the photo) and that that content was connected in appropriate ways to desires and preferences of the individual. Phillips disagrees, stating among a variety of reasons that it is not the contents of a state that determine its attributability, but rather its role in the guidance of voluntary control (which he argues is a role the states in Jiang et al. lack).[19]

---

[17] For a sampling of these phrases, see Phillips and Block (2017, 181) and Phillips (2018, 495, 496, 498, 499).

[18] One obvious worry with this approach is that, if you think voluntary control is synonymous with *conscious* voluntary control, then we're back to a notion of perception that presupposes consciousness. Thus, this conception of individual attributability runs the risk of, as Robert Kendridge warns, "slipping in a requirement equivalent to 'perception must be conscious' through the back door" (Peters et al. 2017, 4).

[19] See Phillips and Block (2017, 173–174) for discussion.

This is just a small sampling of a rich discussion regarding the relationship between action, behavior, agency, and attributability to the individual.[20] There's a lot more to say about the notion both within and independent of the debate about unconscious perception. Both Burge and Phillips acknowledge that these concepts need further development than is provided by either of their works.[21]

I believe it was a mistake to place so much weight on the notion of attributability to an individual within Burge's characterization of perception. Contrary to what Phillips reports, attributability to the individual is not a necessary feature of *all* perception according to Burge.[22] While it's true that Burge states, "fundamentally, it is the individual that perceives," he prefaces that statement with "I do not claim that *all* perceptions are perceptions by an individual."[23]

Phillips (and Block) may diverge from Burge on this point too. Their doing so will seemingly bring us back to a dialectical impasse, unless we can find some independent motivation for a neutral characterization of the attributability requirement. I take it that the most compelling reasons to prefer an attributability requirement is that, in the absence of it, there would be no clear criteria for calling something perception. Phillips often makes statements like this when responding to claims that coordinated central agency is not required for perception (Phillips and Block 2017, 181). In the absence of this feature, what positive reason could we provide for regarding some state as perception? Echoing this concern, in discussion of

---

[20] The notion of attributability to the individual is intended to correspond to a more general distinction that is echoed in work far beyond Burge's. There have been, throughout the history of philosophy of mind, many attempts to characterize a distinction between two levels of states within a creature's psychology. For Burge (2010, 2022), the distinction is between being by the individual and not being by the individual. For Dennett (1969), the distinction was between being personal and being subpersonal. For Sellars (1956), it was belonging to the space of reasons vs the space of causes. For Stich (1978), it was being doxastic vs subdoxastic. For Fodor (1983), it was being modular vs belonging to central cognitive capacities. As Block says, all such characterizations come with an air of postulation (Peters et al. 2017, 8).

[21] Burge (2010, 335, fn. 62); Phillips (2018, 499, fn. 45). For impressive work dedicated to the development of these concepts, see Buehler (2014).

[22] Phillips (2018, 481, fn. 19) states that he, Block, and Burge all agree that attributability to the individual is a necessary feature of perception. On this, he says that while Burge maintains that some "perceptual representations" might not be attributable to the individual, perception always (and constitutively) is. Here, Phillips is resting on a distinction made by Burge between perceptual representations and perception proper. It is true that Burge will make this distinction (recall in my discussion of the necessity and sufficiency of the four elements of Burge's characterization that perceptual anticipation and memory are perceptual but not perception). But he does not do so when stating his view that perception need not be by the individual.

[23] Burge (2010, 369; emphasis in original). This point is even more explicit in Burge's direct criticisms of Phillips's misinterpretation of his view. See Burge (2020, fn. 45, and 2022, 19).

why individual attributability is important, Phillips (2018, 498) quotes psychologists Klotz and Neumann (1999, 976), who reason the following: "In ordinary usage, perceiving is something that a person or animal does, not something that can be properly ascribed to stages, subsystems, brain areas, or the like. The triggering of a sneeze by an external stimulus does not imply that the reflex center that controls it 'perceives' the stimulus."[24] It seems then the concern boils down to this: in the absence of clear criteria for individual attributability, there will be no way to distinguish clear cases of non-perception, like the brute causal and transduction mechanisms of the brain, from genuine perception. Put another way, there will be no way to distinguish the kind of robust intentional content we were interested in as a mark of the mental from the more superficial statistical notions of aboutness demonstrated by the rock and shadow.[25]

But distinguishing between brute causal mechanisms of sensory registrations and genuine representational states is precisely what the other criteria of Burge's characterization do. We already have other resources required to overcome this challenge, without resorting to controversial criteria of individual-level attributability. By focusing instead on the attribution of content, understood as some states being both *objective* and *representational* (grounded in scientists' attributions of constancy mechanisms), we have a clear criterion for distinguishing states that are genuine perception from mere sensory registrations. In fact, I think we can bolster this line of reasoning by ruminating on what importance perception's being by the individual was initially intended to capture within Burge's theory. This will simultaneously give us a more nuanced understanding of the content attribution problem and clarify strategies for overcoming it in particular cases.

---

[24] In similar spirit, Quilty-Dunn (2019, 462) states, "mere sensory processing of this sort [transduction] is arguably insufficient for genuine perception" (citing in that context Prinz 2015 and Phillips 2015).

[25] This motivation is related to what Krickel (2022) describes as "the unconscious mind worry": in the absence of consciousness, what reason do we have for regarding some state mental (as opposed to merely biological). Likewise comparing the two debates of unconscious perception and unconscious bias, she offers a mechanistic response wherein what determines whether some process is mental turns on to what extent some mechanistic difference-makers are present in explanations of some behavior in both conscious and unconscious instances. Insofar as both her and my view turn on how some state features in explanations, the two views are congenial to one another. As a biographical note, Krickel's paper was published as I was finishing the final edits of this chapter. I regret not being able to offer a more sustained engagement with it here. No doubt the present chapter would have benefited greatly had I encountered it earlier in the writing process.

What's important in perception's being fundamentally (though not always) attributable to the individual, as discussed by Burge (2010, 370), is that the *kinds* that are eligible to be the objects of representational states are tied to whole-individual function, e.g. eating, mating, flourishing. Going back to the berry example, it's important that we're able to represent distal features of the environment, like the berry and its constant reflectance, because this capacity contributes to whole-individual function. It is, for example, berries that are edible or inedible (not light just before it hits the retina), and it is the berries' reflectances that give us clues about their being edible or inedible. The white berry of Mistletoe is poisonous to humans, even if observed under blue light. These distal features (and our ability to represent them objectively) are what factor into whole-individual functioning. This isn't to say that representational function can be reduced to biological function.[26] However, whole-individual function does help delineate what kinds can factor into representational capacities. Some kind's being a candidate for representational content (as evidenced by our ability to represent those kinds) is enough to link it up in significant and important ways to the goals and desires of the individual. Crucially, none of this depends on overly demanding notions of individual actions, such as that they be within deliberate control of the individual or that they be available to consciousness. Rather, these considerations bring us back to central notions of objectification and a state's having the representational content that it does.

As this discussion brings out, our impetus for content attribution will be tied in fundamental ways to the *kinds* that factor into a state's veridicality conditions. Regarding a state as genuinely contentful (as opposed to reducing it to mere causal, non-representational information processing) will depend on the kinds and properties we think are being tracked by the information processing capacity. When an explanation of this capacity's operation is restricted to properties and kinds instantiated by the proximal stimulus, this will be reason to avoid attributions of genuine representational content. This is why we don't attribute content in the case of sensory registrations: we can make sense of their operation by only ever citing properties of the proximal stimulus. However, when in an explanation of some capacity we

---

[26] Burge (2010, 292–308) goes to great lengths to distinguish between mere biological functions and representational functions. Likewise, not all whole-individual function (even apart from representational function) will be biological and in principle creatures without biological function (like robots) might still have perception (Burge 2022, 26; see also his fn. 46 and p. 280).

must make reference to robust distal kinds, those that are tied in fundamental ways to whole-individual function, then that will be a reason to attribute genuine representational content. This also explains why constancy mechanisms are such good hallmarks of genuine perception: these just are capacities that allow us to track constant distal kinds in the face of ever-changing proximal stimulations. This is not something we can fully explain without making reference to the distal kinds themselves.

I believe this is a better condition of content attribution than one tied to individual attributability as offered by Phillips. What's special about perception is that its content is what it is in virtue of objective, representational capacities that are fundamentally tied to individual-level function. Those contents are what they are (pick out the kinds that they do) in virtue of this connection. Constancy mechanisms are the hallmark of these representations (and misrepresentations) of distal features of the environment. They enable us to get beyond the veil of appearances to objective representation of the world. This is philosophically central.

If this is one's interpretation of the attributability problem, then many cases of purportedly unconscious perception will avoid the content attribution problem. For example, the Jiang et al. (2007) cases cited by Block appear to meet this condition for the reasons stated by Block: that the content is tied in fundamental ways to individual-level pursuits. Likewise, for Burge, many instances of blindsight involve grasping behavior explained only by reference to shape properties of the objects being grasped (i.e., distal properties). Even Phillips admits of the existence of empirical priming studies that satisfy the more rigorous demands of the conscious criterion problem (demonstrated by the employment of SDT) and that involve constancy mechanisms, thereby satisfying the demands of this refined content attributability problem.[27]

3.5 Summary of Insights

This review of the debate about unconscious perception has highlighted two problems any purported case of unconscious content must address, while simultaneously outlining strategies for addressing each. The problems are

---

[27] Phillips offers Norman et al. (2014) as such a case, though he ultimately denies it as a case of unconscious perception since, according to him, it does not meet the individual-attributability requirement. See Phillips and Block (2017, 168–169) for discussion.

the conscious criterion problem and the content attribution problem. The first demands that we distinguish purported cases of unconscious content as those that are truly unconscious, as measured by some objective conscious criterion, and not merely the byproduct of interaction effects with some subjective response criterion. To address this issue, empirical work can adopt sophisticated (psychophysical) metrics such as SDT that can adjudicate effects of the two. The second demands that we distinguish purported cases of unconscious content as those that truly attribute content, as measured by capacities that track distal features of the environment, and not merely causal, non-representational information processing. To address this issue, empirical work can carefully delineate those cases where their attributions of content essentially involve robust distal kinds and properties that feature fundamentally in whole-individual function (such as when visual psychologists posit constancy mechanisms). These cases cannot be reduced to mere causal descriptions involving low-level properties of proximal stimulations.

These will serve as extendable insights into the debate about social bias, which I turn to next.

4. Is Unconscious Bias Unconscious Bias?

Debate about unconscious bias, though still in its infancy, mirrors many aspects of the preceding debate about unconscious perception.[28] Following the path laid out by that debate, I'll address first whether we can characterize bias in a consciousness-neutral way; second, whether there are instances of bias that are unconscious (keeping in mind the consciousness criterion problem); and third, whether there are instances of bias that involve genuine attributable content (keeping in mind the content attribution problem).

---

[28] Often scholarship on unconscious biases calls them "implicit biases" or "implicit attitudes." The word *implicit* is used in many ways in the literature. For many, it means unconscious. For others, it is associated with other properties themselves associated with so-called *system 1* processes, e.g. being fast, automatic, and subpersonal. More recently, there's been a push in the literature on implicit bias to use *implicit* to describe the indirect tests for mental states (like the Implicit Association Test (IAT)) rather than the mental states themselves. In my own work, I use it more aligned with philosophical theories of representational content, where *implicit* is taken to mean not explicitly represented, i.e. merely encoded in the operation of the computational system. Thus, I claim that some "implicit biases" are "truly implicit." See Johnson (2020c, 1201–1205) for discussion. Here, I will as much as possible use "unconscious bias" rather than "implicit bias" to avoid further confusion.

4.1 What Is Bias?

As in the case of unconscious perception, for the question of whether unconscious bias is possible to make sense, we need some notion of bias that does not presuppose conscious accessibility. In my work, I've argued for a general, functional account of bias.[29] In a functional account of bias, we specify what bias is by the functional role that it serves: roughly, by its input-output behavior or, rougher still, the ways that it guides transitions between informational states.[30]

According to this account, bias exhibits a functional profile (that is, it interacts with other mental states in ways) that mimics inductions on the basis of environmental regularities. Part of what defines bias's functional role is its response to underdetermination present in induction. Bias originates for the purpose of overcoming this underdetermination, and it does so by tracking environmental regularities. Thus, bias is embodied in the reality-tracking rules that guide induction. In short, biases are assumptions (heuristics, tendencies, norms) that allow us to limit the inductive hypothesis space to a tractable size by assuming what is normal in our environment.[31]

Consider again the discussion above of perceiving the white berry. This case illustrates a perceptual bias. Because the sensory registration of light underdetermines the possible distal objects that can cause the sensory registration, it also underdetermines the possible representational contents that can be formed on the basis of that registration. In order to overcome this underdetermination, the visual system adopts the bias to subtract surrounding light. This bias, together with the sensory input, allows the visual system to output a representation of a white berry. In this way, the assumptions embedded in constancy mechanisms throughout the visual system are all biases that encode regularities of one's normal physical environment (e.g., that illumination is uniform, that light comes from above, that patterns are homogenous). When a person has a perceptual bias, their visual system has built-in constancy mechanisms that take them from underdetermining two-dimensional informational states to three-dimensional representations of the world.

---

[29] See Johnson (2020a, 2020b, and 2020c).
[30] This is opposed to an account that would specify what bias is by, for instance, a specific neural mechanism in the brain, a particular representational content or format, or by a simple behavioral disposition.
[31] In its focus on induction and underdetermination, my account owes much intellectual debt to Louise Antony's (2001, 2016) work on bias.

Crucially, as previously discussed, the biases illustrated in cases of visual perception are not realized by states with representational content that is attributable to the individual. The assumptions encoded in these transformation processes are not obviously explicitly represented, but arguably tacitly built into how the computational processes operate.[32] However, the flexibility of the functional account allows for variation here. Crucially, the functional account remains agnostic about what sorts of mental entities bridge the gap between the underdetermining inputs and outputs, ultimately highlighting the diversity of candidates that can serve the role and allowing those that are genuinely contentful. These differences can be seen by extending the notion of bias to cases of social bias.[33]

Social bias, like perceptual biases, facilitate inductions made on the basis of regularities within the environment. However, in the case of social induction, the relevant features of the environment will be social groups and the properties taken to be prevalent among their members. When a person has a social bias, they have some combination of states and processes that take them from underdetermining inputs (in the form of beliefs that someone belongs to a social group) to outputs (in the form of beliefs that that person has some characteristics stereotypical of the social group). Social biases, then, encode assumptions about which properties are stereotypical of a social group (e.g., a stereotype that elderly people are bad with computers).[34] Crucially, these states and processes that realize the bias can take many forms. They could be a generic belief, some complex association between solitary concepts, or some other mental construct altogether.

---

[32] See Johnson (2020c) for a full defense of this point.

[33] This general notion of bias can likewise be extended to the biases that exist in machine learning programs, where just as with psychological biases (perceptual or social), algorithmic biases mimic inductions made on the basis of regularities in the environment too. These algorithms imbibe regularities in the environment (e.g., that people type *male* after typing *doctor*; that images of a particular luminance correspond to depth; that people raised in single-parent households are more likely to recidivate) and use them to inductively label new data points. See Johnson (2020a and 2020b) for more discussion.

[34] Here, I'm using *stereotypical* in a neutral way to include social stereotypes as we normally understand them, but to also include broad regularities that are not taken to be social. To draw an analogy with the visual perceptual case, we can speak loosely about the "stereotypical" conditions wherein illumination is uniform. Thus, perceptual biases, like social biases, function to track stereotypes loosely speaking. Of course, they could ultimately fail in this function, i.e. some regularity assumed by the system might not obtain. A system might assume some loose regularity between the properties *being elderly* and *being bad with computers*, but it might turn out that no such regularity actually exists. Moreover, I'm not intending to beg any questions against different views about what is distinctive about social stereotypes. For sophisticated discussion of this question, see Beeghly (2015).

In order to walk through how different elements might correspond to our notion of *bias*, it will help to again have a concrete (though idealized) example.[35]

Imagine a scenario where a person E has a bias against the elderly that causes him to negatively evaluate elderly individuals he encounters. In this case, let's imagine E runs into his fellow colleague Jan, and forms a negative evaluation of her, i.e. he dislikes Jan. When asked why he dislikes Jan, he explains that it's because Jan is elderly and that he dislikes elderly people in general. Here, E has an explicit bias, and the inference he's making seems straightforward:

(i) Jan is elderly.
(ii) I dislike elderly people.
∴ (iii) I dislike Jan.

Although it's clear there's a bias here, it's less clear which mental states and actions correspond to *the bias*.[36] Just focusing on the mental states involved, the bias could be the generalizing belief corresponding to (ii) or the specific conclusion he draws about Jan, which corresponds to (iii). The functional account allows us to distinguish between these. On the functional account, we call the belief about a particular person on the basis of which a discriminatory judgment is formed—in this case, E's belief that Jan is elderly—*the bias-input*. Next, we call the collection of states and processes that—in tandem with the bias-input—cause a discriminatory judgment *the bias-construct*; the bias-construct in E's case is his generalizing belief that he dislikes elderly people (together with whatever inferential processes are necessary to derive the conclusion). Additionally, we call the discriminatory

---

[35] Much of the example and discussion to follow is borrowed (with slight modifications) from Johnson (2020c, 1196).

[36] The word *bias* is often ambiguous. We could refer to someone's acting in discriminatory ways toward members of social groups as their "bias". This would suggest a more behavioral interpretation of bias, one that is becoming increasingly popular in the literature (see, for example, De Houwer 2019). Gawronski et al. (2006) famously distinguished between three different focal points in discussions of social bias awareness: source awareness, content awareness, and impact awareness. These distinctions have now become standard when discussing in what ways, if any, social bias might be unconscious. In fact, these distinctions are not between different types of awareness, but rather different objects that could be the target of awareness. They correspond roughly to the environmental and psychological causes of someone's acquiring a bias (source), the bias itself (content), and the behaviors and psychological states that result from the bias (impact). For reasons to follow, there are important distinctions to be made among the mental states and processes that are seemingly collapsed under Gawronski et al. (2006)'s notion of *content*.

Figure 4.3 The functional model of social bias.

judgment that bias-constructs and bias-inputs together cause—like E's belief that he dislikes Jan—*the bias-output*. Finally, we can call actions that are performed on the basis of bias-outputs—like E's avoiding Jan in the hallway—*bias-actions*.[37] *Bias* simpliciter, then, is reserved for bias-constructs. They're what lead us from bias-inputs to bias-outputs, resulting in bias-actions.

In E's case, his bias (bias-construct) is instantiated by an explicit belief. Thus, the bias takes the form of a consciously accessible and fully attributable representational content. However, it needn't be the case that all biases take this form. It might be that in other cases, the bias-construct is either unconscious or not constituted by representational content attributable to him. The functional account leaves room for flexible bias-constructs, wherein many different states and processes can map the same kinds of inputs to the same kinds of outputs.[38] In this way, all biases can be characterized along the following tripartite, functional model (see Figure 4.3).

The debate about unconscious social bias to follow, then, will center around what sorts of states and processes constitute the bias-construct, whether those states and processes are truly unconscious, or whether they're bona fide attributable representational contents.

4.2 What Is Unconscious Bias?

In its early stages, literature exploring the existence of so-called "implicit" biases often characterized them as unconscious.[39] In their landmark paper,

---

[37] A similar three-part functional distinction can be made in the case of stereotype implicit biases, as I originally discuss in Johnson (2020c). However, since the data on the conscious accessibility of bias deal almost exclusively with evaluative implicit biases, I discuss only that case here.

[38] A point I argue for at length in Johnson (2020c).

[39] This describes at least one prominent strand of the literature. Another strand tended historically to characterize implicit bias in terms of automaticity rather than consciousness.

Greenwald and Banaji (1995, 8) define *implicit attitudes* as "introspectively unidentified (or inaccurately identified) traces of past experience that mediate favorable or unfavorable feeling, thought, or action toward social objects." On this characterization, "implicit biases" are arguably attitudes that are unconscious.[40]

In the standard cases, evidence of unconscious social bias comes from comparing results on two types of tests: direct and indirect. Direct tests involve asking subjects to report their social attitudes toward others. Social attitudes can be split into either evaluative attitudes (roughly, warm or cold feelings toward members of social groups) and stereotypical attitudes (roughly, whether they think some properties are stereotypically associated with members of social groups). Some of the most standard measures for evaluative attitudes are the Modern Racism Scale (where subjects are asked questions thought to reveal evaluative social attitudes, like "Discrimination against [social group X] is no longer a significant problem in the United States") and a "feelings thermometer" (where subjects are asked to rate their feelings toward members of particular social groups on a range of 0 "cold and unfavorable feelings" to 100 "very warm and favorable feelings"). In the case of direct measures of stereotype attitudes, subjects might be asked directly to what extent they agree with stereotypical statement (e.g., "do you agree that elderly people are bad with computers?").

Indirect measures are intended to test attitudes without asking subjects to directly report and instead measuring their results on some behavioral task. The most famous test of this sort is the Implicit Association Test (or IAT). In the IAT, subjects are asked to quickly sort stimuli presented to them on a computer screen to the left or to the right. The stimuli fall into four categories, and whether two among the four of those categories are "associated" with one another compared to the other categories is determined by how well a subject can quickly sort them to the same side of the screen. For example, if I wanted to test to what extent a person associated "elderly people" with the stereotypical property of being "bad with computers," I might give them an IAT that has four kinds of stimuli: pictures of

---

See Gawronski and Payne (2010, 2)'s discussion of "two roots of implicit social cognition." Thanks to Alex Madva for urging me to highlight this alternative historical framing.

[40] In a footnote, Greenwald and Banaji explain the parenthetical of "inaccurately" identified traces as intending to include instances where an individual remembers particular experiences, but is unable to identify how those experience shape further processing, e.g. "a student may be aware of having been graded highly in a course, but not suspect that this experience influences responses to the course's end-of-term course evaluation survey" (p. 8, fn. 2).

elderly people, pictures of non-elderly people, pictures of computer-related objects (like a keyboard), and pictures of non-computer-related objects (like a legal pad). If when asked to sort the pictures of elderly people and non-computer-related objects to the same side of the screen (sorting the other objects to the other side), they are faster and make fewer mistakes than when I ask them to sort elderly people and computer-related objects to the same side of the screen (sorting the other objects to the other side); then this is taken as good evidence that they harbor some bias that pairs the social group *elderly* with the property of *bad with computers*.

Evidence for unconscious bias then comes in two varieties: first, divergent results on the two kinds of tests (direct and indirect); and second, surprise and shock when being confronted with results on indirect tests. Diverging results on the two kinds of test occurs when, for example, an IAT provides evidence that a subject harbors a social attitude, say a stereotype that elderly people are bad with computers, but yet reports on a direct test that they do not. Imagine that a subject responds "no" when asked if elderly people are bad with computers, but they're slower at sorting elderly faces with computer-related objects. This is taken as evidence that they have a mental state with the content that elderly people are bad with computers (evidenced by the IAT), but they don't have conscious awareness of that mental state (evidenced by the direct subjective report). Meta-analyses suggest that correlations between results on direct and indirect measures are low in just the sort of way that would suggest divergence (Hofmann et al. 2005; Cameron et al. 2012). Likewise, people often demonstrate surprise and shock when confronted with their indirect test results. This sort of experience can be self-administered by taking an IAT online, but they have also been empirically codified in studies that demonstrate the same point.[41]

Taken together, these two sorts of results suggest that people harbor social biases that they are not aware of. But, as with the case of unconscious perception, this evidence is subject to both the conscious criterion problem and the content attribution problem. In what follows, I discuss each in turn.

---

[41] Hillard et al. (2013); Howell et al. (2015); and Howell and Ratliff (2017). More precisely, these studies show that strength of pro-white preferences is predictive of negative affect including surprise (Hillard et al. 2013, 506), where most subjects demonstrate pro-white preferences and that, in general, "people responded defensively to feedback indicating they were biased" (Howell and Ratliff 2017, 125).

4.3 Is Unconscious Bias Really Unconscious?

Evidence against the claim that the above reported social attitudes are really unconscious come either as criticisms of the evidence cited above or, more recently, positive evidence that subjects can in fact report the attitudes once thought unreportable.

Starting with the criticisms of the above methodology, perhaps the most looming concern (as with the discussion of unconscious perception above) is response bias. In the aforementioned cases, it might be that although subjects report not harboring social biases, they are in some sense aware that they do, they just don't admit it.[42] But we needn't assume that subjects are purposely trying to deceive experimenters. It might simply be that (again, as with unconscious perception) they are only weakly aware of their social biases, and their subjective response criterion is conservative enough that they do not feel confident in reporting these attitudes when asked. Indeed, divergences are minimized in conditions where subjects additionally report low motivations to control prejudice (e.g., Dunton and Fazio 1997), suggesting quite liberal response criteria can mitigate divergence.

There are also concerns that the divergence between direct and indirect measures are due to a variety of other methodological inconsistencies.[43] For example, often experimenters, wanting to avoid exactly the kind of response bias discussed above, use questions in direct measures that are not so obviously about the subjects' evaluative attitudes. For example, questions from direct measures like the Modern Racism Scale tend to focus on evaluative attitudes concerning, in addition to the social groups in question, some governmental policy or other (e.g., affirmative action). Thus, reports in response to these questions will be a combination of the subject's evaluation of both the social group and their perception of whether the policy is valid. Another concern is that often direct and indirect measures are asking questions about members of social groups at different levels of

---

[42] There's reason to think response bias (and, thus, the criterion problem) will be significantly harder to overcome in the domain of social psychology. Subjects likely have a more vested interest in hiding their socially unacceptable prejudices than whether they see some innocuous visual stimulus. Indeed, it was precisely the concern that individuals harbored negative social biases that they didn't want to admit to that prompted the shift in empirical psychology from direct to indirect measures in the first place (Banaji and Greenwald 2013, 170–184). It's hard to see how, then, empirical methods in this domain could ever fully avoid conscious criterion concerns.

[43] See Gawronski (2019, 578–580) and Hahn and Gawronski (2014, 28–29) for careful discussion of the points that follow.

granularity. Whereas direct measures typically ask subjects to report on group-level, generic attitudes ("do you think elderly people are bad with computers?") the behavioral tasks measured by indirect tests are almost always at the individual-member level (sorting the faces of particular elderly people). And finally, measures of social attitudes have been demonstrated to exhibit wide contextual effects, such that direct and indirect measures differing in context (either the context embedded in the tests or the subject's context when taking the tests) might limit the sorts of conclusions one can draw about their results. The thought is that in all of these cases, until we better calibrate direct and indirect tests to be targeting the very same attitudes (with the very same types of representational contents), there's no reason to think that divergence between the tests is indicative of unconscious social bias.

The evidence for shock and surprise is similarly explained away by methodological mismatches. Results on indirect tests like the IAT are typically conveyed using a scale that compares the individual taking the test to the wider population.[44] For example, the IAT results are reported as *slight preference*, *moderate preference*, or *strong preference* for one group over another as compared to the general population. When a subject is confronted with the result that their IAT demonstrates a "strong" bias, they might be surprised and shocked not because they were unaware of the bias itself, but because they wouldn't have regarded it as strong or because they took themselves to be less biased than those around them.[45]

In addition to the arguments intended to undermine evidence against the conscious accessibility of bias, there's also been a recent surge in literature that purports to give positive evidence in favor of consciously accessible bias. By and large, these data come in the form of experiments designed to test how well subjects can predict their results on indirect measures like the IAT. For example, Monteith et al. (2001) demonstrate that individuals can accurately describe how they did on an IAT before their results are shared

---

[44] See Hahn and Gawronski (2014, 29; 2019) and Hahn and Goedderz (2020) for careful discussion of the points that follow.
[45] While compelling, with this explanation it would seem to be a struggle to account for those cases where subjects are surprised by even the slightest result indicating bias on the test. Consider, for example, the surprise demonstrated by individuals who receive a *slight preference* result on an IAT when they belong to the very same social group that they demonstrate a bias against (see Banaji and Greenwald 2000 for an example of such a reaction). Still, an even more obvious explanation might simply be that people feel bad when told they harbor problematic biases, and so cognitive dissonance compels them to deny it.

with them.[46] Crucially, it's possible that in these cases, individuals are not introspecting their attitudes, but rather inferring the existence of such attitudes on the basis of behavioral data they gather from themselves while taking the test. In this case, their ability to predict would be no more evidence of their own conscious awareness than the experimenter's ability to infer on the basis of the behavioral results. In order to address this weakness, Hahn and Gawronski (2019) ran a series of studies testing whether subjects could predict their results before taking an IAT, sometimes merely instructing subjects to direct their attention to their "gut feelings" or "spontaneous reactions" to IAT stimuli (which they provided them with). In these cases too, subjects seemed able to predict whether the test would indicate bias against members of particular social groups. Likewise, after being asked to predict their results while attending to their gut feelings, they reported on a direct feelings thermometer (administered before taking the IAT) results more aligned with their IAT results. These results all seem to indicate that, in fact, subjects do have conscious awareness of the biases measured by the IAT. As Hahn and Gawronski (2019, 24) state, "the current findings are consistent with theories suggesting that implicit evaluations are subjectively experienced as spontaneous affective reactions.... Based on these conclusions, we deem it problematic to present implicit biases as attitudes that people are...unable...to report."[47]

However, just as response bias loomed large in the critique of evidence against conscious accessibility, so too it looms large here. While it's true that subjective reports became more aligned with their IAT results, it's also true that, on the whole, subjects reported more bias on direct measures compared to before. Taking lessons from SDT discussed above, one might wonder if in fact these results of alignment are demonstrating true sensitivity to subject's internal states, or whether they're the result of subjects merely adopting a different response criterion for prediction. In the face of uncertainty, it's possible that subjects simply preferred to err on the side of saying they had a bias when they didn't, instead of saying they didn't have a bias when they did. In both the Hahn and Gawronski (2019) study and similar studies presented by Nier (2005), subjects were arguably primed to expect that they might have attitudes toward social groups that they wouldn't normally express. As the instructions presented to subjects before prediction explained, "you may have a more positive affective reaction toward a picture

---

[46] See also Hahn et al. (2014) and Rivers and Hahn (2018).
[47] Such tests also have potential confounds regarding interaction effects between consciousness and memory. I thank Uriah Kriegel for raising this point.

of a skinny top model than toward a picture of a regular woman, even though you may not think or say that skinny top models are better people than regular women." They were again reminded just before the prediction task that "your first reaction could be different from a general opinion you may have" (Hahn and Gawronski 2019, 789). In the case of the Nier (2005) studies, subjects were shown a clip of an *NBC Dateline* special on the IAT, where throughout, explanations of the test were given that presupposed it would reveal to subjects attitudes that would be surprising to them. It's possible that in light of cues suggesting they might get their predictions wrong, they believed false positives (saying they were biased when they weren't) would be less socially stigmatizing than false negatives (saying they weren't biased when they were), and so erred on the side of the former.[48] As we saw above in the discussion of SDT, this combination of erring on the side of false positives when combined with a scenario where you are more likely to have positive instances (i.e., in cases where biases against social groups are more prevalent, as they tend to be in results on IATs) will merely give the illusion of accuracy. Thus, it's not obvious that direct measures and indirect measures aligning on average is sufficient to indicate conscious awareness. To know for sure would require more detailed analyses of the correlations between direct and indirect studies than are presently available.[49,50]

---

[48] Indeed, Howell et al. (2013, 716) report that participants of their study "indicated that learning that they were more implicitly biased than they expected would be distressing...but that learning they were less implicitly biased than they expected would make them happy."

[49] I know of only one study that addresses this potential confound. Nier (2005, 48) states the following: "[A]nother alternative interpretation that could potentially explain the increased implicit–explicit relationship is that people simply reported more negative attitudes in the Accurate condition, regardless of their level of implicit prejudice. However, the data are not consistent with this interpretation. If all participants in the Accurate condition simply elevated their MRS scores to a similar degree, the relationship between post-test MRS scores and IAT scores would not have been any stronger in the Accurate condition. An increase in the implicit–explicit relationship requires, by definition, that those who had more negative IAT scores reported negative explicit attitudes to a greater degree than those who had more positive IAT scores. Therefore the stronger implicit–explicit relationship observed in the Accurate condition is not consistent with the notion that everyone simply reported more negative MRS scores in the Accurate condition." The idea here is that in order for correlation between direct and indirect results to increase, not only would those who demonstrated more bias on the IAT need to report more bias on the Modern Racism Scale, but also those who demonstrated no bias (or bias in the opposite direction) on the IAT would need to report no bias on the Modern Racism Scale. What this fails to take into account is that base-rates of bias tend to be, on average, higher than base-rates of no bias. So, in fact, it is possible that everyone on average reporting more bias would indeed raise average correlations. As far as I know, no study provides the more nuanced breakdown of correlations that would be needed to demonstrate that *only* those who demonstrated biases on the IAT predicted higher scores or reported more bias through direct measures.

[50] I do not intend this chapter as a comprehensive literature review addressing all the data that might speak to conscious accessibility. Rather, I intend it as a small survey of some of the most prominent work cited in the debate. Doubtless other studies exist that investigate

Thus, evidence for conscious accessibility seems just as victim to the conscious criterion problem as evidence for conscious inaccessibility. But the philosophical debate canvassed above regarding unconscious perception highlights empirical paths to progress here. While it's ultimately within the purview of social psychology to choose precise experimental designs, philosophical reflection suggests that minimally, such designs must adjudicate between objective and subjective criteria effects. Incorporating the lessons from SDT, we need an experimental paradigm that can track objective discriminatory capacities (in subject's reports of their own attitudes) while controlling for subjective response bias combined with high base-rates. One way to do this might be to test for reportability in domains that are likely to have low base-rates of bias.[51] In any case, until empirical methodology is available to disentangle these two effects, it remains subject to the conscious criterion problem. Thus, while I'm happy to allow that for some, the preponderance of evidence will compel them to one side of the debate over the other, I caution against forming any strong conclusions that suggest the empirical evidence is conclusive on the question of whether social bias is unconscious.

Setting this issue of conscious accessibility aside, however, there are likewise independent concerns about whether the evidence in favor of unconscious content really is tracking bona fide attributable representational contents. Thus, we turn to the content attribution problem next.

4.4 Is Unconscious Bias Really Attributable Content?

Let us turn to evaluating the aforementioned empirical studies for the attribution problem. Ultimately, I argue that, even if such studies did indicate that some aspect of a bias's operation is consciously (in)accessible, without being clear about which aspect and what the status of that aspect is as a contentful state, they leave unaddressed the question of whether these are

---

manipulations of implicit-explicit correlations and that avoid some of the priming concerns I raise here. Unfortunately, I lack the space to address them in full. I am confident that existing studies are unlikely to fully address both the conscious criterion problem raised here and the content attributability problem raised in the next section. Thanks to Alex Madva for pressing me on this point.

[51] I owe this suggestion to Alex Madva. Though, as he suggests, these domains seem intuitively likely to exhibit high implicit-explicit correlations more generally, generating ceiling effects.

genuine instances of unconscious content. To fully evaluate, we'll need to get even clearer about which aspects constitute the bias.

It helps to work out how the distinctions between components of a bias's operation in the psychological models map onto distinctions made within the functional account described above. The empirical literature above assumes the Associative-Propositional Evaluation (APE) model of social bias presented by Gawronski and Bodenhausen (2006, 2014). The model suggests that implicit biases and explicit biases involve two distinct processes: associative processes and propositional processes, respectively. Gawronski and Bodenhausen (2014, 449) hold that the associative processes of implicit biases operate on a network of concepts. These associations then culminate in an evaluative response based on the aggregate valence of the concepts involved in the activation chain. Consider Figure 4.4, borrowed from Gawronski and Bodenhausen (2006, 697).

In this case, both implicit and explicit social biases mimic social kind inductions. This model would explain E's dislike of Jan as an output of propositional reasoning (at the upper level of Figure 4.4). According to the APE model, "propositional processes are defined as the *validation* of the information implied by activated associations, which [is] guided by the principles of cognitive consistency."[52] Essentially, the associative processes go through a process of "propositionalization," resulting in representations that take the form of propositional statements.[53] To return to the example above, E's negative affective reaction toward Jan is the result of the associative network "transformed into propositional statements such as 'X is bad' or 'I dislike X'."[54] This propositional representation is then checked for consistency against the other propositions being considered. If all the propositions are consistent, then the newly formed proposition is validated. If the propositions are inconsistent, then the inconsistency is resolved by the rejection of one of the propositions.[55]

---

[52] Gawronski and Bodenhausen (2014, 449, emphasis in original).
[53] Bodenhausen and Gawronski (2013, 958).
[54] Gawronski and Bodenhausen (2014, 450). In this case, it's unclear whether X represents Jan or elderly individuals more generally. For reasons discussed, I charitably interpret them as claiming the latter.
[55] The processes underlying *propositionalization* are never formally laid out by the theory; it says only that the propositions are formed on the basis of the information "implied by activated associations." So, it's unclear how propositions are formed on the basis of the activation networks alone. It's even more unclear when we try to extend the model beyond evaluative biases to stereotype biases, since in those cases there is no valence to aggregate. Thanks to Alex Madva for helpful discussion of this point. See also Madva (2017, 103, fn. 31).

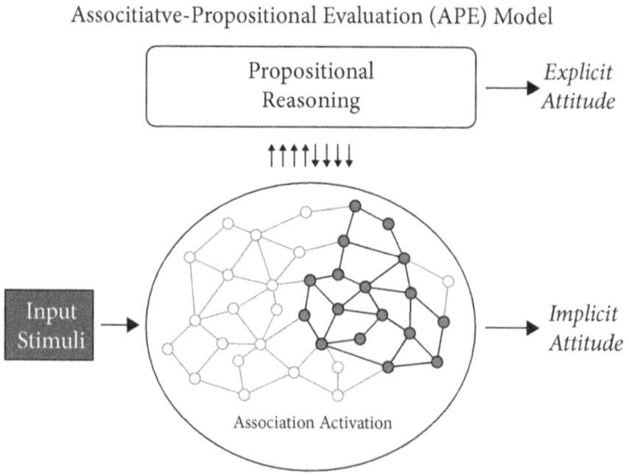

Associtiatve-Propositional Evaluation (APE) Model

Figure 4.4 The associative-propositional evaluation model of social bias. Borrowed from Gawronski and Bodenhausen (2006: 697).

Implicit biases, on the other hand, do not involve explicit propositional reasoning. For example, say another individual P has a purportedly unconscious bias. P visually perceives Jan who is elderly. This visual perception necessarily activates the mental concept *elderly*. This activation then spreads by way of associative processes to other mental concepts, e.g. *wise, frail*, and *forgetful* might all activate. The aggregate valence of these concepts then "elicit[s] a spontaneous affective response that is in line with the net valence of these concepts."[56] In this case, the aggregate valence of the activated concepts is negative, so P would have a negative affective reaction, or what the authors call a "spontaneous affective response." This negative spontaneous affective response is what is then measured by indirect tests. In such a case, the visual perception is the bias-input, the whole associative network then serves as the bias-construct, and the spontaneous affective response serves as the bias-output.

We can now ask whether the Hahn et al. experiments above suggest evidence in favor or against the existence of bona fide attributable content, thereby addressing the content attribution problem. To reiterate the main strategy of the experiments, they attempt to determine whether subjects have conscious access to their biases by asking them to predict their results on indirect methods such as the IAT. Let's say, setting aside criterion concerns, that in general results demonstrate that subjects are fairly accurate in these predictions (even before taking the IAT, so their accuracy cannot be

---

[56] Gawronski and Bodenhausen (2014, 449).

based on bias-actions). Recall that in the Hahn and Gawronski (2019) studies, subjects were asked to predict their results by merely instructing subjects to direct their attention to their "gut feelings" or "spontaneous affective reactions." When doing so, "reactions toward minority members increased acknowledgement of bias to the same extent as IAT score prediction (Study 6), providing further evidence for the functional equivalence of IAT score prediction and attention to spontaneous affective reactions" (p. 23). Here, the researchers are borrowing the notion of "spontaneous affective reaction" from the APE model discussed above, which, for reasons stated above, should be interpreted as what I've been calling a bias-output, i.e. the result of a bias-construct's operation. Crucially, this means the aforementioned evidence for the conscious accessibility of bias is evidence only that an individual has conscious access to the result of a bias-construct's operation—not that they have access to whatever states and processes mediate the negative affective response (see Figure 4.5).

Which should we be concerned about when we evaluate the claim that social bias is unconscious—the bias-output or the bias-construct? Hahn and colleagues seem to be interested in the question of whether a bias-output is consciously accessible. This is in part because they recognize that extent psychological models fail to conceptualize bias in ways that fully distinguish bias-outputs from bias-constructs. On this, Hahn and Goedderz (2020, S127–S128) say the following:

> [T]here is a lack of consensus for how the spontaneously activated cognitions...are best conceptualized....To us, it sounds equally plausible to propose that the gut reaction *is* the underlying cognition (and one may then discuss how to conceptualize a gut reaction scientifically), as it would be to propose that the underlying cognition is something else that *produces* a gut response. We hope that continuous advancement in theorizing will shed further light on this question.

Figure 4.5 The combined associative-propositional evaluation model and functional model of social bias.

This is the perfect opportunity for philosophers of mind to help provide conceptual clarity. On the functional view, bias guides induction. Thinking of social bias in this way helps to secure its place within a broader, unified kind (including other cases of computational bias, like perceptual bias and algorithmic bias). In all the cases of social biases we've discussed (including implicit and explicit biases), the existence of a social bias explains why in the face of underdetermining information about the social group one belonged to, individuals cognitively transition to outputs that paired those individuals with properties stereotypical of the social group. This helps us to explain, for example, why when presented with various individuals belonging to the same social group, the individual is apt to make the same sort of induction. So, while there could be legitimate theoretical interest in the spontaneous affective response (i.e., bias-output), there should also, and perhaps more fundamentally, be theoretical interest in whatever states and processes systematically lead to that response.[57] For any particular response, it seems appropriate to ask why the subject reacts the way they do to particular members of a social group (i.e., what prompts their systematically having the spontaneous affective reactions that they do). And, in ordinary language, it seems perfectly appropriate to respond "because they have a bias against that social group." We then ask whether *that bias* is something the individual was aware of. These sorts of questions seem to me to be at the center of discussions about the conscious accessibility of bias and need to be answered for an account of bias to be genuinely explanatory. This places theoretical priority on the bias-construct.

The empirical evidence so far reviewed does little to suggest positive answers to the question of whether the bias-construct is either conscious or contentful. Indeed, they might even serve as unacknowledged evidence for a negative answer to the former.[58] If it turned out that in the standard pre-

---

[57] Moreover, as a minor exegetical point, Banaji and Greenwald's original definition of an implicit attitude suggests interest in whatever state *gives rise to* the affective response, not the affective response itself: "introspectively unidentified...traces of past experience *that mediate* favorable or unfavorable feeling, thought, or action toward social objects" (Greenwald and Banaji 1995, 8; emphasis added).

[58] It is important to note that even if subjects are able to predict accurately their results on the IAT, this still is not conclusive evidence that they are accessing representational states that are responsible for their results. As I've discussed elsewhere (Johnson 2020c, fn. 24), a sufficiently reflective thinker might be able to deduce the rules that guide their cognitive transitions. For example, a sufficiently reflective logic student might, upon learning about the rule *Modus Ponens*, reflect on their own personal habits and conclude that they often follow the rule in reasoning. This won't be evidence that that content *as it functioned in producing the inferences themselves* was thereby consciously accessed. Here we might draw a distinction between

diction cases, subjects could *only* predict their IAT results when confronted with concrete stimuli that produced bias-outputs, then that would be a reason to think that they lack conscious accessibility to their bias-constructs. In such cases, subjects must produce bias-outputs in order to have any evidence of the existence of bias-constructs at all. In the absence of such bias-outputs, they lack any evidence whatsoever for the mechanism that systematically produces bias-outputs or bias-actions, i.e. the bias-construct.[59] As it turns out, this is precisely what emerging data suggest. On this, Hahn and Goedderz (2020, S122) state, "interpretation of the findings presented here suggests that the biases reflected on implicit measures may often be state-unconscious until people are confronted with concrete stimuli that trigger affective response." This is precisely what one would expect if the bias-construct were consciously inaccessible. Here, we see philosophical conceptual analysis leading to tangible empirical prediction.

However, if the above APE model of implicit bias is correct, none of this would serve as evidence of a consciously inaccessible state that has attributable representational content. This is because associative networks are not standardly regarded as representing the relations between concepts. This relates to a long-standing debate about whether implicit biases could be propositional or associative, with the general consensus among philosophers being that they must be propositional.[60] This discussion makes clear why this question matters. If the bias-construct is an associative network, then these cases would not serve as evidence for unconscious representational content attributable to the individual harboring the bias. Rather, they would be no different from the unconscious, "built-in" biases of the visual perceptual system.[61] If instead, the bias-construct is propositional, then in light of subjects' inability to report that generalizing content, it seems like we would have evidence of an unconscious mental state with

---

some content being consciously accessed versus being consciously accessible. These bias contents might be accessible in some loose sense, but that isn't conclusive evidence that they were directly accessed. Thanks to Uriah Kriegel for raising the importance of this distinction here.

[59] This is similar to how vision scientists come to understand what assumptions are encoded in the biases of the visual perceptual system by investigating instances of when those biases form (in)accurate perceptions.

[60] Prominent defenders of the idea that implicit biases must be explicitly represented propositions include De Houwer (2014); Mandelbaum (2015); Levy (2015); and Karlan (2022).

[61] Such built-in biases are crucially marked by an in-principle indeterminacy in content. For more on this point, see Burge (2010, 404)'s discussion of perceptual formation principles not having privileged forms. This point is likewise congenial to Madva (2017, 88)'s claim that the content of implicit biases is indeterminate and only interpretable if "understood holistically and relationally, as part of broader cognitive-bodily-socialenvironmental systems."

attributable representational content. These biases would be bona fide cases of unconscious content.

Regardless of where one falls on this debate, though, the insights from the debate about unconscious bias highlight another reason why the question of content attribution within a bias's operation is important. Recall that one important impetus for attributing content was that reference to the relevant distal kinds were essential to explanations of how the capacity was operating. It's important that the representational contents, involving the relevant kinds, are the contents we take them to be. In the case of social bias, there are many potential kinds that could be causing us to treat individuals in ways that are indicative of bias against the social group they belong to, but that wouldn't necessarily indicate bias against that social group per se. This is because many biases toward individuals might be best explained by reference to seemingly innocuous causal features that merely correlate with the socially sensitive features of interest. Imagine, for example, a social media platform hiring workers. To make this decision, they choose an epistemically reasonable feature like candidates' being frequent users of the platform in question. This reasonable-to-use feature might, however, be highly correlated with some socially sensitive feature we think is problematic were they to use it explicitly in decision-making. For example, it might be that no elderly individuals use the platform; only much younger people do. Thus, their hiring decisions will—from a pure, causal, behavioral perspective—look exactly like (or similar enough to) decisions made on the basis of age.[62]

As the discussion about unconscious perception above illustrated, in order to figure out whether reference to particular distal kinds is necessary, we need to identify cases where the two come apart and, in cases of near perfect correlation, this will involve identifying cases of misrepresentation of certain social groups. Again, it is ultimately within the purview of social psychology to choose precise experimental designs. But philosophical reflection suggests that minimally, such designs must adjudicate between when the relevant kinds in a bias's operation (at any stage of the input, output, or construct) involve representations of the relevant social groups as such.[63] In the case of the aforementioned experiments, that these kinds are

---

[62] This is one reason why I object to accounts of bias that reduce it to mere behavioral dispositions (see, for example, De Houwer 2019). The reference to the appropriate representational contents is critical to the bias's being what it is.

[63] These considerations also cause trouble for other expansive notions of bias and prejudice. For example, Munton (2021) presents an extremely compelling view of prejudice that, on the

the relevant kinds will be evidenced by subjects exhibiting bias toward not only members who belong to that social group, but also those who are mistakenly thought to belong to that social group. This is evidence that their bias aims to pick out members of a particular social group and, on the basis of some generalizing mechanism that systematically treats members of that social group differently from non-members, treats those people differently. As in the case of unconscious perception, mere causal explanations to

whole, is quite congenial to the functional account of bias that I offer. In both cases, the explanatory locus comes not in any particular mental attitude constituting the phenomenon in question (beliefs, affect), but rather in how attitudes are manipulated. For me, these manipulations will be realized in systematic transitions between mental states; for Munton, they are realized by salience structures that organize information as more or less readily accessible. For both, the explanatory import of these structures (functional/salience) come from their ability to facilitate non-deductive inference by making it computationally tractable (Johnson 2020c, 1195; Munton 2021, 13) and move to a higher level of abstraction that allows for multiple realizability (Johnson 2020c, 1215; Munton 2021, 12). However, it is on this point about content that her view and mine diverge. While we're both focused on mental processes as opposed to states and neither of us wants to reduce these processes to standalone states, both views will depend in part on the mental states that these processes operate over. And whereas Munton at this point prescinds from details about the contents of those mental states, I believe they are central. (See Johnson 2020c, 1222–1223, for a defense of maintaining representational inputs and outputs.) Reasons for this can be brought out by using Munton (2021, 7–8)'s example of Mark scrolling through PhilPapers and selecting only those articles written by men. This can occur, according to Munton, without Mark "even processing [the information that the papers are written by men and not women]" (p. 8) and despite the fact that "Mark does not form beliefs about the papers with female authors" (p. 7). Still, she claims, Mark would have a prejudice against women. I think the question of whether Mark has a social bias against women depends in part on whether he represents them *as women* (or whether he represents the male authors *as men*). Ultimately, Munton's description of the case never clarifies what's going on in Mark's head when he displays the research patterns that he does, and the reading of her case is consistent with his picking out the male-authored papers because he represents the authors as male. However, the way she describes the case is consistent with another scenario (though admittedly unlikely) where Mark never even registers the names or genders of authors and, instead, he attends only to paper citation counts. If low-citation count is correlated with the author being a woman (as discriminatory practices might entail), then while he's ignoring papers authored by women, it is arguably not because they are written by women. In such a case, Mark does not obviously have a bias against women. Or, at least, his bias is importantly different from cases of psychological bias wherein he does use representations of gender to sort papers. While I'm sure that in cases where discrimination against women ultimately explains why the properties an individual uses picks out the individuals that it does, we would all want to say that something problematic is occurring (see my discussion of "the proxy problem" in Johnson 2020a and 2022). Still, in a case where Mark doesn't know the genders of the authors whose papers he's reading, at least some would reasonably hesitate to say that it is his prejudice against women that explains his behavior. Thus, minimally, I believe Munton (2021)'s account must include in its salience structures representational contents (however minimal) that represent the individuals as members of the relevant social group in the states that psychological operations (of saliency) operate over. Though, admittedly these questions warrant more discussion than I can provide here. I thank Jessie Munton for many insightful conversations about the role (or lack thereof) of representational content in psychological explanations of bias and prejudice.

individuals won't do, since in these cases as we've described them, many of these individuals won't actually belong to the social group in question. So, like the perceptual illusions of a berry's color, only explanations to what the states aimed (but in this case failed) to pick out will do the trick. Representational content is just how we describe the objects and properties that some state aims to pick out. Thus, only in those cases will content attribution be necessary and, therefore, warranted.

5. Conclusion

In this chapter, I have outlined two debates about unconscious content and the parallel problems that plague them both. I have then extended philosophical insights from one to shed light on possible paths for progress in the other. Throughout, the discussion has highlighted how these debates serve as paradigm case studies for investigating the fruitful exchange that can exist between philosophy and empirical science.

References

Antony, L. (2001). Quine as Feminist: The Radical Import of Naturalized Epistemology. In Antony, L. and Witt, C. E., editors, *A Mind Of One's Own: Feminist Essays on Reason and Objectivity*, pages 110–153. Westview Press.

Antony, L. (2016). Bias: Friend or Foe? In Brownstein, M. and Saul, J., editors, *Implicit Bias and Philosophy*, Volume 1: *Metaphysics and Epistemology*, pages 157–190. Oxford University Press.

Banaji, M. R. and Greenwald, A. G. (2000, March 19). *Pride and Prejudice*. In G. Moriba-Meadows (Producer), *Dateline NBC*. New York: National Broadcasting Corporation.

Banaji, M. R. and Greenwald, A. G. (2013). *Blindspot: Hidden Biases of Good People*. Delacorte Press.

Beeghly, E. (2015). What is a Stereotype? What is Stereotyping? *Hypatia*, 30(4):675–691.

Berger, J. (2020). Implicit Attitudes and Awareness. *Synthese*, 197(3):1291–1312.

Berger, J. (2022). Kinds of Consciousness. In Young, B. D. and Dicey Jennings, C., editors, *Mind, Cognition, and Neuroscience: A Philosophical Introduction*, pages 251–266. Routledge.

Block, N. (1995). On a Confusion about a Function of Consciousness. *Behavioral and Brain Sciences*, 18(02):227.

Block, N. (2007). Overflow, Access, and Attention. *Behavioral and Brain Sciences*, 30(56):530–548.

Block, N. (2015). The Anna Karenina Principle and Skepticism about Unconscious Perception. *Philosophy and Phenomenological Research*, 93(2): 452-459.

Bodenhausen, G. V. and Gawronski, B. (2013). Attitude Change. In Reisberg, D., editor, *The Oxford Handbook of Cognitive Psychology*, pages 957–969. Oxford University Press.

Buehler, D. (2014). *Psychological Agency: Guidance of Visual Attention*. Doctoral Thesis, University of California, Los Angeles, Los Angeles, CA.

Burge, T. (2010). *Origins of Objectivity*. Oxford University Press.

Burge, T. (2020). Entitlement: The Basis for Empirical Warrant. In Graham, P. J. and Pedersen, editors, *Epistemic Entitlement*, pages 37–142. Oxford University Press.

Burge, T. (2022). *Perception: First Form of Mind*. Oxford University Press, OCLC: on1227381102.

Cameron, C. D., Brown-Iannuzzi, J. L., and Payne, B. K. (2012). Sequential Priming Measures of Implicit Social Cognition: A Meta-Analysis of Associations with Behavior and Explicit Attitudes. *Personality and Social Psychology Review*, 16(4):330–350.

Carruthers, P. (2017). Implicit versus Explicit Attitudes: Differing Manifestations of the Same Representational Structures? *Review of Philosophy and Psychology*, 9(1):51–72.

De Houwer, J. (2014). A Propositional Model of Implicit Evaluation: Implicit Evaluation. *Social and Personality Psychology Compass*, 8(7):342–353.

De Houwer, J. (2019). Implicit Bias Is Behavior: A Functional-Cognitive Perspective on Implicit Bias. *Perspectives on Psychological Science*, 14(5):835–840.

Dennett, D. C. (1969). *Content and Consciousness*. Routledge and Kegan Paul.

Dunton, B. C. and Fazio, R. H. (1997). An Individual Difference Measure of Motivation to Control Prejudiced Reactions. *Personality and Social Psychology Bulletin*, 23:316–326.

Fodor, J. A. (1983). *The Modularity of Mind: An Essay on Faculty Psychology*. MIT Press.

Gawronski, B. (2019). Six Lessons for a Cogent Science of Implicit Bias and Its Criticism. *Perspectives on Psychological Science*, 14(4):574–595.

Gawronski, B. and Bodenhausen, G. V. (2006). Associative and Propositional Processes in Evaluation: An Integrative Review of Implicit and Explicit Attitude Change. *Psychological Bulletin*, 132(5):692–731.

Gawronski, B. and Bodenhausen, G. V. (2014). Implicit and Explicit Evaluation: A Brief Review of the Associative-Propositional Evaluation Model: APE Model. *Social and Personality Psychology Compass*, 8(8):448–462.

Gawronski, B., Hofmann, W., and Wilbur, C. J. (2006). Are "Implicit" Attitudes Unconscious? *Consciousness and Cognition*, 15(3):485–499.

Gawronski, B. and Payne, K. (2010). *Handbook of Implicit Social Cognition: Measurement, Theory, and Applications*. Guilford Press.

Greenwald, A. G. and Banaji, M. R. (1995). Implicit Social Cognition: Attitudes, Selfesteem, and Stereotypes. *Psychological Review*, 102(1):4–27.

Hahn, A. and Gawronski, B. (2014). Do Implicit Evaluations Reflect Unconscious Attitudes? *Behavioral and Brain Sciences*, 37:28–29.

Hahn, A. and Gawronski, B. (2019). Facing One's Implicit Biases: From Awareness to Acknowledgment. *Journal of Personality and Social Psychology*, 115(5):769–794.

Hahn, A. and Goedderz, A. (2020). Trait-Unconsciousness, State-Unconsciousness, Preconsciousness, and Social Miscalibration in the Context of Implicit Evaluations. *Social Cognition*, 38(Supplement): S115–S134.

Hahn, A., Judd, C. M., Hirsh, H. K., and Blair, I. V. (2014). Awareness of Implicit Attitudes. *Journal of Experimental Psychology: General*, 143(3):1369–1392.

Hillard, A. L., Ryan, C. S., and Gervais, S. J. (2013). Reactions to the Implicit Association Test as an Educational Tool: A Mixed Methods Study. *Social Psychology of Education*, 16(3):495–516.

Hofmann, W., Gawronski, B., Gschwendner, T., Le, H., and Schmitt, M. (2005). A MetaAnalysis on the Correlation between the Implicit Association Test and Explicit SelfReport Measures. *Personality and Social Psychology Bulletin*, 31(10):1369–1385.

Howell, J. L., Collisson, B., Crysel, L., Garrido, C. O., Newell, S. M., Cottrell, C. A., Smith, C. T., and Shepperd, J. A. (2013). Managing the Threat of Impending Implicit Attitude Feedback. *Social Psychological and Personality Science*, 4(6):714–720.

Howell, J. L., Gaither, S. E., and Ratliff, K. A. (2015). Caught in the Middle: Defensive Responses to IAT Feedback Among Whites, Blacks, and Biracial Black/Whites. *Social Psychological and Personality Science*, 6(4):373–381.

Howell, J. L. and Ratliff, K. A. (2017). Not Your Average Bigot: The Better-than-Average Effect and Defensive Responding to Implicit Association Test Feedback. *British Journal of Social Psychology*, 56(1):125–145.

Irvine, E. (2013). *Consciousness as a Scientific Concept: A Philosophy of Science Perspective*. Springer.

Jiang, Y., Costello, P., and He, S. (2007). Processing of Invisible Stimuli: Advantage of Upright Faces and Recognizable Words in Overcoming Interocular Suppression. *Psychological Science*, 18(4):349–355.

Johnson, G. M. (2020a). Algorithmic Bias: On the Implicit Biases of Social Technology. *Synthese*, 198(10):9941–9961.

Johnson, G. M. (2020b). Are Algorithms Value-free? Feminist Theoretical Virtues in Machine Learning. Unpublished Manuscript.

Johnson, G. M. (2020c). The Structure of Bias. *Mind*, 129(516):1193–1236.

Johnson, G. M. (2022). Proxies Aren't Intentional; They're Intentional. Unpublished Manuscript.

Karlan, B. (2022). The Rational Dynamics of Implicit Thought. *Australasian Journal of Philosophy*, 100(4):774–788.

Kentridge, R. W. (2015). What Is It Like to Have Type-2 Blindsight? Drawing Inferences from Residual Function in Type-1 Blindsight. *Consciousness and Cognition*, 32:41–44.

Klotz, W. and Neumann, O. (1999). Motor Activation without Conscious Discrimination in Metacontrast Masking. *Journal of Experimental Psychology: Human Perception and Performance*, 25(4):976–992.

Krickel, B. (2018). Are the States Underlying Implicit Biases Unconscious?—A Neo-Freudian Answer. *Philosophical Psychology*, 31(7):1007–1026.

Krickel, B. (2022). The Unconscious Mind Worry: A Mechanistic-Explanatory Strategy. *Philosophy of Science*, 1–45. Online First, doi:10.1017/psa.2022.18.

Kriegel, U. (2009). *Subjective Consciousness: A Self-Representational Theory*. Oxford University Press.

Levy, N. (2015). Neither Fish nor Fowl: Implicit Attitudes as Patchy Endorsements. *Nous*, 49(4):800–823.

Madva, A. (2017). Social Psychology, Phenomenology, & the Indeterminate Content of Unreflective Racial Bias. In Lee, E. S., editor, *Race as Phenomena: Between Phenomenology and Philosophy of Race*, pages 87–106. Rowman & Littlefield International.

Mandelbaum, E. (2015). Attitude, Inference, Association: On the Propositional Structure of Implicit Bias. *Nous*, 50(3):1–30.

Marshall, J. C. and Halligan, P. W. (1988). Blindsight and Insight in Visuo-Spatial Neglect. *Nature*, 336(6201):766–767.

Monteith, M. J., Voils, C. I., and Ashburn-Nardo, L. (2001). Taking a Look Underground: Detecting, Interpreting, and Reacting to Implicit Racial Biases. *Social Cognition*, 19(4):395–417.

Munton, J. (2021). Prejudice as the Misattribution of Salience. *Analytic Philosophy*, 1–19. Online First, https://doi.org/10.1111/phib.12250.

Nier, J. A. (2005). How Dissociated Are Implicit and Explicit Racial Attitudes? A Bogus Pipeline Approach. *Group Processes & Intergroup Relations*, 8(1):39–52.

Norman, L., Akins, K., Heywood, C., and Kentridge, R. (2014). Color Constancy for an Unseen Surface. *Current Biology*, 24(23):2822–2826.

Peters, M. A. K., Kentridge, R. W., Phillips, I., and Block, N. (2017). Does Unconscious Perception Really Exist? Continuing the ASSC20 Debate. *Neuroscience of Consciousness*, 3(1):1–11.

Phillips, I. (2015). Consciousness and Criterion: On Block's Case for Unconscious Seeing. *Philosophy and Phenomenological Research*, 93(2):419–451.

Phillips, I. (2018). Unconscious Perception Reconsidered. *Analytic Philosophy*, 59(4):471–514.

Phillips, I. (2021). Blindsight Is Qualitatively Degraded Conscious Vision. *Psychological Review*, 128(3):558–584.

Phillips, I. and Block, N. (2017). Debate on Unconscious Perception. In Nanay, B., editor, *Current Controversies in Philosophy of Perception*, pages 165–192. Routledge.

Prinz, J. J. (2015). Unconscious Perception. In Matthen, M., editor, *The Oxford Handbook of Philosophy of Perception*, pages 371–392. Oxford University Press.

Quilty-Dunn, J. (2019). Unconscious Perception and Phenomenal Coherence. *Analysis*, 79(3):461–469.

Rivers, A. M. and Hahn, A. (2018). What Cognitive Mechanisms Do People Reflect on When They Predict IAT Scores? *Personality and Social Psychology Bulletin*, 45(6):878–892.

Rosenthal, D. (2005). *Consciousness and the Mind*. Clarendon Press.

Sellars, W. (1956). Empiricism and the Philosophy of Mind. *Science, Perception and Reality*. Routledge and Kegan Paul.

Stich, S. P. (1978). Beliefs and Subdoxastic States. *Philosophy of Science*, 45(4):499–518.

5
Aphantasia and Conscious Thought

Preston Lennon

Take a moment to answer the following question: how many windows are there in your kitchen? Once you've reached an answer, reflect on how you arrived at it. If you are like most, then you might have called up a visual image of your kitchen and used this image to arrive at the correct number. If this is you, then it might come as a surprise to learn that some subjects, when asked to answer this question, do so successfully without performing this process of visual imagination. If you did not invoke mental imagery to answer this question, fear not, for you are not alone. Some subjects with *aphantasia* report never experiencing anything like visual mental imagery at all.

Visual mental imagery allows us to "see" things in our mind's eye. Psychologists have long been aware that visual mental imagery can vary in vividness between different subjects (Galton 1880). Beginning with studies by Adam Zeman and coauthors (2010, 2015, 2016, 2020), however, there has recently been a flurry of new research on aphantasia. For purposes of this chapter, I define aphantasia as the reduced ability to generate mental imagery, although aphantasics can lack mental imagery altogether in extreme cases.

Aphantasia has implications for a number of live issues in psychology and philosophy of mind, including the function of mental imagery (Pylyshyn 2002; Kosslyn et al. 2006) and the nature of dreams (Whiteley 2020). In this chapter, I explore the consequences of aphantasia for debates over the nature of conscious thought. Some philosophers have argued that our thoughts are conscious *only* insofar as they are reducible to sensory experience, broadly construed to include mental imagery and inner speech (Lormand 1996; Wilson 2003; Prinz 2007, 2011). I argue that the existence of aphantasia presents a counterexample to this sensory constraint on conscious thought.

My argument against the sensory constraint on conscious thought has two premises. First, the *positive premise*: aphantasic thoughts are phenomenally conscious. Second, the *negative premise*: aphantasics have some thoughts, aphantasic thoughts, that have no *sensory reduction base*, i.e. no accompanying sensory experience that serves as a plausible candidate to constitute the cognitive experience of thinking. These premises entail that the sensory constraint is false.

Though my main goal is to argue for this negative thesis, my argument also supports a positive thesis that has two conjuncts: (1) there is a non-sensory phenomenology of thinking; and (2) it partially determines the content of thought, i.e. what we are thinking about. In holding that conscious thoughts must be reducible to sensory mental imagery, proponents of the sensory constraint on conscious thought deny (1). Moreover, they are also motivated to reject (2), as it is not clear how sensory phenomenology alone is rich enough to determine thought content.

Here is the plan. In §1, I characterize the sensory constraint on conscious thought, and explain why philosophers who accept the sensory constraint typically deny that there is any thought content determined by its phenomenal character. In §2, I show that the negative premise has empirical support from the psychological literature on aphantasia. In §3, I show that the positive premise has theoretical and introspective support. I close in §4 by suggesting two conclusions we can draw from the existence of aphantasic thought: first, there is a non-sensory phenomenology of thinking; and second, arguments for this non-sensory phenomenology can be extended to show that it partially determines what we're thinking about. Finally, I tentatively suggest that some of the disagreement about these two conclusions may be explained by interpersonal variation in mental imagery.

1. The Sensory Constraint on Conscious Thought

A mental state is phenomenally conscious when there is something it's like for the subject to have that state. The visual experience I have as I glance outside my window, the experience of bitterness upon taking a swig of coffee: these are recognizable instances of phenomenal consciousness. Our familiarity with phenomenal consciousness, however, is not just limited to the kind associated with the senses. We are no less familiar with instances of conscious thought, such as the one I have when I consciously calculate that a dime and a quarter give me thirty-five cents, or when it suddenly occurs to me that I've locked my keys inside my apartment (Siewert 1998).

It thus seems uncontroversial from the first-person point of view that we sometimes have conscious experiences when we think. But the nature of our thoughts—in particular, whether our thoughts are themselves conscious—is disputed. Some philosophers hold that the *only* kind of phenomenal consciousness that exists is *sensory* (Prinz 2007, 2011; Carruthers and Veillet 2011; Tye and Wright 2011). According to these philosophers, a mental state is phenomenally conscious only if it has a kind of phenomenal character had by sensory perception, broadly construed to include bodily sensation, perceptual imagery, and inner speech. Others demur, holding that there is a kind of phenomenal character had by conscious thoughts and other cognitive experiences that is different in kind from sensory phenomenology (Strawson 1994; Siewert 1998; Horgan and Tienson 2002; Pitt 2004).

A brief clarification on what I mean by "phenomenal": some hear "phenomenal" as meaning more or less the same thing as "sensory." If this is what is meant by "phenomenal," then any non-sensory phenomenology is excluded by fiat. Instead, I use "phenomenal" to mean "there is something it's like." In this way, we do not prejudge the issue of whether non-sensory phenomenology exists.

Those who claim that phenomenal consciousness is exhausted by sensory phenomenal consciousness must explain the experience of thinking in terms of associated sensory episodes. Consider the following passage from Eric Lormand (1996):

> One's standing belief that snow is white may cause one to think that snow is white, by causing one to form an auditory image of quickly saying the words 'Snow is white' (or 'I believe snow is white')...At least normally, if there is anything it's like for me to have a conscious belief that snow is white, it is exhausted by what it's like for me to have such verbal representations, together with nonverbal imaginings, e.g., of a white expanse of snow, and perhaps visual imaginings of words. (246–7)

Our conscious thoughts are often accompanied by a certain kind of sensory phenomenology, namely, *mental imagery*. As Lormand notes, when I have the conscious thought that snow is white, this might be accompanied by a state of *visual* mental imagery as of a white snowbank. I might also have *auditory* mental imagery, such as hearing myself saying the English words "snow is white" in inner speech. Once we account for this accompanying sensory mental imagery, Lormand and others claim that there is nothing left over, phenomenologically: the thought's phenomenal properties are exhausted by its sensory phenomenal properties (see also Wilson 2003).

Jesse Prinz also thinks that thoughts are conscious only insofar as they are reducible to sensory mental imagery. He explains away putative cases of imageless thought as failures on the part of introspectors to notice broadly sensory mental imagery (2007, pp. 348–9; 2011, pp. 183–9). When faced with a conscious thought that appears to arrive, unbidden, without any accompanying imagery, Prinz's strategy is to find some sensory mental imagery present that has been left out of the case's description: "On any plausible... view, the phenomenology of thought is underwritten by both verbal and non-verbal imagery. Thus, [my opponents] face the difficult challenge of having to find cases in which the phenomenal character of a thought transcends these rich sources" (Prinz 2011, p. 189). According to Prinz, careful introspection will reveal some visual, verbal, or emotional mental imagery that might initially go undetected. Prinz thus accepts:

The sensory constraint on conscious thought: for any thought, if it is phenomenally conscious, then it has a sensory reduction base.

A phenomenally conscious thought has a *sensory reduction base* when it is accompanied by some sensory mental imagery that can serve as a plausible candidate to constitute the experience of thinking. For example, my experience of thinking that snow is white might be constituted by a mental image of a white expanse of snow, or the auditory imagery of saying the words "snow is white."

Proponents of the sensory constraint on conscious thought must deny the following:

Anti-reductionism: there exists a non-sensory phenomenology of thinking, a *sui generis* cognitive phenomenology had by conscious thoughts.[1]

Philosophers who accept the sensory constraint hold that the experience of thinking is fully constituted by some accompanying sensory phenomenology. They must therefore deny the possibility of conscious thoughts having some non-sensory phenomenology that can come apart from this sensory phenomenology (Carruthers and Veillet 2011; Tye and Wright 2011).

---

[1] Philosophers who argue that there is a non-sensory cognitive phenomenology include Strawson (1994); Siewert (1998); Horgan and Tienson (2002); Pitt (2004); Kriegel (2015); Chudnoff (2015); and Montague (2016).

Proponents of the sensory constraint also typically deny the following claim about the role of cognitive phenomenology:

The determination thesis: thought has content that is determined by its phenomenal character alone.

Determination is the converse of supervenience: if thought has a content that is determined by its phenomenal character, then this thought content supervenes on its phenomenal character. If phenomenal character is *narrow* in the sense that it supervenes on intrinsic properties of the subject, then it follows that thought has some narrow content. The determination thesis is consistent with conscious thoughts also having wide content determined partly by causal or functional roles (Horgan and Tienson 2002). To leave this open, I'll say that the non-sensory phenomenology of thought *partially* determines the content of thought.

Why do proponents of the sensory constraint reject the determination thesis? According to the sensory constraint, the experience of thinking is constituted by sensory phenomenology. It is implausible, however, that sensory phenomenology alone is rich enough to determine the content of thought (Tye 2006). For instance, two people might experience exactly the same sensory phenomenology while thinking completely different thoughts. This motivates these philosophers to sideline the role of phenomenal consciousness in determining thought content in favor of purely causal or functional theories of thought content. As will emerge, my argument against the sensory constraint provides support for both anti-reductionism and the determination thesis.

The sensory constraint on conscious thought has been challenged by phenomenological arguments for *unsymbolized thoughts*, thoughts that are conscious, yet occur in the absence of visual or auditory mental imagery (Siewert 1998; Heavey and Hurlburt 2008; Hurlburt and Akhter 2008). The goal of this chapter is to develop an empirical challenge to the sensory constraint by appealing to the psychological phenomenon of aphantasia.

2. Aphantasic Thoughts Do Not Have a Sensory Reduction Base

In this section, I argue for the negative premise that aphantasics have some thoughts, *aphantasic thoughts*, that have no sensory reduction base.

The negative premise best explains the introspective reports, performance on psychological tasks, and neural activity of aphantasics.

Zeman et al. (2010) initially presented the case of a single subject, MX, who reported losing the capacity to generate any visual mental imagery at all after undergoing a heart procedure. A surveyor by trade, MX was able to remember and describe visual details of landmarks around Edinburgh but reported being unable to "see them" (p. 147). After undergoing a variety of psychometric tests, it was concluded that MX had no underlying cognitive deficits; his results on these tests were consistent with a control group for general intelligence and memory. Notably, MX also performed normally on a number of cognitive tasks that are thought to require sensory mental imagery. For example, when MX was given the "famous face feature test," MX successfully answered questions that require judgments about visual details of familiar faces (e.g., does Tony Blair have a moustache?).

After the initial MX study was publicized in the popular press (Zimmer 2010), a growing number of people have recognized this total imagery deficit in themselves.[2] Unlike the case of MX, many have reported that their lack of visual imagery is a congenital rather than acquired syndrome. This led Zeman and coauthors to do a follow-up study, showing that aphantasia is a regularly occurring phenomenon (2015, 2016). Studying a group of twenty-one subjects who reported similar imagery deficits to MX's, they found that aphantasics rated much lower on the Vividness of Visual Imagery Questionnaire (VVIQ) than a control group of 121. The VVIQ (first developed by Marks 1973) asks subjects to perform certain imaginative tasks and to quantitatively rate the vividness of their imagery during these tasks. Subjects are asked, among other things, to visualize a rising sun and notice any surrounding clouds or blue sky, and to think of a storefront and rate the vividness of "the overall appearance of the shop from the other side of the road" (Zeman, Dewar, and Della Sala 2015, supplementary data).

In addition to this questionnaire data, there is psychological data replicating MX's initial performance on tasks thought to require imagery. In Zeman et al. (2020), aphantasic patients were asked to mentally count the number of windows in their house or apartment. Aphantasics were much less likely to use visual imagery strategies to perform the task than the control group (see Figure 5.1).[3]

---

[2] Faw (2009) suggests that extreme aphantasia may affect up to 5% of people. Zeman, Dewar, and Della Sala (2016) report that "thousands" of aphantasics have made contact with his group at Exeter, which attests to its frequency.

[3] They were also far less likely to use visual imagery strategies than the *hyperphantasia* group, consisting of subjects reporting especially vivid mental imagery.

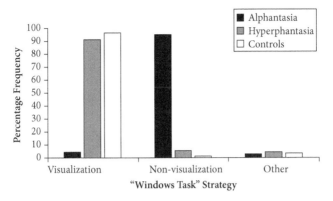

Figure 5.1 Adapted from Zeman (2020).

If they do not rely on visual mental imagery, how do aphantasics complete the windows task and other VVIQ tasks? They use non-imagery strategies, including "amodal knowledge" (Zeman et al. 2020, p. 430). Zeman writes that the success of aphantasics on tasks like the windows task was achieved by drawing on what study participants described as "knowledge, memory, and subvisual" models (Zeman, Dewar, and Della Sala 2015).

A major question for those relying on the VVIQ concerns its reliability. It seems quite plausible that what some subjects describe as "vivid" visual imagery, others will not. What one rates as a 9 out of 10 on a vividness scale, another might rate a 4 out of 10. Or, perhaps some subjects are simply not as good at attending to the vividness of their own visual imagery. The VVIQ results suggest that there might be considerable interpersonal variation in how much imagery people have, but how can we rule out the possibility that there might also be a large degree of variation in people's vividness thresholds? In other words, might the variances in reported mental imagery more likely reflect people's different criteria for reporting it?

This worry can be alleviated by the increased development of objective techniques for measuring mental imagery. These techniques, developed by Joel Pearson and coauthors, exploit the binocular rivalry illusion (Pearson et al. 2008; Pearson 2014; Chang and Pearson 2017; Keogh and Pearson 2018). Binocular rivalry is a process wherein one image is presented to a subject's left eye while a different image is presented to the right eye. One might expect this to cause a fusion of two percepts in the subject. For example, if the left eye is presented with a blue swatch, and the right eye is presented with a red swatch, we might expect the resulting image to be a fusion of these two images (i.e., what is present to the subject's awareness is a purple swatch). Interestingly, what in fact happens is that one of the images becomes dominant, while the other image is not present in awareness. Previous work has shown that which image becomes dominant is subject to a priming effect: when the subject is presented with a weak visual copy of one of the images before a binocular rivalry presentation, this makes it more likely that this image will be the one seen in the illusion (Brascamp et al. 2007; Pearson et al. 2008).

Notably, studies by Pearson found that a similar pattern of priming results from visually imagining some image before being presented with a binocular rivalry presentation. Pearson thus writes that "this imagery paradigm has been referred to as a measure of the sensory strength of imagery, as it bypasses the need for any self-reports and directly reflects more sensory priming from the mental image" (Keogh and Pearson 2018, p. 55). The natural next step, then, was to see if aphantasics were subject to this imagery priming effect in binocular rivalry. Keogh and Pearson (2018) found that aphantasics show *almost no* imagery-based rivalry priming. The image that the aphantasics saw after priming was not significantly different from chance, whereas the image subjects from the general population see is significantly different from chance. These same aphantasics also self-rated their visual imagery very low on the VVIQ and other imagery self-assessments.

A more recent study by Wicken, Keogh, and Pearson (2021) gives further evidence for aphantasia being a genuine lack of imagery. This study compared the skin conductance level of aphantasics with that of a control group of general population subjects when reading fictitious scenarios designed to elicit frightening imagery. Skin conductance levels generally increase when responding to frightening stimuli, including imagined stimuli. The data show that aphantasics show a significantly lower fear reaction (witnessed by the lower skin conductance levels) than control participants who retained the ability to visualize. Notably, there was no significant difference in conductance level between the two groups in a control experiment in which both groups were shown frightening perceptual images (see Figure 5.2).

Aphantasia also has objective grounding in the form of functional magnetic resonance imaging (fMRI) techniques. Zeman et al. (2010) designed a set of tasks to examine patterns of brain activation in MX and in a control group.[4] The participants were subjected to a "perception condition" in which they viewed famous faces, as well as an "imagery condition" in which they were

---

[4] The tasks are adapted from tasks originally performed in Ishai, Haxby, and Ungerleider (2002).

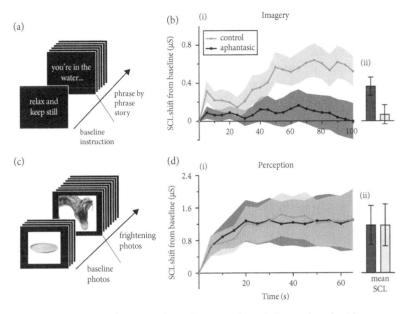

Figure 5.2 From Wicken, Keogh, and Pearson (2021). Reproduced with permission of The Royal Society.

presented with the name of a famous person and asked to attempt to visually imagine the person's face. They also viewed control stimuli for both perception and imagery conditions: scrambled face stimuli and nonsense letter strings, respectively. In both MX and the control participants, face perception activates specific areas, including the inferior occipital and the fusiform gyri (Ishai et al. 2002). There were no differences in brain activation detected between MX and the control group when subjected to the perception condition. There were differences of brain activation, however, between MX and control participants in the imagery condition. While the control participant group employed the posterior visual network when imaging, MX used a predominantly frontal network when attempting to imagine, including the frontal and anterior cingulate gyri. These areas are associated with different cognitive functions, and are activated by different executive tasks; the inferior frontal gyrus has been associated with semantic retrieval (Moss et al. 2005). Zeman et al. (2010) suggests that this relative increase in frontal activation for MX reflects the difficulty in attempting to visually imagine and the search for alternative cognitive strategies. In all, the fMRI data corroborate MX's subjective reports of loss of visual imagery. Another fMRI study lead by Fulford et al. (2018) measured a group of aphantasics, and the findings were consistent with that of MX's: "The increased frontal activation in MX… is mirrored by our current finding that a range of frontal activations, including activation of the anterior cingulate, are negatively correlated with imagery vividness" (p. 37). Taken together, these fMRI studies show that MX and other aphantasics' subjective reports have empirical corroboration.

Now that I've presented empirical support for the negative premise, I'll defend it against the objection that it leads us to be guilty of neglecting various kinds of sensory mental imagery: faint imagery, auditory imagery, involuntary imagery, and unconscious imagery. I'll consider each of these in turn.

First, it might be objected that aphantasics do not have a complete lack of sensory mental imagery, but merely a reduced amount of imagery. If aphantasics do have only an impoverishment of mental imagery, then perhaps there is some very faint sensory mental imagery accompanying their thoughts that can serve as a reduction base for their cognitive experience of thinking.

What the burgeoning aphantasia literature has shown is that there is a large degree of variation in mental imagery across subjects. There seems to be a continuum of imagery vividness: on one end of the spectrum, there are *hyperphantasics*, subjects who report especially vivid imagery (Zeman et al. 2020); at the other end of the spectrum, there appear to be some subjects without *any* sensory mental imagery. Call this complete lack of mental imagery "extreme aphantasia." Dawes et al. (2020) found that up to 26.2% of aphantasics have this extreme form, reporting a *total* absence of imagery. The VVIQ has a range of 16 to 80, where a score of 16 is recorded when a subject answers "no image at all" on all questions in the questionnaire. Zeman et al. (2020) found that a number of subjects achieved the minimum score of 16/80 on the VVIQ. Many subjects in the aphantasia studies do experience reduced mental imagery. Some with extreme aphantasia, however, have none.

Proponents of the sensory constraint might insist that even if aphantasics lack visual imagery, they have other kinds of imagery to serve as a sensory reduction base, e.g. inner speech. In response, many aphantasics lack auditory imagery as well as visual imagery. If aphantasics lack auditory mental imagery, this is good evidence that they lack inner speech, since most views of inner speech agree that it has an auditory-phonological component (Langland-Hassan 2018; Carruthers 2018), even if it has other components as well, such as motor imagery.[5]

---

[5] For the current state of play on inner speech, see the essays in Langland-Hassan and Vicente (2018).

Some initial studies on aphantasia reveal that impoverishment of imagery is not limited to visual imagery. In the (2015) study, Zeman and coauthors write that "10/21 [aphantasic participants] told us that all modalities of imagery were affected" (p. 378; see also Zeman 2021, who reports that half of their participants report imagery reduction in all sensory modalities). Dawes et al. (2020) found that "individuals with aphantasia not only report being unable to visualize, but also report comparatively reduced imagery, on average, in all other sensory modalities," and that 26.2% of subjects report a lack of imagery in *all* sensory modalities (Blomkvist forthcoming). More targeted studies attempting to isolate auditory imagery in aphantasic studies would help to confirm these initial results.[6]

Does extreme aphantasia also occur in the case of auditory imagery? Many anecdotal reports suggest so. In the last decade, as the number of people recognizing aphantasia in themselves has steadily grown, several online communities (aphantasia.com, reddit.com/r/aphantasia) have sprung up as people come together to discuss their shared experience (and lack thereof). These communities feature a number of users who report that they experience no visual imagery and no inner speech when they think. A sampling of these reports:

> I can think in sequences of ideas, but there is no running voice or perceptible characteristic to my inner thinking at all.[7]

> I have Aphantasia and no inner monologue. I discovered the aphantasia first, and the fact that other people have an (often) constant voice in their head soon after. Both things (in that other people do not think like me) were just as surprising to me. My thoughts are generally concepts, that only get put into words when I want to externalise them (talk or write). This makes sense to me as thoughts are thoughts, a different thing from words and pictures![8]

---

[6] A recent study by Hinwar and Lambert (2021) found that most self-reported visual aphantasics also reported weak or entirely absent auditory imagery; and participants lacking auditory imagery tended to be (visually) aphantasic. Blomkvist (forthcoming) argues that we have reason to believe that the data reporting how many people have impairments across sensory modalities is actually underestimated, as the extant data is only taken from a subset of those who have a visual imagery impairment; it would not capture a subject who is only impaired when it comes to non-visual mental imagery.

[7] Accessed from: https://www.reddit.com/r/Aphantasia/comments/9t58jj/what_is_an_inner_monologue/

[8] Accessed from: https://www.reddit.com/r/Aphantasia/comments/c62t5d/aphantasia_lack_of_internal_monologue/

> I have Aphantasia and no inner monologue. I can force words in my head—e.g., if you ask me to repeat a sentence in my head, I can do that (although it feels a bit weird and unnatural)—but I don't think with it and it's never spontaneous. I don't narrate my day, work things out, talk to myself about something, or comment on things I see with words in my head. My thinking is all unsymbolized conceptual thoughts.[9]

> I think in words but don't hear a voice or anything, it's just abstract words, the same as 'visualising', there's nothing there but the abstract concept. It's really hard to explain though... when I'm conscious there's nothing.[10]

> I have no internal monologue but I also don't see pictures... I can't see much but I just "know" what it is. As for thoughts that I have to make concrete, I will 100% think in all words but it's very painstaking because it's like squeezing a bunch of stuff through a strainer to get the right words...[11]

These first-personal reports suggest that a deficit of visual mental imagery and a deficit of auditory mental imagery often go hand in hand. Aphantasics thus sometimes have thoughts without either visual or auditory mental imagery.

Some aphantasia studies indicate that some aphantasics can form *involuntary* mental imagery in the form of daydreaming (Dawes et al. 2020), dreaming (Zeman et al. 2020; Dawes et al. 2020), and "flashes" (Zeman, Dewar, and Della Sala 2015). Many of our conscious thoughts are involuntary, seeming to occur to us suddenly and unprompted. One might be tempted to think that involuntary mental imagery suffices to explain all the conscious thoughts that aphantasic subjects have.[12]

The studies on offer, however, also reveal that many aphantasics have a deficit of involuntary imagery as well (Zeman et al. 2020; Dawes et al. 2020). Moreover, even among those who do have involuntary sensory mental imagery, these episodes could not explain the apparent conscious thoughts

---

[9] Accessed from: https://www.reddit.com/r/Aphantasia/comments/jmvepu/aphantasia_and_inner_speec

[10] Accessed from: https://www.reddit.com/r/Aphantasia/comments/jmvepu/aphantasia_and_inner_speech/

[11] Accessed from: https://www.reddit.com/r/Aphantasia/comments/odskh5/how_does_your_stream_of_consciousness_work/

[12] Thanks to Dan Cavedon-Taylor for raising this possibility.

aphantasics have without accompanying imagery when answering questions on the VVIQ, as these thoughts are voluntarily generated (e.g., "Tony Blair does not have a moustache").

Finally, Bence Nanay argues that aphantasia can be explained by the presence of *unconscious* sensory mental imagery (Nanay 2021). Just as there can be conscious and unconscious perception, so too can there be conscious and unconscious perceptual imagery. Nanay argues for the presence of unconscious visual imagery in order to explain the performance of a single aphantasic studied in Jacobs et al. (2018). If this is right, then there may be some sensory imagery accompanying the conscious thoughts of aphantasics: it's just that the sensory mental imagery is unconscious.

There may indeed be unconscious mental imagery present in aphantasics as Nanay suggests. This is no consolation for proponents of the sensory constraint, however, since an unconscious sensory state cannot serve as a reduction base for a conscious thought. A conscious thought has a sensory reduction base when there is an accompanying sensory experience that can serve as a plausible candidate to explain the cognitive experience of thinking. If aphantasic thoughts are phenomenally conscious, then *unconscious* sensory imagery is not a plausible candidate to explain these thoughts. Showing that aphantasic thoughts are phenomenally conscious is the task of the next section.

3. Aphantasic Thoughts Are Phenomenally Conscious

In this section, I argue for the positive premise that aphantasic thoughts are phenomenally conscious. I give two arguments for this premise. The first argument is from introspective report: aphantasic subjects report that their own thoughts are conscious, and it seems reasonable to take these reports at face value in the absence of strong evidence to the contrary. The second argument is abductive: the best explanation for how aphantasics know what they are thinking is that their thoughts are phenomenally conscious.

First, then, the argument from introspective report. The introspective reports given by aphantasics seem to indicate that their thoughts are conscious. When describing how they think, aphantasics in online communities appear to be describing their subjective experience. The following quotes from aphantasics describing their thinking are instructive:

> I don't have a good way to describe what goes on in my head. I FEEL my thought, in a more abstract way.[13]
>
> Most of the time my mind feels blank, with an occasional thought zipping through it...not in visual form, but not in an auditory form either.[14]
>
> I don't have an inner monologue, although I can force one if I want to but it feels like a slower extra step. To me it feels like thinking in abstract concepts...[15]
>
> Unless I'm actually thinking very specifically about something, a lot of how I think feels very abstract and hard to explain. It's like my own thoughts are on the tip of my tongue.[16]
>
> I just think. There aren't words or images that go with it. I just rapidly go through scenarios in my head, like if I do A then B will happen.[17]

We can distill four distinct points from these reports. First, when aphantasics make reports to the effect that they "feel" their thoughts "zipping" through their mind, they are describing their stream of consciousness: there's something it's like for them to experience their thoughts. Second, what it's like for them to experience the thought is non-sensory in that it's "not in visual form, or in auditory form either." Third, the experience of thinking is not the mere occurrence of non-intentional phenomenal qualities, such as "cognitive qualia." On the contrary, it is an experience *of thinking*: it feels like "thinking in abstract concepts."[18] Finally, what it is like to have a thought with one content is different from what it is like to think a thought with another content in the same external circumstances: for example, the experience of having a conditional thought ("if I do A then B will happen")

---

[13] Accessed from: https://www.reddit.com/r/Aphantasia/comments/penjjt/whats_your_inner_thoughts_language/

[14] Accessed from: https://www.reddit.com/r/Aphantasia/comments/9t58jj/what_is_an_inner_monologue/

[15] Accessed from: https://www.reddit.com/r/Aphantasia/comments/penjjt/whats_your_inner_thoughts_language/

[16] Accessed from: https://www.reddit.com/r/Aphantasia/comments/ad5cl8/thinking_by_using_language_only/

[17] Accessed from: https://www.reddit.com/r/Aphantasia/comments/ccsb7m/how_do_you_think_most_times/

[18] In personal communication, Alexei Dawes writes that the majority of the aphantasics studied in Dawes et al. (2020) reported thinking "semantically" but without sensory phenomenology. When thinking about an apple, for example, they think about the apple concept abstractly, are able to describe an apple, know that it tastes sweet, but do not have any accompanying sensory detail.

feels different from, say, having a conjunctive thought ("I will do A and B will happen").

These introspective reports from aphantasics thus provide defeasible evidence that their aphantasic thoughts are phenomenally conscious. In the absence of defeaters, we should take these introspective reports at face value. It is therefore reasonable to conclude that these thoughts are phenomenally conscious.

Now let's turn to the abductive argument for the positive premise that aphantasic thoughts are phenomenally conscious. The first premise of the abductive argument is that aphantasics have introspective knowledge of their own thoughts. Aphantasics will report that they "just know" that they are thinking and that they are thinking about some things rather than others. As a popular aphantasic YouTube personality says, "my thoughts are manifesting in a *knowing* way...I just *know* they're there..."[19] When asked to describe the contents of their "inner monologue," a member of an online aphantasia community writes, "My internal monologue has no sound or anything *I just know what I'm thinking*."[20]

When aphantasics report that they "just know" their own thoughts, and that their thoughts manifest in a "knowing way," they seem to mean that they know their thoughts directly, rather than indirectly based on inference. When we know a conclusion by inference, and we're asked how we know it, we can usually answer by citing our premises. When our knowledge is non-inferential, however, it's more natural to answer, "I just know." For example, this is the natural answer to give when someone asks you how you know you're in pain. After all, when we know that we're in pain, we do not typically infer this conclusion from further premises. Rather, we "just know" in the sense that we have a direct and non-inferential way of knowing our own minds. And what goes for pain goes equally for aphantasic thoughts. Not only do people with aphantasia report that their thoughts are conscious, but their reports also suggest that they have non-inferential knowledge of their thoughts.

It is standard to use the term "introspection" as a label for this first-personal way of knowing our own minds without inference (Smithies and Stoljar 2012). Philosophers give different theories of introspection,

[19] Accessed from: https://www.youtube.com/watch?v=drFuO81sI5g
[20] Accessed from: https://www.reddit.com/r/Aphantasia/comments/f926eg/what_are_your_internal_monologues_like_asking/

but we need not decide between them here. All that is needed is the idea that there is a distinctly first-personal way of knowing about our own minds without inference, however its nature is ultimately explained. Taking the introspective reports from aphantasics seriously suggests that this first-personal way of knowing our own minds does not just apply to sensations, such as the feeling of pain, but extends to the experience of thinking as well.

The second premise of the abductive argument is that the best explanation of how aphantasics have introspective knowledge of their thoughts is that their thoughts are phenomenally conscious. More generally, phenomenal consciousness seems relevant for explaining our introspective knowledge of the contents of our conscious states. For example, I can know by introspection not only that I'm visualizing, rather than seeing, but also that I'm visualizing an orange, rather than an apple. Moreover, there is a phenomenal difference between seeing and visualizing and between visualizing an apple and visualizing an orange. It is plausible that these phenomenal differences are relevant to explaining how I can know by introspection that I'm visualizing an orange.

Notice that the same points hold true in the case of thought. We can know by introspection not only *that* we are thinking, but *what* we are thinking. For example, one of the aphantasics above reports thinking a conditional thought: *if I do A then B will happen*. Moreover, there is a phenomenal difference between thinking this conditional thought and thinking a conjunctive thought, e.g. *I'll do A and then B will happen*. And, crucially, this phenomenal difference seems relevant to explaining how we can know by introspection that we're thinking a conditional thought, rather than a conjunctive one. The abductive premise thus offers a kind of explanatory unification: in the same way that they can know their conscious sensations and perceptions, aphantasics (and non-aphantasics) can know their own thoughts directly through introspection *because* these thoughts are phenomenally conscious.

We can now state the abductive argument for the positive premise as follows:

Epistemic premise: Aphantasics have introspective knowledge of their own thoughts.

Abductive premise: The best explanation of this introspective knowledge is that aphantasic thoughts are phenomenally conscious.

Conclusion: Therefore, aphantasic thoughts are phenomenally conscious.

Both premises of the abductive argument face objections. First, some argue that the abductive premise is false because we need not appeal to phenomenal consciousness in order to explain our introspective knowledge of our own thoughts. Rather, all that is needed is to posit a reliable introspective mechanism, which takes as an input the thought that p and produces the belief "I think that p" as an output (Levine 2011). So long as this mechanism is sufficiently reliable, it can generate introspective knowledge as output, whether or not its inputs are phenomenally conscious.

In response, let me concede that we have some reliable introspective mechanism. Without such a mechanism, it is hard to see how introspective knowledge is possible at all, since reliability is a necessary condition for knowledge. Plausibly, however, introspection is reliable only in certain conditions and given certain kinds of inputs: in particular, it makes us reliable about our conscious states and not our unconscious states. In optimal conditions, introspection gives us *some* degree of reliable introspective access to our conscious states, like pains, itches, and thoughts (Bayne and Spener 2010). It does not, however, seem to give us *any* degree of reliable introspective access to our unconscious states, like our implicit biases or implicit knowledge of syntactic rules. In order to have knowledge of these unconscious states, we must engage in inference to the best explanation.

Moreover, even if we did have reliable access to our unconscious states, this would not obviously be enough to deliver introspective knowledge. This is because, while reliability is generally agreed to be necessary for knowledge, it is much more controversial whether it is sufficient for knowledge. Consider, for instance, Smithies' (2019, pp. 147–8) discussion of the "super-duper-blindsighter," who has a reliable mechanism that generates true higher order beliefs about the contents of unconscious vision without inference. The super-duper-blindsighter's higher order beliefs are unjustified, despite having a reliable mechanism. And it looks like phenomenal consciousness is the missing element that is needed for such beliefs to be justified. To see this, notice that the feeling of pain doesn't merely reliably cause us to believe that we are in pain; it also *justifies* our believing that we are in pain. The same holds true for experiences of thinking: my conscious thought that a dime and a quarter gives me thirty-five cents doesn't just reliably cause me to believe that I have this thought, it also justifies my belief that I have this thought.

The epistemic premise of the abductive argument also faces an objection. Peter Carruthers (2011, 2015) denies that our knowledge of our own thoughts is non-inferential. When it comes to Siewert's (1998) case of suddenly realizing one has locked one's keys inside one's house, he argues, one's knowledge of this thought isn't directly based on introspection, but is rather the result of a swift process of self-interpretation. Whereas introspective knowledge is direct and non-inferential, self-interpretation is an inferential process that yields knowledge of conclusions about our thoughts from sensory and behavioral premises. Siewert's mistake, according to Carruthers, is to infer the false conclusion that our thoughts are conscious from the true premise that we cannot have non-inferential knowledge of our unconscious mental states together with the false premise that we have non-inferential knowledge of our thoughts. Wrongly judging that our knowledge of our own thoughts is direct leads us to think that our thoughts are conscious. But this is a mistake, according to Carruthers.

Carruthers' objection applies not only to Siewert, but also to the entire community of aphantasics. Aphantasics seem to report having non-inferential knowledge of their thoughts. The reports suggest their knowledge of their thoughts is direct in the same way that they know their feelings and sense perceptions. As one aphantasic says:

I don't have inner seeing or inner hearing, but I do have feelings in the present, sensory awareness, and unsymbolized thoughts. So I can have the feeling of hunger or thirst, walk to the fridge, at same time look outside, seeing a mailman and I be aware of a future action that needs to be done, without any symbolism: words, pictures or anything, it is just knowing.[21]

Here, this aphantasic seems to describe her knowledge of a thought, namely, a thought about some future action that needs to be done, in the same way that she describes knowing her feelings and visual perceptions: she "just knows" that she is having them.

If Carruthers is right, however, then aphantasics are wrong that they have non-inferential knowledge of their minds. What's more, if they were to have non-inferential knowledge about their own thoughts, then those thoughts would be conscious. Carruthers thinks this linking principle is a part of our universal folk psychology (2011, p. 32). This error about how aphantasics know their own minds thus brings in its train a second: they are also wrong about the contents of their own streams of consciousness. As he says about the case of unsymbolized thought:

---

[21] Accessed from: https://www.reddit.com/r/Aphantasia/comments/penjjt/whats_your_inner_thoughts_language/

subjects who report unsymbolized or partly-worded thoughts...may actually be relying on self-interpretation, grounded in prior imagistic activity, current imagery of a non-symbolic sort, and/or knowledge of current behavior and circumstances...[they] will simply find themselves with the powerful intuition that they were entertaining a specific thought.... (2011, p. 221)

It is perhaps not surprising that aphantasics might be wrong about how they know their own minds. But it is the second error that Carruthers imputes to aphantasics, that they are all massively mistaken about their own streams of consciousness, that is more surprising. To motivate this kind of error theory, Carruthers needs a very strong argument.[22] It is a cost of his view of self-knowledge that it seems to be at odds with many introspective reports of aphantasics (and non-aphantasics) when describing their thinking. This is not to say that the introspective judgments of aphantasics are infallible, but rather that the default view should be that aphantasics are not all collectively mistaken about their own streams of consciousness.

Both the argument from introspective report and the abductive argument support the positive premise that aphantasic thoughts are phenomenally conscious. When MX judges that Princes Street is in the New Town part of Edinburgh, it is plausible that this thought is present to him in phenomenal consciousness. And, as I argued in §2, the best explanation of the introspective reports, performance on tasks thought to require sensory mental imagery, and neural activity of aphantasics is that aphantasics sometimes have thoughts without a sensory reduction base. MX's thought about New Town thus need not have any accompanying sensory mental imagery constituting his experience of thinking. In other words, the existence of aphantasic thoughts shows that the sensory constraint on conscious thought is false.

---

[22] Carruthers (2011) does give an argument that we are always mistaken in thinking that we have direct knowledge of our thoughts, but it is beyond the scope of this chapter to evaluate this argument. The argument is a rather complex abductive argument that relies on the comparative advantages of his theory in explaining the pattern of psychological data where we sometimes confabulate. Details aside, the key question is whether we can better explain the data with a mixed theory that says we have two different ways of self-ascribing our own thoughts, one inferential and one non-inferential. This mixed view is defended by Nichols and Stich (2003) and Goldman (2006).

4. Conclusion

What do we learn from the argument against the sensory constraint on conscious thought? Here are the conclusions of the chapter.

First, the existence of aphantasic thought supports anti-reductionism, i.e. there exists a non-sensory phenomenology of thinking, a *sui generis* kind of cognitive phenomenology. Aphantasic subjects sometimes have thoughts without a sensory reduction base, and yet their thoughts are phenomenally conscious. This suggests there must exist some phenomenal character that is proprietary to cognitive experiences, such as conscious thoughts: a phenomenology that is different in kind from the phenomenal character of sensory experiences. It might be quite difficult to describe this cognitive phenomenology in language; we might reach, as aphantasics do, for certain phrases like "it feels like thinking in abstract concepts." But just because an experience is difficult to describe does not mean it doesn't exist at all.

Second, the arguments that support anti-reductionism can be extended to support the determination thesis. When it comes to the argument from introspective report, recall that aphantasics don't just report having the experience of thinking; they also report the experience of thinking thoughts with specific contents, e.g. conditional contents, rather than conjunctive contents. This provides defeasible evidence that the experience of thinking varies depending on what you are thinking about, just as the experience of visualizing varies depending on what you are visualizing. When it comes to the abductive argument, we can know by introspection not just *that* we are thinking, but *what* we are thinking, e.g. I can know I'm thinking a conditional thought, rather than a conjunctive thought. The best explanation of how we can have this introspective knowledge is that the experience of thinking varies depending on what you're thinking about: for example, there's a phenomenal difference between thinking a conditional thought and a conjunctive thought. The case of aphantasic thought thus supports the determination thesis, which says that any difference in the phenomenal character of thought will reflect some difference in its content (Siewert 1998; Horgan and Tienson 2002).

Much of the debate over the existence of cognitive phenomenology trades on introspective arguments. While some claim that we "cannot miss" the cognitive aspects of phenomenology if we "simply pay attention" (Horgan and Tienson, p. 522–3), others report being able to detect only sensory phenomenology.[23] The large degree of variation in imagery illustrated by aphantasia offers a potential diagnosis of this impasse.[24] It may be that opponents of cognitive phenomenology have particularly vivid and ubiquitous sensory phenomenology. Conversely, it may be that proponents of cognitive phenomenology tend to think in imagery less than their opponents: the conceptual or semantic features of their conscious thoughts may stand out to them because they are typically less likely to be accompanied by sensory imagery. I put this forward as a tentative hypothesis regarding this disagreement, one which merits a fuller treatment elsewhere.[25]

References

Bayne, T. and M. Spener. 2010. 'Introspective humility.' *Philosophical Issues* 20 (1): 1–22.

Blomkvist, A. Forthcoming. 'Aphantasia: In search of a theory.' Unpublished manuscript.

Brascamp, J., T. Knapen, R. Kanai, R. v. Ee, and A. van den Berg. 2007. 'Flash suppression and flash facilitation in binocular rivalry.' *Journal of Vision* 7 (12): 1–12.

Carruthers, P. 2011. *The Opacity of Mind: An Integrative Theory of Self-Knowledge*. Oxford: Oxford University Press.

---

[23] Siewert (1998), Pitt (2004), and Strawson (2011) appeal to introspection to argue for cognitive phenomenology. Wilson (2003), Nichols and Stich (2003), Robinson (2005, 2011), Tye and Wright (2011), Carruthers and Veillet (2011), and of course Prinz (2011) doubt the appeal to introspection for cognitive phenomenology.

[24] Schwitzgebel (2008) and Spener (2011) argue that this introspective stalemate amongst participants in the cognitive phenomenology debate shows that introspection cannot be relied on to settle the debate over cognitive phenomenology's existence. Smithies (2013) suggests that arguments for or against cognitive phenomenology should thus instead turn on what theoretical role it might play.

[25] Thanks to Dan Cavedon-Taylor, André Curtis-Trudel, Alexei Dawes, Scott Harkema, Rachel Harris, Tristram McPherson, Erin Mercurio, Joel Pearson, Alex Petrov, Daniel Olson, Richard Samuels, Adam Zeman, and especially Declan Smithies for comments and discussion. An earlier version of this chapter was presented at the 2021 Extremes of Mind Wandering Conference at the University of Edinburgh, and I'm grateful to the organizers and audience for their feedback, including Adriana Alcaraz-Sánchez, Amy Kind, Zachary Irving, Valentina Martinis, and Jodie Russell. Thanks to Uriah Kriegel for very helpful feedback on the penultimate draft. This work was generously supported by a Summer Research Award from the Center for Cognitive and Brain Sciences at The Ohio State University.

Carruthers, P., 2015. *The Centered Mind: What the Science of Working Memory Shows Us about the Nature of Human Thought*. Oxford: Oxford University Press.

Carruthers, P., 2018. 'The causes and contents of inner speech.' In *Inner Speech: New Voices*, edited by P. Langland-Hassan and A. Vicente, 31–52 New York: Oxford University Press.

Carruthers, P. and B. Veillet. 2011. 'The case against cognitive phenomenology.' In *Cognitive Phenomenology*, edited by Tim Bayne and Michelle Montague, 35–56. Oxford: Oxford University Press.

Chang, S. and J. Pearson. 2017. 'The functional effects of prior motion imagery and motion perception.' *Cortex* 105, 83–96.

Chudnoff, E. 2015. *Cognitive Phenomenology*. New York: Routledge.

Dawes, A., R. Keogh, T. Andrillon, and J. Pearson. 2020. 'A cognitive profile of multi-sensory imagery, memory, and dreaming in aphantasia.' *Scientific Reports* 10 (1): 1–10.

Faw, B. 2009. 'Conflicting intuitions may be based on differing abilities: Evidence from mental imaging research.' *Journal of Consciousness Studies* 16 (4): 45–68.

Fulford, J., F. Milton, D. Salas, A. Smith, A. Simler, C. Winlove, and A. Zeman. 2018. 'The neural correlates of visual imagery vividness: An fMRI study and literature review.' *Cortex* 105: 26–40.

Galton, F. 1880. 'Statistics of mental imagery.' *Mind* 5: 301–318.

Goldman, A. 2006. *Simulating Minds*. New York: Oxford University Press.

Heavey, C. and R. Hurlburt. 2008. 'The phenomena of inner experience.' *Consciousness and Cognition* 17 (3): 798–810.

Hinwar, P. and A. Lambert. 2021. 'Anauralia: The silent mind and its association with aphantasia.' *Frontiers in Psychology* 12: 744213.

Horgan, T. and J. Tienson. 2002. 'The intentionality of phenomenology and the phenomenology of intentionality.' In *Philosophy of Mind: Classical and Contemporary Readings*, edited by David Chalmers. New York: Oxford University Press.

Hurlburt, R. and S. Akhter. 2008. 'Unsymbolized thinking.' *Consciousness and Cognition* 17 (4): 1364–1374.

Ishai, A., J. Haxby, and L. Ungerleider. 2002. 'Visual imagery of famous faces: Effects of memory and attention revealed by fMRI.' *Neuroimage* 17 (4): 1729–41.

Jacobs, C., D. Schwarzkopf, and J. Silvanto. 2018. 'Visual working memory performance in aphantasia.' *Cortex* 105: 61–73.

Keogh, R. and J. Pearson. 2018. 'The blind mind: No sensory visual imagery in aphantasia.' *Cortex* 105: 53–60.

Kosslyn, S., W. Thompson, and G. Ganis. 2006. *The Case for Mental Imagery.* New York: Oxford University Press.

Kriegel, U. 2015. *The Sources of Intentionality.* New York: Oxford University Press.

Langland-Hassan, P. 2018. 'From introspection to essence: The auditory nature of inner speech.' In *Inner Speech: New Voices*, edited by P. Langland-Hassan and A. Vicente, 78–104. New York: Oxford University Press.

Langland-Hassan, P. and A. Vicente. 2018. *Inner Speech: New Voices.* New York: Oxford University Press.

Levine, J. 2011. 'On the phenomenology of thought.' In *Cognitive Phenomenology*, edited by T. Bayne and M. Montague, 103–120. Oxford: Oxford University Press.

Lormand, E. 1996. 'Nonphenomenal consciousness.' *Noûs* 30 (2): 242–261.

Marks, D. 1973. 'Visual imagery differences in the recall of pictures.' *British Journal of Psychology* 64 (1): 17–24.

Montague, M. 2016. *The Given: Experience and its Content.* Oxford: Oxford University Press.

Moss, H., S. Abdallah, P. Fletcher, P. Bright, L. Pilgrim, K. Acres, and L. Tyler. 2005. 'Selecting among competing alternatives: Selection and retrieval in the left inferior frontal gyrus.' *Cerebral Cortex* 15: 1723–1735.

Nanay, B. 2021. 'Unconscious mental imagery.' *Philosophical Transactions of the Royal Society* B 376: 1–9.

Nichols, S. and S. Stich. 2003. *Mindreading: An Integrated Account of Pretence, Self-Awareness, and Understanding Other Minds.* New York: Oxford University Press.

Pearson, J. 2014. 'New directions in mental imagery research: The binocular rivalry technique and decoding fMRI patterns.' *Current Directions in Psychological Science* 23 (3): 178–183.

Pearson, J., C. Clifford, and F. Tong. 2008. 'The functional impact of mental imagery on conscious perception.' *Current Biology* 18: 982–986.

Pitt, D. 2004. 'The phenomenology of cognition, Or, what is it like to think that P?' *Philosophy and Phenomenological Research* 69: 1–36.

Prinz, J. 2007. 'All consciousness is perceptual.' In *Contemporary Debates in Philosophy of Mind*, edited by B. McLaughlin and J. Cohen, 335–357. Oxford: Wiley-Blackwell.

Prinz, J. 2011. 'The sensory basis of cognitive phenomenology.' In *Cognitive Phenomenology*, edited by T. Bayne and M. Montague, 174–196. Oxford: Oxford University Press.

Pylyshyn, Z. 2002. 'Mental imagery: In search of a theory.' *Behavioral and Brain Sciences* 25 (2): 157–182.

Robinson, W. 2005. 'Thoughts without distinctive non-imagistic phenomenology.' *Philosophy and Phenomenological Research* 70: 534–561.

Robinson, W. 2011. 'A frugal view of cognitive phenomenology.' In *Cognitive Phenomenology*, edited by T. Bayne and M. Montague, 197–214. Oxford: Oxford University.

Schwitzgebel, E. 2008. 'The unreliability of naïve Introspection.' *Philosophical Review* 117 (2): 245–273.

Siewert, C. 1998. *The Significance of Consciousness*. Princeton, NJ: Princeton University Press.

Smithies, D. 2013. 'The nature of cognitive phenomenology.' *Philosophy Compass* 8 (8): 744–754.

Smithies, D. 2019. *The Epistemic Role of Consciousness*. New York: Oxford University Press.

Smithies, D. and D. Stoljar. 2012. 'Introspection and consciousness: An overview.' In *Introspection and Consciousness*, edited by D. Smithies and D. Stoljar, 3–26. Oxford: Oxford University Press.

Spener, M. 2011. 'Disagreement about cognitive phenomenology.' In *Cognitive Phenomenology*, edited by T. Bayne and M. Montague, 268–284. Oxford: Oxford University Press.

Strawson, G. 1994. *Mental Reality*. Cambridge, MA: MIT Press.

Strawson, G. 2011. 'Cognitive phenomenology: Real life.' In *Cognitive Phenomenology*, edited by T. Bayne and M. Montague, 285–325. Oxford: Oxford University Press.

Tye, M. 2006. 'Nonconceptual content, richness, and fineness of grain.' In *Perceptual Experience*, edited by T. Gendler and J. Hawthorne. Oxford: Oxford University Press.

Tye, M. and B. Wright. 2011. 'Is there a phenomenology of thought?' In *Cognitive Phenomenology*, edited by T. Bayne and M. Montague, 326–344. Oxford: Oxford University Press.

Whiteley, C. 2020. 'Aphantasia, imagination, and dreaming.' *Philosophical Studies* 178: 2111–2132.

Wicken, M., R. Keogh, and J. Pearson. 2021. 'The critical role of mental imagery in human emotion: Insights from fear-based imagery and aphantasia.' *Proceedings of the Royal Society* B 288: 1–6.

Wilson, R. 2003. 'Intentionality and phenomenology.' *Pacific Philosophical Quarterly* 84 (4): 413–431.

Zeman, A. 2021. 'Blind mind's eye.' *American Scientist* 109: 109–117.

Zeman, A., M. Dewar, and S. Della Sala. 2015. 'Lives without imagery: Congenital aphantasia.' *Cortex* 73: 278–80.

Zeman, A., M. Dewar, and S. Della Sala. 2016. 'Reflections on aphantasia.' *Cortex* 74: 336–7.

Zeman, A., S. Della Sala, L. A. Torrens, V. E. Gountouna, D. J. McGonigle, and R. H. Logie. 2010. 'Loss of imagery phenomenology with intact visuo-spatial task performance: A case of "blind imagination."' *Neuropsychologia* 48 (1): 145–155.

Zeman, A., F. Milton, S. Della Sala, M. Dewar, T. Frayling, J. Gaddum, A. Hattersley, B. Heuerman-Williamson, K. Jones, M. MacKisack, and C. Winlove. 2020. 'Phantasia—The psychological significance of lifelong visual imagery vividness extremes.' *Cortex* 130: 426–440.

Zimmer, C. 2010. 'The brain: Look deep into the mind's eye.' *Discover Magazine*, March, <https://www.discovermagazine.com/mind/the-brain-look-deep-into-the-minds-eye>.

6
The Introspective Method

Maja Spener

1. Introduction

In both philosophy and psychology, the term 'introspection' is used in at least two different ways, and these are not clearly distinguished. It is used to talk about both a mental capacity and a form of inquiry. As a mental capacity, introspection concerns a mental or psychological kind on all fours with, e.g. perception or memory. Introspection in this sense refers to a first-person mode of cognitive access to the conscious mind—*introspective access*. As inquiry, introspection is a certain type of question-guided investigation. Introspection in this sense refers to a method of investigation that employs introspective access to gather data or information about the conscious mind—an *introspective method*.[1]

The distinction between introspective access to consciousness and the use of such access in an investigation of consciousness is crucial to a proper assessment of introspective methods in philosophy and psychology. This is because the scope and limits of an introspective method depend in large measure—yet not exclusively—on the nature of introspective access employed in it. Unfortunately, the notions of introspective method and introspective access are often run together and they are seriously underdeveloped in contemporary psychology and philosophy. As I will show in this chapter, the distinction between them is of central importance: ignoring it, or giving it short shrift, results in significant problems for our theorizing with introspection about the mind.

My route to showing this goes via the history of psychology: I will discuss the views about introspective methods of two central figures in mid-nineteenth- to early-twentieth-century German experimental psychology, namely Wilhelm Wundt (1832–1920) and Georg Elias Müller (1850–1934).

---

[1] For an interesting, related distinction, see Feest (2012).

Wundt is widely recognized to be one of the founders of psychology as an experimental academic discipline, establishing the first laboratory dedicated to psychological research at the University of Leipzig in 1879. Müller, a pioneer in the empirical study of memory and attention, is not generally known to contemporary English scholarship in this area. He founded the second such laboratory in Göttingen in 1887, focusing on the experimental study of memory. Both Wundt and Müller had extensive views about introspective methods in empirical psychology.

I look at these two figures from the history of psychology for two reasons. Firstly, this earlier period is seriously misrepresented in mainstream textbooks and relevant literature and my discussion aims to correct the standard narrative. According to that narrative, psychology was founded in the second half of the nineteenth century, more or less with the establishment of Wundt's laboratory in Leipzig, who sought to distinguish the new discipline from physiology on the one hand and philosophy on the other. Psychology is held to be thoroughly and uniformly 'Introspectionist' during this early period, lasting until the rise of behaviourism in the first decades of the twentieth century. Psychologists of this era are typically treated as a cohesive group, united not only in their pursuit of a common psychological project, but also in their endorsement of introspection as the core scientific methodology in service of this project. They are taken to have conducted experimental investigations of consciousness by employing subjects who were asked to introspect their experiences (induced in various ways) and then to provide detailed reports about them. The trouble, so the narrative goes, is that introspection is private and cannot be independently calibrated. It is, moreover, known to be highly susceptible to theory infection, due to interference from background expectation, suggestion, etc. The unreliability of such introspective reports at the heart of this method thus meant that Introspectionist psychology led to diverging and theory-infected results. The standard picture regards the subsequent behaviourist critique of Introspectionist psychology to have successfully and fatally revealed all of these flaws, leading empirical psychology to abandon the—widely considered naive—Introspectionist approach.

This mainstream narrative is grossly mistaken in a number of important respects.[2] One of these is the treatment of earlier psychologists as all

---

[2] My own views have benefitted greatly from the work by a small group of historians of psychology and philosophers of (the history of) psychology, who have provided important reappraisals of early scientific psychology. See, especially, Mischel (1970); Blumenthal (1975);

employing a shared—and obviously problematic—introspective method (e.g. Smith and Kosslyn 2007, 4–5). Such treatment is so far off the mark that it is puzzling how it even could have got going. Wilhelm Wundt, whose central status in early German experimental psychology is still widely recognized, has been particularly misrepresented in this respect. Critics of the standard narrative have therefore naturally focused on him (see Blumenthal 1975; Danziger 1980a, 1980b).

In this chapter, I present Wundt's views on introspective methods in some detail, elaborating on them in the context of other practices involving introspective methods. Historical reappraisals typically present Wundt as a critical opponent of his students' views and practices—especially those of Edward B. Titchener and Oswald Külpe. I widen the focus to include discussion of G. E. Müller's views alongside Wundt's. This allows me to make a more persuasive case for the truly sophisticated state of debate surrounding the use of introspection in theorizing more generally during this period.

Secondly, Wundt and Müller exemplify the fact that, even if they did not explicitly talk in these terms, many of the early German experimentalists were keenly aware of the importance of distinguishing between introspective method and introspective access. The period was marked by intense debates about the merits of different introspective methods. A major factor in these debates was the recognition of different modes of introspective access and the different roles they can play in empirical inquiry. Drawing on this earlier debate, I show that an understanding of how the different modes of introspective access help shape introspective methods offers a better basis for assessing the scope and limits of these methods more generally, inside and outside psychology.

To illustrate this by way of contrast, I briefly consider an example of uses of introspection in the present-day science of consciousness. An appreciation of the history helps in articulating significant methodological problems with recent uses. Extant criticism of contemporary introspective methods in scientific psychology is typically targeted at the employment of introspection *simplicter*, motivating a wholesale rejection of it. This is misguided: once we understand the distinction between introspective access and introspective method, our assessment of the scientific uses of introspection can be more nuanced and less pessimistic in general.

Danziger (1979, 1980a, 1980b); Leahey (1981); Hatfield (1997, 2005, 2020); Araujo 2012, 2016). For examples of the standard narrative, see, e.g., Smith and Kosslyn (2007, ch. 1.1) Braisbyand Gellatly (2012).

The plan for this chapter is as follows. In section 2, I lay out my overall framework for the assessment of introspective methods. I do that by engaging with a question frequently posed in this context: is introspection reliable? I explain how we can transform the seemingly unsurmountable worry about the reliability of introspection into something more tractable. The resulting framework structures the next two sections on the history of psychology and on contemporary science of consciousness. In section 3, I show how Wundt's and Müller's views on introspective methods aim to address the reliability question in different ways. Their views, and the larger debate they were engaged in, can be usefully compared in terms of the proposed framework. In section 4, I demonstrate the value of the framework outlined in section 2 and vindicated by the historical lessons of section 3, by applying it to critically discuss an example of an introspective method from present-day science of consciousness.

2. Is Introspection Reliable?

There is no doubt that introspection is widely used in both psychology and philosophy to acquire information about the conscious mind. Introspective data about consciousness forms the basis of theorizing in a variety of areas in these disciplines. The main reason for this is that it is generally acknowledged that introspection provides the most direct access to consciousness: we appreciate the reality of consciousness primarily from the first-person perspective we all have on our own conscious situation. Third-person observation of consciousness is at best indirect, typically involving inferences or bridge principles connecting perceptually available data about behaviour, agency, neural activity, etc., with conscious features. Introspection seems to offer a more primary—evidentially more direct—source of data about consciousness.

Such employment of introspection has not been without critics, however (for recent ones, see, e.g., Schwitzgebel 2008; Irvine 2012). The critics typically claim that introspection is unreliable and thus ill-suited to the job (Overgaard and Sandberg 2012, 1288). One way to put the concern is that introspection is highly susceptible to interference, which in turn skews its deliverance. Interference might be due to background expectations, habits, the demand character of introspective tasks, suggestion by experimenter, etc. Whatever the source of interference, the worry is that it leads to contaminated introspective data. The interference worry is then compounded by the widespread agreement that interference cannot be controlled for or filtered out because introspection is private. This contrasts sharply with publicly available data which can be cross-checked.

The interference worry may seem to show how deeply problematic the continued use of introspection is in theorizing: introspection is irredeemably unreliable. But we should ask, for any given claim that introspection is unreliable, which sense of 'introspection' is at issue—introspection as mental capacity or introspection as inquiry? As we will see, once we distinguish clearly between introspective methods and introspective access, not only does the question about unreliability become more complex, it also becomes less devastating.

Let us ask first about the reliability of introspective access. This question concerns the epistemic potential of such access. Introspective access involves the attainment of awareness concerning our own conscious situation from the first-person perspective. We need to recognize different modes of such access—different ways in which we can be introspectively aware. There are at least three different modes of introspective access:

Inner Attention: This is an active, typically deliberate intention-guided focus on one's current experience, producing judgements about one's current conscious situation. For example, you might focus on the precise location and intensity of a pain in your shoulder, finding that it hurts acutely somewhere between the spine and shoulder blade. Or, sick of not getting anywhere, you might attend to the fact that your thoughts keep drifting away from your attempts to understand the text before you—'back to thinking about the text you go!'

Inner Apprehension: This is a passive, automatic, and non-focal or peripheral awareness of one's current experience which (typically or constitutively) comes along with having the experience—no special mental effort is required to obtain it.[3] For example, you are aware of your visual experience when focusing your binoculars on a bird in the distance—you are not attending to the experience but instead to the seen bird, yet your lens is adjusted by exploiting peripheral awareness of the experience of the bird.

Retrospection: This is an active, typically deliberate form of episodic recall, producing judgements about one's past experiential situation. For example,

---

[3] This mode of self-awareness is usually associated with Brentano (1874), who called it 'Innere Wahrnehmung', usually translated as 'inner perception'. See also, e.g., Armstrong (1980, 59–63)'s 'reflex introspective consciousness' which he described as having a 'watching brief' over our experiences.

after coming out of a scary tunnel on a fair ground ride, you remember with a shudder the exhilaration and terror you felt a moment ago.

In this chapter, I take for granted that these three modes of introspective access are part of our mental repertoire. So I am not offering a defence of this claim other than to say that when one looks at a wide range of discussions involving introspection in philosophy and psychology, there is an overall classificatory convergence on the above modes of awareness. Such convergence does provide motivation to take the three-fold classification seriously. Moreover, my labels for these modes of introspective access are not meant to prejudge theoretical accounts of them. I am merely pointing to generally recognized mental phenomena. The three modes of access—all routinely classed as introspective—reflect different ways of being or becoming aware of one's conscious mind from the first-person perspective. Introspection as a mental capacity includes deliberate attention to ongoing experience, episodic recall of experiences just past, and passive peripheral apprehension of ongoing experiences 'out of the corner of one's mental eye' (to borrow Lyons' (1986, 4) apt phrase). These assumptions ultimately require a fuller defence, but here I rely on their initial plausibility (see Spener forthcoming for such a defence).

Let us begin with the moderate view that, within certain limited ranges of application anyway, all these introspective mental capacities are reliable in day-to-day business. Making a principled case for this, and determining the range of reliability for each introspective mode is difficult (see Spener 2015 and forthcoming for specific proposals and discussion) but not relevant to our discussion. The important point here is that the three modes of introspective access have distinctive epistemic profiles. Even given their general reliability within specified ranges of application, these distinctive epistemic profiles generate distinctive interference vulnerabilities.

Consider, for instance, that inner apprehension is a passive and non-focal awareness of ordinary first-order experiences. Inner apprehension automatically comes with having experiences and, according to some views, it is even constitutive of such experiences. As such, the immediate upshot of this introspective mode of access is some non-judgemental form of awareness—at least it is not a self-standing judgement that can be used straightforwardly in further reasoning. So, while the upshot of inner apprehension itself is plausibly highly reliable, it is unclear how the content of such awareness can be captured in any explicit judgements based on it downstream. It would seem that vulnerability to interference enters at this later stage without contaminating the upshot of inner apprehension itself.

Retrospection, by contrast, is a form of episodic memory and as such it is prone to well-documented failures, e.g. to incomplete recall or mistaken representation of previously experienced events. Almost everyone has worried about merely seeming to remember something instead of really doing so. One's memory is also often hazy on details, especially if the event remembered happened quickly. The longer the temporal gap between the target experience and the occasion of recall, moreover, the more likely and the more pronounced these failures become. While the upshot of retrospection is a self-standing judgement, it is directly vulnerable to interference in various memory-specific ways.

Inner attention, finally, typically involves a deliberate act of attention to ongoing experience, generating a judgement about one's current conscious situation. One particular concern here is that the act of inner attention itself—either the selection or information attended to or the intention driving such selection contributes to or modulates the ongoing conscious situation. So, for example, when focusing on my shoulder pain, or my rush of elation about something, the very fact that I direct attention to this aspect of my current conscious condition might heighten it (in the case of pain) or lessen it (in the case of elation). There is a long-standing debate, going back to Auguste Comte in 1830, about whether this modulating effect constitutes a distorting or even destructive interference in the upshot of inner attention (Comte 1830; but see also Kant 1787, Mill 1907/1865).

We will come back to Comte's worry about inner attention and the other interference vulnerabilities in subsequent sections. But we can see clearly already that when we are asking about the reliability of introspection as a mental capacity, each mode of access poses different interference concerns.

If the question is about the reliability of introspection as *inquiry*, however, the answer concerns the soundness and legitimacy of introspective methods. An introspective method is a type of question-guided investigation: the targets of such an investigation are aspects of consciousness, and the method employs modes of introspective access to obtain information about consciousness. To assess its reliability, we need to consider the distinctive interference profile of the particular mode of introspective access employed.

Importantly, though, the reliability of an introspective method depends not only on the reliability of the mode of introspective access used, but also on how it interacts with the observational or experimental context in which that mode is employed. In fact, experimental contexts are designed with an eye to correcting for modes' weaknesses and protecting against their vulnerabilities. It is the whole set-up which individuates a given introspective method and which must be considered when asking about the reliability of introspection-based inquiry. As will be clear from section 3, the set-up includes at least: (i) the specific mode of introspective access employed (inner attention, inner apprehension, retrospection); (ii) the specific target of investigation (the aspect of consciousness that is being investigated, together with the theoretical background framing the investigation); (iii) preparation of the subjects (prior training, instructions for the experiments); (iv) the stimulus presentation (the practical details of how the subject is triggered to have the experience under investigation, including the local setting of the experiment, timing of stimulus, etc.); (v) the type of report (e.g. button pressing, yes/no answers, detailed descriptions); (vi) the elicitation of the report (the timing and prompting of the reports); (vii) the handling, assessment, and interpretation of the data (repetition of experiments, quantitative treatment of data, interpretation of reports, use of data in theory construction).

Once we consider the entire set-up, it is obvious that evaluating the reliability of a given introspective method is complex. It depends on how a particular mode of introspective access is put to work in the set-up: apart from the specific epistemic profile of the mode of introspective access, the evaluation must take into account which target the mode of access is meant to deliver information about, how that mode is embedded in the other aspects of the experimental situation, and so on. A corollary of this is that the data collected by such a method—introspective data—are *not* equivalent to the upshots of the mode of introspective access employed in the method.

Having laid out a basic framework for assessments of the reliability of introspection in the context of theorizing about the mind, let us now turn to an earlier period in psychology characterized by endorsement of introspective methods to questions about the mind. We will see that the basic distinctions of our framework are reflected in this earlier work and that it allows us to understand the sophisticated state of play during that period.[4]

3. Wundt and Müller on Introspective Methods

I will begin by briefly canvassing an approach popular especially in the first two decades of the twentieth century—so-called 'systematic introspection'— practiced by a new generation of psychologists some of whom had studied with Wundt and Müller. The method of systematic introspection is

---

[4] For a full development and defence of this framework of assessment built on the distinction between introspective access and introspective method, see Spener (forthcoming).

what most people these days have in mind when they talk, typically derisively, about 'Introspectionist psychology' and which they mistakenly take to be representative of early psychology as a whole. Wundt and Müller explicitly rejected this introspective method. They differed, however, in their critical diagnosis and in their own positive proposals for an introspective method. Looking in detail at their views and their critical engagement with systematic introspection is instructive: each proposes different introspective methods and these turn on their different assessment of the epistemic potential of introspective access.[5]

3.1 The Method of Systematic Introspection

Systematic introspection was practiced by the Würzburg school founded by Oswald Külpe, who was a student of both Wundt and Müller. There are two key characteristics of this method: the use of detailed qualitative reports elicited by experimenters in extensive dialogue with the subjects, and the ambitious targets of investigation (complex high-level psychological features, such as the development of thought and judgement, and volitional mental activity and its influence on thought).[6] In the following brief sketch, I will focus mainly on Ach (1905) and Bühler (1907) since they form the targets of Wundt's and Müller's critiques. But in addition to Külpe, Ach, and Bühler, further central early figures of the Würzburg school—and of the psychology of thinking—are Karl Marbe, Henry Watt, Johannes Orth, and Otto Selz.

In terms of the framework from section 2, the central modes of introspective access employed in systematic introspection are deliberate inner

---

[5] The presentation of systematic introspection before discussing Wundt's and Müller's views is anachronistic and must not be taken to suggest that these two psychologists developed their own views about psychological method in response to their critical engagement with systematic introspection. Far from it. Systematic introspection flourished between 1903 and 1913 (Danziger 1980b). Wundt and Müller were already active in experimental psychology many decades earlier than that. Some key proponents of systematic introspection, e.g. Oswald Külpe and E.B. Titchener, were in fact former students of Wundt, who came to disagree with the views and scientific practices of their teacher. Müller, too, was of an earlier generation than those at the centre of systematic introspection, and his critique of the latter is firmly based on his extensive mature work on these matters.

[6] In my brief exposition of the method of systematic introspection, I will concentrate on the Würzburg school. To avoid complicating an already complicated dialectic, I will not talk about Titchener in this chapter, who, while sharing the general approach of systematic introspection in certain respects, differed from the Würzburgers along many other theoretical dimensions.

attention, and in a secondary manner, retrospection. The experimental set-up then determines the characteristic nature of this employment, given the aim to gather data about the phenomena under investigation.

Subjects are given instructions that prime them with an intention to attend to their experiences in certain ways. In a typical case, the experimenter instructs subjects that they will first perform a particular task in response to a stimulus and that they will then be asked in detail about their conscious mental activity involved in performing the task (Ach 1905, 9; Bühler 1907, 310). In addition, subjects are sometimes briefed about what sort of conscious features specifically to watch out for, or which segment or phase of the mental activity they ought to prioritize in order to be prepared to answer questions about them (Watt 1904, 316; Störring 1908, 2).

Stimulus conditions and the tasks connected to them can vary widely. The goal is to get the subject to have the conscious episodes that form the target of the investigation. The tasks might involve an external stimulus (e.g. presentation of one of two possible letters) and a forced choice (selecting which one is presented on a given trial) (Ach 1905) or the experimenters themselves trigger the relevant conscious episodes by asking the subject to undertake certain thinking tasks, typically in the form of answering a question (e.g. 'How many works did Anaximander write?' (Marbe 1901) or 'Was the theorem of Pythagoras known in the Middle-ages?' (Bühler 1907); see Hoffman and Stock 1996 for descriptions of these set-ups). The target conscious episode is the thinking or mental activity involved in coming to select the letter or answering the question posed with a specific number or yes/no.

Once the conscious episodes are triggered, and the subject attends to them as instructed, the experimenter elicits subjective reports from the subjects. Systematic introspection involves experimenters interrogating subjects in lengthy sessions, drawing out reports about the subject's experiences through in-depth questioning. The chief aim is to leave nothing out, to get a systematic and complete description of the conscious event from the subject. The reports are detailed and qualitative, not antecedently fixed by a simple format or structured response options. There is considerable variation on the timing of report elicitation. In some cases, the report elicitation phase sequentially follows the stimulus presentation phase, so the experimenter begins their interrogation immediately after the triggered conscious response has taken place (e.g. Ach 1905). The subject thus reports on the basis of their memory of the target conscious episodes. In others, the stimulus presentation phase and the report elicitation phase overlap: the experimenter may begin interrogation of the subject during the presentation of the target conscious experience, e.g. during the ongoing conscious activity of the mental task (e.g. Bühler 1907). In this case, the subject reports what they are attending to at a given moment, and their inner attention is guided in part by the experimenters' questions.

This, in very basic outline, forms the method of systematic introspection at least as practiced by these central figures. As noted, Wundt and Müller were both fiercely critical of this way of conducting experimental work in psychology. On the surface, their criticisms lament similar problems with systematic introspection, namely that it is prone to deliver heavily contaminated data due to interference of various kinds. However, the two psychologists also provide a significantly diverging overall assessment of what these problems mean for introspective methods more generally.

Müller does not object to the use of inner attention as such in the method of systematic introspection, as evidenced by his own employment of it in his investigations of memory. Nor does he object to the use of retrospection—on the contrary, according to him, retrospection constitutes the most promising route to access conscious experience in a scientifically respectable manner. But he distances himself sharply from work such as Ach's. Müller's criticisms thus concern the perceived failure to embed these modes of introspective access that are in principle acceptable for employment in theorizing in an adequate experimental method. His positive proposals show how to do so.

In contrast, Wundt's assessment is far more trenchant and negative. It comes with a rejection of the central mode of introspective access at work in systematic introspection, i.e. inner attention, as having any plausible employment in empirical psychology. He is also fairly doubtful as to whether retrospection is suitable for psychological work, at least in the way employed by the Würzburgers. In turn, that means that for Wundt, providing a scientifically respectable alternative requires employment of a different mode of introspective access to form the core of his method.

We will discuss the details of their views below, beginning each time with their critiques of systematic introspection in order to bring into focus the kinds of concerns that their own methods are meant to overcome or avoid.

3.2 Müller and the Methods of Direct Introspection and Careful Retrospection

In his seminal three-volume work *Zur Analyse der Gedächtnistätigkeit und des Vorstellungsverlaufes* ('on the analysis of the activity of memory and the course of representations'), Müller offers a comprehensive study of memory and learning. His treatment engages with extant literature on memory and other relevant areas of psychology, not only from Germany but also from other European countries and the US. The first volume, published in 1911, includes a detailed exposition and discussion of the role of introspection in the experimental study of memory (Müller 1911, 61–176). Here, too, Müller discusses contemporary practices and views, including systematic introspection.

3.2.1 Müller's Critique of Systematic Introspection

On Müller's view, psychological experiment relies on inner attention and retrospection to elicit important data. According to him, *any* questioning of subjects about their experience by an experimenter raises concerns about the potential contamination of the data so elicited. Good experimental practice in psychology seeks to mitigate these as much as possible at various stages of the scientific endeavour. But systematic introspection centrally involves extended dialogue between experimenter and subject, structured around the experimenter's probing questions about the subject's experience. This interrogation practice renders the introspective data acquired via inner attention and retrospection particularly vulnerable to interference and confabulation. Thus, while the interference worries themselves are present in any introspective method available to psychologists, the extensive interrogation practice of systematic introspection means that a number of general dangers of interference are increased rather than mitigated (Müller 1911, 138).

Müller meticulously discusses the many of the general dangers of interference. The most relevant to systematic introspection is what we now call 'the demand character' of the experiment: putting the subject under pressure to provide an answer, or even an answer of a specific type (e.g. positive rather than negative for the presence of a given feature) (Müller 1911, 122, 128–9). But there are other pitfalls as well. Any question posed by the experimenter can evoke associated thoughts and images in the subject, which the subject might then mistake for genuine memories of the original conscious episode (Müller 1911, 117). In addition, these associations can affect the very conscious episodes the subject is having in subsequent trials of the experiment (Müller 1911, 95fn). Another important source of potential interference comes from the introspecting subject's intention to self-observe, which can modulate the natural flow of experience in at least four different ways (Müller 1911, 76).

Each of these general dangers of interference are increased by the lengthy, in-depth questioning of systematic introspection. But worse, Müller points out, they compound each other. For instance, the fact of quickly fading memory raises the pressure of demand character and, together, facilitates mistaking associated thoughts and images introduced by the questions to be mistaken for genuine retrospective memory of the original experience (Müller 1911, 137–43).

The interrogation practice of systematic introspection is also grounded in mistaken empirical assumptions about attention and memory, according to Müller. Subjects are expected to recall the target conscious episode in a manner that remains stable and within reach of examination for a considerable time after the original conscious episode has ceased—a phenomenon called 'perseverance' by proponents of systematic introspection (e.g. Ach 1905). Müller bristles at such claims, which in his view not only lack any empirical support but actually run counter to the available empirical evidence about, e.g., the demonstrated fairly quick fading of episodic memory in many cases: 'I would banish a subject in disgrace, on account of obvious fibbing, if they declared that they could answer all, or even many of the questions mentioned [by Ach], in turning their attention, now towards this part, and now towards that part of the persevering [remembered conscious] content' (Müller 1911, 140-1). The expectation of perseverance thus turns interrogation situations into hotbeds for interference, further increasing the concerns noted above (Müller 1911, 142-3).[7]

3.2.2 The Methods of Restricted Inner Apprehension and Careful Retrospection

Müller's own proposals for adequate introspective methods start with a clear-eyed acceptance of the basic situation faced by any experimental psychologist using inner attention or retrospection: there is an ever-present danger of data contamination due to disturbance, confabulation, or interference. The key is to minimize the sources of likely interference, to mitigate effects one cannot avoid, and to understand the evidential limitations of the introspective data collected under these conditions.

Müller (1911, 73) distinguishes between *natural* conscious episodes and *forced* conscious episodes (*natürliche und gezwungene Bewusstseinszustände*).

---

[7] Müller's discussion of retrospection more generally makes a detailed, empirically grounded case that the strength—or even the availability—of any memory of a given aspect of experience, depends on having attended to the experience at the time it occurred. However, attention is capacity limited and will only support an incomplete recall at best. Ach's key claim that the intention to observe prior to the experience increases the tendency of episodic memory to persevere overall is, according to him, wholly without empirical merit.

Forced conscious episodes are experiences that are produced at least in part in response to an intention to self-observe and which then form the object of inner attention. Natural conscious episodes, by contrast, are experiences that are produced and that unfold without this influence. To use the examples from earlier again, my shoulder pain or my rush of elation are natural consciousness episodes, part of the flow of experience. But once I deliberately attend to my pain, or to the powerful, sweeping elation, the flow of experience changes to include my deliberate intentional focus, shifting salience patterns and modulating intensity. The resulting heightened pain sensation and the muting of elation are forced conscious episodes because they are shaped in part by the effects of attention on them.

In Müller's hands, Comte's worry about the use of inner attention is focused on the interfering influence of the subject's intention which drives deliberate inner attention. He does not seem to think that there is a particularly pressing threat due modulation by the act of inner attention itself (Müller 1911, 86–7). Put in terms of the above distinction, the specific worry is rather that the subject's intention to attend to ongoing experience will interrupt the natural flow of experience and bring about forced experiences. Inner attention, actively guided by the intention to observe, thus does not allow for an observation of natural experience 'as it is'. This means that any introspective method that tasks the subject to observe their ongoing experience is deeply problematic—as we have seen, systematic introspection falls under this rubric.

By contrast, Müller argues, forced experiences are open to direct and deliberate attentional inspection since 'as they are' includes the very effects of the intended attentional focus. In some cases, he suggests, we wish precisely to investigate the experiences which are intentionally produced or heightened by the intention to focus on it (Müller 1911, 80). An everyday example is the description of aches and pains during a visit to the doctor. In many cases, the heightening of sensation in the affected areas under intense and deliberate inner focus is a welcome effect, because it helps describing the affliction to the physician. An example from psychology comes from tasks to deliberately imagine or visually represent something. On being presented with a grey consonant, one might ask subjects whether they can imagine the consonant to be purple (see Müller 1911, 77–8, for discussion of these and other examples).

Inner attention therefore can be used in an introspective method, so long as it is restricted to investigate forced experiences—call this 'the method of restricted inner attention'. Of course, the experimenter must still be alert to the dangers of interference due to, e.g., demand character, uncontrolled intentional influences, habits, etc. Unchecked, these lead to contamination of the introspective data collected. Müller (1911, 90–6) makes many detailed practical recommendations in order to minimize these factors, or at least lessen their effects. They include: the provision of neutral, demand-character-free instructions, so that nothing is suggested as normal, standard, expected, preferred, etc.; reminders of the capacity limits of attention in that one cannot attend to the whole content of consciousness at a given moment all at once; the need for various kinds of training for experimental subjects; asking control questions right after subjects have given responses to probe their level of accuracy.[8]

The method of restricted inner attention thus may be used to collect data about forced experience but not about natural conscious episodes. Importantly, this restriction extends to the use of the data in theorizing about experience. In the first instance, the introspective data collected by this method is indicative of forced experience. It therefore must not be used to generalize to natural experience—at least not without further work that makes such a move reasonable.

Natural experiences are amenable to investigation as well, according to Müller, but only via retrospection. Let us call the method he proposes 'the method of careful retrospection'. The involvement of memory introduces significant concerns about the accuracy of any introspective data so procured. Drawing on his work on memory and attention, Müller holds that attention facilitates memory in that we remember things better if we have attended to them at the time. Good retrospective recall thus depends on prior attention to the experiences.[9] This means that retrospective recall of experience is seriously incomplete (Müller 1911, sect. 14).

Firstly, a significant proportion of conscious episodes unfold rapidly and with low intensity (pp. 100–1). They are so fleeting and peripheral that they do not provide the basis for retaining them in memory and thus are not available to recall later on, even if the temporal gap between experience and

---

[8] Müller calls these sorts of control questions the 'tricks of the trade' (*Kunstgriffe*) of a seasoned experimenter. Incidentally, his own specific example would not work anymore in modern contexts where almost everything one reads is printed in Latin script. He recounts asking subjects who report that their visual representation of an imagined word is very clear, whether the imagined word was handwritten in the old German script or in Latin script (p. 91).

[9] It is important to keep Müller's very different assessment of Comte's worry in mind here. There is nothing essentially distorting about inner attention for him, so long as it is not driven by deliberate intention. In fact, he thinks that spontaneous inner attention due to a kind of 'catching out' can provide useful information.

attempted recall is kept very short. Secondly, practical life has only a limited interest in experiences themselves (pp. 101–2). Many of the aspects and parts of conscious episodes that are of interest to the psychologist are hardly ever the focus of spontaneous (non-deliberate) inner attention. For instance, in the case of conscious acts of memorizing something (e.g. a row of numbers) we are typically interested only in what we are memorizing, not how we consciously memorize it. But without attention to them specifically, these conscious aspects are not retained well and often are beyond the reach of retrospection. Thirdly, Müller notes that our capacity to attend to experience underlies significant limitations (pp. 106–7). We cannot attend fully to everything characterizing the conscious situation in a given moment. The more we attend to at a given time, the more diffuse the focus becomes. But if retaining aspects of a given experience is proportional to how much it was attended to at the time, then a focus on some aspects brings with it weak or no capacity for retrospective recall on other aspects. In addition, highly focused attention is also easily fatigued and we are not able to serially focus on many different aspects of a quickly unfolding conscious episode.

In light of these limitations of retrospective recall, it is almost certainly an incomplete source of information about experience. Indeed, the more complex the conscious episode, the more incomplete retrospective recall will be of it. Any investigation of experience carried out by means of retrospection, must take note of this.

In addition, standard interference worries need to be taken into account. Müller offers detailed practical recommendations for experimenters (1911, sect. 15). In addition to some of those mentioned above for the method of restricted inner attention, they include: retrospective activity should take place immediately after the target experience has passed, since the longer the gap, the more incomplete and unreliable the retrospective reports; instructions should raise the bar for subject's answers by inducing a conservative bias in subjects' tendencies to respond with positive claims; experimenters must cultivate a conservative attitude in evaluating and interpreting subjects' reports. The experimenter is cautioned to treat their own behaviour in giving instructions and during the experiment as susceptible to bias and hence as a source of suggestion.

Müller (1911, 108–9) emphasizes two maxims concerning the further use of introspective data gathered by a method of careful retrospection:

1. Retrospection does *not* supply negative evidence. If retrospection fails to deliver information about a certain aspect of conscious episodes,

this does not constitute evidence that such an aspect is lacking. At best (i.e. with a practiced subject; short temporal gap; relatively simple target experience) it provides some reason for holding it unlikely that such an aspect was a part of the target experience that was the focus of inner attention at the time.
2. Retrospection supplies merely *fragmentary* evidence. To obtain a view of the conscious episodes under investigation, one must collect retrospective data via many different trials and experiments involving the target episodes and then see how to integrate the fragments of information that retrospection delivers, together into an overall coherent picture.

In sum, Müller's methodological views and practice show that psychology must and can use subject's introspective access to acquire data about the mind. But the two available modes—inner attention and retrospection—have to be used with painstaking care. Concerns about distortion caused by the deliberate use of inner attention are mitigated in several ways, central to which is the distinction between forced and natural experience. Concerns about interference from habit, demand character, etc., are addressed by limiting the ambitions of inquiry to relatively simple targets: by minimizing distractions during the experiments; by inducing a conservative bias in subjects' reporting and experimenters' interpreting of the reports; and, finally, by severely curtailing the evidential power of the introspective data vis-à-vis theorizing about the psychological phenomena under investigation.

3.3 Wundt and the Method of Controlled Inner Apprehension

Wundt's methodological views were developed and honed over the course of his long career in conjunction with his conception of psychology as a science (see, e.g., Danziger 1980a, 1980b; Hatfield 1997, 2020; Araujo 2016). He wrote frequently and in detail about the methods of psychology, including the role of introspection in experimental psychology. Here, I will focus mainly on Wundt (1888, 1908, ch. 3, sect. 2), as well as Wundt (1907) which contains a detailed critique of systematic introspection.

3.3.1 Wundt's Critique of Systematic Introspection
Wundt called the experiments of systematic introspection 'interrogation experiments' (*Ausfrageexperimente*) (Wundt 1907, 334). He considered

them to be pseudo-experiments—'experimental' only in an ordinary, extended sense, but not in a scientifically rigorous sense. A scientific experiment, for him, is in essence an investigation by empirical observation, where the observation satisfies the four Baconian conditions (1907, sect. 2):

1. The observer must be able to bring about the onset of the target phenomenon.
2. The observer must be able to focus their attention on the target phenomenon.
3. Results must be confirmed by repeated observations under the same conditions.
4. Onset conditions must be determinable by varying accompanying conditions, and onset conditions themselves must be further explored by systematically varying them in turn.

According to Wundt, satisfaction of these Baconian conditions amounts to 'planned observation' (*planmässige Beobachtung*)—the kind of controlled and hence exact and systematic observation that is at the heart of any rigorous experimental science. The Baconian conditions are not always fully satisfied in the natural sciences, Wundt notes. For example, astronomy often depends on simply waiting for certain phenomena to occur, or botany involves setting out and trying to chance upon new species of plants. But the key is that proper scientific method—in essence, controlled and exact observation and subsequent theorizing based on the data so delivered—must aim for at least approximate satisfaction of as many of the four conditions as possible.

Insofar as psychology is a natural science, it is conducted by use of an experimental method. That is, it involves planned observation of conscious phenomena. Because of the different subject matter, the type of observation is not perceptually based but introspectively based (1907, 306; 1908, 163–4). This is 'self-observation' (*Selbstbeobachtung*) and when undertaken as part of a scientific investigation, it must be a regimented and controlled self-observation. Psychological experiments—for them to count as scientific experiments—are bound by the same rules as those governing adequate experiments in other natural sciences. On Wundt's view, the experimental studies of Bühler, Marbe, and Ach do not qualify as *bona fide* scientific experiments because they do not satisfy even in an approximate sense any of the four Baconian conditions defining systematic scientific observation.

Wundt diagnosed the failure of systematic introspection to comply with the conditions for a proper experiment as being due to three characteristic aspects this method. Firstly, and most importantly, systematic introspection centrally involves inner attention. Wundt held that deliberate inner attention cannot support observation in the scientific sense: 'If you tell yourself each time: now I will [self-]observe, then this aim is already undermined upfront' (1888, 296). He accepted Comte's worry that the act of deliberate attention to one's conscious episodes itself modulates the overall conscious situation, thus leading to a change in—or even distortion or destruction of—the initial target of inner attention (1907, 331; 1908, 164). This means that systematic introspection inevitably delivers misrepresentative data about consciousness.

But the inevitable conscious change resulting from the act of attention contributing to the conscious situation has more foundational consequences for Wundt. Importantly, it is part of his concept of observation that the object of observation must exist at the time of being attended to: observation is a genuine relation between an observer and the thing or state of affairs observed. Observation, self-observation included, thus cannot take place in absence of the object of observation (1888, 296). The change in consciousness—likely distorting and destructive of the original episode—brought about by inner attention, together with the fact that conscious phenomena are fleeting by nature, mean that inner attention results in an object of attention that is different from the conscious episode targeted by the observational intention. Inner attention, then, cannot serve in scientific self-observation.

Secondly, the targets of investigation chosen by proponents of systematic introspection tended to be conscious phenomena of a type that Wundt held to be out of bounds for *experimental* psychology (1907, 330; 1908, 174).[10] Wundt's reason was that such conscious phenomena—e.g. the unfolding of high-level, complex thinking and judgement—are not reliably connected with any objective external stimuli. Without such an external objective grip on them, however, there is no possibility to control observation in any way—neither the subject's introspective activity nor the presentation of the conscious episode can be guided or stabilized with the help of objective measures (1907, 309). We will discuss these ideas in more detail below in the context of Wundt's positive proposals.

Thirdly, Wundt strongly objected to the extensive involvement of the experimenter in the experimental procedure (1907, 335; 1908, 174–5). As

---

[10] On Wundt's view, these mental phenomena were amenable for investigation by other branches of psychology (see Hatfield 2020 for an in-depth discussion).

he pointed out, the experimenter injects themselves at every phase in the process, by priming the subject with instructions, by providing the stimulus in the form of a verbally posed mental task, by asking probing questions during and after the task completion. Each of these injections, according to Wundt, either disrupts the natural flow of the conscious episodes under investigation or determines it by exerting suggestive influences on the subject. The rampant suggestive and interrupting influences are bound to contaminate the data delivered via systematic introspection. Further, echoing Comte's concerns once more, Wundt thought that the experimental procedure is almost deliberately frustrating the subject in carrying out the very tasks they are asked to undertake, constantly preventing them from doing so by getting them to do engage in other mental activity at the same time.

Wundt also objects to the use of retrospection in systematic introspection (1907, 337–40). Insofar as the interrogation proceeds after the conscious episodes have taken place and therefore relies on memory, this opens up a new source of mistakes—especially in light of the suggestive questioning by the experimenter. But more importantly, Wundt argues that although systematic introspection sometimes involves the use of memory by interrogating the subject after the conscious episode in question has passed, this does not then count as an instance of a genuinely *retrospective method*. Retrospection proper involves reproduction of the experience by episodic recall which can then be examined. But systematic introspection typically primes, or outright instructs, subjects to use inner attention to observe the target conscious episodes as it happens, even if they are to report on their experiences only afterwards. It is therefore really a method of delayed reporting of the results of inner attention to ongoing experience. Memory recall concerns the deliverance of earlier inner attention on experience, not the experiential episode per se. This then makes null and void any putative advantage of retrospection in relation to worries about interference from inner attention—if anything, it makes the situation worse by adding potential interference due to memory gaps in the delayed reports (1907, 331–2, 334–5).

Altogether, for Wundt, systematic introspection is at best a kind of everyday (unscientific) self-observation 'under aggravating circumstances' (*unter erschwerenden Bedingungen*) (1907, 337).

3.3.2 The Method of Controlled Inner Apprehension

How is scientific psychology possible given that it must use an introspective method? For Wundt, the mode of introspective access that secures such a method is inner apprehension: 'The whole of psychology rests on inner apprehension' (1908, 163). Inner apprehension offers non-distorting epistemic access to the ongoing natural flow of experience. It thereby satisfies a pre-condition for proper observation: awareness of the object of observation (i.e. the target experience) while it is present.

But proper scientifically valid observation also requires attention—this is the second of the Baconian conditions. Yet, inner apprehension is passive and non-attentive. Any deliberate attempt by subjects to actively engage and control their inner apprehension, in the context of systematic observation of target conscious episodes, leads to the subject inadvertently using inner attention instead, with its detrimental modulating effect on consciousness. This is the conundrum raised by Comte's worry. The framework of section 2 helps us to understand Wundt's solution to it: even though the attention necessary for scientific observation cannot be provided by the mode of introspective access itself, the introspective method can accomplish this—at least in an approximate sense, as we shall see—by embedding inner apprehension appropriately in an experimental set-up.

By Wundt's own lights, this is a tricky needle to thread. The overall introspective method must satisfy the Baconian conditions for scientific observation, including the possibility to attend to the object of observation. But it also must allow for inner apprehension to happen without the subject trying to make it happen deliberately—without the subject forming the intention to self-observe and thus attending to their experience in a destructive manner (1908, 164).

Wundt held that the control and regimentation required for scientific self-observation in psychology can be achieved by using methods that had been developed in physiology and psychophysics. These neighbouring disciplines use objective measuring techniques for different theoretical purposes, i.e. to investigate and explain aspects of bodily physiology that are held to be pre-requisites for psychological features, or to figure out the dependence of certain basic or elementary psychological aspects (e.g. simple sensations) on physiological processes or stimulus conditions. They involve external stimuli as well as publicly available and measurable effects or responses, such as reaction times, button presses, and autonomic responses. In the context of psychology, many of these objective methods can be applied to investigate different theoretical issues, namely those concerned with the nature and organization of psychological features themselves (1908, 166–70; see also Danziger 1980b, esp. 113–16, for discussion).

Psychological experiments use these objective methods as aids (*Hülfsmittel*) to force the individual subject's inner apprehension of consciousness into yielding answers to precisely put questions about its psychological nature (1908, 167, 169–70 and 1893, 85). Objective methods can be used to regiment and control self-observation in two ways. One is systematically to *manipulate the targets of observation*, i.e. the conscious episodes under investigation in line with Baconian criteria for proper observation. The other is to *guide inner apprehension* of the conscious phenomenon without getting the subject actively trying to do so but nonetheless harnessing it so that the attentional requirement can be navigated.

Together, these two ways allow the threading of the needle in a range of cases (Wundt 1907, 309). Wundt distinguishes two categories of experiment, differing in how close they come to satisfying the Baconian conditions. Let me briefly explain these, highlighting in each case satisfaction of the second condition, the possibility of attention to the target experience.

Complete experiments manage to approximate very closely all four Baconian conditions (1907, 312–18; 1908, 172–3). These kinds of experiments concern cases that feature an extremely tight connection between the external stimulus (visual, auditory, or haptic) and the conscious episode under investigation. Specifically, they concern basic perceptual sensations and experiences, the content of which involves the perceptible or sensible properties of the external stimulus object (1907, 313–14). Wundt holds that this intimate connection between external stimulus and conscious content allows for almost direct control over the target of observation. We can deliberately present the external object to perceptual attention and vary the conditions of its perceptual presentation. In manipulating the stimulus conditions, we are almost immediately manipulating the perceptual experience. Furthermore, Wundt holds that this intimate connection between stimulus and conscious episodes allows for guiding inner apprehension and the necessary attentional focus on the target of observation. This is because when perceptually attending to the external stimulus, the subject thereby also fixes the conscious content of the perceptual experience or sensation as apprehended in inner apprehension. Self-observation can literally piggyback on perceptual attention to the external stimulus object: by attending to the stimulus object and its properties, inner apprehension of the experience of the stimulus is guided and stabilized onto the target experience without the subject actively trying to self-observe by using inner attention (1907, 309, 314; 1908, 172).

The range of psychological phenomena that complete experiments allow us to investigate is rather narrow, however, and confined to aspects of perceptual phenomena that are tightly tethered to external stimuli both in terms of occurrence and content. Examples are chronometric experiments on auditory experience of the temporal duration and rhythm of beats, or experiments on haptic and spatial experience of basic geometric position and length perception, involving, e.g., an examination of Muller-Lyer lines (1907, 314–17, for specific empirical studies mentioned by Wundt; 1908, 172–3). Subjects can report the conscious content of the episode, say, by tapping out a rhythm, or drawing the lines of a Muller-Lyer illustration. The kind of non-qualitative report data expressive of conscious content can then furthermore be compared with the objective stimulus properties during manipulations.

Incomplete experiments, by contrast, do not manage to approximate all four conditions, though they do approximate at least some (1907, 319–27; 1908, 172–3). They deal with psychological phenomena that can still reasonably be assumed to have a tolerably stable connection to external stimuli or, more specifically, with the sensory and perceptual experiences immediately brought about by external stimuli. For instance, we expect simple feelings of pleasure or repulsion, or certain basic thoughts, to be strongly associated with particular perceptual experiences or sensations: 'We can, e.g., assume that when quinine is placed on the tongue (provided the olfactory system functions normally) this causes not merely a bitter sensation, but also brings about a feeling of aversion (*Unlustgefühl*)' (1907, 326). Given their more tenuous relationship to external stimuli these psychological phenomena do not submit to direct external manipulation in the manner of the complete experiments. To gain control over these 'subjective psychological processes', as Wundt calls them, the basic set-up of the external stimulus-based reaction experiments must be augmented. In addition to an external stimulus and the report response by the subject, incomplete experiments involve measuring something externally available that is taken to be symptomatic of the target psychological phenomenon. The additional measures concern dynamic and temporal aspects of processes after the onset of stimulus presentation up to and including the report response. They are measures of autonomic responses (e.g. breathing patterns or blood pressure), or the latency between stimulus presentation and report response (1907, 323–4). According to Wundt, these measurements provide a further indirect external control on the target of observation: 'The temporal relationships of the internal or external reactions that accompany or follow the stimulus event, serve in both cases as control measures of the course and the nature (*den Verlauf und die Beschaffenheit*) of the subjective processes which in turn are available to self-observation at the same time' (Wundt 1907, 324).

Such additional external control measures, however, cannot overcome the fundamental limitation of these experiments. The manipulation of the target psychological phenomenon is always indirect and dependent on basic assumptions about standard associative or affective psychological reactions to perception of external stimuli, and about correlations between such psychological reactions and certain physiological processes.

Another limitation of incomplete experiments in comparison to complete experiments relates to the second Baconian condition, i.e. the requirement of attention to the target of observation. Incomplete experiments do not allow for the exploitation of perceptual attention to the stimulus as a means of fixing inner apprehension on the target psychological phenomena, since their content does not concern the stimulus object directly. Instead, inner apprehension must be guided and strengthened in other ways. According to Wundt, this can be done by running repeated trials under the same stimulus conditions not only with different subjects but also with the same subjects. When the same subject repeats the trials closely together, inner apprehension can have several turns at apprehending the same, or almost the same, relatively simple conscious phenomenon. Such repeated exposure means that inner apprehension of a given experience can be improved or heightened in some way that still avoids the deleterious slide into the deliberate act of inner attention (1908, 171). However, this does require extra precaution—experimental subjects need to be significantly practiced to prevent this from happening.

There is a lot more to say about Wundt's introspective method, as manifested in these two kinds of experiments. But the basic set-up involving the employment of Wundt's preferred mode of introspective access—inner apprehension—is clear from the above. Nonetheless, it is worth noting that all experiments, though they aim to exploit inner apprehension to provide the key observational data about the mind, are supplemented by retrospection. A given target experience is captured in inner apprehension and only then can it be reported by recalling it as apprehended (1908, 164, 169). It is part of the experimental challenge to keep the gap between apprehension and recall as small as possible, something that is easiest in the case of complete experiments, and aided by repetition in the case of incomplete experiments (1908, 171–2). The important point is that despite this involvement of retrospection, the core mode of introspective access is inner apprehension and the primary experimental efforts are geared towards employing it in the most controlled and systematic manner. The need to employ retrospection, while it does introduce problematic elements that need to be addressed in the experimental set-up, is in support of the exploitation of inner apprehension in the first instance.

Wundt, like Müller, is clear about the limitations of the introspective data collected even when the utmost care is taken. This is especially true of incomplete experiments, which are weakened by the need to simply trust that the basic relation between external stimuli and subjective psychological processes under investigation persists, the merely indirect external control over target and inner apprehension, and the greater reliance on memory. This means that the experimental results are much less exact than those deriving from complete experiments (1907, 322 and 326). But in all cases, the interpretation of the data and their use in theorizing need to be carefully distinguished from the provision of the data in terms of the experimental results (1908, 314–15).

3.4 The Complexity of Introspective Methods

Wundt and Müller were firmly convinced that psychology needs to use introspection to obtain data about the mind. This section has made amply clear that neither of them took this to be an easy thing to do properly. As we have seen with the help of the framework set out in section 2, their views—developed in concert with their experimental practice—involve different proposals about how to use introspection. But those proposals share a structure: their introspective methods embed modes of introspective access in an observational setting, shaped in various ways to suit the target of inquiry, and to deal with potential sources of interference. Their introspective methods are worked out in great detail. They are aimed at minimizing interference, confabulatory influences, and distortion, and at getting clear on the evidential limitations of the introspective data generated by them.

There is room for disagreement on the specific details of these proposals, of course, but the sort of care and complexity they involve is not optional, if introspection is to be used legitimately in theorizing. We will see in the next section that difficulties arise when introspection is used more casually.

4. Introspective Measures of Consciousness

In the last three decades especially, consciousness has been a renewed focus of research in cognitive science. The science of consciousness is a thriving and increasingly diversified field. Much of the work, e.g. on the relationship between consciousness and perception (in particular, whether there is unconscious perception) and on neural correlates of consciousness, is marked by a distinction between objective and subjective measures of consciousness. Objective measures rely on externally observable indices of consciousness (e.g. discrimination behaviour or neural activity taken to be correlated with consciousness). Subjective measures rely on participating subjects' verbal or non-verbal reports about consciousness. Sometimes subjective measures are held to be introspective measures, though the extent to which all subjective measures (especially those involving confidence ratings) are introspective is an open question (Spener 2020). Here I concentrate on the explicitly introspective Perceptual Awareness Scale (PAS), first developed and employed by Ramsøy and Overgaard (2004).

PAS was originally designed to investigate the degree of conscious experience involved in perceiving visual stimuli but it is meant to be more widely applicable (Sandberg and Overgaard 2015). In keeping with most set-ups for subjective measures in this area, employment of PAS involves a combination of two measures. There is an objective measure of performance in a perceptual discrimination task (detection of an external stimulus or identification of specific stimulus features) and a subjective measure of conscious awareness attending the discrimination event (subjects' reports of their awareness of the stimulus or its features during the objective task).

In (Ramsøy and Overgaard 2004), the basic set-up includes a computer-based external stimulus presentation followed by a mask. Stimuli are simple shapes (squares, triangles, circles) of different colours (red, blue, green) presented at three different (non-centre) locations. Subjects are asked first to identify the stimulus according to the three features, guessing if necessary. They are then asked to rate the 'degree or clearness of experience' of each of the specific stimulus features, using a response scale that offers participants four categories: *no experience, brief glimpse, almost clear image,* and *absolutely clear image*. The awareness reports obtained, together with the results about objective performance, are then analysed in various ways to gain insight about the conscious-unconscious threshold in human visual perception (see Sandberg and Overgaard 2015 for a description of different statistical approaches).

PAS is explicitly meant to address concerns about the reliability of introspective methods: 'The essential problem [with introspective measures] seems to be that there is no possible way for the scientist to determine 'from the outside' which 'report categories' make sense for a participant and, accordingly, how to avoid introducing confounds' (Sandberg and Overgaard 2015, 181-2). For proponents of PAS, key to overcoming these reliability worries and to achieve PAS aims 'for a situation where reports stand in a "1:1 relationship" with relevant inner states', is to develop the scale categories together with the participating subjects in a kind of calibration procedure. The idea is that this interactive procedure fits the scale to participants' actual introspective awareness of their experience and ensures that the scales are used and understood in the same way across participants and experimenters (Ramsøy and Overgaard 2004, 10-12 and 20).

This calibration procedure is the main innovative aspect of PAS. In practice, the suggestion is to begin with a 'lengthy instruction phase' (Sandberg and Overgaard 2015, 188-9). During this phase participants are told in detail about the point of the exercise, namely 'to find out how many and which kinds of report categories could best live up to the ideal of having 1:1 matches between reported categories in experiences difference in perceptual clarity'. Open discussion with participants is invited about the best range and order of response categories. Participants are free to choose the number of scale points and they are always asked to provide descriptions of their meaning. Only end points are provided by reference to the concept of clarity ("nothing at all" and "completely clear"). Over a large number of trials involving representative stimuli and in constant discussion with the experimenter, participants construct a scale that best achieves the 1:1 match.

After that, a pilot trial phase is recommended of at least thirty trials, during which participants get used to the specific experimental set-up, tasks, and responses. To ensure correct use of the PAS scale, the experimenter is encouraged to interrupt the participants, asking them to articulate the reasons for their specific response choice at the time and to remind them of the agreed meaning of the response categories. Sandberg and Overgaard (2015, 188) note that not doing this risks participants using the scale differently and to more conservative responses especially around the threshold.

How does PAS compare with the older introspective methods discussed in the previous section? What sticks out most is that there is scarcely any engagement with the specific mode of introspective access to be employed in the method. Asking a subject to report on their experience (as opposed to, e.g., asking them for a confidence judgement about their perceptual discrimination performance) is all it takes, it seems, to ask them to introspectively access their experience (Overgaard and Sandberg 2012, 1291; Sandberg and Overgaard 2015, 187). Accessing one's experience involves either 'a self-reflective, retrospective process in which one's memory trace of the original target mental state is inspected' or '"on-line" inspection of current and ongoing mental states' (Overgaard and Sandberg 2012, 1288). Curiously, *both* are taken to involve attention to one's experience (Ramsøy and Overgaard 2004, 10; Overgaard and Sandberg 2012, 1288).

Two concerns immediately arise. Firstly, as has been made amply clear in the last two sections, inner attention is a difficult mode of introspective access to exploit in an introspective method. According to the worry raised by Comte, attending to one's experience modulates the ongoing conscious situation. Wundt and Müller each dealt with this worry in different ways, either avoiding inner attention entirely or reserving it for investigations where such changes do not matter. Both of their methodological solutions involve severe restrictions on the targets of investigation and attempts to mitigate any potential for interference coming from inner attention by carefully controlling the experimental set-up in which their preferred mode of introspective access is embedded. The question is how Comte's worry is addressed by PAS, assuming as its proponents clearly do, that introspective access is attentional.

Indeed, something like Comte's worry has a modern expression in the so-called 'observer paradox': 'The observer paradox simply refers to the fact that asking people to produce subjective reports or to reflect in any way on their own performance may change the very processes that are being monitored' (Timmermans and Cleeremans 2015, 35). A standard reaction to the observer paradox is that it points to an inherent, unavoidable problem of all subjective measures of consciousness, which consequently ought to be abandoned altogether. Against the historical background, we can see that this is an overreaction. There are different modes of introspective access available and not all modulate ongoing experience by virtue of using it, for instance, retrospective access does not do so. Of course, if, with PAS and many contemporary psychologists, all introspective access is held to be attentional, then the observer paradox is more worrying.

Nothing in the experimental set-up described above deals with this worry. The calibration procedure of PAS designed to attain a 1:1 match between introspective reports and internal states involves collaboration between experimenter and participant to configure the response scale so that it best matches the participant's conscious awareness. But the point of Comte's worry is that conscious awareness is modulated by the use of inner attention. Even with the most finely calibrated response scale to capture conscious awareness upon attending to it, such awareness would constitute forced experience, rather than the natural flow of experience, to use Müller's terminology. This would not be an issue if the target of investigation is forced experience, or if it is indifferent to there being modulations in the conscious situation due to inner attention. But this is patently not the case in the case of PAS, which is a method to investigate the graded nature of perceptual consciousness.

Secondly, according to the characterization by proponents of PAS, retrospective access involves attention to experience as well. This does not distinguish it properly from inner attention. In section 3, we saw that both Wundt and Müller were very careful to ensure that participants use the right mode of introspective access. This requires a strict experimental discipline, imposed by instructions given to participants prior to the trials and by careful overall set-up of the experimental procedure. For instance, if the introspective method employs retrospection and the goal is to investigate the natural flow of experience, participants must not slip into inner attention during the presentation of the stimulus. Recall Wundt's criticism of systematic introspection, where he pointed out that retrospective application of systematic introspection involves merely delayed report of a remembered introspective judgement made on the basis of inner attention at the time of having the experience. This, Wundt argued, merely adds worries about faulty memory to the methodological problems connected to the use of inner attention. Insofar as retrospection is involved in contemporary measures of consciousness, the question is therefore whether it commits a similar methodological sin.

In line with the theoretical characterization above, which does not clearly distinguish between inner attention and retrospection, PAS's experimental practice also does not differentiate between them. The relevant part of the instructions seems to be neutral on the introspective mode employed, merely 'asking participants to report about their experience'. The reports collected reflect this: 'Typically, a subject would report "red square up there (points); the position was clear, the colour was a glimpse, I had no experience of the shape"' (Ramsøy and Overgaard 2004, 12). It does seem that the reports are post-presentation, that they are elicited after the stimulus experience has passed. However, given the lack of provision to avoid the participants using inner attention during the stimulus presentation, there is no reason to think that the reports are based on retrospection rather than remembered introspective judgements obtained via inner attention during the experience event. They might also be a mixture of both.

Furthermore, the above report also indicates that participants are asked to perform very complex introspective and reporting tasks. They have to attend to, or remember, and then report on, their experience with respect to three different features, as well as the degree of clarity or strength of each—all in one go. This, too, contrasts with the views and practices of the early psychologists, who were adamant that such tasks need to be as simple as possible, especially with respect to retrospection, to minimize gaps and interference typical for memory.

Finally, considering PAS's calibration practice itself, it is hard to see how it could do offer much reassurance about the reliability of introspective methods, specifically with respect to avoiding confounds in the report data. Experimenters are reminded that throughout these calibration phases they must avoid suggestions, examples or feedback to participants. This is to ensure that participants' ideas about how to set and describe scale points are not influenced by the experimenter (Sandberg and Overgaard 2015, 189–90). But at the outset, experimenters explain the purpose of the study to participants—achieving a 1:1 match—which does already create a strong demand character. Experimenters also emphasize to participants that '*any* subjectively notable differences should be reported, whether it may be hunches, feelings, glimpses, thoughts about certainty, etc. as long as they, for the subject, are directly related to the presentation of the stimulus.' On the one hand, this instruction cultivates a very liberal bias, on the other hand, the list of potentially relevant reactions is open to radically different interpretations. When combined with the extensive discussion in which participants develop response categories, it is not reasonable to hold that the concern about confounds in the resulting response data has been minimized.

In the end, it does seem that the heavy lifting with respect to reliability is done by the objective performance data (Irvine 2012). Introspective measures use external controls (stimuli and objectively measurable responses) to ensure that they are on the right track. This is not new, we saw that Wundt especially is clear about the central importance of such external controls: the best experiments (complete experiments) feature the tightest external control.

The lack of a clear distinction between retrospection and inner attention in theoretical discussions and experimental practice is a manifestation of the fact that the notion of introspective access at work in PAS (and other introspective methods) is undertheorized. This leads to imprecision at the heart of these introspective methodological approaches, making them less resilient to criticism than they might otherwise be. Despite frequent assertions to the contrary (e.g. Nelsons and Narens 1990, 127–8) contemporary subjective measures do not present a clear advance over 'classical' uses of introspection in early psychology. Of course, measuring technologies have greatly advanced and in line with this, our understanding of neural anatomy and function, and the structure of cognition more generally. These advances do offer methodological opportunities that were not available back then. But when it comes to the employment of introspection specifically, many of the ideas—promoted as improvements over the old 'Introspectionism'— were already anticipated and often even worked out better by earlier psychologists such as Wundt and Müller.

To make the most of modern advances in understanding and technology when configuring introspective methods in the science of consciousness, the notion of introspection should be developed carefully.[11] Distinguishing sharply between introspective methods and introspective access allows us to clarify the different modes of such access and to specify how they can be employed in experimental contexts. This approach provides the basis for detailed and constructive assessments of the methodological potential of introspection in the science of consciousness.[12]

References

Ach, Narziß. 1905. *Die Willenstätigkeit und das Denken*. Vandehoedt und Ruprecht.

Araujo, Saulo de Freitas. 2012. 'Why did Wundt abandon his theory of the unconscious? Towards a new interpretation of Wundt's psychological project'. *History of Psychology*, 15, 33–49.

Araujo, Saulo de Freitas. 2016. *Wundt and the Philosophical Foundations of Psychology: A Reappraisal*. Springer.

Armstrong, David. 1980. *The Nature of Mind and Other Essays*. Cornell University Press.

Blumenthal, Arthur. L. 1975. 'A Reappraisal of Wilhelm Wundt'. *American Psychologist*, 30, 1081–1088.

Braisby, Nick and Gellatly, Angus. 2012. 'Foundations of Cognitive Psychology'. In *Cognitive Psychology*, edited by Nick Braisby and Angus Gellatly, pp. 1–28, 2nd ed. Oxford University Press.

---

[11] On my view, report-based, or subjective measures are best thought of as introspective measures (Spener 2020, forthcoming). If they are not, then non-introspective subjective measures of consciousness still need to distinguish between subjective method and subjective access and provide more detailed conceptions of whatever modes of subjective access are at employed in a given method.

[12] I am grateful to Uriah Kriegel, Scott Sturgeon, and Gary Hatfield for comments on the chapter, or on ancestors of it.

Brentano, Franz. 1874. *Psychologie vom empirischen Standpunkt*. Duncker & Humblot.

Bühler, Karl. 1907. *Tatsachen und Probleme zu einer Psychologie der Denkvorgänge*. Würzburger Habilitationsschrift.

Comte, Auguste. 1830. *Cours de philosophie positive*, vol. 1. Rouen.

Danziger, Karl. 1979. 'The Positivist Repudiation of Wundt'. *Journal of the History of Behavioural Sciences*, 15, 205–230.

Danziger, Karl. 1980a. 'The History of Introspection Reconsidered'. *Journal of the History of Behavioural Sciences*, 16, 241–262.

Danziger, Karl. 1980b. 'Wundt's Psychological Experiment in the Light of His Philosophy of Science'. *Psychological Research*, 42, 109–122.

Feest, Uljana. 2012. 'Introspection as Method and Introspection as a Feature of Consciousness'. *Inquiry*, 55, 1–16.

Hatfield, Gary. 1997. 'Wundt and Psychology as Science: Disciplinary Transformations'. *Perspectives on Science*, 5, 349–382.

Hatfield, Gary. 2005. 'Introspective Evidence in Psychology'. In *Scientific Evidence*, edited by Peter Achinstein, pp 259–286. Johns Hopkins University Press.

Hatfield, Gary. 2020. 'Wundt and "Higher Cognition": Elements, Association, Apperception, and Experiment'. *History of Philosophy of Science*, 10, 48–75.

Hoffmann, Joachim and Stock, Armin. 1996. 'The Würzburg School'. Unpublished manuscript.

Irvine, Elizabeth. 2012. 'Old Problems with New Measures in the Science of Consciousness'. *British Journal for the Philosophy of Science*, 63, 627–648.

Kant, Immanuel. 1787. *Metaphysische Anfangsgründe der Naturwissenschaft*, 2nd ed. Johann Friedrich Hartknoch.

Leahey, Thomas. 1981. 'The Mistaken Mirror. On Wundt's and Titchener's Psychologies'. *Journal of the History of Behavioural Sciences*, 17, 273–282.

Lyons, William. 1986. *The Disappearance of Introspection*. MIT Press.

Marbe, Karl. 1901. *Experimentell-psychologische Untersuchungen über das Urteil. Eine Einleitung in die Logik*. Wilhelm Engelmann.

Mill, John Stuart. 1907/1865. *Auguste Comte and Positivism*. Kegan.

Mischel, Theodore. 1970. 'Wundt and the Conceptual Foundations of Psychology'. *Philosophy and Phenomenological Research*, 31, 1–26.

Müller, Georg Elias. 1911. 'Zur Analyse der Gedächtnistätigkeit und des Vorstellungsverlaufes'. *Zeitschrift für Psychologie*, I: 1–408.

Nelsons, Thomas and Narens, Louis. 1990. 'Metamemory: A Theoretical Framework and New Findings'. *The Psychology of Learning and Motivation*, 26, 125–173.

Overgaard, Morten and Sandberg, Kristian. 2012. 'Kinds of Access: Different Methods for Report Reveal Different Kinds of Metacognitive Access'. *Philosophical Transactions of the Royal Society of Biological Sciences*, 367, 1287–1296.

Ramsøy, Thomas. Z. and Overgaard, Morten. 2004. 'Introspection and Subliminal Perception'. *Phenomenology and the Cognitive Sciences*, 3, 1–23.

Sandberg, Kristian and Overgaard, Morten. 2015. 'Using the Perceptual Awareness Scale (PAS)'. In *Behavioral Methods on Consciousness Research*, edited by Morten Overgaard, pp. 181–195. Oxford University Press.

Schwitzgebel, Eric. 2008. 'The Unreliability of Naive Introspection'. *Philosophical Review*, 117, 245–273.

Smith, Edward E. and Kosslyn, Stephen M. 2007. *Cognitive Psychology: Mind and Brain*. Pearson Prentice Hall.

Spener, Maja. 2015. 'Calibrating Introspection'. *Philosophical Perspective*, 25, 300–321.

Spener, Maja. 2020. 'Consciousness, Subjective Measures, and Introspection'. In *The Oxford Handbook of the Philosophy of Consciousness*, edited by Uriah Kriegel, pp. 610–634. Oxford University Press.

Spener, Maja. Forthcoming. *Introspection in Science*. Oxford University Press.

Störring, Gustav. 1908. 'Experimentelle Untersuchungen über einfache Schlussprozesse'. *Archiv fur die gesamte Psychologie*, 11, 1–127.

Timmermans, Bert and Cleeremans, Axel. 2015. 'How Can We Measure Awareness? An Overview of Current Methods'. In *Behavioral Methods on Consciousness Research*, edited by Morten Overgaard, pp. 21–46. Oxford: Oxford University Press.

Watt, Henry. 1904. 'Experimentelle Beiträge zu einer Theorie des Denkens'. *Archiv für die gesamte Psychology*, 4, 289–437.

Wundt, Wilhelm. 1888. 'Selbstbeobachtung und innere Wahrnehmung'. *Philosophische Studien*, 4, 292–309.

Wundt, Wilhelm. 1893. 'Hypnotismus und Suggestion'. *Philosophische Studien*, 8, 1–85.

Wundt, Wilhelm. 1907. 'Über Ausfrageexperimente und über die Methoden zur Psychologie des Denkens'. *Psychologische Studien*, 3. 301–360.

Wundt, Wilhelm. 1908. *Logik. Eine Untersuchung der Prinzipien der Erkenntnis und der Methoden wissenschaftlicher Forschung*, vol. 3, 3rd ed. Ferdinand Enke.

PART II
SENSORY EXPERIENCE
Perception, Imagination, Pleasure

7
Right Here, Right Now
On the Eudaimonic Value of Perceptual Awareness

Dorothea Debus

1. Setting the Scene

Perceptual experiences provide us with a fundamental form of awareness, or consciousness: In perceptual experience we are aware, or conscious, of our own current environment. But then, what does it take to *be* perceptually aware of the world around us? What is the *nature* of perceptual experience, and how *could we possibly be* conscious of our environment when we perceive it? These questions usually stand at the centre of recent (and not so recent) debates in the philosophy of perception, and often, philosophers have attempted to answer these questions by offering one of two competing accounts of perceptual experience: Some defend a 'Direct Realist' account (at times, relevant accounts are also called 'naive realist' or 'relationalist' accounts), others argue that we should accept a 'Representationalist' account of perceptual experience.[1]

Various arguments for and against both positions have been developed. Usually, relevant debates are based on the shared assumption that any convincing account of perceptual awareness will have to meet various 'desiderata'. More specifically, all participants in the debate usually agree that, amongst other things, a plausible account of perceptual experience should (1) be compatible with contemporary science; that it should (2) account for the fact that perceptual experiences are characterized by the phenomenological feature of 'transparency';[2] that it should (3) explain how perceptual experiences enable demonstrative reference and demonstrative thought;[3] and that it should (4) explain how perceptual experience might provide the experiencing subject with (new) knowledge about the world.

---

[1] For a comprehensive and authoritative recent survey of the relevant literature, see Crane and French (2021).
[2] See, e.g., Martin (2002).   [3] See, e.g., Campbell (2002).

Being in agreement on relevant desiderata, defenders of the two competing positions then offer claims and counter-claims as to which of their respective accounts might be better placed to meet those desiderata; and while at first sight some of these desiderata might be more easily met by one, some by the other account, ultimately defenders of either account will argue that, maybe with some careful extra work, their respective account can meet all relevant desiderata. Indeed, a substantial amount of relevant work in developing the two competing accounts in such a way that they meet all relevant desiderata has meanwhile been done, so that at present, relevant arguments seem rather well-balanced, and one might well think that the debate between Direct Realists and Representationalists about perceptual experience has currently reached some sort of stand-off.[4]

The present chapter aims to offer a new vantage point from which to consider these issues afresh. We will reach this new vantage point by exploring a new (and maybe surprising) question about perceptual awareness, namely the question as to whether perceptual experience might have 'eudaimonic' value, that is, value with respect to a subject's well-being. Indeed, or so I will argue, a subject's being perceptually aware of her environment does have such eudaimonic value, and this new insight might in turn help us to resolve the stand-off between Representationalism and Direct Realism about perceptual experience, as I will show at the end of the chapter.

Quite independently of the dispute between Direct Realists and Representationalists, however, somewhat more fundamentally and thus presumably also more importantly, the insight that a subject's perceptual awareness of her environment is good for the subject's (mental) well-being, which I will develop in the main body of the following chapter, should also further our understanding of the phenomenon of perceptual awareness itself in new and important ways. It should contribute to our understanding of an important axiological implication of perceptual awareness, and it should also contribute to our understanding of the wider philosophical question of what it might take for a subject's mental life to go well.

2. Nozick's 'Experience Machine'

When thinking about the *value* of our ability to perceive the world around us, philosophers traditionally think about *epistemological* issues. Perceptual

---

[4] Of course, I assume there will be proponents of either view who are firmly convinced that 'their side' has decisively 'won' the debate, but I doubt such assessments are very realistic.

experiences, so they rightly say, are very important with respect to our knowing about the world—a vast amount of the knowledge we have about the world we live in would be impossible (or at least much more difficult to have) without our being able to be perceptually aware of our environment. Thus, the view that perceptual awareness has *epistemological* value seems widely shared. However, I here hope to show that our ability to be perceptually aware of our environment is not only of epistemological, but also of *eudaimonic* value.

In order to develop this claim, we might begin by considering Nozick's famous thought experiment of the 'experience machine'. Nozick writes:

> Suppose there were an experience machine that would give you an experience you desired. Superduper neuropsychologists could stimulate your brain so that you would think and feel you were writing a great novel, or making a friend, or reading an interesting book. All the time you would be floating in a tank, with electrodes attached to your brain. Should you plug into this machine for life, preprogramming your life's experiences?[5]

Most people considering this thought experiment, so Nozick surmises, will be rather reluctant, and will ultimately say that they would rather not plug into the experience machine.[6] But then, how can we explain this refusal?

In the literature, relevant intuitions about the 'experience machine' are normally used to refute a 'hedonist' account of well-being.[7] However, the thought experiment might also provide us with some more *positive* ideas about what we value in our lives—for presumably, there is something about our 'real' lives that is important to us which we wouldn't have in the experience machine, and which explains why we might not want to plug in. Indeed, in the relevant literature on well-being, people often take our response to Nozick's experience machine to support the 'desire-satisfaction

---

[5] Nozick (1974: 42).

[6] For a brief discussion of this passage, see also Chalmers (2022: 15f.). Recent anecdotal evidence suggests that today, more people might be ready to plug into the experience machine than when Nozick first presented his thought experiment in 1974. There is no time to explain this possible trend, but in an attempt to do so, one would presumably have to consider the fact that today, very 'smart' machines are integrated into people's daily lives, people do spend a lot of their time interacting with others online, and that, for at least some people, 'virtual worlds have', in Chalmers' (2022: 15f.) words, 'become more and more a part of [their] lives'.

[7] According to the hedonist, our lives go well if we can maximize the pleasure and minimize the pain we experience; if hedonism was true, so the argument usually runs, we should all want to plug into the experience machine, because we could preprogramme it such that we'd have a maximum amount of pleasure and a minimum amount of pain—so, according to hedonism, our lives would go *much* better in the experience machine than in our ordinary environments; the fact that most people seem reluctant to plug in is taken to indicate that hedonism must be false.

theory' of well-being, which says that our lives go well if our desires are satisfied. Given that most of our desires are to do with things happening in our actual environment, in the experience machine, most of our desires would remain unsatisfied, so defenders of a desire-satisfaction account conclude that our intuitive responses to the experience machine scenario support their theory of well-being.

However, the experience machine might yet reveal some other feature of our everyday situation, a feature which lies a little 'deeper' than the idea that desire satisfaction contributes to our well-being. For thinking about the experience machine and our reluctance to plug in might also be used to show that we simply deem it to be good to be *connected* with people and things beyond our own mental lives. Indeed, this seems Nozick's own take on his thought experiment when he suggests that 'perhaps what we [value] is to live (an active verb) ourselves, in contact with reality. (And this, machines cannot do *for* us.)'[8] Elsewhere, he elaborates on this thought as follows:

> What we want and value is an actual connection with reality. [...] To focus on external reality, with your beliefs, evaluations and emotions, is valuable *in itself*, not just as a means to more pleasure or happiness. And it is this connecting that is valuable, not simply having within ourselves true beliefs. [...] [T]he connection to actuality is important whether or not we desire it—that is why we desire it—and the experience machine is inadequate because it doesn't give us *that*.[9]

Clearly, these quotations are rich and suggestive in various different ways, and there is no room to consider all relevant implications here.[10] Instead, I suggest that for present purposes we extract just one fairly specific claim from Nozick's comments, which we might call the 'Intrinsic Value Claim': We value our being in *perceptual contact* with reality, our having an *actual perceptual connection* with reality; indeed,

---

[8] Nozick (1974: 45).

[9] Nozick (1989: 106f.); for a brief discussion of this passage, see also Allen (2020: 641f.).

[10] One interesting observation is that Nozick's examples of ways in which we might value being connected to reality are *not* cases of perceptual experience (which is what we will concentrate on here) but rather 'beliefs, evaluations and emotions' (as quoted above). In addition to the material presented in the present chapter, it should therefore be illuminating to consider the question as to why beliefs, evaluations, and emotions might also be intrinsically valuable ways of being connected to reality, as Nozick claims them to be.

(**Intrinsic Value Claim**) Our being in *perceptual contact* with reality, our having an *actual perceptual connection* with reality is *intrinsically* valuable, that is, it is valuable *in itself*.

With the help of this claim, we might in turn also be able to explain why many people seem intuitively reluctant to plug into the experience machine: In the experience machine it would not be possible to be in perceptual contact with reality, and if perceptual contact with reality is of intrinsic value, people might not want to give up on that value and thus might not want to plug into the experience machine.

Thus, once we have come to see that standing in an actual perceptual connection with our environment might be intrinsically valuable, we can also understand people's reluctance to plug into Nozick's experience machine. This seems an important claim, but it has not found much attention in the literature, nor is it developed much further by Nozick himself. In order to do so ourselves, we should ask: What precisely does it mean to say, and why should we hold that, a subject's perceptual contact with reality *is* intrinsically valuable?

3. The Intrinsic Value of Perceptual Contact

In talking of perceptual contact with reality being *intrinsically* valuable, we implicitly presuppose a distinction between intrinsic and instrumental value. In the present context, I will draw this distinction simply by assuming that something is *instrumentally* valuable if it is valuable for reaching some other goal, that is, if it is a means to an end, whereas something is *intrinsically* valuable if it is valuable *not* (just) for reaching another goal, but is (also) valuable *for its own sake*.

Now, perceptual contact with a mind-independent world is certainly *instrumentally* valuable: As we saw earlier, our standing in perceptual contact with our environment might be instrumentally valuable because it provides us with *knowledge* about our environment; our standing in perceptual contact with our environment is also often of instrumental value because it helps us in reaching various other goals. For example, you might want to drink some water, and you've got a bottle of water to hand; in order to open the bottle and drink some water, you will (amongst other things) rely on your perceptual awareness of the bottle. Just as in this exemplary case, in very many everyday situations perceptual contact with a mind-independent world enables us to *do* things which we would like to do and is thus instrumentally valuable.

However, the Intrinsic Value Claim suggests that our having perceptual contact with reality is also *valuable in itself*, and in order to see why this should be so, I propose that we here consider the following train of thought:

> (**Openness Claim**) In being in perceptual contact with a mind-independent world, the perceiving subject finds herself open to the world,

and this openness to the world is of *eudaimonic* value for the subject, that is, it increases the subject's *well-being* to find herself open to her environment. This in turn means that

> (**Eudaimonic Value Claim**) A subject's being in perceptual contact with reality, a subject's having an actual perceptual connection with reality, has *eudaimonic* value, that is, a subject's being in perceptual contact with reality has value with respect to her (mental) well-being,

which in turn explains why

> (**Intrinsic Value Claim**) Our being in *perceptual contact* with reality, our having an *actual perceptual connection* with reality is *intrinsically* valuable, that is, it is valuable *in itself*.

Thus, in a nutshell, the train of thought I propose to develop in the following runs as follows: A subject's being in perceptual contact with reality is intrinsically valuable because her being in perceptual contact with reality has a certain kind of *eudaimonic* value, that is, it contributes to her (mental) *well-being* in a certain way.

4. Openness

In order to *develop* this train of thought, we should begin by considering the Openness Claim and the concept of 'openness' which it relies upon, which we might introduce as follows: Subjects can be, and are, related to the world in different ways. Thinking about the world, imagining the world, desiring the world to be a certain way—all these activities might well count as ways of being related to the world in some way, for in order to engage in any of the relevant activities, the subject does need to be aware of what the world is like to *some* degree. However, in each of these ways of relating to the world—thinking, imagining, desiring—the subject herself also imposes her *own* ideas, her *own* interests, in short, her *own will*, onto her engagement with the world. Indeed, in those respects in which her *own* ideas and her *own* interests guide the subject's engagement with the world in cases of thinking, imagining, or desiring, the subject might well be said to be 'closed' to the world—in those respects, her *own* ideas and her *own* interests structure and characterize her engagement with the world, while the world itself and what it might be like become secondary for her. Thus, in thinking about the world, imagining the world, or desiring the world to be a certain way, the subject will be related to the world in some way, but because her own ideas and interests stand in the foreground of her engagement with the world in these contexts, the subject is also closed to the world in some important respects in those cases.

By contrast, it seems that in standing in *perceptual contact* with the world, subjects can take up an attitude of maximal *openness* to their environment. Of course, it is possible, and probably even plausible, to argue that a human being's openness to her environment never is, and could not possibly be, *perfect*, and that there will always be respects in which we (healthy mature human beings) are closed to the world, even in perceptual experience. This, as I say, does seem plausible—after all, we are limited creatures: Someone who has weak eyesight will only see things in a blurry way without glasses, we can't see what goes on inside the tree which we stand in front of, and in each case in which we encounter our environment, we will already bring some of our understanding of the world to the encounter (which might skew things somewhat), even in contexts where we try to be as open to the world around us as at all possible. Thus, when I say here that subjects who stand in perceptual contact with the world take up an attitude of 'openness' to the world, I do not mean to suggest that the relevant openness is *perfect*; rather, the claim under consideration is just that in standing in perceptual contact with a mind-independent world, and compared to other ways in which a subject might be related to her environment (such as thinking about the world, imagining the world, or desiring the world to be a certain way), in being perceptually aware of her environment the perceiving subject finds herself *as* open to her environment as she possibly *could be*, given her limited, species-specific as well as subject-specific, capacities. Thus, following

McDowell, I think we do have reason to 'urge [...] that [perceptual] experience can be conceived as openness to the world'.[11]

A subject who is open to the world is ready to encounter the world, she is ready and available, right here, right now, for the world to present itself to her—that is, the attitude of a subject who is open to the world is an *attitude of receptivity* to the world. By contrast, a subject who has a hallucinatory experience—say, a subject who hallucinates a pink elephant in front of her (while there is no such creature anywhere in her vicinity at all), that is, a subject who has an experience as of a pink elephant while not standing in any perceptual contact with any such creature should not be said to be 'open' to the world either. On the contrary, in a case of hallucination, the subject's receptivity to the world is most seriously damaged and diminished, and a subject in such a situation could not plausibly be characterized as taking up an attitude of receptivity towards her environment.

Thus, I here presuppose a 'factive' understanding of the term 'openness': In order for a subject to be said to be 'open' to the world, it is necessary that the subject actually *be* open to the world. Cases in which the subject has experiences which do in fact mislead her in important respects about the actual world as it is around her at the time, such as cases of hallucination, are cases where the subject's receptivity is seriously diminished if not completely obstructed by the relevant misleading experiences, and accordingly, in the present context those cases should *not* count as cases in which the subject could be said to be 'open' to the world either.[12] In order for a subject to be said to be 'open' to the world, it is necessary that her contact with the world *not* be obstructed by experiences which *mis*represent the world in important respects.[13]

---

[11] McDowell (1996: 111).

[12] This in turn should clarify that and how the term 'openness' as used in the present context differs from French and Crane's (2021) conception of 'openness'; French and Crane take their concept of 'openness' to apply to cases of veridical perceptual experience, but also to 'experiences which don't involve perceptual contact with the world' (2021), e.g. hallucinatory experiences. By contrast, in the context of the present chapter, a subject should only be said to be 'open' to the world if she actually *is* open to the world, and not in cases in which it might *seem* to her as if she were, but she in fact is not open to the world after all. Of course, in cases of the latter kind, the subject herself might still be under the *mistaken impression* that she is open to her environment, and such cases are considered further in Section 9 below. (Thanks to Uriah Kriegel for prompting me to add the last sentence here.)

[13] Such openness to the world is prototypically realized in veridical perceptual experience, but one might argue that subjects who have experiential (or 'recollective') memories stand in 'memorial contact' with their own past and are thus also 'open' to the world. More specifically, one might argue that subjects who recollectively remember a particular past event are open to the past. Indeed, when we vividly remember particular past events, we sometimes say that it is as if we were to see or hear the relevant past events again; it might well seem plausible to say that in these cases, we are 'open' to the relevant past events, or that we have an attitude of 'maximal

Perceptual experiences' feature of openness is in turn closely linked with another feature of perceptual experience which, in the relevant literature, is usually referred to as the 'transparency' of perceptual experience: When one considers the phenomenon of perceptual experience one does, in Mike Martin's words, find that 'introspection of one's perceptual experience reveals [not sense-data, or any other "inner" entities; instead, introspection reveals] only the mind-independent objects, qualities and relations that one learns about through perception'.[14] Thus, perceptual 'experience is, so to speak, diaphanous or transparent to the objects of perception, at least as revealed to introspection'.[15] The fact that based on self-observation and introspection, perceptual experiences seem 'diaphanous or transparent to the objects of perception'[16] can in turn be further elucidated with the help of the Openness Claim: If, as the Openness Claim has it, a subject who stands in perceptual contact with a mind-independent world finds herself *open* to the world, then it also seems plausible to assume that those objects and events in the mind-independent world which the perceiving subject does find herself to be open to in perceptual experience will be revealed to her in a way that in turn should strike her as 'diaphanous' and 'transparent'.

Thus, the suggestion that in standing in perceptual contact with a mind-independent world, the perceiving subject finds herself open to the world also fits with other intuitions about perceptual experience which are currently widely shared. More generally, our present considerations will, or so I hope, have elucidated and given us reason to accept the claim that

(Openness Claim)   In being in perceptual contact with a mind-independent world, the perceiving subject finds herself open to the world.

---

receptivity' towards the relevant past events. This, in any case, would be an implication of the 'relational' account of the nature of recollective memory which I defend in Debus (2008). Thus, it might well be argued that in recollective memory we are open to our own past environment, just as in perceptual experience, we are open to our present environment. Obviously, these two forms of openness to the world do differ with respect to their 'subject matter'—in the one case, the subject is open with respect to her *past* environment, in the other case, the subject is open with respect to her *present* environment—but while openness to the world might well be prototypically realized in perceptual experience, recollective memory might provide us with yet another (maybe less prototypical, but maybe no less important) way of being open to the world.

[14] Martin (2002: 378).
[15] Martin (2002: 378). Martin himself carefully analyses the role which this observation usually plays in debates about the nature of perceptual experience, but for present purposes, we should focus on the observation itself, namely the observation that perceptual experience is 'transparent' with respect to the objects perceived.
[16] Martin (2002: 378).

5. The Eudaimonic Value of Openness

Next, we should now explore the core suggestion of the present chapter, namely the suggestion that a subject's openness to the world is of *eudaimonic* value for the subject, that is, that it contributes to the subject's *well-being* to find herself open to her environment when being perceptually aware of it. In support of this suggestion, I would here like to offer three complementary lines of thought. I will briefly sketch those three lines of thought in the present section, and will then develop them in greater detail in the section that follows.

First, then, a train of thought which we might call '**Availability**': It seems that sometimes, we can be 'lost in thought', or gone off into our own fantasy world. In these situations we encounter ourselves and our own thoughts and fantasy creations, and while this might be fun at times, at other times it might also be quite an isolating experience. By contrast, in finding ourselves open to our environment, we are *not* 'lost in thought' or gone off into our own fantasy world; rather, in finding ourselves open to our environment, we are *available* for the people, objects, and events in our environment here and now; and to find ourselves available for the people, objects, and events in our environment here and now contributes to our mental well-being, that is, it is of *eudaimonic* value for the relevant subject.

A second train of thought might be called '**Belonging**' and be sketched as follows: In finding ourselves open to our environment, we experience ourselves as *belonging* to something, somewhere, at a certain time—to whatever presents itself to us, *here and now*; thus, a subject who finds herself open to the world is *rooted* or *grounded* in the here and now, and to experience oneself as being rooted and grounded in the here and now contributes to one's mental well-being, that is, it is of *eudaimonic* value for the relevant subject.

A third line of thought which we might call '**Accepting Contingency**' runs as follows: We sometimes experience ourselves as 'thrown into' this world, and at least sometimes, in certain moods, the stark contingency of our existence can be quite bewildering: That I did come into existence at all seems rather contingent, that I was born at this particular time in this particular country to these particular parents is contingent, and so are, in many respects, the views I hold, the work I do, the friends I have, the life I lead. Being aware of how contingent one's own life is might at times feel rather uncomfortable, one might feel lost and anxious and unsure of one's place in the world, wondering why one exists and what one is meant to do. But then, in finding ourselves open to our environment, we are ready and fully available, right here, right now, for *other* contingent particulars—objects and people—to present themselves to us; in being open to other contingent particulars in the here and now we are open to other particular objects and people whose existence is just as contingent as our own, which in turn renders our own contingent particularity somewhat less bewildering; thus, in finding ourselves open to our environment we can be a little more *at peace* with our own contingent particularity, and being at peace with our own contingent particularity contributes to our (mental) well-being, that is, it is of *eudaimonic* value to the relevant subject.

All three lines of thought as just sketched aim to support the suggestion that a subject's openness to the world is of *eudaimonic* value for the subject, that is, that it increases the subject's *well-being* to find herself open to her environment when being perceptually aware of it. But then, given that, as the Openness Claim has it, a subject who is in perceptual contact with a mind-independent world does find herself open to the world, we also have reason to hold that

> **(Eudaimonic Value Claim)** A subject's being in perceptual contact with reality, a subject's having an actual perceptual connection with reality, has *eudaimonic* value, that is, a subject's being in perceptual contact with reality has value with respect to her (mental) well-being.

6. Availability, Belonging, and Accepting Contingency

Next, we should look a little more carefully at the three lines of thought just offered. The core claims of those three arguments each describe one characteristic feature which openness is said to have and which is said to contribute to a subject's mental well-being: Being open to the world is said to be a form of being *available* to one's environment, a form of *belonging* to one's environment, and a way of *accepting one's own contingent particularity*, and each of these three features is said to be of *eudaimonic* value. All three lines of thought might seem intuitively plausible, but as our argument in support of the main claim of the present chapter, namely the claim that perceptual awareness is of eudaimonic value, ultimately does rest on these three lines of thought, it might seem appropriate to consider them in greater detail and ask why precisely they should be true.

Now, each of these three lines of thought make claims about 'our' mental well-being, that is, about the mental well-being of healthy, mature human subjects. In order to do full justice to those three arguments, we would therefore have to offer a philosophical account of what it takes for healthy mature human subjects to have mental well-being, but there is no time to do so here. Instead, I suggest that we here simply presuppose a rough, everyday understanding of mental well-being, and then focus on a critical assessment of the three *more specific* philosophical claims about mental well-being under consideration, namely the 'Availability Claim', the 'Belonging Claim', and the 'Accepting Contingency Claim'.

First, then, according to the Availability Claim,

> (**Availability Claim**) In finding ourselves open to our environment, we are *not* 'lost in thought' or gone off into our own fantasy world; rather, in finding ourselves open to our environment, we are *available* for the people, objects, and events in our environment here and now; and to find ourselves available for the people, objects, and events in our environment here and now contributes to our (mental) well-being, that is, it is of *eudaimonic* value.

But then, so someone might ask, *why* precisely should finding ourselves available for the people, objects, and events in our environment here and now contribute to our mental well-being? In response, we might point out that according to the Availability Claim as formulated so far, 'being available' is contrasted with 'being lost in thought' or 'gone off into one's own fantasy world'; the implication here seems to be that being lost in thought or having gone off into one's own fantasy world might *sometimes* be isolating, which in turn might be bad for a subject's mental well-being, so that a subject's being available to her environment might be thought of as having eudaimonic value simply because it is a situation in which the subject is *not* isolated.[17]

Somewhat more positively, however, it would also seem plausible to accept that taking up an attitude which makes you available to the people, objects, and events in your environment, that is, taking up an attitude which enables others (broadly construed: people, objects, or events) to 'get at you' and to have an effect on you, makes your mental life go better than it would

---

[17] This is compatible with the plausible claim that at other times, going off into one's own fantasy world might well be immensely enjoyable and relaxing and might even connect one with other people (for example, if these other people are currently not present in one's own physical environment, but appear in one's daydreams, one might well feel a greater connection with them than one might otherwise do). Thus, sometimes, going off into one's own fantasy world might well also be good for one's mental well-being.

otherwise go. The fact that a subject *is* available for her environment is of value, because it is good for the subject herself to *be* available, sometimes (rather than not to be, that is, to be permanently *closed off* from her environment). For in being available to the world to present itself to her, the subject is ready to stand in a relation to something 'outside of herself', and being ready to stand in such a relation is itself healthy and thus valuable; it is *intrinsically* valuable to take up this sort of attitude sometimes. Being available to the world is an attitude to have with respect to the world which is of eudaimonic value of an *intrinsic* kind.

What is more, it seems good for our mental well-being that we sometimes find ourselves in specific situations where the world can and does 'get at us' on a conscious, personal level. For example, it seems good for one's mental well-being to find oneself addressed by others—finding oneself greeted in a simple, ritualized way when arriving at work in the morning might offer stability, and being sought out by a friend who has some exciting news to share might offer a sense of being valued—and being so addressed by others does depend on our being *available* for such an address in the first place, which indicates that a subject's finding herself available for her environment might also be said to be of *instrumental* value, because it enables the subject to be available to the people in her environment here and now, which in turn will contribute to her mental well-being.

Similarly, it seems good for our mental well-being to be available for other elements of our environment. For example, cycling home from work in the rain and in a bit of a sullen mood, it might be good for you to be suddenly confronted with a gorgeous rainbow in the distance, and being confronted with that rainbow does, once more, depend on your being available for such a 'confrontation' in the first place.

Thus, we find that being available to our environment in being open to it is of both intrinsic and instrumental value. It is *intrinsically* valuable just to be available to our environment, and it is also of *instrumental* value in particular situations to be so available, because being so available might enable valuable encounters.[18]

Of course, there will be ways in which our environment might affect us that are of great disvalue, so it is clear that the eudaimonic value of being 'available' for one's environment might be outweighed in certain cases by

---

[18] Thanks to Uriah Kriegel for prompting me to consider the distinction between eudaimonic values of an *intrinsic* and of an *instrumental* kind as it applies in the present context more explicitly.

the disvalue created by a particular situation, but this does not speak against the suggestion that, all things equal, to find ourselves available for the people, objects, and events in our environment here and now does contribute to our mental well-being and is therefore of eudaimonic value, just as the Availability Claim has it.

Second, according to the Belonging Claim,

> (**Belonging Claim**) In finding ourselves open to our environment, we experience ourselves as *belonging* to something, somewhere, at a certain time—to whatever presents itself to us, *here and now*; thus, a subject who finds herself open to the world is *rooted* or *grounded* in the here and now, and to experience oneself as being rooted or grounded in the here and now contributes to one's mental well-being, that is, it is of *eudaimonic* value to the experiencing subject.

The Belonging Claim does strike me as intuitively plausible, but maybe the first part of the claim as just set out will benefit from some further discussion. In finding ourselves open to our environment, so we are told, we experience ourselves as *belonging* to something, somewhere, at a certain time, which in turn means that a subject who finds herself open to the world is *rooted* or *grounded* in the here and now. Indeed, in finding myself open to my environment, I will find myself confronted with people, objects, and events, and I can't but experience myself as related to the relevant people, objects, and events, if only in a spatio-temporal sense. For example, standing by a lake in the summer, being open to my environment I find myself confronted with children playing in the water, pebbles under my naked feet, and sailing boats passing by in the distance, and I can't but experience myself as related to the children, pebbles, and boats passing by, if only in a spatio-temporal sense. In being open to my environment, I do experience myself as a part of the situation, that is, I experience myself as belonging to the situation as it presents itself. Thus, somewhat more generally, it seems that we have reason to accept that in finding ourselves open to our environment, we experience ourselves as *belonging* to something here and now (i.e., at the time and place at which the experience is had), and a subject who experiences herself as belonging to something here and now will experience herself as *rooted* or *grounded* in the here and now, just as the Belonging Claim suggests.

The second part of the Belonging Claim, namely the suggestion that belonging to something, and feeling rooted and grounded in the here and now contribute to a subject's mental well-being, is, or so I hope, uncontentious, and so we find that we have good reason to accept the Belonging Claim.

However, so someone might ask, is the eudaimonic value as described by the Belonging Claim of an *intrinsic* kind, or is it only a value of an *instrumental* kind?[19] In response, I think we find that while it might well often be of *instrumental* value for a subject to experience herself as belonging to something here and now in being open to her environment, the experience of belonging which is realized by a subject's being open to her environment is also of an *intrinsic* kind, that is, it is an *intrinsic* value of her openness to her environment.

An opponent might hold against this that a subject's openness to her environment only *provides* the subject *with an opportunity* to experience herself as belonging to something, that it only *enables* the intrinsically valuable experience of belonging, and that this in turn indicates that the eudaimonic value of a subject's openness in perceptual awareness itself is only of an *instrumental* kind.[20]

However, I think this objection misses the point somewhat. The core idea of the 'Belonging Claim' rather is that, in a slogan, 'openness *is* belonging'—that is, it is *in* being open to her environment that the subject does experience herself as belonging to whatever presents itself to her in being so open. The core idea here is that in being open to something—anything!—the subject does experience herself as belonging. This in turn implies that, while the eudaimonic value of being open to one's environment as described by the Belonging Claim might often be of an *instrumental* kind, it is also a eudaimonic value of an *intrinsic* kind.

Third, as we said earlier, the Accepting Contingency Claim departs from the observation that at least sometimes, in certain moods, the stark contingency of our existence can be quite bewildering. But then, so the Accepting Contingency Claim has it,

(Accepting Contingency Claim)   In finding ourselves open to our environment, we are ready and fully available, right here, right now, for *other contingent particulars*—objects and people—to present themselves to us; in being open to *other* contingent particulars in the here and now we are open to other objects and people whose existence is just as contingent as

---

[19] Thanks to Uriah Kriegel for prompting me to consider this question here.
[20] I here presuppose that to experience oneself as belonging to something is of intrinsic value; I discuss and support this claim further in Section 8 below.

our own, which in turn renders our own contingent particularity somewhat less bewildering; thus, in finding ourselves open to our environment we can be a little more *at peace* with our own contingent particularity, and being at peace with our own contingent particularity contributes to our mental well-being, that is, it is of *eudaimonic* value.

Now, it seems obvious that in perceptual experience, we are aware of other contingent particulars. Indeed, as Ranalli puts it, '[c]ognitive contact with reality is contact involving relation. It marks an essentially existence entailing relation between the cognizer and reality, as something which implies the actual *existence* of the object cognized [...]'.[21] However, so someone might ask, why should being open to other contingent particulars make my own bewilderment in the face of my own contingent particularity any less pressing? In fact, so our interlocutor might say, isn't it likely that if I find myself in a mood where I do already find my own contingent particularity bewildering, I will be even more bewildered and anxious once I find myself open to other, similarly contingent particulars? Shouldn't such openness to other contingent particulars *increase* the bewilderment, rather than reduce it, as the Accepting Contingency Claim suggests?

In response, it seems plausible to grant our interlocutor that in *some* cases, things might indeed develop as she suggests. However, it also seems plausible that most of the cases in which things develop for a subject in this way will be clinical cases, that is, cases in which the relevant subjects' mental health is damaged in some important way; such clinical cases are very complex and often very difficult to understand, which is why the present investigation is restricted to *healthy* mature human subjects only. And it would seem plausible to assume that for *healthy* mature human subjects, it is usually soothing to encounter other people (or objects) who (or which) *share* certain features with them, quite independently of whether relevant shared features are deemed to be problematic, or welcome and worth having.

We might think here of gentlemen's clubs, AA meetings, specific online groups such as Ravelry (for people with a passion for knitting), groups of families whose children are deaf or autistic, or groups of young widows. The assumption behind such groupings and organizations seems to be that subjects whose lives have certain specific features—e.g., being autistic or deaf, having being widowed early on in life or, indeed, simply enjoying

---

[21] Ranalli (2021: 151).

knitting—can gain from encountering other people whose lives are characterized by similar features. In cases in which the relevant feature is unproblematic (such as a passion for knitting), the benefit of encountering others whose lives have the same feature might primarily be in emphasizing and celebrating the relevant feature by highlighting that the relevant feature is shared with others. In cases in which the relevant feature is deemed to be problematic (for example, having been widowed early in life), encountering others whose lives have the same feature might be beneficial because such encounters help the subject to realize that while difficult to deal with, the relevant feature is less exceptional and in some ways more 'normal' than she might have thought when thinking about her own situation to begin with. Relevant encounters might also be beneficial because seeing how the relevant feature plays out in the lives of others might prompt one to discover regularities that are characteristic of the relevant feature, and might thus help one in understanding better what happens in one's own life with respect to the relevant feature. This in turn is bound to be soothing, it is bound to reduce anxiety in the face of the relevant predicament, and it can also help with simply *accepting* that the relevant feature is presently characterizing one's life, whether one likes it or not.

Now, the feature that stands at the heart of the Accepting Contingency Claim—namely, the fact that for each of us, it is true that our existence is contingent, and that we might just as well not have existed at all—is obviously a somewhat more abstract and general feature than having a passion for knitting, and it is also a more abstract feature than having been widowed early in life. Nevertheless, it seems plausible to hold that, just as encountering others who have been widowed early in life might help someone come to accept their own having been widowed early in life, so being open to other particulars whose existence is just as contingent as one's own will help with *accepting* one's own contingent particularity, just as the Accepting Contingency Claim says.

In being open to her environment, the subject is open to other particulars around her, right here, right now, which (or who) might not have been around *here*, or might not have been around here *now*, or might not exist anymore now, or might not have ever existed *at all*. Openness to other contingent particulars, right here, right now, is comforting partly because these other contingent particulars *share* the feature of contingent particularity with the subject, and *sharing* a certain feature with others will, for a healthy subject, usually be calming and help them to accept the relevant feature in their own case. Relevant encounters help the subject to realize that while maybe bewildering at first sight, her being a contingent particular is less exceptional and in some ways more 'normal' than she might have thought when bewilderment first struck. This in turn is bound to be soothing, it is bound to reduce anxiety, and it can also help with simply *accepting* the fact that one is a contingent particular, whether one likes it or not, which in turn contributes to a subject's mental well-being, and this is precisely what the Accepting Contingency Claim says.

Once more, however, someone might ask whether the eudaimonic value described by the Accepting Contingency Claim is of an *intrinsic* kind, or whether it is only an *instrumental* value.[22] And indeed, with respect to the Accepting Contingency Claim, we might simply grant, at least for the sake of the argument, that the eudaimonic value of a subject's openness to her environment as described here might be of a purely *instrumental* kind.[23] As the Accepting Contingency Claim says, being open to other contingent particulars when being open to our environment *renders* our own contingent particularity somewhat less bewildering; that is, being open to one's environment *enables* acceptance of one's own contingency, and given that acceptance of one's own contingency is valuable, and is *enabled* by openness to one's environment, openness to one's environment should count as instrumentally valuable in this respect.

Thus, while we earlier argued that the eudaimonic values described by the Availability Claim and the Belonging Claim are both of an *intrinsic* kind, we might grant that the eudaimonic value described by the Accepting Contingency Claim is only of an *instrumental* kind. However, accepting one's own contingency seems a central and fundamental value in each and every one of our lives, so it seems important to point out that a subject's openness to her environment can indeed contribute to her gaining such greater acceptance.

More generally, we find that we have good reason to accept the Accessibility Claim, the Belonging Claim, and the Accepting Contingency Claim; each of these claims support the suggestion that a subject's openness to the world is of *eudaimonic* value for the subject, that is, that it increases the subject's *well-being* to find herself open to her environment when being perceptually aware of it, and that this eudaimonic value is of an intrinsic kind with

---

[22] Uriah Kriegel prompted the following set of considerations; thanks, Uriah!
[23] In fact, I think we should also hold that the eudaimonic value described by the Accepting Contingency Claim is an *intrinsic* feature of the subject's openness to her environment; however, this claim is bound to be rather controversial, and as we do not need to rely upon it in order to develop the overall argument of the present chapter, I will not try to defend it here.

respect to the features described by the 'Availability Claim' and the 'Belonging Claim'. But then, given that, as the Openness Claim has it, a subject who is in perceptual contact with a mind-independent world does find herself open to the world, we also have reason to hold that

> (**Eudaimonic Value Claim**) A subject's being in perceptual contact with reality, a subject's having an actual perceptual connection with reality, has *eudaimonic* value, that is, a subject's being in perceptual contact with reality has value with respect to her (mental) well-being.

7. On Shutting the World Out

However, the Eudaimonic Value Claim might not remain uncontested. Indeed, so an opponent might say, while the argument offered and developed above does seem to speak in its favour, something must be wrong with this argument, for the Eudaimonic Value Claim could not possibly be true. While the claim proposes that standing in perceptual contact with reality is eudaimonically valuable, it seems that sometimes, quite on the contrary, it is of great (eudaimonic) value *not* to be in perceptual contact with reality. Think, for example, of people who use noise-cancelling headphones—clearly, someone who wears noise-cancelling headphones does quite explicitly try to shut the world out in some way, and they quite explicitly do not want to be in perceptual contact with reality in the relevant way (namely, acoustically). But then, so our opponent asks, why would people do this, if standing in perceptual contact with reality was of eudaimonic value? More generally, people often shut the world out by blocking their senses in various ways (by closing their eyes when presented with a gruesome scene, for example, or by withdrawing their hand from a slimy surface), and this, so our opponent concludes, clearly indicates that something must be wrong with the Eudaimonic Value Claim.

In response, it would seem sensible to grant that our 'shutting the world out' by blocking our various senses is an ordinary and everyday occurrence, and that people do indeed *value* their ability to 'shut the world out' in these ways in relevant situations. However, this is compatible with the truth of the Eudaimonic Value Claim. For example, whilst I sit on the train and try to do some work, all things considered it might well be best for me to use those noise-cancelling headphones and 'shut the world out', because I need to focus on the work I want to do, and the noise in the carriage is very distracting. A defender of the Eudaimonic Value Claim will say that being open to the world in such a situation *is* of eudaimonic value, but the eudaimonic value of my being open to the world in this situation is heavily outweighed by the value of my being able to concentrate on my work, and given that I can concentrate on my work much better if I am able to block out the noise with the help of noise-cancelling headphones, it is most sensible to use those headphones.

There might also be other circumstances where the value of standing in perceptual contact with the world is outweighed by circumstantial factors; for example, there might be situations where perceptual contact with one's environment might lead to serious trauma, or other serious damage to one's well-being, and in those contexts, once more, it might be plausible to say that while the subject's standing in perceptual contact with her environment *is* of eudaimonic value—after all, in those situations the argument from 'Availability', the argument from 'Belonging', as well as the argument from 'Accepting Contingency', as developed earlier, should all still apply—this value is (in some cases heavily) outweighed by the disvalue which her standing in perceptual contact with her environment in those specific situations would also have, and thus, all things considered, her standing in perceptual contact with her environment in those situations is *not* valuable *overall*.

Thus, in response to the opponent's objection, we find that we can continue to endorse the Eudaimonic Value Claim, while we also do have good reason to grant that there might be circumstances where the eudaimonic value of perceptual contact is outweighed by other values, so that *not* standing in perceptual contact with the world is more valuable in those contexts, *all things considered*. We can agree that it is sometimes valuable to 'shut the world out', but this is compatible with our continuing to endorse the Eudaimonic Value Claim.

8. Taking Stock

We find that we have reason to accept the claim that a subject's being in perceptual contact with her environment has eudaimonic value. But then, or so I suggested earlier, this insight might also explain why, as Nozick holds, a subject's being in perceptual contact with her environment has *intrinsic* value: A subject's being in perceptual contact with reality is intrinsically valuable because her being in perceptual contact with reality is of a certain eudaimonic value which is of the intrinsic kind—namely, the sort of eudaimonic value spelled out by the 'Availability Claim' and the 'Belonging Claim'.

However, someone might question whether the relevant eudaimonic value is really of an *intrinsic* kind, or whether it should not rather count as an instrumental value only. Indeed, so our opponent might hold, to say that being in perceptual contact with reality is of eudaimonic value is to say that standing in the relevant perceptual contact is good for the subject's mental well-being, which means that rather than being valuable for its own sake, standing in the relevant perceptual contact is valuable because it promotes another goal, namely the subject's mental well-being. Thus, so our opponent concludes, the relevant eudaimonic value actually turns out to be only an *instrumental* (and not an intrinsic) value.

In response, we should point out that the subject's perceptual experiences are themselves a constitutive part of the subject's wider mental life. It would seem plausible to assume that a subject's wider mental well-being is improved if mental events which have intrinsic value do occur in the relevant mental life, rather than such events not occurring, and *this*, or so I would like to suggest, is how a subject's wider mental well-being is improved by the occurrence of perceptual experiences in it: Relevant perceptual experiences have *eudaimonic* value for the subject—as we said earlier, being open to the world in perceptual experience is a form of being *available* to one's environment, a form of *belonging* to one's environment, and a way of *accepting one's own contingent particularity*, and it seems plausible to hold that at least the first two of these three features of perceptual experiences are valuable *for their own sake*, that is, the relevant features of perceptual experiences are *intrinsically* valuable. As we said earlier (see Section 6 above), one might argue that with respect to accepting one's own contingency (which itself is intrinsically valuable), openness might only be valuable in an *instrumental* way, but we also saw that with respect to the features described by the Availability Claim and the Belonging Claim, openness to one's environment itself has eudaimonic value of an *intrinsic* kind. Given that the relevant perceptual experiences are mental occurrences, their intrinsic value means that elements of the subject's mental life—namely, relevant perceptual experiences—do have intrinsic value. What is more, to say that these features contribute to the subject's wider mental well-being is *compatible* with this claim. For the relevant features are features of the subject's mental life, so if relevant features instantiate certain intrinsic values, it seems plausible to hold that the mental life of which they are a constitutive part will, as a whole, also gain in value.

At the same time, there might be some situations where a subject opens up to her environment in perception with the *goal* of improving her mental well-being *overall* by *adding* some eudaimonic, intrinsic value to this wider mental life. For example, being caught in a bit of a low mood, someone might go for a walk looking at the spring flowers in their local park, thereby opening up to their environment in perception with the explicit goal of improving their mental well-being *overall*. In such a case, we might want to say that relevant perceptual experiences also do have instrumental value, in that they are quite explicitly sought out in order to increase overall mental well-being. However, they can only do so in virtue of their having the relevant *intrinsic* eudaimonic values as described earlier (namely, the values of being *available* to one's environment, and of *belonging* to one's environment), so that even in those situations in which relevant experiences are sought out with another goal, such as the goal of improving one's overall well-being, the fact that relevant perceptual experiences might have instrumental value in the context of the subject's pursuing such a goal is compatible, and indeed presupposes, that relevant perceptual experiences have intrinsic eudaimonic value in the first place. Thus, we can continue to hold that a subject's perceptual awareness of her environment has *eudaimonic* value of an *intrinsic* kind.

The idea that a subject's perceptual awareness of her environment might be not just of epistemological, but also of *eudaimonic* value does not seem to have received much attention in contemporary Philosophy of Mind.[24] Indeed, the Eudaimonic Value Claim might seem rather surprising at first sight. But as we have meanwhile seen, the argument from 'Availability', the argument from 'Belonging', and the argument from 'Accepting Contingency' give us good reason to accept the Eudaimonic Value Claim. Any account of perceptual experience should therefore be able to accommodate the fact that a subject's perceptual awareness of her environment has value with respect to her (mental) well-being, just as the Eudaimonic Value Claim has it.

---

[24] Ranalli (2021) is a notable exception here, and Allen (2020: 641f.) also briefly discusses the issue. Indeed, Ranalli does formulate the view that conscious perception might have eudaimonic value—that maybe, 'having contact with reality is fundamentally part of the good life' (Ranalli 2021: 142), but in the context of his argument which is related to *epistemological* issues, the main goal of his considerations is to show that the value of perceptual contact is *not only eudaimonic*, but rather, that contact with reality also has *epistemological* value; thus, Ranalli does not address the question which stands at the centre of our considerations here, namely how we might *explicate* and *develop* the claim that perceptual contact has eudaimonic value.

9. Direct Realism vs. Representationalism, Again

Philosophers who attempt to account for the nature of perceptual experience do, as we said in the introduction, often offer one of two competing accounts: Some defend a Direct Realist account, others argue that we should accept a Representationalist account of perceptual experience, and usually, relevant debates are based on the shared assumption that any convincing account of perceptual awareness will have to meet various 'desiderata'—I listed four relevant desiderata in the introduction—and both Direct Realists as well as Representationalists have meanwhile developed accounts that probably can (more or less elegantly) meet all relevant desiderata.

However, our present considerations give us reason to hold that there is a new, further desideratum which any account of the nature of perceptual experience has to meet, and which so far has not been tested in those debates between Direct Realists and Representationalists, namely the need to (5) explain the fact that a subject's perceptual awareness of her environment has eudaimonic value. This is, as we have meanwhile seen, grounded in the fact that a subject who is perceptually aware of her environment is *open* to the world, and the Availability Claim, the Belonging Claim, and the Accepting Contingency Claim set out that and why such openness to the world is of eudaimonic value to the subject.

A Direct Realist about perceptual experience will be able to explain this very easily. For the Direct Realist holds that a subject who perceives an object stands in a *relation of direct awareness* to the relevant object. This claim seems easily compatible with the Openness Claim. For it seems plausible to hold that the core Direct Realist assumption, namely the assumption that a subject who perceives an object stands in a relation of direct awareness to the object perceived, simply *entails* the Openness Claim, namely the claim that

(**Openness Claim**) In standing in perceptual contact with a mind-independent world, the perceiving subject finds herself open to the world.

But then, with the Openness Claim in place, the Direct Realist can also meet our newly discovered desideratum, that is, she can account for the eudaimonic value of perceptual experiences which is grounded, in the ways specified by the Availability Claim, the Belonging Claim, and the Accepting Contingency Claim, in the subject's openness to the world.

By contrast, for the Representationalist it might be more difficult to explain all this. According to them, perceptual experiences, illusory experiences, and hallucinatory experiences are essentially representations, and thus they are all ultimately experiences of the same kind. But then, *hallucinatory* experiences are certainly *not* experiences which could plausibly be characterized as experiences in which the subject finds herself open to her environment (at least not in the *factive* sense of 'openness' which I presuppose here)—quite on the contrary, hallucinatory experiences are characterized by the fact that the world is *not* as the experience represents it as being, so we might well want to say that a subject who has hallucinatory experiences is in relevant ways *closed* to the world. But then, if perceptual and hallucinatory experiences are experiences of the same kind, as the Representationalist holds, it seems difficult to see how one might plausibly claim that in perceptual experience, the subject is open to the world.

The Representationalist might point out that the Openness Claim speaks of the subject *finding herself* open to the world in perceptual experience, and the Representationalist might hold that it is possible for a subject to be wrong about her situation in that respect—that is, a subject might well have the (mistaken) *impression* that she is open to the world in perceptual experience, even though such openness *could not possibly be* a feature of perceptual experiences, that is, whenever a subject is, in perceiving the world, under the impression that she is open to the world, the subject is *wrong* about that aspect of her situation.

Thus, the Representationalist might develop an *error theory* of openness in perceptual experience. She might agree that in standing in perceptual contact with a mind-independent world, the perceiving subject *finds* herself open to the world, just as the Openness Claim says, but hold that 'to find oneself' open to the world just means to be *under the impression* of being open to the world; whenever a perceiving subject does 'find herself' open to the world, the subject is *wrong* in having this impression—she isn't open to the world in these situations, because she could not possibly be. Thus, so the Representationalist concludes, while it seems quite plausible to accept that subjects are *under the impression* of being open to their environment in perceptual experience, and while it might well also be plausible to hold that it is of eudaimonic value to the subject to *be* under this impression, in truth this is some sort of illusion, because Representationalism is true, and according to Representationalism we could not possibly ever *be* open to our environment in the way suggested by the Openness Claim. The best we can offer in accounting for the observation formulated by the Openness Claim, so the Representationalist might conclude, is an *error theory*.

However, an account on which we have to assume that we are *constantly in error* when (apparently) finding ourselves open to the world in perceptual experience might be less appealing than an account on which we do *not* have to assume this. Thus, if the Representationalist has to resort to an error theory in order to account for the fact that perceptual experience has eudaimonic value, then the Direct Realist view of perceptual experience might well seem preferable, for it can account for this *without* the assumption of some such constant error.

In response, a Representationalist might offer an alternative way of accommodating the Openness Claim. Indeed, so the Representationalist might say, while hallucinatory experiences and perceptual experiences are ultimately experiences of the same kind, there is clearly an important difference between cases of hallucination and cases of perceptual experience with respect to the *context* in which these experiences occur: For in cases of perceptual experience, there is a *causal link* which obtains between the perceived object and the perceiving subject (and, more specifically, the subject's perceptual experience), whereas in (the vast majority of) cases of hallucinatory experiences, no such causal link could possibly obtain between any relevant object in the subject's environment and the subject (or, more specifically, the subject's hallucinatory experience), because there just is no relevant such object in the subject's environment in the first place. But then, so the Representationalist might conclude, what we mean to say when we say that a subject is 'open' to her environment in perceptual experience is simply that in perceptual experience, the subject is causally affected by her environment in the relevant ways. The 'openness' to the world which perceptual experience provides us with is based on this *causal* connection—a subject is 'open' to the world if she stands in the right causal connection to her environment, and in perceptual experience, the subject should be said to be 'open' to her environment, because in those cases she does stand in a relevant causal relation to her environment.

Now, if one was already committed to a Representationalist view of perceptual experience, then presumably this would be the best one could possibly say about our 'openness' to the world in perceptual experience, and so one should be satisfied with the present suggestion. However, for anybody who is *not* yet committed to Representationalism, the current suggestion might seem less than satisfactory. Indeed, anybody *without* any antecedent commitment to Representationalism might well hold that the current suggestion does not account for the feature of perceptual experience which the Openness Claim originally tried to capture, namely an openness to the world which is characterized by some sort of immediacy and directness, which is of eudaimonic value to us in virtue of this immediacy and directness. We do not, or so it would seem, value standing in an appropriate *causal* relation to the world; rather, we value being *in contact* with the world, and arguably, the kind of contact we value is not just our being causally affected by it, but our standing in some sort of *experiential* contact with our environment. Of course, at this point the Representationalist might retort that whatever we might try to point at when talking about 'experiential' contact will ultimately be *nothing but* some sort of causal contact, because this, or so the Representationalist will hold, is the *only* sort of relation we can stand in a relation to anything in. But again, the Representationalist here obviously already assumes the truth of her theory, which renders her effort less than satisfactory in the present context.[25]

In an attempt to consider the issues at hand without presupposing the truth of either a Representationalist or a Direct Realist account of perception, it seems plausible to hold that even if the Representationalist can offer *some* account, the Direct Realist will be able to offer a *better* account of our

---

[25] One might make a similar point on behalf of the Representationalist by insisting that the question as to whether perceptual awareness has eudaimonic value or not is 'orthogonal' to the question as to whether we should accept Direct Realism or Representationalism about perceptual experience. Indeed, so Uriah Kriegel suggests, 'the Representationalist and the Direct Realist [can] agree that veridical perceptual experiences have [...] eudaimonic value [...] while nonveridical perceptual experiences [do not]; their only disagreement is on whether [veridical and nonveridical perceptual experiences] belong to the same kind or not, which seems completely orthogonal. If they [are of] the same kind, it just means that it's not belonging to the [relevant] kind [of experience] that makes certain experiences have eudaimonic value, but belonging to a subset of that kind' (personal communication).—In response, it would seem important to emphasize that, as I said earlier, the Representationalist certainly *can* offer an account of the eudaimonic value of perceptual awareness; for a start, the Representationalist can certainly hold that those experiences which belong to the relevant *subset* of the relevant kind of experience do have eudaimonic value, while other experiences which belong to the relevant kind, but *not* to the relevant *subset*, do *not* have eudaimonic value. As soon as one accepts Representationalism, this is what one will have to say, and for anybody who already does endorse Representationalism it would seem sensible to do so. However, the Representationalist then still has to offer an explanation as to *why* experiences which belong to the relevant subset do have eudaimonic value; and it seems that the best the Representationalist can offer in reply to this question is to say that in the case of experiences which belong to the relevant subset, the experiencing subject stands in a *causal* relation to an object of the kind which her experience represents. But then, as I tried to explain above, intuitively it seems that what is of eudaimonic value about perceptual awareness is a connection between the perceiving subject and the object perceived which goes *beyond* such a causal relation, a connection which is more *direct*, more *immediate* than a causal relation, and this, or so I tried to argue above, cannot be accounted for by the Representationalist, while it *can* be accounted for by the Direct Realist. This in turn suggests that the Direct Realist can offer a *better* account of the eudaimonic value of perceptual awareness than the Representationalist, which is what I have tried to show in the text above.

openness to the world in perceptual experience and its intrinsic eudaimonic value, which might give us reason to prefer a Direct Realist account of perceptual experience over a Representationalist one. Somewhat more generally, we find that consideration of the novel suggestion that perceptual experience has eudaimonic value might in turn help to get the debate between Representationalists and Direct Realists about perceptual experience unstuck. Indeed, if our considerations here are on the right track, we might have reason to conclude that a Direct Realist account of perceptual experience can account for perceptual experience more successfully than a Representational account, and a Direct Realist account of the nature of perception should therefore be preferred.

10. Conclusion

Thus, one conclusion of the present chapter is that we might have reason to prefer Direct Realism over Representationalism when trying to account for the nature of perceptual experience. However, this conclusion is probably not the most important result of the present chapter. I think the more fundamental and more important contribution of the present chapter is to have shown that and why perceptual experience does have eudaimonic value.

As we have seen,

(**Openness Claim**) In being in perceptual contact with a mind-independent world, the perceiving subject finds herself open to the world.

But then, a subject's being thus open to the world is a form of being *available* to her environment, a form of *belonging* to her environment, and a way of *accepting her own contingent particularity*, and each of these three features is of *eudaimonic* value. This in turn means that we have reason to hold that

(**Eudaimonic Value Claim**) A subject's being in perceptual contact with reality, a subject's having an actual perceptual connection with reality, has *eudaimonic* value, that is, a subject's being in perceptual contact with reality has value with respect to her (mental) well-being.

This observation in turn has not found much attention in the philosophy of mind so far, but it strikes me as true and important. For it seems remarkable that perceptual experiences do have intrinsic eudaimonic value, and it also seems remarkable that our mental lives can have value simply in virtue of our being, right here, right now, perceptually aware of our present environment. In this chapter, I have made a first attempt at elucidating this phenomenon, but in order to understand the nature of our mental lives better, we should certainly give the eudaimonic value of perceptual awareness further careful consideration.[26]

References

Allen, K. (2020). 'The Value of Perception', *Philosophy and Phenomenological Research* 100 (3). 633–656.

Campbell, J. (2002). *Reference and Consciousness*. Oxford: Oxford University Press.

Chalmers, D. (2022). *Reality+: Virtual Worlds and the Problems of Philosophy*. London: Allen Lane.

Crane, T. and French, C. (2021). 'The Problem of Perception', *The Stanford Encyclopedia of Philosophy* (Fall 2021 Edition), Edward N. Zalta (ed.). Stanford, CA: Stanford University Press, https://plato.stanford.edu/archives/fall2021/entries/perception-problem/

Debus, D. (2008). 'Experiencing the Past: A Relational Account of Recollective Memory', *Dialectica* 62. 405–432.

Martin, M.G.F. (2002). 'The Transparency of Experience', *Mind and Language* 17. 376–425.

McDowell, J. (1996). *Mind and World*. Harvard: Harvard University Press.

Nozick, R. (1974). *Anarchy, State, and Utopia*. New York, Basic Books.

Nozick, R. (1989). 'Happiness', in his *The Examined Life: Philosophical Meditations*. New York: Touchstone. 99–117.

Ranalli, C. (2021). 'The Special Value of Experience', *Oxford Studies in the Philosophy of Mind* 1: 130–167.

---

[26] I would like to thank audiences at the University of Hamburg and at Rice University, Houston, for their very helpful feedback on earlier versions of the material presented here. I am especially grateful to Uriah Kriegel, the editor of this series, for encouraging me to think about the topic of this chapter in the first instance, for his great patience in waiting for my work on it to be completed, and for some very helpful comments on its penultimate version.

8
Imagination, Fiction, and Perspectival Displacement

Justin D'Ambrosio and Daniel Stoljar

1. The Puzzle of Perspectival Displacement

The verb 'imagine', like a number of other cognitive and perceptual verbs, admits of perspectival modification. Consider the following sentences:

(1) Zeno imagines the battlefield from above.[1]
(2) Alex imagines the battlefield from a distant point of view.
(3) Sarah imagines the situation in Ukraine from the point of view of a Russian.

In (1), the perspectival modifier is 'from above'; it apparently gives us information about the perspective or point of view from which Zeno imagines a battlefield. In (2), the relevant modifier is 'from a distant point of view', which tells us that the battlefield is being imagined from a perspective or point of view distant from it. In (3), the perspectival modifier is 'from the point of view of a Russian', although in this case the literal connotations of the notion of a 'point of view'—a point in space from which something is viewed—have been dispensed with. What (3) reports, intuitively, is that Sarah is representing the desires, preferences, beliefs, and emotions of a Russian and somehow imagining the situation in Ukraine in their light.

When combined with the verb 'imagine', however, perspectival modification is puzzling. Perspectives are perspectives *of* someone; they do not float

---

[1] In order to maintain uniformity among our examples, we will use the simple present throughout. If readers find the simple present awkward in the case of 'imagine', we invite them to substitute either the progressive—'is imagining'—or the past perfect: 'imagined'. Nothing in our discussion will turn on the tense or aspect of the embedding verb.

free. There is always someone to whom a perspective belongs. Yet on the face of it, the perspectives specified by the modifiers in (1)–(3) need not belong to anyone at all. In (1) for example, there need not be anyone, either real or imagined, who is above the battlefield and who takes a perspective on it. And in (3) while Sarah may imagine the situation in Ukraine from the point of view of a Russian, there need not be a Russian, and certainly no particular Russian, whose perspective this is.

We may bring out the issue by contrasting 'imagine' with another verb that admits of perspectival modification, namely, 'see'. Consider (4) and (5):

(4)   Zeno sees the battlefield from above.
(5)   Alex sees the battlefield from a distant point of view.

In (4), 'from above' tells us that the perspective or point of view from which the battlefield is seen is one above it, and entails that the point of view is Zeno's—Zeno is above the battlefield. Likewise, (5) tells us that the perspective from which the battlefield is seen is one that is distant from it, and entails that the perspective is Alex's. It follows from (5) that Alex is distant from the battlefield.

In the linguistics literature, the technical term for this phenomenon is *argument orientation*.[2] Modifiers such as 'from above' are oriented towards certain of the verb's arguments in that they generate entailments about them: the presence of 'from above' makes (4) entail that Alex is above the battlefield, while the presence of 'from a distant point of view' makes (5) entail that Alex is distant from the battlefield. In particular, the modifiers in (4) and (5) have what is called 'subject-object' orientation: they entail that a certain relation holds between the subject and the object of the verb.[3]

But in the case of 'imagine', there are no such entailments. In (1), Zeno may imagine the battlefield from above while he is sitting quietly in his study at home in Western Massachusetts. In that case, Zeno is not above the battlefield, and so the perspective specified is not his. Concerning (2), Alex may be in the midst of the battle, fighting on the front line, and yet imagine the battlefield from a distance, wishing he were far away. Alex need not be distant from the battlefield, and so again, the modifier is not oriented towards him. Finally, while (3) does not contrast with 'see' in the same way as (1) and (2), (3) again tells us that Sarah imagines the Ukraine situation

---

[2] See Keenan and Faltz (1985), Nam (1995), and Kracht (2002) for discussion.
[3] See Nam (1995), among others.

from a point of view that she need not occupy: the point of view of a Russian. Sarah herself may have no Russian connections at all.

Let us call this the phenomenon of *perspectival displacement*. In perspectival displacement, a perspectival modifier specifies a perspective that appears to be altogether unowned or unoccupied, because it is missing an argument toward which it is oriented. This phenomenon gives rise to what we will call the *puzzle of perspectival displacement*: while a perspective is always someone's perspective—one of the sentence's arguments must be the bearer of the perspective—in many reports of imagination, there appears to be no one to whom the imaginative perspective belongs, since there is no appropriate argument in the sentence to which the modifier applies. In cases of perspectival displacement, the subject needed to anchor the perspective is ghostly.

A satisfactory understanding of perspectival modification, and so of sentences (1)–(3) above, requires a solution to the puzzle of perspectival displacement. Without such a solution, we will not understand why those sentences mean what they do, or what exactly is required for their truth. Our goal in this chapter is to set out and defend such a solution. The key element of our proposal draws on the idea that reports of imagining conceal questions, and that such concealed questions have an extra argument place for (what we will call) an *experiencer*. We will begin (section 2) with some remarks about the generality of the puzzle before criticizing two solutions to it that may be gleaned from the existing literature (sections 3 and 4). We will then present our own solution to the puzzle and distinguish it from rivals (sections 5–7). We will end (sections 8–9) by drawing out two consequences of our proposal for various issues that have emerged in recent philosophy of imagination.

2. Language and Mind

We have introduced the puzzle as a problem about language, and we will often talk that way in what follows, but the issue we are concerned with generalizes from language to mind. It cannot, therefore, be dismissed as merely a 'semantic puzzle', unrelated to the facts about imagination philosophers are properly interested in.

To see the mistake in this attitude, forget for the moment about the English sentences (1)–(3) and sentences like them, and think instead about various states of imagining, states that exist and have a nature independently of how anybody talks about them. In philosophy of mind, there is a view about these states that is common enough in various guises to be called 'the standard view'; see, e.g., Yablo (1993). On this view, when you imagine something, you are in a state that represents a possible situation in which various things are true. Hence, when Zeno imagines a battlefield, he represents a possible situation. One thing that is true in this situation is that there is a battlefield. Other things that are true will include various details or specifications of the battlefield he is imagining.

No proponent of the standard view can reasonably deny that there is a difference between imagining the battlefield from above and imagining the battlefield but not from above, for example, from the perspective of the poor sod on the front line. If you do the latter, you might well find yourself flinching or ducking. If you do the former, by contrast, you would do none of these things. What then is the difference? The standard view seems unable to answer this question. On that view, the difference must be located either in the content of the imagining—that is, in what is true in the imagined situation—or in the way the subject represents that situation. But on the face of it neither of these options is right. In particular, in the situation Zeno imagines, there need not be anyone above the battlefield, nor is Zeno himself above it. As we noted above, Zeno may be safely far away in his study. Nor does it seem that there are any other good candidates for being the bearer of the perspectives that differentiate these episodes.

Thus the problem of perspectival displacement is both a problem concerning the semantics of 'imagine' and its attendant modifiers, as well as one concerning the nature of imagination and imaginative perspective. This tells us that both our semantic and our metaphysical understanding of imagination are far from complete. It also provides an important constraint on any solution, namely, that such a solution must address the problem in both linguistic and nonlinguistic form.

3. Vendler and Peacocke

We have introduced the puzzle of perspectival displacement, and noted that it generalizes from language to mind. How then to solve it? Before turning to our proposal, let us review two lines of thought already present in the literature and explain why they are implausible.

The first of these is due to Zeno Vendler and Christopher Peacocke (see Vendler 1979, 1982 and Peacocke 1985; see also Martin 2002). Considered as a thesis in philosophy of language, the Vendler-Peacocke view (as we will call it) is that, (1) is elliptical for (6), (2) for (7), and (3) for (8):

(6) Zeno imagines seeing the battlefield from above.

(7) Alex imagines seeing the battlefield from a distant point of view.

(8) Sarah imagines seeing the Ukraine situation from the point of view of a Russian.[4]

This ellipsis hypothesis provides us with at least two candidates for being the thing above the battlefield: the event of seeing and the agent who sees. Whichever of these we choose, the proposal solves our puzzle, construed either as a puzzle about language or about mind. Instead of modifying 'imagine', the perspectival modifiers in (6)–(8) modify 'see', and tell us about some relationship between the subject of the event of seeing—the person who sees—and what they see. Thus, the Vendler-Peacocke view solves our puzzle by positing that the complements of (1)–(3) elide a perceptual verb. When the elided verb is made apparent, as in (6)–(8), it provides an argument towards which the perspectival modifier is oriented, and so provides a bearer for the perspective.

On the Vendler-Peacocke view, whose perspective do perspectival modifiers specify? Who, in (6)–(8), is the subject of the seeing? The most natural response in the case of (6) is to treat the subject of the seeing as Zeno himself. From a syntactic point of view, a sentence like (6) would normally be treated as containing an unarticulated constituent, PRO, which acts as sort of pronoun. Standardly, PRO is interpreted as co-referring with the subject of the main clause.[5] What this means is that (6) should be read as saying something like this: Zeno imagines he himself seeing the battlefield from above. Hence, since (6) simply spells out the material allegedly elliptical in (1), (1) likewise means this. The point applies, *mutatis mutandis*, to (2) and (7), and to (3) and (8).

But the problem is that this gets (1)–(3) wrong. On the Vendler-Peacocke view, when (1) is true, and Zeno imagines the battlefield from above, he is imagining he himself seeing the battlefield; Zeno himself, in other words, is present in the situation he is imagining. But as we have seen, (1) can be true without anything like this being the case. Suppose, for definiteness, that Zeno is imagining a battlefield from the distant past, the battle of Thermopylae,

---

[4] Similarly to the case of (3), in the complement of (8), 'see' is used in a nonvisual sense. But nothing about this changes the basic Vendler-Peacocke proposal, which is that there is some verb elided in the complements of (1)–(3).

[5] For discussion of PRO and its motivations, see Chomsky (1981); Carnie (2006); and Moltmann (2006).

say. Does it follow that he is imagining a situation in which he himself is above the battlefield at Thermopylae, looking down on it, or somehow floating above it? Surely not; but that would have to be so on the Vendler-Peacocke view.

Nor does this problem go away if we transpose the Vendler-Peacocke view from language to mind. Considered as a proposal in philosophy of mind, their view is that when Zeno imagines the battlefield from above, he represents a situation in which he, Zeno, sees the battlefield from above. But again this need not be the case. Zeno can imagine the battlefield from above without imagining a situation in which he is above the battlefield.

The problem here is no news to Vendler or Peacocke; at any rate, it is no news to Peacocke. On the contrary, Peacocke (1985) explicitly notes this consequence of the view, and notes it is connected to a classical problem in philosophy, namely, the problem of whether it is possible to imagine a tree unseen. As Peacocke points out, Berkeley denies that this is possible in the course of defending his distinctive idealist world-view, on which 'esse est percipi', to be is to be perceived. Peacocke has no brief for idealism in general, but he defends Berkeley's idea that it is impossible to imagine a tree unseen, on the ground that imagining a tree is imagining seeing a tree, in which case you cannot imagine a tree unseen.

Peacocke is right that his view has this Berkeleyan consequence, as we will call it, but that does not remove its underlying implausibility. As against Berkeley, surely you *can* imagine a tree unseen. Take the tree outside your window, and imagine that life on earth had evolved differently so that, while plants evolved, animals never did. In such a situation, that tree might well have existed unseen by anyone. Or suppose a neutron blast happens, wiping out all life on earth but with minimal damage to buildings. One can still imagine the Sydney Opera House in such a case, in the same place as it always was, on the harbour foreshore, but with nobody around it. That is to imagine it unseen.

Peacocke's embrace of this consequence does not render it plausible, but there is a different reply that might be made to the objection that the Vendler-Peacocke view is mistaken in representing (1) as equivalent to (6). We have so far interpreted the view as entailing that (6) requires that Zeno himself is doing the seeing, on the ground that the unarticulated constituent, PRO, is controlled by, or co-refers with, the subject of the main clause. However, there is a different interpretation of PRO that is available here, sometimes called the 'generic interpretation'. On a generic interpretation of PRO, (3) is equivalent to something like this: Zeno is imagining someone seeing the battlefield from above. This seems an improvement since we are no longer maintaining that Zeno must imagine himself above the battlefield, but rather only some arbitrary person who serves as the subject of the event of seeing. However, while this is better, the underlying problem still remains. One can imagine the battlefield from above not only without imagining Zeno seeing the battlefield, but without imagining any episode of seeing at all. One can imagine the battlefield from above completely unseen. If so, the generic interpretation of PRO provides no support to the Vendler-Peacocke view.[6]

4. Camp

The Vendler-Peacocke view is elegant, but it represents a sentence like (1) as having a Berkeleyan consequence that it does not have. A different possible solution to the puzzle of perspectival displacement may be extracted from a recent important paper by Elizabeth Camp (2017). Camp does not approach the issues quite as we have done, but as we will understand her, her view is that the puzzle may be solved not by looking at what you imagine, but at how. Vendler-Peacocke ask us to concentrate on the contents of imagination, Camp asks us to concentrate on the mode.

Let us focus again on what the difference is between imagining the battlefield from above, and imagining it but not from above. On Camp's view, the difference here is not in the imagined situation—in both cases you imagine a situation in which the same things are true. The difference is rather in *how* you imagine or represent the situation. In particular, to imagine the battlefield from above is to imagine the battlefield and to be disposed to focus on certain aspects of the scene or to elaborate what is imagined in

---

[6] In the text, we are presuming that the sentence 'Zeno is imagining seeing the battlefield from above' reports a state in which what is being imagined—the content of the imagining—is *seeing the battlefield from above*. But Uriah Kriegel points out to us that, in principle, one might understand the attitude as a particular mode of sensory imagining: 'imagining-seeing'. On that view, what is imagined-seen is the battlefield from above. We won't attempt to address this in detail here beyond making the following two points. First, this is not the view that Vendler and Peacocke have in mind. On the contrary, they think that the content clause of (6) involves a gerund that denotes an event of seeing. Second, as a proposal about the semantics of reports of imagining, it is implausible, for it does not generalize to other cases. For example, in 'John is imagining dancing Swan Lake with Barysnikov', what John is imagining is surely an event of dancing, modified by the prepositional phrase 'with Baryshnikov'. There is no special kind of imagining—'imagining-dancing'—that John bears to the denotation of 'Swan Lake with Baryshnikov', whatever that would be.

certain ways. This is what Camp calls 'characterization'. On her view, perspectives are dispositions to characterize what you imagine in certain ways. To imagine the battlefield from above is, roughly, to be concerned with some of its features rather than others—less with the swords and blood, for instance, and more with the distribution of soldiers, the areas of most intense combat, and perhaps the strategic positions of the armies.

Camp's view is not a semantic proposal, but it does provide a solution to the puzzle of perspectival displacement construed as an issue in the philosophy of mind. Points of view or perspectives are, on her view, psychological dispositions that go along with various states of imagining. The difference between one point of view and another is the difference between these dispositions. When Zeno imagines the battlefield from above, he imagines it in a particular way—namely, from above—which is understood as analogous to imagining the battlefield intently or feverishly. Thus there is a sense in which the perspective at issue here is Zeno's, but his having this perspective is not something that requires him to be above the battlefield.

If we were to transpose Camp's proposal from mind to language, it would be as follows. In a sentence like (1), the perspectival modifier 'from above' is not oriented towards any of the arguments of 'imagine'. Unlike when x sees y from above, where x must be above y, Camp's view, roughly, is that for Zeno to imagine the battlefield from above is for him to imagine-from-above the battlefield. This does not entail that any argument of the verb 'imagine' must be above any other—it modifies the verb in a different way entirely. Thus Camp's proposal solves the problem by altogether eliminating the need for an argument position occupied by something that is above the battlefield.

One thing that is right in Camp's proposal is that, when you imagine the battlefield from above, you do indeed have a disposition, or a set of dispositions, that you would not have if you imagined the battlefield from some other perspective. But there are nevertheless several major weaknesses in her view.

The first weakness is that it is mysterious on Camp's view why the particular dispositions constitutive of perspectives go together with the cases of imagining that they do. To bring out the problem, contrast her view with that of Vendler and Peacocke. They can agree with Camp that when you imagine the battlefield from above you will have various dispositions, including the disposition to focus on certain properties of the battlefield rather than others. But the Vendler-Peacocke view has an account of why you have these dispositions, namely, because of what you imagine. You imagine seeing the battlefield from above, and that is why you focus on the areas of heaviest fighting and the strategic positions of the armies, rather than the gorier aspects of the melee. Likewise, you imagine seeing the battlefield from the perspective of someone in it, and that is why you focus on the lance-wielding horseman approaching, and so flinch and duck.

The second weakness in Camp's view is that having a disposition to characterize imagined contents does not seem to be sufficient for adopting a perspective on what is imagined. One can be disposed to characterize what is imagined in a variety of ways, but these dispositions are not always rightly considered perspectives. Suppose Zeno is disposed to characterize some aspects of the battlefield as more important than others—suppose, for instance, that he is disposed to focus on or treat as important the aspects of the battlefield most relevant for the purposes of philosophical argumentation. This is a disposition to characterize, but it is not yet a perspective. What is needed is something further that connects characterization with what is imagined—mere dispositions to characterize are not themselves perspectives.

A third weakness emerges when we interpret Camp's proposal (as she admittedly does not) as one in the philosophy of language. The idea that 'from above', in (1), does not specify a relation between any of the verb's arguments is highly implausible as a general proposal about the semantics of perspectival modifiers. When one sees something from above, it follows that one is above that thing. But Camp's view entails that 'from above', when used to specify an imaginative perspective, has an altogether different and unrelated function. Thus, while Camp's proposal has some attractive features, there are reasons to seek an alternative.

5. Three Observations

Neither the Vendler-Peacocke view nor the Camp view provides a plausible solution to the puzzle of perspectival displacement. The time has come to formulate our own positive view. To do so, we may start with three observations about 'imagine'.

Observation #1 is that 'imagine' can take *wh*-complements. It is well known that a distinction may be drawn between knowing-that and knowing-how, though the precise contours of the distinction remain a matter of dispute.[7] Much less well known is that a parallel distinction may be drawn in the case of imagination. You may imagine that your car keys are on the roof, for example, and also how to get them down. Indeed, not only may you imagine how to such and such, almost the whole gamut of 'imagination-*wh*' is in principle available: you may imagine where you last saw your keys, who put them on the roof, what they will be like when you get them back, and so on. In what follows we will be concerned with one sort of construction in particular, namely, 'imagining what something is like'. Just as one can imagine a battlefield, one can imagine what the battlefield is like, and this is a case of imagining-*wh*.

In general, *wh*-clauses have two readings, an interrogative reading and a free relative reading—and when embedded under 'imagine', *wh*-clauses can receive either interpretation. In the case of the interrogative reading, the semantic value of the clause is a set of propositions each of which is an answer to the question expressed by the corresponding interrogative. So, for example, on its interrogative reading, 'what the battlefield is like' has as its semantic value a set of propositions each of which is an answer to the question 'what is the battlefield like?' Given the close semantic connection—if not outright equivalence—between the interrogative clauses 'what it is like' and 'how it is', we may equally say that the semantic value of the *wh*-clause is a set of propositions each of which is expressed by a sentence of the form 'the battlefield is way W'. Here we will focus on the interrogative reading of such embedded clauses.

Observing that 'imagine' embeds interrogatives of the form 'what X is like' and that such interrogatives denote sets of propositions is not yet to provide a full semantics for such constructions. In order to do that, we need to answer a range of further questions. For instance, are the propositions that answer the questions true answers? Or should we allow the set to include both true and false answers? In order to imagine what the battlefield is like, must Zeno imagine only some way that it is? Or need he imagine all of the ways that the battlefield is? How is the semantics of interrogatives embedded under 'imagine' derived compositionally? Since we have discussed these questions elsewhere, we will set these points aside.[8] The main thing for our purposes is that, when 'imagine' takes a 'what X is like' complement, the resulting ascription is true if and only if the subject of the

---

[7] For discussion of this distinction, see Stanley and Williamson (2001) and Stanley (2011).
[8] See D'Ambrosio and Stoljar (2021) for extended discussion of the semantics of interrogatives embedded under 'imagine'.

ascription stands in a relation to one or more of the propositions in the answer set denoted by the interrogative. 'Imagine' is, to use terminology common in the literature on the semantics of embedded questions, a *responsive* embedding verb.[9]

Observation #2 is that 'imagining what X is like' has more structure than is apparent at first, and that is because the *wh*-clause here has more structure than is apparent at first. We may ask, for example, not only 'what is getting home late like?' and 'what is Sally's getting home late like?' but also 'what is Sally's getting home late like to Mary?' (Suppose for example Mary is Sally's mother sitting up concerned about Sally's getting home late.) Thus, at least in cases where interrogatives concern what certain events are like, we must keep separate both the agent of the event with which we are concerned, and the subject to whom that event is like something.[10]

This entails that in constructions that embed 'what it's like' interrogatives, there will sometimes be three subjects to keep track of that are in principle distinct. In cases where a subject imagines what a particular event is like, such as 'Suzy imagined what Sally's getting home late was like', there is, first, the subject doing the imagining, namely, Suzy; second, the agent of the imagined event—in this case, Sally; and third, the person to whom Sally's getting home late was like something—in this case, Sally's mother Mary. We can call this last subject the *experiencer*, for it is this person to whom the event or object is like something.[11]

Observation #3 is that imagining what things are like is more widespread than you might think. Some nominals, when they appear as the complements of certain verbs, conceal questions. 'Sarah knows the capital of Vermont', for example, is naturally interpreted as 'Sarah knows what the capital of Vermont is', and '*The Guardian* exposed the corrupt member of cabinet' is naturally interpreted as '*The Guardian* exposed who the corrupt member of cabinet is'.[12] Something similar is true in the case of 'imagine', though here the question at issue is very often a 'what it is like' question, rather than a 'what it is' or 'who it is' question. For example, 'Zeno imagined the battlefield' is naturally understood as 'Zeno imagined what the battlefield

---

[9] For this terminology, see Lahiri (2002) and George (2011).
[10] For discussion of this point, see Stoljar (2016) and references therein.
[11] For an example of the use of the experiencer role in semantic theorizing, see Gisborne (2010).
[12] The topic of concealed questions is a large one in semantics. For two recent discussions, see Nathan (2006) and Frana (2017).

is like'. Likewise, 'Sarah imagined the situation in Ukraine' is naturally heard as 'Sarah imagined what the situation in Ukraine is like'.

This observation entails that many reports in which 'imagine' is complemented by a nominal expression are in fact semantically equivalent to constructions involving a 'what it's like' interrogative. This equivalence can be stated schematically as the equivalence between (9) and (10):

(9)   Zeno imagines NP.

(10) Zeno imagines what NP is like.

Given our semantic assumptions above about the nature of embedded 'what it's like' interrogatives, (10) is true just in case Zeno imagines that P, for some P among the answers to the question 'what is NP like?' Thus there is a general equivalence between what we is sometimes called 'objectual' imagining and propositional imagining. Imagining NP is always, in fact, to imagine that something is the case.

6. Our Proposal

In the light of these observations, our proposal about perspectival modification may be stated very simply. Considered as a thesis in philosophy of language, our view is that (1) is semantically equivalent to (11), (2) is equivalent to (12), and (3) to (13):

(11) Zeno imagines what the battlefield is like to someone above it.

(12) Alex imagines what the battlefield is like to someone distant from it.

(13) Sarah imagines what the situation in Ukraine is like to someone with a Russian point of view.

Like the Vendler-Peacocke approach, on this view, perspectival modifiers modify the clause that specifies the content of an event of imagining—such modifiers change what is imagined. To imagine the battlefield from above, as opposed to from any other perspective, is to be the agent of an event of imagining with a certain propositional content. And like the Vendler-Peacocke view, our proposal provides an argument towards which the perspectival modifier 'from above' is oriented: 'someone'. This argument is analogous to Mary in our case above—it is the experiencer. Just as Sally's getting home late is like something for Mary, the battlefield is like something to someone above it.

What is distinctive about our proposal is that in the case of (11), for example, 'someone' need not pick out a specific, existent person. Just as you can seek someone to lead your team to a championship without there being a particular existent person whom you seek, so you can imagine what the battlefield is like to someone without there being some particular existent person to whom you imagine it being that way. Hence the argument place associated with the experiencer, towards which perspectival modifiers are oriented, can be occupied by NPs that are nonspecific and existence-neutral. This is why perspectives seem ghostly: they are ghostly in exactly the same way that the objects of intentional states such as searches and desires are ghostly. I might seek or want a puppy, but not a particular one. Analogously, I might imagine what the situation in Ukraine is like to a Russian, but without there being a Russian to whom I imagine it being that way.

A final point concerns the default reading of (1). The most natural understanding of (1) is that Zeno is *visualizing* the battlefield; that is, he is imagining what it looks like, rather than what it sounds or smells like. On our proposal, however, (1) tells us only that he is imagining what it *is* like, without specifying the sensory mode in which he imagines it. How, then, on this view, is this default reading generated? Our proposal is that this has nothing to do with the semantics of sentences like (1), or the equivalent (11). Rather, there is a default pragmatic connection between imagining what an object is like and imagining what it looks like.

Such default pragmatic connections are both extremely common and well understood in pragmatics. In fact, they form one component of Horn's (1986) 'division of pragmatic labour'. According to the division of pragmatic labour, when a speaker's utterance contains a general term that can be specified in various ways, the speaker is standardly understood as conveying the stereotypical strengthened reading. For instance, suppose I utter:

(14) I am drinking a glass of milk.

Here, 'milk' admits of many different specifications: I might be drinking, for instance, cow's milk or goat's milk. But given the relative prevalence of cow's milk, and the relative paucity of goat's milk, the division of pragmatic labour tells us that the general, 'unmarked' term will come to convey the stereotypical, 'unmarked' meaning. So when I utter (14), I will implicate that I am drinking a glass of cow's milk. In order to convey that I was drinking goat's milk, when cow's milk is overwhelmingly prevalent, I would need to say something more specific. I would have to say that I am drinking a glass of goat's milk.[13] But in a context in which goat's milk was overwhelmingly prevalent, the opposite would hold.

Much the same is true, we maintain, for imagining what an object is like. When you tell me that you are imagining what the battlefield is like, the default or stereotypical interpretation, given the background frequencies of use, is that you are visualizing the battlefield—you are imagining what it *looks* like. By contrast, to convey that you are imagining what the battlefield *smells* like, you would need to say so. The general construction 'imagining what the battlefield is like' conveys, pragmatically, the stereotypical visual interpretation. But in other cases, the stereotypical interpretation may be different. Suppose that I imagine winning the 100 metres (m) at the Olympics. In this case, it is very natural to understand me as imagining not what winning the 100 m at the Olympics looks like, but rather what it feels like.

7. Comparisons

The proposal we have just set out has advantages over both the Vendler-Peacocke view and Camp's view. Unlike Vendler-Peacocke, our proposal has no Berkeleyan consequence. When Zeno imagines what the battlefield is like to someone above it, it does not follow that there is someone above the battlefield, nor does it follow that he imagines someone seeing the battlefield. This is because our view makes available a distinction between there being a particular person to whom the battlefield is like something, and the battlefield being like something to someone, but no one in particular. Again, the perspectival argument place can be occupied by noun phrases that are nonspecific and not existence-entailing.

Unlike Camp's view, on our proposal, to imagine from a particular perspective is to be the agent of an event of imagining with a particular propositional content, and it is this content that explains why we have the dispositions that standardly accompany events of imagining. If I imagine the battlefield from the perspective of someone on the front line, the reason that I am inclined to flinch is that I am imagining what the battlefield is like to him: horses whinnying in terror, lanced riders charging, infantrymen approaching with swords, etc. Such imagining has all of the power one

---

[13] For extensive discussion of Horn's division of pragmatic labour, see Franke (2013).

could possibly need to generate dispositions to attend to certain features and have certain emotional or affective responses.

Not only does our view avoid the problems we presented for Camp's view, it also allows us to avoid Camp's own objections to the propositional-attitude view of imagining of which ours is a version. According to Camp (2017: 77–9), merely representing how things are cannot account for the perspectives that we take on the worlds we imagine. How could propositions that simply state how things are with some object incorporate a perspectival element? Our answer is that Camp underestimates the complexity of the propositions that are true in the imagined situation and so serve as the contents of our imaginings. The propositions that serve as the contents of states of perspectival imagining, on our view, are propositions concerning what things are like *to* people of particular kinds. To imagine the battlefield from above is to imagine that the battlefield is a particular way to someone above it. This is a proposition like any other, but it incorporates perspectival information by making mention of a person to whom the battlefield is or looks a certain way.

Finally, our proposal is also an improvement on a different approach to perspectival displacement that we have not encountered in print but which has been suggested to us by David Chalmers. On this proposal, a sentence like (1) is equivalent to:

(15)   Zeno imagines the battlefield as seen from above.

This proposal faces several problems which ours does not. First, it is unclear why (1) should be interpreted as containing a covert 'as'-phrase, and so unclear why (1) should be equivalent to (15). There is no syntactic evidence for the presence of such a phrase, and the 'as'-phrase is merely posited to solve the semantic puzzle. Thus the proposal appears unmotivated. Our own proposal, by contrast, is that (1) is equivalent to (11), a claim which is motivated by the literature on concealed questions, and follows from the general idea that 'imagine NP' is equivalent to 'imagine what NP is like'.

Second, as it stands, the proposal is crucially underspecified. To defend it properly requires a theory of 'as'-phrases. Depending on which theory is adopted, however, the proposal may face the same objections that doomed the Vendler-Peacocke view. In (15) the 'as'-phrase employs the passivization of the perceptual verb 'see'. But the verb 'see', in all other cases, requires a specific, existent person as a subject. If this is required here as well, the proposal will entail that there is a specific, existent subject in the world imagined who sees the battlefield—i.e. it will have the Berkeleyan consequence. In order to avoid this consequence, the proponent of this view needs an account of 'as'-phrases that does not entail the existence or particularity of the subject doing the seeing. But if (15) is understood in this way, and the qualifier is taken to mean something like 'as seen by someone above it', with 'someone' construed nonspecifically, then the proposal will be all but indistinguishable from our own.[14]

Third, (15) cannot be equivalent to (1) since it has entailments that (1) does not have. (1) requires Zeno to imagine the battlefield from above. But, as noted before, he may do this by imagining how it looks, smells, or sounds; his imagining need not be visual. By contrast, (15) requires Zeno's imagining to be visual, and rules out imagining in other sense modalities. Thus the proposal cannot be right as it stands. Our own proposal does not have this consequence, since while the 'what it is like' phrase is typically interpreted in visual terms, it need not be: the connection between imagining what the battlefield is like and imagining what the battlefield looks like is pragmatic rather than semantic.

8. Application 1: Fiction

In this chapter we have offered and explored a solution to the puzzle of perspectival displacement. The picture of imaginative perspective that emerges from our solution is one on which, whenever you imagine something from a perspective, you imagine what that thing is like to someone with that perspective. As we have seen, this does not require you to imagine that there is a person from whose perspective the object is imagined, or to whom it is like something—one can imagine things completely unperceived. This approach solves the puzzle of perspectival displacement by providing an argument towards which perspectival modifiers are oriented. But because of the distinctive nature of this argument—it is nonspecific and existence-neutral—our proposal does not have the Berkeleyan consequence of the Vendler-Peacocke view. At the same time, unlike the Camp view, it provides an explanation of the dispositions and affective responses that are associated with episodes of perspectival imagining.

---

[14] Existing accounts of 'as'-phrases in the literature include Landman (1989b, 1989a); Szabó (2003); and Loets (2021); among many others. To our knowledge none of these views vindicate, or even raise the possibility that the subject of 'see' in (14) is an intensional position.

We will close the chapter by noting two ways in which our view advances discussions in contemporary philosophy of imagination. First, our proposal satisfies three desiderata laid out by Camp on an adequate account of perspective in fiction. Second, our account provides a novel solution to a persistent puzzle discussed by Peter Langland-Hassan concerning how imagination interacts with desire.

In her (2017), Camp sets out three conditions of adequacy on any theory of perspectival engagement with fiction. She phrases the first as follows:

> [A] reader's emotional and interpretive responses are not simply a function of the focal character's mental state: they also depend upon his beliefs about the fictional world as a whole, including facts of which that character is ignorant. Thus, I fear for the heroine fixing a late-night cup of hot chocolate because I know, as she doesn't, that a burglar is hidden in the pantry. (Camp 2017: 78)

Our proposal concerning perspective straightforwardly accommodates this feature. On our view, one can imagine the heroine making hot chocolate not only from her perspective, but from the perspective of someone who knows that the heroine is in danger. Such perspectival imagining, on our view, will be to imagine what the heroine's making a late-night cup of hot chocolate is like to someone who knows that there is danger afoot. In turn, this will be for the imagining subject to imagine that there is some way it is to someone who knows that danger is afoot. Thus, by giving us the resources to target propositions that specify what the heroine making a late-night cup of cocoa is like to people other than the heroine herself, our view captures the way in which our reactions to fiction are sensitive to things that we or others may know that the characters in the fiction may not.

Camp states her second desideratum as follows:

> [I]n reading fiction I don't only locate myself imaginatively inside each successive scene. In addition, I often also adopt an acentral and external perspective on the fictional world as a whole. As a result, even as I rehearse a scene through the eyes of a specific character, my responses are modulated by how sympathetically the author presents that character—that is, by the degree to which the author 'deputizes' them as someone whose perspective is to be adopted. (Camp 2017: 78)

Again, our account is well placed to accommodate this form of perspective-taking. On our view, one can imagine not only what the objects and events of a work of fiction are like to characters in the fiction, but also what they are like to someone who knows everything about the fictional world, and who is unsympathetic to the characters. This is yet another form of imaginative perspective-taking licensed by our view.

Camp states her third desideratum as follows:

> Finally, and most importantly, an adequate account of perspectives must explain how a perspective can apply to multiple situations or even multiple worlds. Many theorists... have argued that we read fiction to acquaint ourselves with new perspectives on the real world... To make sense of these claims, we need to analyze perspectives in a way that allows them to be extracted from particular scenes. (Camp 2017: 78)

Here again, our account is well placed to meet Camp's challenge. One can imagine not only a battlefield from above, but the ocean from above, a desk from above, or the street-plan of Chicago from above. The perspective *from above* can be extracted from a particular instance of imagining, and can instead apply to a whole range of objects and situations. Likewise, we need not only imagine the situation in Ukraine from the perspective of a Russian. We might also imagine what post-Soviet policing is like to a Russian, what the renewal of the Orthodox church is like for a Russian, or what the vestiges of Soviet propaganda are like for a Russian. On our view, the Russian perspective is extractable, and the modifier 'from the perspective of a Russian' makes a particular compositional contribution to the content-specifying clause of a report of imagining.

Beyond just meeting these three desiderata, our proposal provides an attractive general account of how we engage with fiction, and do so from different perspectives. Fiction is naturally understood as a collection of instructions to imagine. Authors describe various objects and events, and implicitly instruct those who engage with them to imagine these objects and events. Tolstoy describes Anna and Vronsky, the events of their courtship, and the climactic event in which Anna throws herself on the tracks. Given our second observation above, to imagine these objects and events—Anna, Vronsky, and the events in which they are involved—is to imagine what these things are like. Readers of *Anna Karenina* are instructed to imagine what Anna is like, what her meeting Vronsky is like, and what her throwing herself on the tracks is like.

But Tolstoy does not just instruct us to imagine what these people and events are like. He also asks us to undertake certain perspectives on them. He might, for instance, ask us to imagine Anna throwing herself on the tracks from the perspective of someone standing on the platform, or from the perspective of Karenin, her husband. On our view, this amounts to asking the reader to imagine what Anna throwing herself on the tracks is like to a person standing on the platform or to Karenin. This kind of instruction accounts in a simple and intuitive way for fiction's emotional and affective consequences. If we imagine what Anna throwing herself on the tracks is like to someone on the platform, we might naturally imagine what it looks like and feels like to that person, and so imagine the horror, sadness, or disgust that such a person would feel. Thus, viewing fiction as primarily a set of instructions to imagine what various things are like to some person or other yields an attractive overall view of what authors are doing in creating fiction.

9. Application 2: Desire

The second and final application of our proposal is to a persistent puzzle concerning how desire interacts with imagination. The following example due to Peter Langland-Hassan serves to make the problem vivid:

> In the HBO mini-series *The Wire*, Wallace is a sixteen-year-old caregiver to his younger siblings and cousins, and occasional drug dealer. At the end of Season One, he is murdered by his peers on the off chance that he'll become a police informant. I felt anxiety and distress as the scene unfolded, having grown attached to Wallace.
> (Langland-Hassan 2020: 212)

The puzzle here is the following: why do you, as a viewer, feel distress or anxiety at Wallace's death? Langland-Hassan discusses three potential answers to this question. The first is what he calls the Simple View: you feel anxiety because (a) you imagine that Wallace will die, and (b) you want him not to die. This view is not at all plausible. Wallace doesn't exist, he is a fictional character; and you know these things perfectly well. So it is not rational for you to want him not to die.

The second view is what Langland-Hassan call the Change of Content view. On this view, you feel anxiety about Wallace because (a) you imagine that he will die and (b) you want him not to die *in the fiction*. This also seems an inadequate account of why you feel anxiety. Is the reason you feel anxiety that you want the fiction to be different than it in fact is? If Wallace didn't die, the fiction wouldn't have the power that it does; without confronting deaths of sympathetic characters, *The Wire* would be far less emotionally engaging, and would hardly be able to teach us the lessons it aims to teach. Thus, the Change of Content view is inadequate.

The third view is that you feel anxiety concerning Wallace's fate because you (a) imagine that he will die and (b) you *I*-want him not to die, where to *I*-want Wallace not to die is to be in a state that is satisfied if he does not die in the fiction, but is distinct from wanting him not to die in the fiction. The problem with this view is that it's hard to see what the difference between it and the previous view is supposed to be. If *I*-desiring is a state that is satisfied just in case Wallace does not die in the fiction, it seems to be equivalent to wanting him not to die in the fiction. But as we saw, that is not what you want.

Unlike any of these three views, our view provides an immediate and intuitive answer to the question of why you feel anxiety about Wallace's death. On our view, you don't just imagine that Wallace dies. Rather, you imagine what his dying is like to someone who cares about him deeply and so wants him not to die. In doing so, it is natural to imagine what Wallace's death feels like to such a person: it would produce incredible anxiety and sadness. But in imagining someone feeling this way, you are apt to feel these emotions yourself, or at least empathize with the person you imagine feeling them, and that is why you feel the way you do.[15]

References

Camp, Elizabeth. 2017. "Perspectives in Imaginative Engagement with Fiction." *Philosophical Perspectives: Philosophy of Mind* 31 (1): 73–102.

Carnie, Andrew. 2006. *Syntax: A Generative Introduction*. Second Edition. Malden, MA: Blackwell Publishers.

Chomsky, Noam. 1981. *Lectures on Government and Binding*. Vol. 9. *Studies in Generative Grammar*. London: Foris Publications.

---

[15] We presented earlier versions of this chapter to the Global Consciousness Conference and the Bochum Language Colloquium; we are very much indebted to the audiences on those occasions for their helpful and encouraging input. We are particularly grateful for comments from David Chalmers, Matt Duncan, Uriah Kriegel, Adriana Renero. Kristina Liefke, and Markus Werning.

D'Ambrosio, Justin, and Daniel Stoljar. 2021. "Vendler's Puzzle About Imagination." *Synthese* 199 (5–6): 12923–44.

Frana, Ilaria. 2017. *Concealed Questions*. Oxford Studies in Theoretical Linguistics. Oxford: Oxford University Press.

Franke, Michael. 2013. "Game Theoretic Pragmatics." *Philosophy Compass* 8 (3): 269–84.

George, B. R. 2011. "Question Embedding and the Semantics of Answers." PhD thesis, University of California, Los Angeles.

Gisborne, Nikolas. 2010. *The Event Structure of Perception*. Oxford: Oxford University Press.

Horn, Laurence. 1986. "Presupposition, Theme and Variations." In *CLS 22 Part 2: Papers from the Parasession on Pragmatics and Grammatical Theory*, edited by Karl-Erik McCullough and Anne M. Farley Peter Farley, 168–92. Chicago: Chicago Linguistics Society.

Keenan, Edward L., and L. M. Faltz. 1985. *Boolean Semantics for Natural Language*. Amsterdam: Springer Netherlands.

Kracht, Marcus. 2002. "On the Semantics of Locatives." *Linguistics and Philosophy* 25 (2): 157–232.

Lahiri, Utpal. 2002. *Questions and Answers in Embedded Contexts*. Oxford: Oxford University Press.

Landman, Fred. 1989a. "Groups 2." *Linguistics and Philosophy* 12: 723–744.

Landman, Fred. 1989b. "Groups I." *Linguistics and Philosophy* 12: 559–605.

Langland-Hassan, Peter. 2020. *Explaining Imagination*. New York: Oxford University Press.

Loets, Annina J. 2021. "Qua Qualification." *Philosopher's Imprint* 27: 1–24.

Martin, M. G. F. 2002. "The Transparency of Experience." *Mind and Language* 17 (4): 376–425.

Moltmann, Friederike. 2006. "Generic One, Arbitrary Pro, and the First Person." *Natural Language Semantics* 14 (3): 257–81.

Nam, Seungho. 1995. "The Semantics of Locative Prepositional Phrases in English." PhD thesis, University of California, Los Angeles.

Nathan, Lance. 2006. "On the Interpretation of Concealed Questions." Dissertation, Massachusetts Institute of Technology, Cambridge, MA.

Peacocke, Christopher. 1985. "Imagination, Experience, and Possibility." In *Essays on Berkeley: A Tercentennial Celebration*, edited by John Foster and Howard Robinson. Oxford: Oxford University Press.

Stanley, Jason. 2011. *Know How*. Oxford: Oxford University Press.

Stanley, Jason, and Timothy Williamson. 2001. "Knowing How." *Journal of Philosophy* 98 (8): 411–44.

Stoljar, Daniel. 2016. "The Semantics of 'What It's Like' and the Nature of Consciousness." *Mind* 125 (500): 1161–98.

Szabó, Zoltán. 2003. "On Qualification." *Philosophical Perspectives: Language and Philosophical Linguistics* 17: 385–414.

Vendler, Zeno. 1979. "Vicarious Experience." *Revue de Métaphysique et de Morale* 84e Année (2): 161–73.

Vendler, Zeno. 1982. "Speaking of Imagination." In *Language, Mind, and Brain*, edited by T. W. Simon and R. J. Scholes. Reprinted as chapter III of *The Matter of Minds*. Oxford: Oxford University Press.

Yablo, Stephen. 1993. "Is Conceivability a Guide to Possibility?" *Philosophy and Phenomenological Research* 53 (1): 1–42.

9
The Dilemma for Attitude Theories of Pleasure

Daniel Pallies and Alexander Dietz

1. Introduction

You open the kitchen cabinet, and you are pleased to see that it contains coffee grounds. You brew yourself a cup of coffee, and you get pleasure from drinking it. What makes it the case that you have these episodes of pleasure? According to the *phenomenological* theory of pleasure, your pleasure is explained by your phenomenology: the way you feel, or "what it is like" to be you. According to the *attitude* theory of pleasure, your pleasure is explained by your having certain pro-attitudes: you *desire*, *like*, or *favor* having coffee grounds, as well as your experience of drinking coffee.[1] These theories can be naturally extended to cover unpleasant experiences, as well: the phenomenological theorist will say that unpleasantness is explained by feelings; the attitude theorist will say that it is explained by our attitudes.

In this chapter, we show that the attitude theory faces a dilemma. The attitude that is relevant to pleasure—the desire, liking, or favoring—is either *necessarily co-instantiated* with certain phenomenology, or not. If the attitude theorist denies that the relevant attitudes are *phenomenologically enriched* in this sense, then their theory has the problematic implication that pleasure can come radically apart from phenomenology. This leads to a scenario that Guy Kahane calls *hedonic inversion*.[2] If the attitude theorist instead affirms that the relevant attitudes are phenomenologically enriched, then they

---

[1] For defenses of the phenomenological theory, see Smuts (2011) and Bramble (2013); for defenses of the attitude theory, see Feldman (1988) and Heathwood (2007). For an introduction to the contemporary debate on the nature of pleasure, see Bramble (2016a).

[2] Kahane (2009). Daniel Haybron uses the phrase "hedonic inversion" in the same way. He presents but does not ultimately endorse the view that total hedonic inversion is possible (Haybron 2008a, 2008b: 71–73).

undermine their main objection to the phenomenological theory of pleasure. This is the so-called *heterogeneity problem*, according to which pleasures do not feel alike.

We conclude that in debates between attitude theorists and phenomenological theorists, the prospects for attitude theorists are worse than is typically supposed. Either they must abandon their most important objection to the phenomenological theory (the heterogeneity objection) or they must confront a serious objection of their own (the objection from hedonic inversion). Either option is a serious setback for attitude theorists in their debate with phenomenological theorists. There are ways of trying to split the difference between the two horns of our dilemma, but in the end there is no way for attitude theorists to avoid both of the problems.

2. Preliminaries

In this chapter we will be principally concerned with two views about the nature of pleasure: the phenomenological theory, and the attitude theory. The phenomenological theory can be stated in terms of *phenomenal properties*, which are properties that characterize "what it is like" to be a given subject. We define the phenomenological theory as follows:

Phenomenological Theory of Pleasure:
- There is a non-empty set of phenomenal properties of pleasure. Necessarily, one enjoys an episode of pleasure iff one instantiates any phenomenal property which is a member of that set. (*Phenomenology-Pleasure Extensional Claim*)
- For each episode of pleasure and each subject, that subject has that episode of pleasure in virtue of instantiating a pleasant phenomenal property. (*Phenomenology-Pleasure Grounding Claim*)

The basic idea here is simple. The Extensional Claim tells us that there are certain kinds of phenomenology which are closely linked with pleasure: necessarily, you enjoy an episode of pleasure just in case you experience some phenomenology of one of those kinds. The Grounding Claim tells us that the connection between pleasure and phenomenology is not *merely* extensional; rather, you have episodes of pleasure *in virtue of* having pleasant phenomenology. So, if you are getting pleasure from drinking some hot coffee, then (i) you must be having an experience with some pleasant phenomenology, and (ii) you are getting pleasure in virtue of this pleasant phenomenology. Different versions of the phenomenological theory of pleasure correspond to different views about which phenomenal properties are pleasant in this sense.

The attitude theory of pleasure, in contrast, makes no reference to phenomenal properties. It instead makes reference to *pro-attitudes*: ways of "favoring" or "being into" certain states of affairs. Different versions of the attitude theory correspond to different views about which pro-attitudes are relevant. For ease of presentation, we will appeal to a simple version of the theory according to which the relevant attitude is *attraction*. Being attracted to something is a way of "favoring" or "being into" it, but beyond that we will not fill in the details of how the attitude should be understood. There are many ways in which the details could be filled in—perhaps being attracted to something is like *desiring* it, or *wishing* for it, or *favoring* it—but the details do not matter for our purposes. We want to show that the attitude theorist faces a dilemma *no matter how* they understand the pro-attitude that is implicated in their preferred version of the theory. For our purposes, then, "attraction" is merely a placeholder for whichever pro-attitude features in the best version of the attitude theory. The details can be filled in however the attitudinal theorist sees fit.

We define the attraction-based attitude theory as follows:

Attraction Theory of Pleasure:

- There is an attitude of *attraction*. Necessarily, one enjoys an episode of pleasure iff one is attracted to something. (*Attraction-Pleasure Extensional Claim*)
- For each episode of pleasure and each subject, that subject has that episode of pleasure in virtue of being attracted to something. (*Attraction-Pleasure Grounding Claim*)

Again, the basic idea here is simple. The Extensional Claim tells us that a certain attitude—"attraction"—is closely linked with pleasure: necessarily, you enjoy an episode of pleasure just in case you are attracted to something. The Grounding Claim tells us that the connection between pleasure and attraction is not *merely* extensional; rather, you enjoy episodes of pleasure *in virtue of* being attracted to things. So, if you are getting pleasure from drinking some hot coffee, then (i) you must be attracted to some state of affairs (presumably sipping the coffee, or getting a certain kind of gustatory experience), and (ii) you are enjoying an episode of pleasure in virtue of being attracted to the relevant state of affairs.

According to an especially influential version of the attitude theory, pleasures are grounded in a *combination* of desire and belief. On Chris Heathwood's version of this theory, the relevant attitudes are (roughly) *intrinsically desiring a certain state of affairs in a "genuine-attraction sense,"* and *believing that the relevant state of affairs obtains* (2006, 2019). We intend for our attraction theory of pleasure to cover this kind of theory, as well. If one prefers this desire-plus-belief version of the attitude theory, one can understand attraction as involving a combination of desire and belief.

Our dilemma arises when we bear down on the question of whether or not attraction—or whichever attitude features in the attitude theory—is *phenomenological*, in the following sense:

Phenomenology of Attraction Thesis:
- There is a non-empty set of *phenomenal properties of attraction*. Necessarily, one is attracted to something iff one instantiates any phenomenal property which is a member of that set. (*Phenomenology-Attraction Extensional Claim*)

Notice that this thesis which concerns us is *merely* extensional; we are not concerned with the issue of whether or not one is attracted to things *in virtue of* one's phenomenology. The extensional thesis alone gives rise to the dilemma for attitude theorists. If they accept the thesis—if they accept what we will call the *enriched attraction theory*—then they must give up their heterogeneity objection against phenomenological theorists. If, on the other hand, the attitude theorist rejects the thesis—if they accept what we will call the *unenriched attraction theory*—then they face the objection from hedonic inversion.

Although we appeal to the particular attitude of *attraction* for ease of presentation, it will be clear that the dilemma applies to all versions of the attitude theory. No matter which attitudes are implicated in one's preferred version of the attitude theory, they must be either enriched or unenriched, in the sense that they either are or are not necessarily co-instantiated with certain phenomenal properties. If the attitude theorist tells us that the relevant attitudes are enriched, then they must give up the heterogeneity objection against phenomenological theories of pleasure. If they tell us that the relevant attitudes are unenriched, then they are vulnerable to an objection from hedonic inversion.

3. Unenriched Attraction

Suppose the attraction theorist opts for an unenriched theory. They claim that attraction is to be understood in non-phenomenological terms, and there is no phenomenology with which attraction is necessarily co-instantiated. There are many ways such a theory might be developed; for ease of presentation, we will consider just one version: the *dispositional* theory. According to this theory, you count as being attracted to a given state of affairs just in case you are *disposed to try to continue it*. And you enjoy an episode of pleasure just in case and because you are disposed to try to continue a certain state of affairs. This theory is admittedly simplistic; we do not mean to imply that actual attitude theorists accept it. We focus on the dispositional theory because it clearly qualifies as "non-phenomenological," in our sense. The relevant disposition is not necessarily co-instantiated with any phenomenology; subjects with the same phenomenology can differ with respect to whether or not they have the disposition.

The problem with this view—and all other versions of the unenriched attitude theory—is that it suggests, counterintuitively, that two subjects could have exactly the same experiences while differing *radically* in their levels of pleasure. Or, as Kahane puts it, that they could be *hedonic inverts* (2009).

We can state this problem in the form of the following argument:

P1. If the unenriched attitude theory of pleasure is true, then it is possible for there to be phenomenal duplicates with radically different levels of pleasure.

P2. It is not possible for there to be phenomenal duplicates with radically different levels of pleasure.

C. Therefore, the unenriched attitude theory of pleasure is false.

Kahane and other philosophers have suggested this objection, but its force and scope have not been properly appreciated.[3]

To illustrate the problem, we will consider the following pair of cases:

---

[3] For examples of papers in which the problem has been broached, see Haybron (2008a, 2008b); Kahane (2009); Labukt (2012: 183); Bramble (2016b: 92); Lin (2020: 521).

Amy at the Amusement Park: Amy spends a tremendously enjoyable day at an amusement park riding rollercoasters, eating delicious food, and joking with her friends.

Twin Amy at the Amusement Park: Twin Amy also spends the day at an amusement park riding rollercoasters, eating delicious food, and joking with her friends. Over the course of this day, Twin Amy is a phenomenal duplicate of Amy: that is, Twin Amy's total phenomenology, or conscious experience, is exactly like Amy's.

An attitude theorist of pleasure will claim that Amy's pleasures are to be explained partly in terms of some attitude that she has, and on the proposal under discussion here, this attitude is to be understood in non-phenomenological terms. Let's suppose again that the attitude is taken to be a disposition to try to continue certain states of affairs. This means that we could imagine Twin Amy having a day that is exactly like Amy's in every respect, except that Twin Amy does not have the relevant disposition. Since the disposition is stipulated to be non-phenomenological, this means we can assume that Twin Amy has exactly the same phenomenology as Amy— the same rush from the rollercoasters, the same juicy taste from the food, the same warm tingle from the jokes. But Twin Amy is not disposed to try to continue the relevant states of affairs, so the attitude theorist must conclude that her day is entirely devoid of pleasure. Despite the fact that Amy and Twin Amy are phenomenal duplicates—there is no difference between "what it is like" to be Amy, and "what it is like" to be Twin Amy—they differ significantly with respect to the pleasantness of their experiences: Amy's day is extremely pleasant and Twin Amy's day is not at all pleasant.

This, we think, is already an implausible result. But in fact, the attitude theorist is committed to an even more implausible result. Attitude theorists explain the *unpleasantness* of our experiences in the same way that they explain the pleasantness of our experiences: by appealing to our attitudes.[4] They claim that unpleasant experiences consist in our having attitudes which are in some sense *opposites* of those which are relevant to pleasure.

---

[4] See Heathwood (2007: 40–44). Might the attitude theorist avoid this problem by explaining unpleasantness in terms of something other than (non-phenomenological) desire? They could, but they would only be delaying the inevitable. Whatever is implicated in their explanation of unpleasantness, it must be either phenomenological or non-phenomenological. So the dilemma arises all over again: if unpleasantness is explained in terms of something non-phenomenological, the attitude theorist faces the problem of hedonic inversion; otherwise, they face the heterogeneity problem (introduced in the next section).

The dispositional theorist might claim that you suffer an episode of displeasure just in case, and because, you are *averse* to something, where aversion consists in a disposition to *end* certain states of affairs. Since the relevant attitudes are again non-phenomenological, we can imagine that Twin Amy has those attitudes throughout the day at the amusement park, but is nevertheless a phenomenal duplicate of Amy. Although she has all the same sorts of experiences as Amy, phenomenologically speaking, she is disposed to *end* the various states of affairs which Amy is disposed to continue. So the attitude theorist must conclude that Twin Amy is a *hedonic invert* of Amy—despite the fact that there is no difference between "what it is like" to be Amy, and "what it is like" to be Twin Amy, they differ radically with respect to the pleasantness of their experiences: Amy's day is extremely pleasant, and Twin Amy's day is *miserable*. We find this suggestion very hard to make sense of.

A second pair of cases serves to drive the point home:

Bob's Bad Day: Bob has a tremendously unpleasant day. He has extremely itchy and painful hemorrhoids. He is fired from work, which fills him with feelings of anxiety and self-loathing. He gets caught in the freezing rain on his way home. Upon arriving home, he stubs his toe so hard that he breaks his toe bone. Finally, his girlfriend breaks up with him. He succumbs to despair and cries himself to sleep.

Twin Bob's Bad Day: Twin Bob's day is just like Bob's day. Twin Bob is a phenomenal duplicate of Bob: that is, Twin Bob's total phenomenology, or conscious experience, is exactly like Bob's.

Just as the attitude theorist must allow that Twin Amy could be a hedonic invert of Amy, they must also allow that Twin Bob could be a hedonic invert of Bob. They must allow that Twin Bob's day could be extremely pleasant, despite the fact that he has experiences which feel *exactly like* Bob's experiences of itchiness, self-loathing, pain, and despair.[5] Again, we find this suggestion very hard to make sense of.

---

[5] Notice we are *not* claiming that Twin Bob's feelings are in fact feelings of itchiness, self-loathing, pain, and despair. Nor are we claiming that Twin Bob's feelings are *not* in fact feelings of itchiness, self-loathing, pain, and despair. Given that Twin Bob is a hedonic invert of Bob, both claims are implausible. If Twin Bob *does* feel itchiness, despair, etc., then we must accept that there can be *pleasant* feelings of itchiness, despair, etc. That is deeply implausible. If Twin Bob *does not* feel itchiness, despair, etc., then we must accept that there can be "pseudo-itches" and "pseudo-despair"—experiences which are not feelings of itchiness

It is important to keep in mind that Bob and Twin Bob are exactly alike with respect to their *total* phenomenology, and not merely with respect to some set of particular feelings. Consider the thoughts that might be running through Bob's head as he walks home after being fired. He might think to himself: "Why did I ever think that I could succeed at that job? I'm just a fraud, and I'm sure all of my co-workers knew it. They'll be glad I left, if they even notice." If this self-belittling monologue has any impact on Bob's phenomenology—and surely it does!—then Twin Bob is impacted in exactly the same way. For Twin Bob, it is *exactly as if* a self-belittling monologue is running through his head as he trudges through the freezing rain. Now consider the claim that those experiences, taken as a whole, are pleasant. It seems to us that this claim strains the concept of pleasure to the breaking point. We do not know what it would mean for it to be true. So we regard P2 as extremely plausible: hedonic inversion is impossible.

As a reminder: there *is* a straightforward way for attraction theorists to avoid committing themselves to hedonic inversion. They can embrace the *enriched* attraction theory. According to that theory, attraction is necessarily co-instantiated with certain phenomenology—a *feeling of attraction*, perhaps. This theory, we think, is not without some initial plausibility. And if it is true, then hedonic inversion is impossible—in virtue of the differences in their attitudes, Amy's overall phenomenology *must* differ from Twin Amy's. Similarly, if aversion is necessarily co-instantiated with certain phenomenology, then Bob's overall phenomenology must differ from Twin Bob's. We consider enriched versions of the attitude theory in the next section.

For attraction theorists who want to maintain an *unenriched* version of the theory, there are two ways to respond to our argument. First, they could deny P1: in other words, they could deny that their theory has the implications that we have just described. Second, they could deny P2: that is, they could insist that it is not so implausible to think that phenomenal duplicates could have radically different levels of pleasure.

In order to deny P1, attitude theorists might first claim that even if attraction and aversion are to be understood in terms of non-phenomenological dispositions, these dispositions will tend to affect what our experiences are like. For example, we might think that if Amy is disposed to continue riding rollercoasters, then we would expect her also to be disposed, for example, to

---

and despair, despite feeling exactly like them. That, too, is deeply implausible. The only way to avoid an implausible result is to reject the idea that Twin Bob is a hedonic invert of Bob. We take this as further evidence that hedonic inversion is implausible.

find herself wondering about which rides might have the shortest lines. In contrast, attitude theorists might argue, if we are supposed to imagine a "twin" who really does not have this disposition, then we would expect this twin not to think about such things; and if she is in fact disposed not to *stop* riding rollercoasters, then we would expect her instead, for example, to find herself imagining how it will feel to finally be back home.

However, this is not enough to undermine P1. At most it shows that, on the dispositional theory, hedonic inversion is *unexpected*, or *highly unlikely*. It does not show that, on the dispositional theory, hedonic inversion is *impossible*. So it does not show that P1 is false. Of course the attraction theorist could make a stronger claim: they could claim that the difference in Amy and Twin Amy's dispositions *necessarily* makes for differences in their phenomenology. That would be enough to show that P1 is false. But if the attitude theorist claims that the relevant dispositions are phenomenologically enriched in this way, then they are accepting an enriched version of the attraction theory, and fall on the second horn of our dilemma. We consider the second horn in the next section.

As an alternative response to P1, the attitude theorists might reject the particular non-phenomenological theory of attraction that we have been considering, and instead opt for a different non-phenomenological theory. According to the theory we have been considering, attractions are dispositions to choose certain states of affairs. Attitude theorists may suspect that the problem of hedonic inversion is a problem for *this* theory, but not for *all* unenriched versions of the attitude theory. Motivated by this suspicion, they may go in search of a more sophisticated attitude to employ in their theory.

It is true that the theory of attraction we have been considering is not very sophisticated. But it is hard to see how a more sophisticated theory would help. Posit the most sophisticated theory you like—in terms of attention, or functional role, or representational content, or whatever else. If the resulting theory entails that the relevant attitudes are unenriched in the relevant sense—if it entails that those attitudes are not necessarily co-instantiated with any phenomenal properties—then the problem of hedonic inversion arises all over again. Given that the relevant attitudes are unenriched, phenomenal duplicates can differ with respect to those attitudes. And so, if the unenriched attitude theory is true, phenomenal duplicates can differ with respect to their pleasures. The structure of the problem is the same, no matter what we say specifically about the unenriched attitudes which feature in the theory.

Let's next consider how attitude theorists might challenge P2. Perhaps, attitude theorists could argue, we should not really find the idea that there could be phenomenal duplicates with radically different levels of pleasure so implausible. After all, attitude theorists might argue, consider ordinary cases of differences in tastes. Attitude theorists typically appeal to such cases as *prima facie* evidence for their view. Chris Heathwood points out that whereas some people love spicy food, others hate it (Heathwood 2007: 35–36). Fred Feldman claims that two people might differ with respect to whether or not they enjoy the taste of a certain beer (Feldman 2004: 82–83). And Feldman suggests that, at least in many cases, beer lovers and beer haters might be having more or less the same taste experience. So doesn't this show that two people can in fact have the same phenomenology, but different levels of pleasure?

Our first response is that even if beer lovers and beer haters have the same *taste* experience, this does not mean that they have the same *total* experience. The attitude theorist needs to claim that "what it's like" to *drink beer as a beer lover* is the same as "what it's like" to *drink beer as a beer hater*, despite the fact that the former experience is very pleasant and the latter experience is very unpleasant. *This* claim is not obviously true. It is natural to suppose that the beer hater experiences disgust, for example. If so, then their total experiences are different. So the claim that there can be hedonic inverts receives no strong support from our common sense judgments regarding differences in taste.

The friend of hedonic inversion might point out that they only need to endorse a *possibility* claim: it's *possible* that the beer lover's and beer hater's total experiences are exactly alike with respect to phenomenology, despite the fact that the lover and hater bear very different attitudes towards those experiences, and despite the fact that those experience differ radically with respect to pleasantness. It is true that the friend of hedonic inversion only needs to make this possibility claim. But what supports it? If they are *merely* making a claim about a *possible* difference, and *not* making a claim about *actual* differences in taste, then clearly they are not appealing to our common sense judgments about differences in taste. On what basis, then, does the friend of hedonic inversion insist that some possible taste differences have the structure they describe?

A natural thought is that the friend of hedonic inversion is appealing to Hume's Dictum. The idea is that our attitudes are "distinct" from our experiences, so there are no necessary connections between them: as a matter of metaphysical possibility, our attitudes and experiences can be mixed and matched in every which way.[6] In particular, then, it must be possible for the beer lover to love the exact same kind of total experience which the beer hater hates. And given that *love* and *hate* are to be understood in terms of the kinds of attitudes that can ground differences in pleasantness, it follows that the beer lover and beer hater's experiences differ radically in pleasantness despite sharing the same total phenomenology.

The trouble is that, despite appearances, Hume's Dictum has no direct implications for differences in taste or hedonic inversion. We can accept Hume's Dictum while rejecting the conclusion about differences in taste, simply by denying that pleasure is "distinct" from phenomenology. We might say that *part of what it is* to feel pleasure is to feel certain phenomenology, either because pleasure itself or the attitudes relevant to pleasure are grounded in some sort of phenomenology. In either case, Hume's Dictum does not forbid that there may be necessary connections between pleasure and phenomenology. More generally, it is not clear that there are any plausible metaphysical principles which entail the possibility of hedonic inversion.

Of course, one who wishes to reject P2 should not insist upon the bare *possibility* that differences in taste may involve radical differences in pleasantness without differences in total phenomenology. This is simply to insist that, in cases like that of Amy and Twin Amy, hedonic inversion is possible. If this insistence is not supported by some further argument—by an argument from *actual* differences in taste, for example—then it will not convince anyone who finds hedonic inversion implausible.

Rather than trying to resist our intuitions regarding hedonic inversion, the attitude theorist would do better to grant that hedonic inversion is indeed *prima facie* implausible. By extension, P2 is *prima facie* plausible. They might nevertheless resist it by arguing that it leads to implausible results. In particular, the attitude theorist might claim that accepting P2 commits us to a tendentious phenomenological theory of pleasure. Here is one such tendentious theory: pleasure consists in a certain sort of warm tingling feeling. If this naïve theory is correct, then obviously hedonic inversion is impossible, because hedonic inverts would differ with respect to this warm tingle. But the reverse is not true—P2 does not entail the warm tingle theory, nor any other specific and tendentious theory of pleasure. It entails only a modest claim about pleasure: there cannot be *extreme* differences in

---

[6] Thanks to a reviewer for suggesting this line of response.

pleasantness, without *some* difference in phenomenology. This claim, we think, is quite plausible, and for exactly the same reason that P2 is plausible.

As a final response to the argument from hedonic inversion—one which has often been suggested to us in conversation—the attitude theorist might make a dialectical point. They might point out that the desire theory is standardly presented in contrast to the phenomenological theory: attitude theorists claim that the pleasantness of an experience is explained not by the way it feels, but instead by the fact that the subject desires it. But if attitude theorists deny that pleasure is a matter of phenomenology, then it is *obvious* that they must claim that phenomenological duplicates could have different levels of pleasure. In other words, we should not be *surprised* by the attitude theorist's commitment to hedonic inversion.

It is hard to see how far this response goes. Perhaps attitude theorists will not be surprised to hear that they are committed to hedonic inversion, but that does not make hedonic inversion less counterintuitive. Similarly, if attitude theorists claim that hedonic inversion is not counterintuitive, we can only remind them of the cases we have described. Think about Bob as he ruminates on his failures, and as he cries himself to sleep. Think about *what it is like* to be Bob—that is, to experience intense itchiness, fear, despair, and self-loathing. It makes no sense to claim that *those very experiences*—in all of their qualitative detail—might be instances of pleasure. Some attitude theorists might be able to convince themselves otherwise, but we doubt that many will share this judgment.

4. Enriched Attraction

Given the issues raised in the last section, the attitude theorist might embrace an *enriched* theory of attraction, according to which attraction is necessarily co-instantiated with some phenomenology. Just as there are many possible unenriched attraction theories, so too are there many possible enriched theories. Once again it will be best to focus on a simple and specific version. We will consider the *simple feeling* theory, according to which there is a single and homogenous *feeling of attraction*.[7] This theory is

---

[7] See Lin (2020: 518–522). Presumably, the attitude theorist who opts for this strategy will say something similar about unpleasant experiences. Aversion is necessarily co-instantiated with a *feeling of repulsion*, so one who suffers from an episode of displeasure will invariably experience this feeling. For ease of discussion, we will focus on the proposed reduction of

neutral about whether or not attraction is grounded in, or constituted by, the feeling of attraction. The claim is merely that the feeling and attitude are necessarily co-instantiated.

The simple feeling theory avoids the problem of hedonic inversion. On the simple feeling theory, the Amusement Park cases will *not* produce the result that pleasure can be radically disconnected from phenomenology. Since Amy is attracted to various states of affairs—riding rollercoasters, eating delicious food, and joking with her friends—she must experience the feeling of attraction. Since Twin Amy is not attracted to those states of affairs, she must *not* experience the feeling of attraction. This amounts to a phenomenological difference in their overall experiences, so Amy and her counterpart will not be phenomenal duplicates. Similar considerations apply to Bob's Bad Day. The problem of hedonic inversion does not arise.

However, the simple feeling theory faces a different problem. The theory—along with every other version of the enriched attraction theory—is subject to the most famous argument against the phenomenological theory of pleasure: the *heterogeneity problem*. It faces this problem because it predicts that there are certain kinds of phenomenology which are common to every instance in which we enjoy pleasure. But many philosophers have thought that pleasure is entirely *heterogeneous*; they have claimed there are no phenomenological commonalities among pleasures.

The heterogeneity problem is standardly taken to be a problem for the *phenomenological* theory of pleasure, so we can start by considering how the objection applies to that theory. Phenomenological theorists accept that whenever we enjoy pleasure, we do so in virtue of our phenomenology. Relatedly, they accept an extensional claim about the instantiation of pleasure and phenomenal properties:

Phenomenology-Pleasure Extensional Claim: There is a non-empty set of *phenomenal properties of pleasure*. Necessarily, one enjoys an episode of pleasure iff one instantiates any phenomenal property which is a member of that set.

The *phenomenal properties of pleasure* may or may not be a singleton set. If it is a singleton set, then this would straightforwardly imply that there is a phenomenological commonality among all instances on which we enjoy

---

pleasure to feelings of attraction. But everything we say in this section applies equally to the reduction of unpleasant experiences to feelings of repulsion.

pleasure. Even if it is not a singleton set,[8] it is natural to ask what the members of that have in common, and the most natural answer is that the phenomenologies resemble one another. This, too, would imply that there is a phenomenological commonality among all instances on which we enjoy pleasure. This is presumably why many philosophers have found it natural to suppose that, if the phenomenological theory of pleasure is true, then we feel the same or similar feelings whenever we enjoy pleasure.

Many philosophers have also supposed that there are no such feelings. And this supposition is *prima facie* plausible. Consider Amy's amusement park experiences: the rush she gets from the rollercoaster ride, the juicy taste she gets from the delicious food, the warm tingles she gets from joking with friends. These experiences are pleasurable—for Amy—but it is at least *not obvious* that they all involve the same or similar feelings.

Many attitude theorists have taken the heterogeneity problem to provide an extremely forceful objection against phenomenological theorists. For example, here is Derek Parfit:

Narrow Hedonists assume, falsely, that pleasure and pain are two distinctive kinds of experience. Compare the pleasures of satisfying an intense thirst or lust, listening to music, solving an intellectual problem, reading a tragedy, and knowing that one's child is happy. These various experiences do not contain any distinctive common quality. (Parfit 1984: 492)

Here is Thomas Carson:

The heterogeneity of pleasures is a serious problem for the felt-quality theory. Consider the pleasures of orgasm, the pleasure of being rubbed or massaged during sexual activity, the pleasure of warming oneself by a fire, the pleasure of eating delicious food... [...] It is not obvious that there is any common felt quality they all share. [...] My own introspection and that of many others fails to discern a feeling tone of pleasantness that is shared by all pleasant experiences. (Carson 2000: 14)

Here is Chris Heathwood:

---

[8] Admittedly, as we saw earlier, we might distinguish between different kinds of pleasure, such as sensory and attitude pleasures. And one might claim that "pleasure" is in fact ambiguous, and that these different kinds of pleasure do not in fact have anything in common. Even then, it is plausible that there must be something that unites each particular kind of pleasure.

There are well-known arguments against Felt Quality Theories, and, suffice it to say, the phenomenology just doesn't bear it out—there doesn't seem to be any one feeling (or even "hedonic tone") common to all occasions on which we experience pleasure or enjoyment. (Heathwood 2007: 26)

And here is David Sobel:

A great many philosophers have introspected in vain for such a phenomenological commonality involved in the full range of pleasurable experiences such as taking a warm bubble bath, winning a tense tennis match, and sexual excitement. (Sobel 2019: 162–163)

These quotations are representative of the general consensus among attitude theorists. The above quotations target different theories—"Narrow Hedonism," "Felt-Quality Theories," the "Benthamite Theory"—but these are all versions of the phenomenological theory.

It is *dialectically* significant, then, that the heterogeneity problem applies as much to the enriched attraction theory as it does to the phenomenological theory. The enriched attraction theory includes the following extensional claims:

Attraction-Pleasure Extensional Claim: There is an attitude of *attraction*. Necessarily, one enjoys an episode of pleasure iff one is attracted to something.

Phenomenology-Attraction Extensional Claim: There is a non-empty set of *phenomenal properties of attraction*. Necessarily, one is attracted to something iff one instantiates any phenomenal property which is a member of that set.

These claims jointly entail the Phenomenology-Pleasure Extensional Claim. The only difference is the name given to the relevant phenomenal properties: *phenomenal properties of attraction*, as opposed to *phenomenal properties of pleasure*. So it would seem that, insofar as the phenomenological theorist gets in trouble for saying that there are phenomenal properties common to every instance on which we enjoy pleasure, the enriched attraction theorist gets in trouble for the same reason. The heterogeneity problem is the same problem either way.

We are not claiming that the heterogeneity problem is a decisive objection to either the enriched attraction theory or the phenomenological theory. In fact, we will ultimately suggest that the problem is less pressing than many philosophers have thought. We are chiefly interested in making a *dialectical point*. As we have seen, attitude theorists have often suggested that the heterogeneity problem is decisive against the phenomenological theory. In fact, the heterogeneity problem is often invoked as the main reason to accept the attitude theory over the phenomenological theory. But the heterogeneity problem applies to the enriched attitude theory in the same way that it applies to the phenomenological theory. So if the heterogeneity problem is a cogent objection to the phenomenological theory, it's an equally cogent objection to the enriched attitude theory.

We can formulate the dialectical point as the conclusion of a simple argument:

P1b. If the phenomenological theory of pleasure implies that we experience phenomenologically similar feelings on every occasion on which we enjoy pleasure, then the enriched attraction theory of pleasure also implies that we experience phenomenologically similar feelings on every occasion on which we enjoy pleasure.

P2b. If P1b is true, then the heterogeneity problem has the same strength against the enriched attitude theory of pleasure as it has against the phenomenological theory of pleasure.

C2. The heterogeneity problem has the same strength against the enriched attitude theory of pleasure as it has against the phenomenological theory of pleasure.

If attitude theorists accept C2, then they should admit that they do not enjoy what *they* take to be the strongest advantage of their theory over their chief rival. They should admit that *by their own lights*, their theory has a decisive problem—or that they have been wrong to think that the phenomenological theory faces a decisive problem.

In an effort to avoid this result, the attitude theorist might deny P1b or P2b. Suppose they deny P1b. They might start by suggesting that, even if pleasures are necessarily co-instantiated with some *phenomenal properties of attraction*, this does not imply that we experience phenomenologically similar feelings on every occasion on which we enjoy pleasure. For the phenomenal properties of attraction might not be phenomenologically similar to one another. They might be phenomenologically *heterogeneous*. To take a simple proposal along these lines, perhaps there are two phenomenal properties of attraction—a *feeling of enthusiasm* and a *feeling of yearning*—and these feelings do not resemble each other phenomenologically. Then the enriched attitude theory of pleasure could be true, and yet we do not experience phenomenologically similar feelings on every occasion on which we enjoy pleasure.

Of course, the attitude theorist cannot merely leave things there. They must also claim that, if the phenomenological theory of pleasure is true, then this *would* imply that we experience phenomenologically similar feelings on every occasion on which we enjoy pleasure. And here the attitude theorist faces a problem, for it seems as though the phenomenological theorist can make more or less the same claim that the attitude theorist has just made. If it's legitimate to suppose that *phenomenal properties of attraction* are phenomenologically heterogeneous, then it also seems legitimate to suppose that *phenomenal properties of pleasure* are phenomenologically heterogeneous. Perhaps there are two phenomenal properties of pleasure—a *feeling of satisfaction* and a *feeling of excitement*—and these feelings do not resemble each other phenomenologically. Then the phenomenological theory of pleasure could be true, and yet we do not experience phenomenologically similar feelings on every occasion on which we enjoy pleasure.

The challenge for the attitude theorist, then, is to find a strategy for explaining heterogeneity which cannot be appropriated by the phenomenological theorist. And we do not believe that this challenge can be met. Thus far we have been considering quite simple strategies for explaining heterogeneity, but the same considerations apply to more sophisticated strategies. Whether simplistic or sophisticated, the same moves are available to both the enriched attitude theorist, and the phenomenological theorist. Whatever can be said about phenomenal properties of attraction can also be said about phenomenal properties of pleasure.

To illustrate, consider a sophisticated strategy that the enriched attitude theorist might adopt. They might claim that attraction is to be understood as a disposition (along the lines sketched in the previous section) and phenomenal properties of attraction are the *categorical grounds* of that disposition. On the resulting view, the phenomenal properties of attraction are unified not by phenomenological similarity, but by their shared role in grounding the disposition of attraction. So there is no *phenomenological* resemblance among the experiences we have when we enjoy pleasure, but those experiences do have something genuinely in common.

This is, we think, an interesting and *prima facie* plausible view about the relationship between our phenomenology and pro-attitudes. But it is not exclusively available to attitude theorists; it is available to phenomenological theorists as well. The phenomenological theorist can claim that the *phenomenological properties of pleasure* are unified not by phenomenological similarity, but by their shared role in grounding the disposition of attraction. So there is no *phenomenological* resemblance among the experiences we have when we enjoy pleasure, but those experiences do have something genuinely in common.

In saying all this, the attitude theorist and the phenomenological theorist are telling more or less the same story about the relationship between phenomenology and attraction. They differ in how they describe the relevant phenomenology: "phenomenal properties of attraction" versus "phenomenal properties of pleasure." But the story is still more or less the same. The real difference between the theories concerns the grounds of pleasure *itself*. According to the phenomenological theorist, each episode of pleasure is grounded in the instantiation of some phenomenal properties of pleasure. You count as enjoying pleasure, on a particular occasion, because your experiences feel the way that they do. According to the attitudinal theorist, by contrast, each episode of pleasure is grounded in some particular attitude of attraction. You count as enjoying pleasure, on a particular occasion, because you are attracted to some state of affairs—you "favor it," or are "into it." So there does seem to be a real difference between the theories here.

The crucial point, for our purposes, is that these versions of the attitude and phenomenological theories of pleasure are alike with respect to their implications for the heterogeneity of pleasure. If the proponent of the enriched attitude theory has succeeded in showing that their view is consistent with the phenomenological heterogeneity of pleasure, then the proponent of the phenomenological theory has *also* succeeded in showing that their view is consistent with the phenomenological heterogeneity of pleasure. And vice versa. The theories have the same resources for accommodating the supposed phenomenological heterogeneity of pleasure. P1b is secure.

Suppose the enriched attitude theorist concedes all this. They might nevertheless try to show that the heterogeneity problem is more of a problem for their opponents, the phenomenological theorists. That is, they might try to show that P2b is false. If so, this could only be because *both* theories imply that we experience phenomenologically similar feelings on every occasion on which we enjoy pleasure, but somehow this commitment is less damaging for the attitudinal theory than it is for the phenomenological theory.

They might claim that we have introspective evidence which favors the enriched attraction theory over the phenomenological theory. The claim would then be that whereas introspection militates against the view that there are *phenomenal properties of pleasure*, introspection does *not* militate against the view that there are *phenomenal properties of attraction*. Thus, the heterogeneity problem is specifically a problem for the view that pleasures share phenomenal properties of pleasure, and not a problem for the view that pleasures share phenomenal properties of attraction. This line of thought seems to be endorsed by Eden Lin, who seems to advocate a version of the enriched attraction theory (Lin 2020: 518–522).

The line of thought does not seem very plausible to us. We know what it is like to ride rollercoasters, to eat delicious food, and to laugh with our friends. We are uncertain as to whether or not we detect phenomenologically similar feelings on each of these occasions.[9] But certainly it is *not* the case that, while we *cannot* detect a shared phenomenology of pleasure, we *can* detect a shared phenomenology of attraction. The alleged phenomenology of attraction is at least as elusive as the phenomenology of pleasure.

This is not to say that there is no such phenomenology. It might be that we experience phenomenologically similar feelings on every occasion on which we enjoy pleasure, even if we fail to detect these feelings introspectively. There are various stories we might tell about why we fail to detect this feeling. Perhaps the feeling is ephemeral and hard to pin down. Perhaps whenever we feel it, our attention is elsewhere—we attend to the things which are sources of pleasure for us, rather than the phenomenology which always accompanies pleasure. But these responses are available to both enriched attitude theorists *and* phenomenological theorists. Indeed, phenomenological theorists have endorsed precisely these sorts of responses to the heterogeneity objection (Smuts 2011: 256–257; Bramble 2013: 210–211). So, once again, the attraction theory is on par with the phenomenological theory with respect to the heterogeneity objection. Enriched attitude theorists and phenomenological theorists have all the same resources for responding to the objection. If it is a cogent objection to the phenomenological theory of pleasure, it is a cogent objection to the enriched attraction theory as well.

On balance, we are inclined to doubt that the heterogeneity problem is a decisive problem. We are inclined to endorse some combination of the responses outlined in this section. But if the heterogeneity problem is not a serious problem, then it is not a serious problem for anyone—for attitude theorists, or for phenomenological theorists. And *that* would be a problem

---

[9] Notice this is not to say that the heterogeneity objection succeeds against the phenomenological theory or enriched attraction theory; those theories might be developed in a way that accommodates heterogeneity.

for attitude theorists, because they claim to be at an advantage with respect to the heterogeneity problem. Indeed, it is often cited as a central reason, if not *the* central reason, to reject the phenomenological theory in favor of the attitude theory.

5. Escaping the Dilemma?

Is there any way in which the attitude theorist might escape the dilemma? One strategy would be to find a middle ground between the enriched attraction theory and the unenriched attraction theory. According to the enriched attraction theory, there is a set of phenomenal properties necessarily co-instantiated with attraction: instantiating any or all of those properties is *necessary and sufficient* for being attracted to something. According to the unenriched attraction theory, there is no such set of phenomenal properties. On the most extreme version of this theory, there are no necessary connections between phenomenology and attraction. But there are other possible views according to which there is some phenomenology which is *necessary but not sufficient* for attraction, or *sufficient but not necessary*. These views might seem to present a middle ground.

On closer inspection, however, the middle ground is not particularly promising. Consider first the view that some phenomenology is *necessary but not sufficient* for attraction. This view is vulnerable to the heterogeneity problem to whatever extent the phenomenological theory is vulnerable to that problem, and for the same reason: both theories entail that some particular phenomenal property or properties always accompany pleasure. Furthermore, the *necessary-but-not-sufficient* view faces the problem of hedonic inversion as well. During her day at the amusement park, Amy must have whatever phenomenology is necessary for pleasure—but since that phenomenology is not *sufficient* for enjoying pleasure, Twin Amy's day might not be pleasant despite being phenomenologically just like Amy's day.

Consider next the view that some particular phenomenology is *sufficient but not necessary* for attraction. (Perhaps the theory tells us that attraction is a disjunction of feeling and disposition: instantiating at least one of the feeling or disposition is necessary for being attracted, but instantiating either is sufficient for being attracted.) This strategy has a little more initial promise. With respect to hedonic inversion, the attitude theorist might stipulate that Amy experiences the feeling of attraction. In that case Twin Amy must also experience it, and so Twin Amy cannot fail to be attracted to things, and enjoy pleasures. This is a good result on the first horn of our dilemma. Furthermore, if the feeling of attraction is not *necessary* for enjoying pleasure, then the theory does not entail that some particular phenomenal property or properties always accompany pleasure. This is a good result on the second horn of our dilemma.

In the end, however, this *sufficient-but-not-necessary* strategy is unstable. The attitude theorist can stipulate whatever they like about Amy, but we can make stipulations too. We can stipulate that Amy's friend Cara does *not* experience the feeling of attraction, despite having a tremendously pleasant day at the amusement park. And then we can construct another hedonic inversion case with Cara and Twin Cara, in the same way that we did with Amy and Twin Amy. If the attitude theorist rejects these stipulations—if they insist that a tremendously pleasant day at the amusement park *must* involve the feeling of attraction—then they are in effect claiming that the feeling of attraction is not only *sufficient* but also *necessary* for enjoying pleasure. In that case they have endorsed the enriched attraction strategy, and they face the second horn of our dilemma. They must admit that the heterogeneity objection has as much force against their view as it does against the phenomenological theory.

We conclude that there is no way for attitude theorists to simply *avoid* the dilemma. Rather, they must face the dilemma head on, by choosing either the enriched attraction theory or the unenriched attraction theory. And so they will have to either address the problem of hedonic inversion or abandon the heterogeneity objection to the phenomenological theory of pleasure.

We do not claim to have shown that the attitude theory is false. We do claim to have shown that the theory is importantly *ambiguous*, because the enriched and unenriched attitude theories are importantly different theories, with different costs and benefits. The enriched version avoids the challenges faced by the unenriched theory, and vice versa. Insofar as we fail to disambiguate, this can mislead us into thinking that there is a unitary theory—*"the attitude theory"*—that avoids *both* sets of challenges. But this is a mistake. There is no way to develop the attitude theory such that it avoids both sets of challenges. Recognizing this, and pressing attitude theorists to get clear about *which* version of the theory they accept, will lead to more productive discussions regarding the prospects of particular attitude theories.

References

Bramble, Ben. 2013. "The Distinctive Feeling Theory of Pleasure." *Philosophical Studies* 162 (2): 201–217.

Bramble, Ben. 2016a. "The Role of Pleasure in Well-Being." In *The Routledge Handbook of the Philosophy of Well-Being*, edited by Guy Fletcher. London: Routledge, 199–208.

Bramble, Ben. 2016b. "A New Defense of Hedonism About Well-Being." *Ergo: An Open Access Journal of Philosophy* 3: 85–112.

Carson, Thomas L. 2000. *Value and the Good Life*. London: University of Notre Dame Press.

Feldman, Fred. 1988. "Two Questions About Pleasure." In *Philosophical Analysis*, edited by D. F. Austin, 59–81. London: Kluwer Academic Publishers.

Feldman, Fred. 2004. *Pleasure and the Good Life: Concerning the Nature, Varieties, and Plausibility of Hedonism*. Oxford: Oxford University Press.

Haybron, Daniel M. 2008a. "Happiness, the Self and Human Flourishing." *Utilitas* 20 (1): 21–49.

Haybron, Daniel M. 2008b. *The Pursuit of Unhappiness: The Elusive Psychology of Well-Being*. Oxford: Oxford University Press.

Heathwood, Chris. 2006. "Desire Satisfactionism and Hedonism." *Philosophical Studies* 128 (3): 539–563.

Heathwood, Chris. 2007. "The Reduction of Sensory Pleasure to Desire." *Philosophical Studies* 133 (1): 23–44.

Heathwood, Chris. 2019. "Which Desires Are Relevant to Well-Being?" *Noûs* 53 (3): 664–688.

Kahane, Guy. 2009. "Pain, Dislike and Experience." *Utilitas* 21 (3): 327–336.

Labukt, Ivar. 2012. "Hedonic Tone and the Heterogeneity of Pleasure." *Utilitas* 24 (2): 172–199.

Lin, Eden. 2020. "Attitudinal and Phenomenological Theories of Pleasure." *Philosophy and Phenomenological Research* 100 (3): 510–524.

Parfit, Derek. 1984. *Reasons and Persons*. Oxford: Oxford University Press.

Smuts, Aaron. 2011. "The Feels Good Theory of Pleasure." *Philosophical Studies* 155 (2): 241–265.

Sobel, David. 2019. "The Case for Stance-Dependent Reasons." *Journal of Ethics and Social Philosophy* 15 (2): 146–174.

10
Seeing through Transparency

Davide Bordini

1. Introduction

Drawing on some well-known remarks by G. E. Moore (1903),[1] in the 1990s Gilbert Harman (1990) and Michael Tye (1995, 2000) famously claimed that experience is transparent: in introspecting what it's like for you to undergo an experience, the only things you are aware of are the (apparently) worldly objects your experience is of and their properties, and nothing else—in particular, no property of your experience itself is revealed to you by introspection.

This claim has crucially impinged on core debates in the contemporary philosophy of mind, notably concerning perceptual experience and consciousness more generally. Standardly, transparency has been appealed to as twofold evidence in favor of *externalist accounts* of experience—roughly, views according to which the conscious aspects of experience are determined by one's being in the appropriate relation with things in the external environment and their properties (e.g., Harman 1990; Tye 1995, 2000; Dretske 1996; Martin 2002; Kennedy 2009)—and against their *internalist* competitors—views that deny that the external environment plays a constitutive role in consciousness.

The recent developments of the literature, however, have made transparency itself quite opaque. The very idea of *transparent experience* has now become quite elusive and fuzzy. Some theorists (e.g., Kind 2003, 2007; Soteriou 2011, 2013; Gow 2016; Aydede 2019) have called into question Harman's and Tye's claim and distinguished different senses of transparency, as well as transparency theses (e.g., strong vs. weak transparency;

---

[1] See also Reid (1764/1970). However, it is a matter of debate whether Moore and Reid had in mind the same strong claim made by Harman and Tye (see, e.g., Kind 2003).

metaphysical vs. phenomenological transparency). Absent a unified logical space where these notions and theses can be mapped and confronted, we are left with an overall impression of conceptual chaos. In this context, both insiders and outsiders have a hard time getting oriented in the existing transparency literature. That is a problem, given the constant and ubiquitous references to transparency in the literature and its prominent position in contemporary philosophy of mind. My goal in this chapter is to restore clarity.

By offering a systematic reconstruction of the debate on the transparency of experience, I aim to give it structure. The key is a proper analysis of the mutual relations between the different transparency theses (§§3–4). Upon closer inspection, I will suggest, they help identify different *dimensions* along which transparency views can vary and differ. This allows me to uncover a unitary multidimensional logical space where existing (as well as possible) views can be properly singled out and located (§§5–6). Thereby, I hope to turn a fragmented and chaotic mosaic of notions and claims into a unitary and coherent picture. My discussion begins with reconstructing Harman's and Tye's takes on transparency, which may be considered the *standard* way of understanding transparency (§2).

2. The Standard Understanding of Transparency

After reviewing Harman's and Tye's understanding of transparency (§2.1) and its (alleged) consequences (§2.2), I will highlight the motivations that have recently led some to revise Harman's and Tye's claims on transparency (§2.3).

2.1 Harman's and Tye's Transparency Thesis

Let us consider two famous passages from Harman and Tye:

> When Eloise sees a tree before her, the colors she experiences are all experienced as features of the tree and its surroundings. None of them are experienced as intrinsic features of her experience. Nor does she experience any features of anything as intrinsic features of her experiences. And that is true of you too.... When you see a tree, you do not experience any features as intrinsic features of your experience. Look at a tree and try to turn your attention to the intrinsic features of your visual experience.

> I predict that you will find that the only features there to turn your attention to will be features of the presented tree. (Harman 1990: 39)
>
> Focus your attention on a square that has been painted blue. Intuitively, you are directly aware of blueness and squareness as out there in the world away from you, as features of an external surface. Now shift your gaze inward and try to become aware of your experience itself, inside you, apart from its objects. Try to focus your attention on some intrinsic feature of the experience that distinguishes it from other experiences, something other than what it is an experience of. The task seems impossible: one's awareness seems always to slip through the experience to blueness and squareness, as instantiated together in an external object. In turning one's mind inward to attend to the experience, one seems to end up concentrating on what is outside again, on external features or properties. (Tye 1995: 30)

The idea is clear. Consider your current visual experience and try to introspectively focus on what it's like for you to have it, its *phenomenal character*. Harman and Tye maintain that, in so doing, you only seem to be aware of features of the externally located objects that you see—their color, shape, location (relative to other things in the environment), and so on. In short, what you see exhausts what you introspect. If you were originally looking for some conscious features of the experience over and above those involved in *what* you experience, you will be disappointed: nothing like that seems to be revealed by introspection.

The lesson that Harman and especially Tye draw is summarized clearly by Tye himself:

> [T]he key transparency claims are as follows: in a case of normal perception, if we introspect:
>
> (1) We are not aware of features of our visual experience.
>
> (2) We are not aware of the visual experience itself.
>
> (3) We cannot attend to features of the visual experience.
>
> (4) The only features of which we are aware and to which we can attend are external features (colors and shapes of surfaces, for example).
>
> (Tye 2014: 41)

Moreover, at least according to Tye, the same remarks apply *across the board*. As he writes: "visual experience...is transparent or diaphanous, as is *phenomenal consciousness generally*" (1995: 31; my emphasis).

All this can be condensed in the following twofold claim:

(HT Transparency) In introspecting one's own experience, (a) one is *not* aware of/cannot attend to features of the experience itself. Rather, (b) one is only aware of/can *only* attend to features of the externally located objects one's experience is of.

This is the *standard understanding of transparency*. This is not meant to suggest that Harman's and Tye's characterization of transparency is correct or is the point of convergence of a general and widespread consensus—a standard understanding of transparency in this sense is quite hard to find. Rather, I mean to convey the idea that it has been the *center of gravity* of the debate on transparency. That is, over the last three decades, it has been the way of characterizing transparency that almost everyone would quote and critically discuss—in short, the view to be endorsed, attacked, revised, or fine-tuned.

2.2 The Argument from Transparency

HT Transparency has been used as an introspective premise in an argument for a twofold conclusion with a negative and a positive element. The *negative element* speaks against internalist accounts, which cast phenomenal character as fully determined by certain introspectable qualitative properties that experience possesses independently of what goes on in the external environment.[2] The *positive element* (allegedly) speaks in favor of some version of externalism—the view according to which phenomenal character

---

[2] Traditionally, some internalists have construed phenomenal character in terms of *qualia* understood as non-representational or only contingently representational qualitative features of the experience (e.g., Block 1996, 2003). That view, known as *qualia* theory, is the view that Harman and Tye originally meant to attack. However, there are also representationalist versions of internalism, so I prefer not to cast those features as non-representational by definition. (Also, I will avoid *qualia*-talk to avoid any non-representationalist connotation.) For example, they might be manners or ways of representing a certain content (Chalmers 2004), attitudes toward a content (Crane 2006, 2009), or phenomenal contents that do not depend constitutively on one's relation to the environment (Horgan and Tienson 2002; Horgan, Tienson, and Graham 2004; Kriegel 2007, 2011; Mendelovici 2018). HT Transparency can be used as evidence against these internalist versions of representationalism, too. Briefly, if qualitative features are ways of representing a content, then the thought is that introspection does not reveal any way of representing, but only ways in which things are represented as being or even *are*. If they are phenomenal contents, they are ruled out, as long as it is true that we are introspectively aware only of properties of external objects, as HT Transparency states.

(at least in part) depends on one's being somehow directly related to the external environment. Here is one way to put the argument:[3]

Argument from Transparency

(P1)   If internalism is true, then one should be introspectively aware of features of the experience itself.

(P2)   In introspecting one's experience, one is not aware of features of the experience itself (but only of features of the externally located objects one's experience is of). Therefore,

(C)   Internalism is false (and some version of externalism is true).

P1 is typically accepted by internalists. So, they react by rejecting P2, namely, HT Transparency.

As it stands, the argument says that *some* version of externalism is true. Now, at least as far as perceptual experience is concerned, externalism about phenomenal character comes in two main versions. According to *externalist representationalism*, experience is a representation relation, understood in terms of tracking (Dretske 1981, 1988; Fodor 1990). *Naïve realism* casts experience as an even more direct relation to worldly properties and things, usually spelled out in terms of a non-representational relation of acquaintance. One might then wonder whether the argument can be pushed a little further to claim that HT Transparency supports one version of externalism over the other.[4] That is a delicate issue and settling it goes beyond the scope of this chapter. So, I will set it aside.

The argument claims that HT Transparency supports an externalist take on phenomenal character. However, this does not mean that *any* externalist *accepts*, or *should* accept, HT Transparency (see also §3.1). For example,

---

[3] For the sake of simplicity, I am formulating the argument in terms of awareness. A formulation in terms of attention might involve further complications not relevant for our present discussion (cf. Tye 2014).

[4] Originally, the argument was put forward to support Harman's (1990) and Tye's (1995, 2000) externalist representationalism. Partly, that was due to the original setting of the debate, in which naïve realism did not feature as an option—Harman and Tye used HT Transparency to attack the internalist construal of phenomenal character in terms of introspectable qualitative features or sense data. One more principled reason might be that if HT Transparency holds across different experiential domains, then representationalism has an advantage: representationalism is a theory of consciousness in general, while naïve realism is a theory of perception only. Another reason might be that representationalism has been traditionally taken to offer a better explanation of the phenomenal continuity between veridical and non-veridical cases of perception, which both seem to be transparent. However, those are far from conclusive reasons, and naïve realists have their own replies to offer.

some externalists (often naïve realists) construe phenomenal character as involving more than just external objects or properties—e.g., the experiencer and their standpoint (Campbell 2009) or features of the experiential relation itself (Martin 2004; Richardson 2010, 2014; Soteriou 2011, 2013). Now, this seems in tension with HT Transparency (see French 2018: 155). Thus, some externalists may want to reject HT Transparency (though they may accept other understandings of transparency).

The take-home message is this: internalists have obvious reasons to reject HT Transparency. However, some externalists might find it unsatisfying, too. So, interestingly, the acceptance/rejection of HT Transparency does not (perfectly) map onto the externalist/internalist opposition.[5] Criticisms of HT Transparency might come from within the externalist camp, too.

2.3 Revising Transparency

To block the Argument from Transparency, one must reject HT Transparency. In the early stages of the debate, the general strategy was to produce (putative) counterexamples. Opponents of HT Transparency appealed to cases such as afterimages, phosphenes, or blurry vision, as well as itches, pains, orgasms, and moods to argue that we are directly aware of certain qualities of the experience (e.g., Boghossian and Velleman 1989; Block 1996, 2003). Notice: implicit in the debate was the assumption that HT Transparency is the *only* way to look at transparency. So, in that context, the rejection of HT Transparency went hand in hand with the more radical claim that experience is *not* transparent. Consequently, a *rejectionist* attitude toward transparency was generally adopted by opponents of HT Transparency.

Recently, a subtler strategy has emerged that incorporates a more *revisionist* attitude: instead of focusing on counterexamples and concluding that experience is not transparent, many theorists have argued that HT Transparency simply gets transparency wrong.[6] The general structure of

---

[5] So, interestingly, while a commitment to HT Transparency seems built into Harman's and Tye's externalist representationalism (Kind 2003, 2007; Aydede 2019), this does not seem to be true of externalism in general.

[6] The rejectionism/revisionism distinction is meant to capture a difference in attitude and interest rather than in substance. Once the more fine-grained distinctions are in place, some rejectionists might be happy to accept that experience is transparent *in some sense* (or to some extent), if that implies a rejection of HT Transparency. After all, a subtler criticism might just be a way of refining previously advanced, more coarse-grained critiques. I think this is true of views like Block's and Kind's, which are often very close to each other—but Block has a rejectionist attitude while Kind adopts a revisionist one.

their response is something like the following. First, they distinguish and contrast two notions of transparency—e.g., *strong* vs. *weak* transparency (Kind 2003; Soteriou 2011, 2013); *metaphysical* vs. *phenomenological* transparency (Gow 2016); *s-transparency* vs. *transparency datum* (Aydede 2019). Second, they claim that one of the two notions, typically the stronger, captures the notion of transparency presupposed by HT Transparency. Third, they argue that the phenomenon we observe introspectively is the other, typically weaker, one. Thereby, they block the Argument from Transparency without denying transparency altogether.

My aim here is not to critically assess this line of reply. I just want to stress that the adoption of a revisionist attitude in response to the Argument from Transparency is the main source of the multitude of transparency theses we currently find in the literature. With that in mind, we can now set aside the motivations behind revisionism to focus on its *products*: the different transparency theses. In what follows, I will not take a stance on what (if any) is the right view on transparency or what (if anything) transparency suggests about consciousness. Rather, my main goal will be to give structure to the debate. The first step in that direction was to clarify the standard understanding of transparency and lay out the background that led to the current proliferation of transparency theses. The next step is to build up a unitary logical space, where the different views can be mapped.

3. Distinctions and Transparency Theses

In this section, I present the main distinctions between transparency theses drawn in the literature, highlighting the dialectical import of each. To keep things simple, I set aside considerations about the scope of transparency until §6. So, I conduct the discussion having in mind mainly perceptual experience—and, in particular, veridical visual experience.

3.1 Strong vs. Weak Transparency

Amy Kind (2003) distinguishes between *strong* and *weak* transparency:

> *Strong Transparency*:   it is *impossible* to attend directly to our experience, i.e., we cannot attend to our experience except by attending to the objects represented by that experience.

> *Weak Transparency*: it is *difficult* (but not impossible) to attend directly to our experience, i.e., we can most easily attend to our experience by attending to the objects represented by that experience. (Kind 2003: 230)

Matthew Soteriou (2011, 2013) also distinguishes between a stronger and a weaker version of transparency:

> According to the stronger version [of the transparency thesis], introspection of one's perceptual experience reveals *only* the objects, qualities, and relations one is apparently perceptually aware of in having the experience. According to the weaker version, when one introspectively attends to what it is like for one to be having a perceptual experience, it seems to one as though one can only do so by attending to the sorts of objects, qualities, and relations one is apparently perceptually aware of in having that experience. (Soteriou 2011: 193–4)

The two distinctions are similar but do not perfectly overlap. Kind's Strong Transparency claims that we can only attend to our experience by attending to what experience is of. But that, *per se*, does *not* exclude that something about the experience itself, other than what it is of, is introspectable. In principle, then, Kind's strong thesis is compatible with the following two mutually exclusive interpretations:

(Interpretation 1) We can only introspect what the experience is of. So, we cannot introspectively attend to anything other than that.

(Interpretation 2) We can introspect *some* features of the experience (other than what it is of), but it is impossible to attend to them without (or in isolation from) attending to what the experience is of.

Interpretations 1 and 2 look very much like (respectively) Soteriou's stronger and weaker thesis. In this respect, Soteriou's distinction is more fine-grained than Kind's. At the same time, it seems to leave out Kind's Weak Transparency. One natural move, then, is to combine the two distinctions. Thus:

(Ultra-Strong Transparency) Introspection only reveals what experience is of. It is impossible to introspectively attend to anything other than that.

(Strong Transparency) Some features of the experience (other than what it is of) are introspectable, but it is impossible to introspectively attend to them without (or in isolation from) attending to what the experience is of.

(**Weak Transparency**)   Some features of the experience (other than what it is of) are introspectable, and it is not impossible (though it might be difficult) to introspectively attend to them without (or in isolation from) attending to what the experience is of.

These three theses take different stances on (a) what and (b) how we introspect. They are built around two main contrasts: (i) direct vs. indirect introspective attention;[7] (ii) what the experience is of vs. features of the experience *other than* what it is of.[8]

Ultra-Strong Transparency is in line with Harman's and Tye's views on transparency. However, it can find supporters in the internalist camp, too. For example, so-called phenomenal intentionality theorists—internalist representationalists who construe phenomenal character as phenomenal content (e.g., Horgan and Tienson 2002; Loar 2003; Kriegel 2007, 2011; Mendelovici 2018)—might happily accept that we can only introspect what the experience is of—its content in this case.

Strong Transparency is not compatible with Ultra-Strong Transparency, insofar as it claims that there is more to attend to in introspection than what the experience is of. However, it also claims that the extra bit cannot be discerned in isolation from the objects and properties experience presents us with. Hence, it is incompatible with Weak Transparency, too.

Externalist representationalists *à la* Harman and Tye should reject Strong Transparency, as in their view phenomenal character just is what the experience is of—and that is all we can introspect. However, other externalists (representationalists of a different sort or naïve realists) can accept Strong Transparency. For example, Soteriou (2011, 2013; but see also: Martin 2004; Richardson 2010, 2014) claims that, by attending to the objects of the experience, we can introspectively discern certain invariant *structural* features, such as the visual field or its boundaries, which remain constant as objects and properties change. Such structural features are modality-specific and are responsible for *how* we experience things within that modality. Consequently, they are not properties of *what* we experience but of the

---

[7] Importantly: this should *not* be understood as a contrast rooted in the distinction between awareness of / awareness that, along the lines of what supporters of introspection as displaced perception argue (e.g., Dretske 1994, 1999; Tye 2000; Byrne 2018). That view makes our epistemic contact with phenomenal character indirect, and it counts as one way of supporting Ultra-Strong Transparency.

[8] For the sake of brevity, sometimes I will refer to features of the experience other than what it is of using shorter labels such as "features of the experience", "experiential features", "experience itself", and the like.

experience itself.[9] And indeed, according to Soteriou, we do not seem to be aware of them in the same way we are aware of the objects of our experiences—they cannot be targets of independent attention or scrutiny. Nonetheless, they are constituents of phenomenal character, and we can notice them *by* performing proper introspective reflection on the objects of the experience and their properties. An externalist supporter of Strong Transparency might then argue that, when properly understood, transparency supports this view and not Harman's and Tye's.

However, Strong Transparency is compatible with internalist views, too. For example, Siewert (2004), who defends a version of internalist representationalism, endorses it:

> I would endorse this general formulation of transparency:
>
>> T3: You cannot attend to how it appears to you, by turning your attention away from something that appears to you, and towards your experience....
>
> We should recognize that directing attention to experience is not like directing attention from one sensorily apparent thing to some other. You can turn your attention away from one visually apparent thing, and to another, so as to ignore the first, in favor of the second. Directing attention to the second thing excludes attending to the first. But if you turn your attention to how some object looks to you on some occasion, you don't (and can't) do so, by turning your attention away from it or diminishing how much attention you devote to it, while increasing your attention to its looking to you as it does. (Siewert 2004: 35–6)

Likewise, an internalist representationalist who construes phenomenal character as constitutively involving, say, manners or ways of representing or attitudinal features (e.g., Chalmers 2004) might well accept Strong Transparency and claim that we can only attend to those features by attending to what the experience presents us with.

What about Weak Transparency? It is incompatible with both Strong and Ultra-Strong Transparency. Clearly, it is at odds with accounts,

---

[9] The idea that features of the experiential relation partly constitute phenomenal character, thereby shaping our awareness of worldly objects and properties, is often voiced by naïve realists. However, it is also compatible with versions of externalist representationalism that accept that modality-specific manners of representing contribute to phenomenal character. This is *not* Harman's and Tye's externalist representationalism.

externalist or internalist, that construe phenomenal character as exhausted by what the experience is of. Instead, it sits well with internalist non-representationalist views, which explain phenomenal character by appealing to non-(essentially-)representational qualitative features of the experience (e.g., Block 1990, 1996, 2003; Kind 2003, 2007). But it is also compatible with internalist representationalist accounts that appeal to extra-content attitudinal features (e.g., Crane 2006).[10]

Kind argues that Weak Transparency is the right way to look at transparency. Given the above, *if* she is right, then the Argument from Transparency is blocked and the situation is turned around: when properly understood, transparency would not only be compatible with internalism but would also be at odds with at least some versions of externalism.[11]

3.2 Metaphysical vs. Phenomenological Transparency

Laura Gow (2016) distinguishes between *metaphysical* and *phenomenological* transparency:

> Perceptual experience is phenomenologically transparent if and only if it is true that the properties we are aware of during a perceptual experience all *seem* to us to be externally located.
>
> Perceptual experience is metaphysically transparent if and only if all the properties we are aware of *are in fact* externally located. (Gow 2016: 723)

The distinction is built around two main oppositions: (i) what *seems* to be the case vs. what *is* the case; (ii) external vs. internal. Some remarks are in order. First, "seem" (or "appear") is to be read *phenomenologically*. Second, "externally located" is to be read in light of the internalism/externalism opposition. So, it alludes to what is "outside one's head," namely, worldly,

---

[10] An interesting question is whether Weak Transparency is compatible with some version of naïve realism that construes phenomenal character as including more than just the objects of the experience and their features. The reply depends on whether, within a naïve realist framework, non-objectual experiential features can be construed as introspectable in isolation from, and independently of, what the experience is of. As far as the extant views are concerned, it is quite safe to say that naïve realism rejects Weak Transparency. I leave it open here whether that is a matter of principle or just by accident.

[11] Or *all* versions of externalism, if naïve realism involves a commitment to either Ultra-Strong Transparency or Strong Transparency (see previous footnote).

mind-independent features located in the environment. I will use these labels interchangeably. Third, "the properties we are aware of during a perceptual experience" is a bit vague—we can be aware of many things during a perceptual experience that are not relevant for what (I think) Gow is aiming at here. So, I will understand it as something like "the properties of which we are aware *in virtue of* having a perceptual experience". Fourth, the distinction concerns perceptual experience and the target-properties of perceptual awareness that constitutively contribute to perceptual phenomenal character. However, in principle, it can be extended to other experiential domains. Finally, because transparency is an (alleged) introspective datum, introspection is to establish which (if any) of the two conditions stated in the quote is met (Gow 2016: 725). However, as Gow points out, introspection can only tell us how things appear to us, not what they are. So, it can only establish whether experience is phenomenologically transparent, remaining silent on metaphysical transparency.

We can now state the following two theses:

(**Phenomenological Transparency**) [Introspection shows that] the properties we are aware of in virtue of having an experience of a certain kind all *seem* to us to be externally located/worldly.

(**Metaphysical Transparency**) All the properties we are aware of in virtue of having an experience of a certain kind *are in fact* externally located/worldly.

Phenomenological Transparency tells us how the targets of experiential awareness *appear* to us and is taken to state an introspective datum. Metaphysical Transparency is a stronger claim concerning the *nature* of the targets of experiential awareness and needs more than introspective observation to be established. Neither thesis (explicitly) comments on whether introspection reveals more than the targets of experiential awareness.[12]

Now, Gow maintains, HT Transparency presupposes Metaphysical Transparency, so it is *not* the right rendition of transparency. This blocks

---

[12] So, Phenomenological Transparency is not obviously incompatible with a view on which the target of introspective awareness and the target of experiential awareness do not coincide (see §§4.2–4.4). One might then think that Phenomenological Transparency, alone or combined with Metaphysical Transparency, does not fully capture Harman's and Tye's view, on which the target of introspective awareness and the target of experiential awareness coincide. Ultimately, I agree: I do not think that the phenomenological/metaphysical distinction, alone, exhausts the logical space of the debate.

the Argument from Transparency. For unlike Metaphysical Transparency, Phenomenological Transparency is compatible with at least some representationalist versions of internalism. For example, on the phenomenal intentionality theory, experiences possess certain qualitative properties independently of the external environment that are also essentially representational. Phenomenological Transparency would then be explained by experience's instantiating those properties and, in virtue of that, representing a certain phenomenal content. Hence, when properly understood, transparency does *not* rule out internalism.

Regarding entailment relations between the two: Phenomenological Transparency *does not entail* Metaphysical Transparency. In general, a deductive inference from appearance to reality does not look good. One might try to argue that the transition can be justified otherwise, perhaps by appealing to an inference to the best explanation—Metaphysical Transparency would best explain Phenomenological Transparency (Tye 2000). But inferences to the best explanation can be resisted (Gow 2016: 731–6), and anyway these are not entailment relations. So, accepting Phenomenological Transparency does not force one to accept Metaphysical Transparency.

Metaphysical Transparency *does not entail* Phenomenological Transparency either. If appearance and reality can come apart, then it is not clear why we should rule out the possibility that what *is* in fact an external property fails to *appear* external. Gow, too, makes a similar point and mentions phosphenes as a candidate-case where one might hold Metaphysical Transparency and reject Phenomenological Transparency.[13] She claims that an externalist might concede that the color-quality involved in the experience does not appear to be externally located; and yet, she suggests, an externalist explanation of this case—e.g., in terms of uninstantiated property—is still a coherent option.[14] One can then coherently hold Metaphysical Transparency and reject Phenomenological Transparency.

The upshot is: Metaphysical and Phenomenological Transparency are *logically independent* claims. However, they are *not* mutually exclusive—so,

---

[13] Smells too, one might think, fail to be *phenomenologically* transparent without failing to be *metaphysically* transparent. (For a discussion, see, e.g., Lycan 1996, 2000, 2014; Batty 2010; Richardson 2013.) More on olfaction and transparency in §6.

[14] However, this is not the path typically taken by externalists: they insist that phosphenes, afterimages, and blurry vision are phenomenologically *and* metaphysically transparent. By the way, in another paper (2019), Gow herself defends the claim that phosphenes, afterimages, and blurry vision are all phenomenologically transparent experiences.

they can be held together. That seems in line with the view of many externalist representationalists, including Harman and Tye.

As they stand, both Phenomenological and Metaphysical Transparency are universally quantified claims. So, they hold *unrestrictedly* within the domain of a certain kind of experience. However, in some cases, one might not want to commit rather to an unrestricted thesis. In these cases, one endorses a *restricted* version of Phenomenological or Metaphysical Transparency:

(**Restricted Phenomenological Transparency**) [Introspection shows that] *some* of the properties we are aware of in virtue of having an experience of a certain kind seem to us to be externally located/worldly.

(**Restricted Metaphysical Transparency**) *Some* of the properties we are aware of in virtue of having an experience of a certain kind are in fact externally located/worldly.

These are logically independent claims. Each restricted thesis is of course entailed by, but does not entail, the corresponding unrestricted version.

3.3 S-Transparency vs. Transparency Datum

More recently, Murat Aydede (2019) has distinguished between what he calls "S-Transparency" and "Transparency Datum":

(**S-Transparency**) "Experiences have no introspectable features over and above those implicated in their representational contents" (Aydede 2019: 685).

(**Transparency Datum**)

(LOCATION) The qualities that we are aware of in virtue of having a (perceptual) experience...all *appear* to be qualities of extra-mental objects (particulars), including bodily parts....

(FOCUS) If there are intrinsic qualities of experiences, it seems impossible to attend to or focus on these qualities *without* attending to or focusing on the qualities that these experiences present as belonging to the extra-mental particulars. (Aydede 2019: 683)

These are claims about the phenomenological aspects of what we introspect, as well as what we can attend to introspectively and how we do that. It should not be difficult to see, then, that they can be reconducted to some of the theses already encountered. Abstracting away from the specific formulation in terms of content, S-Transparency claims that we can only introspect what an experience is of. So, it corresponds to Ultra-Strong Transparency.

Transparency Datum involves two elements. LOCATION, Aydede (2019: 683) stresses, "is supported by introspection. It describes *how* your (perceptual) experiences present the qualities they do: they present them as qualifying extra-mental *particulars/objects*". So, it is (a version of) Phenomenological Transparency with a slightly different wording. FOCUS is either Strong Transparency or Weak Transparency, depending on how one reads it: setting aside the representationalist jargon, it claims that we cannot (or it is at least very difficult to) attend to features of the experience without attending to what experience is of.[15]

Finally, following a usual pattern, Aydede argues that, when properly understood, transparency does not rule out, but indeed supports, internalism against Harman's and Tye's externalist representationalism (he does not consider naïve realism). He maintains that S-Transparency is Harman's and Tye's transparency, but what we really gather from introspection, and hence the best rendition of transparency, is Transparency Datum. Since the latter is compatible with, and best explained by, internalist accounts (Aydede 2019: 696–705), the Argument from Transparency is blocked.

4. Logical Relations across Distinctions

Transparency Datum combines (a version of) Phenomenological Transparency with another thesis from the weak/strong distinction. That is interesting as it suggests that theses from different distinctions *can* be combined. Ultimately, this is no accident: the two distinctions are largely independent. To see the point, let us have a closer look at (some of) the relations between theses across distinctions. For convenience, I focus on Phenomenological Transparency and its relations with theses from the weak/strong distinction.

---

[15] I read Aydede as supporting Strong Transparency, as he seems to consider attending to what the experience is of as crucial to our capacity to introspect features of the experience (Aydede 2019: 701).

4.1 Phenomenological Transparency and Ultra-Strong Transparency

It is perfectly okay to say that (a) all the properties we are aware of in virtue of having an experience of a certain kind *seem* to be externally located; (b) those seemingly externally located properties are what the experience is of; and (c) that is all we can introspect about that experience. Therefore, Phenomenological Transparency is *consistent* with Ultra-Strong Transparency. Moreover, the two are often held together. One natural question, then, is whether Phenomenological Transparency is *entailed* by Ultra-Strong Transparency. I tend toward a negative reply: one can coherently hold Ultra-Strong Transparency and deny Phenomenological Transparency.

For example, consider phosphenes or afterimages. One might admit that the color-quality we experience in virtue of undergoing such experiences does not appear to qualify any externally located object; nor does it appear to be located anywhere in the outside space or more generally mind-independent.[16,17] Perhaps, one might add, in these cases we are just confronted with a peculiar "in-between" phenomenology whereby it is not clear where the color-quality really belongs—that would be enough for Phenomenological Transparency to fail.[18] And yet, one might insist, there are independent (plausibly, theoretical and non-introspective) reasons to think that that quality *is* represented by the experience. The proponent of such a view can still accept Ultra-Strong Transparency—i.e., that the represented color-quality an experience is of is all that we can introspectively attend to about the experience.[19]

---

[16] For instance, afterimages are usually described as violating some of the constraints for appearing worldly—e.g., they do not appear to move independently from us, they cannot be inspected from different perspectives, they remain there when we close our eyes, they lack size-constancy, etc. (Siegel 2006, Farkas 2013, Masrour 2013; for a critique, see Phillips 2013 and Gow 2019).

[17] Other cases might be the so-called "brain-gray" (Johnston 2004) and *ganzfeld*-experiences (Frey 2013).

[18] One might complain that there is no such thing as an "in-between" phenomenology of this sort. For example, Batty (2010: 116) writes: "if properties do not appear to be those of external things, then they must appear to be properties of the experience itself. Experience must attribute properties to *something*."

[19] Lycan (1996, 2000, 2014) suggests that different versions of representationalism might agree that smell-qualities do not appear external or worldly, identify them with contents, and yet claim that they exhaust the phenomenal character of olfaction (see, e.g., Lycan 2014: 2 fn10). Those contents would thus be all that there is to introspect about experience. Phenomenological Transparency would then fail, but Ultra-Strong Transparency would not.

To my mind, however, better examples come from accounts of non-perceptual experiences such as moods. Rephrased to cover these cases, Phenomenological Transparency maintains that the properties we are aware of in virtue of being in a certain mood all seem to be externally located. Now, at least sometimes, the peculiar affective qualities involved in these experiences do not seem to be properties of anything in outside space, or located in outside space—including the subject's body. Nonetheless, one might argue, they can still be accounted for in terms of what the experience is of. For example, accepting this phenomenological description, Mendelovici (2013a, b) casts some moods as representing unbound affective properties (*sui generis* properties represented by affective states, but without being represented as bound to, or exemplified by, some object). Barlassina and Hayward (2019a, b) seem to accept that the distinctive affective component involved in mood phenomenology, valence, appears to qualify the experience itself—e.g., in depression, it is the experience that feels bad and not (things in) the external world. Still, they cash out this component as a kind of content—(self-reflexive) imperative content. On such accounts, there would still be nothing to introspect and attend to over and above what the experience represents (in accordance with Ultra-Strong Transparency), and yet that would not appear external or worldly (failure of Phenomenological Transparency).

In short, how what the experience is of appears does not impinge on whether it is the only introspectable aspect in experience. So, nothing in Ultra-Strong Transparency seems to force one to accept Phenomenological Transparency.[20] The two theses often go together, but that does not seem to be because of some internal connection; rather, it seems to be the result of the work of some (hidden) extra assumption—something like:

(Extra Assumption #1) If an experience is of a certain property P, then P seems externally located/worldly.

However, as we have seen, the supporter of Ultra-Strong Transparency is not forced to accept this.

---

[20] If one rephrases Ultra-Strong Transparency as a claim about what it *seems* to one in introspection, then failure of Phenomenological Transparency might indeed lead to a failure of Ultra-Strong Transparency. However, Ultra-Strong Transparency is a stronger claim about what one *can* or *cannot* introspect—where "can"/"cannot" might express psychological or epistemic (and not necessarily metaphysical) possibility/necessity.

4.2 Phenomenological Transparency and Strong Transparency

Like Ultra-Strong Transparency, Strong Transparency makes *no claim* about how the targets of our experiential awareness appear. Instead, it imposes a constraint on how we manage to introspectively attend to features of experience. Thus, Strong Transparency stands in conflict with Phenomenological Transparency *only if* one also accepts the *conjunction* of the following two assumptions:

(Extra Assumption #2) The features of the experience we can introspectively attend to are among those we are aware of in virtue of having that experience; *and*

(Extra Assumption #3) The features of the experience we can introspectively attend to do not seem to be externally located properties.

But the supporter of Strong Transparency does not have to accept this conjunction—they might reject either assumption, or both.

Concerning Extra Assumption #2, a supporter of Strong Transparency could accept that the targets of (say) perceptual awareness, and indeed what the experience is of, are all seemingly externally located sensory qualities. However, they might believe that the scope of introspection is simply larger than the scope of perceptual awareness. So, in principle, nothing prevents them from endorsing the following claim: when we switch to an introspective mode, we attend to the seemingly externally located properties our experience is of and, by doing that, we also manage to become aware of, and thereby attend to, some other features of our perceptual experience that contribute to its phenomenal character.

Concerning Extra Assumption #3, a supporter of Strong Transparency might respond that it misconceives what it is to introspect the features of the experience and what it means that they do not *seem* external. Recall, supporters of Strong Transparency often stress that there is a difference between experiential (perceptual) awareness of / attention to seemingly external features and awareness of / attention to the experience and its features.[21] So, some could argue that introspecting the experiential features does not amount to discovering some seemingly "internally located"

---

[21] Importantly, the relevant difference here is not (just) *quantitative* but *qualitative*: a difference in the way we are aware of / attend to things in perception and in introspection. Recall Siewert's (2004: 36) comment that "we should recognize that directing attention to

properties of an "internal" object in addition to the seemingly externally located ones.

How to positively develop this further will depend on one's specific account of introspection. One option is to say that introspecting the experience consists in the specific capacity to deploy the right cognitive resources—e.g., the right sort of recognitional concepts or thoughts—to focus on and recognize the *ways* in which the properties we are perceptually aware of appear or are presented by the experience (Siewert 2004: 35–7, 2012: 148f; Aydede 2019: 696–705). So, introspecting the features of the experience is focusing on the very appearance of externally located properties, and clearly appearances do not themselves appear—internal, external, or otherwise.[22] Thus, the sense in which experiential features do not *seem* external has to do not with their *appearing* internal, but with the way in which we *conceptualize* them. So, Extra Assumption #3 is false; or if true, it must be read in a way that does not presuppose a phenomenological reading of "seem". Thus, Strong and Phenomenological Transparency can be consistently combined.

4.3 Phenomenological Transparency and Weak Transparency

Often theorists have supported Weak Transparency because of a putative failure of Phenomenological Transparency in cases like phosphenes, afterimages, blurry vision, itches, moods, or orgasms. The thought is that the qualities involved in such experiences do *not* seem to be worldly properties but properties of the experience itself. And indeed, that is what they are, according to these theorists: intrinsic qualitative features of the experience to which we can introspectively attend directly, i.e. in isolation from what the experience is of (e.g., Block 1996, 2003; Kind 2003, 2007)—as per Weak Transparency.

But what about Weak Transparency and the *unrestricted* version of Phenomenological Transparency? The two can be held together. For one

---

experience is not like directing attention from one sensorily apparent thing to some other" (see also Kennedy 2009: 586; Soteriou 2013: 119; Aydede 2019: 701).

[22] I am following Siewert (2004, 2012) here. But I suspect others might make claims in the vicinity. For example, Aydede (2019: 700), who casts experiential features as ways in which the experience presents sensory qualities, writes: "my experience presents a certain extra-mental particular to me as F, and then, my phenomenal knowledge consists of my applying a phenomenal concept to an 'object' conceived by me only as *the way Fness is experientially/perceptually presented to me now*.... I do not sense, perceive, or in any other way experience, this 'object', i.e., the *way F*ness is presented to me in my experience."

can coherently (a) accept that all the properties we are aware of in having a visual experience *seem* to be externally located; (b) deny that they are what the experience is of; and (c) maintain that they are, instead, features of the experience itself. That would cast experience as phenomenologically transparent not because of *what* it is *of*, but because of *how* it *is* in itself—perhaps, due to the internal arrangement of its qualitative features or some such (Farkas 2013; Masrour 2013; Papineau 2021). At least some mental-paint-friendly views might accept that (e.g., Loar 2003; Molyneaux 2009; Papineau 2021). They construe phenomenal character as constituted by qualitative features of the experience that are not represented, some of which represent things and properties in the external environment in virtue of some contingent causal-covariation relation. As Molyneaux (2009: 131) stresses: "we can...experience the properties of experience itself (mental paint) as properties of external objects and surfaces even though the former are *not* properties of external surfaces and objects." So, I see no principled compatibility issue with Weak Transparency: if one believes that it is possible to bring "mental paint" to the foreground of one's introspective attention while leaving what the experience is of in the background, then one can combine the two theses.

Loar (2003) seems to suggest something along those lines. He claims that introspection involves different ways of framing attention. When we take a naïve introspective attitude, which he calls *transparent reflection*, our attention is oriented toward the external properties the experience represents and "passes through" the qualities of the experience itself. However, Loar maintains, we can perform introspective reflection of a "deeper" sort, which he dubs *oblique reflection*. And *that*, on his view, reveals the real nature of visual phenomenal character. When in this introspective mode, we consider experience in isolation from its referential relations to the external world. Thereby, we appreciate what remains constant across different veridical and non-veridical scenarios.[23] What oblique reflection discloses is still a phenomenology of *seemingly* worldly objects and their properties—so, Phenomenological Transparency is preserved. However, now, we no longer take such a phenomenology as consisting in a relation to external objects

---

[23] To do that, one must deploy some sophisticated introspective (or introspection based) techniques: variation of some of the features of the actual scenario, consideration of possible scenarios like inverted spectrum cases, etc.

and their properties—Metaphysical Transparency is dropped. Rather, we take it as something non-relational, namely, the way our experience is internally constituted (and represents). So, according to Loar, in shifting to oblique reflection, a shift in our introspective attention occurs: we manage to attend directly to the qualitative features of the experience itself, in isolation from what it is of—thus, Weak Transparency is endorsed.

4.4 Upshot

Here is the upshot. Phenomenological Transparency, both in its restricted and its unrestricted version, is compatible with *all* the theses from the weak/strong distinction. So, it does not entail any of them. Nor is it entailed by *any* of them. Extra assumptions are needed to generate entailment relations or inconsistencies. *Mutatis mutandis*, considerations along the same lines apply to Metaphysical Transparency, too. The principled reasons are these. First, each distinction revolves around two main contrasts: (i) direct vs. indirect introspective attention and (ii) what the experience is of vs. features of the experience (other than what it is of), in the case of the weak/strong distinction; (iii) appearance vs. reality and (iv) external vs. internal, in the case of the phenomenological/metaphysical distinction. None of these contrasts overlap. Moreover, each distinction includes theses that take a stance on different issues. Phenomenological and Metaphysical Transparency are theses about the targets of experiential awareness constitutively involved in phenomenal character—how they appear and what they are. They do not comment on whether (and in case how) introspection reveals more than the target of experiential awareness, as do Ultra-Strong, Strong, and Weak Transparency.

5. A Unitary Multidimensional Logical Space

Since transparency theses across the strong/weak and metaphysical/phenomenological distinctions are largely compatible, I suggest that the two distinctions should be *integrated* to compose a unitary logical space. To a first approximation, the idea is that a view on transparency results from combining different transparency theses, in a way that respects the (few) constraints on the possible combinations highlighted by our discussion in §4.

5.1 Four Dimensions

The transparency theses take different stances on different questions. In particular, four questions can be singled out:

(Q1) What is introspectable about experience?
(Q2) Can we attend to it directly?
(Q3) How does what we are experientially aware of appear?
(Q4) What is it?

Q1 is a question about the *target of introspection*; Q2 is about the *focus of introspection*; Q3 is about *phenomenology*; Q4 is about *metaphysics*. Ultra-Strong, Strong, and Weak Transparency take a stance on both Q1 and Q2.[24] Phenomenological Transparency takes a stance on Q3, while Metaphysical Transparency takes a stance on Q4.

So, *qua* combinations of different transparency theses, views on transparency are the overall result of taking a stance on the whole set of questions Q1–Q4 with respect to a certain experiential domain. Thereby, Q1–Q4 individuate four *dimensions* along which views on the transparency of experience (can) vary:

Dimension 1: Introspective target. It is captured by the weak/strong distinction and consists in the reply one gives to Q1. The choice to be made is as to whether we can introspect only what the experience is of or also other features of the experience.

Dimension 2: Introspective focus. It is captured by the weak/strong distinction and consists in the reply one gives to Q2. The choice to be made is as to whether we can attend *directly* to features of the experience (other than what it is of).

Dimension 3: Phenomenology. It is captured by the phenomenological/metaphysical distinction and consists in the reply one gives to Q3. The choice to be made is as to whether the properties one is aware of in virtue of having an experience of a certain kind *appear* external/worldly or internal/experiential.

---

[24] Notice: Ultra-Strong Transparency claims that we cannot introspect anything other than what the experience is of (Q1). Thereby, it also (trivially) replies to Q2: we can only attend to the experience by attending to what it is of.

Dimension 4: Metaphysics. It is captured by the phenomenological/metaphysical distinction and consists in the reply one gives to Q4. The choice to be made is as to whether the properties one is aware of in virtue of having an experience of a certain kind are *in fact* external/worldly or internal/experiential.

These four dimensions provide us with the essential coordinates to individuate and locate different points in the logical space—each of those points corresponding to a (possible) view on transparency. They are thus the basic structure of a unitary and multidimensional logical space where the different (existing as well as possible) views on transparency can be mapped.

Typically, *every* view takes a stance on introspective target, introspective focus, and phenomenology, while some (but not all) take a(n explicit) stance on metaphysics. However, this does not make the metaphysical dimension idle. First, it is useful to capture fine-grained differences between at least *some* views. Second, even neutrality on it is a feature of a view. Thus, a view on transparency combines *at least* two transparency theses: one thesis (or negation thereof) from the phenomenology/metaphysics distinction (typically the phenomenological thesis) and one from the weak/strong distinction.

5.2 Mapping the Views on Visual Transparency

With this at hand, by way of example, we can map the main existing views on the transparency of visual experience and see how they interact with views on the nature of visual experience. In particular, we can single out the following main views in the debate.

Externalist camp:
- *Externalist representationalists à la* Harman and Tye typically hold a combination of Ultra-Strong, Phenomenological, and Metaphysical Transparency.
- *Other externalists* (naïve realists or representationalists) combine Strong Transparency with (Restricted or Unrestricted) Phenomenological Transparency, and at least Restricted Metaphysical Transparency (e.g., Martin 2002, 2004; Kennedy 2009; Richardson 2010, 2014; Soteriou 2011, 2013).

Internalist camp:

- *Internalist representationalists* hold different views. Some combine Ultra-Strong Transparency and Phenomenological Transparency (e.g., Horgan and Tienson 2002; Horgan, Tienson and Graham 2004; Kriegel 2007; Mendelovici 2018). Others embrace Strong Transparency and (Restricted or Unrestricted) Phenomenological Transparency (e.g., Chalmers 2004; Siewert 2004; Aydede 2019). Still others support Weak Transparency in combination with Restricted (e.g., Crane 2006) or Unrestricted (e.g., Loar 2003) Phenomenological Transparency.
- *Internalist anti-representationalists* typically hold Weak Transparency in combination with Restricted Phenomenological Transparency (e.g., Block 1996, 2003; Kind 2003, 2007).

Internalists are not always explicit on Metaphysical Transparency. That is not crucial for our present discussion. However, in passing, we can note the following: insofar as versions of Metaphysical Transparency are claims about the nature of properties constitutively involved in phenomenal character, plausibly an internalist *should* reject any version of this thesis.

One final remark. The proposed mapping shows something like a convergence on (at least) Restricted Phenomenological Transparency, which seems to support the claim that visual perception is largely (or normally) phenomenologically transparent. Theorists disagree on whether it is metaphysically transparent and on introspective target and focus—and these seem more theoretically oriented disagreements, plausibly rooted (at least in part) in the underlying metaphysics of visual experience one embraces or in the view of introspection one presupposes.

Interestingly, relevant differences emerge not only among views from different camps, but also among views from the same camp. For example, supporters of different versions of externalism tend to accept different theses from the weak/strong distinction. Acceptance of Strong (as opposed to Ultra-Strong) Transparency seems to go along typically with a construal of phenomenal character as including features of the experiential relation as opposed to just worldly objects and/or properties. Likewise, in the internalist camp, phenomenal intentionality theorists tend to endorse Ultra-Strong Transparency, whereas the others tend to endorse Strong or Weak Transparency. So, at least *prima facie* and to some extent, the differences between the various transparency views seem to go together with differences in views of the underlying metaphysics of visual experience. Plausibly, similar remarks apply to views of introspection, too.

Defending, investigating, or explaining these *prima facie* correlations is not my aim here. To be sure, assuming that they are real, they suggest a deep level of theoretical penetration of the "raw" introspective data—transparency views seem to be built into descriptions of the data from the very beginning. Transparency seems to have a dual structure: a very thin pre-theoretical core—plausibly captured by the phenomenological dimension—is largely supplemented and permeated by more theory-laden considerations—plausibly linked to the other dimensions. In a way, it is as if transparency demanded supplementation and interpretation almost all the way down, to be brought to full philosophical significance.[25] Whether this is really the case, how it should be properly explained, and what (if anything) it tells us about the phenomenon of transparency itself and its significance are interesting questions that cannot be addressed here but deserve to be dealt with in future work.

6. Scope

In the previous section, I characterized a transparency view as the result of taking a stance on Q1–Q4 *with respect to a certain experiential domain*. In this section, I say more about "with respect to a certain experiential domain".

6.1 A Fifth Dimension

Zooming out of the visual domain and taking a broader perspective on experience, a further question arises:

(Q5) Does transparency hold across different experiential domains and in what form?

A reply to Q5 specifies the relevant domain of application of a transparency view, i.e. its *scope*. Scope can be seen as a *fifth dimension* along which transparency views vary, with the following qualification: while the other four dimensions capture *intra*domain variations between views, scope captures *inter*domain variations.

---

[25] Although I will not argue for this here, I suspect that this is at least partially linked to the largely ostensive, elusive, and scarcely descriptive way the phenomenon has been singled out originally (e.g., by Moore).

When it comes to scope, a first opposition is between *global* and *local* transparency views. A global view is one with *maximal scope*: it holds in *all* experiential domains. A local view holds in only *some* experiential domains. Clearly, local views can take different scope, so a second opposition is among local views with larger or narrower scope.

6.2 Relevance of Scope

In addition to providing a further element to mark out fine-grained differences between transparency views, scope is relevant for other reasons. Let me quickly survey some of them.

6.2.1 Pervasiveness and Significance of Transparency

Indicating scope spells out whether (and in what form) transparency is a widespread phenomenon. This reflects importantly on the significance of transparency for the study of consciousness. If the scope of transparency is large enough, then arguably there are good reasons to take it as a constraint on theories of consciousness (or perception): something that those theories must explain. By contrast, the narrower the scope, the easier it is for one to deflate the relevance of transparency for evaluating theories of consciousness (or perception). It is indeed not by accident that, e.g., Tye combines the strongest transparency theses in a view with global scope. As we have seen, when so understood, transparency can be claimed as strong evidence in favor of radically externalist views, such as Harman's and Tye's representationalism.

From the opposite angle, internalist anti-representationalists have often tried to neutralize this line of argument by offering very deflationary (if not rejectionist) views of the phenomenon, not just by endorsing the weakest transparency theses, but also by narrowing its scope. For example, Block's overall view seems to be that experience is largely *non*-transparent— though he might accept Restricted Phenomenological and Weak Transparency for visual experience. In a similar vein, Kind (2007: 423) suggests that transparency is "*inapplicable*" outside of the perceptual domain (see also Kind 2013), while defending a combination of Restricted Phenomenological and Weak Transparency in the case of perceptual experience. When so understood, transparency looks like an exception rather than the rule—or anyway, it does not look like an impressive phenomenon.

6.2.2 Transparency as a Guide to Differences between Experiences

Differences or similarities in the way experiences are transparent across experiential domains, or even presence versus lack of transparency across domains, are often taken as a guide to underlying differences or similarities among experiences themselves. To put it somewhat boldly, the idea would be that transparency might help us draw distinctions that (purportedly) carve experience at its joints.

A shared thought is that transparency—whatever it boils down to—is a distinctive feature of perceptual experience, hence something that an adequate theory of perception should explain. Many theorists of perception are persuaded that some fairly strong transparency view is true of perceptual experience, without extending such a view across the board to all experience. For example, naïve realists defend fairly strong views of transparency encompassing Metaphysical Transparency limited to perceptual (and visual in particular) experience.

Other theorists have treated the differences between perceptual transparency and what we observe in non-perceptual domains as revealing something important about the nature of non-perceptual experience. For example, Deonna and Teroni (2012) sharply contrast perceptual with emotional experience:

> Try...to describe the content of the visual experience of a vase of flowers on a table. You will realize that it is very difficult to mention anything other than the properties exemplified by the objects that you see.... [In contrast,] the felt quality of fear is not clearly experienced by us as a feature of the spider that frightens us, nor is that of gratitude given as a property of such and such a benefactor. If you are to describe how it feels to be frightened by a spider, you would not do so in terms of the spider's qualities, but rather in terms of how it feels to experience a jolt up your spine, your hair standing on end, your teeth clenching, muscles freezing, heart jumping, etc. And these felt changes in your body are definitely not what you apprehend as dangerous in the circumstances.
> (Deonna and Teroni 2012: 68–9)

So, they seem to endorse different local views in different domains: while perceptual experience is phenomenologically and (ultra-)strongly transparent, emotions would be only weakly and perhaps non-phenomenologically transparent. This difference is used by Deonna and Teroni to support their account of emotions as attitudes toward values.[26] Moreover, as stressed by Tappolet (2016), it can be used to question theories that cast emotions as perceptions of values.

Some have contrasted *moods* with both perception and emotions, as an even more straightforward failure of Phenomenological Transparency, and some have concluded that moods are not representational (Deonna and Teroni 2012; Kind 2013; Bordini 2017).[27]

Other theorists have looked at differences in transparency between sensory and affective phenomenology rather than perceptual and non-perceptual experiences. For example, Aydede (2019: 684, 694) maintains that perceptual and bodily experiences, pain and pleasure included, are phenomenologically and strongly transparent, insofar as they are considered from the point of view of the *sensory* aspects involved in their phenomenology, but doubts that such a combination can be extended to the distinctively *affective* bit involved in at least some of those experiences—e.g., the painfulness of pain (see also Barlassina 2020). Aydede and Fulkerson (2014) argue against such an extension.[28] This might suggest a deep difference between sensory and affective components of phenomenal character, regardless of their being involved in perceptual or non-perceptual experiences.

However, differences in transparency have been highlighted within the sensory domain, too, to stress relevant differences between sensory modalities. For example, Lycan (2000: 281) claims that, unlike visual and auditory qualities, "a smell seems a modification of our own consciousness rather than a property of a perceptual object that would exist unperceived."

6.2.3 Cross-Modal Phenomenological Differences and the Core of Transparency

However, variations in transparency across different sensory modalities might also lead one to argue that Phenomenological Transparency misses the real phenomenological core of transparency, failing to capture the relevant phenomenon.

---

[26] See also Deonna and Teroni (2015). de Sousa (2004) defends a similar view. Mitchell (2020) argues for a combination of Weak and Restricted Phenomenological Transparency in the case of emotion. Tye (2008) argues that emotions are as transparent as perception. Mendelovici (2013a, b) argues that emotions (but not moods) and perception are phenomenologically on a par: both present us with qualities that are experienced as properties of worldly object, and that exhausts their phenomenal character.

[27] For an argument to the effect that moods represent despite their phenomenology, see Mendelovici (2013a, b).

[28] For views that the affective component of pain/pleasure experience is transparent, see, e.g., Tye (2006); Cutter and Tye (2011); Carruthers (2018).

For example, Frey (2013) acknowledges phenomenological variations among sensory experiences—e.g., at least some of them would involve qualities that do not appear externally located, worldly, or mind-independent. His diagnosis is that standard formulations of Phenomenological Transparency are too metaphysically loaded, in that they categorize sensory qualities by making use of descriptors such as "external", "mind-dependent", "objective", etc. On top of exposing them to counterexamples, this makes them incapable of rendering the deep phenomenological lesson that transparency has to teach, namely, that in all cases, we appreciate sensory qualities as *other* than ourselves:

> [W]hen we phenomenally appreciate a sensuous element in an experience, we appreciate it as being both something other than ourselves and as standing in opposition to ourselves. This view, which I call *Core Transparency* (CT), can be formulated in two interdependent ways.
>
> (CT1) The sensuous elements that one phenomenally appreciates in an experience are always appreciated as other.
>
> (CT2) The sensuous elements that one phenomenally appreciates in an experience are never appreciated as being, being instantiated in, or being about the self qua experiential subject (or a state/mode thereof).
>
> (Frey 2013: 76)

Discussing olfactory experience and objecting to both Lycan's and Tye's views, Batty (2010: 113) makes a very similar suggestion:

> *Generalized Transparency:*
> An experience is generally transparent iff all of the modality-salient properties of which you are aware appear to be properties of something other than the experience itself.

Notice: Phenomenological Transparency, so revised, is meant to extend over the entire sensory domain but *not* beyond that domain—so, not to affective phenomenology (Frey 2013: 77). Hence, as it stands, this is a localist proposal. It would be an interesting project to explore the possibility of using the model offered by Batty and Frey to try and overcome differences between sensory and affective phenomenology, too, or alternatively to pin down more precisely the phenomenological differences between sensory and affective phenomenology (Bordini 2014: ch. 4).

7. Conclusion

My aim in this chapter has been to give structure to the debate on the transparency of experience by constructing a unitary logical space where the different views could be identified, mapped, and confronted. According to the reconstruction I have offered here, such a logical space is complex and multidimensional. In particular, it involves five dimensions: introspective target, introspective focus, phenomenology, metaphysics, and scope of the view.

The discussion suggests that the recent developments of the debate, and the distinction of many different transparency theses and notions, have not led to a merely verbal dispute but involve substantial disagreement. Theorists do not disagree on the meaning of the word "transparency", but on what it is for an experience to be transparent and what (if any) experiences are transparent in the relevant sense.

Given my reconstruction, one might wonder whether transparency is a single, unitary phenomenon or a cluster of somehow parented phenomena. Such questions are importantly connected to the crucial questions of what is the right view of transparency and what (if any) is its significance for the study of consciousness and the mind more generally. I have not addressed these issues here, but I take the work done in this chapter to be preliminary and preparatory for properly framing and assessing them.[29]

References

Aydede, Murat (2019). Is the Experience of Pain Transparent? *Synthese*, 196: 677–708.

Aydede, Murat and Matthew Fulkerson (2014). Affect: Representationalists' Headache. *Philosophical Studies*, 170(2): 175–98.

Barlassina, Luca (2020). Beyond Good and Bad: Reflexive Imperativism, not Evaluativism, Explains Valence. *Thought*, 9: 274–84.

---

[29] For extremely useful conversations on these topics, I would like to thank Luca Barlassina, Arnaud Dewalque, Anna Giustina, Uriah Kriegel, Gianfranco Soldati, and Giuliano Torrengo. I am grateful to Isabel Käslin and Uriah Kriegel for their extensive comments on previous drafts of this chapter. The research that led to this chapter was generously funded by the Belgian Fund for Scientific Research (F.R.S.-FNRS, project T.0095.18, "The Phenomenology of Mental States") and the Swiss National Science Foundation (SNSF, project 100019E_177538, "L'Expérience des États Mentaux").

Barlassina, Luca and Max K. Hayward (2019a). Loopy Regulations: The Motivational Profile of Affective Phenomenology. *Philosophical Topics*, 47(2): 233–61.

Barlassina, Luca and Max K. Hayward (2019b). More of Me! Less of Me! Reflexive Imperativism about Affective Phenomenal Character. *Mind*, 128(512): 1013–44.

Batty, Clare (2010). Scents and Sensibilia. *American Philosophical Quarterly*, 47(2): 103–18.

Block, Ned (1990). Inverted Earth. *Philosophical Perspectives*, 4: 53–79.

Block, Ned (1996). Mental Paint and Mental Latex. *Philosophical Issues*, 7: 19–49.

Block, Ned (2003). Mental Paint. In M. Hahn and B. Ramberg (eds.), *Reflections and Replies: Essays on the Philosophy of Tyler Burge*, Cambridge, MA: MIT Press.

Boghossian, Paul and David Velleman (1989). Color as a Secondary Quality. *Mind*, 98(389): 81–103.

Bordini, Davide (2014). *The Transparencies and the Opacities of Experience: Intentionalism, Phenomenal Character, and Moods*. PhD Dissertation. University of Milan.

Bordini, Davide (2017). Not in the Mood for Intentionalism. *Midwest Studies in Philosophy*, 41: 60–81.

Byrne, Alex (2018). *Transparency and Self-Knowledge*. Oxford: Oxford University Press.

Campbell, John (2009). Consciousness and Reference. In B. P. McLaughlin, B. Ansgar, and W. Sven (eds.), *The Oxford Handbook of Philosophy of Mind*. Oxford: Oxford University Press.

Carruthers, Peter (2018). Valence and Value. *Philosophy and Phenomenological Research*, 97(3): 658–80.

Chalmers, David (2004). The Representational Character of Experience. In B. Leiter (ed.), *The Future for Philosophy*. Oxford: Oxford University Press.

Crane, Tim (2006). Is There a Perceptual Relation? In T. Szabo Gendler and J. Hawthorne (eds.), *Perceptual Experience*. Oxford: Oxford University Press.

Crane, Tim (2009). Is Perception a Propositional Attitude? *The Philosophical Quarterly*, 59(236): 452–69.

Cutter, Brian and Michael Tye. (2011). Tracking Representationalism and the Painfulness of Pain. *Philosophical Issues*, 21(1): 90–109.

de Sousa, Ronald (2004). Emotions—What I Know, What I'd Like to Think I Know, and What I'd Like to Think. In R. C. Solomon (ed.), *Thinking about Feeling*. Oxford: Oxford University Press.

Deonna, Julien and Fabrice Teroni (2012). *The Emotions: A Philosophical Introduction*. London: Routledge.

Deonna, Julien and Fabrice Teroni (2015). Emotions as Attitudes. *Dialectica*, 69(3): 293–311.

Dretske, Fred (1981). *Knowledge and the Flow of Information*. Cambridge, MA: MIT Press.

Dretske, Fred (1988). *Explaining Behavior: Reasons in a World of Causes*. Cambridge, MA: MIT Press.

Dretske, Fred (1994). Introspection. *Proceedings of the Aristotelian Society*, 94: 263–78.

Dretske, Fred (1996). Phenomenal Externalism, or If Meanings Ain't in the Head, Where Are Qualia? *Philosophical Issues*, 7: 143–58.

Dretske, Fred (1999). The Mind's Awareness of Itself. *Philosophical Studies*, 95(1–2): 103–24.

Farkas, Katalyn (2013). Constructing a World for the Senses. In U. Kriegel (ed.), *Phenomenal Intentionality*. Oxford: Oxford University Press.

Fodor, Jerry (1990). *A Theory of Content and Other Essays*. Cambridge, MA: MIT Press.

French, Craig (2018). Naïve Realism and Diaphaneity. *Proceedings of the Aristotelian Society*, 118(2): 149–75.

Frey, Christopher (2013). Phenomenal Presence. In U. Kriegel (ed.), *Phenomenal Intentionality*. Oxford: Oxford University Press.

Gow, Laura (2016). The Limitations of Perceptual Transparency. *The Philosophical Quarterly*, 66(265): 723–44.

Gow, Laura (2019). Everything is Clear: All Perceptual Experiences Are Transparent. *European Journal of Philosophy*, 27: 412–25.

Harman, Gilbert (1990). The Intrinsic Quality of Experience. *Philosophical Perspectives*, 4: 31–52.

Horgan, Terence and John Tienson (2002). The Intentionality of Phenomenology and the Phenomenology of Intentionality. In D. Chalmers (ed.), *Philosophy of Mind: Classical and Contemporary Readings*. Oxford: Oxford University Press.

Horgan, Terence, John Tienson, and George Graham (2004). Phenomenal Intentionality and the Brain in a Vat. In R. Schantz (ed.), *The Externalist Challenge*. Berlin: Walter De Gruyter.

Johnston, Mark (2004). The Obscure Object of Hallucination. *Philosophical Studies*, 120: 113–83.

Kennedy, Matthew (2009). Heirs of Nothing: The Implications of Transparency. *Philosophy and Phenomenological Research*, 79(3): 574–604.

Kind, Amy (2003). What's So Transparent about Transparency? *Philosophical Studies*, 115: 225-44.

Kind, Amy (2007). Restrictions on Representationalism. *Philosophical Studies*, 134: 405-27.

Kind, Amy (2013). The Case against Representationalism about Moods. In U. Kriegel (ed.), *Current Controversies in the Philosophy of Mind*. London: Routledge.

Kriegel, Uriah (2007). Intentional Inexistence and Phenomenal Intentionality. *Philosophical Perspectives*, 21: 307-40.

Kriegel, Uriah (2011). *The Sources of Intentionality*. Oxford: Oxford University Press.

Loar, Brian (2003). Transparent Experience and the Availability of Qualia. In Q. Smith and A. Jokic (eds.), *Consciousness: New Philosophical Perspectives*. Oxford: Oxford University Press.

Lycan, William G. (1996). *Consciousness and Experience*. Cambridge, MA: MIT Press.

Lycan, William G. (2000). The Slighting of Smell. In N. Bhushan and S. Rosenfeld (eds.), *Of Minds and Molecules: New Philosophical Perspectives on Chemistry*. New York: Oxford University Press.

Lycan, William G. (2014). The Intentionality of Smell. *Frontiers in Psychology*, 5: 436.

Martin, Michael G. F. (2002). The Transparency of Experience. *Mind and Language*, 17(4): 376-425.

Martin, Michael G. F. (2004). The Limits of Self-Awareness, *Philosophical Studies*, 103: 37-89.

Masrour, Farid (2013). Phenomenal Objectivity and Phenomenal Intentionality. In U. Kriegel (ed.), *Phenomenal Intentionality*. Oxford: Oxford University Press.

Mendelovici, Angela (2013a). Intentionalism about Moods. *Thought* 2: 126-136.

Mendelovici, Angela (2013b). Pure Intentionalism about Emotions and Moods. In U. Kriegel (ed.), *Current Controversies in the Philosophy of Mind*. London: Routledge.

Mendelovici, Angela (2018). *The Phenomenal Basis of Intentionality*. Oxford: Oxford University Press.

Mitchell, Jonathan (2020). The Attitudinal Opacity of Emotional Experience. *The Philosophical Quarterly*, 70(280): 524-46.

Molyneaux, Bernard (2009). Why Experience Told Me Nothing about Transparency. *Noûs*, 43(1): 116-36.

Moore, G. E. (1903). The Refutation of Idealism. *Mind*, 48: 433-453.

Papineau, David (2021). *The Metaphysics of Sensory Experience*. Oxford: Oxford University Press.

Phillips, Ian (2013). Afterimages and Sensation. *Philosophy and Phenomenological Research*, 87(2): 417–53.

Reid, Thomas (1764/1970). *An Inquiry into the Human Mind*, ed. T. Duggan. Chicago: University of Chicago Press.

Richardson, Louise (2010). Seeing Empty Space. *European Journal of Philosophy*, 18(2): 227–43.

Richardson, Louise (2013). Sniffing and Smelling. *Philosophical Studies*, 162: 401–19.

Richardson, Louise (2014). Space, Time and Molyneaux's Question. *Ratio*, 27(4): 483–505.

Siegel, Susanna (2006). Subject and Object in the Contents of Visual Experience. *Philosophical Review*, 115(3): 355–88.

Siewert, Charles (2004). Is experience transparent? *Philosophical Studies*, 117: 15–41.

Siewert, Charles (2012). On The Phenomenology of Introspection. In D. Smithies and D. Stoljar (eds.), *Introspection and Consciousness*. Oxford: Oxford University Press.

Soteriou, Matthew (2011). The Perception of Absence, Space, and Time. In H. Lerman and N. Eilan (eds.), *Perception, Causation, and Objectivity*. Oxford: Oxford University Press.

Soteriou, Matthew (2013). *The Mind's Construction: The Ontology of Mind and Mental Action*, Oxford: Oxford University Press.

Tappolet, Christine (2016). *Emotions, Values, and Agency*. Oxford: Oxford University Press.

Tye, Michael (1995). *Ten Problems of Consciousness*. Cambridge, MA: MIT Press.

Tye, Michael (2000). *Consciousness, Color, and Content*. Cambridge, MA: MIT Press.

Tye, Michael (2006). Another Look at Representationalism about Pain. In M. Aydede (ed.), *Pain: New Essays on Its Nature and the Methodology of Its Study*. Cambridge, MA: MIT Press.

Tye, Michael (2008). The Experience of Emotion. *Revue Internationale de Philosophie*, 62: 25–50.

Tye, Michael (2014). Transparency, Qualia, and Representationalism. *Philosophical Studies*, 170: 39–57.

PART III
BOOK SYMPOSIUM ON DAVID PAPINEAU'S *THE METAPHYSICS OF SENSORY EXPERIENCE*

11
Précis of *The Metaphysics of Sensory Experience*

David Papineau

My book defends the *qualitative* view that conscious sensory experiences are intrinsic states of people that are not essentially related to any further objects or properties.

There are affinities between my view and the defence of "qualia" by philosophers like Ned Block and Christopher Peacocke. But my position is more thoroughgoingly qualitative than theirs. Block and Peacocke argue that there are non-relational qualitative aspects to colour and shape experiences—Block calls them "mental paint"—*in addition* to the relational aspects of those experiences. As I see it, however, the qualitative aspects of experience are not add-ons to putatively relational features of experience. Rather they exhaust the nature of experience. In my view, *it's all paint*.

In defending the view that experience is qualitative, I set myself at odds, not only with such explicitly relational views as naïve realism and sense datum theories, but also with *representationalist* theories that equate experiential states with the relational possession of representational contents.

I make it clear, though, that I do not deny that sensory experiences *are* representational. I certainly accept that conscious sensory experiences are typically caused by environmental conditions, and that they guide subjects' behaviour in ways appropriate to those conditions. And, given that I accept a broadly naturalist view of representation, I take those systematic correlations with environmental conditions to suffice for those conscious experiences to *represent* those conditions.

However, those who identify themselves as "representationalists" in the philosophy of perception hold far stronger commitments than this. They maintain that the representational contents of sensory experiences are *essentially* tied to their conscious nature. They don't think, as do I, that this connection derives from the way certain intrinsic conscious properties are contingently correlated with environmental conditions. Rather they hold that the contents and the conscious characters necessarily go together.

I offer an analogy with words. The sentence "Elvis once visited Paris", taken as a sequence of marks or sounds, represents a certain possible circumstance all right. But it doesn't represent that circumstance essentially. It could well have represented something different, or nothing at all. I view conscious sensory experiences as akin to sentences. They represent contingently. But representationalists in the philosophy of perception deny this. In their view, it is built into the nature of conscious experiences, though not of sentences, that they represent as they do.

Chapter 1

I explain these general features of my position in the Introduction to the book. Chapter 1 then maps out the ground in more detail. I discuss both sense datum theories and naïve realism, and give my reasons for laying them aside. Sense datum theories are dealt with relatively briefly and dismissed as difficult to reconcile with physicalism. Naïve realism is treated at greater length. After making some general points about the explanatory differences between factive and non-factive mental states, I offer three objections to naïve realism: first, it has difficultly with the timing of perceptions of temporally distant events; second, similarities between sensory states seem to go with intrinsic cerebral similarities rather than with similarities in objects perceived; and, third, naïve realism seems unable coherently to maintain its fundamental commitment to the possibility of conscious differences that are not apparent to introspection.

In chapter 1 I also explain that representationalists fall into two quite different camps, which I distinguish as *naturalist representationalism* and *phenomenal intentionalism*. Naturalist representationalists aim to explain sensory consciousness in terms of representation, and then to explain representation in naturalist terms, by reducing it to correlations between internal states and environmental conditions. The phenomenal intentionalists reverse the direction of explanation, and aim to explain sensory representation in terms of sensory consciousness. As they see it, naturalist correlations with environmental conditions can only account for mechanical relations of "detection", where representation properly so-called needs to derive from the inherent structure of consciousness.

Chapter 2

Chapter 2 is devoted to a critique of representationalist views. It begins by putting pressure on the assumption, common to both naturalist representationalism and phenomenal intentionalism, that the conscious characters and representational contents of sensory experiences are necessarily tied together. I observe that conscious character—how an experience feels—and representational content—the accuracy condition of the experience—are very different things, and that most of the arguments normally offered in support of representationalism suffice at best to show that sensory experiences contingently happen to be representations, not that they possess their representational contents essentially.

I then turn to naturalist representationalism. At first pass, I observe, this seems a counter-intuitive view. According to naturalist representationalism, the conscious character of a sensory experience is fixed, not by the relevant intrinsic state of the subject, but by whatever distal environmental condition that state happens to be correlated with—with the implication that a given intrinsic state would feel different if it had a different distal correlate, while a different intrinsic state would feel the same if it had the same distal correlate.

Despite the oddity of this stance, naturalist representationalists typically commandeer the support of intuition by appealing to the "transparency" of experience, that is, to the way that introspection apparently shows worldly properties like *yellowness* and *roundness* to be constituents of experiences (from which it is then taken to follow that experiences essentially represent the environmental presence of such properties).

However, this appeal to transparency raises its own difficulties. In what sense can naturalist representationalists take properties like *yellowness* and *roundness* to be constituents of experience? I point out that this idea is far less straightforward for naturalist representationalists than it is for naïve realists or sense datum theorists. At least the latter views hold that worldly properties like *yellowness* and *roundness* feature in experiences in virtue of being *instantiated* by the objects or sense data that the experiences involve. But naturalist representationalists are "common factor theorists", and so hold that the same conscious sensory properties obtain in "bad cases" of illusion and hallucination as well as in "good cases" of veridical perception. So they must hold that worldly properties like *yellowness* and *roundness* are constituents of experiences even when uninstantiated, and so feature in experience as pure properties abstracted from any objects that might possess them. And this, I then argue, is surely inconsistent with the concrete causal nature of conscious states. Conscious states are here-and-now, concrete facts with causes and effects. This seems incompatible with their being constituted by some non-instantiation relation to abstract properties with no local embodiment.

At the end of chapter 2 I generalize this form of argument so that it is directed, not just at those who think that uninstantiated worldly properties are present in experience, but at any representationalists who equates the conscious character of a sensory experience with the experience's possession of accuracy conditions. I point out that the possession of accuracy conditions is itself an abstract state, a relation to a possibly uninstantiated *possibilium*, and so cannot constitute a concrete conscious state with causes and effects.

At this point I note that a number of philosophers who are normally placed in the phenomenal intentionalist camp, including Brian Loar, Uriah Kriegel, and Angela Mendelovici, are prepared to abandon the claim that conscious sensory character relationally determines accuracy conditions without the assistance of contingent environmental embedding, and to content themselves with the claim that sensory consciousness is at least intrinsically *directed*, somehow pointing to a world beyond itself. It is a nice question, I point out, how far this "non-relational phenomenal intentionalism" differs from my own qualitative view, and I postpone further discussion until I have developed my qualitative view further.

Chapter 3

I begin the positive elaboration of my qualitative view in chapter 3. I start by pointing out that my view evades many of the challenges facing representationalism; in particular, since it does not aspire to any necessary connection between sensory character and sensory content, it is happily free to ascribe "broad contents" to sensory experiences.

In the light of these advantages, I ask why there seem to be no other defenders of my straightforward qualitative view in the contemporary literature. I suggest that this might be due to the way that those writers who are prepared to countenance "qualia", like Block and Peacocke, also tend to run "functional" properties together with "representational" ones, and so misguidedly take the functional nature of many sensory properties to show that they are related to representational contents.

I then stress that my own qualitative view does not deny that sensory experience has a rich internal structure. Following Katalin Farkas (2013), I note how certain experiential properties, such as those correlated with shapes and colours, display a coherence and predictability that distinguishes them from those associated with pains, say, or after-images. Moreover, I observe, our experience is further characterized by stable clusters of such properties that behave in an object-like manner. I suggest the terminology of "quasi-objects" and their "quasi-properties" for these features of experience.

Farkas observes that the constancy and coherence of these "quasi-objects" and their "quasi-properties" makes it attractive to think of them as somehow *mind-independent*. I do not deny this attraction. But in truth—and Farkas does not claim otherwise—there is nothing in her observations to show that sensory experience is genuinely related to anything mind-independent. She is pointing entirely to structures *within* experience, and that alone is not enough to show that experience is related to anything outside it.

The temptation to view sensory experience as essentially relational, however, is compounded when Farkas's observations are combined with the notion that sensory states have "intentional objects". A commitment to "intentional objects" is one response to the challenge of understanding the manner in which representational mental states are *about* objects (whether essentially or contingently). At first pass, if you are *thinking of King Arthur*, or *visually experiencing a white rabbit*, it looks as if your mental state is related to an object, namely, King Arthur, or a white rabbit. But what if there is no such king or rabbit? Some philosophers say that in such cases your mental state is still related to an object—albeit one that doesn't exist. As they see it, representational mental states always point beyond themselves to their "intentional objects." In most cases, these will be ordinary constituents of reality, but sometimes they will be non-existent items. (After all, who would deny that people sometimes think about things that don't exist?)

While I myself would opt for a different account of the structure of representational mental states, I have no great objection to the doctrine of possibly non-existent intentional objects as such. However, once intentional objects are on the table, it is very tempting to take the further step of identifying them with the "quasi-objects" present in sensory experience—and this can then be the source of great confusion. Brian Loar expresses the temptation perfectly:

> Now imagine having one of the lemon-experiences without knowing whether it is veridical. You are strongly tempted to say 'that object'... you seem both to commit yourself, by using a demonstrative, and to take it back at the same time: 'that object may or may not exist'. The phenomenology gives you the feel of a sort of ontologically neutral object that could have the property of existing or not-existing... (2003: 54)

Loar here invites us to start with the "quasi-object" ("the phenomenology gives you the feel") and then to identify that with the "intentional object" at which the experience is directed ("may or may not exist"). But once we succumb to this invitation, we are inevitably seduced into a relational view of experience. For the identification implies that in the good cases, where we are really seeing a lemon, the quasi-object is identical to a real lemon, and so will enjoy such worldly properties as yellowness and lemon-shapedness. But the quasi-object will be no less part of experience in the bad cases as well, and so these worldly properties will be displayed there too, although in those cases they will not be instantiated by any real object...

And thus we end up with the "transparency" view, the focus of much of my chapter 2, according to which possibly uninstantiated worldly properties are present in experience, and thereby represent themselves to be instantiated in the subject's environment. (It is noteworthy how many of those who trade in "transparency" seek to assuage worries about the experiential presence of uninstantiated worldly properties by appeal to their supposed possession by non-existent "intentional objects".)

This whole path to "transparency", however, is quite broken-backed. It makes no sense to assimilate "quasi-objects" to intentional objects. The former are items *within* experience, and as such definitely exist, both in the good veridical cases and in bad hallucinatory cases. The latter are putative items *beyond* experience, which might or might not exist, depending on whether the case is good or bad. Something which definitely exists cannot be identified with something that might or might not exist.

It should be said that Brian Loar does not endorse this identification. The passage quoted above is not intended to show that experience is essentially related to anything beyond itself, but only that, even so, it is inherently *directed*—in Loar's phrase, it is "paint that points". As Loar sees it, this pointing is inherent in the way that the structure of experience "strongly tempts" us to view it as reaching beyond itself.

Still, is there anything in the structure of conscious experience to show that it is *really* essentially directed outwards? Experience is certainly organized in a way that renders it suitable for representing aspects of our environment, and this structure has no doubt been selected by evolution for this purpose. But does this mean that the conscious experiential state is essentially directional, even in abstraction from these environmental connections?

Farkas might show that the constancy and coherence of "quasi-objects" and their "quasi-properties" creates an intuitive impression that they are "mind-independent." And Loar might show that this impression is reinforced when we are "strongly tempted" to identify "quasi-objects" with the putative worldly referents of sensory experiences. However, none of this shows experience is genuinely directed beyond itself. After all, as Farkas and Loar both allow, they are offering reasons why people *mistakenly* come to view experience as relational. But that experience is such as to induce people to *mischaracterize* it as relational is scarcely enough to show that it is really somehow inherently directed beyond itself. In the end, I argue, we have been given nothing to substantiate the "non-relational phenomenal intentionalism" considered at the end of chapter 2.

Chapter 4

In the final chapter of the book I explore the implications of my qualitative view for a range of related issues.

First, I return to "transparency", and in particular to the psychological circumstance that we seem unable to shift our introspective focus onto the specifically qualitative elements in our experience. I observe that this is scarcely surprising, given my view that sensory experience contains nothing but qualitative "paint". I explain that introspection is a *cognitive* act, and that (once we put some complications about the workings of sensory attention to one side) we should not expect our sensory consciousness to be altered just by our starting to think about it.

Having invoked the possibility of sensory introspection, I then address the question of how it works. I suggest that in the general run of cases we cognitively characterize our sensory experiences by noting what beliefs they incline us to form. This of course leaves us with questions about how we introspectively know what beliefs we have and what experiences they stem from, but I note that the literature already contains well-developed answers to these questions.

I then consider whether this model of sensory introspection is consistent with the "phenomenal concept" response to Frank Jackson's "knowledge argument" against physicalism. Phenomenal concepts are normally introduced as directly recognitional ways of introspectively identifying sensory states. But my suggested account of sensory introspection implies that it characterizes sensory states indirectly, in terms of the representational contents of the beliefs they prompt, which are in turn characterized in terms of the worldly properties they involve. In response, I observe that this more complex account is still able to preserve the general spirit of the phenomenal concept response to Jackson's argument, by appealing to the way that new experiences will lead to subjects forming new directly recognitional *perceptual* concepts of worldly properties (like *redness*), and hence derivatively to forming new *phenomenal* concepts of *experiences of redness*.

There are affinities between my qualitative view and the "adverbialist" view of sensory experience defended in the middle of the last century. Given this, I discuss some issues about sensory experience *reports* that are widely viewed as invalidating adverbialism. I first survey the range of rough-and-ready devices that everyday discourse uses to characterize sensory states. I then consider the prospects for a more regimented language that is faithful to the qualitative nature of sensory states. It turns out that some of the traditional challenges to adverbialism correspond to ways in which such a language would be constrained, but I argue that these constraints are indeed ones that should be respected by a regimented language for sensory reports.

Finally, I explore the implications of my view for the debate about "rich sensory contents". I note that nearly all participants in this debate assume that sensory contents derive from the "presence" of worldly properties in conscious experience, and so do not countenance the possibility of consciously similar subjects enjoying different sensory contents. Since my qualitative view is not constrained in this way, I am happy to allow some very rich sensory contents indeed, including sensory representation of biological kinds and particular people. I show that there is plenty of independent reason to accept such strongly rich contents, once we free ourselves from the idea that sensory content is essentially tied to conscious sensory character. I point out that, once we recognize the full range of rich sensory contents, we face a number of further empirical questions about the workings of sensory representation. Rather than pursuing these further, however, I content myself with the observation that any answers should respect the metaphysical independence of sensory content and conscious sensory character.

References

Farkas, K. 2013. "Constructing a World for the Senses" in Kriegel, U. ed *Phenomenal Intentionality* Oxford: Oxford University Press 99–115.

Loar, B. 2003. "Phenomenal Intentionality as the Basis of Mental Content" in Hahn, M. and Ramberg, B. eds *Reflections and Replies: Essay on the Philosophy of Tyler Burge* Cambridge, Mass: MIT Press 229–58.

12
Papineau on Sensory Experience

Alex Byrne

David Papineau's characteristically clever, original, and forthright *The Metaphysics of Sensory Experience* is a pleasure to read.[1] From my perspective, the book presents a kind of looking-glass world where black is white and up is down. Naturally from Papineau's perspective my own views look equally bonkers.

I will touch on three topics: Papineau's case against property-awareness, his diagnosis of the phenomenon of "transparency," and his account of colour similarity.

1. Consciousness and Awareness of Properties

Consider Papineau's signature example: "I am looking at a yellow ball in the middle of my garden lawn." "In so doing," he continues, "I am having a conscious visual experience, constituted by my instantiating certain conscious properties, properties that I would cease to possess if I closed my eyes" (1).

Switching to myself for convenience, what are these "conscious properties" that I possess when I look at the yellow ball? Well, I see the yellow ball, and the ball looks yellow to me. So here are two candidates: *seeing the yellow ball*, and *being such that the ball looks yellow to me*. Neither of those are what Papineau has in mind, since without the ball, I could have neither property, and on Papineau's view,

> conscious sensory properties are intrinsic qualitative properties of people. When I have a visual experience of a yellow ball, for example, I have a certain conscious property, a certain feeling, which does not essentially

---

[1] Papineau 2021; all page references are to this book unless otherwise noted.

involve any relations to anything outside me. Taken purely in itself, my state does not guarantee the presence of an actual yellow ball .... (1)

This quotation shows why substituting 'a ball' for 'the ball' doesn't help: *seeing a yellow ball* can't be a Papineau-style conscious property, because it is not intrinsic. Let's try something even less committal. I *seem* to see a yellow ball. Hallucinating a yellow ball is one way of seeming to see one, so this looks more promising. Perhaps hallucinations *do* involve relations to things "outside me," but it is standardly assumed that they don't, and anyway we want to characterize sensory experiences in a way that leaves this issue open.

Seeming to see a yellow ball, understood in the natural way, is one of Papineau's "conscious sensory properties." If I see a yellow ball in good light, and imagine someone having a "phenomenologically identical" experience, then (in the intended interpretation) I am imagining someone who "seems to see a yellow ball." In Papineau's preferred formulation, this conscious sensory property is *"visually experiencing a yellow ball"* (15).

It is important to add a caveat. If someone seems to see a yellow ball on the lawn, one might think she is inclined to believe that there is a yellow ball on the lawn, or at least before her. Moreover, this is not a contingent connection: seeming to see a yellow ball necessarily suggests the presence of a yellow ball, even though it is a suggestion than can be resisted. That, however, is not Papineau's view. Consider the words 'Hay una bola amarilla'. Inscribed by some purported truth-teller, they do suggest the presence of a yellow ball—but only to someone who understands Spanish. To a monolingual Chinese speaker, they suggest nothing. And those very same orthographically individuated marks, appearing in a world in which language users never evolved, have no semantic connection to balls, the colour yellow, or anything else. Papineau thinks that *seeming to see a yellow ball* is analogous:

> Imagine a cosmic brain in a vat, a perfect duplicate of my brain that coagulates by cosmic happenstance in interstellar space, together with sustaining vat, and proceeds to operate just like my brain for some minutes, with the same sensory cortical inputs, motor cortical outputs, and intervening neuronal processes. I take it that this being would share all my conscious sensory experiences. Yet its sensory states would represent nothing. They would lack the kind of systematic connections with worldly circumstances required for representational significance. They would no

more have a representational content than would the marks 'Elvis Presley once visited Paris' traced out by the wind on some mountain on Mars. (6)

On Papineau's view, seeming to see a yellow ball has no more connection to yellowness and sphericity than it does to blueness and triangularity. When a cosmic brain in a vat seems to see a yellow ball, it is not inclined in the slightest to form beliefs about the presence of a yellow ball.

On a rival view, when someone seems to see a yellow ball, she may not see a ball, but she is aware (or is in a position to be aware) of some worldly items, yellowness and sphericity—those properties are "present in" her experience. There is thus an intimate connection between seeming to see a yellow ball and yellowness, a connection that is absent between seeming to see a yellow ball and blueness. We can call this the *Moorean view*, since it can be found in Moore's "The Refutation of Idealism" (1903).[2]

On the Moorean view, seeing a yellow object in good light is one way of becoming aware of yellowness. But someone can be aware of yellowness even though she is not aware of any yellow object, as in illusion or hallucination. Papineau thinks this is completely wrong: "I don't see how *any* worldly properties can be present in experience. The whole idea strikes me as quite misplaced" (60).

Does Papineau think that *any* properties, worldly or unworldly, can be present in experience? He does: "The only properties 'present in' experience are conscious properties of people, not worldly properties" (118). People are just as worldly as beachballs and lemons, so in that sense conscious properties are also worldly, but it's clear what Papineau means. When I look at the yellow ball, the only properties present in my experience are properties of *me*—specifically, conscious sensory properties like *seeming to see a yellow ball*.

Papineau has two lines of objection against the Moorean view. First, he thinks that the idea "that uninstantiated properties can be *present* in sensory experience" is "inconsistent with the here-and-now nature of conscious experience" (65). He explains his reasoning in this passage:

> As I see it, when I instantiate the property of *visually experiencing a yellow ball*, this results in a local fact, a state which is here-and-now, in line with the immediate nature of my sensory consciousness. By contrast, if I am

---

[2] Papineau cites Moore's paper in connection with the famous passage about "transparency" (73, fn. 12).

mentally related to some property, but without instantiating it, then *the resulting relational fact is by no means local, but extended into whatever distal realm the property in question inhabits.* That is why I say that mental relations to properties as such, abstracted from their instances, cannot constitute the here-and-now nature of sensory experience.

(66; second emphasis added)

Suppose I see a yellow ball on the lawn, and am thereby mentally related to yellowness (instantiated by the ball, not by me). Here is a relational fact: I am visually aware that a yellow ball is on the lawn. That fact involves a relation between me and another fact, the latter itself involving a relation between the yellow ball and the lawn. The fact that I am visually aware that a yellow ball on the lawn is not "local" to me, in the sense that it does not supervene on facts about how I am intrinsically. Let us grant, for the sake of the argument, that this means that this fact "cannot constitute the nature of sensory experience," because sensory experience is local, confined to the "here-and-now."

But what about the (ostensible) fact that I am aware of yellowness? That is a relational fact, but it involves a relation to a property. According to the Moorean, that very fact obtains in a counterfactual situation in which the ball isn't yellow but merely looks that way, or in which I am hallucinating a yellow ball. The relational fact that I am aware of yellowness does not involve a relation to a ball, or an "instance" of yellowness (understood as a trope or particularized property). Admittedly, if the property or universal yellowness is spatially located in yellow objects, then when I am aware of yellowness (even when hallucinating) I am aware of an entity that is multiply located, with some locations being very distant. But the fact that I am aware of yellowness does not depend on the existence of these remote yellow objects; for all that has been said, that I am aware of yellowness may be a "local" fact, concerning how I am intrinsically—what is going on in the "distal realm" is irrelevant.[3]

Even granted the premise about the "here-and-now" nature of sensory experience, Papineau's first argument against the Moorean view seems to me not to succeed. (I do not grant the premise, but that is another story.)

Papineau's second objection turns on considerations of causation. Some facts are "*concrete*":

---

[3] See the exchange between Pautz 2019 and Block 2019, and Pautz 2021: 170–85.

> constituted by some spatio-temporal particular (or particulars) instantiating some first-order property (or relation). *A ball being yellow* (or *on the table*) are concrete facts. These concrete facts are the kinds of items that can enter into causal relations. They are localized in space and time and have causes and effects. (66–7)

Non-concrete facts, for instance facts of pure arithmetic, are not "eligible to enter into causal relations" (71). The fact that I seem to see a yellow ball is not one of those, because: "it can result from concrete causes, such as the yellow ball being nearby, and can give rise to concrete effects, such as my kicking the ball" (67). However,

> relations between human subjects and properties as such, abstracted from their instances, do not amount to concrete facts. If I bear some mental relation to the property of yellowness as such, even though yellowness is not instantiated anywhere nearby, this cannot be the kind of concrete local fact that is capable of entering into causal relations. Since yellowness as such lives in the realm of abstract properties, this relational fact involves me, the abstract property of yellowness, and some mental relation joining the two. This relational fact is by no means here-and-now. (67)

If the ostensible fact that I am aware of yellowness is not concrete, and so causally impotent, there is no reason to believe in such a thing.

But why is that ostensible fact not "here-and-now"? The "realm of abstract properties" is not literally a *distal* realm, *outside* the perceiver. Notice that Papineau (rightly) countenances relational facts among the concrete, for instance *that the ball is on the table*. Some relational facts involving numbers also appear to be concrete (or, at any rate, eligible to enter into causal relations). The fact that the number of bangs = 3 could be causally explained by the fact that a single explosion occurred in an echo-producing cavity, or that the number of explosions = 3. If relations to abstracta like numbers don't prevent a fact from being concrete, why can't the fact that I am related to yellowness be concrete? Papineau insists that it isn't, but he gives no argument.

Here's a related point, which I will mention but not defend: deciding between theories by wielding an abstract principle about causation almost always fails, either because it is unclear that the principle excludes any theory, or else because it is unclear that the principle is true.

2. Transparency

On Papineau's view, seeming to see a yellow ball amounts to instantiating an "intrinsic qualitative property" which does not in any way point towards the subject's environment. When I see a yellow ball in good light, on Papineau's view I am instantiating the intrinsic property *seeming to see a yellow ball.* That is where my conscious experience ends. The ball and the colour yellow have nothing to do with it. How can that be right? To amend a frequently reproduced quotation from Harman (58):

> When you see a [yellow ball], you do not experience any features as intrinsic features of [yourself]. Look at a [yellow ball] and try to turn your attention to intrinsic features of [yourself]. I predict you will find that the only features there to turn your attention to will be features of the presented [ball]...

There are two claims in this passage. First, when I see a yellow ball I can attend to its features—its colour, shape, texture, and so on. (To that list we can add the ball itself.) Second, when I see a yellow ball I can't attend to any intrinsic features of myself, for instance *seeming to see a yellow ball.* (The actual quotation from Harman has "intrinsic features of your experience.")

This is not to deny that I instantiate the property *seeming to see a yellow ball.* It is not even to deny that this property is intrinsic, or that I can know that I have it. But I'm not aware of it and I can't attend to it, as I am aware of the ball and its features, and can attend to them. That property of myself is curiously elusive. If I know that I seem to see a yellow ball, it is somehow *by being aware of, or attending to, my environment.*[4]

Papineau's response to this piece of phenomenology is not to write it off entirely. The Harmanesque passage contains an important truth, namely that the attempt to attend to one's experience (or oneself) does not reveal the internal realm that we usually ignore. The attempt does *something*: it might "induce heightened contrasts," for example (119). But sensory attention only sharpens what we are sensorily aware of anyway. Harman's mistake is to think these include "features of the presented ball":

> I don't accept that any worldly properties are 'present in' experience to start with. Sensory experience is constituted entirely by intrinsic

---

[4] See 121–5, an interesting discussion that deserves to be treated at length.

qualitative properties. It's all paint. So of course, when we try to shift our introspective focus from worldly to qualitative properties, we fail. After all, as I see it, there's nothing except intrinsic qualitative properties to focus on. Our inability to shift focus does not show that we can't introspect qualia. It just shows that there's nothing else in experience to introspect. (118)

Suppose I see a yellow ball. I turn my attention to (what I naïvely take to be) the colour of the ball. Then, unbeknownst to me, God intervenes, vaporizing the ball but keeping my visual system in the same state. We may suppose that I notice no change: "Still attending to the colour of the ball!," I report.

I think Papineau would agree that there is a single feature that occupies my attention throughout this process. Let us call that feature *yellow†*. The ball is not yellow†, because I am sensorily aware of that feature after the ball has been destroyed, and on Papineau's view I am not aware of uninstantiated properties. Something must be yellow†, but what? It can't be a sense datum, because Papineau has no truck with such things (28–30). An obvious candidate is myself: *I* am yellow†.

Let us run with that idea. By the same token, since I see the spherical ball, I am spherical†. I am also orange†, since I see an orange ball next to the yellow one. Can I really be yellow† *and* orange†? Naïvely, I would take these two properties to exclude each other.

These "daggered" properties of myself appear to be the same as Papineau's "starred" properties.

> ...*yellow*★ [is] the property present in experience that represents worldly *yellow*, and *round*★ the experiential property that represents *round*. In my view, *yellow*★ and *round*★ are quite distinct from, and only contingently related to, *yellow* and *round* After all, it is central to my view that, in cases of illusion and hallucination, the former starred mental properties are instantiated, even though nothing nearby instantiates the unstarred worldly properties. When I misperceive a ball to [be] yellow, I instantiate the mental *yellow*★ property all right, but nothing in the vicinity, and certainly not my mental state, instantiates *yellow*. (115)

I will assume that yellow† = yellow★. The extra notation is useful because this equation may not be correct. A naïve perceiver would take yellow† to be a property of external objects, not herself. Indeed, I would think that a naïve perceiver would take yellow†ness to be *yellowness*, but I doubt that

Papineau wants to commit himself to this kind of error theory. On the other hand, he does say:

> I do not dispute that sensory experience has a rich and distinctive introspectable structure. Nor do I dispute that this structure makes it extremely natural to think of sensory experience as intrinsically pointing to a world beyond. But from my point of view this intrinsic directedness is a kind of illusion. (75)

What is Papineau's explanation of this "illusion"? Why would the "structure" of what are in fact intrinsic non-representational properties of myself make me think of experience as pointing to "a world beyond"?[5] But let us pass over that and focus on another issue.

If I see a banana, and then see a lemon, and finally a yellow ball, I instantiate yellow★ on each occasion. If I see a banana next to a lemon, I also instantiate yellow★. In this case, my experience represents a yellow curved object to my left, and another yellow ovoid object to my right. But there's only *one* relevant property present in experience, namely yellow★. I can't instantiate it twice over! How do *two* yellow objects get into the picture?

A section called "Quasi-Objects and Their Quasi-Properties" suggests that there is an "element of my experience" that represents the yellow banana, and another that represents the yellow lemon (95). But what does this mean? I am yellow★, and curved★, and ovoid★, but what we apparently want are *two* objects, one yellow★ and curved★, the other yellow★ and ovoid★. Papineau invokes an analogy with "clusters of visible properties moving around [a television] screen and standing in various visible relations to other such clusters" (94), but I don't see that he is entitled to it. The analogy fits with the rejected sense datum theory, on which there are two objects, representing the banana and the lemon respectively. Papineau only has one.[6]

---

[5] Papineau appeals to Farkas 2013 at this point (see 91–3, 108–9). As Papineau puts the basic idea, it is the "relative coherence of certain elements of experience" that explains why "we intuitively think of certain experiences, but not others, as relating us to mind-independent aspects of the world" (92, 91). Here's one worry with this explanation. Why would this "relative coherence" make us think that sensory experience *intrinsically* (i.e. non-contingently) points to the world beyond? The relative coherence of a series of messages in Morse code might make us think that they point to the world beyond, but not intrinsically.

[6] For the suggestion that Papineau could take "populations of neurons" to be the bearers of the starred properties, see Pautz 2021: 84–90.

3. Colour Similarity

Papineau endorses the argument from similarity against the identification of colours with physical properties of objects (say, reflectances):

> Physically speaking, blue and green go together and are unlike purple. In particular, the reflectance profiles of blue surfaces closely match those of green surfaces but are markedly different from those of purple surfaces.
>
> At the level of conscious colour experiences, though, blue goes with purple, not with green. Experiences of blue surfaces are much more like those of purple surfaces that those of green surfaces. This argues that the conscious character of colour experiences is determined, not by subjects' relation to worldly surface properties like reflectance profiles...but rather by intrinsic properties of subjects. (20)

Since Papineau is a physicalist, and thinks that the "conscious character of colour experiences"—blue★, green★, and so on—has to be instantiated, he is committed to finding colour similarities mirrored "physically speaking" *in subjects*. Imagine an alien scientist with alien perceptual modalities, examining the intrinsic physical properties of human subjects when they are exposed to a variety of stimuli that differentially reflect light in a narrow band of wavelengths. The alien would notice that these intrinsic physical properties stand in various similarity relations, and in fact these "physical" similarities would perfectly recreate colour similarities. In particular, the alien would classify some of these physical properties as "unique," and others as "binary," recreating the unique/binary distinction between the hues.

Good luck with that.[7] More importantly, the argument from similarity is dubious in the first place. The problem is that similarity is always similarity *in a respect*. If we make that explicit, then the premises of the argument from similarity can be put this way:

P1. Blue is more similar to purple than it is to green in chromatic respects.

---

[7] See Mollon 2009. As Papineau notes, other modalities need to be treated in a similar fashion. On pain, for example, see Hilbert and Klein 2014: fn. 3, 301, and Pautz 2014: fn. 4, 312–13. One particularly mystifying problem concerns *dissimilarities* between modalities. If the experienced similarities between colours, and between sounds, are to be explained in terms of the similarities in physical respects between "patterns of neural activation" (21), then colours and sounds should be experienced as *more* similar than we actually experience them. Two different patterns of neural activation are still *patterns of neural activation*, rather than patterns in the weather or in galaxies. On Papineau's view, seeing red should literally be like hearing a trumpet.

P2.   Reflectance^B is not more similar to reflectance^P than it is to reflectance^G in physical/optical respects.

From these premises nothing exciting follows. In particular, P1 and P2 are compatible with an identity theory: blue=reflectance^B, and so on. (See Davies 2014; Byrne and Hilbert 2020.)

There is much more to be said, but I'll leave it there. That there is much more to be said is a testament to the importance of *The Metaphysics of Sensory Experience*.[8]

References

Block, N. 2019. Arguments pro and con on Adam Pautz's external directedness principle. *Blockheads!*, ed. A. Pautz and D. Stoljar. Cambridge, MA: MIT Press.

Byrne, A., and D. R. Hilbert. 2020. Objectivist reductionism. *The Routledge Handbook of Philosophy of Colour*, ed. F. Macpherson and D. Brown. London: Routledge.

Davies, W. 2014. The inscrutability of colour similarity. *Philosophical Studies* 171: 289–311.

Farkas, K. 2013. Constructing a world for the senses. *Phenomenal Intentionality*, ed. U. Kriegel. Oxford: Oxford University Press.

Hilbert, D., and C. Klein. 2014. No problem. *Consciousness Inside and Out: Phenomenology, Neuroscience, and the Nature of Experience*, ed. R. Brown. Dordrecht: Springer.

Mollon, J. 2009. A neural basis for unique hues? *Current Biology* 19: R441–2.

Moore, G. E. 1903. The refutation of idealism. *Mind* 7: 1–30.

Papineau, D. 2021. *The Metaphysics of Sensory Experience*. Oxford: Oxford University Press.

Pautz, A. 2014. Ignoring the real problems for phenomenal externalism: A reply to Hilbert and Klein. *Consciousness Inside and Out: Phenomenology, Neuroscience, and the Nature of Experience*, ed. R. Brown. Dordrecht: Springer.

Pautz, A. 2019. How can brains in vats experience a spatial world? A puzzle for internalists. *Blockheads!*, ed. A. Pautz and D. Stoljar. Cambridge, MA: MIT Press.

Pautz, A. 2021. *Perception*. London: Routledge.

---

[8] Many thanks to E. J. Green and David Hilbert.

13
Truth and Content in Sensory Experience

Angela Mendelovici

David Papineau's *The Metaphysics of Sensory Experience* is deep, insightful, refreshingly brisk, and very readable. In it, Papineau argues that sensory experiences are intrinsic and non-relational states of subjects; that they do not essentially involve relations to worldly facts, properties, or other items (though they do happen to correlate with worldly items); and that they do not have truth conditions simply in virtue of their conscious (i.e., phenomenal) features.

I am in enthusiastic agreement with the picture as described so far. But Papineau also argues that sensory experiences are in no interesting sense essentially representational and that what is responsible for their truth conditions is their correlations with the environment. Here, I disagree. Indeed, I think Papineau does not follow his arguments to their proper conclusions. For if sensory experiences are intrinsic, non-relational, and only contingently correlated with worldly conditions (as Papineau and I agree they are), then the phenomenal features of sensory states are representational in an important sense: they constitute what we think, perceptually experience, or otherwise entertain, making up how things seem to us from a first-person perspective. Because of this, the truth conditions of perceptual experiences cannot be entirely independent of their phenomenal features—they cannot merely be a matter of environmental correlations. If we follow Papineau's arguments to their proper conclusions, we end up with a view much closer to a version of representationalism that Papineau dismisses, a view he calls "pure phenomenal intentionalism." Or so I will argue.

I proceed as follows: Section 1 overviews Papineau's picture of sensory experience and his main lines of argument. Section 2 distinguishes between two ways of understanding the notion of mental representation. Section 3 argues that even if sensory experiences are intrinsic, non-relational, and only contingently correlated with worldly conditions, as Papineau claims, there is an important sense in which they are essentially representational. Section 4 argues that the truth or veridicality of sensory experiences is a matter of conforming to their essentially represented contents. Section 5 considers Papineau's picture of introspection of phenomenal properties, which might be thought to preclude the picture of experiential truth suggested in Section 4. The upshot is that if sensory experiences are intrinsic, non-relational, and independent of worldly correlations—as, again, Papineau and I agree they are—then reaching the world in an epistemically meaningful way is much more challenging than Papineau makes it out to be.

1. Book Summary

The Metaphysics of Sensory Experiences is about *sensory experiences*, which are phenomenally conscious experiences of the sort involved in perception. Sensory experiences include genuine cases of perception as well as illusions and hallucinations. Papineau is not overly concerned with how to distinguish sensation from cognition (11–14),[1] and rightly so since he eventually argues that everything he says about sensory experiences also applies to cognitive experiences, if there are any (128–9). So, although his focus is on *sensory* experiences, we may take his discussion to pertain to conscious experiences more generally. Papineau takes sensory properties to be properties of subjects, though he accepts that there can be alternative ways of setting things up on which it would be correct to say that they are properties of mental or neural particulars (14–16).

The main theses of the book are that "conscious sensory properties are intrinsic qualitative properties of people" (1) and that "sensory consciousness is one thing and sensory representation another" (152).

Papineau's argument for this view mostly consists in arguments against alternative naive realist, sense-datum, and representationalist views of experience, which take conscious sensory experiences to constitutively involve relations to facts, mental particulars, and properties, respectively. Let us quickly go over some of these arguments, focusing, with Papineau, on the arguments against representationalism.

---

[1] Unless indicated otherwise, all page references are to Papineau's *The Metaphysics of Sensory Experience* (2021).

Naive realism is the view that sensory experiences at least sometimes (i.e., in cases of genuine perception as opposed to illusion or hallucination) constitutively involve relations to worldly facts (or perhaps to objects and their properties). A consequence of naive realism is that a genuine perceptual experience, on the one hand, and a hallucination or illusion, on the other, cannot involve the very same conscious properties, since the perceptual experience constitutively involves a relation to worldly facts while the hallucination or illusion does not. This, Papineau claims, is unacceptable because it posits conscious differences that go beyond anything subjects can introspectively discern, which "threatens to loosen our hold on the very concept of consciousness itself" (17).

The *sense-datum theory*, like naive realism, maintains that conscious sensory properties are relational but that they are relations to mind-dependent sense-data rather than worldly facts. Unlike naive realists, sense-datum theorists can accept that perceptual experiences, hallucinations, and illusions can involve the same conscious properties. But Papineau rejects the sense-datum view because he takes it to be inconsistent with physicalism since, presumably, sense-data are non-physical entities (29).

Papineau's treatment of naive realism and sense-datum theories is mainly intended to clear the ground before he engages his main opponent, the representationalist. Papineau takes *representationalism* to be the view that conscious sensory properties are identical to representational properties (30). For example, according to representationalism, what it is to have a sensory experience as of a red square is to mentally represent (perhaps in a certain way) a red square. While Papineau accepts that sensory experiences can "happen contingently to be representations" (31), he rejects the stronger representationalist claim that they are "essentially representational" (32). What he means by this is that although sensory experiences can have representational features, these representational features are not metaphysically connected to their phenomenal features—the two sets of features don't bear any relations of identity, grounding, metaphysical necessitation, constitution, etc., to one another. Papineau likens sensory experiences to marks on a piece of paper, which might happen to represent various propositions but do not represent simply in virtue of being the typographical marks that they are (they might have had the same typographical features but represented differently).

At this point, it is pertinent to ask what Papineau means by "representation." Papineau understands representation as being a matter of having truth conditions, where truth conditions are to be understood broadly so as to include conditions of accuracy, veridicality, and satisfaction:

Throughout this book I shall understand representational contents in terms of the possession of *truth conditions*. The essential feature of any representational state is that it lays down a condition for the world to satisfy. It portrays the world as being a certain way, by drawing a line in logical space between the possibilities that verify it and those that do not. (36, italics in original, footnote suppressed)

We will return to this understanding of representation in the next section, where I will suggest that there is another notion of representation at play in some debates over representationalism.

Papineau distinguishes between two kinds of representationalist views: naturalist representationalism and phenomenal intentionalism. *Naturalist representationalism* combines the basic representationalist thesis with a naturalistic theory of mental representation. The view aims to offer an account of phenomenal properties in terms of representational properties, which are accounted for in terms of "naturalistic" ingredients like correlations between internal states and worldly items.[2] Papineau himself accepts a teleological correlational account of mental representation on which the relevant correlations are specified in part by the behavioral effects of internal states (48–9; see also Papineau 1984, 2017). In *The Metaphysics of Sensory Experience*, Papineau does not argue for this correlational view of mental representation but he does take it on board as part of his overall position. While he accepts the naturalist representationalist's general picture of representation, he rejects the additional claim that conscious sensory properties are metaphysically connected to representational properties.

The second version of representationalism that Papineau considers, *phenomenal intentionalism*, aims to offer an account of representational properties in terms of phenomenal properties. According to phenomenal intentionalism, instantiating the right phenomenal properties metaphysically necessitates representing a particular content. For example, a sensory experience as of a red square might represent a red square simply in virtue of its phenomenal character. This kind of "phenomenal intentionality" is the most basic or fundamental kind of representation, the kind from which any other kinds ultimately derive.[3] My sympathies lie with phenomenal

---

[2] This kind of naturalist representationalism combining representationalism with a correlational picture of mental representation is sometimes called "tracking representationalism." Dretske (1995) and Tye (2000) are well-known proponents of this view. See Bourget and Mendelovici (2014) for an overview.

[3] This view, or something near enough, has been defended by Pitt (2004, 2009); Farkas (2008, 2013); Siewert (1998); Kriegel (2011); Horgan and Tienson (2002); Woodward (2019,

intentionalism, though I do not entirely agree with Papineau's characterization of the view (see below).

Papineau's characterizations of naturalist representationalism and phenomenal intentionalism gloss over many details. For instance, some (arguably *all*) naturalist representationalists take phenomenal properties to be identical to properties of representing contents *in a particular way* (as Papineau recognizes; 33); phenomenal intentionalists do not generally aim to identify *every* sensory property with a representational property; both naturalist representationalism and phenomenal intentionalism are sometimes characterized in terms of supervenience, determination, constitution, metaphysical necessitation, and other relations apart from identity (as Papineau recognizes; 38); and some phenomenal intentionalists—and perhaps also some other representationalists—do not understand representation in terms of truth conditions (as Papineau also seems to recognize (75)—more on this shortly). For ease of discussion, Papineau skates over many of these nuances. In most cases, this is unproblematic.

Papineau offers an extended discussion of representationalism in which he urges readers to seriously consider the metaphysical consequences of various versions of the view. Naturalist representationalism, for instance, takes our here-and-now sensory experiences to constitutively involve distant correlations, which, depending on the specifics of one's correlational view of mental representation, may be neither "here" nor "now." This is a consequence Papineau finds hard to take seriously (51). Against representationalists appealing to transparency observations, who maintain that abstract properties like redness and squareness are literally present in sensory experience, Papineau suggests the view is "little better than magic" (63) and, again, that it is "inconsistent with the here-and-now nature of conscious experience" (65).

Papineau's urgings culminate in an argument that he takes to apply to all versions of representationalism:

1. Instantiations of conscious sensory properties constitute concrete facts with causes and effects.
2. Instantiations of representational properties constitute abstract facts that cannot feature as causes or effects.
3. Conscious sensory properties are not representational properties. (72)

2016); Bourget (2010); and yours truly (2018). For overviews, see Kriegel (2013) and Bourget and Mendelovici (2016).

The basic idea is that representing a content constitutively involves bearing relations to abstract items, while instantiating a conscious sensory property does not. So, instantiating a conscious sensory property is not representing a content. Although there are potential concerns with seeing how this argument applies to non-identity versions of representationalism, I am largely sympathetic to Papineau's worries. If, along with many of the representationalists Papineau targets, we take representation to be a relation to abstract properties, conditions, propositions, or the like, it is utterly mysterious how representing a content can be identified with—or, arguably, otherwise interestingly metaphysically related to—having a concrete phenomenal experience.

According to Papineau's alternative view, which he dubs the *qualitative view*, "conscious sensory properties are intrinsic qualitative properties of subjects. It is not essential to sensory experiences that they relate subjects to objects or properties beyond themselves" (83). He likens his view to the adverbialist views of Ducasse (1942) and Chisholm (1957), on which sensory experiences are modifications of subjects rather than relations to mental, physical, or abstract items. (Papineau wisely distances himself, though, from the adverbialists' linguistic project of paraphrasing apparently relational descriptions of sensory experiences into adverbial constructions.)

Papineau does not think that sensory experience is an amorphous blob of mish-mashed qualia. He recognizes that sensory experiences exhibit particular structural and organizational features and even that they can be divided into object-appearing and property-appearing components. He calls these components "quasi-objects" and "quasi-properties." Drawing on Farkas (2013), Papineau argues that quasi-objects and quasi-properties are purely phenomenal constructions that are not constituted by any worldly objects or properties. Papineau also takes care to emphasize that these quasi-objects and quasi-properties do not constitute or somehow specify our sensory experiences' truth conditions. As mentioned earlier, Papineau instead accepts a correlational picture of representation, i.e. of the having of truth conditions. Thanks to how we are embedded in our environments, our sensory properties happen to correlate with certain worldly conditions. Sensory experiences are true just in case the conditions with which they are correlated in fact obtain.

Put figuratively, we have an internal movie playing in our heads in which we experience quasi-objects as having quasi-properties. This internal movie is constitutively independent of any worldly objects, properties, or facts. But bits of this internal movie are correlated in particular ways with the external world, and in virtue of these correlations they have truth conditions. When the external condition with which a bit of the internal movie is correlated obtains, that bit is true.

I agree with a lot of the picture presented so far. I agree that conscious properties are not relations to worldly objects, facts, properties, or other items. I agree that they are structured and organized in a way that results in something like "quasi-objects" and "quasi-properties." And I agree that conscious properties do not (usually) determine their own truth conditions. But I think there are ways of understanding the notion of representation on which quasi-objects, quasi-properties, and other quasi-items qualify as represented contents: these items are what we think, experience, or entertain. Once we recognize this representation-like feature of quasi-items, it becomes clear that truth is a matter of conforming to these represented contents and not just a matter of correlated worldly conditions obtaining.

2. Two Notions of Representation

As we saw in the previous section, Papineau uses "representation" to mean the having of truth conditions. But this way of defining "representation" is not universally accepted. In this section, I want to suggest that there are at least two related representation-like notions at play in the relevant debates: first, the notion of there being something that is thought, believed, perceptually presented, or entertained; and, second, the notion of connecting with the world, perhaps by securing or constituting truth conditions. I will later suggest that the having of Papineau's quasi-objects, quasi-properties, and other quasi-items satisfies the former representation-like notion even though it does not secure truth conditions. I will also later suggest that as a result of this, truth requires conformity with our quasi-contents, not merely that correlated environmental conditions obtain. If all this is right, then Papineau's picture is incomplete, in that it neglects to describe some representation-like features of sensory experiences, and incorrect, in that it mistakenly takes experiential truth to be a matter of worldly correlations.

Let us first consider the two representation-like features. Contemporary discussions of the mind's ability to represent the world can be largely traced back to a well-known passage from Brentano:

> Every mental phenomenon is characterized by what the Scholastics of the Middle Ages called the intentional (or mental) inexistence of an object,

and what we might call, though not wholly unambiguously, reference to a content, direction toward an object (which is not to be understood here as meaning a thing), or immanent objectivity. Every mental phenomenon includes something as object within itself, although they do not do so in the same way. In presentation, something is presented, in judgment something is affirmed or denied, in love loved, in hate hated, in desire desired and so on. (Brentano 1874: 88, notes suppressed)

Brentano's talk of "intentional (or mental) inexistence" refers to the phenomenon of a mental state having "something as an object within itself." This object need not be constituted of worldly objects, facts, abstract properties, propositions, or truth conditions. Arguably, the representation-like notion at play in this passage need not essentially involve truth conditions or relations to anything.

Let us call the phenomenon Brentano's passage points to *intentionality* and the contents it involves *intentional contents*. Intentional contents are the "objects" of mental states—they are that which is thought, that which is entertained, that which is believed, that which is perceptually experienced, etc. Contents in this sense are what we are in some sense aware of or entertain when we think and reason and when it perceptually appears to us that things are a certain way. When we wonder what to have for dinner, believe that $2+2=4$, or sensorily experience a fluffy brown and white dog, we are entertaining intentional contents. These are the contents that characterize our first-person perspective on the world, how things seem or appear to us. When we try to imagine what someone is thinking or perceptually representing, we are trying to imagine their contents in this sense, the contents that they are entertaining. When thought bubbles in comic books are used to depict the contents of a character's thoughts and experiences, it is their intentional contents that they are depicting.

Arguably, many of Papineau's representationalist opponents intend to be using "representation" to mean intentionality, the phenomenon described above. This is most clearly true of phenomenal intentionalists (as Papineau appears to recognize; 33),[4] though there is also a case to be made that

---

[4] Most phenomenal intentionalists, as far as I know, do not specifically understand the relevant notion of mental representation in terms of truth conditions but instead rely on something like the intuitive Brentanian characterization, and some are rather explicit in this (see especially Kriegel 2011, ch. 1; and Mendelovici 2018, ch. 1).

naturalist representationalists like Fodor (1987) and Dretske (1995) also aim to at least be covering the phenomenon of intentionality.[5]

The notion of truth might be taken to be connected to that of intentionality in the following way: If an intentional state "says" that things are a particular way, then it seems to follow that they might be that way or they might fail to be that way. So, it is natural to think that intentional states have truth conditions just in virtue of having intentional contents. This brings us to the second representation-like notion, that of having truth conditions (and, similarly, conditions of reference—but I will focus on truth conditions in what follows). Papineau uses the term "representation" to pick out the having of truth conditions.

It is a common assumption that intentional contents are or determine truth conditions, that a single thing plays both the role of being what is thought, entertained, etc., and that of constituting or otherwise determining truth conditions. Arguably, many naturalist representationalists and phenomenal intentionalists accept this assumption.[6] But it is a substantive claim that a single thing plays both of these roles. The intentional contents we think and experience might not be identical to or otherwise determining of truth conditions. What we think *in* might not specify conditions for the world to satisfy.

3. Papineau's Disagreement with Phenomenal Intentionalism

At this point, one might worry that Papineau's arguments do not make contact with some of his opponents' views. Although Papineau defines representationalism using the notion of representation as the having of truth conditions, he does consider a view, which he calls *pure phenomenal intentionalism*, that denies that phenomenal properties constitutively involve relations to abstract items or other worldly items. He recognizes that the version of pure phenomenal intentionalism that denies that phenomenal properties determine truth conditions is not susceptible to his

---

[5] See my 2018: 14–16.

[6] Naturalist representationalists making this assumption arguably include Dretske (1995) and Tye (2000). Many phenomenal intentionalists also assume this, such as Chalmers (2006), Pautz (2009), and Bourget (2019a, 2019b).

main line of argument against representationalism. But he dismisses the view, claiming it effectively collapses into his own view:

> [P]erhaps [the pure phenomenal intentionalist's] best move at this point would be to abandon the idea of a constitutive tie between [conscious] character and truth conditions. And indeed an increasing number of philosophers who identify themselves as phenomenal intentionalists do just that. They rest their case entirely on the internal structure of sensory consciousness itself, and make no attempt to claim any essential tie to further worldly conditions. Their position is that sensory experience is intrinsically directed, pointing out to a world beyond itself, even if this directedness fails to fix any definite truth conditions without the assistance of the subject's environment. (See Loar (2003), Kriegel (2008: Section 7), and Mendelovici (2018: Part 5) for versions of this position.)
>
> This is a viable position, but the obvious question is what distinguishes it from the kind of purely qualitative view that I am defending. As I said at the end of the last chapter, once it is granted that conscious character fails to fix truth conditions on its own, the claim that it is essentially representational is called into question. After all, my own view also takes conscious sensory character to determine truth conditions once it is given an environmental setting, yet on my view conscious sensory character in itself is representationally dumb. (75)

Papineau is right to say that the pure phenomenal intentionalist who denies that phenomenal states by themselves secure their own truth conditions holds a view quite similar to his own. However, there are two important differences, which he appears to neglect. First, the pure phenomenal intentionalist insists that there is an important sense in which sensory experiences are essentially representational: they are essentially *intentional* (in the sense outlined in the previous section). Second, the pure phenomenal intentionalist need not (and generally does not) take truth conditions to be determined by environmental factors.[7]

---

[7] Papineau's attribution of the view that truth conditions are determined by environmental factors to me in the above passage is inaccurate. It is true that some versions of phenomenal intentionalism like those of Horgan and Tienson (2002), Bourget (2010), myself (2018, 2020), and Pautz (2021) aim to accommodate externalist contents—and externalist truth conditions—with a picture of *derived* representation. But these externalist contents and truth conditions are in some way or other indirectly determined by *phenomenally* represented contents. They are not determined by mere correlations with the environment or by the mere fact of being embedded in a particular environment.

In the next two sections, I will consider the two points of contention between pure phenomenal intentionalism and Papineau's view. I want to suggest that Papineau's view of sensory experience as intrinsic, non-relational, and involving structured quasi-objects and quasi-properties leads us to a view much closer to the pure phenomenal intentionalist view he rejects.

4. Quasi-Items as Intentional Contents

I want to suggest that Papineau's quasi-objects, quasi-properties, and any other related quasi-items (quasi-propositions?) qualify as intentional contents. They are among what we think, perceptually experience, or entertain. I'm not sure if Papineau would agree with this claim—he neither makes such a claim nor denies it, since he does not employ the relevant notion of intentionality. But, in any case, this is a claim worth making because it highlights an important feature of quasi-items: they are intentional contents.

If Papineau takes on board this claim about quasi-items, his overall view bears even more similarity to the pure phenomenal intentionalist view he claims collapses into his own than he acknowledges. We can read him as arguing, against many of his representationalist opponents (but along with the pure phenomenal intentionalist), against the assumption that a single phenomenon plays both the roles of intentional contents and of truth conditions. Our intentional contents—what we think, experience, or entertain—do not constitute or determine their own truth conditions; there is no fact of the matter stemming from their nature as intentional contents as to how the world must conform to them in order for them to be true. Put figuratively, our internal movie constitutes our first-person perspective on the world. These are the contents we think, experience, and entertain. But there is no fact of the matter as to how this internal movie is *supposed* to correspond to the world arising from the intrinsic features of the movie itself.

If Papineau does not reject the claim that quasi-items qualify as intentional contents, his view is compatible with construals of representationalism alternative to his own that take phenomenal properties to be identical to (or in some way metaphysically determined by or determining of) intentional properties (rather than truth conditions), including pure phenomenal intentionalism. Such a construal of representationalism would take phenomenal properties to be essentially connected to intentional properties but remain neutral on how these properties are related to the having of truth conditions.

So far, I've made the (friendly, I think) suggestion that Papineau's quasi-items qualify as intentional contents, where intentional contents are what is thought, believed, experienced, entertained, etc. While many theorists will identify intentional contents with truth conditions or take them to otherwise determine truth conditions, this is not obligatory, and the resulting overall view would reject this further claim.

5. Where Do Truth Conditions Come From?

Now I want to make a less friendly suggestion: If quasi-items qualify as intentional contents, this casts doubt on Papineau's correlational picture of the truth conditions of sensory experiences.

Let us again consider Papineau's picture of sensory experiences. One of the most agreeable features of Papineau's book, in my opinion, is that it seems to take consciousness seriously. On Papineau's view, consciousness is a real, concrete, here-and-now phenomenon (see his argument against representationalism), a phenomenon that cannot lie beyond the realm of introspective discernibility (see his arguments against naive realism). The structure of consciousness is real and significant, painting our internal life with quasi-objects and quasi-properties. It constitutes a rich multimodal internal movie, an immersive quasi-world that captures our first-person outlook, that is what we experience and entertain, and that guides our behavior. This quasi-world is not a mere window onto an external world beyond but rather is wholly constituted by a subject's own consciousness. It's a full-blown, purely mental phenomenal world, in something like the Kantian sense, a phenomenal world that is divorced from the noumenal world beyond. All this applies equally to cognitive states, too, insofar as they have phenomenal features. The conscious mind is rich, real, metaphysically substantive, constitutively independent of the external world beyond, a world unto itself.

If this right, then when we ask whether our sensory experiences are true or false, it is clear that what we care about is whether the world conforms in the right way to the quasi-world in our minds—whether the noumenal world corresponds in the right way to the phenomenal world, whether the external world is as our intentional contents "say." When we care about truth, we do not generally care about whether the conditions that our quasi-items correlate with in such-and-such a way obtain now. Of course, this is not to deny that our quasi-world correlates with the external world in various ways. Presumably, there are many such correlations, some of which might play interesting roles in the explanation of why our behavior is sometimes successful.[8] But once we become convinced that consciousness constitutes an all-encompassing quasi-world of quasi-objects and quasi-properties, we can recognize that such correlations do not bear on the question of *truth*. What matters for truth is conformity with our phenomenal world, not with conditions assigned by some environmentally determined correlation.

That mere correlations are neither metaphysically necessary nor metaphysically sufficient for the having of truth conditions is supported by consideration of cases where intentional contents and worldly correlations come apart in interesting ways. Consider a brain in a vat worried that they are a brain in a vat. The brain would not be comforted to know that most of their sensory experiences are "true" because their internal states are caused so very reliably by states of a computer. Such correlations do not make contact with the brain in a vat's internal picture of the world, their quasi-world of experience. And it is *this* world of phenomenal appearances that the brain hopes conforms to the world beyond. What the brain in a vat wants to know is whether the world beyond their mind conforms to the world as it phenomenally appears to them, as their intentional contents depict, not whether some mind-world correlation generally obtains. Indeed, the brain in the vat might agree that if they were a brain in a vat, the worldly conditions correlated with their phenomenal states generally obtain. But they might still wonder if the world is as their intentional contents depict. What they'd be wondering is whether they veridically represent the world or whether they instead reliably *mis*represent the world. If all this is right, then mere correlations are not metaphysically sufficient for truth conditions.

Mind-world correlations are also not metaphysically necessary for truth conditions. Consider the well-known swamp person who suddenly comes into existence with all the internal states of some person with a normal history. This swamp person has the very same types of phenomenal states as their historically normal twin and hence, on Papineau's view, experiences the very same quasi-world as their twin. But this swamp person has no history, so on correlational views that take historical factors to determine the relevant correlations (like Papineau's), their sensory experiences do not have truth conditions. But the fact that no such correlations have been

---

[8] Papineau himself holds that the explanatory role of such correlations is limited to explaining why behavior is likely to be successful and not the generation of behavior itself (23).

established would not by itself thwart the swamp person's pursuit of truth.[9] What the swamp person cares about is whether their internal quasi-world, a world considered purely in terms of its phenomenal features and the quasi-items they constitute or determine, adequately corresponds to the world beyond, not whether some (perhaps historically mediated) correlation obtains. If this is right, then mere correlations are not metaphysically necessary for truth conditions.

Earlier, I agreed with Papineau that representationalist views that take mental representation (understood as the having of truth conditions) to be a relation to abstracta, propositions, or the like fail as views of phenomenal properties. However, it is noteworthy that they do get one thing right: they take sensory experiences' truth conditions to be determined by their subject's phenomenal features (in most cases). Internal states themselves specify the conditions that must be met for their own truth. So, while I agree with Papineau that such views are inadequate as views of phenomenal properties, they are better placed than Papineau's view to offer a satisfactory account of how the mind makes an epistemically meaningful connection with the world.

And so, given his other views, I think Papineau should reject the correlational theory and accept, along with many representationalists (particularly pure phenomenal intentionalists), that *if* sensory experience makes any meaningful epistemic contact with the world, this must be secured by consciousness itself. Nothing short of that would do.

This is not to say that we *can* secure meaningful epistemic contact with the world beyond consciousness. Indeed, there are deep problems with the idea that we can secure a connection with the world out of elements that are not already thus connected, which Papineau recognizes:

> A medium that is not intrinsically representational [i.e., that does not intrinsically have truth conditions] cannot render itself representational by somehow trying to say that it is. Content [i.e., truth conditions] can't be manufactured simply by adding contentless arrows to a set of marks that are not themselves contentful. (108)

---

[9] We can construct similar examples where there is a breakdown of the relevant type of correlations for other correlational views. For example, for a correlational view taking an internal state's truth conditions to be the worldly conditions it is most reliably caused by, we could imagine a (perhaps momentarily existing) brain that is causally disconnected from the world or equally connected to too many things such that there is no worldly condition meeting the requirements of the view.

You can't get truth conditions out of states that lack truth conditions, no matter what they "quasi-say." That's because quasi-saying (having intentional contents) does not amount to *saying* (having truth conditions). The worry is reminiscent of the basic idea behind Putnam's (1977) model-theoretic argument against internally determined standards of truth and reference: A theory, understood as a mere uninterpreted set of sentences or strings of symbols, cannot specify its own interpretation, since any attempt to do so from within the theory would merely add further uninterpreted sentences to the theory—it would be "just more theory." The same holds for any items that do not themselves have conditions of truth or reference. Nothing in the internal movie that constitutes our intentional contents can specify how the external world is *supposed* to correspond to the movie since nothing in the internal movie can reach out beyond the movie to specify what the required kind of correspondence is. Everything that goes on in the movie is "just more movie," never reaching the world beyond.

And so, it seems, if a non-relational picture of sensory experience of the sort accepted by Papineau and the pure phenomenal intentionalist is correct, we are truly stuck in our minds. We have no way of imposing conditions on the world, no way of reaching beyond and making any kind of meaningful epistemic contact with it. This, I think, is the fundamental challenge facing such non-relational views of intentionality, and I don't think it has been adequately appreciated.[10] We are trapped in a phenomenally constituted quasi-world, wanting to make cognitive contact with the noumenal world beyond, but unable to claw our way out of our phenomenal prison.

For what it's worth, I think that we might be able to specify truth conditions for our sensory experiences from within consciousness itself without running afoul of problems of self-interpretation. We might be able to do this if we have conscious experiences that directly and immediately pick out their referents. The most obvious candidates for such directly referential conscious experiences are conscious experiences of our own conscious states and their intentional contents, the features of such states and contents, and perhaps even some of their relations to one another. For example, perhaps we can directly refer to our own present experiences, their intentional contents, and the relations of similarity and difference that they exemplify (or at least instances of these relations). From these directly referential ingredients, we might be able to specify, from the inside, conditions the

---

[10] But see Ott (2016) and Bourget (2019b).

world would have to satisfy for our sensory experiences (and perhaps also our other mental states) to be true. Whether we can indeed do so remains to be seen. My point here is that on a picture of sensory experience like Papineau's, truth conditions must be specified from within. Mere correlations won't do.

6. Introspection

I doubt that Papineau would be sympathetic to the above-mentioned approach. For one, it would be in tension with his view of introspection of sensory experience, which does not generally permit the kind of immediate awareness of our own conscious states and intentional contents that would allow us to directly refer to them. In this section, I briefly consider this view of introspection and argue that it is both in tension with Papineau's other views and independently implausible. Someone attracted to Papineau's overall view of sensory experience would do best to avoid taking on board his view of introspection.

Papineau claims that we introspect our sensory experiences indirectly by "noting what beliefs these experiences incline us to form" (122), which we come to know by noting which propositions we are inclined to accept (122–3). The resulting introspective knowledge of sensory experiences "characterize[s] them in terms of their representational contents, i.e., in terms of their truth conditions" (126) and not by their phenomenal features. For example, suppose you have a sensory experience as of a red triangle. On Papineau's view, you have a sensory experience presenting a red* quasi-property and a triangle* quasi-property as attaching to some quasi-object. To introspect upon this experience, here's what you have to do: You notice that you have a sensory experience that forms the basis of a belief. You also notice that you are inclined to accept that something is red and triangular (where *redness* and *triangularity* are the worldly properties that correlate with red* and triangular*). From this, you come to know that the belief is true just in case there is something red and triangular, and from this you come to know that your sensory experience has those same truth conditions. This is what it is to introspect upon your red* and triangular* experience.

This view of introspection is indirect in more ways than one: First, your way of depicting your sensory experience to yourself is indirect, via its contingent truth conditions rather than its essential phenomenal features.

Second, your way of knowing that you have a sensory experience depicted in this indirect way is by knowing that you have a belief that you take to be caused by it. Third, the way you know that you have the relevant belief is by noting that you are inclined to accept certain represented contents, understood as truth conditions.

This view of introspection of sensory experience is both independently implausible and in tension with Papineau's other views and arguments. It is independently implausible because it takes knowing which proposition we are inclined to accept to require being able to identify the truth conditions of our acceptances, which requires that we know which external conditions they happen (contingently) to be correlated with. So, introspection of our sensory experiences turns out to presuppose substantive worldly knowledge, knowledge with respect to which we are presumably quite fallible. This is an implausible consequence.

Papineau's view of introspection also leads to an odd type of skeptical worry. Our basis for thinking we have particular sensory experiences includes no evidence for our experiences having particular phenomenal features rather than others. For example, from our evidence, we can (let us grant) infer that we have whatever phenomenal property corresponds to our having truth conditions involving, say, the worldly property of redness, but this evidence does not bear on the question of whether that phenomenal property is red* or green*—or even whether there is such a corresponding phenomenal property at all. Two subjects spectrum-inverted relative to one another but embedded in the same environment would introspect alike and have no rational basis for thinking they have one set of phenomenal features rather than another.

This indirect picture of introspection is in tension with Papineau's other views and arguments. In his argument against naive realism, Papineau urged us to reject the view because it accepts conscious differences that are not introspectively accessible. This argument seems to presuppose that we have some kind of direct, privileged, and authoritative access to our conscious experience. But on Papineau's indirect picture of the introspection of sensory experience, it's unclear why we should be bothered by this consequence of naive realism. Indeed, as was illustrated by the case of spectrum inversion, Papineau's picture of introspection also allows for phenomenal differences we cannot in principle discern. To take another example, physical changes in the brain could result in changes in our sensory features without corresponding changes in the environmental conditions with which they correlate, yielding, again, phenomenal changes that we cannot discern. So, it seems that Papineau is himself committed to phenomenal differences that are not introspectively accessible.

More generally, throughout the book, Papineau urges us to take the structure and phenomenology of sensory experience seriously. Sensory experience is a concrete, here-and-now phenomenon, one that can't be explained in terms of insufficiently substantive relations to abstracta and the like. One reason we could have for thinking that sensory experiences are concrete and here-and-now phenomena is phenomenological: something merely abstract cannot account for the very real, substantive, and here-and-now phenomenology of sensory experience. Another reason is that phenomenal features are causally efficacious (something Papineau accepts). But both reasons are undercut by Papineau's picture of introspection. If our only access to sensory experience is indirect via knowledge of how distinct internal states are correlated with the environment, we have no strong phenomenological reasons for thinking we have phenomenal features at all. Any reasons stemming from the causes of behavior for thinking we have such concrete phenomenal features would need to be a reason for thinking that non-phenomenal features of the mind aren't likely candidates for playing the requisite causal roles—a tall order, indeed!

In short, Papineau's indirect theory of introspection undercuts whatever confidence we would otherwise have in Papineau's overall picture. The good news is that this picture of introspection can be excised from Papineau's overall view without any downstream consequences. Indeed, it occurs toward the end of the book, giving the reader the feeling that it simply serves to tie up some loose ends rather than forming a core part of the view, and Papineau himself ends his discussion by admitting that it might not account for introspection of sensory experiences that are not even contingently representational, allowing for alternative and more direct ways of introspecting upon at least some of our sensory experiences (135–6). I would recommend that someone attracted to Papineau's overall position reject the claim that most of the relevant introspective episodes are indirect in the way Papineau suggests and instead adopt a view on which we often do have direct and immediate access to the phenomenal features of our sensory experiences. This is independently more plausible and makes for a better fit with many other aspects of Papineau's overall position, and it gives us a glimmer of hope for specifying our truth conditions from within our quasi-world.

7. Conclusion

My overall reaction to *The Metaphysics of Sensory Experience* is that it is largely correct but that it does not go far enough in the direction in which it sets off. The book takes consciousness seriously; exposes the problematic commitments of many versions of representationalism, which have been largely neglected in the rush to naturalize the mind; and correctly recognizes, against the philosophical mainstream, the distinctness of phenomenal consciousness and truth conditions. But, I have argued, if sensory experiences are more or less as Papineau says they are, then we should also say, along with the pure phenomenal intentionalist, that they are essentially intentional and that their truth conditions are determined from within consciousness itself (if they are determined at all). If sensory experience is an intrinsic, non-relational feature of subjects, then what we are directly aware of is our own phenomenal world of intentional contents and reaching the external world beyond is much harder than Papineau makes it out to be.

References

Bourget, D. (2010). Consciousness is underived intentionality. *Noûs*, 44(1):32–58.

Bourget, D. (2019a). Implications of intensional perceptual ascriptions for relationalism, disjunctivism, and representationalism about perceptual experience. *Erkenntnis*, 84(2):381–408.

Bourget, D. (2019b). Relational vs adverbial conceptions of phenomenal intentionality. In Sullivan, A., editor, *Sensations, Thoughts, Language: Essays in Honor of Brian Loar*, pages 137–66. Routledge.

Bourget, D. and Mendelovici, A. (2014). Tracking representationalism. In Bailey, A., editor, *Philosophy of Mind: The Key Thinkers*, pages 209–35. Continuum.

Bourget, D. and Mendelovici, A. (2016). Phenomenal intentionality. In Ed Zalta, editor, *The Stanford Encyclopedia of Philosophy*. Stanford University Press.

Brentano, F. (1874). *Psychology from an Empirical Standpoint*. Routledge.

Chalmers, D. J. (2006). Perception and the fall from Eden. In Gendler, T. S. and Hawthorne, J., editors, *Perceptual Experience*, pages 49–125. Oxford University Press.

Chisholm, R. M. (1957). *Perceiving: A Philosophical Study*. Cornell University Press.

Dretske, F. (1995). *Naturalizing the Mind*. MIT Press.

Ducasse, C. J. (1942). Moore's refutation of idealism. In Schilpp, P. A., editor, *The Philosophy of G. E. Moore*, pages 232–3. Open Court.

Farkas, K. (2008). Phenomenal intentionality without compromise. *The Monist*, 91(2):273–93.

Farkas, K. (2013). Constructing a world for the senses. In Kriegel, U., editor, *Phenomenal Intentionality*, pages 99–115. Oxford University Press.

Fodor, J. A. (1987). *Psychosemantics: The Problem of Meaning in the Philosophy of Mind*. MIT Press.

Horgan, T. and Tienson, J. (2002). The phenomenology of intentionality and the intentionality of phenomenology. In Chalmers, D. J., editor, *Philosophy of Mind: Classical and Contemporary Readings*, pages 520–33. Oxford University Press.

Kriegel, U. (2011). *The Sources of Intentionality*. Oxford University Press.

Kriegel, U. (2013). The phenomenal intentionality research program. In Kriegel, U., editor, *Phenomenal Intentionality*. Oxford University Press.

Mendelovici, A. (2018). *The Phenomenal Basis of Intentionality*. Oxford University Press.

Mendelovici, A. (2020). Propositional attitudes as self-ascriptions. In Oliveira, L. R. G. and Corcoran, K., editors, *Common Sense Metaphysics: Themes from the Philosophy of Lynne Rudder Baker*, pages 54–74. Routledge.

Ott, W. (2016). Phenomenal intentionality and the problem of representation. *Journal of the American Philosophical Association*, 2(1):131–45.

Papineau, D. (1984). Representation and explanation. *Philosophy of Science*, 51(December):550–72.

Papineau, D. (2017). Teleosemantics. In Smith, D. L., editor, *How Biology Shapes Philosophy: New Foundations for Naturalism*, pages 95–120. Cambridge: Cambridge University Press.

Papineau, D. (2021). *The Metaphysics of Sensory Experience*. Oxford University Press.

Pautz, A. (2009). A simple view of consciousness. In Koons, R. C. and Bealer, G., editors, *The Waning of Materialism*, pages 25–66. Oxford University Press.

Pautz, A. (2021). Consciousness meets Lewisian interpretation theory: A multistage account of intentionality. In Kriegel, U., editor, *Oxford Studies in Philosophy of Mind*, Vol. 1. Oxford University Press.

Pitt, D. (2004). The phenomenology of cognition: Or what is it like to think that P? *Philosophy and Phenomenological Research*, 69(1):1–36.

Pitt, D. (2009). Intentional psychologism. *Philosophical Studies*, 146(1):117–38.

Putnam, H. (1977). Realism and reason. *Proceedings and Addresses of the American Philosophical Association*, 50(6):483–98.

Siewert, C. (1998). *The Significance of Consciousness*. Princeton University Press.

Tye, M. (2000). *Consciousness, Color, and Content*. MIT Press.

Woodward, P. (2016). Conscious intentionality in perception, imagination, and cognition. *Phenomenology and Mind*, *10*:140–55.

Woodward, P. (2019). Phenomenal intentionality: Reductionism vs. primitivism. *Canadian Journal of Philosophy*, *49*(5):606–27.

14
An Argument against Papineau's Qualitative View of Sensory Experience

Adam Pautz

> Visual experience is intrinsically spatial...if we do not use spatial properties in characterizing visual [experience], we omit a subjective feature of experience.
> —Christopher Peacocke (2008)

> When I see a yellow ball to the left of a red cube the relation that I am aware of is not itself a spatial relation...However it may first seem, what we are aware of when we introspect are properties of ourselves.
> —David Papineau (2021)

In his excellent book *The Metaphysics of Sensory Experience*, David Papineau argues against standard theories of sensory experience: the sense datum view, representationalism, naïve realism, and so on. The only view left standing is his own "qualitative view." On Papineau's physicalist version, all experiences are nothing but neural states, and the only features essentially involved in experience are intrinsic neural properties (2021: 29–30, 95–97).

In previous work I have developed an *argument from spatial experience* against this kind of view (Pautz 2010a, 2017, 2021). Here I will elaborate on that argument in the light of Papineau's discussion.

1. The Spatial Character of Visual Experience

Suppose you experience an orange moving slowing to the right (Figure 14.1). Let's say you have the *orange-experience*.

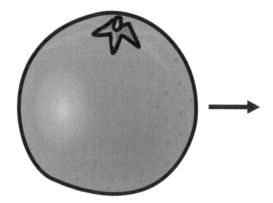

Figure 14.1 The orange-experience.

A goal of the philosophy of perception is to arrive at a "real definition" or "identification" of the form: for a subject to have the orange-experience is for the subject to _____ (Pautz 2010a: 255ff; Papineau 2021: 14ff). At the start of the inquiry, we don't know the *full* real definition. Does it involve an *actual* round item, such as a physical object, or perhaps a "visual field region"? Or does it merely involve *representing* a round item, so that such an item *seems* present?

But from the start we know *something* about the correct real definition. In particular, we know (or at least we have strong reason to believe) that spatial terms will show up in a correct real definition:

Spatial claim. Spatial terms such as *round* and *moving to the right* will show up in a correct definition of what it is to have the orange-experience. That is, there is a correct identification of the following form: for person *x* to have the orange-experience is for *x* to...*round*...*moving to the right*.

Here's an analogy. Consider the Japanese flag. From the start we know the following:

Spatial claim. Spatial terms such as *round* will show up in a correct definition of what it is to be the Japanese flag. For *x* to be the Japanese flag is for *x* to be a rectangular white banner with a *round* and red area at its center, etc.

Pretheoretically, the spatial claim about the orange-experience is equally plausible.

In fact, all the major theories satisfy this pretheoretical constraint. For example:

Visual field theory. For you to have the orange-experience is for you to experience an orange and literally *round* and *moving* "sense datum" (Russell, Moore) or "visual field region" (Peacocke) in a private space.

Externalist representationalism. For you to have the orange-experience is for it to experientially seem to you (for you to "experientially represent") that an orange and *round* object is *moving to the right*. And that is for you to be in some internal (e.g. neural) state or other that suitably tracks this type of object in the external environment. The availability of representationalism shows that the spatial claim doesn't require that the orange-experience involve an *actual* round item (a physical object, sense datum, or visual field region).

Internalist representationalism. For you to have the orange-experience is for it to experientially seem to you that an orange and *round* object is *moving to the right*. That is fixed by a neural state regardless of environmental connections; but it is something more than a neural state. In an "illusionist" or "Edenic" version, these color and shape properties are nowhere instantiated, and the orange-experience is a relationship to them.

Naïve Realism. For you to have the orange-experience is *either* for you to see an orange and *round* and *moving* physical object *or* for you to be in a state indiscriminable from seeing such an object. That is enabled by a neural state but it is something more than a neural state.

Indeed, it is hard to point to explicit denials of the spatial claim in the writings of *any* philosophers, including "adverbialists" (Pautz 2021: 92, n. 9).

By contrast, Papineau's qualitative view is inconsistent with the spatial claim, as we shall now see. This will be the basis of my argument against it.

2. The Spatial Argument against the Qualitative View

My *spatial argument* against Papineau's qualitative view (Pautz 2010a, 2017, 2021) is simple:

1. Papineau's qualitative view is inconsistent with the spatial claim.

2. We have an extremely strong pretheoretical reason to accept the spatial claim and there is no sufficiently strong reason to reject it ("defeater").
3. *Conclusion*: We should reject Papineau's qualitative view.

Let me explain these two premises in turn. First, why accept premise 1? What is Papineau's qualitative view, and why is it inconsistent with the spatial claim?

Papineau's qualitative view is opposed to all views listed in §1 that accommodate the spatial claim. Representationalism accommodates the spatial claim. But a central theme of Papineau's book is that representationalism is metaphysically problematic (more on this in §3). There are anti-representationalist theories that accommodate the spatial claim. For instance, Peacocke (2008) holds that having the orange-experience essentially involves a literally *round* "visual field region," where the visual field is not something to be found in the brain. But Papineau finds this view to be metaphysically weird as well (2021: 95, n. 9).

In the end, Papineau opts for the qualitative view. To have the orange-experience is simply to have a certain "intrinsic property." Moreover, the experience does not essentially "relate the subject to objects or properties beyond itself" (2021: 83). Throughout I will focus on Papineau's *physicalist version* of the qualitative view (although nothing will hang on this):

Papineau's qualitative view. For you to have the orange-experience is simply for you to have a certain neural property (2021: 29–30, 95–97). A *neural property* is one that can be defined in terms of types of neurons and the times, directions, and intensities at which they fire. It doesn't essentially involve representing *round* and *moving to the right*, or a *round* visual field region, or anything like that.

Unlike the representational view and the visual field view, Papineau's qualitative view is inconsistent with the spatial claim. The spatial claim says that the spatial terms *round* and *moving to the right* will show up in a definition of what it is to have the orange-experience. By contrast, Papineau's qualitative view implies that what it is for you to have the orange-experience can be defined in terms of *types of neurons* and the *times*, *directions*, and *intensities* at which they fire. And the spatial terms *round* and *moving to the right* will not show up in a definition of any of these things *at any level*. Thus, Papineau must hold, contrary to the spatial claim, that neither *an actual round item*

AN ARGUMENT AGAINST PAPINEAU'S QUALITATIVE VIEW 343

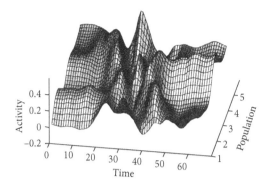

Figure 14.2 A representation of the temporal pattern of firing of several different neurons in the visual cortex.

(e.g. round visual field region) nor *representing a round item* will show up in the definition of what it is to have the orange-experience.

Here is another way of verifying premise 1. *If* we assume the spatial claim, we can construct a Leibniz's law argument against his qualitative view. The spatial claim says that the spatial terms *round* and *moving to the right* show up in a correct definition of what it is to have the orange-experience (Figure 14.1). But, as just argued, this is not true of what it is to have a neural property (Figure 14.2). Therefore, to have the orange-experience is not merely to have a neural property.

Given the spatial claim, then, having the orange-experience might *involve* undergoing a neural property, but it is *something more* than undergoing a neural property. For instance, perhaps it is to be presented with a literally round visual field region, *where the visual field is not to be found in the brain* (Peacocke 2008). Or perhaps it is for it to *experientially seem* to you (for you to "experientially represent") that a round thing is present, where this is merely contingently *realized by* a neural property.

So much for premise 1. Now you might think: "Ok, Papineau's qualitative view is inconsistent with the spatial claim, but it is consistent with *something close*. In particular, he can say that certain *neural features* show up in a definition of what it is for you to have the orange-experience, and he can call those neural features '*quasi*-roundness' and '*quasi*-moving-to-the-right'. Isn't that close enough?"

The trouble is that the spatial claim says that genuine *spatial features*, such as *round* and *moving to the right*, show up in a definition of what it is to have the orange-experience, where those are features that could be instantiated in the external world. Therefore, they are *evidently nothing like the relevant neural features instantiated in your brain*.[1] Of course, there is nothing like an object moving to the right in your brain when you have the orange-experience! Further, undergoing a mere neural state doesn't essentially involve *representing* a round object moving to the right (2021: 84–85), so it doesn't even essentially involve the *appearance* of such an object. Therefore, Papineau's qualitative view doesn't even *come close* to accommodating the spatial claim about the orange-experience. This is something he appears to concede (2021: 29–30, 95–97).

This means that Papineau's view implies a radical error theory about visual phenomenal character. It seems to you that the phenomenal character of your orange-experience is such that spatial terms like *round* and *moving to the right* will show up in its definition (Figure 14.1). Its phenomenal character essentially involves a real or apparent spatial field in which there is a *round* item. Even anti-representationalist theories such as Peacocke's (2008) accommodate this. But Papineau's view does not. It implies that in reality the phenomenal character of your experience can be fully defined without using spatial terms such as *round* and *moving to the right* (Figure 14.2). It does *not* essentially involve a real or apparent spatial field in which there is a *round* item. So Papineau's view implies *your orange-experience doesn't have the phenomenal character it seems to have*. I think that, if you understand Papineau's view, you see that it flies in the face of what is obvious.

Now let us turn to premise 2. In §1, I supported the first part of this premise: we have a strong pretheoretical reason to accept the spatial claim. In §§3–4, I will support the second part: there is no sufficiently strong reason to reject it.

3. Papineau's Reason for Rejecting the Spatial Claim?

In his book, Papineau doesn't directly address my spatial argument against his qualitative view (Pautz 2010a, 2017, 2021). But, given what he says, I think that he would accept premise 1 but reject premise 2. Contrary to

---

[1] Even if it turns out that the spatial features involved in the orange-experience are not actually instantiated in the external world because some radical quantum ontology is correct (they are "Edenic"), they at least *could be* instantiated in the external world in a basic way (e.g. in a world where space is Newtonian). Therefore, even in that case, they cannot be identified with neural features instantiated in the brain. See Pautz (2021: 92, n. 6).

premise 2, he would say that there is a sufficiently strong reason to reject the spatial claim.

But what is that reason? His discussion suggests the following argument:

1. If the spatial claim is correct, then one of the theories listed in §1 must be correct: representationalism, the visual field theory, or naïve realism.
2. But representationalism fails (ch. 2).
3. And the visual field theory (2021: 28–30; 95, n. 9) and naïve realism (2021: 20–22) fail for other reasons.
4. *Conclusion*: the spatial claim is false.

Call this the *theoretical argument* against the spatial claim because the idea is that we should reject it because there is no good theoretical account of it. If this argument is good, then it would save Papineau's qualitative view from my argument against it based on the spatial claim. But is it good?

I agree with premise 3: the visual field theory and naïve realism fail. But I reject premise 2. I defend a representational account of the spatial claim (Pautz 2010a, 2021). Papineau devotes much space to arguing against representationalism but I think that his argument is unconvincing.

Here is what Papineau calls his "general" master argument against any form of representationalism (2021: 71–74):

A. Representationalism holds that "instantiations of experience properties are instantiations of representational properties."

B. But "instantiations of representational properties constitute abstract facts."

C. If so, then "they cannot feature as causes or effects" because only concrete facts "are eligible to enter into causal relations."

D. So: representationalism implies that instantiations of experience properties cannot have causes and effects.

E. But "the difficulties facing epiphenomenalism are well known."

F. Therefore "conscious sensory properties are not representational properties."

Call this the *epiphobia argument* against representationalism. I think that the argument has a couple of questionable steps.

To begin with, I question B. I am open to a *nominalist* interpretation of representationalism (for references, see Pautz 2021: 129). To illustrate, let's consider my own favorite form of representationalism, *internalist* representationalism. On this view, there is a neural state that is necessarily sufficient for experientially representing that there is before you a thing that is orange, round, and moving to the right. The nominalist now adds a negative claim: experientially representing that something is round (etc.) is not to be further analyzed. In particular, it is not to be analyzed as a relation to the proposition *that something is round*, or the universal property *being round*, or any other abstract entity. There are no such abstract entities. Therefore, this representational view agrees with Papineau's own qualitative view that "the experience does not essentially relate the subject to external properties" (2021: 83), because it holds that there are no such entities as properties. This view would block Papineau's epiphobia argument at the start by rejecting B.

In reply, Papineau might argue that representationalists are *committed to* an "abstract entities" interpretation of their view, but nominalists have found ways of resisting such arguments. Predicates like "is round" can be meaningful even if there don't exist properties understood as abstract entities.[2]

Even if we grant B, Papineau's epiphobia argument is unconvincing because there are two problems with C.

First, Papineau doesn't give any reason for accepting C. If we grant B, then representationalists hold that your experientially representing that there is before you a thing that is orange, round, and moving to the right is to be analyzed as your standing in a relationship ("experientially representing") to the abstract entity, <being round, being orange, moving to the right>. Now this abstract entity *itself* doesn't have causes and effects. But what is Papineau's reason for thinking that the state of experientially representing this abstract entity cannot have causes and effects, as C implies?

And what is the strength of the "cannot" in C? Cannot as a *matter of metaphysical necessity*? That is, are there no possible worlds where relationships to abstract entities have causes and effects? Does Papineau think that this is known through *a priori* intuition?

Second, C is inconsistent with all theories of causation and "causal efficacy." In the 1990s there was a general outbreak of epiphobia concerning all macro

---

[2] I note in passing that the spatial argument against the qualitative view presented in §2 is likewise not committed to the idea that the orange-experience involves spatial properties understood as abstract objects.

properties. A standard solution is that, if macro properties suitably "supervene on" or are "grounded in" physical properties, then they might pass some counterfactual-proportionality test (sufficient condition) for being "causes" or "causally efficacious." Of course, the analysis of causation is tricky, but presumably there is *some* such sufficient condition.

Given this solution, representationalists can now co-opt it to undermine C, even if they accept B. For instance, return to the kind of internalist representationalism that I favor, but now assume (in line with B) a "relations to abstract entities" interpretation of it. In a way, this view is like Papineau's: the orange-experience is necessitated by a neural state mediating between stimulus and response. But whereas Papineau holds that the orange-experience is *identical with* the neural state, this view holds that it is a matter of experientially representing <being round, being orange, moving to the right>, where this is distinct from but *grounded in* the neural state. On this internalist representationalism, *even if* the experience is a relationship to an abstract entity, it might (contrary to C) count as a cause of your behavior, thanks to being grounded in the neural state and *satisfying the relevant counterfactual/proportionality sufficient condition*. It is hard to see how Papineau might show that it *couldn't* satisfy the relevant sufficient condition, just because it is a relation to an abstract entity.[3] Papineau may have other objections to internalist representationalism (more on this in §4); but he cannot object that it necessarily implies epiphenomenalism.[4]

A final point. The spatial claim is extremely plausible (§1). So even if we were to reject a *representational* account of it (accept premise 2), we should fish around for *another* account of it (that is, question premise 3). For example, Papineau rejects Peacocke's visual field theory in a brief footnote (2021: 95, n. 9), but perhaps this kind of view deserves more discussion (Pautz 2021: 49, 57–58, 134–135).

---

[3] Even on a "primitivist" theory of causation, Papineau's constraint C is implausible if he intends it as a necessary truth. Why couldn't your standing in a mental relation to an abstract entity stand in a primitive causal necessitation relation to certain of your behaviors?

[4] Papineau has other arguments against representationalism. One concerns the question: (i) what are the contents? (78). I think Papineau neglects a natural response (Pautz 2009: 499). Another challenge (apparently distinct from his epiphobia argument): (ii) why are *having the orange-experience* and *experientially representing a content* "necessarily connected"? (Papineau 2021: 39, 74, 84). My answer is that they are identical, and identities don't call for explanation. The best argument for the identity takes the form of an inference to the best explanation (Pautz 2010a, 2021)—not any of the arguments Papineau criticizes in his book (2021: sect. 2.2).

4. Another Potential Reason to Reject the Spatial Claim?

So I find Papineau's own reason for rejecting the spatial claim unconvincing. Let me now turn to another potential reason for rejecting the spatial claim not considered by Papineau.

In my essay "How do Brain's in Vats Experience Space?" (2019), I developed the following *"brain-in-the-void" (BIV) argument:*

1. Phenomenalism internalism is correct: experience is determined by neural states.
2. Therefore, a hypothetical BIV duplicate of your brain that formed by chance in an otherwise empty universe could have the same orange-experience as you.
3. If the spatial claim is also true, then (assuming realism about properties) you and your BIV duplicate are somehow *perceptually related* to the spatial properties *being round* and *moving to the right*, even though in the case of BIV they are not instantiated in the environment.
4. But the BIV stands in no interesting *physical relationship* to these properties: the BIV has never physically interacted with *round* or *moving* objects.
5. Therefore, if the spatial claim is true, the orange-experience involves a perceptual relationship to spatial properties that cannot be identified with any physical relationship—an irreducible, non-physical relationship.

To illustrate the argument, consider my own internalist representational account of the spatial claim. In particular, I will assume the "relation to abstract entities" version discussed at the end of §3. This view accepts the "internalist" premises 1 and 2. It also accepts a version of premise 3: given the spatial claim, you and your BIV duplicate stand in the dyadic "experiential representation relation" to <being round, being orange, moving to the right>. But the BIV stands in no interesting dyadic physical relationship to these properties. For instance, it doesn't have any states with the *historical function of indicating the instantiation* of these properties. So the experiential representation relation is an irreducible, non-physical relationship. Our brains have an innate capacity to enable us to stand in this relationship to spatial and other basic properties that are not instantiated *in* our brains.[5]

---

[5] The phenomenal internalist cannot answer the BIV argument by reductively explaining how the BIV experientially represents spatial properties in terms of what spatial properties the

In my view, the BIV argument is sound. If so, then the spatial claim has a surprising consequence: it requires rejecting *identification physicalism*. Roughly, this is a strong form of physicalism on which every instantiated property is a physical or functional property definable in terms of a basic list of physicalistically acceptable properties. However, it is compatible with more liberal *ground physicalism* (Schaffer 2013; Pautz 2020). For instance, we might say that there is a neural state N such that, necessarily, the fact that one undergoes N grounds the fact that one stands in the irreducible experiential representation relation to <being round, being orange, moving to the right>. Perhaps such grounding connections can be systematized (Pautz 2021: 182–184).[6]

Now Papineau's arguments in his book don't rely on any form of physicalism (90). But Papineau (2016) does favor a strong identity form of physicalism over more liberal forms. Since the BIV argument shows that the spatial claim is incompatible with identification physicalism, he could therefore argue that the reasonable course is to apply *modus tollens* and reject the spatial claim. As he once said to me in some comments on the BIV argument, "I'd rather drop [the spatial claim] than accept an irreducible experiential representation relation" (personal correspondence, 2014). This would block my spatial argument against his qualitative view.

To show that this is indeed reasonable, Papineau would have to show that we should have higher credence in a controversial metaphysical theory (identification physicalism) than in a pretheoretical datum about experience (the spatial claim).

But this is not the case. As I said in §1, the reason for accepting the spatial claim is extremely strong—indeed it seems obvious. By contrast, the overall case for identification physicalism is not very strong at all. It may explain the dependence of experience on the physical in a simple way (Pautz 2020: sect. 4). But today many philosophers reject it based on multiple realizability (Schaffer 2013) and other considerations (Pautz 2020: sect. 2.3). They instead

---

BIV *would* track *were* it embodied (Pautz 2019: 401–402; Papineau 2021: 112–113). Nor would it help her to hold that spatial properties are response-dependent (Pautz 2010b: 48–49, 2021: 167–169; Papineau 2021: 80–82). Of course, we might block the BIV argument at the start by rejecting phenomenal internalism and denying that the BIV could have visual experiences at all. Then we might reductively explain our experiential representation of spatial properties along the lines of "externalist representationalism" (an option listed in §1). But externalist representationalism is empirically implausible (Pautz 2010b; Papineau 2021: 59–60) and violates "phenomenal localism" (Pautz 2014: 172–174; Papineau 2021: 51–52).

[6] Another option for accommodating the spatial claim in the light of the BIV argument would be to say that both you and your BIV duplicate are *presented with* an orange' and literally round visual field region, where this is *grounded in but distinct from* neural goings on (Pautz 2021: 49, 134–135).

favor a form of ground physicalism on which some grounding connections cannot be explained in terms of identities. It's hard to see how Papineau could be certain *a priori* that there cannot be such grounding connections.

So if the BIV argument shows that the spatial claim is incompatible with identification physicalism, the reasonable course is to *keep* the spatial claim *and reject* identification physicalism—for identification physicalism is a speculative view that we probably should reject anyway.

5. Conclusion

Papineau may be unmoved by my spatial argument against his qualitative view. He may reject the spatial claim about the orange-experience. Then he might try to explain why we find it irresistible even though it is mistaken (2021: 91–92, 110–112).

But, before giving such an explanation, Papineau must give a sufficiently strong reason to think that the spatial claim is mistaken in the first place.[7] I have raised the following question for Papineau: *isn't our reason for accepting the spatial claim stronger than our reasons for accepting the questionable metaphysical assumptions driving the arguments against it considered in §3 and §4 (viz. the causal constraint C and "identification physicalism")?*

After all, don't we have strong (albeit defeasible) reasons to accept *some* things about our experiences? For instance, everyone will agree that we have a strong reason to believe that two reddish color experiences essentially resemble each other more than they resemble the smell of chocolate. No one would give *that* up in the name of a philosophical theory. Isn't our pretheoretical reason to accept the spatial claim about the orange-experience equally strong? (Indeed, if we *know* the spatial claim about the Japanese flag, why not the spatial claim about the orange-experience?) Isn't the spatial claim more than a common opinion? Isn't it something we have

---

[7] I would also like to know the details of Papineau's psychological explanation of why the spatial claim is irresistible even though in his view it is radically mistaken. Some of his remarks (2021: 92, 95) suggest the following explanation: (i) we know that the orange-experience (in his view, merely a neural pattern) is caused by *round* objects; and (ii) we mistakenly infer from this that *round* shows up the definition of what it is to have the experience (we "confuse causation with constitution"). But this explanation is insufficient. After all, if head-pains were systematically caused by the presence of variously shaped objects, we wouldn't be inclined to mistakenly think that those shapes show up in the *definitions* of what it is to have those head-pains. In my view, the spatial claim about the orange-experience is irresistible because it is true in this case (as in the case of the Japanese flag).

excellent reason to believe on the basis of introspection and reflection? Therefore, isn't our reason for accepting the spatial claim stronger than our reason for accepting the questionable metaphysical assumptions behind Papineau's arguments against it?

References

Papineau, D. 2016. Grounds and Gaps. Presentation at the University of Birmingham. Available at https://www.davidpapineau.co.uk/unpublished-talks.html

Papineau, D. 2021. *The Metaphysics of Sensory Experience*. Oxford: Oxford University Press.

Pautz, A. 2009. What Are the Contents of Experiences? *Philosophical Quarterly* 59: 483–507.

Pautz, A. 2010a. Why Explain Experience in Terms of Content? In B. Nanay (ed.), *Perceiving the World*. Oxford: Oxford University Press, 254–309.

Pautz, A. 2010b. A Simple View of Consciousness. In R. C. Koons and G, Bealer (eds.), *The Waning of Materialism*. Oxford: Oxford University Press, 25–66.

Pautz, A. 2014. The Real Trouble for Armchair Arguments against Phenomenal Externalism. In M. Sprevak and J. Kallestrup (eds.), *New Waves in Philosophy of Mind*. London: Palgrave Macmillan, 153–181.

Pautz, A. 2017. Experiences are Representations. In B. Nanay (ed.), *Current Controversies in the Philosophy of Perception*. London: Routledge, 23–42.

Pautz, A. 2019. How Can Brains in Vats Experience a Spatial World? A Puzzle for Internalists. In A. Pautz & D. Stoljar (eds.), *Blockheads! Essays on Ned Block's Philosophy of Mind and Consciousness*. MIT Press, 379–420.

Pautz, A. 2020. How to Achieve the Physicalist Dream: Identity or Grounding? Available at https://philpapers.org/rec/PAUHTA-2

Pautz, A. 2021. *Perception*. London: Routledge.

Peacocke, C. 2008. Sensational Properties: Theses to Accept and Theses to Reject. *Revue Internationale de Philosophie* 62: 7–24.

Schaffer, J. 2013. Metaphysical Semantics Meets Multiple Realizability. *Analysis* 73: 736–751.

15
Responses to Mendelovici, Pautz, and Byrne

David Papineau

I am grateful to my commentators for their thoughtful discussions of my book. I have learned much from reading them and am pleased to have the opportunity to respond.

1. Mendelovici

It will be convenient to discuss Angela Mendelovici's comments first. Mendelovici agrees with much of the story I tell. Her only complaint is that I do not develop it far enough. As she sees it, I am much closer to her own positive views than I think. If only I would follow my argument a bit further, she urges, I would be able to join her in endorsing them.

I would be very happy to accept this invitation, if only I could understand it better. I get the general idea of what Mendelovici is after. But when I try to make it precise I am afraid it seems to dissolve away.

Let me begin with our points of agreement. Mendelovici shares my view that sensory experience is purely qualitative. Conscious sensory properties, such as having a visual experience "as of" a yellow ball, are intrinsic to subjects, and have no necessary connections to any objects or properties in the world beyond the mind ("wordly" objects and properties henceforth). In particular, sensory experiences do not, in virtue of their nature, determine truth conditions involving such worldly items. To the extent that such external truth conditions can be associated with types of experience, this is only due to the way experiences are contingently associated with conditions in the environments of specific subjects.

This does not mean, Mendelovici and I further agree, that sensory experience is not richly structured internally. The realm of sensory experience displays a range of "quasi-objects" and "quasi-properties", elements of experiences that display a continuity over time as clusters of sensory features. Invoking a useful analogy—though one that needs to be treated with care—Mendelovici likens sensory experience to an internal movie playing in our heads. But the quasi-objects and quasi-properties in the movie have no constitutive connection with the world beyond.

Still, while Mendelovici agrees with me about all this, she urges that there is a further species of representation that I ignore, and that this underpins a different sense of truth, one which owes nothing to contingent associations with environmental conditions. It is this suggestion that I find difficult to make good sense of.

Mendelovici first introduces her alternative idea by quoting Brentano:

> Every mental phenomenon is characterized by what the Scholastics of the Middle Ages called the intentional (or mental) inexistence of an object, and what we might call, though not wholly unambiguously, reference to a content, direction toward an object (which is not to be understood here as meaning a thing), or immanent objectivity.

I must say I do not find this idea of "intentional inexistence of an object" helpful. What object? If it is just what I call a "quasi-object", then that is straightforward enough. It's an element of experience, the element that (contingently) represents, let us say, an external yellow ball. But why does it have "inexistence"? It's perfect real. There's no question of its not existing. Of course there is also the further possibility of an external yellow ball—and relative to the experience such a worldly ball might or might not exist. But this possible real ball is not at all the same thing as the mental quasi-ball. There should be no question of identifying them. In the book I spend some time on this, and point out that it must be a confusion to identify the quasi-ball, which definitely exists in the experience, with some possible real ball whose existence isn't guaranteed by the experience. And on this point too I take it that Mendelovici agrees. Quasi-objects have no constitutive connection with anything beyond the mind. So all we are left with are the internal mental items with their phenomenological structure. If we want to refer to this structure as "intentionality", then I am prepared to let the terminology pass. But we have so far been given nothing that looks representational, nothing that involves mental items laying claim to something beyond themselves.

Mendelovici then introduces the idea of "intentional contents", items that are thought, or perceptually experienced, such as that *2 + 2 = 4* or the apparent *presence of a yellow ball*. Mendelovici is prepared to take the ontology of such "contents" at face value, but from my perspective an ambiguity threatens. In chapter 4 of the book, I distinguish two sorts of properties involved in the possession of mental states: *vehicle* properties and *content* properties. When I have a visual experience as of a yellow ball, say, I instantiate both properties. In the first instance, I house a certain vehicle of representation, an intrinsic state that in itself is representationally dumb. But along with that, in virtue of that state's (contingent) representational power, I also instantiate the property of representing the presence of a yellow ball.

As far as I can see, Mendelovici's initial introduction of "intentional contents" only gives us vehicle properties. She points us to the intrinsic items we think and experience *with*, to our internal vehicles of representation. But nothing so far has been said to explain why these items should be other than representationally dumb. They have a phenomenology, sure, purely in virtue of their nature as vehicles. But the challenge we are facing is to explain why such phenomenological entities should by their nature lay claim to matters beyond themselves, and this challenge still seems to remain unanswered.

Perhaps Mendelovici is still agreeing with me. Towards the end of her comments she says: "I don't think it has been adequately appreciated… [how we] are trapped in a phenomenally-constituted quasi-world, wanting to make cognitive contact with the noumenal world beyond, but unable to claw our way out of our phenomenal prison."

Even so, Mendelovici clearly has faith that it is *somehow* possible for intentional contents to point beyond themselves. She gives the example of a brain in a vat hooked up to computer. As far as contingent representational contents go, she observes, the thoughts of this being will generally be true. When it visually experiences a yellow ball, the computer's registers will generally be in their "yellow ball" state. When it thinks *I am not a brain in a vat*, it will again be right, given that that the computer's registers won't "locate it in" any computer "vat". But even so, insists Mendelovici, this brain in the vat is clearly mistaken about something. As she puts it, the real world does not *conform* to its phenomenological understanding of its situation. So we need some more basic notion of representation, in terms of phenomenal intentionality, and not just contingent environmental truth conditions, in order to accommodate the poor envatted brain's misapprehension.

I share the intuition, but I doubt Mendelovici is pointing to the right kind of explanation. I just don't see how this basic idea of "conformity" to the phenomenology can be made good. I can understand representation in terms of contingent environmental truth conditions, but I can't make any good sense of Mendelovici's more basic phenomenological representation.

The most immediate way of understanding "conformity" would be in terms of some primitive notion of *resemblance*. But I presume that Mendelovici would not want to go this way. She distinguishes clearly between the phenomenal world of experience and the noumenal world beyond. I would have thought there is no question of items from the noumenal world primitively resembling elements of the noumenal world. (It would be different if we embraced an idealist metaphysics, and arguably this has been one of the main motivations for idealism. But I take it that this is not what Mendelovici has in mind.)

Towards the end of her comments, Mendelovici suggests a different line. Perhaps we can directly refer to our own experiences, and somehow parlay this into a specification of worldly conditions that would render our experiences true. Presumably the idea would be that our experiences answer to those powers in the world that typically cause *these* experiences in us. I must say I don't find this programme particularly attractive. Note that it would require a *dispositional* account of all worldly referents. Mendelovici wouldn't want us to end up referring to whichever items in our environment (contingently) cause our experiences, because then the referents would once more depend on environments and not just our intrinsic phenomenology. So we would need to make all worldly referents response-dependent, dispositional properties to produce experiential results in us. As I observe at the end of chapter 2, while this isn't a crazy account of colours and other secondary qualities, it seems a very odd view of primary qualities.

In any case, it's not clear that this line will fit Mendelovici's bill. Go back to the brain in the vat that she used to motivate the idea that we need some other notion of representation than that deriving from environmental correlations. Her thought was that the world did not conform to the envatted brain's phenomenological picture, and that we need a notion of basic representation that will account for this. But the response-dependent option just broached is not going to deliver this. If the brain in the vat's experience as of a yellow ball answers to the presence of *a power that typically produces these experiences*, then the experience will come out veridical (since the computer does embody just such a power)—which is not the answer that Mendelovici wants.

The hankering for a primitive mode of phenomenological representation seems to have got us nowhere. I say that we should recognize that naturalist representation is the only kind of representation there is. (And if we are still worried about the intuition that the brain in the vat is mistaken, the literature on naturalist representation offers various ways of accommodating it.)

2. Pautz

I turn now to Adam Pautz's comments. Central to these is what he calls the *spatial claim*. He imagines a visual experience of a round orange moving to the right, and urges that spatial categories will have to play some role in any metaphysical analysis ("real definition") of this experience.

> *Spatial claim.* Spatial terms such as *round* and *moving to the right* will show up in a correct definition of what it is to have the orange-experience. That is, there is a correct identification of the following form: for person x to have the orange-experience is for x to . . . *round* . . . *moving to the right*.

By way of analogy, he gives the example of the Japanese flag. As he observes, any satisfactory account of the nature of the Japanese flag will need to specify that it contains a *round* circle on a white background.

As Pautz observes, I do not accept the spatial claim for visual experiences of oranges and other similar examples. I deny that the elements of experience themselves instantiate the spatial properties and relations in question. Pautz notes that, as a physicalist, I am likely to identify elements of experience with neural activations in the brain, which will themselves have spatial properties. But of course, he further observes, while these neural processes might have spatial properties, they won't have the right ones. The neural processes that constitute my seeing something round are not themselves round. (For what it is worth, I do not commit myself to physicalism in the book. But that does not matter here. In my view, even if sensory experiences were made of some distinctive mind-stuff, they still wouldn't involve the relevant spatial properties and relations.)

How bad is it to deny the spatial claim? That certainly runs counter to initial common sense. To switch examples slightly, suppose I see a round orange to the left of a white box. Now consider the elements of my experience corresponding respectively to the orange and the box. It will strike most people as pretty obvious that the former element of experience is itself to the left of the latter. Or suppose I see the orange above the box. Again it seems clear that the orange element of my experience of the orange is itself above the white-box element.

However, attributing spatial properties to elements of experience is by no means as straightforward as it seems. After all, our visual experience also involves a dimension of depth, along with the left-right and up-down dimensions. Should we then think that depth relations also apply to elements of experience? Suppose I now see the box to be some distance further away from me than the orange. Does this mean that the box element of my experience is itself further away from me than the orange element? I take it that this does not strike us as nearly so obvious.

Similar points arise in connection with the way vision represents absolute size and shape and the associated phenomena of size and shape constancy. Consider the familiar "moon illusion" which makes the moon look much bigger when viewed near the horizon than when directly overhead. One might initially think that this results from the element of visual experience that corresponds to the moon itself being bigger when the moon is viewed near the horizon. But not too fast. A coin that exactly occludes the overhead moon when held at arm's length will do the same for the horizon moon, even though the coin itself seems the same size in both cases. No easy equation of apparent size with experiential size can accommodate this. (Cases involving shape perception can be used to make similar points.)

Examples like these put pressure on the idea that the elements of visual experience themselves have spatial properties. As it happens, I would not expect Pautz to object to my line of argument so far. This is because his *Spatial Claim* is not committed to the thesis that spatial properties and relations like *round* and *left of* (and *further away* and *bigger than*) are themselves *instantiated* in visual experience. This thesis is upheld, it is true, by naïve realist and sense datum accounts of experience. But Pautz intends his *Spatial Claim* to cover the idea that experiences essentially involve spatial properties and relations, not by instantiating them, but by *representing* them.

What is more, Pautz's representationalism is significantly less ontologically committed to spatial elements in experience than is mainstream representationalism. The mainstream, but not Pautz, holds that worldly properties, including spatial ones, are in some sense literally "present" in experiences, even when nothing actually bears them. Such versions of representationalism typically appeal to the "transparency" of experience, pointing to the way that, even in illusions and hallucinations, introspection apparently reveals no properties in experience other than normal worldly colours, shapes, textures, and so on.

It is arguable that such transparency-based versions of representationalism will also have difficulty accommodating some of the spatial aspects of experience. Is it plausible that such spatial relations as *further away* or *bigger than* are literally present in our visual experiences, even as possibly uninstantiated relations, given the oddities I pointed to above? It is not obvious to me how transparency-inspired representationalists can happily explain these.

Still, I shall not press this point here, given that Pautz takes care to distance his own representationalism from the idea that uninstantiated worldly properties can literally be present in experience. As we shall see, he opts for a primitivist version of experiential representationalism which does not explain representation as deriving from the presence of represented properties in experience—and indeed does not explain experiential representation at all.

So the ellipses in Pautz's *Spatial Claim* are doing a lot of work. His insistence that an analysis of his orange experience must include "...*round... moving to the right*" does not require that these spatial properties are in any sense contained in the experience, but only that the experience primitively represents them.

Pautz says that my own view implies a "radical error theory" about visual phenomenal character, adding that "it flies in the face of what is obvious." Maybe so. I am happy to grant that it strikes many people as obvious that elements of experience *possess* spatial properties, or at least that spatial properties are *present in* experience, albeit as possibly uninstantiated universals. And my account certainly denies these claims. But so does Pautz's. By his own account, spatial properties are not possessed by or even present in experience. Rather they are related to experiences via some further unexplained primitively representational mode. It is not clear to me why Pautz's account isn't itself a radical error theory.

Still, I don't rest anything much on this. As I see things, divergences from common sense are in themselves neither here nor there. If philosophical analysis requires us to reject assumptions that have been baked into common sense, then so be it. What matters in a philosophical theory is whether it explains all empirical data and makes good metaphysical sense, not that it respects untested ideas that have been handed down to us by tradition.

In the book, I offer an argument against all representationalist theories of sensory experience, Pautz's primitivist version included. Pautz maintains that his version of representationalism evades this argument. But in my view he has to work hard to get round it, and I would say that he manages to maintain metaphysical coherence in response to my argument only by abandoning all explanatory ambitions.

The argument is simple enough. As I put it in the book, it goes:

1. Instantiations of conscious sensory properties constitute concrete facts with causes and effects.
2. Instantiations of representational properties constitute abstract facts that cannot feature as causes and effects.
3. Conscious sensory properties are not representational properties.

Pautz has two objections to premise 2. He denies that representational properties are abstract, and adds that, even if they were, that wouldn't stop them featuring in causes and effects.

It will be convenient to take the second point first. Pautz here appeals to the rich tradition of recent work on supervenient causation. As he points out, it is widely agreed that mental properties can be causally efficacious even if they cannot be identified with physical brain properties, as long as they are supervenient on or metaphysically grounded in the physical realm. Moreover, he observes, many essentialist representational theories, including his own, will take mental representational properties to be so physically grounded. So he urges that there is no barrier to representational properties featuring as causes. He cites the availability of counterfactual or proportionality criteria that will secure such causal claims.

I do not think that this serves. I have no objection to the general idea of supervenient causation being vindicated by appeal to criteria of counterfactual dependence or proportionality. Still, as will be familiar from work connecting causation to such criteria, we need to be careful about what kinds of properties we apply the criteria to. If we allow properties that are metaphysically intertwined with one another, or otherwise metaphysically inappropriate, we will end up with causal nonsense.

I take the same view about applying counterfactual or proportionality criteria to abstract representational properties. The idea that some non-instantiation relation to an abstract entity might feature in a causal relationship should be off the agenda from the start. It's just not the kind of thing that enters into causal relationships.

Pautz asks about my basis for this claim. I certainly don't base it on *a priori* intuition. Rather I infer it from the fact that none of the other causes and effects uncovered by science feature non-instantiation relations to abstract entities. In particular, none of the mental properties upheld as efficacious in the debate about supervenient causation need to be viewed in this way. Nor do causes and effects in the precise physical sciences. It is a familiar point that, even though physical causes and effects are often picked out via their relations to abstract mathematical objects, we need to switch to non-abstract nominalist versions in order to find items capable of entering into causal relations. (I shall return to this point when discussing Alex Byrne's comments below.)

I turn now to Pautz's other objection to my argument. He is not ready to accept that representational properties involve non-instantiation relations to abstract entities, and says he would prefer a nominalist approach to representation. I am not sure I understand this. It is hard to see what it would be for something to *represent* anything, if it doesn't do so by determining a truth condition, or a proposition, or a property, or a value of some higher order variable, or some such. Pautz says that he is going to stipulate that *representing that something is round* does not involve any such entities, but I am not sure that he can—at least not without stipulating away representation itself. (After all, how do constructions like "that something is round" work? The compositional structure of representational attributions would seem to demand some account of what such phrases refer to.)

Having said this, I am old enough to remember Donald Davidson's heroic attempts to give an account of meaning that was free of any reference to propositions, or properties, or so on. This austerely nominalist project unsurprisingly foundered on a range of technical problems, but even if it hadn't, there are further reasons for thinking it would be no help in our current content. Suppose that Davidson has succeeded in devising some way of conveying the significance of sentences, or mental states, without referring to any abstract entities. He still faced the meta-semantic challenge of explaining what made it the case that those sentences, or mental states, bore the meanings they did. Davidson would have answered that those meanings were the ones that best allowed us to understand the utterances and behaviour of the subjects in question, or something along those lines. Perhaps some other meta-semantic account could serve the nominalist project better. But any such account will make the property of representing something to be thus-and-so a very messy property, even if it doesn't involve any relations to abstracta. And then I will argue, as before, that such messy properties just don't look like things with causes and effects, or at least not the causes and effects that we take conscious sensory states to have.

I suspect that Pautz would be unmoved by these objections to his nominalist evasion of my causal argument. I have been challenging him to explain what it is for one thing to represent another, and why such relationships should obtain. But Pautz's eventual position explicitly precludes any such explanations. At the end of his comments Pautz commits himself to a *primitivist* view of experiential representational relations. Certain conscious subjects stand in an irreducible non-physical experiential representational relationship to certain contents. Perhaps we can systematically specify which neural states ground these relationships, but beyond that no explanation of experiential representation is possible.

Pautz defends this position by appeal to brain-in-vat considerations. He takes it that a cosmic brain-in-vat would have the same experiences as its normal counterpart, and hence (via his spatial claim) would be related to properties like *round* and *moving to the right*. But at a physical level the brain-in-vat bears no identifiable relationship to those properties. So the experiential representational relationship must transcend anything physical. As it happens, certain neural states ground certain conscious feelings, and these conscious feelings by their nature represent the physical properties *round* and *moving to the right*, even though grounding neural states are quite unconnected with those properties.

I grant that this position is coherent. But at the same time it is explanatorily empty. Its experiential representation is a kind of magic, and it evades my causal argument only by refusing to explain the nature of this experiential representation. If this is where the spatial claim drives us, so much the worse for the claim. By rejecting it, I think I am able to develop a theory that delivers detailed explanations for everything that needs explaining. If the price I must pay is to reject some small part of common sense, that seems well worth it.

3. Byrne

Alex Byrne is also unpersuaded by my arguments. In particular, he is unpersuaded by my arguments (1) that the presence of uninstantiated properties in sensory experience is inconsistent with the causal role of experience; (2) that introspection reveals only the presence of intrinsic properties of subjects; and (3) that considerations of colour similarity argue against both naïve realism and representationalism. I shall take these in turn.

First, then, is my causal argument against the presence of uninstantiated properties in sensory experience. But, before I discuss the argument, I would like to clarify one point. When he explains my view, Byrne says that I deny that sensory experiences necessarily incline subjects towards beliefs. But I do not deny this. In section 2.2.2 ("Conscious Character Fixes Belief"), I explicitly allow that there might well be "essential links between experiences and the vehicles of belief". I deny only that this is enough to make experiences essentially representational. In support of his reading of me, Byrne cites a passage in which I say that the sensory states of a cosmic brain-in-vat would represent nothing. I do say this, but that is not because the brain-in-vat would lack beliefs. By its nature, the brain-in-vat will have physical states matching its normal counterpart's beliefs, and moreover in my view those states will share the phenomenology, if any, of those normal beliefs. Moreover, those brain-in-vat belief-like states could well have constitutive functional connections to brain-in-vat experiences. Of course, given its lack of any systematic links to any environment, I will say that none of the cosmic brain-in-vat's states, neither sensory experiences nor belief-like states, would have representational contents. But, to repeat, that's not because the experiences wouldn't be linked to the belief-like states.

To return to the issue at hand, Byrne takes me to offer two different arguments against the presence of uninstantiated properties in sensory experience, one appealing to the local "here-and-now" nature of sensory experience, and the other appealing to causal considerations. But in fact I only have one argument. As I take care to explain, I don't view the rhetorical appeals to "here-and-now" as having any dialectal substance independent of the causal argument. ("I have expressed my puzzlement... that uninstantiated properties can be *present* in sensory experience. As I have said, this strikes me as inconsistent with the here-and-now nature of conscious experience... Still, puzzlement is not an argument... So, in this section and the next two, I shall develop my puzzlement into an argument"; p. 65.)

As to the argument itself, Byrne sees no reason why mental relations to abstract entities should not enter into causal relations. In support, he draws an analogy with causal explanations involving numbers. Can't we causally explain a series of three noises by the fact that the preceding explosions were enumerated by the natural number 3?

Perhaps I should have said more about this in the book, but I take it to be obvious that we cannot so explain the noises, precisely because abstract facts can't be causes. A relation to a natural number outside space and time can't figure in a causal explanation. To get a cause for the series of noises, we have to switch to the concrete "nominalist" fact that $(E_3!x)(x$ *was an explosion*)—that is, there was an explosion, and another, and another, and they were all different, and anything that was an explosion was one of them—a fact that does not itself incorporate the abstract object 3.

I take this to be a familiar point from the philosophy of mathematics. As Hartry Field argues in *Science without Numbers*, extrinsic physical explanations citing relations between objects and abstract numbers (the length-in-metres relation, the mass-in-grams relation, and so on) ought always to be replaceable by explanations in terms of intrinsic lengths, masses, and other nominalist quantities. After all, how could a relation to an abstract object make a causal difference in the spatiotemporal world? Surely we ought to be able to understand the concrete realm without bringing in numbers from outside space and time. Such numbers might provide useful models for the structure of the concrete world, but they can't be an essential part of it.

One can accept these points without endorsing Field's fictionalist scepticism about numbers. The present issue is the exclusion of abstract objects from the concrete world, not whether or not they exist in some further realm. (Correspondingly, I am happy to accept the existence of abstract representational facts, as I make clear in section 2.11, contrary to Byrne's suggestion that in my view "there is no reason to believe in such a thing".)

Sometimes it is not obvious how to articulate nominalist descriptions of scientific facts that we normally refer to via their relationships to abstract objects. But few take this to discredit the principle that only concrete facts can enter into causal relations. Rather the consensus among philosophers of mathematics and physics is that such cases pose an interesting challenge. What exactly is the intrinsic physical structure that we are pointing to via our use of abstract mathematical models? The development of representation theorems for different branches of science can be seen precisely as answers to such challenges.

I now turn to the second of Byrne's issues, my argument that introspection reveals only intrinsic properties of subjects. Byrne notes that, on my view, this intrinsic realm is itself richly structured, in a way that encourages us to think that it points to a world beyond itself. But he doubts that I have the resources to explain certain kinds of experience, for example an experience of a yellow banana next to a yellow lemon.

Before addressing this example, let me quickly respond to one issue Byrne raises. He asks in passing why I think that the intrinsic structure of experience should make us think it points to "a world beyond", and observes that the mere coherence of certain elements of experience is itself no explanation of this.

I intended the second half of chapter 3, from sections 3.5 to 3.10, to be an answer to this query of Byrne's. An initial point, drawn from Kati Farkas's work, is that the coherence to be found within experience is not just any coherence, but involves a contrast between those elements within experience that move as I do and those "quasi-objects" that don't. This gives us an initial sense in which the latter elements can appear to be independent of us. I then discussed the temptation to identify these "quasi-objects" with the possibly existing "intentional objects" of experience—an identification which then has the consequence that, in the good cases of veridical perception, the "quasi-objects" do genuinely exist outside the mind, and moreover, even in the bad cases, incorporate the kind of worldly properties that external objects possess. Of course, I argued throughout that this mind-independence is all an illusion induced by bad thinking. But it is not as if I do not address the issue.

Now for Byrne's example of seeing a yellow banana next to a yellow lemon. As Byrne says, I regard the properties found in experience as properties of subjects, and thus not the kinds of properties possessed by physical objects. Somebody seeing a yellow lemon will thus instantiate *yellow** rather than ordinary *yellow*. Byrne's worry is then that this apparatus will be inadequate to account for someone seeing two yellow objects, given that there will be only one subject to singly instantiate yellow*.

This is reminiscent of Frank Jackson's well-known objection to adverbialism, and my response will draw on my discussion of that objection in chapter 4 of the book. In line with the complexity of sensory experience, I will have complex starred properties* of subjects. Thus the subject in Byrne's example will have a complex property along the lines of yellow*-banana*-next*-to*-yellow*-lemon*.

In the literature on adverbialism, the introduction of such "fused" properties is met with the worry that we will now lose the inference from "X is seeing something yellow and lemon-shaped" to "X is seeing something yellow". In the book, I respond that such inferences are not to be taken for granted. Whether they are acceptable will depend on the "syntax" of sensory vehicles. "Seeing something yellow" will follow from "seeing something yellow and lemon-shaped" only to the extent that the vehicle for the latter state is composed of repeatable elements corresponding to "yellow" and "lemon-shaped". While this seems likely in this example, it is not to be taken for granted for all sensory representations of conjunctive facts. (Incidentally, as I observe in footnote 16 of chapter 4, representationalists like Byrne are ill-placed to object to these moves, since they too have "fused" properties of subjects—*representing*-a-yellow-banana-next-to-a-yellow-lemon—and so face just the same questions about their implications.)

Byrne's third and final objection was to my argument from colour similarity against naïve realism and representationalism. I am not sure I understand this objection. Byrne takes me to be arguing "against the identification of colours with physical properties of objects (say reflectances)" and points out that this identification is not undermined by a divergence between subjective colour similarities and objective physical similarities. Quite so. However, I wasn't arguing against the identification of colours with physical properties at all. I'm all for that. My target was rather the claim that the conscious character of sensory experiences derives from their literal incorporation of physical properties. And this claim does still seem to me to be undermined by a divergence between subjective and objective similarities.

PART IV
HISTORY OF PHILOSOPHY OF MIND
Cavendish and Strong

16
Cavendish and Strawson on Emergence, Mind, and Self

David Cunning

In a series of provocative papers Galen Strawson defends the view that mental states never emerge or arise from the behavior and interaction of bodies that exhibit no trace of mentality themselves. Strawson then leverages the view in support of panpsychism. Macroscopic bodies like the human brain do possess mental states—*clearly*—and so the matter of which they are composed must not be entirely absent of mentality. At the very least it must contain a kind of proto-mentality, and on the assumption that the matter that resides at the most elemental level of the human brain is not entirely dissimilar to the matter that composes the rest of the universe, mentality—or at least proto-mentality—abounds.[1] Here I engage a comparative discussion of the materialism of Strawson and the materialism of the seventeenth-century philosopher Margaret Cavendish. The discussion is to some degree preliminary, as there is a lot more to be said than can be addressed in a single chapter, and I hope and expect that others might notice connections and contestations that I have missed. I focus on the view in Cavendish and Strawson that the mental cannot emerge or arise from the material, and on the panpsychist implications that both take to follow almost immediately.

As monists, Cavendish and Strawson suppose that there is just one kind of thing that exists—*matter*—but at the same time they attribute an extremely wide range of properties and features to it. To be sure, both will need to explain why all of these properties and features are properly identified as material, and they will need to explain why any *new* kinds of being— whether they are discovered via physics or other disciplines of study—are to be identified as material as well. Both will also need to provide reasons for

---

[1] Below there is a discussion of the specific Strawson passages and texts.

thinking that mentality is ubiquitous in nature and is not restricted to the bodies that compose the human brain. Cavendish and Strawson take steps to do all three, and they also attempt to square their understanding of matter with other views that they advance—for example, on the nature of the thinking self. Cavendish does better on the latter count, or so I shall argue.

1. Strawson on Mind and Matter

In "Realistic Monism: Why Physicalism Entails Panpsychism," Strawson argues that mental states do not emerge from the behavior and interaction of unminded bodies and that, if so, mentality is ubiquitous in nature. Strawson first points to a textbook case of emergence that might seem to prove him wrong—the emergence of liquidity from the interaction of bodies that are not liquid themselves. He allows that liquidity is a textbook case of emergence, if what we have in mind is a purely physical phenomenon and we bracket any reference to our experience of it. He writes:

> We can easily make intuitive sense of the idea that certain sorts of molecules are so constituted that they don't bind together in a tight lattice but slide past or off each other (in accordance with Van de Waals interaction laws) in a way that gives rise to—is—the phenomenon of liquidity.
> (Strawson 2008b, 61)

The same applies in the case of heat, so long (again) as we have in mind "utterly non-experiential phenomena" like "surface tension, viscosity and other forces governing the motion of molecules" (61). But in the case of the *experience* of liquidity or heat—or any other mental phenomenon—Strawson argues that things are very different. This is because part of what it means for a phenomenon Y to emerge from a phenomenon X is for Y to owe the entirety of its existence to X from moment to moment:

> It seems plain that there must be a fundamental sense in which any emergent phenomenon, say Y, is wholly dependent on that which it emerges from, say X. It seems, in fact, that this must be true by definition of 'emergent'; for if there is not this total dependence then it will not be true after all, not true without qualification, to say that Y is emergent from X. For in this case at least some part or aspect of Y will have to hail from somewhere else and will therefore not be emergent from X. (62)

Liquidity and heat considered as non-experiential phenomena do not depend for their existence on anything other than patterns of motion in bodies, but mentality would appear to be different, at least if we are talking about experiential phenomena or the kind of mentality that is exhibited in episodes of conscious awareness.[2] There is no way to understand how *it* would emerge or arise from entities that admit of zero trace of mentality themselves. The emergence of mind from (non-mental) body would be magic and would be "unintelligible even to God" (Strawson 2008b, 65). For the emergence of mind from non-mind to be intelligible there would have to be some conceptual link—however slight—between non-mind and mind, but that is exactly the sort of link that is ruled out from the start.

What Strawson seeks from the physicist or chemist is an instance of emergence in which Y wholly depends for its existence on X, but Y is as different from X as experiential phenomena are different from non-experiential phenomena. He himself does not locate one. The closer he gets, the more he worries that the instance in question is merely phantastical. He considers, for example, the view that dimensional spatiality is in some respect an emergent property of the configuration of mathematical points that have no dimension themselves. He writes,

> Suppose someone...proposes that all ultimates, all real, concrete ultimates, are in truth, wholly unextended entities: that this is the truth about their being; that there is no sense in which they themselves are extended; that they are real concrete entities, but are nonetheless true-mathematical-point entities. And suppose [this someone] goes on to say that when collections of these entities stand in certain (real, concrete, natural) relations, they give rise to or constitute truly, genuinely, concrete entities; real concrete extension being in this sense an emergent property of phenomena that are, although by hypothesis real and concrete, wholly unextended.[3]

---

[2] Strawson does not define 'experiential phenomena' but instead supposes that any human being that has a mind knows experiential phenomena immediately and directly (Strawson 2008a, 22, 25). Presumably there are other sorts of mentality that we do not know as well, but like Strawson I am not sure how to communicate with an opponent who denies the existence of first-person conscious states. There just aren't any further definiens that would help to identify such states in the case of an opponent who does not already recognize their existence.

[3] Strawson (2008b, 63). Note the clear connection to the view in Leibniz (1714, sects. one to three, 213) that monads are unextended but are the fundamental building blocks of reality, bodies included. See also the discussion in Garber (2009, 127–80). Note also the apparent opposition to Hume (1739–40, I.iii.3, 78–82), who seems to hold that it is possible for anything to come from anything (or even from nothing). I say 'apparent' just because Strawson (2008b, 66) says that that is a "gross misunderstanding of Hume."

Strawson does not have in mind the hypothesis that a field, or a quantity of energy, or some "area of influence or influenceability," gives rise to dimensional extension; any such thing "*ipso facto* has extension" already (64). He accordingly concludes that the "suggestion [that dimensional extension emerges from dimension-less mathematical points] should be rejected as utterly absurd" (63).

He then argues that we should also reject as absurd the suggestion that the thinking that takes place in our brain arises from real, concrete, and natural relations in which utterly non-mental phenomena stand toward each other. If he is right, our brains are composed of bodies that exhibit mentality themselves—either mentality that is very much like the conscious and reflective thinking in which we sometimes engage, or mentality that is very different but that is still sufficiently fortified. But it cannot be *that* different.[4] It might be something that we cannot specifically conceive: "there is no more difficulty in the idea that the experiential quality of micro-experientiality is unimaginable by us than there is in the idea that there may exist sensory modalities (qualitatively) unimaginable by us" (72). However, it would have to be not wholly unlike the mentality of which we are intimately familiar. It would have to be similar enough to that mentality to give rise to it.

Strawson supposes that a kind of micro-experientiality is had by the bodies that make up the human brain. Those bodies—things like protons, electrons, and quarks—are smaller than the brain, and perhaps the mentality that they exhibit is more slight as well. But as he puts it, "Real physicalists must accept that at least some ultimates are intrinsically experience-involving" (71), and in a literal sense. On the assumption that there would not be "radical heterogeneity at the very bottom of things" (71), Strawson adopts panpsychism as well. He supposes that at the most basic level of reality there is mentality and experiential being. If he is right, there is no obstacle at all to understanding how human beings and other creatures think. There is a kind of thinking that we human beings know—the kind "whose existence is more certain than the existence of anything else" (53)[5]—and there exist kinds of thinking that (different or not)[6] are its source.

---

[4] Strawson writes, "if experience like ours (or mouse experience, or sea snail experience) emerges from something that is not experience like ours, then that something must already be experiential in some sense or other. It must somehow already be experiential in its fundamental and essential nature" (70).

[5] Here Strawson is showing his Cartesian hand with respect to questions of knowledge and justification. At the end of this chapter there is a discussion and critique of Strawson's view on the primacy of conscious experience as part of the self.

[6] Again, it is consistent with Strawson's view that bodies like protons and quarks have the highly reflective mental states that are sometimes exhibited by human beings.

To his credit, Strawson does not conclude that we understand very much when we posit the existence of a kind of mentality that is ubiquitous. Indeed he does not think that we understand much of anything when we study the bodies that are the subject matter of physics. He writes:

> A lot of us think we know that gravitational attraction between two objects a and b decreases as a function of the square of the distance between them, and if we are right, then again we have some very substantial and not merely referential descriptive or characterizational knowledge of an aspect of the nature of reality as it is in itself, even if the referring expressions 'grativational attraction', 'a', 'b', and even 'distance' pick out entities that we are, given our grasp of the nature of spacetime, and matter, in some ways hopelessly wrong about.   (Strawson 2008c, 99)

A theme across much of Strawson's writing is that the understanding that we take ourselves to have of bodies is nothing close to the understanding of bodies that we have in fact.[7] After concluding that bodies exhibit mentality (or at least proto-mentality) at a very basic level, he does not throw a big epistemic parade or suppose that we have thereby understood very much. A less committal philosopher might argue that we should not take any stand at all on the relationship between things like size, shape, force, dimensionality, temporality, fields, particles, waves, energy, and mentality. But if we are in the business of taking a stand—and the *opponents* of Strawson are in the business of taking a stand—then at least for now, and for the foreseeable future, we should be materialist monists, or so Strawson argues. He would then add that there is a commonality across the entities that monists (and dualists) are attempting to categorize: for example, whatever we or anyone else (e.g. the physicist) uncovers and makes the object of study will be spatio-temporal, "on the assumption that space-time is indeed a fundamental feature of reality" (Strawson 2008b, 73), and so spatio-temporality will be a feature of whatever is most basic. Otherwise the spatio-temporal would

---

[7] See Strawson (2008a, 26, 33, 39, 42, and 2008b, 64, 73). He writes, for example, that "we are as inescapably committed to the discursive, subject-predicate form of experience as we are to the spatiotemporal form of experience, but the principal and unmistakable lesion of the endlessness of the debate about the relation between objects and their propertiedness is that discursive thought is not adequate to the nature of reality: we can see that it doesn't get things right although we can't help persisting with it. There is in the nature of the case a limited amount that we can do with such insights, for they are, precisely, insights into how our understanding falls short of reality, but their general lesson—that the nature of reality is in fundamental respects beyond us—needs always to be borne in mind" (73).

in some instances emerge from the non-spatio-temporal, but that is absurd. Strawson also points to a number of other reasons for putting mind and body into the same category of being—reasons that were prominent in the early modern period and before.[8] He notes, for example, that minds and bodies causally interact, but it is impossible for two things to stand in causal relations if they had nothing in common (Strawson 2008a, 50); he also references considerations like simplicity and Ockham's Razor (50). And thinking, like the activity of bodies, clearly takes place "in spacetime" (33). Strawson adds that there is much about spatially extended body that is at least as wondrous and puzzling as anything that we would attribute to mind—for example, that it is sometimes both a particle and a wave (33, 38), that it exhibits gravitational attraction (32), and that space might have as many as ten dimensions. He is not suggesting that we have a good grasp of the properties and features of bodies and that we recognize exactly how mentality is among these. Instead, we understand very little about body, and we benefit from "diluting or undermining features of our natural conception of the physical that make non-experiential phenomena appear *toto coelo* different from experiential phenomena" (42).

Strawson might be on stronger ground still. A mantra across his corpus is (again) that we barely know reality at all. He also supposes that the intuitions that undergird a philosophical theory (like materialist monism) do not have the epistemic pedigree that philosophers have traditionally attributed to them. For example, he says in one passage that to convert to the view that mind and body are not dissimilar "involves a profound reseating of one's intuitive theoretical understanding of nature" (37), but then he adds immediately:

> I say 'intuitive theoretical understanding of nature', but it isn't as if there is any other kind. For (briefly) what we think of as real understanding of a natural phenomenon is always at bottom just a certain kind of *feeling*, and it is always and necessarily relative to other things that one just takes for granted, finds intuitive, feels comfortable with. This is as true in science as it is in common life. (37)

Here Strawson is intimating a meta-philosophical view according to which philosophical intuitions, no matter how compelling, are fallible and

---

[8] See, for example, Gassendi (1641, 238–39); Princess Elisabeth (1643, 9–10); de la Mettrie (1747, 5–9); and Lucretius (1995, 95).

malleable.⁹ If he is right, then he (and we) would be wise to remain open to the possibility that with experience and time we might come to have intuitions that are very different from those we have at the moment—perhaps even intuitions that are wholly dualistic.¹⁰ And then we would update our metaphysics accordingly. But in that case Strawson might say that for *now* our best bet is to identify experiential phenomena as material.

If I am reading him correctly, Strawson would have us return to the earliest moments at which the dualist began to divert experiential phenomena into the category of invisible, intangible, and indivisible as opposed to the category of the visible, tangible, and divisible.¹¹ He would then have us present a list of the characteristics that we attribute to body in the twenty-first century. We would talk the dualist back from the ledge, and we would return to a present in which the language of dualism had never taken root.¹²

Still, it can be maddening to read passages in Strawson's corpus like this:

> What, after all, is matter? As a materialist, I take it that it is whatever we are actually talking about when we talk about concrete reality. I fix the reference of the term matter in this way—giving a chair a kick, perhaps—independently of any reference to theories. I can be certain that there is such a thing as matter, as a realistic materialist monist—one who takes it that experience is wholly material in nature—because I can be certain that there is such a thing as concrete reality: experience, at the very least. What a materialist may still wish to add to this is the insistence that nothing can count as matter unless it has some sort of non-experiential being.... I sail close to the wind—by which I mean the charge of vacuousness, and the charge that it may be hard to distinguish my position from idealism—in my use of the word 'matter' because that is exactly what one has to do at

---

⁹ In another part of "Real Materialism" he refers to the "general principles of ignorance defended in this paper" (Strawson 2008a, 48), for example in the section entitled "Knowledge of Ignorance."

¹⁰ And Strawson is very clear that he does not "rule out the theoretical possibility that substance dualism—or pluralism—is in fact the best view to take about our universe for reasons of which we know nothing" (50).

¹¹ For example, in Plato (1992, 116–19).

¹² Or Strawson might wish that we could go back and make an intervention in the case of Henry More, who argued (in 1671) that minds are immaterial even though they are extended: "I will evince with Mathematical certainty, That God and our Soul, and all other Immaterial Beings, are in some sort extended... [T]he operations wherewith the Soul acts on the Body, are in the Body.... Wherefore if the Operation of the soul is somewhere, the Soul is somewhere" (More 1671, 188). Strawson is very familiar with the work of More; see, for example, Strawson (2008a, 31).

this point.... In some moods I am prepared to call myself an experiential-and-non-experiential?-ist and think no more about the word 'monist'; there is no decidable issue here.... At the moment, though, the physics idea (the ancient idea) that everything is made of the same ultimate stuff... seems to me as compelling as it is remarkable, and I choose to register my attraction to it with the word 'monism'.

(Strawson 2008a, 48–51)

Strawson spends page after page critiquing those who reject materialism and monism, but he is a bit cagey with regard to providing a definitive articulation of the two views and a definitive statement of his commitment to them. It is also maddening to consider the wide range of discrete properties and features that he takes to apply to bodies (for example, 42, 49–50, 70), and then to read him assert that there is no "radical heterogeneity at the very bottom of things" and that panpsychism is true. Perhaps there is a wide range of properties and features that apply to bodies, and some of these are not particularly common. Perhaps mentality is one of the latter. For all we know it is found only in the bodies that compose the brains of human beings and other sophisticated animals, and it is only such creatures that think.[13]

Nor is Strawson able to do very much to ground the intuition that undergirds the whole of his panpsychism—the intuition that a property or feature Y cannot emerge from X unless X exhibits some incarnation or variant of Y already. It is tempting to side with Hume and argue that we are presumptuous to put such a constraint on reality *a priori*.[14]

In fairness, however, Strawson is not assuming that his view of materialist panpsychism is once and for all correct or that the intuitions that undergird that view are infallible. Instead, he owns and encourages a kind of humility

---

[13] See also the discussion in McGinn (2006, 95–7). McGinn presents a number of other objections to Strawson's panpsychism—for example, that Strawson provides no account whatsoever of how the proto-mentality of microscopic bodies gives rise to the unity that is exhibited in the minds that emerge from them.

[14] But again Strawson thinks that this is a "gross misunderstanding of Hume." See footnote 3 above. I do wonder if part of Strawson's intuition is fueled by connotations around the term 'emergence'—when we think, for example, about the very literal kind of case in which a character emerges from behind a screen, and the character was already present beforehand. I wonder what Strawson would say instead about supervenient properties that would appear to be wholly dissimilar to the base properties on which they supervene. I assume that he would insist that the base properties have to be similar to the supervenient properties, but replacing the language of 'emergence' with the language of 'supervenience' raises interesting questions I think.

and playfulness that is appropriate in the case of any investigation into the ultimate nature of reality. In settling on panpsychism, he is banking on an intuition, and his attitude toward intuitions is quite humble. In settling on monism, he appears to be assuming that "independently of any reference to theories" the term 'body' was invented to pick out things like tables and water and brains and thus that whatever it is that we discover in them—for example, properties and features—ought to be identified as bodily also.[15] But that is not to say that we fully understand those properties and features, or that we even understand what a property or feature is. As we have seen, there are passages in which Strawson is quite cagey with respect to the language of monism and body. But if one has to choose between saying that it is a *body* that has features like spatio-temporality, extension, force, and proto-mentality, and saying that it is some other entity, I do not take issue with him for erring on the side of the first.[16] He appears to hold that we have a lot less of a handle on body than we think we do and that if we recognized just how puzzling some of the features of body are that we take to be unproblematic, we would include experiential phenomena as part of the subject matter of physics straightaway.

2. Cavendish on Mind and Matter

Cavendish is in agreement with Strawson that philosophers have a historical record of superimposing onto bodies a conception of body to which bodies do not answer. For example, according to Descartes the nature of a body includes features like three-dimensional size and shape, and then any additional features that it has are explicable in terms of those.[17] Cavendish and Strawson agree with Descartes that there is no way to explain how mentality would arise from body so construed.[18] But for Cavendish

---

[15] Also Strawson (2008a, 45).

[16] So I am more sympathetic here than other critics of Strawson, for example Melnyck (2009) and Dainton (2011).

[17] Descartes would then add that if we encounter a body that appears to have a feature that is not explicable in terms of size, shape, and motion, we are required to conclude that it is a feature of something else, and something that is not a body. See, for example, *Principles of Philosophy* I.53, which is Descartes (1644, 210–11). Descartes says in a letter to one of his correspondents that "in the case of body and soul you cannot see any...connection, provided you conceive them as they should be conceived, the one as that which fills space and the other as that which thinks....I do not know any other pair of ideas in the whole of nature which are as different from each other as these two" (Descartes 1641a, 188).

[18] All of the relevant Cavendish texts will be discussed below.

(and likewise for Strawson), bodies do think, and so the Cartesian conception of body is broken. Cavendish, like Strawson, embraces the conclusion that at a very basic level the characteristics of body include mentality and cognition.[19] However, Cavendish disagrees with Strawson (and Descartes) that the thinking self is constituted by conscious awareness alone.[20] Strawson excludes from the thinking self[21] the vast amount of proto-mentality that on his view gives rise to the thinking that we know very well. He is mistaken to do so, or that is what I shall argue. We are reckless to limit our conception of *body* to characteristics that are straightforward and familiar, he would allow, but I would insist we should not artificially limit our conception of self either.

Cavendish like Strawson is a materialist, insisting that "all that is a substance in Nature, is a body, and what has a body, is corporeal" (Cavendish 1664, 194). She accordingly holds that "[a]s for the Natural Soul, humane sense and reason may perceive, that it consists of Matter, as being Material" (230).[22] Cavendish also agrees with Strawson that much of our thinking takes place in the brain and is in a literal sense spatial. If our minds have and are in some way interfaced with bodies, they are housed in bodies and are material themselves. She writes:

> I would ask those, that say the Brain has neither sense, reason, nor self-motion, and therefore no Perception; but that all proceeds from an Immaterial Principle, and an Incorporeal Spirit, distinct from the Body, which moveth and actuates corporeal matter; I would fain ask them, I say, where their Immaterial Ideas reside, in what part or place of the Body?... If [the spirit] have no dimension, how can it be confined in a material body?
> (1664, 185–86)

---

[19] Note though that Cavendish holds that bodies are by nature divisible (for example, in Cavendish 1664, 143), and so strictly speaking she does not posit basic bodies, but instead she uses the language of "elemental creatures" (147).

[20] For the view in Descartes, see Descartes (1641b, 18, and 1641c, 171). A discussion of the specific Cavendish and Strawson texts is below.

[21] Strawson grants that there is a distinction between "considering oneself principally as a human being taken as a whole, and one's experience of oneself when one is considering oneself principally as an inner mental entity or 'self' of some sort" (Strawson 2008d, 190). He makes clear that he is focusing on the latter (190). See also Strawson (2009, 69): "the self is figured as something merely mental, or wholly mental, in so far as, and to the extent that, it is expressly figured as something that has mental being…."

[22] Note that Cavendish leaves open the possibility that we might also have a divine immaterial soul (for example, in Cavendish 1664, 186-7), even though it is something of which we have no idea and something of which we cannot think or speak (for example, 1664, 69). In at least one passage she goes farther and argues that finite immaterial substances have no existence whatsoever (Cavendish 1668, 239).

Here Cavendish is asserting that the brain is an important locus of perception and thinking, and that mentality is therefore a feature of the brain.[23] She is not going out on a limb, however, as most of her dualist opponents admit that there is at least some sense in which our minds are interfaced with brains.[24] Otherwise they would need to do the mental gymnastics of arguing that the mind and body of a human being are not in fact united—and that minds exist in some kind of alternate realm and that the activity of a mind is simply correlated or harmonized with the activity of the body that is (in some sense) assigned to it.[25] With Descartes (and also Strawson and Henry More[26]), Cavendish takes seriously the view that thinking has a locus in the human body. She also offers much in the way of a defense of the view. She points, for example, to the (presumptive) phenomenon of mind-body interaction: "it is, in my opinion, more probable, that one material should act upon another material, or one immaterial upon another immaterial, than that an immaterial should act upon a material or corporeal."[27] For Cavendish, minds act upon bodies, but only bodies are able to act upon bodies, and so a mind is material itself.[28] That is not to say that a mind is the

---

[23] Note though that Cavendish does not suppose that in the case of a human being mentality is restricted to the brain. She takes it to be present throughout the entire nervous system. See, for example, Cavendish (1664, 111–12).

[24] And even Descartes would admit *that*. See, for example, *The Passions of the Soul* I.31, which is Descartes (1649, 340).

[25] See, for example, Leibniz, *Discourse on Metaphysics*, sect. 33, which is Leibniz (1686, 64); and Malebranche, *The Search after Truth*, VI.ii.3, which is Malebranche (1674, 446–52).

[26] Again, see footnote 12.

[27] Cavendish (1664, 207). She adds that "Immaterial and Material cannot obstruct each other" (10), but minds and bodies do obstruct each other, and so minds are material.

[28] Note however that Cavendish has an unorthodox view of mind-body interaction according to which a body never transfers motion to a second body, but simply occasions motion that is already in that body. Motion is inseparable from the body that has it, according to Cavendish, and so the only way that the motion of the first body could be transferred is if the second body also transfers some of its substance, but bodies do not grow bigger when other bodies cause them to move (Cavendish 1664, 82). She writes, "In my opinion, there can be no abstraction made of motion from body, neither really, nor in the manner of our conception, for how can I conceive that which is not, nor cannot be in nature, that is, to conceive motion without body? Wherefore Motion is but one thing with body, without any separation or abstraction soever" (97). Bodies never transfer motion to other bodies, but instead are "Occasional causes" of motion that is already present in them (79). Cavendish takes matter to be puzzling and weird—and she and Strawson (2008a, 40–2) would appear to agree on that count—but she does not take it to be *that* weird. Although bodies never transfer motion to a second body, on her view, the first body (of a causal interaction) still plays a critical role in the change in motion of a second body: it redirects motion that is already present in that body, and it does so by contact. She writes, for example, of sensory perception that "Neither is the influence of the Stars performed beyond a certain distance, that is, such a distance as is beyond sight or their natural power to work; for *if their light comes to our Eyes*, I know no reason against it, but their effects may come to our bodies" (301–2). She adds in the very next sentence that a disease can only

"extension, flexibility, and changeability" that survives the wax experiment of Descartes' Second Meditation and that is essential to body as Descartes conceives it.[29] There is more to body than that, Cavendish supposes. It thinks.

Body thinks at the level of the brain, according to Cavendish, and it also thinks at the level of the constituent bodies that make up the brain. She writes,

> I shall never be able to conceive, how senseless and irrational Atoms can produce sense and reason, or a sensible and rational body, such as the soul is.... 'Tis true, different effects may proceed from one cause or principle; but there is no principle, which is senseless, can produce sensitive effects; nor no rational effects can flow from an irrational cause....[30]

Human brains think, but mentality does not emerge or arise from the behavior and interaction of components that are wholly non-mental. The bodies that compose the brain therefore are not wholly non-mental, which is to say that they are somewhat mental, which is to say that they are mental enough that there is no insurmountable gap between the kinds of properties that they possess and the kinds of properties that are had by brains. According to Cavendish, mentality does not arise or emerge from the interaction of bodies that admit of no trace of mentality.[31] Instead, for any intelligence or cognition that we encounter, "life and knowledg is the cause of them, which life and knowledg is animate matter, and is in all parts and all Creatures..." (Cavendish 1664, 514). Cavendish and Strawson subscribe to the view that the material universe is not so heterogenous as to exhibit mental properties only in the case of the human brain. Cavendish also offers reasons in support of the view.

---

infect a body if it comes into contact with that body—by "touch." Note that Cavendish does not hold that the light from a distant body literally travels all the way to our eyes; instead there is a process in which the intermediary air "patterns" the light, which is then patterned by our eyes as well. (See also Cunning 2022, 106–10, and 2023.) For Cavendish, bodies are teeming with motion that we do not notice—along the lines of the motions of electrons, or the violent motions that are contained inside a balloon that otherwise appears to be stationary. We do not notice these, but they are present, and instances of "new" motion are always just instances in which existing motion is redirected.

[29] Descartes (1641b, 18–19).
[30] "Observations upon the Opinions of Some Ancient Philosophers," in Cavendish (1666, 26).
[31] See also Cunning (2016, 72–3) and Shaheen (2021, 637–8).

One is that there is intelligence, purposiveness, and skill—all marks of mentality—that are exhibited throughout the non-human regions of the material universe and that would have to be explained away if mentality were restricted to the constituents of the human brain. She owns that there is a tremendous amount of skill in the case of human activity, for example in the building of a house, but a house is not nearly as intricate or sophisticated as a honeycomb (1664, 147). Nor can a human being build the tree from which a house is built: perhaps we plant a seed, and so there is a sense in which we grow a tree, but most of the real labor is entirely out of our hands.[32] For Cavendish, a human being "cannot work as [Nature] worketh: for though he can extract, yet he cannot make."[33]

She also points to the phenomenon in which a medicine is able to discriminate between the parts of a body that need assistance and the parts of the body that it can ignore:

> none ought to wonder at how it is possible, that medicines that must pass through digestions in the body, should, neglecting all other parts, shew themselves friendly onely to the brain or kidneys, or the like parts; for if there be sense and reason in Nature, all things must act wisely and orderly....[34]

She might also cite current-day language in which viruses and cells are identified as clever or smart.[35] According to Cavendish, intelligent and purposive activity abounds; it exhibits a level of order and organization for which mentality—at least some level of mentality—is a pre-condition.[36]

Rather than do cartwheels to explain away such activity, she understands it in line with her view that mentality does not emerge or arise from bodies that are wholly non-mental. She accordingly says that "the Elemental Creatures are as excellent as Man, and...that I cannot perceive more abilities in Man then in the rest of natural Creatures..." (1664, 147). Elemental bodies are not wholly non-mental, and purposive and skillful behavior in non-human bodies would be expected to be the norm.

---

[32] Cavendish (1664, 147).
[33] Cavendish (1664, 45). We might point out that in the twenty-first century our technology is much better, but Cavendish would then respond that Nature has had the corresponding skills a lot longer than we have.
[34] "Further Observations upon Experimental Philosophy," in Cavendish (1666, 78).
[35] See the discussion in Figdor (2018, 19–59).   [36] Cavendish (1666, 141–2, 1668, 7).

Cavendish likes to talk in particular about ants and bees (and by extension the bodies that constitute them). For example, she highlights the order that is exhibited in the material structure of an ant colony, along with the way in which ants almost ritualistically treat their dead: "they are careful of Repairs, lest Ruin should grow upon them; insomuch that if the least grain of Dust be misplaced, they stop, or close it up again.... [T]heir care and affection is not less to bury their Dead" (Cavendish 1671, 281–2). She also speaks with wonder and admiration of the work that bees put into the creation of a honeycomb and into the protection of the larger group and its home (1664, 152–3). We might strike a hive with a bat and then run like mad as the swarm of the bees zips our way. We run in response to the datum that the bees are protecting the hive; and they are doing so deliberately. To use any other language is preposterous, Cavendish would be right to say. Nor is there a need to use any other language if bees and the bodies that enter into them exhibit mentality as a matter of course.

Cavendish and Strawson agree that minds and bodies have far too much in common to be partitioned into separate categories of being. Minds and bodies are both spatial, Cavendish argues, and they regularly interact. She did not have the benefit of the perspective of modern physics to appreciate other respects in which mind and body might appear to be similar—or at least similarly puzzling and wondrous—but she emphasized two additional points that she thought to be obvious. One is that bodies and minds partake of motion. Another is that the binary of sensible bodies and insensible minds collapses upon inspection.

A tenet (and indeed a mantra) of the Cavendish corpus is that there is no such thing as immaterial motion. Cavendish appeals to this tenet on multiple occasions in defense of the view that minds are material:

Though Matter might be without Motion, yet Motion cannot be without matter; for it is impossible (in my opinion) that there should be an Immaterial Motion in Nature.   (Cavendish 1668, 2)

But put an Impossible proposition, as that there is an Immaterial motion.
(Cavendish 1664, 77)

immaterial spirits, being supernatural, cannot have natural attributes or actions, such as is corporeal, natural motion.   (Cavendish 1666, 126)

In defense of the view that thinking is material, Cavendish appeals to the premise that immaterial motion is impossible. She does not, in every case, articulate the additional" premise that minds move,[37] but it is clearly part of an enthymeme for the conclusion that thinking is material,[38] and the premise is as obvious to her as it was to other philosophers of the era. Locke writes, for example, that

> No Body can imagine, that his Soul can think, or move a Body at Oxford, whilst he is at London, and cannot but know, that being united to his Body, it constantly changes place all the whole Journey, between Oxford and London, as the Coach, or Horse does, that carries him; and, I think, may be said to be truly all that while in motion....
> (Locke 1689, II.xxiii.20, 307)

Note that motion is not literally a change of location or place according to Cavendish. Although she sometimes speaks of the "place" of a mind (for example, in Cavendish 1664, 33), she holds with Descartes and others that strictly speaking the place of a body is in no way distinct from that body itself.[39] But however she analyzes motion she supposes that minds (and bodies) partake of it.[40]

Cavendish also rejects the binary of minds as insensible and bodies as sensible. For example, she agrees with Descartes and others that the material universe is a plenum and that much of what surrounds us is body that we never notice (Cavendish 1664, 521). She indeed supposes that bodies exist on a spectrum from observable to unobservable and that the observability of a body is by no means an indication of its dissimilarity to mind. She writes,

> by reason this matter is not subject to our senses, although our senses are subject to it, as being made, subsisting and acting through the power of its actions, we are not apt to believe it, no more then a simple Country-wench will believe, that Air is a substance, if she neither hear, see, smell, taste, or touch it, although Air touches and surrounds her. (1664, 418).

---

[37] Though she does do that sometimes, for example: "I cannot conceive how it is possible, that...the Soul, being incorporeal, can walk in the air, like a body; for incorporeal beings cannot have corporeal actions" ("Observations Upon the Opinions of Some Ancient Philosophers," in Cavendish 1666, 20). See also Cavendish (1668, 34, 20), Cavendish (1664, 34), Cavendish (1666, 238–9), and Cavendish (1665a, 105).

[38] Here I am disagreeing with Shaheen (2021, n. 27).

[39] See, for example, Cavendish (1664, 67, 521), and Descartes, *Principles of Philosophy* II.11–16, which is Descartes (1644, 227–31). In these passages Descartes defends the view that the material universe is a plenum.

[40] Her understanding of motion is a matter of some debate, but for a compelling defense of the view that she understands it mereologically, see Peterman (2019).

If we treat as a paradigm case of body the macroscopic entity that is tangible and visible, then minds and bodies might appear to be quite different. But a macroscopic body that is tangible and visible is just one incarnation of a body, and there are many others.[41]

Cavendish supposes that mentality is ubiquitous in the material universe.[42] She also holds (as we will see, in opposition to Strawson) that much of the mentality of the self is below the threshold of conscious awareness. She considers, for example, the kind of case where a person is walking or talking, and their behavior is as skillful as it is seamless:

> there is a wise saying, think first, and speak after; and an old saying that many speak first, and think after; and doubtlesse many, if not most do so, for we do not always think of our words we speak, for most commonly words flow out of the mouth, rather customarily than premeditatedly, just like actions of our walking, for we go by custome, force and strength, without a constant notice or observation; for though we designe our ways, yet we do not ordinarily think of our pace, nor take notice of every several step; just so, most commonly we talk, for we seldom think of our words we speak, nor many times the sense they tend to.[43]

I do not want to make too much of what Cavendish is saying here—in terms of attributing to her an account of an entity that is the self—for she does not present herself as offering such an account. Still, I think that her comments point us in the direction of an account of self, and an account of self that is more plausible than what is offered by Strawson. Cavendish makes the not-unobvious point that the behaviors that she is highlighting are the "actions of *our* walking," and *our* talking, and our coming up with the words that

---

[41] See also Conway (1692, 48–50). Conway argues that if we are not paying attention, mind and body might seem like opposites, but they are not opposites in fact. Minds move, have dimension, and are divisible, for example, and they often exhibit resistance and impenetrability; and bodies range from solid to penetrable to misty and ephemeral. See also the discussion in Hutton (2004, ch. four).

[42] One of the reasons why Cavendish thinks that mentality is ubiquitous—and that it is not just present in fingers, seeds, ants, bees, plants, cells, and such—is that she supposes that mentality is a precondition of order and organization, and she takes order and organization to be ubiquitous (Cavendish 1664, 439, 481). Note that in the end she posits three varieties of matter—rational, sensitive, and inanimate—but she holds that these are so intimately blended that it is accurate to say that thinking matter is ubiquitous. See the discussion in O'Neill (2001, xxi–xxv).

[43] Cavendish (1655b, unnumbered between pp. 26 and 27). Similar passages are at Cavendish (1664, 113–14, and 1671, 625).

make up half of a conversation. She notes more specifically that in cases in which we are walking or talking, or walking and talking, much of what we do is not the product of conscious states.[44] Indeed, conscious reflective thought is often an *obstacle* in the way of skillful functioning, even if there are contexts (like philosophy or math or planning a party) in which it is quite fruitful. Examples abound. We think too hard as we are attempting to put a key into a keyhole—perhaps we are tired or under stress—and we fail to unlock the door; we then distract ourselves and think of something else, and we open the door right away. Or we stare at a word that we have written on the board and wonder if we have spelled it correctly. We think too much, and we have no idea, but then we change the subject and crank out the word just fine. Or we try to recall our member number in line at the Co-op, and the only way that we remember it is if we stop being so reflective. We distract ourselves, and then state the number straightaway. Or as Cavendish highlights in her own two examples, we walk and talk with great skill even if we do not pay attention to every word and step, and *especially* if we do not pay attention to every word and step.[45]

---

[44] Note that as an interpretive matter it is possible that Cavendish holds that in expert walking or talking, the legs and tongue are conscious of their behavior even though the person who is walking or talking is not. However, I do not see any reason to attribute that view to Cavendish, and I think that there are reasons to think that she rejects it. See footnote 45 below. What is undeniable is that Cavendish holds that in cases of expert human behavior our expert bodily movements are below the threshold of our own awareness.

[45] For purposes of this chapter, I am bracketing the question of whether or not Cavendish subscribes to the view that the fingers, legs, and cells of the human body are conscious of their activity even though the larger mind of which they are a part is not. I worry that the view is incoherent (see, for example, Dainton 2011, 245–6), and I also think that there are good reasons for thinking that Cavendish does not subscribe to it. One reason is that she holds (with Hume and others) that reflective ratiocination is too cumbersome and clunky to result in seamless order and organization, and she takes the order and organization of natural productions to be much more seamless and sophisticated than that of (human) artifacts. (See, for example, Cavendish 1664, 500; Hume 1748, sect. nine, 165–7; Dreyfus 1991, 1–9, 45–59; and Cunning 1999.) Another reason is that when she compares the highly reflective thinking that sometimes takes place in a human being with the kind of mentality that (she thinks) is operative in the orderly behavior of (for example) the legs and the tongue, she clarifies that the kind of knowledge had by each of these is different and that "each part hath its sense and reason, and consequently its own sensitive and rational knowledg;...and each hath its own particular and peculiar knowledg" (1664, 113–14). Another reason is that a fixture of the philosophical writing of her contemporary Henry More is that there exists an immaterial spirit of nature which pervades the material universe, and which is without conscious awareness (More 1659, 169), but Cavendish does not take issue with that view in her extended critique of More's system. She is relentless in her critique of More, but she nowhere disputes his oft-stated contention that the spirit of nature is not conscious. Note that the first reason listed above is not just a reason for thinking that Cavendish holds that much of the mentality (or proto-mentality) in the material universe is not conscious; it is also a reason for thinking that she is right. Insofar as we have any model of mental activity that results in the seamless order and organization of bodies, it is the

The view that Cavendish is expressing is quite common in the early modern period, even if it did not overtake the Cartesian view that something is not an aspect of our thinking unless it is an aspect of our thinking of which we are aware.[46] For example, Cavendish's direct contemporary Henry More held that there is ubiquitous in nature a skillful and intelligent mentality that guides the orderly behavior of bodies and is "without Sense and Animadversion" (More 1659, 169). His colleague Ralph Cudworth used different language to describe (what is basically) the same—a "Plastick Nature" that is spread throughout the material universe and that "hath no Animal-Sense or Consciousness" (Cudworth 1678, 679). Cudworth writes:

> But because this may seem strange at the first sight, that Nature should be said to *Act for the sake of ends*, and *Regularly* or *Artificially*, and yet be itself devoid of *Knowledge* and *Understanding*, we shall therefore endeavour to persuade the *Possibility*, and facilitate the Belief of it, by some other Instances; and first by that of *Habits*, particularly those Musical ones, of Singing, Playing upon Instruments, and Dancing. (157)

Here Cudworth is registering that much of the skilled and expert behavior of the musician or dancer is not monitored by conscious reflective attention (also 157–9). With More, Cudworth, and others, Cavendish is in good company defending the seventeenth-century view that much of what we are and do is below the threshold of our conscious awareness. For example, Spinoza held that the human mind perceives all of the states of its body, though not consciously of course.[47] Leibniz held that there is much in a monad (or finite mind) of which it is not aware—for example, all of the mentality that plays a role in the production of its conscious states and without which those states would lack a sufficient cause.[48] We also see different variants of this (seventeenth-century) view in the work of later figures like Hume, Nietzsche, Freud, and Heidegger.[49] The view is dominant in at least some philosophical

---

non-reflective mental activity of being "in the zone." Cavendish posits the existence of that sort of activity, though she also posits mental activity that is highly reflective and perhaps other sorts of mentality as well. For a further discussion, see Cunning (2016, 79–89).

[46] Descartes writes, "As to the fact that there can be nothing in the mind, in so far as it is a thinking thing, of which it is not aware, this seems to me to be self-evident.... [W]e cannot have any thought of which we are not aware at the very moment when it is in us" (Descartes 1641c, 171).

[47] Spinoza (1677, part II, propositions eleven through thirteen, 250–2).

[48] Leibniz (1714, sects. eleven through fourteen and twenty through thirty-two, 214–17), and Leibniz (1686, sects. thirteen and fourteen, 44–7).

[49] See, for example, Hume (1779, part four, 162–3); Nietzsche (1887, sect. 13, 25–7; Freud (1915); and Heidegger (1927, 123–59).

circles, even if it can still feel unintuitive—perhaps because of Descartes—to attribute to ourselves states of which we are not immediately aware.

The example of a conversation is especially telling, Cavendish supposes, where the right words would just seem to materialize, and we come to have an idea that is witty or clever or otherwise responsive to the situation that we inhabit. We might consider the case of the late-night talk-show host who thinks of exactly the right thing at exactly the right time, though it is one of perhaps a hundred million possible thoughts in their wheelhouse.[50] But they think of—and utter—just the one. Cavendish shines a proper light on the phenomenon by positing the existence of cognitive workers that select our thoughts and then set them in order:

> Who knows, but in the *Braine* may dwel / Little small *Fairies*, who can tell?
>
> And by their several actions they may make / Those *formes* and *figures*, we for *fancy* take.
>
> And when we sleep, those *Visions, dreames* we call / By *their* industry may be raised all;
>
> And all the *objects*, which through *sens'es* get, Within the *Braine* they may in order set.[51]

Cavendish does not suppose that there are actual winged fairies flying around in our brain.[52] What she does suppose is that (since something cannot come from nothing[53]) there must be a cause that puts before our mind the intelligent thoughts that we come to have—in the coherent and intelligent order in which we come to have them. Otherwise we would not have those thoughts, or we would come to have them in an order that is jumbled and random. In the course of a conversation, and in the course of any train of thought, there is something of which we are not aware that "in order set[s]"

---

[50] See also the language in Hume (1739–40, I.i.7, 24). He writes, "Nothing is more admirable than the readiness with which the imagination suggests its ideas, and presents them at the very instant in which they become necessary or useful. The fancy runs from one end of the universe to the other, in collecting those ideas which belong to any subject. One would think the whole intellectual world of ideas was at once subjected to our view, and that we did nothing but pick out such as were most proper for our purpose. There may not, however, be any present, beside those very ideas, that are thus collected by a kind of magical faculty in the soul, which, though it be always most perfect in the greatest geniuses, and is properly what we call a genius, is however inexplicable by the utmost efforts of human understanding."

[51] "Of small Creatures, such as we call Fairies," in Cavendish (1653a, 162).

[52] She says in a later text (Cavendish 1664, 500–1) that in the 1653a passage she is using the term 'fairy' as a stand-in for whatever process it is by which our thoughts are set in order.

[53] Cavendish (1664, 53 and 431).

our ideas. This something is cognitive and perceptive and discriminatory by nature. If a comedian or philosopher or witty person is identified as intelligent for articulating a clever idea, the process that generates the idea is properly identified as intelligent—if not more so.

We often engage in organized and purposive behavior that includes among its elements cognitive activity of which we are not consciously aware. We move our legs as we dance; we move our fingers as we play the piano; we dribble the basketball; we seamlessly engage in conversation. Or we engage in activity that is highly reflective but that presupposes cognitive activity that is not. We think of something and we report—"I thought of that." Or someone else exclaims, perhaps in admiration or envy—"*How* did you think of that?" The case of wit is particularly instructive on Cavendish's view. Wit is a constituent of our inner mental life, if we are lucky enough to have it, and indeed Cavendish devotes a lot of the space and time of her plays to the celebration of characters whose fairies (in the brain) are quite active.[54] Wit is a constituent of our inner mental life; to claim otherwise would be absurd. For Cavendish, as for More and Cudworth and Leibniz, there is our cognition and thought, on the one hand, and there is our awareness of our cognition and thought on the other.

3. Cavendish vs. Strawson on the Self

Cavendish is not a dualist. Nor does she hold that thinking is essentially conscious or that activity that is properly attributed to us is always activity of which we are aware. She is in almost no respects a Cartesian.

Enter Strawson again, who is a Cartesian at least with respect to questions of knowledge and justification. He says things like:

> [W]e are inevitably a further step away from the thing with which we are in contact when it is a non-experiential phenomenon .... [E]xperiential phenomena are not only indubitably real; they are also phenomena whose intrinsic nature just is their experiential character; and their experiential character is something with which we are directly acquainted.
>
> (Strawson 2008a, 26–7)

---

[54] For example, in *Wits cabal*, in Cavendish (1662, 294–5), and *Natures three daughters*, in Cavendish (1662, 509–10). It is also tempting in this context to mention the trademark wit of Cavendish herself. See, for example, Grant (1957, 228–39).

> In fact—and it had to come back to this—we don't really know enough to say that there is any non-experiential being. All the appearances of a non-mental world may just be the way that physical phenomena—in themselves entirely mental phenomena—appear to us; the appearance being another mental phenomenon. (44)

Strawson is more or less a Cartesian when it comes to his understanding of self as well. According to his account, the self is a stretch of conscious experience that is episodic in nature. Its beginning and end are marked by conscious awareness, and since we are not conscious at all times, the self is periodic and short-lived. Strawson acknowledges that there is another self that persists much longer—perhaps over the course of a lifetime—but he is not giving an account of that (Strawson 2008c, 190). He is focusing instead on the self as an "inner mental entity" (190)—a self that is "a specifically mental presence of some sort, a mental someone or something. One might say that it's experience of oneself as having nothing more than mental being..." (Strawson 2009, 2). This is an entity whose "persistence conditions are not obviously or automatically the same as the persistence conditions of a human being considered as a whole" (Strawson 2008c, 190). Indeed, it exists in patches, and because it begins and ends with conscious awareness, it is not the same inner self that exists in patches, but a new one at every interval. If we do not have an experience of perpetual rebeginning, we are just not paying attention:

> I think that the sense of being always just beginning is nothing more than an accurate reflection or surfacing in consciousness of the actual nature of all conscious being in time, at least in the human case. I think it may also be an ever-present feature of ordinary human experience that is accessible to everyone but rarely attended to. (192)

Strawson uses the term *I* to refer to the inner mental self that is episodic in nature, but he recognizes that there will be rampant miscommunication if he uses that term and a more traditional understanding of self continues to hold sway. He is therefore happy to speak of I*, and also me*, you*, they*, and so on (194). He also grants that at any moment we might have an *experience* of connectivity to a past self, but that is not a sign of an actual thread; it is just an experience in the here and now (191). He writes:

> I'm well aware that my past is mine in so far as I am a human being, and I fully accept that there's a sense in which it has special relevance to me*

now, including special emotional and moral relevance. At the same time I have no sense that I* was there in the past, and think it obvious that I* was not there, as a matter of metaphysical fact. (195)

What Strawson calls an Episodic self might "have no particular positive experience of perpetual rebeginning" (192), but each stretch of conscious experience and hence each stretch of self is a discrete entity and is entirely new.[55]

Strawson is offering an account of self, and an account that commentators have already gone to great lengths to critique.[56] Here I want to focus on an objection to the account that has not received much attention—that it does not include as part of the self any of the proto-mentality that (on Strawson's view) is present throughout the nervous system and is arguably (and I think obviously) a constituent of the "inner mental entity" or "mental someone or something" that we are.

Strawson does of course allow that there exist regions of mentality that are unconscious. He says, for example, that unconscious states often play a causal role in the formation of (conscious) states that we know more directly (Strawson 2008c, 205-6). He adds that "[t]he conscious/non-conscious border is both murky and porous" (202). But he does not want to include any region of unconscious mentality as part of the self. In a wonderful moment he even considers the kind of case that Cavendish highlights in her discussion of the fairies that "in order set" our thoughts:

> The case of thought in conversation is especially striking. One doesn't act to generate material for one's reply, as the other is speaking. It just comes,

---

[55] See also Strawson (2009, 245-9).

[56] See, for example, the discussions in Melnyck (2009); Dainton (2011); and Lowe 2011. Note for the record that I am assuming that Strawson is offering an account of self—which is what he says he is doing (for example, Strawson 2009, 7)—and not just stipulating his own definition of the word 'self'. If he were doing the latter, it would make no sense for him to attempt to refute accounts of self that are opposed to his—for example, when he says that one piece of evidence against a diachronic view of self is the phenomenological datum that many experience their selves to be episodic (and not continuous) in nature (Strawson 2008d, 194); or when he points out that on a narrative view of self, there is no fact of the matter of the identity of a self across time, but instead the story of what we are is subject to regular (almost unfettered) revision (205); or more generally when he devotes the nineteen pages of Strawson (2008d) and the 400+ pages of Strawson (2009) to a defense of his view. If he were just stipulating a definition of the word 'self', his text would not be nearly that long. There are some passages however in which he does speak as though he is simply stipulating a definition (for example, Strawson 2009, 31-2). If he is just stipulating a definition and usage, then I am not sure what exactly he is doing. And in that event I will not be arguing against his *account*, but instead proposing that his stipulative definition is ad hoc and overly restrictive.

often before the other has finished speaking, and one often knows—in a flash, it seems—both that the essential content of the reply is ready to hand in the mind, and, in some ineffably compressed manner, what its content is, before one has run through its detail in any way.

(Strawson 2009, 187)

But Strawson employs the case to opposite effect. He argues that strictly speaking it is not *we* who come up with the words that make up our half of a conversation. Some aspects of our thinking are due to us, but many are not:

> what actually happens when one wants to think about something or work something out? If the issue is a difficult one, then there may well be a distinct, and distinctive, phenomenon of setting one's mind in the direction of the problem, a setting of it at the problem, and this phenomenon, I think, may well be a matter of intentional action. It may involve rapidly and silently imaging key words or sentences to oneself, or refreshing images of a scene …. What else is there, in the way of action? Well, sometimes one has to shepherd—or dragoon—one's wandering mind back to the previous thought-content in order for the train of thought to be restarted or continued, and this too may be a matter of action…. Sometimes one has a sense that there's a relevant consideration that isn't in play, although one doesn't know what it is. One initiates a kind of actively receptive blanking of the mind in order to give any missing elements a chance to arise…. The rest is waiting, intellectual receptivity; waiting for something to happen—waiting for content to come to mind…. To this extent Philo was radically understating things when he said that 'a man's thoughts are sometimes not due to himself but come without his will'. (190–1)

For Strawson, it is not the *I* that thinks of a witty or clever rejoinder in the course of a philosophical or comedic exchange; it is some other entity. It is an entity that is conceived in abstraction from our conscious thinking. It is an entity that is cognitive but unconscious. He continues:

> [A]ll the cognitive work that thought involves, all the computation in the largest and most human sense, all the essential content-work of reasoning and judgement, all the motion and progress of judgement and thought considered in their contentual essence, as it were—the

actual confrontation and engagement between contents, the collaborations and competitions between them, the transitions between them, and so on—are not only not a matter of intentional action, but are also non-conscious (sub-experiential). (190–2)

I think that Strawson is right that the putting before the mind of an intelligent string of thoughts is for the most part not an intentional action. But he is making an additional contention: that what it is that puts those thoughts before the receptive conscious mind—whatever it is "Within the Braine [that]...in order set[s]" our ideas—is not me. Strawson instead sides with Rimbaud: it is false to say "I think," we ought to say "it thinks in me" (198).

I am hoping that the debate here does not just come down to competing intuitions. If there is an argument it is this: a thing is wholly unrecognizable as the mental entity that is the self if it has none of the states that are "the essential content-work of reasoning and judgement," but those (mental) states are non-conscious. The border between the conscious and the unconscious is indeed porous, Strawson is right to say; and it is porous in ways that have implications for the border that marks the self. In something like the way that a tree is not just the elements that we detect above ground—it also consists of roots that make possible its leaves and branches—I am not just my conscious reflective thinking. Or perhaps a better analogy is a house, which is not just its interior and exterior walls; it also has piping, along with a foundation that is in no sense extraneous. To be sure, if I were a Cartesian, and was concerned to identify those aspects of my self that admit of no possible doubt, then conscious thinking is the first attribute that I would include on the list. But I would not thereby assume that other aspects of the self do not exist that are less well-known.[57] I would want to uncover those (now that I know they are there), and I would want to look into them. I would want to look into them in part because they play a formative role in behavior that is attributable to me. There are a million cases we could cite, but we might start with a consideration of the conscious intentions from which I act when I am feeling uncomfortable, or when I am feeling proud, or when I am feeling protective of another, or when I feel that my life is under threat. In all such cases there is cognition that takes place at

---

[57] So I am more or less siding with Churchland (2013, esp. 11–32 and 195–224).

an unconscious level and that I might prefer not to own.[58] But if my self begins and ends with conscious awareness, then none of that is me, and I can disavow it straightaway.[59] I can figuratively and perhaps even literally get away with murder.[60]

Strawson would likely respond at this point that I am confusing the more contingent and psychological question of *who I am* with the more abstract and philosophical question of *what I am*. He is not asking the first question; only the second (Strawson 2009, 40–1). Fine. The fact remains that much is left out of any realistic conception of the self—as an "inner mental entity" or "mental someone or something"—if it excludes the unconscious cognition by which we do the bulk of our thinking. The trains of thought that unfold, the occurrences of a clever or witty idea, and all the essential content-work

---

[58] Here I am thinking of the kinds of case discussed throughout Yancy (2017)—involving race, and also gender, class, and other categories to which our cognitive system might be responsive—though there are many others of course.

[59] Strawson raises a similar concern about narrative accounts of self, in that they can be extremely selective and suppose "an ideal of control and self-awareness in human life that is mistaken and potentially pernicious" (Strawson 2008d, 205). For example, "the more you recall, retell, narrate yourself, the further you are likely to move away from accurate self-understanding" (205). I am arguing that an analog worry arises for Strawson's view of self. As an aside, I would be curious to know how Strawson theorizes pernicious or "potentially pernicious" behavior. He does not talk much about ethics or value anywhere in his writing. He does speak of moral responsibility in some contexts (for example, in Strawson 2008e, 319–31), but the discussion is more about whether or not there is a meaningful sense in which there exist such things as free will, self-determination, and accountability. The index of *Real Materialism and other essays* does not include entries for 'value' or 'morality'. It does include entries for 'ethics' and 'deontology', but perhaps in a moment of humor, the page references for each are left blank. Those are the only two such omissions in the ten-page index. Part of the reason that I raise the issue is that I assume that if Strawson was going to posit the existence of macro-level features like perniciousness, he would want to say that there exists something like proto-perniciousness at a more basic level. But he does not include such features as part of the subject matter of physics. (I also wonder as an aside why Strawson would not include such features, given that he holds that our grasp of claims about gravitation and other matters of physics is so slight (footnote 7 above), and given that it seems much more clear and obvious that (for example) it is bad to be thrown a child off of a skyscraper.) Note for the record that Cavendish appears to land in the same position. At the level of "Elemental creatures" she posits features like figure, motion, perception, and knowledge (for example, Cavendish 1655a, 105), but not any qualities of the normative variety. So it is hard to see how she would allow that normative properties arise from those, and indeed she suggests as much in at least one passage (Cavendish 1653b, 5). For a reading according to which Cavendish does posit normativity in nature, see Boyle (2018). I suspect that Cavendish and Strawson both subscribe to a version of the view that normativity is to be analyzed in terms of the attitudes and sentiments of cognizers, but that is a topic for another day.

[60] Strawson is right that the happy-go-lucky life of the Episodic self might be very enjoyable (for example, Strawson 2008d, 207), but a worry is that it leaves us open to the charge of reckless or even depraved indifference.

of reasoning and judgment—these would be nothing without the torrent of cognitive activity that goes on behind the scenes. We do not need to include as part of the self all of our conscious ideas, and we do not need to include all of the particular unconscious elements that give rise to these, but if generic self-conscious awareness can be partly constitutive of the self, then generic unconscious cognition can be partly constitutive of the self as well.[61] It is something that we can be sure is there, and it can include elements for which we would want to be on the lookout and that in some cases we would want to hunt down.[62]

References

Note: In the text, I reference the original year of publication.

Deborah Boyle, *The Well-Ordered Universe: The Philosophy of Margaret Cavendish* (Oxford: Oxford: Oxford University Press, 2018).

Margaret Cavendish, *Poems and Fancies* (London: Printed by T.R. for J. Martin and J. Allestrye, 1653a).

Margaret Cavendish, *Philosophical Fancies* (London: Printed by Tho. Roycroft for J. Martin, and J. Allestrye at the Bell in St. Pauls Church-yard, 1653b).

Margaret Cavendish, *Philosophical and Physical Opinions* (London: Printed for J. Martin and J. Allestrye, 1655a).

Margaret Cavendish, *The Worlds Olio* (London: Printed for J. Martin and J. Allestrye, 1655b).

Margaret Cavendish, *Playes* (London: Printed by A. Warren, for John Martyn, James Allestry, and Tho. Dicas, 1662).

Margaret Cavendish, *Philosophical Letters* (London, 1664).

Margaret Cavendish, *Observations upon Experimental Philosophy* (London: Printed by A. Maxwell, 1666).

Margaret Cavendish, *Ground of Natural Philosophy* (London: Printed by A. Maxwell, 1668).

---

[61] But if it is, then Strawson's episodic view is under further strain, as there is no reason to believe that the unconscious region of the mind that is partly constitutive of the self does not continue to exist in-between stretches of conscious awareness. Perhaps it even has "the same persistence conditions of a human being considered as a whole."

[62] Or better—if the language here is too individualistic and Cartesian—we would want to identify such elements and hunt down the structures that engender and feed them. See, for example, the discussion in Yancy (2017, 1–49).

Margaret Cavendish, *Natures picture* (London: Printed by A. Maxwell, 1671).

Patricia S. Churchland, *Touching a Nerve: The Self as Brain* (New York: W.W. Norton, 2013).

Anne Conway, *The Principles of the Most Ancient and Modern Philosophy*, ed. Allison P. Coudert and Taylor Corse (Cambridge: Cambridge University Press, [1692] 1996).

Ralph Cudworth, *True Intellectual System of the Universe* (Stuttgart-Bad Cannstatt: F. Fromann Verlag, [1678] 1964).

David Cunning, "Agency and Consciousness," *Synthese* 120 (1999), 271–94.

David Cunning, *Cavendish*, in the series The Arguments of the Philosophers (London: Routledge, 2016).

David Cunning, "Cavendish, *Philosophical Letters*, and the Plenum," in *Cavendish: An Interdisciplinary Perspective*, ed. Lisa Walters and Brandie Siegfried (Cambridge: Cambridge University Press, 2022), 98–111.

David Cunning, "Ways of Knowing," in *The Routledge Handbook of Women and Early Modern European Philosophy*, ed. Karen Detlefsen and Lisa Shapiro (London: Routledge, forthcoming 2023).

Barry Dainton, "Review of Consciousness and Its Place in Nature," *Philosophy and Phenomenological Research* 88 (2011), 238–61.

René Descartes, "To [De Launay], 22 July 1641," in *The Philosophical Writings of Descartes*, Volume III, ed. and trans. John Cottingham, Robert Stoothoff, Dugald Murdoch, and Anthony Kenny (Cambridge: Cambridge University Press, [1641a] 1991), 188.

René Descartes, *Meditations on First Philosophy*, Volume II: *The Philosophical Writings of Descartes*, ed. and trans. in John Cottingham, Robert Stoothoff, and Dugald Murdoch (Cambridge: Cambridge University Press, [1641b] 1984), 3–62.

René Descartes, *Fourth Replies*, Volume II: *The Philosophical Writings of Descartes*, ed. and trans. John Cottingham, Robert Stoothoff, and Dugald Murdoch (Cambridge: Cambridge University Press, [1641c] 1984), 154–78.

René Descartes, *Principles of Philosophy*, *The Philosophical Writings of Descartes*, Volume I, ed. and trans. John Cottingham, Robert Stoothoff, and Dugald Murdoch (Cambridge: Cambridge University Press, [1644] 1985), 179–291.

René Descartes, *The Passions of the Soul*, in *The Philosophical Writings of Descartes, Volume I*, ed. and trans. John Cottingham, Robert Stoothoff, and Dugald Murdoch (Cambridge: Cambridge University Press, [1649] 1985), 328–404.

Hubert L. Dreyfus, *Being-in-the-World* (Boston: The M.I.T. Press, 1991).

Princess Elisabeth, "Princess Elisabeth of Bohemia to René Descartes, 16 May 1643" in *The Princess and the Philosopher*, ed. Andrea Nye (New York: Rowman and Littlefield, [1643] 1999), 9–10.

Sigmund Freud, "The Unconscious," in *Standard Edition of the Complete Psychological Works of Sigmund Freud*, Volume 14, ed. and trans. J. Strachey (London: Hogarth, 1915), 166–215.

Daniel Garber, *Leibniz: Body, Substance, Monad* (Oxford: Oxford University Press, 2009).

Pierre Gassendi (1641), *Fifth Objections*, Volume II: *The Philosophical Writings of Descartes*, ed. and trans. John Cottingham, Robert Stoothoff, and Dugald Murdoch (Cambridge: Cambridge University Press, 1984), 179–240.

Douglas Grant, *Margaret the First: A Biography of Margaret Cavendish, Duchess of Newcastle, 1623–1673* (Toronto: Toronto University Press, 1957).

Martin Heidegger, *Basic Problems of Phenomenology*, ed. and trans. Albert Hofstadter (Bloomington, IN: Indiana University Press, [1927] 1988).

David Hume, *A Treatise of Human Nature*, ed. P.H. Nidditch (Oxford: The Clarendon Press, [1739–40] 1978).

David Hume, *An Enquiry Concerning Human Understanding*, ed. Tom L. Beauchamp (Oxford: Oxford University Press, [1748] 1999).

David Hume, *Dialogues Concerning Natural Religion*, ed. Norman Kemp Smith (New York: Macmillan, [1779] 1987).

Sarah Hutton, *Anne Conway: A Woman Philosopher* (Cambridge: Cambridge University Press, 2004).

G.W. Leibniz, *Discourse on Metaphysics*, in *G.W. Leibniz: Philosophical Essays*, ed. and trans. Daniel Garber and Roger Ariew (Indianapolis and London: Hackett, [1686] 1989), 35–68.

G.W. Leibniz, *Monadology*, in *G.W. Leibniz: Philosophical Essays*, ed. and trans. Daniel Garber and Roger Ariew (Indianapolis and London: Hackett, [1714] 1989), 213–24.

John Locke, *An Essay Concerning Human Understanding*, ed. P.H. Nidditch (Oxford: Oxford University Press, [1689] 1979).

E.J. Lowe, "Review of *Selves: An Essay in Revisionary Metaphysics*," *Analysis* 71 (2011), 587–92.

Lucretius, *On the Nature of Things*, ed. and trans. Anthony Esolen (London and Baltimore: The Johns Hopkins University Press, 1995).

Nicolas Malebranche, *The Search After Truth*, ed. and trans. Thomas L. Lennon and Paul J. Olscamp (Cambridge: Cambridge University Press, [1674] 1997).

Colin McGinn, "Hard Questions: Comments on Galen Strawson," *Journal of Consciousness Studies* 13 (2006), 90–9.

Andrew Melnyck, "Review of Galen Strawson: Real Materialism and Other Essays," *Notre Dame Philosophical Reviews* (2009), https://ndpr.nd.edu/reviews/real-materialism-and-other-essays/

Julien Offray de la Mettrie, *Man Machine*, in *Man Machine and Other Writings*, ed. and trans. Ann Thomson (Cambridge: Cambridge University Press, [1747] 1996), 1–40.

Henry More, *The Immortality of the Soul*, in *Philosophical Writings of Henry More*, ed. Flora Isabel Mackinnon (Oxford: Oxford University Press, [1659] 1925), 55–180.

Henry More, "The True Notion of a Spirit," in *Philosophical Writings of Henry More*, ed. Flora Isabel MacKinnon (Oxford: Oxford University Press, [1671] 1925), 181–229.

Friedrich Nietzsche, *On the Genealogy of Morality*, ed. Keith Ansell-Pearson and trans. Carol Diethe (Cambridge: Cambridge University Press, [1887] 1997).

Eileen O'Neill, "Introduction," in *Observations upon Experimental Philosophy*, ed. Eileen O'Neill (Cambridge: Cambridge University Press, 2001), x–xxxvi.

Alison Peterman, "Margaret Cavendish on Motion and Mereology," *Journal of the History of Philosophy* 57 (2019), 471–99.

Plato, *Phaedo*, in *Five Dialogues*, ed. and trans. G.M.A. Grube (Indianapolis: Hackett, [1992] 2002), 93–154.

Jonathan Shaheen, "The Life of the Thrice Sensitive, Rational and Wise Animate Matter: Cavendish's Animism," *HOPOS: The Journal for the International Society for the History of Philosophy of Science* 11 (2021), 621–41.

Baruch Spinoza, *Ethics*, in *Spinoza: Complete Works*, ed. and trans. Samuel Shirley and Michael L. Morgan (Indianapolis: Hackett, [1677] 2002), 213–382.

Galen Strawson, "Real Materialism," in *Real Materialism and other essays*, ed. Galen Strawson (Oxford: Oxford University Press, 2008a), 19–51.

Galen Strawson, "Realistic Monism: Why Physicalism Entails Panpsychism," in *Real Materialism and Other Essays*, ed. Galen Strawson (Oxford: Oxford University Press, 2008b), 53–74.

Galen Strawson, "Can We Know the Nature of Reality as It Is in Itself?," in *Real Materialism and Other Essays*, ed. Galen Strawson (Oxford: Oxford University Press, 2008c), 75–100.

Galen Strawson, "Against Narrativity," in *Real Materialism and Other Essays*, ed. Galen Strawson (Oxford: Oxford University Press, 2008d), 189–207.

Galen Strawson, "Mental Ballistics: the Involuntariness of Spontaneity," in *Real Materialism and Other Essays*, ed. Galen Strawson (Oxford: Oxford University Press, 2008e), 233–53.

Galen Strawson, *Selves* (Oxford: Oxford University Press, 2009).

George Yancy, *Black Bodies, White Gazes: The Continuing Significance of Race in America*, second edition (Washington, DC: Rowman and Littlefield, 2017).

17
'Actions of a Body Sentient'
Cavendish on the Mind (and against Panpsychism)

Alison Peterman

Introduction

Margaret Cavendish has been hailed a heroine of panpsychism: she allegedly 'takes thinking agents as her basic causal model in explanation' (Duncan 2012: 19), endorses 'a form of panpsychism in the strong sense that every part of nature contains the same rational principle as humans' (Shaheen 2021: 636), holds that 'bodies [are] intelligent and thoughtful from the start' and that 'mentality is already among their immediate properties' (Cunning 2016: 73). I do not think these are right. Cavendish does not hold that matter thinks in anything like the sense that humans do, nor do plants, minerals, or other things that aren't animals.

Cavendish's account of matter is revisionary, but it is not a panpsychist one. Instead of mind, Cavendish takes what we might call the *organic* to be pervasive. Matter, which is substance structured by parthood and composition, is self-moving. Humans and other animals, plants, and minerals—all of which Cavendish calls 'creatures'—are composed of parts that act so that they can survive, self-regulate, act, and interact with their environments. Cavendish calls all these capacities of creatures 'knowledge' and 'perception', and she argues that all creatures have them. But, I'll argue, we have no reason to think that the knowledge and perception that kidneys, rocks, tables, and trees have has anything further in common with human and animal cognition.

Animal cognition encompasses just a handful among infinite such ways that the infinite varieties of creatures live in the world, and philosophers make a very deep mistake, Cavendish argues, when they project onto other creatures our own ways of doing that. In addition to warning generally against anthropomorphizing in natural philosophy, Cavendish warns against imagining that matter or creatures are minded in the specific way that animals are. What is distinctive about the kinds of animal perception that we are likely to classify as cognitive, including sense perception, imagination, and reasoning, is that they involve creating inside the animal's body something like internal representations, maps of the environment, or isomorphisms with external things. These processes are enabled by the material structures specific to animal bodies, especially sense organs and the brain. While Cavendish does not rule out the possibility that some non-animal creatures perceive and know in this way, she does not think we have reason to believe that they do, and she does rule out that all creatures do, and that matter does.

I cannot stress enough that while Cavendish thinks that these capacities are, as far as we know, unique to animals, this is not in order to mark them out as special in any other way. Cavendish provides a naturalized account of these kinds of perception and knowledge: they are adaptive capacities just like any others, highly dependent on the particular matter and structure of a creature, and they provide us no special window onto reality. Like non-animal perception and knowledge, and like non-cognitive kinds of animal perception and knowledge, Cavendish evaluates them in terms of how good they are at keeping us living and thriving. Sometimes they do better for us than a worm's knowledge of rain or wood's knowledge of how to be hard, but sometimes they don't, and in those cases, the worm and the wood are more knowing than Marie Curie and wiser than the Dalai Lama. They are not, however, thinking.

'Mind' is said in many ways, and as I'll suggest in the conclusion, there may be some definitions of mind on which it may count as pervasive for Cavendish. But these are not what people mean when they say that Cavendish is a panpsychist. Most people, especially scholars of Cavendish, mean that Cavendish thinks that all natural phenomena require explanation in terms of representational, informational, or epistemic states. Some others, especially contemporary panpsychists wishing to recruit Cavendish to the cause, mean that she thinks that conscious experience or proto-experience is pervasive. I argue in this chapter that neither is true.

Instead, the lessons that Cavendish has to teach us about philosophy of mind include: that the mind cannot be understood in abstraction from its organic basis, both in the body and in the environment; that to understand it we have to appreciate both the specificity of the brain and sense organs as well as what we have in common with other natural systems; that what we understand about the mind, we understand in structural terms; that we should not allow a theory of what kind of metaphysical stuff there is dictate our theorizing about mind; that the mind should in the first instance be understood as a set of capacities, among others, that animals have to survive and act, rather than a window onto things in themselves or eternal truths; and that humans are no closer to gods than any other natural things.

1. Matter, Materialism, Monism

Cavendish holds that everything in nature is matter and that explanations in natural philosophy should be given in terms of the motions of that matter. She is hijacking the polemics of the so-called mechanical philosophy, according to which natural-philosophical explanations should be given in terms of sized, shaped bits of matter, spatially arranged, subject only to changes in their location in space and rearrangement. But she is putting this rhetoric to her own use, because 'matter' and 'motion' do not mean in her system what they do for mechanical philosophers like Descartes and Boyle.

Matter, according to Cavendish, is necessarily (1) substance; (2) divisible; and (3) self-knowing. Substance is what cannot be created or destroyed but only changed. All and only matter is divisible, and parthood and composition is the only metaphysical structure there is (GNP 45, 65). Matter's divisibility is a fundamental feature of it and not a consequence of its extension; more generally, Cavendish does not think, as many of her contemporaries did, that spatial facts carve nature at its joints. Putting aside for now the question of what self-knowledge is, we can define matter simply as divisible stuff.[1]

Beyond this, matter is (4) self-moving; (5) sensitive; and (6) rational, but it might not have been.[2] Cavendish articulates the contingency of (4), (5), and (6) by claiming there are in fact three 'constitutive parts' or 'degrees' of matter: inanimate matter, and sensitive and rational matter, which are both self-moving. However, these degrees are so thoroughly mixed that every part of nature contains all three. For Cavendish, matter is what the Aristotelians called a '*mixis*,' or perfect mixture: it is a homogeneous substance from which the components cannot be recovered, but whose nature is nonetheless grounded in those components. So we may follow Cavendish in treating matter as homogeneous, with all three capacities (PL 1.33, 1.35, 2.4, 4.29).

---

[1] Peterman (forthcoming) defends this.
[2] 'This 'triumvirate' of the degrees of matter, is so necessary a constitutive principle of all natural effects, that nature could not be without it: I mean; nature considered, not what she might have been, but as she is, and as much as we are able to perceive by her actions."

That matter is self-moving means that it causes changes in itself. Cavendish seems to think that there is something incoherent in the idea of one thing's acting *on* another. One thing can influence or occasion another thing to act, so that, for example, a hand tossing a ball serves as the occasion for the ball to move itself skyward. And, as we will see in Section 2, a thing can act toward and with other things in virtue of being composed with them. But strictly speaking, a thing can only act on itself.

Cavendish distinguishes the constitutive parts of matter from the 'effective parts' of nature, which are creatures, including you, Lassie, the sun, livers, and whatever might make up those things. While matter is essentially divisible, Cavendish holds that the actual parts of nature are generated by self-motion (OEP 70). This sounds like Descartes's claim that individual bodies are generated in homogeneous matter by local motion, but it is very different. For Cavendish, generating parts and the changes in those parts is something that matter *does*, while for Descartes it is something that matter *undergoes*. Also, according to Cavendish, motion is not local motion, or change of place, but rather change in facts about parthood and composition.[3] While there are many kinds of changes at the level of effective parts, Cavendish analyzes all fundamental change in terms of division and composition, so that 'the chief actions of nature, are composition and division, which produce all the variety of nature' (OEP 140). So the connection between motion and the variety of parts is clearer for Cavendish than it is for Descartes: self-motion diversifies matter because self-motion is matter dividing itself.

The intrinsic divisibility of matter, the complete mixture of the kinds of matter, and the ability of matter to act diversely are important sources of metaphysical structure, for Cavendish, especially because she hates properties. The natures of things and the changes in them should never be explained in terms of properties, qualities, forms, or the like, because they are 'half-beings' and are therefore not matter, and the distinction between a thing and its properties, not being a distinction between parts of matter, does not exist.[4]

Cavendish's characterization of matter as divisible stuff and her rejection of properties are very important for understanding what she means when she claims that only matter exists. She means that there is stuff, and that stuff has a precise kind of part-whole structure, which is all the structure

---

[3] Peterman (2019) defends this.   [4] Peterman (forthcoming) defends this.

that there is. Since there is change, matter is self-moving, or causes changes by composing and dividing itself. Matter is not a physical posit but a metaphysical one, and Cavendish's materialism is not the claim that there is only physical substance, be that extended stuff or stuff with size, shape, or spin, or stuff with whatever properties are mentioned in a completed physics. It is not the claim that there is one specific kind of substance at all, especially not if the kind is characterized in terms of property types.[5]

This makes Cavendish unusual in a tradition where much metaphysics of mind is carried out in terms of property types. Monism, dualism, idealism, and even panpsychism and panprotopsychism are characterized, among both Cavendish's contemporaries and ours, in these terms. In his 1729 *Philosopisches Lexicon*, J. G. Walch defines materialism as the position that 'all the occurrences and operations of natural bodies are derived from the bare properties of matter, as from its dimension, shape, weight, confrontation and mixing.'[6] In our own *Philosopisches Lexicon*, the *Stanford Encyclopedia of Philosophy*, Daniel Stoljar couches most of the versions of physicalism he entertains in terms of the relationship between physical and non-physical properties. Most of them are claims that, for example, all non-physical processes are identical, supervene on, or are grounded by physical properties.[7]

But Cavendish does not allow her account of the mind to be constrained by what kind of stuff there is. She is committed to the view that the structure and behavior of what there is, at the very deepest level, will explain rock behavior as well as human minds. But she neither argues from the nature of the stuff to the nature or minds, nor from the nature of minds to the nature of the stuff—other than that minds, since they are matter, must be structured the way that matter is.

So far I've ignored Cavendish's claims that matter is sensitive and rational. This is one of three main reasons that people read Cavendish as some kind of panpsychist. The other two reasons are that Cavendish argues that all

---

[5] Peterman (forthcoming).

[6] As cited in Wolfe, 'Materialism.' 'Materialism' wasn't a widely used term until the end of the seventeenth century, where it appeared primarily as an ill-defined term of abuse and was run together with similarly ill-defined polemical terms like 'mechanism', 'Spinozism', 'necessitarianism', 'atheism', and 'Epicureanism'. It became increasingly common in the eighteenth and nineteenth centuries but was still extremely polysemous.

[7] Today there are other characterizations of physicalism on offer, but even those don't explicitly reject property talk; it just isn't front and center. See, e.g., Ney ('Physicalism") or Dowell ('Formulating the thesis of physicalism').

creatures are perceptive and knowing, and that she frequently describes Nature and matter, along with creatures, in anthropomorphic terms. Section 3 argues that we should not take Cavendish's anthropomorphic characterizations of non-humans literally. Section 4 argues that the knowledge and perception of creatures in general is not mentalistic. And Section 5 argues that Cavendishian sense and reason are not mentalistic.

Part of the argument that perception and knowledge in general are not like animal mental states requires understanding how Cavendish explains animal mental states. This is the topic of the next section.

2. Animal Perception and Knowledge

Creatures are effective parts of nature that are made up of other creatures, or effective parts. Cavendish's model of humans, animals, plants, and even minerals is that of organism—each creature is some ordered parts which are themselves ordered, and the matter that constitutes those parts is self-moving. Cavendish frequently claims that nature's order requires that all creatures must perceive and know: '[K]nowledge and perception...are general and fundamental actions of nature; it being not probable that the infinite parts of nature should move so variously, nay, so orderly and methodically as they do, without knowing what they do, or why, and whether they move' (OEP 139). Perception is a species of knowledge—specifically, 'knowledge of exterior parts and actions' (OEP 16). Cavendish does not define knowledge.

Like all other creatures, animals perceive and know in a wide variety of ways. But Cavendish details two specific kinds of animal perception and a variety of non-perceptual mental states like memory and imagination. So what follows does not exhaust animal perceiving and knowing, which, as we will see, includes, for example, knowledge of digestion and respiration. Instead it represents Cavendish's attempt to say what is distinctive about how creatures with brains and sense organs interact with the world.

An animal mind, like every part of nature, 'is matter moved' and thoughts are 'nothing else but corporeal motions' (OEP 53). Besides claiming in general that the mind is just so much matter, Cavendish constantly describes states like knowledge, wisdom, memory, love, fear, and disagreement in terms of the structure and dynamics of matter (e.g. OEP 163).

2.1 Animal Perception

In an animal, the 'perception of its exterior senses, as Seeing, Hearing, Tasting, Touching, Smelling... is properly made by way of patterning and imitation, by the innate, figurative motions of those Animal Creatures' (OEP 15). In vision, for example, the matter of the eye 'patterns out' or 'imitates' the 'figure, motion, or action' of an external object (OEP 150, 169, 173). The object must exist and be in some sense present to a perceiver to occasion this patterning (OEP 171). It does not cause the patterning either by a purely physical process, as in the mechanical theories of Descartes and Hobbes, or via information-carrying intermediaries like ideas or scholastic sensible species (OEP 148, 174). Patterning is just what some parts of an animal do when the animal is around the relevant objects.

Sense perception happens entirely in the matter of the sense organ: the eyes see, the ears hear, and there is no need for what happens in a man's eye, say, to be passed along to the brain or processed in any way for seeing to occur (OEP 151, 154, 175). There is also a kind of perception that Cavendish calls 'rational perception,' which she characterizes as 'purer,' 'more general,' and 'more penetrating' than sense perception; it also accounts for cross-modal integration (OEP 83).

It seems to me that this kind of animal perception is Cavendish's attempt to account for the fact that some of the ways that animals interact with the world involve mapping it in their bodies.

Patterns are isomorphic, to some extent, with their objects and they are, to some extent, truth-evaluable. The re-patterning of sensitive perceptions by the rational parts looks something like a mechanism for abstraction. To that extent, patterning involves representing the external world.

At the same time, Cavendish is intent on naturalizing these processes in some interesting ways.

First, the perception is an action of an animal's matter. It is not an idea in the Cartesian sense of a mind-dependent object of perception: '[I]n those perceptions which are made by patterning, the action of patterning, and the perception, are one and the same' (OEP 178).[8] Perception is a direct relationship with an object that exists without intermediary (GNP 8, 69).

---

[8] Michaelian also makes this point nicely (2009: 40).

Sometimes Cavendish describes perception as a dance that a perceiver does with the object that is perceived.

Second, perceptions are highly dependent on the animal's structure, on their role in the animal, and on the part of the animal that they occur in. Cavendish repeatedly stresses that the perceptions that a thing can have depend on how it is structured and what kinds of motions it can make (e.g. OEP 166). The dependence of the meaning of perceptions on their role is suggested by Cavendish's fascinating discussion of patternings that are not perceptions. Like sense perception, she writes, echoes, reflections, and pictures are 'made by the self-moving matter, by way of patterning and copying out.' Nonetheless, 'I cannot guess what their perceptions are, onely this I may say, that the air hath an elemental, and the glass a mineral, but not an animal perception' (PL 1.24). Both the human eye and a mirror pattern the face of a man, but this may be a perception in the human but not a perception in the mirror. This means that any so-called 'information' contained in the patterns is not easily abstracted from that context and realizable in some other kind of thing—or even, she claims, in a very similar individual like another human being.

Perceptions are similarly dependent on the particular parts of the animal: 'the Eye doth not know what the Ear knows, nor the Ear what the Nose knows...because they are composed differently' (OEP 185). So while Cavendish's account of re-patterning is a way to capture, to some extent, the fact that animals sometimes go on to use perceptual representations in different ways, patterns are not easily abstracted from the part of the body they occur in. So re-patterning is perhaps better thought of as a way that the parts of an animal work together, rather than on the model of information-processing.

Third, Cavendish is far, far more likely to characterize sense perceptions as natural or unnatural than to characterize them as true or false. Her epistemic norm is naturalness, not accuracy. In one of my absolute favorite parts of the *Observations*, Cavendish critiques experimental philosophers who think that optical lenses give us special insight into the natures of things. In fact, they deform our natural sight, presenting creatures as 'misshapen rather than natural: For example; a louse by the help of a magnifying glass appears like a lobster' (OEP 51). And under a microscope 'If the edge of a knife, or point of a needle were naturally and really as the microscope presents them, they would never be so useful as they are; for, a flat or broad plain-edged knife would not cut, nor a blunt globe pierce so suddenly another body' (OEP 51). Do our natural eyes present a knife more accurately? No—just as the way the glass patterns the louse reflects the structure of the glass, the way my eye patterns the louse reflects the structure of my eye. But my eye, and not the microscope, is tuned to see things in ways that are natural to me. That naturalness is in turn important because it tracks usefulness: 'if a Painter should draw a Lowse as big as a Crab, and of that shape as the Microscope presents... what advantage would it be to the Beggar? for it doth neither instruct him how to avoid breeding them, or how to catch them, or to hinder them from biting' (OEP 11). Human perception is for the 'Subsistence, Consistence, and use of the Whole Man' (GNP 51). It is the same for other animals. The different species of birds, for example, are 'better discerned by those that eat their flesh, than by micrographers that look upon their colours and exterior figures through a magnifying glass' (OEP 52).

To summarize: the patterning account of animal sense perception is Cavendish's attempt to explain how animals come to have something like maps, isomorphisms, or representations in their bodies. At the same time, she's always concerned to stress that these are first and foremost just some ways that animal bodies ensure their survival. I'll argue in Section 4 that non-animal perceptions are like animal sense perceptions in being ways of ensuring a creature's survival, but that we have no reason to think that non-animal perceptions are like animal sense perceptions in being representations of their environments.

2.2 Animal Knowledge

First, however, let us consider Cavendish's account of non-perceptual animal knowledge, under which Cavendish includes 'Thoughts, Conceptions, Imaginations, Fancy, Understanding, Memory, Remembrance, and whatsoever motions are in the Head, or Brain' (PL 2.18). An important difference between these actions and perception is that these are not occasioned, but 'voluntary' or made 'by Rote, and not by Example' (GNP 5.11).

In non-animal contexts, Cavendish is fairly consistent that there are two exclusive and exhaustive kinds of knowledges: perception, which is 'exterior' or concerns other parts and actions, and what she calls a creature's self-knowledge, which is internal and concerns the creature itself. But an ambiguity arises in the case of animal knowledge. Conceptions and so on are not 'exterior' in the sense that they are not occasioned by external objects, but can they nonetheless be *of* anything outside the animal's body?

Cavendish is quite aware of this ambiguity:

> [T]his is the difference between exterior perceptions, and interior voluntary actions:... perceptions are properly concerning foreign parts, figures and actions, and are occasioned by them: but, the voluntary actions are not occasioned by any outward objects, but make figures of their own accord, without any imitation, patterns, or copies of foreign parts, or actions... the reason why I call the voluntary actions, interior, is, b*ecause they have no such respect to outward objects, at least, are not occasioned by them*, as perceptions are, but are the figurative actions of sense and reason, made by rote; whereas perceptions do tend to exterior objects, and are made according to the presentation of their figures, parts or actions.
> (OEP 170–171; my emphasis).

Texts can be marshaled that suggest that some interior, voluntary conceptions can be of outward objects, and others can be marshaled that suggest that they cannot. I prefer the latter reading. I believe that Cavendish has the sense that perception grounds all the cognitive contact that animals have with the external world. Here are some reasons to think that.

First, Cavendish sometimes suggests that to the extent that certain non-perceptual states like dreams or memories are *of* anything at all, it is only in virtue of some original patterning. For example, remembrances are not occasioned, but they do 'repeat some former actions' and so to that extent are connected with original patternings (GNP 101).

Similarly dreams are 'those Corporeal Motions of Sleep, [which] make the same pattern of that Object in Sleep, as when that Object was present' (GNP 112). While dreaming happens strictly speaking by rote,

> if the Self-moving Parts move after their own inventions, and not after the manner of Copying; or, if they move not after the manner of Human Perception, then a Man is as ignorant of his Dreams, or any Human Perception, as if he was in a [Swoon]; and then he says, he did not dream; and, that such Sleeps are like Death. (GNP 112)

Without the connection to any human perception, a dream has no content.

In the case of other non-perceptual mental states, it is rare for Cavendish to characterize them in terms of what they are of. Instead, she usually describes them in non-representational terms, like this:

When [the] Rational Parts...divide in divers sorts of Actions, Man names it, Arguing, or Disputing in the Mind. And when those divers sorts of Actions are at some strife, Man names it, A contradicting of himself. And if there be a weak strife, Man names it, Consideration...When all the Parts of the Mind move regularly, and sympathetically, Man names it, Wisdom. (GNP 101)

Perhaps the non-perceptual mental state that most interests Cavendish is creation. 'Man' has the ability to 'enjoy Worlds of his own making' and to 'govern and command those Worlds; as also, dissolve and compose several Worlds, as he pleases' (GNP 103). But Cavendish is very much inclined to talk of these conceptions in the sense of begettings rather than in the sense of concepts, even playing on the word's polysemy in a discussion of miscarriage (GNP 87). Conceptions are the offspring of brains.

What about the possibility that non-perceptual knowledge is of eternal truths, or numbers, or something else? Cavendish doesn't think too highly of abstract or mathematical reasoning.[9] She does say that we have some knowledge of God, but she is sometimes inclined to classify this as self-knowledge and sometimes as perception, which further suggests that she thinks of self-knowledge and perception as exhaustive (OEP 193). Other times she says the idea has no real content. It is wise to avoid worrying too much about God in thinking about Cavendish's natural philosophy, since she tells us repeatedly that this should be left to theologians.

So Cavendish seems to have the hunch that our representations all have their roots in perception, or in actual interactions with external objects. This doesn't mean that she is an empiricist, since there are non-sensory rational perceptions, although she does say that in a properly functioning animal the sensory and rational perceptions work together, which suggests that she appreciates the special role that the sense organs have in generating our mental contents (OEP 179).

Non-perceptual animal knowledge like memory, hope, imagination, and love are some kinds of internal actions that we have in virtue of being structured the way we are—specifically, in virtue of having a brain. They are no better than other kinds of knowledge, and there is no sense in which humans represent the most complex or developed version of this: 'Man may

---

[9] For more detail about this, see Peterman (2019).

have a different Knowledg from Beasts, Birds, Fish, Flies, Worms, or the like; and yet be no wiser than those sorts of Animal-kinds' (GNP 148). Locating them in the brain is not an attempt to unify consciousness. In fact Cavendish regards it as absurd to think that 'the mind chiefly resides but in one part of the body' (OEP 154) or that 'one single part should be King of the whole Creature,' for a creature is 'a Republic and not a Monarchy' (PL 3.24). Among the arguments she gives for this is that if blood 'were the seat of the Soul, then in the circulation of the blood...it would become very dizzy by its turning round' (PL 4.2)—a most colorful critique of homuncular thinking. Indeed, 'every particular Creature hath numerous souls' (PL 4.3) which are moreover not very distinct from other souls, since souls are matter, and no matter is fully distinct from other matter (PL 4.2). This includes us: 'one man may have numerous souls, as well as he has numerous parts and particles' (OEP 191).

Sense perceptions, conceptions, and so on are only a few among many kinds of perception and knowledge in an animal body; others include 'the motions of digestion, growth, decay, etc.' which

> are as sensible, and as rational, as those five sensitive organs; and the heart, liver, lungs, spleen, stomach, bowels, and the rest, know as well their office and functions, and are as sensible of their pains, diseases, constitutions, tempers, nourishments, etc. as the eyes, ears nostrils, tongue, etc. know their particular actions and perception. (OEP 151)

There are also countless perceptive and knowing processes in other creatures. I'll turn to those in Section 4, but it will be helpful to first consider those metaphors of thoughtful teleology.

3. Anti-Anthropomorphism

In addition to attributing knowledge and perception to all creatures, Cavendish frequently describes nature as a Wise and Provident Lady 'who governs her parts very wisely, methodically, and orderly' (OEP 105). Rational matter is the 'architect' or the 'most prudent and wisest part of Nature, as being the designer of all productions' (OEP 3). Many readers take these literally and think that for Cavendish, we cannot explain natural phenomena without appealing to the 'ends of thinking, reasoning beings.'[10]

---

[10] Goldberg (2017: 80); see also Jorati (2019: 487) and Detlefsen (2007: 188).

This is very puzzling, given that an important normative dimension in Cavendish's system is the natural (thumbs up) vs the artificial (thumbs down). Specifically relevant here is her observation that art 'is but a natural creature or effect, and not a creator of anything' (OEP 193). If art is not a creator of anything, and matter and Nature are, why liken them to artificers? You might think that the limitation of our artifice is a matter of degree, as it is for Leibniz, and that the problem with art is just that humans are limited planners while Nature has all the power and sees the whole picture. But this doesn't feel right. Leibniz doesn't call art names like 'Nature's mimic or fool,' 'nature's foolish changeling child,' and 'the insnarled motions of nature' (PL 2.13, 1.26, 2.12). For Cavendish, there is nothing intrinsically wrong with art: humans do stuff and make things, like spiders make webs. What she seems to think is bad about human artifice is that we assume that creatures, Nature as a whole, and matter itself act the same way. In contrast, Leibniz encourages us to think of God as an infinitely powerful workman.

The solution to this puzzle is pretty simple: Cavendish explicitly tells us not to take these literally. Of the notion that the actions of God or Nature may be understood by analogy with our own, she writes:

> I am not of the opinion...that all natural effects may be called artificial, nay, that nature herself may be called the 'art of God'...for art is as much inferior to nature, as a part is inferior to the whole, and all artificial effects are irregular in comparison to natural; wherefore to say, God or Nature works artificially, would be as much as to say, they work irregularly.
> (OEP 198)

When Cavendish contrasts the wisdom of Nature with 'Divine Wisdom,' it may sound like she does think that God, at least, is such an artificer. But 'divine', for Cavendish, often means something like 'whatever thing that humans think makes them super-natural.' Cavendish connects the view that God is an artificer with mechanism: 'And as for 'mechanical motion'; that seems but a mechanic opinion: nor have those, who make God the 'First Mechanical Mover,' any other but an irreverent concept of the 'divine nature" (OEP 21-22). Cavendish is attacking specifically the view that matter is inert and God, working from outside of matter, sets it in motion. That that irreverent concept is 'but a mechanic opinion' sounds like another allusion to an argument against analogizing with human activity.

Here is another warning against conceiving of Nature's wisdom on analogy with our own:

It is absurd to conceive the Generality of wisdom according to an Irregular effect or defect of a particular Creature; for the General actions of Nature are both life and knowledg, which are the architects of all Creatures, and know better how to frame all kinds and sorts of Creatures then man can conceive. (PL 2.4)

And just as Nature is not literally a wise lady, rational and sensitive matter is not literally a builder. We should not imagine 'that as a builder erects a house according to his conception in the brain, the same happens in all other natural productions or generations...if all Animals should be produced by meer fancies, [then] a Man and a Woman should beget by fancying themselves together in copulation' (PL 4.2). Here, Cavendish tells us precisely what the difference is between the literal and metaphorical builder. While a human builder erects a house 'according to a conception in the brain,' rational and sensitive matter does not.

We might wonder why Cavendish uses analogies of thoughtful teleology so much if she doesn't want us to take them literally. Cavendish is indeed trying to emphasize the continuity between human beings and other natural things, down to minerals and planets. But the fact that we are made of matter, and that we are just one manifestation of nature's action, should cause us to reinterpret how we do things in light of how nature does things, and not the other way around.

What do we learn from this shift in perspective? One thing that we know about nature's actions is that they are all corporeal motions, so that is one lesson: our own willing, perceiving, and thinking are just so many corporeal motions. Beyond that, however, we do not have much insight into the infinite variety of ways that nature acts. In one place, Cavendish explains that when she analogizes the powers that matter has to human powers, she does so 'to make my meaning more intelligible to weaker capacities.' But it is not only weaker capacities that must rely upon anthropomorphism. Cavendish thinks that it is extremely difficult—often impossible—to avoid, because we are, after all, human. To avoid it entirely would be to transcend our partial and particular human natures, which we cannot do, and a philosopher who pretends that she can will just end up relying on anthropomorphism unawares. By oversaturating her philosophy with obvious—and obviously inadequate—anthropomorphism, Cavendish makes us more sensitive to the widespread but often hidden reliance on it in natural philosophy.[11]

---

[11] We should also consider that terms like 'perception' and 'knowledge' are less anthropomorphic than we might think. 'Perception' was used before Cavendish in a way that did not

4. Perception and Knowledge

As a natural philosopher, what is salient to Cavendish are not trajectories and collisions but digestion, respiration, generation, and growth; not solid bodies but animals, trees, and other self-moving, self-regulating systems of organized parts. Cavendish, similar to her mechanist contemporaries like Descartes and Boyle, wants to ground the creature level in fundamental metaphysical structure. However, the structure that she finds both at the creature level and the fundamental level is not spatial and geometrical structure, but compositional structure. Cavendish does not seem to take physics to be a bridge between the creature level and the foundational facts. She is interested in a theory of organism, not a theory of local motion.

I will argue in this section that her account of creaturely perception and knowledge should be understood in this context. In brief: an organism's perception is its ability to interact with its environment, and its knowledge is the ability to regulate itself. Ultimately, Cavendish thinks that these abilities are grounded in matter's self-motion. We have no reason to think that perception and knowledge at the level of creatures, or the perceptual and knowing abilities of matter, involve the internalization of information in the sense that animal sense perception and knowledge do.

4.1 Creaturely Perception

Every effective part of nature perceives, including plants, stars, and mud, and the way that a creature perceives depends on how its body is constituted: '[E]very several kind and sort of Creatures, have several kinds of sorts of Perception, according to the nature and property of such a kind of sort of Composition, as makes such a kind or sort of Creature' (GNP 69). What is shared by every kind of perception is that it is (1) a knowledge of external parts, and (2) a kind of corporeal motion; (1) is just the definition of

---

require a mind (see, e.g., Jalobeanu 2021). In recent work, Jody Azzouni has argued that the ordinary notion of knowledge presupposes something 'cognitive' but in a sense that might apply to things like thermostats and gas gauges (he draws the line at tables and chairs; it's less clear whether Cavendish does—that depends on whether they count as 'creatures' or not) (Azzouni 2020). Azzouni argues that at least some aspects of this ordinary notion of knowledge stretch back to Cavendish's period (Azzouni, forthcoming), raising the possibliity that Cavendish does not see the word 'knowledge' as obviously anthropomorphic. Finally, as Azzouni contrasts this vernacular use of 'knowledge' with the 'historically shifty and wavering philosophical notion of knowledge' (forthcoming, 4). This would be especially intriguing given her resistance to philosophical jargon and her preference for plain language and 'natural' sense and reason.

perception, and (2) is true because every natural action is a kind of corporeal motion (OEP 170).

What is *not* shared by every perception is that it is a kind of patterning or imitation:

> there are as many different sorts of perceptions, as there are of motions; because every particular motion has a particular perception; and though in a composed figure or Creature, some motions may work to the patterning out of exterior objects, yet all the rest may not do so, and be nevertheless, perceptive: For, as a man, or any other animal creature, is not altogether composed of eyes, ears, noses, or the like sensitive organs: so, not all perceptive motions are imitating or patterning .... (OEP 173)

If, as I argued in Section 2, patterning is Cavendish's account of how animals create something like naturalized representations, then Cavendish denies that ability to non-animal creatures. It is possible, of course, that they represent in some other way that counts as cognitive or mental, but it seems significant that she provides a detailed account of how animal bodies specifically achieve that, which is moreover specific to organs that non-animals lack.

Elsewhere, Cavendish makes clearer that we should not conclude, from the fact that animals perceive by creating representations, that this is how other things perceive. Cavendish poses this question to her account of animal perception:

> Q: *How is it possible that any perception of outward object, can be made by patterning, since patterning doth follow perception? for, howe can anyone pattern out that which he has no perception of?*

Cavendish claims that perception is necessary to ensure order, which makes it sound like it guides motion. But she also makes clear that perception, particularly in the patterning case, is caused by motions. That seems to imply that for the eyes, for example, to pattern an external object, the parts of the eyes must first perceive the object.

Given what I've argued so far, this is not strictly circular: the matter of the eyes, in rearranging to pattern an object, does perceive, but its perceptions are different from the perception of the eye and of the whole animal. However, if you are thinking of the perceptions of matter as like animal sense perceptions, you will find this account unsatisfying. If matter can perceive in the way that an animal does *without* patterning, then why does Cavendish need patterning to account for animal sense perception? She seems to be giving a corporeal-motion-based account of sense perception, but she is actually relying on some more basic capacity that matter has.

The reply to this is that the perceptions of matter are *not* like animal sense perceptions:

> I answer, Natural actions are not like artificial; for art is but gross and dull in comparison to nature: and, although I allege the comparison of a painter, yet it is but to make my meaning more intelligible to weaker capacities: for, though a painter must see or know first what he intends to draw or copy out; yet the natural perception of exterior objects is not altogether after the same manner; but, in those perceptions which are made by patterning, the action of patterning, and the perception, are one and the same.   (OEP 178)

Human seeing, or patterning, is just one human way of acting with relation to an external objects. Specifically, it involves the creation of representations of objects in animal bodies. Natural perception is not a 'seeing' or a 'knowing' in this sense.

Cavendish sometimes characterizes perception without mentioning knowledge at all, for example, as an 'exterior action, because it is occasioned by an object that is without the perceiving parts' (OEP 171). So while we don't yet know what 'knowledge' means, for Cavendish, we have a candidate way of understanding perception that does not rely on it: a creaturely perception is an action of that creature toward an external object.[12] We have no reason to think that this action always reproduces, even in a very abstract sense, the figure of the object in the perceiver, or that every perceiving creature assimilates information about what it perceives.

4.2 Matter's Perception

Cavendish defines perception as the knowledge that one part has of another part, and so far, I've treated this as the claim that perception is the knowledge that one creature has of another. But it is very important that these creatures are *parts* of the body of nature. To be part of nature, for Cavendish, is to be connected in a unique way to the other parts of nature. Parts that

---

[12] The editor of this volume asks: 'So kicking a tree is a way of perceiving it? That sounds a bit strange. Maybe it is a specific kind of action?' But for Cavendish there is only occasional causation between parts of matter. The kicker kicks, and the tree is damaged, but in fact any change in the tree is self-caused. Both are indeed perception, although kicking the tree and seeing the tree are not the same ways of perceiving it.

were not connected to each other in this way ('single parts,' as Cavendish calls such parts) would actually not be parts at all, but atoms, which is the same as to say, so many independent worlds.

An organism's perceptions are the ways that it has of orienting itself to other parts of nature. Cavendish grounds this in matter's overall tendency to orient itself toward other parts. It has this tendency because matter has part-composition structure, and it is in the nature of this structure that parts are oriented to other parts. It is also in the nature of material parthood, according to Cavendish, that there are no completely divided parts or entirely composed units. Material parthood and composition is, you might say, metaphysically unstable, and this is the most basic metaphysical structure that there is. There is no question of part-composition priority: it is precisely the sort of structured relationship in which the question of priority does not arise, and this is an example of Cavendish's non-hierarchical metaphysics and resistance to dependence relations.

Cavendish strongly associates knowledge with composition and ignorance with division: 'ignorance is caused by division, and knowledge by composition of parts' (OEP 20). To the extent that one part is divided from another, it is ignorant of that part; knowledge can only be recovered—and never completely—to the extent that the parts form a composite. Laura Georgescu has beautifully argued that we can understand Cavendishian perception as just the ground of relations between parts of a composite, and there is no reason to think of this as 'epistemic' in the usual sense (Georgescu 2021). I resist characterizing the connection between parts as a relation, but I agree that perception, for Cavendish, is the recovery of a connection between two divided parts of matter. And there is no reason to think of it as requiring thought, cognition, or consciousness.

4.3 Creaturely (Self-)Knowledge

I have offered a characterization of creaturely perception: it is the action of a creature toward other parts, which it has in virtue of being composed with them. In doing so, I put aside the question of what 'knowledge' means, for Cavendish, given that she defines perception as exterior knowledge. We must now ask what 'knowledge' means. Since Cavendish does not define 'knowledge', we'll have to look at how she uses it, starting with how she describes the knowledge that creatures have. As I mentioned in Section 2.2, Cavendish usually treats perception, or exterior knowledge, and self-knowledge, or interior knowledge, as exclusive and exhaustive kinds of knowledge. Having treated perception, let us consider creaturely self-knowledge.

A composed creature as a whole has self-knowledge, which is knowledge of itself and of its parts.

> A Whole may know its Parts...but no particular part can know its whole...I say, no particular part; for, when parts are regularly composed, they may by a general Conjunction or Union of their particular Knowledges and Perceptions, know more, and so judg more probably of the Whole; and...by the division of parts, those composed knowledges and perceptions, may be broke asunder like a ruined House or Castle.
> (OEP 138)

Self-knowledge is 'interior, inherent, innate, and, as it were, a fixt being'; it is 'fixt' in that it exists as long as the creature exists, but being dependent on the structure of the creature, it can 'alter as [its] own parts alter' (OEP 171).

This 'fixt', creaturely self-knowledge is 'the ground of particular knowledges,' or knowings, of the creature, including particular self-knowings and particular perceptions. Particular knowledges are just so many corporeal figurative motions. '[P]articular figures have a variety of knowledge, according to the difference and variety of their corporeal figurative motions' (OEP 177). The corporeal figurative motions that are possible for a creature depends upon the structure of the animal:

> [T]hough the Bell hath not an animal knowledg, yet it may have a mineral life and knowledg...and the Jack-in-a-box a vegetable knowledg...each in its own kind may have as much knowledg as an animal in his kind; onely they are different according to the different proprieties of their Figures. (PL 2.13)

> [A] tree, although it has sensitive and rational knowledge and perception, yet it has not an animal knowledge and perception; and if it should be divided into numerous parts, and these again be composed with other parts, each would have such knowledge and perception, as the nature of their figure required. (OEP 171)

> [T]he Sun, Stars, Earth, Air, Fire, Water, Plants, Animals, Minerals; although they have all sense and knowledg, yet they have not all sense and knowledg alike, because sense and knowledg moves not alike in every kind or sort of Creatures, nay many times very different in one and the same Creature. (PL 2.7)

We may ask: what is this fixt self-knowledge of a creature, beyond its structure? Canvassing these and Cavendish's many other references to creaturely self-knowledge, I think the answer must be: *nothing*. The fixt self-knowledge of a creature is just its structure. To take just one vivid example of this, Cavendish says of a man who is born without the use of his legs that 'his Leggs...have no knowledge of such Properties that belong to such Parts' (GNP 109). Similarly:

> In a Human Creature, those Parts that produce, or nourish the Bones, those of the Sinews, those of the Veins, those of the Flesh, those of the Brain, and the like, know all their several Works, and consider not each several composed Part, but what belongs to themselves; the like, I believe, in Vegetables, Minerals, or Elements. (GNP 81)

In virtue of their compositions, fish know how to swim, songbirds know how to sing, we know how to add and forage but also how to grow, reproduce, and digest; snow knows how to make crystals, how to make you cold, and how to be fun to slide on. The fixt self-knowledge knowledge that creatures have is just the way that they are; the fixt self-knowledge that our legs have of how to move is encoded in their structure. The evaluative terms Cavendish applies to this kind of knowledge are about health, regularity, harmony, and naturalness, not truth, accuracy, or detail.

All of Cavendish's references to creaturely fixt self-knowledge make sense if we understand it simply as structure, and her references to particular self-knowledges make sense if we understand them as the corporeal figurative motions that arise from the self-motion within that structure. Moreover, on my reading of Cavendish, there is nothing else that fixt self-knowledge *can* be. Given Cavendish's picture of nature in terms of self-moving, composite stuff, there is no way for a creature to 'contain information' other than in that structure. In the next sections—4.4 and 5—I argue that Cavendish's claim that matter is self-knowing, sensitive, and rational is consistent with this claim.

4.4 Matter's Self-Knowledge

Cavendish claims that self-knowledge is the 'ground and fountain of all other particular knowledges and perceptions' (OEP 176). Many such passages can be read as concerning creaturely self-knowledge in the sense described in the previous section: the self-knowledge, or structure, of creatures is what grounds their particular knowings.

But sometimes it sounds like Cavendish means something else. Sometimes it sounds like she takes self-knowledge to be some intrinsic, fundamental feature of matter, necessary to explain why composite creatures can have creaturely self-knowledge and particular knowledges and perceptions in the first place. For example:

> [S]elf-knowledge...cannot be divided from its own nature; for, as matter cannot be divided from being matter, or self-motion from being self-motion; so, neither can self-knowledge be divided from being self-knowledge; nor can they be separated from each other, but every part and particular of natural matter, has self-knowledge and perception, as well as it hath self-motion. (OEP 163)

Cavendish also writes that inanimate matter has self-knowledge, and—what amounts to the same—that matter could have lacked self-motion and had self-knowledge (GNP 12). So it seems that self-knowledge is not, like particular knowledges, derived from self-motion, but it is fundamental to matter alongside self-motion.

A number of Cavendish scholars have argued that this kind of self-knowledge should be taken literally, as a body's knowledge of nature's norms (Detlefsen 2007; Boyle 2015), or as 'know-how' (Michaelian 2009: 38). But as we have seen, Cavendish goes to great lengths to show how *particular* perceptions and knowledges are generated by self-motion. Here again, I appeal to Georgescu's detailed defense of a deflationary reading of perception and self-knowledge. A mentalistic account of self-knowledge like this, she writes, 'gets a dependency relation upside-down...self-knowledge is the ground of all particular knowledge, that is, all particular types of knowledge depend on self-knowledge, and not the other way around...On the know-how reading, we get an over-inflated concept of self-knowledge which, I believe, Cavendish does not endorse' (Georgescu 2021: 633–634). I would add to this that readings on which self-knowledge is some kind of intrinsic property or nature runs afoul of what I believe to be at the core of Cavendish's materialism: that talk of intrinsic properties is obscurantist and metaphysically indefensible. The different ways that matter can all involve its composition facts, and the ways it can act involve changing those composition facts.

So, we should not understand matter's self-knowledge on analogy with the particular knowledges and perceptions of creatures. This would include thinking of it as a kind of knowledge of norms or as a kind of know-how. These are only effects of matter's self-knowledge. So then what *is* matter's self-knowledge?

Much of what Cavendish writes about self-knowledge makes it sound like identity. This is true, for example, in the passage cited four paragraphs above, that 'self-knowledge...cannot be divided from its own nature' just as 'matter cannot be divided from being matter' (OEP 45). I believe that this is indeed the right place to start in understanding how Cavendish is thinking about matter's self-knowledge. In the counterfactual case that there were no self-motion and as a result no metaphysical structure, to say that matter is self-knowing is simply to say that it is self-identical.

In a world with parthood and composition, however, self-knowledge, precisely by being the principle of identity, also serves as the principle of composition: it is what identifies some parts with one single composite thing. For Cavendish, composition is identity, namely, the identity of some parts with one thing: 'a whole and its parts,' she writes, are 'yet are one and the same thing, several ways' (OEP 193), and 'a whole is nothing but a composition of parts, and parts are nothing but a division of the whole' (GNP 158).[13] Since there is no thing which is a single or independent part (except nature as a whole), there is no thing which is entirely self-knowing or entirely perceiving:

> As one part cannot be another part, so neither can one parts knowledg be another parts knowledg; although they may have perceptions of each other: When I speak of parts, I mean not single parts; for there can be no such thing. (OEP 196)
>
> [T]he infinite parts of nature have not only interior self-knowledge, but also exterior perceptions of other figures or parts, and their actions; by reason there is a perpetual commerce and intercourse between parts and parts; and the chief actions of nature, are composition and division, which produce all the variety of nature; which proves, there must of necessity be perception between parts and parts. (OEP 140; see also 177)

We now have a way of making sense of Cavendish's frequent claims that 'knowledge and perception...are general and fundamental actions of

---

[13] As Georgescu puts the point: 'Cavendish thus provides an account of self-knowledge and perception as metaphysical notions that allow each body to be simultaneously a whole and a relational part' (Georgescu 2021: 639).

nature' (OEP 139), without granting that matter is minded in anything like the sense that we are. Specifically, we can make sense of this claim without positing that matter does anything like animal representation. Composition and division are the general and fundamental actions of nature; self-knowledge is composition and perception results from the balance of composition and division. Perception is the capacity that a part of matter has to be oriented to the whole, in virtue of being part of it.

5. Sense and Reason

I've argued that Cavendish's claim that all creatures are perceptive and knowing does not mean that non-animals have mental states, and that her claim that matter is self-knowing does not mean that it has epistemic states like know-how or knowledge of norms. However, Cavendish also claims that matter itself is sensitive and rational. This sounds like a version of panpsychism that we might more precisely dub 'hylopsychism', following Cudworth's coinage of 'hylozoism' to describe the view that all matter has life. This section argues that Cavendish is not a hylopsychist. In Sections 5.1 and 5.2, I'll offer an account of sense and reason which is not mentalistic. In Section 5.3, I'll respond to some objections that arise from some of what Cavendish says about rational matter.

5.1 Self-Motion, Sense, and Reason

Cavendish calls sensitive and rational matter 'sensitive' and 'rational', and identifies them as the grounds of creaturely knowledge and perception. She also describes them in terms of an anthropomorphic building metaphor: rational matter is an architect, sensitive matter a laborer, and inanimate matter the building materials. It's natural to think, then, that Cavendish holds a version of panpsychism that we might call 'hylopsychism', following Cudworth's coinage of 'hylozoism' to describe the view that matter is intrinsically living. (This is a useful coinage because unlike 'panpsychism', it makes explicit that it is a claim about the nature of matter, or the physical, as opposed, say, to idealism or world-soul-ism, or to Cavendish's alleged view that all composite creatures have something like mental states.)

However, while these kinds of matter, like the Aristotelian sensitive and rational souls, they do so not because they are themselves sensing or thinking, or because they have some additional feature, beyond self-motion, that makes them suited to sensing and reasoning when they come together in certain ways ('hyloprotopsychism', perhaps?). They do so because they are self-moving; and self-motion, as Cavendish writes, is the 'Life and Soul of Nature.' Cavendish writes in the OEP: 'All parts of nature are living, knowing, and perceptive, because all are self-moving; for self-motion is the cause of all particular effects, figures, actions, varieties, changes, lives, knowledges, perceptions, etc. in nature, *and makes the only difference between animate and inanimate matter*' (OEP 191–192; my emphasis). The *only* difference between animate (which includes sensitive and rational) matter and inanimate matter is that animate matter has self-motion.

This is confirmed by Cavendish's derivation of the 'triumvirate' in the *Grounds*, where she distinguishes sensitive and rational matter from inanimate matter because they are self-moving, and distinguishes them from each other only in the degree to which each couples with inanimate matter:

> Neither can there be more than two sorts of Matter, namely, that sort which is Self-moving, and that which is not Self-Moving. Also, there can be but two sorts of the Self-Moving Parts; as, that sort that moves intirely without Burden, and that sort that moves with the Burdens of those Parts that are not Self-moving: So that there can be but these three sorts; Those parts that are not moving, those that move free, and those that move with those parts that are not moving of themselves: Which degrees are (in my opinion) the Rational Parts, the Sensitive Parts, and the Inanimate Parts; which three sorts of Parts are so join'd, that they are but as one Body; for, it is impossible that those three sorts of Parts should subsist single, by reason Nature is but one united material Body.   (GNP 66)

Cavendish ultimately argues that we are in a world with all three kinds of matter, perfectly mixed together so that every part of matter has all three capacities. The mixture is necessary to explain why change happens over time, why some things move quickly and some move slowly, and why we do not find fully animate things or fully inanimate things in the world: just things that change in some ways and stay the same in others.[14]

So, the fact that matter has 'sensitive' and 'rational' parts arises from the nature of matter combined with its relationship to self-motion, and there is

---

[14] For more detail on the mixture and its role in explaining change, see Peterman (forthcoming).

nothing mentalistic that needs to be added to explain mental phenomena. Indeed, Cavendish often writes that there are just two kinds or degrees of matter: animate and inanimate ('as for matter itself, there are no more degrees but animate and inanimate; that is, a self-moving, active, and perceptive, and a dull, passive and moved degree' (OEP 30; see also 201)). That sense and reason are just self-motion is confirmed by Cavendish's frequent claims that sense and reason follow immediately on self-motion ('wherever there is Self-motion, there is Sense and Reason'; OEP 169), that sense and reason simply are self-motion ('Sense and Reason, which is self-motion'; PL 1.10, see also PPO 1663 298), and that perception is self-motion or that self-motion is the only cause of perception ('self-motion is the action of perception, without which, no perception could be; and therefore perception and self-action are one and the same'; OEP 178).

It is easy to understand the other characterizations of sense and reason in terms of the relative encumbrance of rational and sensitive matter. Rational matter is freer and more 'penetrating' because it is not being mixed with and therefore limited by inanimate matter, so it can move in a wider variety of ways: 'The rational perception, being more general, is also more perfect than the sensitive; and the reason is, because it is more free, and not encumbered with the burdens of other parts' (OEP 166; see also 175, 181).[15]

As for the building metaphor, both the architect and the builder are self-moving and thereby create the variety-in-composition that is the house, but with different degrees of freedom. The sensitive parts of matter are laborers inasmuch as they 'bear the grosser Materials about them, which are the Inanimate Parts' (GNP 67). The architect, being unencumbered, is simply freer in his self-motions. Moreover, just as self-motion is the ultimate source of all the variety of forms and all change, an architect is the ultimate source of the form of the house and the motions toward building it. It has the power to do so because it is self-moving, which is to say, it can divide and compose:

> But yet by reason this life and soul [of Nature] is material, it is divided into numerous parts, which make numerous lives and souls in every particular Creature, but all the parts considered in general, make but one soul of

---

[15] While sometimes Cavendish describes the actions of matter as 'voluntary' or writes that they have 'free will', she writes in a number of places that 'by voluntary actions I understand self actions' (OEP 19), or unoccasioned actions.

Nature; and as this self-moving Rational Matter hath power to unite its parts, so it hath ability or power to divide its united parts. (PL 4.2)

Sensitive and rational matter are both just self-moving matter, and self-motion is the 'Life and Soul of all Creatures' (PL 4.33). Cavendish diagnoses the denial that all matter is self-moving as another case of human hubris:

> Thus some learned... are so much afraid of self-motion, as they will rather maintain absurdities and errors, than allow any other self-motion in nature, but what is in themselves: for, they would fain be above nature, and petty gods, if they could but make themselves infinite; not considering that they are but parts of nature, as all other creatures. (OEP 112)

5.2 Order

Cavendish argues that creaturely knowledge and perception is widespread because 'in all natural actions, there is a commerce, intercourse, or agreement of parts; which intercourse or agreement, cannot be without perception or knowledge of each other' (OEP 172). In order to explain widespread knowledge, perception, and order, matter must be sensitive and rational. Can we understand this order without an ordering mind or minds? Yes.[16]

It is often suggested that Cavendish connects what she calls 'order' and 'regularity' with the law-like or the typical, with conformity to kind or norm, or with predictability. But in fact Cavendish connects order at least as more tightly with *variety*: 'Order and Distinction, are Regularities' (GNP 208). Meanwhile, confusion is associated with a lack of distinction and even with similarity: '[S]everal sorts, kind, and differences of Particular, causes Order, by reason it causes Distinctions: for, if all Creatures were alike, it would cause a Confusion' (GNP 79). The importance of natural variety to Cavendish's system cannot be overstated; she constantly emphasizes the infinite variety of creatures as well as the infinite power of matter to divide and compose. She observes often that nature is 'delighted with variety' and never simplicity or predictability. In fact, she claims, 'there's not anything

---

[16] This is a very brief treatment of order, which as Boyle (2015) argues, plays a central role for Cavendish. Boyle's book is an excellent and comprehensive treatment of order in her system, although I disagree that Cavendish's reliance on order indicates fundamental thoughtful teleology.

that has, and doth still delude most men's understandings more, than that they do not enough consider the variety of nature's action' (OEP 99).

To the extent that order is associated with variety, it is very easy to explain why sensitive and rational matter, understood simply as self-moving matter, are necessary for nature to be orderly: self-motion is what is responsible for variety. Without it, the world be 'a dull, indigested and unformed heap and chaos' (OEP 207).

Now, Cavendish does sometimes suggest that variety alone is not sufficient for order, but rather a variety of 'kinds and sorts.' That does make it sound like some kind of regularity in the sense of similarity is necessary for order, and Marcy Lascano has argued that disorder is relative to kinds (Lascano forthcoming: 120–125). But as Lascano points out, we should be careful not to reify these kinds and sorts: they are just functions of similarities in organisms' bodily structures (Lascano forthcoming: 123). Moreover, Cavendish writes that there is always variety even between individuals of the same kind or sort:

> Nature is so delighted with Variety, that seldom two Creatures (although of the same sort, nay, from the same Producers) are just alike...Nature is necessitated to divide her Creatures into Kinds and Sorts, to keep Order and Method: for, there may be numerous Varieties of sorts; as for example, Many several Worlds, and infinite Varieties of Particulars in those Worlds. (G 149)

This passage also hints that Cavendish has an idiosyncratic conception of kinds and sorts. She assimilates them with worlds, and a world, for Cavendish, is something approximating a self-sufficient whole.

What this all suggests is that Cavendish associates order with a 'poise or balance' between multiplicity and unity: an orderly state is one in which there is a great variety of parts that are distinct from one another, but they are united into a whole. In fact, Cavendish often describes order precisely in this way:

> The reason that variety, division, and composition, runs not into confusion, is, that first there is but one kind of Matter; next, that the division and composition of parts doth balance each other into a union in the whole. (PL 4.3)
>
> Where Unity is not, Order cannot be. (GNP 67)

There is no need for a planning mind to ensure order.

5.3 'Rational Matter Is Really Weird'

Rational matter as I've interpreted it will strike some as too austere to do all the work that Cavendish makes it do. For example, Colin Chamberlain argues that Cavendish relies on the special capacity of rational matter to explain the phenomenological unity of some of our mental representations. To do that, one piece of rational matter must be able to have representational or at least qualitative structure that is not parthood structure: 'a single portion of rational matter can see and hear and smell and taste at the same time.'[17] For Chamberlain and others, rational matter is not just the grounds of perception but is actively perceiving.

I think it is an important part of Cavendish's materialism that there is no structure that is not the structure of matter. Chamberlain will likely agree, and reply that the structure he is describing is the structure of matter, because it is structure that matter has. And I do not want to cling too tightly to one particular interpretation of material structure. I wholeheartedly agree that, as Chamberlain has put it to me, rational matter is really weird.

However, I do not think we can simply define material structure as whatever structure matter turns out to have. The fact is that Cavendish makes many comments that assert that there is 'no variety but of parts' (OEP 18). She gives many explanations of mental life in terms of parthood structure, and is very concerned to emphasize that mental structure requires this kind of structure:

> [T]he rational soul of every particular Creature is composed of parts (I mean parts of a material substance; for whatsoever is substanceless and incorporeal, belongs not to Nature)…not any Creature can have a soul without parts…that which makes so many confusions and disputes amongst learned men is, that they conceive, first, there is no rational soul but onely in man; next, that this rational soul in every man is individable. But if the rational soul is material, as certainly to all sense and reason it is, then it must not onely be in all material Creatures, but be dividable too.
> (PL 4.2)
>
> Action, and variety cannot be without motion, division, and composition.
> (PL 4.3)

---

[17] Chamberlain (2022: 31). Cavendish's treatment of the mixture of the kinds of matter, and her insistence that there are no single parts in nature, should make us suspicious of the idea of a 'single portion of rational matter.'

Actions are divisions and compositions, and creaturely perceiving and knowings are actions.

As for the unity of experiences or of experience in general, Cavendish gives no indication that material composition is not sufficient to account for it: '[N]o Part of the Body, or Mind of a Man, knows each Part's perceptive knowledg, but by Confederacy' (GNP 107). In general, I do not take phenomenology to be an important source of data for Cavendish. It is certainly true that in some respects, 'reflection on one's own mind reveals what matter is like,' as Chamberlain nicely puts it (2022: 41). But what that reflection tells us is very basic: the mental is material and it is divisible. Beyond that, human ways of perceiving are highly dependent on the specificities of human structure and on our situation within our environment, and so we cannot simply attribute to matter whatever qualities we take ourselves to perceive it as having.

One objection to this comes from Cavendish's quality realism. Cavendish argues, for several kinds of perceptions, that if we perceive matter that way, it must be that way. For example, of those who argue that heat is not really in fire, Cavendish writes that

> They are so far in the right, that the heat we feel, is made by the perceptive motions of, and in our own parts, and not by the fire's parts acting upon us: but yet, if the fire were not really such a thing as it is, that is, a hot and burning body, our sense would not so readily figure it out, as it does, which proves it is a real copy of a real object, and not a mere phantasm.
>
> (OEP 148)

Similarly of color: 'Our optic sense could not perceive either the original, or copy of an exterior object, if it did not make those figures in its own parts: and therefore figure and color are both in the object, and the eye; and not, as they say, neither in the object, nor in the eye' (OEP 147). It is not obvious how color and heat, as we experience them, could be patterned by composition and division of parts. So you might think that Cavendish is positing some kind of intrinsic qualitative nature to matter that is at least protopsychic.

But I see no reason to think that Cavendish thinks these are protopsychic qualities. Her arguments show that they are ways that matter must be to explain our experience of them, but there is no suggestion they are any different from, say, shape either in their relationship to matter or in our ability to represent them. As for how to understand them metaphysically, they are only slightly uncomfortable for the view I am proposing. Sure, reality is qualitat*ive*—it is yellow and hot—but that does not mean that there is a metaphysics of qualities underlying that. And while I can't say exactly how color or heat qualify as 'motions,' I appeal to Chamberlain's dictum: matter is weird. But I don't think that means it is psychic or protopsychic.

6. Conclusion

I've offered an account of matter's sense and reason, and the knowledge and perception in nature, that does not rely on there being anything like mental states in matter or in all creatures. Matter is structured by parthood and composition, and it is self-moving. The actions of a part, *qua* part, are a function of its own nature, which is its 'self-knowledge' or compositional structure, and its orientation toward the composition of which it is a part, which is perception.

Humans and animals have many ways of knowing and perceiving, but among them are sense perception and conception, which, I've argued, are Cavendish's attempt to capture the distinctively cognitive. Cavendish does not deny that it is possible for some non-animals to perceive and know in this way—she expresses agnosticism about whether other kinds of creatures pattern. However, she does associate them with animal sense organs and brains, she does write that we have no reason to assume that other creatures perceive by patterning, and she does claim positively that patterning gives way to other kinds of perception in at least some creatures. The fact that other creatures do not or may not pattern makes us in no way superior to them.

Cavendish's account of sensitive and rational matter is not aimed at explaining human psychology. It is aimed at explaining natural order. Natural order requires that creatures be self-regulating, interdependent, self-moving, affective, but it does not require that matter have anything like mental states. And those capacities of creatures, Cavendish thinks, can be explained by self-motion alone.

Is Cavendish a neutral monist? I've argued that calling her a monist already does some damage to our understanding because she simply is not concerned with telling us what kinds of things or properties are possible, and furthermore she is not concerned to thereby constrain her theory of mind. Despite the alleged neutrality of neutral monism, it still begins in the assumption that 'experiential phenomena cannot be emergent from wholly non-experiential phenomena' (Strawson 2019: 24). I do not think that Cavendish is worried about this.

There may be some versions of panpsychism on which the interpretation I've suggested counts. For example, you might think that Cavendish's account of perception sounds like a kind of teleofunctionalism, and the fact that everything perceives means that there is proto-mentality everywhere. Or perhaps it is a version of biopsychism, although I think it is important that Cavendish tries to mark out animal perception and knowledge from other kinds. Or Rovelli, in a recent article, claims that twentieth-century physics vindicates a 'very mild form of panpsychism' inasmuch as

> it is not about how individual entities are by themselves. It is about how entities manifest themselves to one another... This implies that the most effective way of thinking about the world is not in terms of entities with properties, but rather in terms of systems that have properties in relation to other systems. (Rovelli 2021: 32)[18]

This sounds a lot like Cavendish, although I do not think it sounds a lot like panpsychism.

It is not important whether or not Cavendish merits the label. What is important is how to understand Cavendish's diagnosis of man's 'conceited prerogative.' Many readers of Cavendish think that our conceit is that only we have this very special capacity for experiencing and understanding nature that we find in ourselves. I think that our conceit is that it is very special. Instead, it is just one among a dazzling variety of ways that creatures interact with the world.[19]

---

[18] Cavendish also holds that matter has genuine causal powers. Mørch (2020) has recently cataloged and defended arguments that this collapses into something like panpsychism.
[19] For their extremely valuable feedback, many thanks to Colin Chamberlain, Bryce Huebner, Uriah Kriegel, Baron Reed, seminar participants at the University of Rochester, the Philadelphia Cavendish Circle, and audiences at UCSD and Johns Hopkins.

Bibliography

Works by Cavendish

OEP: O'Neill, Eileen (ed). 2001. *Observations upon Experimental Philosophy.* Cambridge: Cambridge University Press.

GNP: Thell, Anne M. (ed). 2020. *Grounds of Natural Philosophy.* Peterborough, Ontario: Broadview Press.

PL: 1664. *Philosophical Letters.* https://quod.lib.umich.edu/e/eebo/A53058. 0001.001. London.

Secondary Literature

Azzouni, Jody. 2020. *Attributing Knowledge.* Oxford: Oxford University Press.

Azzouni, Jody. Forthcoming. 'Smith, Smith and Seth, and Newton on "Taking to be True".' In Schliesser, Smeenk, and Stan, eds. *Theory, evidence, data: The philosophical legacy of George E. Smith.* Springer.

Boyle, Deborah. 2015. 'Margaret Cavendish on Perception, Self-Knowledge, and Probable Opinion'. *Philosophy Compass* 10(7): pp. 438–450.

Chamberlain, Colin. 2022. 'What Is It Like To Be a Material Thing? Henry More and Margaret Cavendish on the Unity of the Mind'. *Oxford Studies in Early Modern Philosophy* XI: pp. 97–136.

Cunning, David. 2016. *Cavendish.* New York: Routledge.

Detlefsen, Karen. 2007. 'Reason and Freedom: Margaret Cavendish on the Order and Disorder of Nature'. *Archiv für Geschichte der Philosophie* 89 (2007): pp. 157–191.

Duncan, Stewart. 2012. 'Debating Materialism: Cavendish, Hobbes, and More'. *History of Philosophy Quarterly* 29(4): pp. 391–409.

Georgescu, Laura. 2021. 'Self-knowledge, Perception, and Margaret Cavendish's Metaphysics of the Individual'. *Early Science and Medicine* 25(6): pp. 618–639.

Goldberg, Benjamin. 2017. 'Epigenesis and the rationality of nature in William Harvey and Margaret Cavendish'. *History and Philosophy of the Life Sciences* 39(2): pp. 1–23.

Jalobeanu, Dana. 2021. 'Francis Bacon's "Perceptive" Instruments'. *Early Science and Medicine* 25(6): pp. 594–617.

Jorati, Julia. 2019. 'Teleology in Early Modern Philosophy and Science'. *Encyclopedia of Early Modern Philosophy and the Sciences.* Ed. D. Jalobeanu and C. Wolfe, Springer.

Lascano, Marcy P. 2023. *The Metaphysics of Margaret Cavendish and Anne Conway: Monism, Vitalism, and Self-Motion.* Oxford: Oxford University Press.

Michaelian, Kourken. 2009. 'Margaret Cavendish's Epistemology.' *British Journal for the History of Philosophy* 17: pp. 31–53.

Peterman, Alison. 2019. 'Cavendish on motion and mereology.' *Journal of the History of Philosophy* 57(3): pp. 471–499.

Peterman, Alison. Forthcoming. 'Cavendish on Matter and Materialism.' *Oxford Studies in Early Modern Philosophy.*

Rovelli, Carlo. 2021. 'Relations and Panpsychism.' *Journal of Consciousness Studies* 28 (9–10): pp. 32–35.

Shaheen, Jonathan. 2021. 'The Life of the Thrice Sensitive, Rational and Wise Animate Matter.' *HOPOS* 11(2): pp. 621–641.

Strawson, Galen. 2019. 'A hundred years of consciousness: "a long training in absurdity".' *Estudios de Filosofía*: pp. 9–43.

18
C. A. Strong—Real Materialism, Evolutionary Naturalism, Panpsychism

Galen Strawson

There is no one to whom I can talk so ***straight*** as to Strong or so profitably... I never knew such an unremitting, untiring, monotonous addiction as that of his mind to truth. He goes by points, pinning each one definitely, and has, I think, the very clearest mind I ever knew... I suspect that he will outgrow us all, for his race accelerates, and he never stands still. He is an admirable philosophic figure, and I am glad to say that in most things he and I are fully in accord.

(James 1904: 394, 1905: 36.)[1]

The difficulty of making people believe that there is in suns and atoms anything of the nature of feeling is so mountainous that I sometimes wish I had devoted my energies to something else, such as writing poetry or helping to bring about the millennium.

(Strong 1936: v)

1. Introduction

The ethics, epistemology, and philosophy of logic and language of the first few decades of the twentieth century have been much studied. (I'll call this period the 'early analytic period', understanding the name in a wide sense.)

---

[1] When I cite a work I give the date of first publication or occasionally the date of composition, while the page reference is to the published version listed in the bibliography. In the case of quotations from languages other than English I cite a standard translation but don't always use it. I use bold italics to mark an author's emphasis and italics to mark my own.

There's been a lot less work on the philosophy of mind—with the exception of the philosophy of perception. There has, perhaps, been a sense that philosophy of mind in the early analytic period is not particularly interesting, together with a presumption that it must by now have been superseded. Both the sense and the presumption are mistaken. When one looks further into this stretch of philosophical time, and considers (for example) the intense and unremitting discussion of the so-called mind–body problem, it seems a high point for philosophy of mind, a golden period before a new twilight begins, a twilight that intensifies from about 1950 on, and falls into a strange darkness around about 1960, a darkness that has in deep ways persisted until the present day (with, let it be said, some fine lights shining out within it).[2]

Things aren't as bad as they were fifteen years ago. There's new interest in the philosophy of mind of British philosophers like C. D. Broad, Arthur Eddington, Samuel Alexander, and Bertrand Russell, and Alfred North Whitehead has always had a devoted if small following. It's mainly the American philosophers who—apart from William James—have continued to be largely ignored: among them Charles Hartshorne, Durant Drake, William Pepperell Montague, James Bissett Pratt, George Santayana, Roy Wood Sellars, Charles Augustus Strong, Donald C. Williams (C. I. Lewis has fared somewhat better, as have John Dewey and C. S. Peirce). These philosophers aren't, perhaps, card-carrying analytic philosophers, but they're all at work in the period, alongside Austrian analytic philosophers like Moritz Schlick, Herbert Feigl, and others in continental Europe.[3]

Certainly it's a myth that the issue of consciousness was not high on the philosophical agenda at that time, just as it's a myth that there was a resurgence of interest in consciousness in philosophy in the late 1990s.[4] Consciousness, understood in the standard, wide, present-day sense that covers any sort of feeling or 'experiential what-it's-likeness' or 'qualia', was in its usual place—right at the top. 'It is undoubted', Sellars writes in 1922, 'that the...mind–body...problem is, as Bergson contends, the most formidable problem that humanity can face' (286). In a reply to Strong published in the same year, Russell says that the 'main purpose' of his theory of the external

---

[2] One should also look further back, to the high days of 'German materialism' in the 1860s, and then, moving forward, include writers like W. K. Clifford, Emil Du Bois-Reymond, T. H. Huxley, Henry Maudsley, Morton Prince, Alois Riehl, G. F. Stout, John Tyndall, and many others.

[3] For a contemporary survey of analytic philosophy, see e.g. Nagel (1936): 'Specifically, I wish to report on the philosophy professed at Cambridge, Vienna, Prague, Warsaw, and Lwow' (6). Nagel himself must count as a fully paid-up analytic philosopher.

[4] See Strawson (2015).

world (including his theories of perception and of physics) 'is to fit our perceptions into a physical context,...to show how they might...become part of physics' (478)—i.e. to solve the mind–body problem. Schlick in 1925 considers 'the central position...the mind-body problem...now occupies in modern metaphysical systems' (304). 'No higher claim could be made for a theory of cognition', according to Strong in 1930, 'than that it permits solution of the problem of the relation of mind and body' (1930a: 160). 'The adequate handling of the mind–body problem [by] any philosophy...is at one and the same time a supreme test and an indication of its power' (Sellars 1938: 461). 'Nothing is more needed in philosophy at present than a correct doctrine of consciousness' (Strong 1939: 393). Pratt is amusing in 1936:

> there has never been a time when so much was written in the attempt to solve...the problem of the relation between the mental and the physical... or when those who consider this discussion an absurd waste of energy spent so much of their time in trying to prove that no one should spend any time upon it.[5]

2. Terminology

Those who want to read philosophy of mind from the early analytic period face a considerable terminological barrier, as will those who try to read our present-day philosophy of mind in a few decades' time. I think our descendants' difficulties with our work will be worse than our difficulties with the early analytic period, because we've descended into a terminological chaos, especially in the philosophy of mind, that is perhaps unsurpassed (although doubtless equalled) in the history of Western philosophy. That said, confusing differences between uses of central terms like 'consciousness', 'sense-datum', 'the given', 'experience', and 'mental' are already virulent a hundred years ago, and further difficulties arise when it comes to less familiar terms like 'ejective'[6] or 'epistemological monism';[7] not to mention

---

[5] Pratt (1936: 144); see also Hatfield (2004, 2010).

[6] Typically used to refer to 'something (viz. a sensation or mental state other than our own) which is neither an actual nor a conceivable object of *our* consciousness, but which is [assumed] to be a real existence analogous in kind to our own sensations or mental states' (*Oxford English Dictionary*).

[7] Epistemological monism 'hold[s] to the presentative rather than to the representative theory of perception' (Holt et al. 1912: 5). It is closely related to or in some versions identical with '(pan)-objectivism' ≈ Mach–James 'neutral monism' ≈ phenomenalism.

'essence' understood in Santayana's (in fact traditional) sense to mean everything there is to a thing other than its actual existence, 'the entire *what* of a thing, without its existence' (Strong 1918: 38), everything about a thing that 'can be conceived as *duplicable*' (Montague 1938: 576).[8]

Much of the terminological puzzlement flows out of a great old debate in the philosophy of perception, parts of which are being recapitulated today. On one side we find the 'New Realists' or 'neo-realists' or direct-realist 'relationalists' or naïve realists of the time. In 1912 their leading representatives published a joint manifesto—a collection of papers—called *The New Realism: Cooperative Studies in Philosophy*.[9] On the other side, the 'critical realists', with Thomas Reid and neo-Kantians like Hermann von Helmholtz and Alois Riehl among their distinguished forebears. In 1920 their leading figures also published a joint manifesto—another collection of papers—in response to the New Realists: *Essays in Critical Realism: A Co-operative Study of the Problem of Knowledge*.[10] They pointed out that they too were direct realists—even as they rightly insisted that all sensory *perception*, as opposed to bare *sensation*, necessarily involves mental representation, and, again quite rightly, that colour in the sense of what Mackie calls 'colour-as-we-see-it' (Mackie 1976: 24) is not 'out there in the world'.

3. Villa le Balze

Charles Augustus Strong (1862–1940) was one of the leading philosophers of the time. He studied under William James.[11] His first publication was in 1892, his last in 1941. He taught psychology at Columbia University from

---

[8] Meinong also opposes a thing's essence to its existence rather than to its accidental qualities: the essence of an Object is 'the *Sosein* [the total 'howness'] attaching to the Object whether the object has being or not' (Meinong 1904: 86).

[9] The contributors were Edwin Holt, Walter Marvin, William Pepperell Montague, Ralph Barton Perry, Walter Pitkin, and Edward Spaulding. The venture was probably inspired by Dewey's *Studies in Logical Theory*, 1903, composed 'with the cooperation of members and fellows of the department of philosophy' of the University of Chicago.

[10] The contributors were Durant Drake, Arthur O. Lovejoy, James Pratt, Arthur Rogers, George Santayana, R. W. Sellars, and C. A. Strong.

[11] 'Strong and I...are at it hammer and tongs all day long....I...have walked and driven with Strong and have had philosophy hot and heavy with him almost all the time.... He gains a great deal from such talks, noting every point down afterwards, and I gain great stimulation, though in a vaguer way. I shall be glad, however, on Monday afternoon, to relax...' (James 1904: 394, 1905: 36).

1903 to 1910, and moved to Italy with his daughter Margaret some years after his wife Bessie Rockefeller died. There he designed, built, and lived in Villa le Balze, a fine house in Fiesole overlooking the city of Florence in which, from 1918 on, he wrote his philosophy. My present aim is to provide a brief introduction to his work, mixed in with some theoretical proposals and terminological provisions of my own and a brief focus on the excellent R. W. Sellars.[12] Since Strong is almost completely unknown I want to *ism-atize* him—sketch his principal 'isms' as I understand them: his (1) materialism; (2) his outright (real) realism about consciousness or experience; (3) his unwavering evolutionary naturalism; (4) his wholly naturalistic panpsychism; which is, more particularly, (5) 'pure' panpsychism; (6) his direct realism about perception; (7) his critical realism about perception; (8) his definitive rejection of the so-called 'myth of the given'; and (9) his sophisticated and thoroughgoing 'enactivism'. I'll try to cover (1)–(5), his metaphysics, in this chapter, and (6)–(9), his epistemology, and in particular his theory of perception, in a companion paper.[13]

Strong is not always easy to read. His grasp of history of philosophy seems to me imperfect, and his terminology shifts somewhat, unsurprisingly, over the fifty years of his publishing career. That said, he is usually extremely clear—difficult at times, certainly, but clear—and extremely economical. I'll draw mainly on his work from 1920 on—e.g. *A Theory of Knowledge* (1923), *Essays on the Natural Origin of Mind* (1930a), 'Nature and Mind' (1930b), *A Creed For Sceptics* (1936), 'The Sensori-Motor Theory of Awareness' (1939), 'Final Observations' (1940).[14]

4. Materialism: 'χ'

C. A. Strong is, then, first,

(1) a materialist

---

[12] Sellars is not Strong's wingman. Durant Drake holds that position.
[13] 'C. A. Strong: critical direct realism, enactivism, anti-Mythism'.
[14] Anyone interested in G. E. Moore's famous 1903 paper 'The Refutation of Idealism' might begin with Strong's elegant 1905 response: 'Has Mr. Moore Refuted Idealism?' (It isn't necessary to have already read William James's no less famous 1904 response to Moore, 'Does Consciousness Exist?')

or if you prefer, a *physicalist*.[15] Both of these terms have been used in so many different ways that they're effectively useless, but one thing is certain: materialists/physicalists are *stuff monists*. They hold, that is, that everything in concrete reality is of a single fundamental kind which is the subject matter of physics and which they call 'physical':

(P)   the stuff of which everything that exists in concrete reality consists is wholly physical stuff.

A good number of twentieth- (and now twenty-first-)century philosophers have supposed, extraordinarily, and I think quite unprecedentedly in the history of philosophy, that a further view, which I call *physics-alism*, the view that

(P*)   the terms of physics can fully capture—express, convey—the nature of everything that concretely exists

is also part of (P)—physicalism. And since they see that physics can't fully capture or express the nature of consciousness (either in its present form or in any imaginable future form), they conclude that to be a materialist (or physicalist) is to deny the existence of consciousness.

In so doing they (i) contradict the previous history of the word 'materialist', and (ii) ignore the origin of the relatively recent word 'physicalist'. As for (i), the heart of philosophical materialism was always understood to be *precisely* its claim that consciousness—real consciousness, *consciousness* no less!—was wholly material. As for (ii), denial of the existence of consciousness (*ontological* reduction of the mental to the non-mental) was no part of the programme initiated under the name 'physicalism' by members of the Vienna Circle in the late 1920s. They were, after all, not crazy.[16]

(P*)—physics-alism—is a truly elementary mistake, for as Russell says 'physics, in itself, is exceedingly abstract, and reveals only certain mathematical characteristics of the material with which it deals. It does not tell us

---

[15] I follow David Lewis (1994: 293) in treating 'physicalist' and 'materialist' as synonymous, in spite of the fact that there's more to physical being than matter. So too I sometimes use 'matter' in a conventional way as a loose general term for all physical being.
[16] See Uebel (2019 and 2021) for discussions of Neurath (on *Verstehen*) and Carnap (on knowledge of other minds) that show their physicalism to be far from eliminativist in intent or in its consequences. See also Stoljar (2010: ch. 1); Strawson (2021b: 240–3).

anything as to the intrinsic [non-structural] character of this material'.[17] Even a completed unified physical theory would be 'just a set of rules and equations... a mathematical model', as Stephen Hawking says (1988: 174).

I call this the 'silence of physics', following Russell:

> Theoretical physics... lays down certain fundamental equations which enable it to deal with the logical structure of events, while leaving it completely unknown what is the intrinsic [i.e. structure-transcendent] character of the events that have the structure. We only know the intrinsic character of events when they happen to us [i.e. in having conscious experience]. Nothing whatever in theoretical physics enables us to say anything about the intrinsic character of events elsewhere. They may be just like the events that happen to us, or they may be totally different in strictly unimaginable ways. All that physics gives us is certain equations giving abstract properties of their changes. But as to what it is that changes, and what it changes from and to—as to this, physics is silent. (1959: 17–18)

There are hundreds of expressions of the point (it also has important Kantian and neo-Kantian forms). It was a commonplace a century ago but it was in effect forgotten by philosophers of mind in the second half of the twentieth century. I regret that I knew nothing of this history when I started lecturing on the philosophy of mind at Oxford in the late 1980s and making essentially the same point; I argued for 'agnostic materialism' (1994: 43), and proposed that '"physical"... is a natural-kind term (it is the ultimate natural-kind term), and we may be very wrong about the nature of the physical' (1994: 1).

The idea that (P), physicalism, is or incorporates (P*), physics-alism, is sufficient evidence of the chaos built into current philosophical use of the word 'physical'. The principal axis of confusion is well described by Daniel Stoljar (2001). A massive and immediate gain in clarity can be achieved simply by replacing 'physical' by 'physics' used as an adjective, or by 'physics-attributed', wherever possible, e.g. in phrases like 'physical description' or 'physical property', to get 'physics description' and 'physics-attributed property'. *There is no such thing* as 'the physical description of the physical' if one is a realistic physicalist in the core sense of (P), someone who uses

---

[17] Russell (1927: 10). I've inserted 'non-structural' before 'intrinsic' because Russell uses 'intrinsic' (not unnaturally, but questionably) in a way that supposes that a thing's structure is not part of its intrinsic character.

'physical' in the straightforwardly metaphysical sense and therefore holds that consciousness (real qualial consciousness) is wholly physical. There is of course the *physics* description of the physical, and there is also the *everyday* description of the physical in non-experiential terms (shape, size hardness, and so on), but these are a different matter.

We have good reason, then, to avoid the word 'physical' as far as possible. The confusion it carries is so deeply entrenched, and so contagious, that I don't expect to be understood,[18] so I'm going to try to avoid it as far as I can by saying that a materialist/physicalist is someone who holds that concrete reality is wholly χ. 'χ' simply replaces '(the) physical'. (I began by using 'ϕ' rather than 'χ', because 'ϕ' indirectly echoed '*ph*ysical' ('$\phi\upsilon\sigma\iota\kappa o\varsigma$'), but it began to seem better to have an unconnected term.)

On the present terms, then, Strong is a χ-ist: a stuff monist who uses 'χ' as a name for the single kind of fundamental stuff that this universe is wholly made of.

—'If 'χ' simply replaces '(the) physical', how can it help?'

The aim, again, is simply to minimize the use of the actual word 'physical', and the errors—the profoundly disabling confusions—built into most of its uses in this area of philosophy.

—'What errors?'

The central error, I think, is the error of supposing that the term 'physical' has a certain kind of *positive descriptive* content when used in philosophy to refer to the fundamental stuff—the fundamental *stuff nature*—of concrete reality.

—'What do you mean by "stuff" and "stuff nature" '?

---

[18] I was signing copies of *Mental Reality* at the American Philosophical Association meeting in Boston in December 1994, at the request of Teri Mendelssohn of the MIT Press, and with some embarrassment, when David Chalmers, whom I'd just met, and who'd read *Mental Reality* in typescript the previous year, told me that he didn't think my use of 'material(ism)' and 'physical(ism)'—the 'object' use, in Stoljar's (2001) terms—would ever catch on. Well, he has been proved right—and I don't think things will change. And yet it would only be a matter of returning to an earlier understanding, and it could remove a great deal of the confusion in the debate.

I use 'stuff' as a theoretically uncluttered, general term for concrete being that abstracts from all traditional categorial descriptions: 'event', 'process', 'substance', 'object', 'intrinsic categorical property'. All these things are stuff. The relevant intrinsic categorical properties are those of which the following is true. (i) Their nature isn't captured by any true logico-mathematico-structural descriptions of concrete reality (including shape descriptions: shape isn't stuff, stuff comes in shapes). (ii) They're everything in virtue of whose concrete existence those descriptions are true. They constitute the 'stuff nature' of concrete reality.

—'Even if there's something in what you say about physics, it's too sweeping. For physics describes the universe as, specifically, spatiotemporal, and to describe something as spatiotemporal is to give a positively descriptively contentful account of its nature that is essentially more than merely numerico-structural.'[19]

So it may seem. But we go beyond the actual descriptive content of physics insofar as we associate any sort of everyday or otherwise intuitive or imaginative picture of what spatiotemporality is with our logico-mathematical representation of spatiotemporal features of reality. We cannot legitimately claim to know the ultimate, not mathematically characterizable nature of the reality we theorize as spacetime in physics, and experience as space and time in everyday life.[20]

Suppose we put this point aside, and allow that the ascription of spatiotemporality to reality, as a fundamental characteristic, does have some positive descriptive non-mathematico-structural content. If we do, we must then quickly stress—it may surprise some—that the ascription of spatiotemporality doesn't give any support to the view that the fundamental stuff nature of reality is *non-experiential*, either wholly or even only in part.

This last point is difficult, at least initially, but it is what matters here, because the term 'physical' (which is now being taken to be backed by a physics that incorporates some more than merely structural picture of what spatiotemporality is) is standardly taken to have positive descriptive content of a sort that does allow us to take it as given that χ is in its fundamental nature something non-experiential. This quickly leads many to think—for

---

[19] Russell invokes this idea in his answer to Newman's objection to the theory he put forward in *The Analysis of Matter* (Newman 1928; Russell 1928: 393–4).

[20] This point is independent of the fact that some leading present-day cosmologists (e.g. Arkani-Hamed) believe, with Kant, that fundamental reality as it is in itself is not spatiotemporal.

example—that materialism is incompatible with panpsychism, although David Lewis is among those who note that this isn't so: 'a thesis that says [that] panpsychistic materialism...is impossible...is more than just materialism' (1983: 36). It also leads many self-declared materialists/physicalists to full-on eliminativism about consciousness, by a somewhat different route than the route already described (the false route according to which (P) entails (P*)).[21]

In fact there's no scientific justification for the assumption that χ is fundamentally non-conscious. This is so even when we grant that it's fundamentally spatiotemporal, and even when we grant that our intuitive (logico-mathematical-representation-transcending) picture of spatiotemporality gets something fundamental right about the nature of spatiotemporality. There is in fact a strong scientific case against the assumption of the fundamental non-consciousness of χ—in spite of the fact that physics gives us no insight into its (non-structural) intrinsic nature. It's a matter of inference to the best explanation (see the end of §9).

If there's no scientific justification for the view that χ is fundamentally non-conscious, why is it so widely believed? What holds it so fiercely in place in the philosophical community? Nothing but a mighty wall of habit, built high and deep into the standard philosophical use of 'physical', which remains grounded in its everyday use. The habit has deep roots in our natural everyday distinction between the physical and the mental ($\approx$ conscious), but it has no place in science or metaphysics—*philosophy*. Nor is it ineradicable. A hundred years ago, as remarked, many philosophers (including notably Whitehead, Eddington, Calkins, Russell, Strong, Drake) were quite clear that it was a mistake, whether or not they agreed with winners of the Nobel Prize for Physics like Erwin Schrödinger—'the material universe and consciousness are made out of the same stuff' (1931: 16)—or Louis de Broglie—'I regard consciousness and matter as different aspects of one thing' (1931: 15). David Lewis's teacher D. C. Williams made the point nicely: 'the materialist, holding that the world is matter, is not wedded to any one doctrine of the nature of matter...the supposed logical difficulty in saying that a mind is matter (or that matter is mind) is as specious as that in saying that a spoon is silver' (1944: 425, 423–4). The *reference* of the term 'matter' (or 'physical stuff') is sufficiently fixed before we begin. We can

---

[21] The idea is likely to be that if reality is in its fundamental nature wholly and utterly non-conscious, then it is non-conscious through and through, because (a thought Strong endorses, as do I) you can't get consciousness from complex spatiotemporal arrangements of wholly non-conscious stuff, however complex.

sufficiently indicate it, if we wish, by pointing at the world—anything we like. We can kick a stone, like Samuel Johnson 'refuting' Berkeley, or consider a cloud or an experience.[22] We may then as philosophers—metaphysicians—go on to wonder about the intrinsic stuff nature of matter. We may wonder in particular what we can best conclude from the fact (it's beyond all reasonable doubt) that conscious experiences like our own are neural goings-on, which are universally recognized as physical.

Some overt or (more likely) covert eliminativists about consciousness may think they can agree with Williams when he allows that there's no difficulty in the idea that mind is matter. They would, however, be wrong, because Williams, like Strong, is a full-on realist about consciousness, a *real* realist in a sense I'm about to define.

5. The Reality of Consciousness: 'ψ'

Strong is a materialist. He is also, like all materialists until the later nineteenth century, and almost all materialists until about 1960, and almost all materialists even now (even within the analytic-philosophy community, which is of course far larger than the analytic-philosophy-of-mind community),

(2)   a full-on *realist* about consciousness.

He is as I like to say a *real* realist about consciousness, a qualia realist, if you like, an outright realist about the phenomenological or 'qualial' character of seeing colour, tasting tastes, feeling sleepy, listening to a story, and so on; a realist about consciousness of a sort that is most simply specified by saying that he holds the same view about the subjective experiential character of everyday life that everyone holds before they do philosophy (or psychology, or information science, or...).

Here I'm using the word 'consciousness', as before, in the familiar wide way currently standard in philosophy to mean any sort of feeling or 'sentience' at all, however primitive: 'experiential what-it's-likeness' of any sort, anything with any sort of intrinsic phenomenological content. This is *not*

---

[22] 'I refute it THUS', said Dr Johnson in 1763 (Boswell 1791: 292), kicking the stone and inspiring a poem (called 'Epistemology') by Richard Wilbur: 'Kick at the rock Sam Johnson, Break your bones: But cloudy, cloudy is the stuff of stones' (Wilbur 1950).

how Strong (or Calkins, or, usually, Russell) uses it. Like many in his time, he uses 'consciousness' (and 'awareness'—he treats the terms as synonyms) more narrowly. All conscious states are of course and necessarily phenomenologically contentful states, on his view, but they're also essentially intentionally directed at—essentially registrative of—something other than themselves, and are in that sense essentially cognitive, conscious *of* something, in a way in which absolutely primitive feeling-states aren't.[23]

This raises a question about the best way to use 'consciousness' and 'awareness' and their cognates in this chapter. I'm going to continue to use them in the wide present-day, 'qualia-realist' way. I'll give 'consciousness' an asterisk when I use it in the Strong–Calkins–Russell–etc. way and where there is some possibility of confusion. The relation between the two uses is simple. It is taken for granted that consciousness* essentially involves consciousness—Calkins doesn't need to assure us of her qualia realism when she speaks concisely of 'consciousness, the relation of mind to its objects' (1925: 408)—but consciousness needn't involve consciousness*: bare or mere consciousness needn't be consciousness* *of* anything (i.e. of something other than itself).

Having reserved 'consciousness' for consciousness*, Strong uses various words for what I'm calling 'consciousness'. His primary words are 'feeling', 'feelings' (1930a *passim*), 'of the nature of feeling' (1936: v), 'sentience' (1930b: 323), 'sentience, or a raw material out of which animal sentience is made' (1930b: 324); also 'psychical', the 'psychical' (e.g. 1923: 10), 'psychical, that is, of the nature of feeling' (1940: 237). He speaks variously of 'sensations' (1930a *passim*), of 'a sensuous stuff' (1930a: 193), of 'sensation' in the mass-term use (1930a: 99), of 'sentience or sensibility' understood as 'a purely affective state' (1940: 240). In these last cases he uses 'sense'-related words in a standard way as maximally general terms for consciousness (experiential what-it's-likeness) that don't entail possession of sense organs that detect features of the environment.

---

[23] Russell notes the double use when he speaks of consciousness 'conceived either as a relation to objects, or as a pervading quality of psychical phenomena' (1921: 9). The claim that primitive feeling-states lack intentionality needs qualification, because any experiential episode necessarily (trivially) has some phenomenological character or other, say F, and in being a token occurrence of phenomenological character F, it is necessarily (trivially) an experience *of* the phenomenological-character-type F. In this simple (and disputable) sense, all possible experiential episodes may be said to be intentional episodes. This point is closely connected to what G. E. Moore had in mind when he argued in his 'Refutation of Idealism' (1903) that even the simplest sensational state is essentially of or about something other than itself, and is indeed essentially of or about something non-mental (blueness, in his example, considered—if you like—as an abstract object).

In Strong's terms, then, all consciousness* necessarily involves feeling/sentience, but feeling/sentience in its simplest form is not a matter of consciousness* at all. It's not a matter of 'thought, or awareness, or anything implying a subject-object relation' (1940: 240). It is, precisely, 'feeling without awareness', i.e. without consciousness* of something other than itself (1930a: 34). It is 'anoetic, non-cognitive' (1936: 57), 'anoetic sentience' (1936: 46). It is in Asian philosophical terms essentially 'non-dual', 'experience in which there is no distinction of subject and object' (1923: vii).[24]

I think it's sufficiently clear what Strong has in mind, but it's still hard to avoid terminological confusion. For this reason I'm going to adopt another new general term—'ψ'. 'ψ' stands for consciousness in the wide, experiential what-it's-likeness sense. It applies to absolutely all forms of experiential what-it's-likeness—the whole domain of the psychical in Strong's sense.[25]

Since ψ can exist in extremely primitive forms, as just remarked, I propose to introduce a separate term—'ψ*'—for what one might call *interesting* ψ: the complex kind of ψ that (we may assume—I do) only ever arises as a result of processes of evolution by natural selection. I'm going to take it that all ψ* involves *cognition* (and indeed consciousness*) of some sort—without attempting to specify the minimal case of cognition. All ψ* is ψ, but not all ψ is ψ*. Almost all if not all ordinary adult human experience is ψ*.

6. Montague v Strong

Strong's 1939 paper 'The Sensori-Motor Theory of Awareness' is a reply to W. P. Montague's 1938 review of Strong's 1936 book *A Creed for Sceptics*. The two philosophers belong to different epistemological schools, critical realism (Strong) and neo-realism (Montague), but—as Strong says—'we are not far apart in our metaphysics, for we both think that the *brain-process is not*

---

[24] 'I have chosen "sentience"', Strong writes, 'which, coming as it does from *sentire*, may be reasonably held to signify feeling without awareness' (1930a: 34). A point against the choice of this word (and also 'sensuous') is that it's closely connected with 'sensation', which implies sensory organs, which are not only products of evolution but also—essentially—devices of consciousness or awareness in Strong's cognitive sense. If one does choose to use 'sentient' as one's word for basic consciousness, one has to make it clear that sentience is not to be thought of as essentially requiring sensory organs of the (biological) sort we normally associate with sensation.

[25] I'm happy for there to be a natural link between 'ψ' and 'psychical' (unlike 'χ' and 'physical'). Note that 'the psychical' has nothing to do with the supernatural; 'psychical' is simply a general term for experiential what-it's-likeness. When James endorses the principle 'No psychosis without neurosis' (1890: 133), he isn't making a psychiatric claim that most believe to be false. The principle simply says that all conscious goings-on involve neural goings-on.

only physical but also psychical in its nature' (1939: 393). They're both *mind–brain identity theorists*. They are, that is (here one needs to be very clear), *genuine* mind–brain identity theorists; they are in other words mind–brain identity theorists who are real realists about ψ.[26] They're not fake mind–brain identity theorists, like most of those who have recently called themselves mind–brain identity theorists, and who are in fact eliminativists about ψ. (You can't claim to identify two seemingly different things if you deny the existence of one of them.)

So far so harmonious. 'But', Strong continues (I've added asterisks to his uses of 'conscious' and 'aware(ness)' in the quotation)

> we mean something different by 'psychical'. He [Montague] means *conscious**...I mean by 'psychical' something much more modest. I am anxious to avoid the conclusion that wherever there is energy there is consciousness*.[27] I cannot believe that the sun and stars, or that atoms, are conscious*; and yet there must be something in them out of which consciousness* can be evolved.[28] This something I call **sentience**, *without being able to form a very clear idea of it*. It differs from consciousness* in two respects. First, consciousness* is awareness*, and awareness* involves a subject-object relation, but there is no subject-object relation in [mere] sentience; it is aware* neither of other things nor of itself. It is not cognitive, but purely affective. Secondly, in the sun and stars, in waves and rocks, it is unorganized...; but in the brain it is organized and in virtue of its organization takes on functions. Even then, the sentience [considered just as such] contains no subject-object relation, it is not aware* **intrinsically**. Awareness* is a *function* which sentience acquires when it is organized.
> (1939: 393–4)

Do not try too hard to imagine sentience (1934: 317).

Here Strong follows his teacher William James. Both are of course full-on realists about ψ, i.e. consciousness, but they use the word 'consciousness' to

---

[26] Their clearest and most impressive predecessor, in the American tradition of genuine identity theorists, is I believe Morton Prince; see e.g. Prince (1885): 'states of mind and neural activities are identical ....It must be distinctly understood that it is not a question of translation or *transformation* at all, but of *identification*. Physical changes are not transformed into states of consciousness, nor are there "two processes" which occur "side by side" in the same person. *There is only one process*' (pp. 44, 65–6). See also Prince (1891).

[27] This is a reference to a very remarkable and specific feature of Montague's view.

[28] There must be 'a raw material out of which animal sentience is made' (1930b: 324).

mean consciousness*.²⁹ They use it, in fact, as a name for a *function* that ψ states can have, or (in effect equivalently) a *relation* that they can help to constitute. What function? The (evolved, adaptive) function that a particular ψ state ψ_1 has (fulfils) when my being in it constitutes my being aware of something, standing in the relation of intentional contact with something—a cow or a tree, say. ψ_1 is in performing this function a *cognitive* state, i.e. a state whose existence essentially involves a *making of mental contact with*, a mental registration of or knowing of, something other than itself.³⁰

In Strong's and James's use, then, the word 'consciousness' *doesn't name any fundamental quality of being*—unlike 'ψ', or 'consciousness' in its standard present-day wide philosophical use. Once again, it simply names a function that certain ψ states may have, a function that they fulfil precisely when they are states that put organisms like ourselves into a relation of intentional contact with something (they are in so doing ψ^* states, not merely ψ states).

This is a terminological decision with which Russell comes to agree, and it's helpful, here, to compare Russell's similarly limited use of 'mental', according to which any goings-on that are properly called 'mental' are ψ^* goings-on. Most today take it to be true by definition that any sensation— any ψ—whatever, however primitive, is *ipso facto* a mental occurrence. This is not true in Russell's scheme, in which mind, mentality, is something essentially cognitive, essentially systematic, essentially ψ^*. It's something that *essentially* involves 'mnemic' phenomena (i.e. memory phenomena, which are necessary for recognition, conceptualization, and so on), something essentially more complex than mere sensation, which may be merely ψ. If a vivid sensation were somehow to occur in complete isolation from anything else it would not be a mental phenomenon in any sense, for Russell, because it would be merely ψ, not ψ^*. If on the other hand it were part of a human perceptual experience, it would indeed be something indeed mental, part of a ψ^* occurrence.

---

²⁹ See, famously, James (1904), written to confute Moore (1903). Moore offered a picture of consciousness as a kind of arena or medium or 'menstruum' (James 1904) in which particular contents could occur; something which was ontologically over and above its contents.

³⁰ A large part of 'the present confusion of psychological theory is due to treating (1) feelings [and] (2) functions or activities...as "mental" or "psychical" in the same sense' and using some blanket term, such as "consciousness" or "experience", which covers them all without distinguishing them; in disregard of the fact that they belong to entirely different categories' (Strong 1930a: 8).

7. Evolutionary Naturalism

Russell's use of 'mind' and 'mental' is not uncommon in his time, and this, for readers today, is another potential—all too likely—source of misunderstanding. I learnt to use 'mental' in the maximally inclusive way when I took up philosophy in the 1970s, but the more restricted use is undeniably attractive. One of its great advantages is that it allows one to say, plausibly, that all *mind*—all ψ^*—is a product of evolution, although *qualiality*—ψ, *sentience*—is not. ψ is something that had to be there already for mind as we know it to evolve. ψ had to be there already to be put to adaptive use, and so become ψ^*.

This is Strong's view. All ψ^*, all consciousness in Strong's sense, all consciousness*, all awareness of things, is a product of evolution. Strong is as remarked

(3) an evolutionary naturalist

and his evolutionary naturalism is the core of his commitment to panpsychism (the topic of the next section). The overall theoretical situation seems to him—and to James, and Prince, and many others at the time, and many today, including me—clear. We know from our own case that at least some of the consciousness*—awareness of the environment—that exists on earth is intrinsically ψ-involving or qualial in character. The question is this: How (on earth) did this happen—unless ψ was already around?

It's not just that it would have required *radical emergence*, of a sort posited nowhere else in science, for ψ to emerge from stuff that was in itself wholly non ψ. There's a further consideration that we can bring out if we temporarily abandon any semblance of methodological naturalism and suppose that such radical emergence is after all possible. For if we do do this, we're still left with a Very Large Question: if ψ did indeed somehow emerge from something wholly and utterly non-ψ, *why* did it do so? What possible plausible explanation can we give? It's an old thought that it's not possible to give a specifically *evolutionary* explanation of the existence of ψ—of why adaptive, fitness-enhancing sensitivity to the environment like ours is ψ rather than non-ψ. We didn't need *to feel pain or pleasure*, the standard argument goes, in order to avoid or pursue what it's good for us to avoid or pursue, we just needed the right behavioural reactions: no ψ needed. We already have ψ-less machines that can survive in hostile environments and identify different wines far more accurately than any human being.

There's a large irony here. Some philosophers think that the impossibility of explaining the existence of ψ in evolutionary terms constitutes a further argument against its existence. But this is the wrong way round: since ψ certainly exists, the impossibility of explaining its existence in evolutionary terms shows that it must have been there before any evolution took place. It had to be there already for awareness of the environment to evolve in the particular ψ-involving or qualial (technicolour, stereophonic, etc.) way it did.

In general, evolution can only work with what it finds, and this is what happened: already existing ψ was pressed into service in the concrete implementation of the magnificent multimodal adaptive function which is consciousness*. The problem of giving an evolutionary explanation of the existence of ψ disappears.[31]

Suppose we grant this. What can we know of ψ in its primordial state? Not much, according to Strong. Basic 'sentience must not be conceived too much after the model of human feeling' (1930a: 189):

> the notion of sentience [= ψ] is difficult to form—evident though the need for it is if consciousness is to arise naturally and not by a sort of miracle. There must be something in…matter at large which permits the formation of animal organisms that feel. I do not pretend that I can imagine it; but I can conceive it with sufficient exactness, by thinking that it is like my own [mental] nature, with all organization removed.   (1939: 395)

We should I think be satisfied with Strong's caution in this regard.

8. Panpsychism, Archepsychism

We see, then, that Strong is

(4)   a *panpsychist*

in addition to being a materialist and a real realist about ψ. He holds, in the words of the *Oxford English Dictionary* definition of panpsychism, and with

---

[31] Suppose that there could be a universe in which there is no ψ, and in which increasingly sophisticated and living creatures nevertheless come to exist by processes of evolution by natural selection. Here we may suppose that something behaviourally/functionally equivalent to much of our consciousness*-involving mentality has evolved without involving any ψ.

Margaret Cavendish in 1664, and with many—most?—truly rigorous naturalists,[32] that 'there is an element of consciousness in all matter'—all physical being, all χ in the present terms.

This initial definition of panpsychism—which we can restate as

there is an element of ψ in all χ

—leaves open the possibility that χ also has certain non-ψ intrinsic categorical properties, or as I shall say from now on—using the word 'quality' to denote only intrinsic, categorical, stuff-constituting properties—certain non-ψ qualities.[33] And this appears to be Cavendish's view:

> in all parts of nature there is a commixture of animate and inanimate matter: sense and reason, or sensitive and rational corporeal motions...are all one thing with [i.e. are identical with] animate matter...and can no more quit matter, then matter can quit motion.
>
> nature is altogether material...thoughts, ideas, conceptions, sympathies, antipathies,...natural life, and soul, are all material.[34]

One way to express Cavendish's view is to say that while she takes ψ to be a *fundamental and ubiquitous* quality of χ, present in even the most basic forms of χ, she doesn't take it to be the only fundamental quality. If we define *archepsychism* as the view that

ψ is among the fundamental qualities of χ

(*arche* signalling fundamentality) we can call Cavendish's view *ubiquitous archepsychism* in order to distinguish it from all-out or *pure* panpsychism. Ubiquitous archepsychism holds that ψ is a fundamental quality of all χ, but it doesn't rule out the possibility that χ also has non-ψ qualities. On

---

[32] 'Qualia...must...be understood as aspects of nature. That is our commitment to naturalism—the philosophy that asserts that all that exists is part of the natural world science studies' (Smolin 2013). Many self-styled 'naturalists' today are fundamentally anti-naturalistic.

[33] It's unfortunate that the extremely general term 'quality' (Aristotle's third category) has recently come to be used in analytic philosophy of mind in a way that suggests that it applies specially (or even perhaps only) to experiential or phenomenal (conscious) properties. This contributes considerably to the terminological chaos.

[34] Cavendish (1664: 98–9, 12).

these terms, all panpsychists are ubiquitous archepsychists, but the converse is not true.

We can also, it seems, distinguish non-ubiquitous from ubiquitous archepsychists. The non-ubiquitists may (for example) think that all *electrical* phenomena are ψ phenomena and indeed that all ψ phenomena are electrical phenomena. In this case they will presumably hold that while the existence of electrons involves ψ, the existence of neutrinos does not; and go on to claim that ψ is *fundamental* but not *ubiquitous*. It's not, however, clear that this position is compatible with a properly field-theoretic conception of the nature of fundamental particles. (In the final analysis, it's not clear that a consistent panpsychism can stop short of all-out panpsychism.)[35]

9. Strong's panpsychism

Strong's panpsychism is stronger than Cavendish's. He's what one might call a

(5) a *pure* panpsychist.

He holds that the stuff of reality (in this universe at least) is entirely ψ: that $[\chi = \psi]$.[36] He's orthodox among the philosophical panpsychists of his time in having naturalistic and Occamical grounds for his view, and he is as already remarked principally motivated by his unusually clear-eyed *evolutionary naturalism*.[37]

I say that his view is Occamical. He agrees with Eddington when the latter says, so mildly, that it 'seems rather *silly*' for a materialist (a real materialist, a materialist who is a realist about ψ) to assume χ (matter) to be 'something of a so-called "concrete" nature inconsistent with ψ, and then to

---

[35] I endorse archepsychism in *Mental Reality*, arguing that a real (realistic) materialist must at the very least be a non-ubiquitous archepsychist (1994: 60–2).

[36] This is a statement of quality identity, or equivalently stuff-type identity (see Strawson 2021a for an argument that all concrete stuff is concrete quality and conversely).

[37] William James was not the first to observe that evolutionary naturalism more or less obliges a real materialist to accept some form of archepsychism—even as he articulated his famous (but by no means original) challenge to one form of it in the shape of the 'combination problem' (1890: 151–2, 162). James finally stood up to his own challenge in a charming passage in *A Pluralistic Universe* (1909: ch. 5), a book in which he anticipates field-theoretic conceptions of reality.

wonder where the ψ comes from'.³⁸ I have recently, however, learnt to put the point in a different way, and to say, with the Buddhists, not that Strong wields *Occam's razor*, but that he upholds *the Principle of Lightness*, which 'dictates that we choose the "lighter" of two competing [empirically equivalent] theories' (Siderits 2007: 44).

Strong, then, is a *panpsychist materialist*: 'my panpsychism', as he says, 'is only a revised materialism' (1930b: 327). He endorses the then commonplace point (see §4) that physics has nothing (or almost nothing) to say about the intrinsic non-numerico-structural nature of physical reality, i.e. χ. The fact that physics leaves open the question of the non-structural 'stuff nature' or 'stuff being' of χ immediately makes some version of panpsychism the best (Lightest) hypothesis for a materialist, given that we know with certainty that ψ exists and is an entirely natural phenomenon, and given that we find no reason anywhere else in science to posit radical emergence of the sort that would be required to get ψ from unadulterated non-ψ. Inference to the best explanation closes the deal.

To see the force of this argument, one has to overcome various deep thought blockers. First among them, perhaps, is our natural everyday conception of what we think of as physical things—tables and chairs, rivers and mountains. For most of us it takes work and time to come to see that possession of non-experiential *properties* like spatial extension doesn't entail possession of non-ψ *qualities* (i.e. intrinsic categorical *stuff-constituting* non-ψ properties).³⁹ Still less does possession of non-experiential *properties* like spatial extension exclude possession of fundamental ψ qualities.

10. Panpsychism and Power

Two versions of panpsychism are available at this stage, as remarked: all-out strong (Strongian) panpsychism, i.e.

(i) $[\chi = \psi]$

---

³⁸ Eddington (1928: 259), substituting 'ψ' for Eddington's standard Cartesian use of 'thought' to mean consciousness.

³⁹ There's no entailment even given our ordinary everyday conception of the spatial; see e.g. Strawson (2020: 330). The point was quite widely accepted in the eighteenth century, but is still difficult given a standard Western education (*nb*. 'entail' has a non-semantic use: 'to bring on by way of necessary consequence' *OED*).

or some weaker Cavendishian panpsychism, i.e.

(ii) $[\chi = \psi + \omega]$

—where 'ω' denotes some unknown but non-ψ stuff. And now that $[\chi = \psi]$ is in place as an expression of Strongian panpsychism (materialist pure panpsychism), I will sometimes use '$\psi\chi$' (or '$\chi\psi$') instead of 'χ' or 'ψ' for the same single fundamental quality-stuff that, according to Strong, they all three denote; depending on context.[40]

(i) is plainly Lighter than (ii), but (ii) offers relief to those who think, naturally if unwarrantedly, that they can know for sure that ψ can't constitute a star or a nuclear explosion (or indeed a piano), because it isn't—so to say—*solid* or *substantial* or *forceful—powerful*—enough. One may allow, with Strong, that 'sentience is force' (1936: 46). More generally, one may—must—agree with Plato, Leibniz, Schopenhauer, and thousands more that to concretely exist is *ipso facto* to have power; that possession of categorical being is also and *eo ipso* possession of power being. One may also agree with Locke, Newton, Mørch, and others (and contrary to Hume) that we have direct experience of ψ as possessing power in our experience of agency, of desire, of pain, and so on.[41] Even so one may think that 'mere feeling' just hasn't got the *clout* to be the fundamental intrinsic nature of all the uproariousness of matter.

Is there any way to weaken the attraction of this last thought? It may perhaps help a little, if only in a crabwise manner, to look at a small glass of water (say 8 fluid ounces), and reflect that the existence of the water, i.e. a small portion of χ, call it χ_1, is the existence of enough energy to power the city of Los Angeles for three months.[42] We may then naturally say that there's something very remarkable (to us) about the being of χ_1—what one might call its 'power being'—that is not given to us in the appearance of χ_1. In the same general way, we may suppose that there's something very

---

[40] Given the way I use 'χ' and 'ψ', let me say that I follow Descartes, Spinoza, Kant, and others (against Aristotle) in taking the relation between an *object* at any given time and the totality of its *intrinsic categorical propertiedness* (its *qualitiedness*) at that time to be *identity*: there is at bottom no real distinction between qualitativity and stuffhood or substance: all qualities are stuff, all stuff is quality. Note (I'm pessimistic about being understood) that there is no conflict between this view and the fact that something that we identify as the same object or substance over time can change its qualities over time (see e.g. Strawson 2008, 2021a).

[41] See e.g. Locke (1689: §2.21.4); Mørch (2017, 2020).

[42] Assuming 8 US fluid ounces of water = ~236.59 grams = ~5,906 Gigawatt hours (thanks to Brad Saad).

remarkable (to us) about the power being of some particular portion of human ψ, call it ψ_1 (a two-second experience as of a cow standing under a tree) that is not experientially given to the person whose experience it is. We may suppose this even though the case of ψ_1 is epistemologically very different from the case of χ_1, in that there is at least something about the intrinsic nature of ψ_1 that is fully known in the experience of having it, i.e. its phenomenological character (I call the water and the experience 'χ_1' and 'ψ_1' respectively for convenience; both are of course $\psi\chi$).

Suppose ψ_1 is my experience. Whatever else may be said about it, it's a portion of χ ($\psi\chi$), which has a physics and a neurology description as well as a phenomenological description, and has (or consists of) enough energy to power the city of Los Angeles for a certain period of time. Plainly this last property of ψ_1 isn't evident to me in having it. It isn't evident to me even though I believe that the categorical being of a concrete entity like ψ_1 is strictly metaphysically identical with its power being. Equally plainly, then, I don't know everything there is to know about the being or nature of ψ_1 in having it, even though there's something absolutely fundamental about it that I do know, something of which it's true to say that the having is the knowing.[43]

11. Complexity and Simplification

There's another thing I don't know about ψ_1, according to Strong, who is I believe right again. I'll mention it only very briefly here, because it's complicated and needs separate treatment. It relates to the respect in which ψ_1—my cow-experience—is the upshot of a process he calls 'simplification', simplification of astonishingly complex and intricate $\psi\chi$ goings-on in the brain that lead up to and also include ψ_1.[44] We can give pretty good and interesting descriptions of these microcomplexities in neurological terms, and also in physics terms, but we have no access to any description of them in phenomenological terms. In developing—shaping—the $\psi\chi$ of the central control

---

[43] I discuss this issue further in Strawson (2006: 249–62). The knowing in question is non-propositional 'knowledge by acquaintance'.

[44] Strong settles on the term 'simplification' (or 'summation') after surveying a number of other suggestions: 'contraction' (Bergson), 'compression' (Balfour), 'condensation' or 'fusion' (Holt); see Strong (1930a: 30–1, 63–4). He could endorse Andy Clark's vivid description, in 'I am John's Brain', of the vast gap between the character of our experience and the neurophysics description of the functioning of the brain (Clark 1995).

systems of separately embodied self-propelling animals like ourselves into adaptively optimal phenomenological 'GUIs' or 'graphical user interfaces', evolution necessarily hides its workings. It conceals the unsimplified nature of $\psi\chi$ from us. At one point Strong proposes that the process involves 'summation': 'in a sum the elements disappear; but they are lost only to view, and still have their effect in determining the total quantity.... The common characteristic of all cases of this process is that we are aware of a whole without being aware of its parts'.[45]

This is arguably Leibnizian in spirit, and equally—although Strong probably doesn't know it—Nietzschean. But what particularly marks Strong's account is its *enactivism*. Where Bergson (for example) attempts to explain the simplification process principally 'by means of memory', Strong aims to 'show that the agency concerned is not memory, but *action*. We are unaware of the parts because we do not react to them, or are unable to react to them' (1930a: 64). If it had been for some reason adaptive for us to be able to react to smaller elements, we would have been sensitive to them.

I think both Bergson and Strong are partly right—once it is granted that evolution has done all the preparatory work. There is a great deal more to be said about this. Here let me note that the idea of simplification is related to the so-called combination problem for panpsychism: how can unitary, integrated experience of the kind that is adaptive for singly embodied creatures like ourselves be a function or product or aspect of the multifarious intricacies revealed by and neurological descriptions, and *a fortiori* physics descriptions, of the brain? How can it be part of what such multifarious intricacies *are*? I find myself incapable of being worried by the combination problem, but those who are worried may I think safely rely on Orgel's Second Rule: 'Evolution is cleverer than you are'. Sensitivity to the environment was experiential right from the start, on the present view, and coevolved with the evolution of bodily form in the direction of maximum efficacy—maximum effective simplicity.

To Orgel's Second Rule the worriers can add 'the silence of physics' (physics' silence on the question of the intrinsic *non*-structural nature of χ), and the fact that understanding of the *structural* nature of χ is very imperfect; and draw great encouragement from the predominance of fundamentally field-theoretic accounts of χ. Certainly, before reaching any conclusion, they

---

[45] Strong (1930a: 64). Strong suggests that ψ_1 may also be thought of as an *appearance* of the vast number of $\psi\chi$ elements that show up in the physics and neurology descriptions of the processes in my brain that are ψ_1. This raises difficulties that are I believe tractable given an appropriately field-theoretic conception of $\psi\chi$.

should look carefully at electromagnetic field theories of consciousness as developed by Susan Pockett and others.[46]

I set out some of the details of Strong's enactivism in 'C. A. Strong: critical direct realism, enactivism, anti-Mythism', the paper mentioned in §3. Here I will end by introducing Strong's near contemporary R. W. Sellars (1880–1973), the father of Wilfrid Sellars, in order to make a further remark about the connection between evolutionary naturalism and panpsychism.

12. R. W. Sellars

Sellars *père* is, like Strong, a real materialist, a realist about ψ, and a passionate evolutionary naturalist. Using the word 'consciousness' in the current wide way to mean any ψ, he has the same desire as Strong, not only in his book *Evolutionary Naturalism* but throughout his long career: to 'render *intellectually conceivable* the presence of consciousness in the organism' (1922: 288). He also sees what this implies—'we must enlarge our conception of the physical' (313). But he rejects Strong's panpsychism.

I think that Sellars and Strong disagree about panpsychism partly because Sellars is confused about what it is, especially early on (at one point he thinks, quite wrongly, that 'the panpsychist is a phenomenalist' (1917: 181, 262), but also because he can't see how ψ could possibly have the clout of matter, for reasons considered in §10. Panpsychism, he says,

> must make plausible the structure of the brain and the massive properties and relations of the physical world. Mental contents, as I am aware of them or as I introspect them, seem to me incapable of bearing this burden.
> (1922: 318)

> Panpsychism must, I take it, be dismissed, because consciousness is not substantival enough to meet the demands of the categories of external knowledge. Nothing corresponding to nervous structure and mass can be discovered in it. It is more like a qualitative dimension of integral activities of an emergent order. (1932: 475)

This, for him, rules out 'Strong's magnificent attempt to carry panpsychism through' (Sellars 1932: 296). It does leave room for Cavendishian panpsychism,

---

[46] See e.g. Pockett (2012). For a good review article, see Jones (2013).

ubiquitous archepsychism, and also some species of non-ubiquitous archepsychism, but Sellars remains resistant to panpsychism across the board, partly perhaps because the term has for him certain associations that he can't shake off. This doesn't, however, prevent him from recognizing that 'panpsychism must be considered a species of naturalism' (1927: 218), or from holding that 'the psychical is of the very texture of the functioning brain' (1922: 319).

What can realistic evolutionary naturalist materialists like R. W. Sellars do, once they reject any form of psychism or panpsychism? They don't have much room to manoeuvre. It seems that they have to assume some sort of radical emergence of the ψ from the wholly non-ψ—presumably in the course of biological evolution. This, accordingly, is what Sellars does, at least so far as I understand him (I haven't read all his work). Strong, by contrast, thinks, with William James and others, including me, that any such appeal to emergence is irredeemably at odds with a fully naturalistic attitude—apart from facing the further problem mentioned in §7 (the evolutionary inexplicability of ψ).

R. W. Sellars is a beautifully honest thinker, like Strong, and he's constantly preoccupied with the possibility of panpsychism. He feels obliged to return over and over again to his reasons for not accepting it (even as late as 1960, when he is 80, in a paper called 'Panpsychism or Evolutionary Materialism') while developing a positive account of ψ as a wholly physical 'variant' of χ that I don't fully understand. Why does he speak 'of consciousness as a variant? Because', he says,

> I do not think of it as a stuff so much as an ever-changing qualitative component of the functioning of the brain. It is here that I differ from panpsychism. But it is a variant which has for us a unique status, for in it alone are we conscious, in it alone are we on the inside of nature as conscious beings. (1927: 225)

'On the inside of nature'. This fine phrase is Sellars' way of expressing Russell's view that 'we know nothing about the intrinsic quality of physical events *except when these are mental events that we directly experience*' (Russell 1950: 153), and recurs throughout his writings:

> in consciousness we are literally on the inside of being in the case of our brains. *Consciousness is a qualitative dimension of being characteristic of this high level of emergent evolution.* (Sellars 1929: 487)

> Consciousness is the qualitative dimension of a brain-event. It is the patterned brain-event as sentient. It is because of its status that we, as conscious, participate in the being of brain-events. Here, and here alone, are we, as conscious beings, on the inside of reality. It is not a question of equative identification, as with Mr. Russell and the panpsychists generally, but of something more subtle, something intrinsic to synthetic action-patterns or wholes in the brain.[47]
>
> Scientific knowledge, while a disclosure of pattern in an abstracted reproductive fashion, never samples physical existence in the sense of *participating* in it. In such knowing, genuine as it is, we are never literally on the inside of external objects intuiting, or experiencing, their particular 'go', their life and substantial being.... In his own consciousness [by contrast], each of us is on the inside of his own brain. (1938: 471–2)

Panpsychism is still ruled out, but it's not clear how far Sellars is from Strong when he writes that

> I have never taken the term ['emergence'] mystically but have made it ***rational*** by connecting it with the rise of new [physical] relationships and organization.[48] I believe that consciousness emerges ***with*** nervous organization for the reason that I hold it to be intrinsic to it.... As to what ***content of being*** physiological events have below this level, we can have no intuitive knowledge because we cannot participate in them. But I see no reason to hold that such events do not contain an internal content of a qualified sort, perhaps some dimly felt urgency.... If we decide that, in the human organism at least, consciousness is a feature of the content of cerebral events intuited by us because we participate in it, then we are allowed to speak of consciousness as a ***unique co-emergent*** with nervous organization. Out of what internal ***content of being*** it flashes we cannot say, for the simple reason that it is our only contact with the content of existence. We have a right to assert that physical systems are not vacuous in content even though we cannot peer into their being but only gain descriptive knowledge of their structure and behavior. (1938: 483–4)

This is panpsychism, by Strong's lights.

---

[47] Sellars (1932: 414). There is a promising connection here to the electromagnetic field theories of consciousness cited in the previous footnote.

[48] On this, see Brian McLaughlin's (1992) important discussion of British emergentism.

13. Conclusion

There is a great deal more to say about Charles Augustus Strong.[49] There is, in particular, a lot more to say about his epistemology, and in particular his (philosophical) theory of perception—I don't know of a better one. For the moment, I hope that this opinionated introduction to the more metaphysical parts of his work will be of interest. He deserves a new hearing. He's one of the very best philosophers of the twentieth century.[50]

References

Boswell, J. (1791/1906) *The Life of Samuel Johnson* vol. 1 (London: Dent).

Calkins, M. (1925) *The Persistent Problems of Philosophy*, 5th edition (New York: Macmillan).

Cavendish, M. (1664) *Philosophical letters: Or, modest reflections upon some opinions in natural philosophy* (London).

Clark, A. (1995) 'I Am John's Brain', *Journal of Consciousness Studies* 2/2: 144–8.

de Broglie, L. (1931) 'Interviews with Great Scientists: No. 8—Prince de Broglie', *The Observer*, 8 February: 15.

Eddington, A. (1928) *The Nature of the Physical World* (New York: Macmillan).

Hatfield, G. (2004) 'Sense Data and the Mind–Body Problem', in *Perception and Cognition*, ed. R. Schumacher (Paderborn: Mentis): 305–31.

Hatfield, G. (2010) 'Mandelbaum's Critical Realism', in *Maurice Mandelbaum and American Critical Realism*, ed. Ian Verstegen (London: Routledge, 2010): 46–64.

Hawking, S. (1988) *A Brief History of Time* (New York: Bantam Books).

Holt, E. B., Marvin M. T., Montague W. P., Perry, R. B., Pitkin, W. B., and Spaulding, E. G. (1912) 'Introduction', in *The New Realism: Cooperative Studies in Philosophy*, ed. E. Holt et al. (New York: Macmillan).

James, W. (1904/2002) 'Letter to Alice Howe James, April 12, 1904', in *The Correspondence of William James*, vol. 10 (London: University Press of Virginia).

James, W. (1905/2003) 'Letter to Alice Howe James, May 13, 1905', in *The Correspondence of William James*, vol. 11 (London: University Press of Virginia).

---

[49] There is a useful introductory piece by Klausner (1967).
[50] Thanks to David Builes, John Greenwood and Uriah Kriegel.

Jones, M. (2013) 'Electromagnetic-Field Theories of Mind', *Journal of Consciousness Studies* **20/11-12**: 124-49.

Klausner, N. (1967) 'Charles A. Strong: Realist and Panpsychist', *The Monist* **51**: 267-83.

Lewis, D. (1983/1999) 'New Work for a Theory of Universals', *Papers in Metaphysics and Epistemology* (Cambridge: Cambridge University Press).

Lewis, D. (1994) 'Reduction of Mind', in *Papers in metaphysics and epistemology* (Cambridge: Cambridge University Press).

Locke, J. (1689-1700/1975) *An Essay concerning Human Understanding*, ed. P. Nidditch (Oxford: Clarendon Press).

Mackie, J. L. (1976) *Problems from Locke* (Oxford: Oxford University Press).

McLaughlin, B. (1992) 'The Rise and Fall of British Emergentism', in *Emergence or Reduction? Essays on the Prospects of Nonreductive Physicalism*, ed. A Beckermann, A. H. Flohr, and J. Kim (Berlin: Walter de Gruyter).

Meinong, A. (1904/1960) 'The Theory of Objects' ('Über Gegenstandstheorie'), trans. I. Levi, D. B. Terrell and R. M. Chisholm, in *Realism and the Background of Phenomenology*, ed. R. M. Chisholm (Glencoe, IL: Free Press, 1960): 76-117.

Montague, W. P. (1938) 'Mr. C. A. Strong's *Creed for Sceptics*', *The Journal of Philosophy* **35/21**: 572-80.

Mørch, H. (2017) 'The Evolutionary Argument for Phenomenal Powers', *Philosophical Perspectives* **31/1**: 293-316.

Mørch, H. (2020) 'The Argument for Panpsychism from Experience of Causation', *The Routledge Handbook of Panpsychism*, ed. W. Seager (London: Routledge).

Nagel, E. (1936) 'Impressions and Appraisals of Analytic Philosophy in Europe I', *The Journal of Philosophy* **33**: 5-24.

Newman, M. (1928) 'Mr. Russell's "Causal Theory of Perception"', *Mind* **37**: 137-48.

Pockett, S. (2012) 'The Electromagnetic Field Theory of Consciousness: A Testable Hypothesis about the Characteristics of Conscious as Opposed to Non-conscious Fields', *Journal of Consciousness Studies* **19/11-12**: 191-223.

Pratt, J. B. (1936) 'The Present Status of the Mind-Body Problem', *The Philosophical Review* **45**: 144-66.

Prince, M. (1885) *The Nature of Mind and Human Automatism* (Philadelphia: Lippincott).

Prince, M. (1891) 'Hughlings-Jackson on the Connection between the Mind and the Brain', *Brain* 14/2-3: 250-69, https://doi.org/10.1093/brain/14.2-3.250

Russell, B. (1921) *The Analysis of Mind* (London: George Allen and Unwin).

Russell, B. (1922) 'Physics and Perception', *Mind* **31**: 478–85.

Russell, B. (1927) *The Analysis of Matter* (London: George Allen and Unwin).

Russell, B. (1928/2009) 'Letter of April 24 to Max Newman in B. Russell', *Autobiography* (London: Routledge).

Russell, B. (1950/1956) 'Mind and Matter', *Portraits from Memory* (New York: Simon and Schuster): 145–65.

Russell, B. (1959) *My Philosophical Development* (New York: Simon and Schuster).

Schlick, M. (1925/1974) *General Theory of Knowledge*, 2nd edition, trans. A. E. Blumberg with an introduction by A. E. Blumberg and H. Feigl (New York: Springer-Verlag).

Schrödinger, E. (1931) 'Interviews with Great Scientists: No. 4. —Prof. Schrödinger', *The Observer*, 11 January: 15–16.

Sellars, R. W. (1922) *Evolutionary Naturalism* (New York: Russell & Russell).

Sellars, R. W. (1927) 'Why Naturalism and Not Materialism?', *Philosophical Review* **36**: 216–25.

Sellars, R. W. (1929) 'Critical Realism and Substance', *Mind* **38**: 473–88.

Sellars, R. W. (1932) *The Philosophy of Physical Realism* (New York: Macmillan).

Sellars, R. W. (1938) 'An Analytic Approach to the Mind-Body Problem', *The Philosophical Review* **47**: 461–87.

Siderits, M. (2007) *Buddhism as Philosophy* (Indianapolis, IN: Hackett).

Smolin, L. (2013) 'Free Will, Determinism, Quantum Theory and Statistical Fluctuations: A Physicist's Take', *Edge*, 8 July, https://www.edge.org/conversation/carlorovelli-free-will-determinism-quantum-theory-and-statistical-fluctuations-a

Stoljar, D. (2001) 'Two Conceptions of the Physical', *Philosophy and Phenomenological Research* **62**: 253–81.

Stoljar, D. (2010) *Physicalism* (New York: Routledge).

Strawson, G. (1994) *Mental Reality* (Cambridge, MA: MIT Press).

Strawson, G. (2006) 'Panpsychism? Reply to Commentators, with a Celebration of Descartes', in *Consciousness and Its Place in Nature*, ed. A. Freeman (Thorverton: Imprint Academic): pp. 184–280.

Strawson, G. (2008) 'The Identity of the Categorical and the Dispositional', *Analysis* **68**: 271–82.

Strawson, G. (2015) 'The Consciousness Myth', *Times Literary Supplement* **5839** (27 February): 14–15.

Strawson, G. (2017) 'Physicalist Panpsychism', in *The Blackwell Companion to Consciousness*, ed. S. Schneider and M. Velmans, 2nd edition (New York: Wiley-Blackwell).

Strawson, G. (2020) 'What Does "Physical" Mean?', in *The Routledge Handbook of Panpsychism*, ed. W. Seager (London: Routledge): 317–39.

Strawson, G. (2021a) 'Identity Metaphysics', *The Monist* **104**: 60–90.

Strawson, G. (2021b) '"Oh You Materialist!"', *Journal of Consciousness Studies* **28/9–10**: 229–49.

Strawson, G. (forthcoming) 'C. A. Strong: critical direct realism, enactivism, anti-Mythism'.

Strong, C. A. (1905) 'Has Mr. Moore Refuted Idealism?', *Mind* **14**: 174–89.

Strong, C. A. (1918) *The Origin of Consciousness: An Attempt to Conceive the Mind as a Product of Evolution* (London: Macmillan).

Strong, C. A. (1923) *A Theory of Knowledge* (London: Constable).

Strong, C. A. (1930a) *Essays on the Natural Origin of Mind* (London: Macmillan).

Strong, C. A. (1930b) 'Nature and Mind', in *Contemporary American Philosophy: Personal Statements*, ed. G. P. Adams and W. P. Montague, vol. 2 (London: George Allen and Unwin).

Strong, C. A. (1934) 'A Plea for Substantialism in Psychology', *The Journal of Philosophy* **31**: 309–28.

Strong, C. A. (1936) *A Creed for Sceptics* (London: Macmillan).

Strong, C. A. (1939) 'The Sensori-Motor Theory of Awareness', *The Journal of Philosophy* **36**: 393–405

Strong, C. A. (1940/1941) 'Final Observations' *The Journal of Philosophy* **38**: 233–43.

Uebel, T. (2019) 'Neurath on Verstehen', *European Journal of Philosophy* **27**: 912–38.

Uebel, T. (2021) 'Carnap, Knowledge of Other Minds, and Physicalism', *Philosopher's Imprint* **21/34**: 1–27.

Wilbur, R. (1950/2006) 'Epistemology', *Collected Poems 1943–2004* (New York: Harcourt).

Williams, D. C. (1944) 'Naturalism and the Nature of Things', *Philosophical Review* **53**: 417–43; reprinted in D. C. Williams (1966) *Principles of Empirical Realism* (Springfield, IL: Charles C. Thomas): 212–38.

Index

Ach, N. 164–5, 168, 173, 186
acquaintance 267, 388, 453
affect 113, 116, 119–23, 125, 136, 141, 179, 233–4, 237, 279, 290–1, 382, 428, 443, 445 *see also* emotion
agency 17, 95, 102–3, 159, 452, 454
Akins, K. 65, 69, 81–2, 130
Allen, K. 194, 218
Anderson, J. 4, 5, 26
Antony, L. 108, 126
aphantasia vii, 131–55
Araujo, S. d. F. 158, 172, 186
Armstrong, D. 160, 186
Aronowitz vii, 3
attitude viii, 46, 112–20, 125, 127–30, 197–8, 202–3, 225, 241–61, 266, 268, 282, 290, 294, 393
    implicit 107, 112, 120, 122, 126–30, 268 *see also* bias, implicit
    pro viii, 241, 243, 257
    propositional 93, 233, 293, 337
Averill, E. 80–2
Aydede, M. 186, 263, 268–9, 276–7, 281, 290, 292
Azzouni, J. 413, 430

Bayne, T. 147, 151–4
Barlassina, L. 279, 290, 292–3
Batty, C. 275, 278, 291, 293
belief 3, 6, 10, 16–17, 38, 88–9, 93, 109–11, 125, 133, 147, 194, 219, 235, 244, 305–6, 310, 333–4, 362
Benaji, M. R. 112, 114–15, 122, 126, 128
Berger, J. 88, 128
bias vii, 13, 17–19, 23–6, 87–9, 93, 98–101, 107–29, 147, 171–2, 185
    implicit 107, 111, 117, 123–9 *see also* bias, unconscious
    unconscious vii, 87, 104, 107–8, 111–26
Block, N. J. 78, 83, 88, 95–103, 106, 127, 130, 266, 268, 273, 281, 286, 288, 293, 299, 302, 311, 317
Blomkvist, A. 141, 151

Blumenthal, A. 157–8, 186
Bodenhausen, G. V. 119–20, 127–8
Bordini, D. viii, 263, 290–1, 293
Bourget, D. 321–2, 326–7, 332, 336
Boyle, D. 393–4, 419, 424, 430
Boyle, R. 401, 413
Bradley, R. 3, 27
brain in a vat 294, 309–10, 330, 354–6
Bramble, B. 241, 245, 259, 262
Brandom, R. 78, 83–4
Brentano, F. 160, 187, 324–5, 336, 353
de Broglie, L. 441, 458
Bühler, K. 164–6, 173, 187
Burge, T. 59–65, 73–4, 78–9, 83, 91–5, 102–6, 123, 127
Byrne, A. ix, 74–6, 83, 271, 293, 308, 317, 352, 360–5

Calkins, M. 441, 443, 458
Camp, E. 225–7, 232–6, 238
Campbell, J. 61, 83, 191, 218, 268, 293
Canguilhem, G. 40–2, 52
Carruthers, P. 88, 127, 133–4, 140, 147–9, 151–2, 290, 293
Carson, T. 254, 262
categories 26, 74–6, 80, 85–6, 112, 181–2, 185, 356, 382, 393, 455
    perceptual 66–9, 72
Cavendish, M. vi–ix, 367, 369–70, 377–431, 449–52, 455, 458
Chalmers, D. J. 193, 218, 233, 238, 266, 271, 286, 293, 326, 336, 439
Chamberlain, C. 426–30
Chirimuuta, M. 69, 81, 83
Chisholm, R. 323, 336
Chomsky, N. 60, 79–81, 83, 85, 223, 238
Churchland, P. S. 59, 83, 392, 395
cognition ix, 3, 29, 32–9, 44–5, 51, 65, 89, 91, 112, 121, 153, 186–7, 319, 378, 380, 388, 392–4, 399, 416, 434, 444, 446
cognitive phenomenology *see* phenomenology, cognitive

cognitive science 29–33, 37, 39, 50–1, 77, 82, 89, 180
Collins, J. 75, 79, 83
color/colour 66–8, 74–84, 86, 91–4, 275, 278, 293, 299, 303, 308–9, 313–16, 341, 355, 357, 361, 365, 407, 427–8, 435
  perception of 57, 65–9, 73–83, 91–4, 130, 275, 278, 308–9, 313–16, 350, 442
Comte, A. 162, 169–70, 174–6, 183, 187
consciousness 87–91, 96–9, 102, 104–7, 111, 144, 148–9, 156–63, 169, 174, 176, 181–4, 191, 263, 267, 269, 288, 290, 292, 300, 302, 308, 310, 320, 327–32, 336, 386, 389, 410, 416, 433–49, 451, 455–7
  phenomenal 132–3, 135, 146–7, 180, 265, 336
  science of viii, 158–9, 180–6
  sensory 300, 302, 305, 310, 327
content 57, 65, 74, 77–9, 82, 87–93, 97–8, 101–11, 113, 115, 118, 120, 122–6, 132, 135, 144–50, 161, 168, 170, 177–9, 222–33, 236–8, 249, 266, 271–9, 289, 299–302, 306, 310, 318–36, 347, 353–4, 360–2, 385, 391–3, 408–9, 439–43, 446, 455, 457 *see also* intentionality, representation
  unconscious vii, 87–90, 97, 106–7, 118–19, 124, 126, 147
Conway, A. 384, 395–6, 431
correspondence vii, 57, 64, 68–9, 73–82, 332
Cova, F. 37, 39, 52
Cowles, H. vii, 29, 47, 52
Crane, T. 191, 198, 218, 266, 273, 286, 293
Cudworth, R. 386, 388, 395, 421
Cunning, D. ix, 369, 380, 385–6, 395, 399, 430

Dainton, B. 377, 385, 390, 395
D'Ambrosio, J. viii, 219, 228, 239
Danziger, K. 158, 164, 172, 176, 187
Daston, L. 35, 40, 46, 48, 51–2
Dawes, A. 140–2, 144, 151–2
De Houwer, J. 110, 123–4, 127
Debus, D. viii, 191, 199, 218
Dennett, D. C. 6, 27, 103, 127
Deonna, J. 289–90, 294
Descartes, R. ix, 377–83, 386–7, 395–6, 401–2, 405, 413, 452, 460
desire 6, 8, 93, 102, 105, 193–4, 219, 231, 235, 237, 241, 244, 246, 252, 325, 452

Detlefsen, K. 395, 410, 419, 430
Devitt, M. 72, 75, 83, 85
direct realism *see* realism, direct
Douglas, H. 31, 36, 52
Dretske, F. I. 263, 267, 271, 294, 321, 326, 336
dualism 373, 375, 379, 388, 403
Ducasse, C. J. 323, 337
Dupre, G. vii, 57
Durkheim, E. 42–3, 52, 55
Duncan, S. 399, 430

Eddington, A. 433, 441, 450–1, 458
Egan, F. 80, 83–4
Egré, P. 37, 39, 52
emergence ix, 369–71, 376, 429, 447, 451, 455–7
emotion 42, 134, 194, 219, 233, 235, 237–8, 289–90, 390 *see also* affect
evolution 25, 69, 78, 305, 432, 436, 444, 447–8, 450, 454–6
experience 88, 99, 112–13, 122, 132, 141, 157, 160–85, 200, 204–5, 241–61, 263–92, 339–50, 370–5, 378, 389–90, 400, 427, 434–40, 443–6, 452–6
  cognitive 132, 140, 143 *see also* phenomenology, cognitive
  perceptual viii, 177, 191–9, 206, 211–17, 263, 267–74, 280, 288–9, 320, 446 *see also* perception
  sensory vii–ix, 131–2, 143, 150, 299–306, 308–36, 339, 352–3, 358, 361–4
  spatial ix, 178, 339
  subjective 88–90, 99, 116, 144
  transparency of *see* transparency of experience
  visual 132, 160, 264–5, 269, 282, 285–9, 308, 339, 352–7
experience machine 192–5
externalism 80, 263, 266–8, 271–7, 285–8, 327, 341, 349 *see also* internalism

Farkas, K. 278, 282, 294, 303, 305, 307, 315, 317, 321, 323, 337, 364
Faw, B. 136, 152
Feldman, F. 241, 250, 262
Fodor, J. A. 59–61, 71, 76, 78–9, 84, 103, 127, 267, 294, 326, 337
Foucault, M. 41–2, 52
French, C. 191, 198, 218, 268, 294

INDEX 465

Freud, S. 129, 386, 396
Frey, C. 278, 291, 294

Gallistel, C. R. 59, 63, 84
Gawronski, B. 110, 112, 114–21, 127–8
Georgescu, L. 416, 419–20, 430
Glaton, F. 11–12, 19, 41, 43, 53, 131, 152
Gentler, D. 4–5, 27
Gow, L. 263, 269, 273–5, 278, 294
Greenwald, A. G. 112, 114–15, 122, 126, 128

Hacking, I. 40–3, 51, 53
Hahn, A. 114–17, 120–3, 128, 130
Hahn, M. 69, 81–3, 293, 307
Halligan, P. W. 96–7, 129
hallucination 77, 198, 214–15, 301, 304, 309, 311, 314, 319–20, 357
Hardin, C. L. 68, 75, 84
Harman, G. 78, 84, 263–8, 271–7, 285, 288, 294, 313
Hatfield, G. 158, 172, 174, 186, 434, 458
Hawking, S. 438, 458
Haybron, D. M. 241, 245, 262
Hayward, M. K. 279, 293
Heathwood, C. 241, 244, 246, 250, 254–5, 262
Hilbert, D. 74–6, 83, 316–17
Hitchcock, C. 34, 37, 53
Horgan, T. M. 133–5, 150, 152, 266, 271, 286, 294, 321, 327
Horn, L. 231–2, 239
Howell, J. L. 113, 117, 128
Howes, A. 4, 7–11, 27
Hume, D. 250–1, 371, 376, 385–7, 396, 452
Hurlburt, R. 135, 152

Icard, T. 10–13, 22, 27, 37, 39, 53
illusion 63, 76, 92, 94, 117, 126, 137–8, 214, 301, 310, 314–15, 319–20, 357, 364
imagination v, viii, 5, 131, 133, 136–9, 169–70, 196–7, 219–37, 387, 400, 404, 407, 409
information 8, 10, 13–14, 17, 21, 24, 33, 36, 58, 60–4, 67–8, 73, 80–2, 90–5, 98, 101, 105–8, 119, 122, 125, 156, 159, 162–3, 170–2, 233, 400, 405–6, 413, 415, 418, 442
intelligence ix, 136, 381, 386–8, 399
intention 16, 162, 165–70, 174

intentionalism 300–2, 305, 318, 321–2, 325–8, 331–2, 336 see also representationalism
intentionality 90, 325–6, 328, 332, 353, 443 see also content, representation
phenomenal 79, 271, 275, 286, 321, 354
internalism 10, 73, 79–80, 263, 266–77, 286, 288, 341, 346–9 see also externalism
introspection viii, 16, 134, 145–51, 156–68, 172–5, 180, 184–6, 199, 254, 258, 263, 265–6, 270–1, 274–86, 300–1, 305–6, 319, 333–5, 351, 357, 361
introspectionism 157, 164, 186
Irvine, E. 89, 129, 159, 185, 187

James, W. 432–6, 444–7, 450, 456, 458
Jiang, Y. 98, 102, 106, 129
Johnson, G. vii, 77, 82, 84, 87, 107–11, 122, 125, 129

Kahane, G. 241, 245, 262
Kant, I. 46, 162, 187, 329, 435, 438, 440, 452
Keleman, D. 33, 48, 53–4
Kennedy, M. 263, 281, 285, 294
Kentridge, R. W. 99, 129–30
Keogh, R. 137–9, 152–4
Kind, A. 263, 268–70, 273, 281, 286, 288, 290, 295
Klein, U. 46, 54
Klotz, W. 104, 129
Knobe, J. vii, 29, 34, 37–9, 51–5
Kominsky, J. F. 34, 37, 39, 53–4
Kosslyn, S. 131, 153, 158, 188
Krickel, B. 88, 104, 129
Kriegel, U. 26, 57, 82, 88, 116, 123, 129, 134, 151, 153, 186, 198, 203, 205, 208, 216, 218, 225, 238, 266, 271, 286, 295, 302, 321–2, 325, 327, 337, 429, 458

Langland-Hassan, P. 140, 152–3, 235, 237–9
Lascano, M. 425, 431
Leibniz, W. G. 343, 371, 379, 386, 388, 396, 411, 452, 454
Lenoir, T. 33, 35, 54
Levine, J. 147, 153
Lewis, D. 337, 437, 441, 459
Lin, E. 245, 252, 259, 262
Loar, B. 78, 85, 271, 282–3, 286, 295, 302–5, 307, 327

Locke, J. 383, 396, 452, 459
Lombrozo, T. 28, 33–4, 54, 56
Lormand, E. 131, 133, 153
Lycan, W. 65, 85, 275, 278, 290–1, 295
Lyons, W. 161, 187

McDowell, J. 197–8, 218
McGinn, C. 376, 397
Mackie, J. 435, 459
Madva, A. 112, 118–19, 123, 129
Marbe, K. 164–5, 173, 187
Marr, D. 80, 85
Marshall, J. 96–7, 129
Martin, M. G. F. 191, 199, 218, 222, 239, 263, 268, 271, 285, 295
Masrour, F. 278, 282, 295
Materialism ix, 369, 373–8, 393, 401, 403, 419, 426, 432–3, 436–42, 448–52, 455–6 *see also* physicalism
matter ix, 369–70, 373, 375, 377–84, 399–406, 410–29, 437, 441–2, 448–52, 455
Meinong, A. 435, 459
Melnyk, A. 377, 390, 397
memory 24–5, 93, 103, 116, 136–7, 156–7, 162, 165–70, 175, 180–5, 199, 404, 407, 409, 446, 454
Mendelovici, A. ix, 76, 79, 85, 266, 271, 279, 286, 290, 295, 302, 318, 321–2, 325, 327, 336–7, 352–5
mental representation *see* representation, mental
Michaelian, K. 405, 419, 431
Mitchell, J. 290, 295
Molyneaux, B. 282, 295
monism 369–70, 373–7, 401, 403, 428–9, 434, 437, 439
Montague, M. 134, 153
Montague, W. P. 433, 435, 444–6, 458–9, 461
mood 203, 212, 268, 279, 281, 290
Moore, G. E. 263, 287, 295, 310–11, 317, 337, 341, 436, 443, 446, 461
Mørch, H. 429, 452, 459
More, H. 375, 385–6, 397
Müller, G. E. 156–9, 163–72, 180, 183–7
Munton, J. 124–5, 130

Nagel, E. 433, 459
naïve realism *see* realism, naïve

Nam, S. 220, 239
Nanay, B. 143, 153
naturalism 16, 299–301, 321–2, 326, 356, 432, 436, 447, 449–50, 455–6
Neumann, O. 104, 129
Newell, A. 59, 80, 85
Newman, M. 440, 459–60
Nichols, S. 149, 151, 153
Nier, J. A. 116–17, 130
Nietzsche, F. 386, 397, 454
Nozick, R. 192–5, 210, 218

Overgaard, M. 159, 181–5, 188

panpsychism ix, 369–72, 376–7, 399–400, 403, 421, 429, 432, 436, 441, 448–57
Papineau, D. vi–vii, ix, 282, 295, 297, 299, 308–52
Parfit, D. 254, 262
Pautz, A. ix, 311, 315–17, 326–7, 337, 339–41, 344–9, 351–2, 356–61
Peacocke, C. 222–7, 230–4, 239, 299, 302, 339, 341–4, 347, 351
Pearson, J. 137–9, 151–4
Pearson, K. 41–2, 54
Perception vii–ix, 62–77, 80, 133, 138–9, 156, 160, 178–9, 181, 191, 199, 212, 265, 267, 271, 280, 288–90, 299–301, 319–20, 340, 357, 378–9, 393, 399–400, 404–29, 433–6, 458 *see also* experience, perceptual
  color *see* color/colour, perception
  speech 57, 66–75, 79, 82
  unconscious vii, 87–91, 96–108, 113–14, 118, 124–5, 143, 181
  visual 62, 90–6, 109, 120, 286
Pereplyotchik, D. 75, 85
Peterman, A. ix, 383, 397, 399, 401–3, 409, 422, 431
Peters, M. A. 102–3, 130
Phenomenology viii, 135, 150, 191, 241–61, 264, 269, 273–92, 304, 309, 313, 335, 353–6, 362, 390, 426, 442–3, 453–4 *see also* consciousness, phenomenal
  cognitive vii, 134–5, 150–1
  sensory vii, 132–5, 151
Phillips, I. 89, 95–106, 130, 278, 296
Phillips, J. 34, 37, 54–5

Physicalism ix, 300, 306, 316, 320, 339, 342, 349–51, 356, 370, 372, 403, 437–41 *see also* materialism
Pitt, D. 133–4, 151, 153, 321, 337
Plato 375, 397, 452
pleasure viii, 178, 193–4, 241–61, 447
Pockett, S. 455, 459
Poldrack, R. A. 59, 85
Porter, T. M. 35, 40–2, 46, 55
Pratt, J. B. 433–5, 459
Prince, M. 433, 445, 447, 459
Prinz, J. 104, 130–4, 151, 153
pro-attitude viii, 241, 243, 257
Putnam, H. 51, 55, 332, 337
Pylyshyn, Z. A. 79, 85, 131, 154

Quetelet, I. 42–3, 55
Quine, W. V. O. 56, 75, 85, 126

Railton, P. 16, 28
Ramsey, F. P. 16–17, 28
Ramsøy, T. 181–4, 188
Ranalli, C. 206, 212, 218
rationality vii, 3–26, 79–80, 237, 380, 384–5, 399, 401, 403, 405, 409–12, 417–28, 449
realism 348, 427, 435–6, 442–5, 448, 450, 455–6
  direct ix, 191–2, 213–17, 435–6, 455
  naïve viii, 191, 267–73, 277, 285, 289, 299–301, 319–20, 329, 334, 339, 341, 345, 357, 361, 365, 435
reduction 46, 132–5, 140–3, 149–50, 252–3, 348–9, 437
Reid, T. 263, 296, 435
Representation 11, 13, 15, 17, 20, 25, 57–65, 71–2, 75–81, 91–6, 106, 108, 119, 162, 170, 267, 299–300, 306, 318–27, 343, 348–9, 353–8, 361, 421 *see also* content, intentionality
  mental 59, 64–5, 72, 80, 318, 321–2, 325, 331, 435
representationalism 57, 61, 192, 213–17, 266–8, 272, 277–8, 288, 300–1, 318–23, 326–9, 336, 339–42, 345–9, 357–8, 361, 365 *see also* intentionalism
representational theory of mind vii, 57–8, 77, 82, 89 *see also* representationalism
Rescorla, M. 80, 85
Rey, G. 75–8, 85

Richardson, L. 268, 271, 275, 285, 296
Robinson, W. 151, 154
Rovelli, C. 429, 431
Rudoph, J. L. 47, 55
Russell, B. 341, 433, 437–41, 443, 446–7, 456–7, 459–60

Sandberg, K. 159, 181–5, 188
Schlick, M. 433–4, 460
Schwitzgebel, E. 151, 154, 159, 188
Scrödinger, E. 441, 460
self ix, 291, 369–70, 372, 378, 384, 388–94
self-knowledge 149, 401, 409, 416–21, 428
self-observation 167, 169, 173–8, 194, 199
Sellars, R. W. 433–6, 455–7, 460
Sellars, W. 103, 130
Shaheen, J. 380, 383, 397, 399, 431
Shea, N. 59–60, 64–5, 77, 85
Siderits, M. 451, 460
Siewert, C. 132–5, 147–8, 150–1, 154, 272, 280–1, 286, 296, 321, 338
Simon, H. A. 4, 28
Smithies, D. 145, 147, 151, 154
Smolin, L. 449, 460
Smuts, A. 241, 259, 262
Sobel, D. 255, 262
Soteriou, M. 263, 268–72, 281, 285, 296
soul 375, 377–80, 383, 387, 410, 421–4, 426, 449
Spener, M. viii, 147, 151, 154, 156, 161, 163, 181, 186, 188
Spinoza, B. viii, 386, 397, 403, 452
Staffel, J. 3, 28
Stalnaker, R. 77, 85
Stanley, J. 228, 239 40
Stich, S. P. 79–90, 86, 103, 130, 149, 151, 153
Stoljar, D. viii, 145, 154, 219, 228–9, 239–40, 403, 437–9, 460
Strawson, G. vi, ix, 133–4, 151, 154, 369–94, 397–8, 429, 431–3, 450–3, 460–1
Strong, C. A. vi–ix, 367, 432–61

Teroni, F. 289–90, 294
Tienson, J. 133–5, 150, 152, 266, 271, 286, 294, 321, 327
transparency of experience viii, 191, 199, 263–92, 301, 304–5, 308, 310, 313, 322, 357–8
Tye, M. 133–5, 151, 154, 263–77, 285, 288–91, 293, 296, 321, 326, 338

unconscious 36–42, 46–57, 109, 257–61, 265, 268, 289

Veillet, B. 133–4, 151–2
Vendler, Z. 222–34, 239–40
vision, color *see* perception, color

Watt, H. 164–5, 188
Weber, M. 35, 56

Whiteley, C. 131, 154
Wicken, M. 138–9, 154
Wilbur, R. 442, 461
Williams, D. C. 433, 441–2, 461
Wilson, R. 131, 133, 151, 154
Wundt, W. 156–9, 163–6, 172–80, 183–8
Wysocki, T. 37–8, 56

Zeman, A. 131, 136–42, 151–2, 155